Pro DNS and BIND 10

Ron Aitchison

Apress®

Pro DNS and BIND 10

ISBN-13 (pbk): 978-1-4302-3048-9

ISBN-13 (electronic): 978-1-4302-3049-6

Printed and bound in the United States of America (POD)

Trademarked names, logos, and images may appear in this book. Rather than use a trademark symbol with every occurrence of a trademarked name, logo, or image we use the names, logos, and images only in an editorial fashion and to the benefit of the trademark owner, with no intention of infringement of the trademark.

The use in this publication of trade names, trademarks, service marks, and similar terms, even if they are not identified as such, is not to be taken as an expression of opinion as to whether or not they are subject to proprietary rights.

President and Publisher: Paul Manning
Lead Editor: Michelle Lowman
Technical Reviewer: Joe Topjian
Editorial Board: Steve Anglin, Mark Beckner, Ewan Buckingham, Gary Cornell, Jonathan Gennick, Jonathan Hassell, Michelle Lowman, Matthew Moodie, Jeff Olson, Jeffrey Pepper, Frank Pohlmann, Douglas Pundick, Ben Renow-Clarke, Dominic Shakeshaft, Matt Wade, Tom Welsh
Coordinating Editor: Laurin Becker
Copy Editor: Mary Behr
Compositor: MacPS, LLC.
Indexer: Julie Grady
Artist: April Milne
Cover Designer: Anna Ishchenko

Distributed to the book trade worldwide by Springer Science+Business Media, LLC., 233 Spring Street, 6th Floor, New York, NY 10013. Phone 1-800-SPRINGER, fax (201) 348-4505, e-mail orders-ny@springer-sbm.com, or visit www.springeronline.com.

For information on translations, please e-mail rights@apress.com, or visit www.apress.com.

Apress and friends of ED books may be purchased in bulk for academic, corporate, or promotional use. eBook versions and licenses are also available for most titles. For more information, reference our Special Bulk Sales–eBook Licensing web page at www.apress.com/info/bulksales.

The information in this book is distributed on an "as is" basis, without warranty. Although every precaution has been taken in the preparation of this work, neither the author(s) nor Apress shall have any liability to any person or entity with respect to any loss or damage caused or alleged to be caused directly or indirectly by the information contained in this work.

The source code for this book is available to readers at www.apress.com. You will need to answer questions pertaining to this book in order to successfully download the code.

To Jed and Cleo.
Your arrival changed my life. Mostly for the better.

Contents at a Glance

Contents

About the Author

Ronald (Ron) Aitchison is the President of Zytrax, Inc., a Montreal-based company that specializes in wireless and wire-line IP communications. Zytrax develops its own products as well as undertaking specialized consulting, training, system design, and development for clients. Zytrax supports its own and customer-hosted DNS, web, e-mail, and LDAP services on a mixed network of Windows, Linux, and, increasingly, FreeBSD systems, and has been an Open Source user since 1998. The company maintains www.zytrax.com/tech, a collection of more than 5,000 pages of technical information on an eclectic variety of technical subjects as a service to the community.

Prior to founding Zytrax in 1994, Ron worked in senior roles in development, sales, and marketing in both Europe and the US. He started his computer career in 1973 as a grunt systems programmer developing communications software for mainframes in a nineteenth-century palace outside of Edinburgh, Scotland. His major achievement in those years was, as cofounder of the local micro-club, persuading Intel to ship the UK's second 8086 system for club use ahead of minor competition such as IBM and others. He moved into sales and marketing for a number of years before returning to real— technical—work when he established Zytrax. He was educated in mechanical engineering at the University of Strathclyde in Glasgow, Scotland, a long time ago.

About the Technical Reviewer

 **Joe Topjian** has been working in ISP environments for more than 10 years. He currently runs Terrarum IT Services, which provides system administration services specializing in infrastructure support and automation. He lives in Calgary, Alberta, with his wife, Meghan.

Acknowledgments

The author would like to gratefully acknowledge the patience and forbearance of a number of individuals during the writing of this book:

The Apress team of Laurin Becker, Debra Kelly, and Mary Behr, who struggled valiantly with my complete inability to keep to a writing schedule and, since I am someone for whom split infinitives tend to stay split, who edited my writing so that it more closely resembles the English language. The contributions of Michelle Lowman and Joe Topjian were invaluable. My admiration for their diligence and perceptive comments is unbounded. Frank Pohlmann was a constant source of support and creative ideas when all seemed, frequently, to be doom and gloom.

One of the sad things about e-mail is that one never meets the individuals who took the time from busy lives to respond to questions and provide insight and information on numerous obscure topics. I would like to thank, in no particular order, Paul Vixie, Shane Kerr, Michael Richardson, Jeremy C. Reed, Michael Graff, Doug Barton, Bert Hubert and Jakob Schlyter. In spite of all the help, any errors are entirely the responsibility of the author.

Introduction

Every time you get e-mail, every time you access a web page, you use the Domain Name System (DNS). In fact, over 2 billion such requests hit the DNS root-servers alone every day. Every one of those 2 billion requests originate from a DNS that supports a group of local users, and every one of them is finally answered by a DNS server that may support a high-volume commercial web site or a modest, but much loved, family web site. This book is about understanding, configuring, diagnosing, and securing the DNS servers that do the vital work. Many years ago when I set up my first pair of DNS servers, I wasted my time looking for some practical advice and some sensible description of the theory involved. I found neither. I completed the DNS rite-of-passage—this book was born from that experience.

DNS is a complex subject, but it is also unnecessarily cloaked in mystery and mythology. This book, I hope, is a sensible blend of practical advice and theory. You can treat it as a simple paint-by-numbers guide to everything from a simple caching DNS to the most complex secure DNS (DNSSEC) implementations. But the background information is there for those times when you not only need to know what to do, but you also need to know why you are doing it, and how you can modify the process to meet your unique needs.

When the first edition of the book was written, we were on the cusp of a major change in DNS technology—the paint had not quite dried yet on the newly published DNSSEC standards. It is no exaggeration to say that even we who live in close proximity to DNS have been staggered by just how radical a change was brought about by those standards. In part this derives from the increasing focus on general Internet security, but it also comes from the recognition of the fundamental role DNS plays in enabling the Internet.

Among many unanswered questions for the future is, once the DNS is secure, what form and type of information may be safely added to DNS zones? The obvious follow-up question that immediately springs from such speculation is what functionality will be demanded of DNS software? We have already seen increasing specialization, clear separation of the roles of authoritative DNS and resolvers, to name one development, and alternative data sources for zone data such as databases and IP provisioning systems, to name another. But all continue to provide classic DNS look-up functionality. In this respect BIND 10 represents a new and radical approach, not just to the issues of functional separation and alternative data source, though these are provided, but in employing a modular and component-like architecture BIND 10 allows us to contemplate a very different way in which DNS may be used within a rapidly evolving Internet.

Introduction to the Second Edition

The second edition of this book represents a major expansion of material in both depth and breadth. On the theoretical side of the DNS equation a more rigorous separation of the roles of authoritative DNS servers and resolvers (caching name servers) is present throughout the book in keeping with the move to specialized software. A complete update of the material on zone files and BIND 9 statements and clauses means that once again the material provided represents a complete and detailed reference work on BIND 9. New sections now cover a wider range of specialized DNS Techniques under the renamed Chapter 8. The DNSSEC chapter has been significantly expanded to reflect both the additional standards involved as well as the wealth of operational possibilities offered by BIND 9. Significant new material has been provided to illustrate usage and implementation of the BIND extended POSIX library functions, which can provide secure last-mile solutions.

While one of the original objectives of the book was to introduce BIND 10 with all its radical changes, it rapidly became apparent that to commit to a paper version at this stage in the evolution of BIND 10 would be to short-change readers. Consequently, a downloaded version of the BIND 10 material is provided. This method allows the material to be updated as necessary to reflect the increasing functionality of BIND 10 as it moves through its development cycle.

Who This Book Is For

This book is about running DNS systems based on BIND 9.7 and BIND 10. If you run or administer a DNS system, are thinking about running a DNS system, need to upgrade to support IPv6 DNS, need to secure a DNS for zone transfer, dynamic update, or other reasons, need to implement DNSSEC, or simply want to understand the DNS system, then this book is designed to provide you with a single point of reference. The book progressively builds up from simple concepts to full security-aware DNSSEC configurations. The various features, parameters, and Resource Records that you will need are all described and in the majority of cases illustrated with one or more examples. The book contains a complete reference on zone files, Resource Records, and BIND 9's named.conf configuration file parameters. Programmers and the insatiably curious will find BIND 9's Simple Database API, resolver library interfaces, and the gory details of DNS wire-format messages compelling reading.

How This Book Is Structured

This book is about the Domain Name System. Most of the examples used throughout the book are based on the Berkeley Internet Name Domain, universally known as BIND, which is the most widely deployed name server software in current use. BIND version 9.7.1-P2 was used as the baseline version for all the examples. During the course of writing the book, version 9.7.2-P2—a bug clearance–only version—was released. The majority of, but not all, tests were rerun on the new version—no functional differences were noted between the releases. Readers are advised to always obtain and use the latest stable BIND version.

Like most technical books, this is a mixture of descriptive text, reference material, and samples. For those completely unfamiliar with the subject, Part 1 (Chapters 1 to 5) is designed to introduce DNS in a progressive manner and could be read as a classic text on the subject. For those of a hands-on disposition, Part 2 provides an alternative entry point, with the various earlier chapters to be read as needed. Experienced readers would typically head straight for the meat in either Parts 3, 4, or 5, depending on their area of interest. As well as providing help and guidance during your initial endeavors, it is my fervent hope that this book will also provide you with an indispensable reference work for years to come.

Chapter 1, "An Introduction to DNS"

Chapter 1 provides introductory and background material to the DNS as a specific implementation of the general name server concept. The key concepts introduced are the domain name hierarchy, delegation, DNS operational organization, the role of ICANN, and the various components that comprise a DNS eco-system. A clear separation between the roles of authoritative name servers and resolvers (a.k.a. caching name servers) is introduced, and this terminology is used rigorously throughout the book. This chapter is for those who are unfamiliar with the topic or the changes that have occurred in the recent past.

Chapter 2, "Zone Files and Resource Records"

Here you are introduced to the basic Resource Records and directives used to construct zone files. An example forward-mapping zone file is introduced that is used throughout the book and illustrates key DNS operational concepts such as resilience and location diversity. Those with little or no knowledge of zone files and their construction will find this chapter a gentle introduction to the topic.

Chapter 3, "DNS Operations"

This chapter describes the basic operation of a DNS system, including queries, referrals, reverse mapping, zone transfers, and dynamic updates. A brief overview of DNS security is presented to familiarize readers with the potential threats posed when running DNS systems. This chapter is intended to give the reader a thorough grounding in the theory and background to these topics.

Chapter 4, "DNS Types"

The text in this chapter breaks down configuring a DNS into a number of types such as master, slave, resolver (caching only name server), forwarding, Stealth, and authoritative only with the objective of giving the reader a set of building blocks from which more complex configurations can be constructed. This chapter will be useful to those unfamiliar with the range of possibilities offered by the DNS and its BIND implementation, including the view clause introduced with the BIND 9 series.

Chapter 5, "DNS and IPv6"

Chapter 5 focuses on IPv6 and the DNS features that support this increasingly widespread protocol. A brief overview of IPv6 address structure and notation is provided for those currently unfamiliar with this topic.

Chapter 6, "Installing BIND"

This chapter covers the installation of BIND on Linux (Ubuntu Server 10.04), FreeBSD (8.1), and Windows 7 from binary packages. For those cases where a package is not available, building from a source tarball is also described. An increasingly wide range of software configuration options offered by BIND especially means that building from source tarballs may become increasingly common.

Chapter 7, "BIND Type Samples"

The zone and named.conf sample files for each of the DNS types introduced in Chapter 4 are provided. While these samples can be used as simple paint-by-number implementations, explanations are included to allow the configurations to be tailored to user requirements.

Chapter 8, "DNS Techniques"

A number of DNS configurations are described and illustrated with sample files and implementation notes. The items covered include delegation of subdomains, load balancing, fixing sequence errors, delegation of reverse subnets, SPF and DKIM records, DNSBL, split horizon systems, and the use of wildcards.

Chapter 9, "DNS Diagnostics and Tools"

The major utilities supplied with a BIND distribution, including those used for security operations, are covered with multiple use examples. The reader, however, is encouraged—especially with dig and nslookup—to get out and explore the Internet using these tools. A practical example is used to illustrate to some diagnostics techniques and procedures.

Chapter 10, "DNS Secure Configurations"

DNS security within this book is broken into four parts: administrative security, securing zone transfers, securing dynamic update, and DNSSEC. An overview of general cryptographic processes including symmetric and asymmetric encryption, digital signatures, and MACs, which form the basis of DNS security implementations, is provided for readers unfamiliar with this topic.

Chapter 11, "DNSSEC"

This chapter deals exclusively with the DNSSEC security standards and covers both the theory and practical implementation. Zone signing, chains of trust, Zone Signing Keys and Key Signing Keys, DNSSEC Lookaside Validation (DLV), and key-rollover procedures are all covered with practical examples. BIND 9 provides a bewildering variety of DNSSEC implementation options—the final section in this chapter provides some advice and worked examples from which an intelligent choice can be made.

Chapter 12, "BIND Configuration Reference"

As suggested by the title, this is purely a reference section, and it catalogues and describes with one or more examples all the clauses and statements used in BIND's named.conf file. The chapter is organized in a manner that allows the reader to easily find appropriate statements to control specific BIND behaviors.

Chapter 13, "Zone File Reference"

This is purely a reference section that describes each Resource Record in the current IANA list—normally with one or more examples to illustrate usage.

Chapter 14, "BIND APIs and Resolver Libraries"

Designed more for programmers and designers, you will need a reasonable understanding of C to make sense of this chapter. The new BIND Simple Database API and the newly released BIND extended POSIX interfaces from which secure last-mile DNS solutions can be created.

Chapter 15, "DNS Messages and Records"

This chapter covers the gory details of DNS wire-format messages and RR formats. A reasonable working knowledge of decimal, hex, and binary notations are required to make sense of the chapter. Essential reading if you are developing DNS applications, when RRs are not supported by your sniffer application or you are insatiably curious about how this stuff works.

Appendix A, "Domain Name Registration"

This appendix is a collection of material, presented in FAQ format, that may help to answer questions about registering domains in a variety of situations.

Appendix B, "DNS RFCs"

This appendix presents a list of RFCs that define the DNS and DNS-related topics.

Additional Material

In addition, the author maintains a web site about the book (www.netwidget.net/books/apress/dns) that covers additional material, including links to alternative DNS software, resolver language bindings, and background reading on various topics covered in the book, which may be of use to the reader.

Conventions

The following conventions are used throughout the book:

- The # (hash or pound) symbol is used to denote a command prompt and always precedes a command to be entered. The command to be entered starts after this symbol.

- The \ (back slash) is used to denote where lines that are contiguous have been split purely for presentational reasons. When added to a file or entered on a command line the \ should not be present.

- Lines consisting of four dots (....) in zone and configuration files are used to denote that other lines may or may not be present in these files. The dot sequence should not be entered in the actual files.

- When describing command syntax, the following convention is used throughout:

  command argument [option1] **keyword** [option2 [optional3] ...]

  where all items in bold, which include command and keywords, must be entered as is. Optional values are enclosed in square brackets and may be nested. Where repeated options are allowed, a sequence of three dots is used to indicate this.

Contacting the Author

The author may be contacted at ron.aitchison@netwidget.net, and he maintains links and other information relating to this book at www.netwidget.net/books/apress/dns.

## PART I

Principles and Overview

## CHAPTER 1

An Introduction to DNS

The Internet—or any network for that matter—works by allocating a locally or globally unique IP address to every endpoint (host, server, router, interface, and so on). But without the ability to assign some corresponding name to each resource, every time we want to access a resource available on the network, the web site www.example.com for instance, it would be necessary to know its *physical IP address*, such as 192.168.34.166. With hundreds of million of hosts and more than 200 million web sites,[1] it's an impossible task—it's also pretty difficult with even a handful of hosts and resources.

To solve this problem, the concept of *name servers* was created in the mid-1970s to enable certain attributes (or properties) of a *named resource*, in this case the IP address of www.example.com, to be maintained in a well-known location—the basic idea being that people find it much easier to remember the *name* of something especially when that name is reasonably descriptive of function, content, or purpose rather than a numeric address. This chapter introduces basic name server concepts and provides a bit of background regarding the evolution of the Domain Name System from a tool used for managing just a few hundred hosts to a global utility responsible for maintaining smooth operation of the entire modern Internet.

A Brief History of Name Servers

The problem of converting names to physical addresses is as old as computer networking. Even in times long since past, people found it easier to remember they were using a teletype device called "tty2" rather than "port 57 of the MCCU," or whatever the addressing method then in use. Furthermore, administrators wanted the flexibility to reconfigure equipment while leaving users with a consistent way of describing the device they were using. In the preceding example, the user could continue to use "tty2" even if the device had been reconfigured to be on port 23 of the mythical MCCU. Simple configuration files were typically used to perform *address translation*. As networking, rather than simple communications, emerged in the early 1970s, the problem became more acute. IBM's System Network Architecture (SNA), probably the grandfather of networking, contained a rudimentary mainframe database for *name translation* when originally published in 1974. The much-maligned Open Systems Interconnect (OSI) Model, developed by the International Organization for Standardization (ISO—www.iso.org), defined *Address/Name Translation* services at the Transport Layer (Layer 4) when initially published in 1978. NetBIOS provided the NetBIOS Name Server (NBNS) when originally defined in 1984, which later morphed into Microsoft's Windows Internet Naming Service (WINS).

The first ARPANET (the network that morphed into the Internet) RFC, the quaintly named Request For Comments that document and standardize the Internet, on the concept of domain names dates from 1981 (RFC 799), and the definitive specifications for the Internet's Domain Name System as we know it today were published in 1987 (RFC 1034 and RFC 1035).

---

[1] http://news.netcraft.com/archives/web_server_survey.html

Name Server Basics

When a name server is present in a network, any host only needs to know the *physical address* of a name server and the *name* of the resource, a web site for example, it wishes to access. Using this information, it can find the address (or any other stored attribute or property) of the resource by interrogating (commonly referred to as *querying*) the name server. Resources can be added, moved, changed, or deleted at a single location, the name server, and new information will be immediately available to every host using this name server. Our name server is simply a specialized database that translates names to properties—typically IP addresses—and vice versa. Name servers both simplify network management and make networks more dynamic and responsive to changes.

Solutions, however, can also generate problems. If our name server is not available, then our host cannot access *any* resource on the network. We have made the name server a critical resource. So we had better have more than one name server in case of failure.

The initial solution to the problem of name server availability was to introduce *Primary* and *Secondary* name servers. If the Primary name server did not respond to a query, the host would retry using the Secondary name server. So critical is the name server that today it is common to see lists of three, four, or more name servers. The terms *Primary* and *Secondary name servers*, and even *Tertiary*, and *Quartiary name servers*, while still widely used, imply priority of access, which works against availability. Not only would such prioritization cause transaction bunching on the Primary name server, degrading overall performance, but in the case where the Primary name server was inoperable, *every* transaction would have to wait for a timeout before retrying with the Secondary, and so on. Most name server software uses some form of randomized, measured response time or round-robin access to the name server list to try and spread loads and decrease response times.

As our network grows, we start to build up a serious number of names in our name server. This gives rise to three new problems:

- *Organization*: Finding any entry in the database of names becomes increasingly slow as we power through many millions of names looking for the one we want. We need a method to index or organize the names.

- *Scalability*: If every host is accessing our name servers, the load becomes very high. We need a method to spread the load across a number of name servers.

- *Management*: With many name records in our database, the management problem becomes increasingly difficult, as multiple administrators attempt to update records at the same time. We need a method to separate (known as *delegating*) the administration of these name (generally known as *resource*) records.

The need to satisfy these three requirements led to the creation and evolution of the Internet's Domain Name System (DNS), discussed in the next section.

The Internet Domain Name System

The Internet's *Domain Name System* is a specific implementation of the name server concept optimized for the prevailing conditions on the Internet. From our brief history of name servers, we saw that three requisites emerged:

- The need for a hierarchy of names

- The need to spread the operational loads on our name servers

- The need to delegate the administration of our name servers

The Internet DNS elegantly solves all three problems.

Note The standard RFCs that define the basic DNS functionality, RFC 1034 and RFC 1035, were both written close to a quarter of a century ago—1987—and authored by Dr. Paul Mockapetris while at the Information Sciences Institute of the University of Southern California. Although many subsequent RFCs have modified certain DNS behaviors, the core functionality remains intact. This is indeed a remarkable achievement.

Domains and Delegation

The Domain Name System uses a tree (or hierarchical) name structure. At the top of the tree is the root node, followed by the *Top-Level Domains* (*TLDs*), then the *Second-Level Domains* (*SLDs*), and then any number of lower levels, each separated with a dot.

Note The root of the tree is represented most of the time as a silent dot (.), which simply means that although it should be present, it is not always required and can therefore be omitted (silent) simply for convenience. There are times, however, when this trailing dot is *very* important.

TLDs are split into two basic types:

- Generic Top-Level Domains (gTLDs): For example, .com, .edu, .net, .org, .mil, and so on

- Country Code Top-Level Domains (ccTLDs): For example, .us, .ca, .tv, .uk, and so on

Country Code TLDs use a standard two-letter sequence defined by ISO 3166.[2] Figure 1–1 illustrates this diagrammatically.

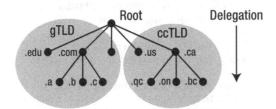

Figure 1–1. Domain structure and delegation

---

[2] www.iso.org/iso/en/prods-services/iso3166ma/02iso-3166-code-lists/list-en1.html

What is commonly called a *domain name*, for instance example.com, is actually a combination of an SLD name and a TLD name and is written from left to right with the lowest level in the hierarchy on the left and the highest level on the right:

sld.tld

The term *Second-Level Domain* is technically precise in that it defines nodes at the second level within the domain name hierarchy, but is long-winded. To be even more long-winded, there can also be Third-Level Domains, which are especially relevant with ccTLDS, and so on. By convention—or perhaps laziness—the term *domain*, or *domain name*, is generally used to describe a delegated entity, for instance, example.com, which consists of the SLD example and the TLD com. Unless precision is required, the term *domain name* will be used throughout the remainder of this book.

Domain Authority

The concepts of *authority* and *delegation* lie at the core of the Domain Name System hierarchy and exactly mirror its hierarchical organization. Each node within the domain name hierarchy is assigned to an *authority*—an organization or person responsible for the management and operation of that node. Such an organization or person is said to administer the node *authoritatively*. The *authority* for a particular node can in turn *delegate* authority for lower levels of that node within the domain name hierarchy. The rules and limitations of the authority are covered by agreements that flow through the various nodes in the hierarchy.

The authority for the root domain lies with the Internet Corporation for Assigned Numbers and Names (ICANN—www.icann.org/). Since 1998, ICANN, a nonprofit organization, has assumed this responsibility from the United States Department of Commerce. When ICANN was established, part of its mandate was to open up that part of the domain name hierarchy for which it is responsible to commercial competition. To facilitate this competition, it created the concept of *accredited registrars*, organizations to which ICANN delegated limited responsibilities for the sale and administration of parts of the domain name hierarchy.

The gTLDs are *authoritatively* administered by ICANN and *delegated* to a series of accredited registrars. The ccTLDs are delegated by ICANN to the individual countries for administration purposes. Figure 1–1 also shows how any authority may in turn delegate to lower levels in the hierarchy; in other words, it may delegate anything for which it is *authoritative*. Each layer in the hierarchy may *delegate* the *authoritative* control to the next or lower level.

In the case of ccTLDs, countries define their own rules for delegation. Countries like the United States (ccTLD .us), Canada (ccTLD .ca), and others have decided that they will administer both at the national level and delegate to each state (U.S.) or province (Canada) using a two-character state/province code (for example, .ny = New York, .qc = Quebec, .md = Maryland, and so on). Thus, example.us is the domain name of example that was delegated from the U.S. national ccTLD administration, and example.md.us is the domain name of example that was delegated from the state of Maryland in the United States.

Other countries, such as the United Kingdom and Brazil, among many others, have opted for functional segmentation in their delegation models. Thus example.co.uk is the domain name of example registered as a company from the UK registration authority, and example.com.br is the domain name of example registered as a company from the Brazilian registration authority.

Delegation within any domain may be almost limitless and is *decided by the delegated authority*. For example, many states in the United States and provinces in Canada delegate cities within state/province domains: the domain name example.nb.us would be the town of Example in the state of Nebraska in the United States, and indeed we could have mycompany.example.nb.us, which would be the domain name of mycompany in the town of Example in the state of Nebraska in the United States.

Reading a domain name from right to left will track its delegation.

So What Is www.example.com?

From our previous reading, we can see that www.example.com is built up from www and example.com. The domain name example.com part was delegated from a gTLD registrar, which in turn was delegated from ICANN.

The owner of the domain chose the www part because they are now the delegated authority for the example.com domain name. They own everything to the left of the delegated domain name; in this case, example.com.

The leftmost part, the www in this case, is called a *host name*. Keep in mind that only by convention do web sites use the host name www (for World Wide Web), but a web site can be named fred.example.com—few users may think of typing this name into their web browser, but that does not invalidate the name!

Every computer that is connected to the Internet or an internal network and is accessed using a name server has a host name. Here are some more examples:

www.example.com	The company web service
ftp.example.com	The company file transfer protocol server
pc17.example.com	A normal PC
accounting.example.com	The main accounting system

A host name must be unique within the delegated domain name, but can be anything the owner of example.com wants.

Finally, consider this name:

www.us.example.com

From our previous reading, we figure the domain name is example.com; the www probably indicates a web site, which leaves the us part.

The us part was allocated by the owner of example.com (who is authoritative) and is called a subdomain. In this case, the *delegated authority* for example.com has decided that their organization is best served by a country-based subdomain structure. They could *delegate* the responsibility internally to the U.S. subsidiary for administration of this subdomain, which could in turn create a plant-based structure; for example, www.cleveland.us.example.com could indicate the web site of the Cleveland plant in the U.S. organization of example.com.

To summarize: the *owner* can delegate, in any way they want, anything to the left of the domain name they own (or were *delegated*). The delegated owner is also responsible for administering this delegation. The unit of delegation is referred to as a *zone* in the DNS specifications.

■**Note** www.example.com and www.us.example.com are commonly—but erroneously—referred to as Fully Qualified Domain Names (FQDN). Technically, an FQDN unambiguously defines a domain name to the root and therefore must terminate with the normally silent dot; for instance, www.example.com. (with the dot) is a valid FQDN, but www.example.com (without the dot) is not.

DNS Implementation and Structure

The Internet's DNS implementation exactly maps the domain name delegation structure described previously. There are name servers (servers that run DNS software) at each level in the delegated hierarchy, and the responsibility for running the name server lies with the authoritative control at that level. Figure 1–2 shows this diagrammatically.

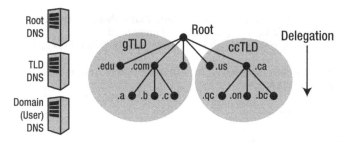

Figure 1–2. *DNS mapped to domain delegation*

The root name servers (hereafter called the *root-servers*) are the most critical resources on the Internet. When any name server worldwide is *queried* for information about a domain name for which it does not currently have information, it first asks (*queries*) one of the root DNS servers. There are currently 13 root-servers worldwide, described in further detail later in this chapter. The root-servers are known to every name server in the world using a special *zone file*, which is distributed with all DNS software.

The TLD name servers (gTLD and ccTLD) are operated by a variety of organizations, termed *Registry Operators*, under ICANN agreements and are described more completely later in this chapter.

The owner of a domain name has been delegated the authority for administering the domain name and therefore has the responsibility for the operation of the user (or domain name) name servers—there must be a minimum of two for resilience. The name *server operational responsibility* may be delegated by the domain owner to an ISP, a web hosting company, or increasingly a domain name registrar. Many companies and domain name owners, however, elect to run their own name servers and even delegate the authority and responsibility for subdomain name servers to separate parts of their organization.

When any name server cannot answer, or *resolve*, a request for a name, for instance, fred.example.com, the query is passed to a root-server (discussed in the next section), which returns a *referral* to the appropriate TLD name server, which in turn provides a referral to the appropriate domain (user) name server which returns the real (*authoritative*) answer. Figure 1–3 illustrates this process.

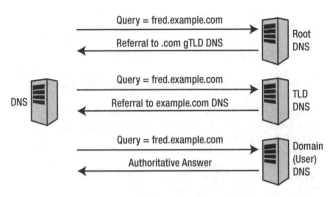

Figure 1–3. *The operational DNS hierarchy*

Root DNS Operations

The root-servers (root DNS) are the responsibility of ICANN, but are operated under an agreement known as the Cooperative Research and Development Agreement (CRADA) that was signed between ICANN and the U.S Department of Commerce (www.icann.org/committees/dns-root/crada.htm). This agreement covers the methods and processes by which updates to the root name systems are carried out. ICANN also created the Root Server System Advisory Committee (RSSAC) to provide advice and guidance as to the operation and development of this critical resource. The IETF was requested by the RSSAC to develop the engineering standards for operation of the root-servers. This request resulted in the publication of RFC 2870.

There are currently 13 root-servers. They occupy a reserved domain name: root-servers.net. Each root-server typically comprises many physical servers but, using a process called *anycasting*, each physical server (called a root-server *instance* in the jargon) shares a single IP address. Root-servers are named from a.root-servers.net through m.root-servers.net, as shown in Table 1–1. As of 2010, while there are 13 named root-servers, there are just over 200 instances throughout the world. Current information about the root-servers can be obtained from www.root-servers.org.

Table 1–1. *Root-servers*

Server	Operator	Location	IP Address
A	VeriSign Global Registry Services	Sites = 6: Los Angeles, US; New York, US *; Frankfurt, DE; Hong Kong, HK; Palo Alto, US *; Ashburn, US *	IPv4: 198.41.0.4 IPv6: 2001:503:BA3E::2:30
B	Information Sciences Institute	Sites = 1: Marina del Rey, US	IPv4: 192.228.79.201, IPv6: 2001:478:65::53
C	Cogent Communications	Sites = 6: Chicago, US; Herndon, US; Los Angeles, US; New York City, US; Frankfurt, DE; Madrid, ES	IPv4: 192.33.4.12

Server	Operator	Location	IP Address
D	University of Maryland	Sites = 1:College Park, US	IPv4: 128.8.10.90
E	NASA Ames Research Center	Sites = 1: Mountain View, US	IPv4: 192.203.230.10
F	Internet Systems Consortium, Inc. (ISC)	Sites = 49: Ottawa, CA *; Palo Alto, US *; San Jose, US; New York, US *; San Francisco, US *; Madrid, ES; Hong Kong, HK; Los Angeles, US *; Rome, IT; Auckland, NZ *; Sao Paulo, BR; Beijing, CN; Seoul, KR *; Moscow, RU *; Taipei, TW; Dubai, AE; Paris, FR *; Singapore, SG; Brisbane, AU *; Toronto, CA *; Monterrey, MX; Lisbon, PT *; Johannesburg, ZA; Tel Aviv, IL; Jakarta, ID; Munich, DE *; Osaka, JP *; Prague, CZ *; Amsterdam, NL *; Barcelona, ES *; Nairobi, KE; Chennai, IN; London, UK *; Santiago de Chile, CL; Dhaka, BD; Karachi, PK; Torino, IT; Chicago, US *; Buenos Aires, AR; Caracas, VE; Oslo, NO *; Panama, PA; Quito, EC; Kuala Lumpur, MY *; Suva, FJ; Cairo, EG; Atlanta, US; Podgorica, ME; St. Maarten, AN *	IPv4: 192.5.5.241, IPv6: 2001:500:2f::f
G	U.S. DOD Network Information Center	Sites = 6: Columbus, US; San Antonio, US; Honolulu, US; Fussa, JP; Stuttgart-Vaihingen, DE; Naples, IT	IPv4: 192.112.36.4
H	U.S. Army Research Lab	Sites = 1: Aberdeen Proving Ground, US	IPv4: 128.63.2.53, IPv6: 2001:500:1::803f:235
I	Autonomica	Sites = 34: Stockholm, SE; Helsinki, FI; Milan, IT; London, UK; Geneva, CH; Amsterdam, NL; Oslo, NO; Bangkok, TH; Hong Kong, HK; Brussels, BE; Frankfurt, DE; Ankara, TR; Bucharest, RO; Chicago, US;	IPv4: 192.36.148.17

Server	Operator	Location	IP Address
		Washington, US; Tokyo, JP; Kuala Lumpur, MY; Palo Alto, US; Jakarta, ID; Wellington, NZ; Johannesburg, ZA; Perth, AU; San Francisco, US; Singapore, SG; Miami, US; Ashburn, US; Mumbai, IN; Beijing, CN; Manila, PH; Doha, QA; Colombo, LK; Vienna, AT; Paris, FR; Taipei, TW	
J	VeriSign Global Registry Services	Sites = 70: Dulles, US (2 sites); Dulles, US (1 sites); Ashburn, US *; Miami, US; Atlanta, US; Seattle, US; Chicago, US; New York, US *; Honolulu, US; Mountain View, US (1 sites); Mountain View, US (1 sites); San Francisco, US (2 sites) *; Dallas, US; Amsterdam, NL; London, UK; Stockholm, SE (2 sites); Tokyo, JP; Seoul, KR; Beijing, CN; Singapore, SG; Dublin, IE; Kaunas, LT; Nairobi, KE; Montreal, CA; Perth, AU; Sydney, AU; Cairo, EG; **Cairo, EG;** Warsaw, PL (2 sites); Brasilia, BR; Sao Paulo, BR; Sofia, BG; Prague, CZ; Johannesburg, ZA; Toronto, CA; Buenos Aires, AR; Madrid, ES; Fribourg, CH; Hong Kong, HK (2 sites); Turin, IT; Mumbai, IN; Oslo, NO; Brussels, BE; Paris, FR (2 sites); Helsinki, FI; Frankfurt, DE; Riga, LV; Milan, IT; Rome, IT; Lisbon, PT; San Juan, PR; Edinburgh, UK; Tallin, EE; Taipei, TW; New York, US *; Palo Alto, US *; Anchorage, US; Moscow, RU; Manila, PH; Kuala Lumpur, MY; Luxembourg City, LU; Guam, US; Vancouver, CA; Wellington, NZ	IPv4: 192.58.128.30 IPv6: 2001:503:C27::2:30

Server	Operator	Location	IP Address
K	Réseaux IP Européens Network Coordination Centre (RIPE)	Sites = 18: London, UK *; Amsterdam, NL *; Frankfurt, DE; Athens, GR *; Doha, QA; Milan, IT *; Reykjavik, IS *; Helsinki, FI *; Geneva, CH *; Poznan, PL; Budapest, HU *; Abu Dhabi, AE; Tokyo, JP; Brisbane, AU *; Miami, US *; Delhi, IN; Novosibirsk, RU; Dar es Salaam, TZAmsterdam, Athens, Doha, Frank- furt, London, Milan	IPv4: 193.0.14.129, IPv6: 2001:7fd::1
L	Internet Corporation for Assigned Names and Numbers (ICANN)	Sites = 3: Los Angeles, US *; Miami, US *; Prague, CZ *	IPv4: 199.7.83.42 IPv6: 2001:500:3::42
M	WIDE Project	Sites = 6: Paris, FR; Seoul, KR; Tokyo, JP (3 sites);Los Angeles, US;	IPv4: 12.27.33, IPv6: 2001:dc3::35

■ **Note** Sites with an * support IPv6. The number 13 is not a perverse desire by anyone to operate a number of servers seen by some cultures as unlucky, but rather a technically determined limit enabling common root-server queries to be answered within a single 512-byte UDP transaction and hence reduce root-server loads. DNS secure transactions (DNSSEC; see Chapter 12) significantly increase the average DNS transaction size; thus, although the root-server limit may remain at 13, there is no longer the same overwhelming block size argument to justify the number.

The job of the root-servers is to provide a referral to the authoritative name servers for the required TLDs (gTLDs or ccTLDs). For example, if a user requests information about fred.example.com, then the root-servers will supply a list of the authoritative name servers for the .com TLD. In 2004, ICANN took over responsibility for the maintenance of the root-servers TLD master file—the file that lists the authoritative servers for each TLD. Distribution of this file to each of the operational root-servers is carried out using secure transactions. To further increase security, the server providing the root updates is accessible only from the operational root-servers. It is not a publicly visible server. Figure 1–4 illustrates this process.

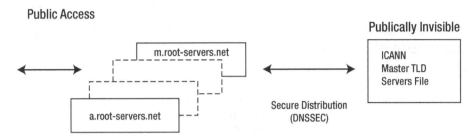

Figure 1–4. Root-servers' update process

Top-Level Domains

As was mentioned earlier in this chapter, Top-Level Domains are split into Generic Top-Level Domains and Country Code Top-Level Domains. Each group is administered slightly differently, but all are controlled by ICANN. ICANN controls the gTLDs by a purely contractual process. In the case of ccTLDs, because multiple countries and national sovereignty issues are involved, the process is essentially consultative rather than purely contractual.

Generic Top-Level Domains

Generic Top-Level Domains, or gTLDs, are controlled by ICANN using a contractual process. When competition was introduced into the registration of domain names, ICANN established two separate entities:

- *Registry Operators*: Registry Operators contract with ICANN to operate the authoritative gTLD DNS servers (see Figure 1–2 earlier). There is a single *Registry Operator* for each of the gTLDs, for example, the U.S. Department of Defense, Network Information Center, is the Registry Operator for the .mil gTLD, but each *Registry Operator* will operate multiple name servers. DNS queries to the root-servers return a *referral* to the authoritative gTLD servers for the specific gTLD; for example, if the query is for example.net, then the root-servers will supply the list of .net authoritative DNS servers. Registry Operators obtain the list of registered domain names for the TLD from one or more *Registrars*. The public has no contact with the Registry Operator. However, a number of Registry Operators are also Registrars; for example, VeriSign, Inc., is the Registry Operator for the .com gTLD but is also a well-known Registrar.

- *Registrars*: Registrars are accredited by ICANN through a contractual process to interact with the public to register one or more gTLDs. When you purchase or renew a domain name, you deal with a *Registrar*. The Registrar maintains all the required details, including owner name, administrative contact, billing contact, technical contact, the authoritative name servers for the domain name, and so on. The Registrar is responsible for providing the *Registry Operator* for the gTLD with an extract of the data, which consists of the registered domain name and the name and IP addresses of the authoritative DNS servers for the domain. This information is exclusively used to answer DNS queries.

■ Note The secure exchange of domain information between *Registrars* and *Registry Operators* is controlled by the Extended Provisioning Protocol (EPP) defined by RFC 5730.

The separation of functionality between the Registry Operator and the Registrar allows the relevant organizations involved to concentrate expertise and—importantly—ensures that specialists handle operation of the TLD name servers. Figure 1–5 illustrates this process.

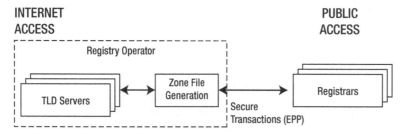

Figure 1–5. Registry Operator–Registrar relationship

ICANN inherited the gTLDs listed in Table 1–2 on its establishment in 1998.

Table 1–2. gTLDs Available Prior to November 2000

gTLD	Use
.arpa	Address and Routing Parameter Area (ARPA) reserved for use in Internet infrastructure
.com	Historically used for abbreviation of *company*
.edu	Special TLD reserved for use by certain U.S. educational institutions
.gov	Reserved exclusively for use by U.S. federal, state, and local government
.int	Reserved exclusively for use by organizations established by international treaty
.mil	Reserved exclusively for use by the U.S. military
.net	Historically for use by network operators
.org	Historically for use by nonprofit organizations

In November 2000, ICANN authorized the new gTLDs you see in Table 1–3.

Table 1–3. gTLDs Authorized by ICANN in November 2000

gTLD	Use
.aero	Reserved for use by the airline industry
.biz	Generic business name domain
.coop	Reserved for use by cooperatives
.info	Generic information resources
.museum	Reserved for use by museums
.name	For use by individuals—vanity domain names
.pro	For use by professional organizations

The ICANN agreements with the Registry Operators covering the post–2000 gTLDs have specified that information registration services and WHOIS services be made more easily available by reserving the use of nic and whois SLD names for each of the gTLDs. For example, to obtain registration information for the .coop gTLD, you need enter only www.nic.coop (or just nic.coop). To obtain WHOIS services for the .museum gTLD, you need enter only www.whois.museum (or whois.museum). Although many of the newer TLDs do support such easy-to-remember names, regrettably not all do.

■**Note** WHOIS is quite literally a service by which anyone can find "who is" the owner, and other pertinent details, of domain names or IP addresses. Registrars and in some cases third parties provide access to the registration databases using the standard WHOIS protocol (RFC 3912).

As can be seen in the list in Table 1–3, some of the gTLDs, such as .aero, have limited registration policies; others do not. During 2004, ICANN undertook a review of gTLD policy, one of the effects of which was to create a new gTLD *subset* called Sponsored TLDs (sTLDs) to clarify the form of registration access to be offered by new gTLDs. The domains .museum, .coop, .aero, .gov, .mil, .edu, and .int are all now classified as sTLDs. Since November 2000, ICANN has authorized six new TLDs, all sTLDs: .travel, .jobs, .mobi, .cat, .tel, and .asia.

Authorizing new gTLDs has always attracted controversy. In June 2008, ICANN adopted a new gTLD policy based on a report by its Generic Names Supporting Organization (GNSO) Working Group. In essence, this policy places no limits on the number of new gTLDs that can be created in the future and allows any competent party to propose a new gTLD that will be judged against an objective set of criteria. As of the date of writing, no gTLD application has been authorized under the new policy.

■ **Note** A full list of all current gTLDs (and sTLDS), together with a description of their use, the date of ICANN authorization, their Sponsors and Registry Operators, as well as further information about and references to the revised ICANN gTLD policy is defined in Appendix A question 4: What TLDs are available?Country Code Top-Level Domains

---

Country Code Top-Level Domains are controlled by ICANN and consist of a two-character code defined by ISO 3166. ICANN has neatly sidestepped the thorny issue of what is a country by the use of ISO 3166. ISO 3166 is controlled by a branch of the United Nations, which is pretty experienced in the matter of defining what is (and what is not) a country!

ccTLDs are delegated by ICANN to a country code manager. *Country code manager* is a historic term reflecting a time when the Internet was a small and intimate place—more often today the country code manager is a branch of government, and the country code has become a valuable economic resource.

The relationship between ICANN and country code managers is complicated by sovereignty and cultural sensitivity, and the process is largely consultative rather than contractual. It is a testament to the good will of all parties that the process works as well as it does. In general, country managers are responsible for administering and operating their delegated country codes and the associated TLD servers with regard to their local circumstances and within the spirit of RFC 1591 and ICANN's ICP-1 (www.icann.org/en/icp/icp-1.htm). As part of the move to make the Internet more accessible worldwide, Internationalized Domain Name (IDN) ccTLDs are being introduced. See Chapter 17 for IDN details and Appendix A for more information on IDN ccTLDs.

The country delegation models are typically based on a federated model; for example, by state or province—example.md.us—or a functional model, for example, example.co.uk or example.com.br. However, many exceptions do exist, reflecting local conditions and needs. The most famous that spring to mind are .tv (Tuvala) and .la (Laos), whereby those countries have sought to optimize the economic value of the domain name resource.

The Internet Assigned Numbers Authority (IANA) maintains a current list of country code managers at www.iana.org/domains/root/db/ on behalf of ICANN.

DNS in Action

So far, we have focused on domain names and authoritative name servers used in DNS. But for the DNS to be useful it must deliver information, in the form of *answers* to *queries,* from an authoritative name server to a user's PC or any application (such as an SMTP [mail] agent or an FTP client) that needs to *resolve* names to IP addresses. Figure 1–6 illustrates how a browser running in a PC uses and accesses the DNS and introduces all the pieces that can make up the operational DNS puzzle.

■ Note Like all systems, DNS has its fair share of terminology, some of which is inconsistently applied. Within the DNS there are essentially two types of systems: *authoritative name servers* that deliver *authoritative answers* (data) in response to *queries.* The queries originate from what are called *resolvers.* A resolver is simply a part of the DNS infrastructure that issues queries in order to *resolve* (translate) names into IP addresses. Resolvers, which can come in all shapes and sizes, are explained further in the next section and throughout the book.

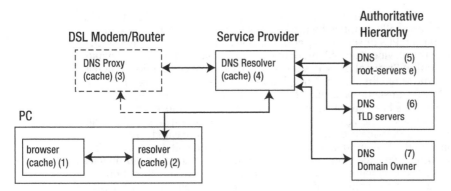

Figure 1–6. A DNS system

As can be seen in Figure 1–6, DNS makes extensive use of caching, which can play a significant role in reducing system complexity and speeding up DNS response times. *Caching* simply means that any results (answers to queries) are saved in temporary storage. If a request for the same data arrives at the resolver, the *cache* is inspected first and if the required data is present the answer is supplied directly from the cache. Thus, unnecessary external communication is avoided, and the result is supplied much more quickly. The process by which stale data is discarded from the cache uses a Time to Live (TTL) value which is explained in Chapter 2.

The numbers used in the following descriptions refer to those in Figure 1–6:

- When users enter a URL, such as www.example.com, into their favorite browser, (1) it first searches its internal cache to see whether it already has the data. If not, the browser calls an internal software library or program called a resolver (2). The normal method, whereby stale data is removed from a DNS cache (the TTL) is not possible within the browser, making this cache only marginally effective or in some cases counterproductive (see Chapter 8).

- A DNS resolver can be a very complex piece of software, but the DNS standards allow for a simplified version called a *stub-resolver*. Stub-resolvers are installed on all platforms such as Windows and *nix systems (for example, Linux, UNIX, and BSD). The majority of modern stub-resolvers also provide caching services, so if you enjoy using long descriptions it could be called a *caching stub-resolver*. As expected, the stub-resolver inspects its cache first and immediately supplies the result if present. If not, it creates a DNS query (a question) and sends it to either a DSL modem (3) or directly to a *DNS resolver* (4) depending on how the PC or server was configured.

- In the majority of residential and small business cases, some form of DSL modem or local router, normally supplied by the Internet service provider, is used to access the Internet. PCs or servers are connected via a LAN (often a wireless LAN) connection to this device. The DSL modem or router typically provides a Dynamic Host Configuration Protocol (DHCP) service. In this style of connection, when a PC or server is powered on, it runs through a startup sequence during which a number of DHCP transactions occur. At the end of this process, configuration parameters will have been supplied notably including an IP address and one or more DNS addresses. Although in some cases the DNS address(es) supplied will point directly to the service provider's DNS resolver (4), increasingly the DNS address points to the DSL modem or local router (3), which will contain a *DNS proxy*. Depending on device manufacturer and Internet service provider policies, DNS proxy functionality varies wildly from a simple pass-through operation (nothing is changed), to caching and other more intrusive operations mostly designed to reduce load and speed up user responses, but they can have unintended side effects. No standards are defined for DNS proxies, but RFC 5625 contains a series of recommendations designed to minimize operational problems. In all cases, if the data is not available in any local cache, the queries are *forwarded* (passed on) to the DNS resolver (4).

- A PC or server can indirectly access the DNS resolver (4) through the DSL modem/router (3), as previously described, or directly through manual configuration or a DHCP service. This resolver is the real deal: a full-featured, heavyweight beast that performs a lot of work on behalf of its clients. It always contains a cache that it first inspects for any available answers to client queries. Just to illustrate the rich range of terminology available to the DNS user, this resolver can be and frequently is referred to as a *caching name server* or even a *recursive name server* (*recursive* is explained in Chapter 3). Because this resolver typically provides services for a very large number of client resolvers and proxies, its cache will likely already contain lots of answers, so the probability of a cache "hit" (the required data exists in the cache) will be high. However, if the answer is not present in its cache, this resolver, unlike all the previous stub-resolvers and DNS proxies we have seen so far, will chase down the DNS authoritative hierarchy (5), (6), and (7) to obtain the *authoritative answer* to the user's query, which it then sends to the user and places in its cache for future use by other queries.

There are many possible tactical variations on the scenario described previously, but for the vast majority of Internet users this is the normal method by which the name of a resource, such as www.example.com, is *resolved* (translated) into one (or more) IP addresses obtained from an authoritative name server. The key points to note in this scenario are the role played by various caches that are largely designed to speed up user response, but can also have unintended consequences, and the functionality of the DNS resolver (4), which reduces the complexity of client resolvers (stub-resolvers) and proxies by concentrating the complex and potentially dangerous job of accessing the DNS authoritative hierarchy. The configuration and functionality of a DNS resolver (4) and DNS authoritative name servers (5), (6), and (7) are explained further in Chapter 4, and detailed configuration samples are provided in Chapter 7.Any DNS program, either a DNS resolver or an authoritative name server, typically does three things:

- It reads one or more *zone files* (described in the following text), which describe the domains for which it is responsible or will use.

- Depending on the DNS software functionality, it reads a configuration file, which describes various required behaviors (for example, to cache or not).

- It responds to questions (queries) from local or remote clients (other name servers, resolvers, or proxies).

Zones and Zone Files

Name servers support what are called *zones*. The term *zone* and its relationship to a *domain name* can be very confusing. A zone is described using a *zone file* that translates the domain name into operational entities, such as hosts, mail servers, services, and other characteristics for use by DNS software. Subdomains delegated by the domain name owner can also be described using separate zone files. The original DNS specifications called them *subzones*—a term that has mercifully disappeared over time. A zone file therefore describes, using textual Resource Records (RRs), that part of the domain name being handled by the DNS software—a zone designates an operational (and *authoritative*) part of a domain name managed by a DNS or name server. The format of zone files and their RRs is standardized in RFC 1035. Zone files are therefore portable across all standard DNS software. A zone file will typically consist of the following types of RRs:

- Data that describes the zone's properties, known as the *Start of Authority (SOA) Resource Record*. This RR is mandatory in all zone files.

- All hosts within the zone—typically defined using Address (A) Resource Records for IPv4 and AAAA Resource Records for IPv6.

- Data that describes global information for the zone—typically *MX Resource Records* describing the domain's mail servers and *NS Resource Records* describing the name servers that are authoritative for the domain.

- In the case of subdomain delegation, the name servers responsible for this subdomain—using NS Resource Records.

- In the case of subdomain delegation, a record (called a *glue* record and described in Chapter 8) that allows the name server to reach the subdomain name server(s)—typically one or more A or AAAA Resource Records.

The following shows a simple example of a zone file showing most of the items mentioned in the preceding list. It is not important at this stage to understand the detail of any line, which is described in the next chapter.

```
; IPv4 zone file for example.com
$TTL 2d    ; default TTL for zone
$ORIGIN example.com.
; Start of Authority record defining the key characteristics of the zone (domain)
@        IN     SOA    ns1.example.com. hostmaster.example.com. (
                       2003080800 ; sn = serial number
                       12h        ; refresh
                       15m        ; retry = refresh retry
                       3w         ; expiry
                       2h         ; nx = nxdomain ttl
                       )
; name servers Resource Records for the domain
          IN     NS     ns1.example.com.
; the second name servers is
; external to this zone (domain).
          IN     NS     ns2.example.net.
; mail server Resource Records for the zone (domain)
```

```
        3w      IN      MX  10  mail.example.com.
; the second  mail servers is
; external to the zone (domain)
                IN      MX  20  mail.anotherdomain.com.
; domain hosts includes NS and MX records defined above
; plus any others required
ns1             IN      A       192.168.254.2
mail            IN      A       192.168.254.4
joe             IN      A       192.168.254.6
www             IN      A       192.168.254.7
```

The individual RRs are described in Chapter 2; many more sample zone files are presented in Chapter 7, and a complete RR reference is provided in Chapter 13.

Master and Slave DNS Servers

Early in this chapter, you saw that more than one authoritative name server is required to increase reliability and performance. It is not uncommon nowadays to see sites with four, five, or more name servers, each of which may be in a physically different location, and each of which must have access to the zone file. In order to reduce the management overheads involved in synchronizing zone files, the DNS specifications allow for a single DNS server to own a *master* copy of the zone file and to allow *zone transfers* (described in Chapter 3) to the other (*slave*) name servers. The terms *zone master*, or *master DNS*; and *zone slaves*, or *slave DNS*, are commonly applied to the respective name servers. The terms *master* and *slave* simply define which name server has the *master* copy of the zone file (loaded from a local file system) and which has a copy (loaded via zone transfer); they do not imply any priority of access. Both *masters* and *slaves* answer authoritatively for the zone. The master-slave relationship is illustrated in Figure 1–7.

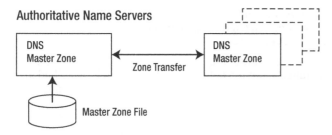

Figure 1–7. *Zone master and slave relationship*

Note In a perfect world, all terminology is unambiguous. The original DNS specifications used the terms *Primary* and/or *master* and *Secondary* (called *slave* previously) to describe the zone transfer process. The terms *Primary* and *Secondary* are still widely used to describe the order of DNS in many places such as registration of domain names and when defining network properties on PCs or hosts. In an attempt to reduce confusion, Berkeley Internet Name Domain (BIND) introduced the terms *master* and *slave* in the context of zone transfers, as shown earlier. This book will use these terms throughout. When reading other documents and purely in the context of zone transfers, Primary = master and Secondary = slave.

DNS Software

There is a dizzying choice of DNS software tailored to suit a range of user requirements. Berkeley Internet Name Domain—always referred to as BIND—is an Open Source implementation currently developed by the Internet Systems Consortium, Inc. (`www.isc.org`). It is probably the most widely known and deployed of the DNS implementations, and indeed most of this book documents BIND features. BIND, however, is by no means the only DNS solution available or for that matter the only Open Source DNS solution.

BIND has historically been viewed as the high-quality reference implementation of the Internet Engineering Task Force (IETF) RFCs that specify DNS functionality. As a consequence, BIND has generally traded performance for generic functionality. BIND, including the current production versions of BIND 9, is a "one size fits all" solution providing both DNS resolver and authoritative name server functionality within the same software package.

Microsoft Windows users are well provided with DNS solutions. The Microsoft Server packages come bundled with a native DNS server (providing DNS resolver and authoritative name server functionality). The production versions of BIND 9 provide a binary package that will run on Windows XP, Windows 2003 Server, and Windows 2008 Server.

But the world of DNS has undergone a serious transition, especially in the last five years or so, from being an essential, stable, perhaps even boring service to being now recognized as a critical (if not *the* critical) resource that keeps the Internet alive.

DNS software is changing to reflect the forces at work within the larger Internet, in particular:

- *Data sources*: Increasingly IP provisioning and management systems mean that larger organizations especially, but not exclusively, maintain IP and name data in other formats. DNS software needs to be more flexible in providing alternate data sources such as from transactional databases and LDAP as well as its traditional text-based zone file format.

- *Complexity*: DNSSEC particularly has added considerably to the complexity of DNS functionality. One of the classic responses to complexity is to increase specialization. DNS software is increasingly following this trend with separation of resolver functionality from authoritative name server functionality. In most cases, the happy consequence of this specialization is also an increase in performance.

- *Management*: Traditional DNS software has supplied clunky command-line style management interfaces. Increasingly users are demanding modern web-based management interfaces, both to improve responsiveness and to decrease errors.

- *Dynamic data*: One of the major criticisms leveled over the years against many of the DNS software implementations is the lack of ability to dynamically add or remove zones without having to stop and start the DNS server. This criticism reflects both the increasingly dynamic nature of the Internet—more changes, more frequently—and the increased volume of traffic involved. Many users are reluctant to stop answering queries for even the seconds needed to stop and restart DNS software. Although Dynamic DNS (DDNS), supported by BIND and described in Chapter 3, allows editing of individual RRs within zones, it cannot add or remove entire zones. Such a limitation is increasingly less acceptable; zones need to be added and removed dynamically without interrupting service.

Historically, all the root-servers used BIND software. In order to encourage diversity, some of the root-servers now run the NSD (www.nlnetlabs.nl/projects/nsd) software, which provides a Open Source, DNSSEC-ready, implementation optimized for high performance when acting as an authoritative name server only; it does not provide DNS resolver functionality. It has traded generic functionality for raw performance, which may be up to twice that offered by an equivalent BIND 9 configuration.

Unbound is an Open Source DNS resolver solution (www.unbound.net) that provides a high-performance C implementation of an original Java–based design exercise that also fully supports the latest DNSSEC standards.

Even BIND is not invulnerable to changes. BIND 10 is a multiyear radical restructuring program designed to bring significant functional and performance benefits to the extensive BIND user base. The first release of this new BIND 10 generation of products is an authoritative-only name server that is fully described in Chapter 14 with the configuration samples in Chapter 7 updated to cover both BIND 10 and BIND 9 where appropriate. A BIND 10 resolver–only product and a BIND 10 multifunction product (equivalent to today's BIND 9) will be released progressively over the coming years. BIND 9 will continue to be aggressively maintained throughout this multiyear period and will continue to be used in many environments for years to come.

Which DNS solution best works for any user will reflect the functional and organizational requirements and—as always—will require clear understanding of the trade-offs and limitations that may be involved.

It is important to remember that the format of zone files used by DNS software is standardized by RFC 1035. Migrating from one implementation of DNS software to another can thus be considerably eased. Where a feature is unique to BIND (not standardized), it will be clearly indicated in the text.

Summary

This chapter introduced a lot of terminology and concepts that will be used throughout the rest of the book. The text described the need for name servers, which translate the descriptive name of a resource to its physical network address, and identified them as being essential for the operation of a dynamic and flexible network of any size.

The Internet's Domain Name System (DNS) was introduced as being a specific implementation of the name server concept. You learned about the Internet's DNS domain name hierarchy, in particular the separation of the Top-Level Domains into Generic TLDs, for which ICANN is fully authoritative, and Country Code TLDs, which are administered by the individual sovereign countries. You now also know the component parts of a domain name; for instance, www.example.com consists of a host name (www), an SLD (example), and a TLD (.com). You also encountered the key concepts of an authority, the entity or person responsible for a particular node in the domain name hierarchy; and delegation, the process by which the authority at a higher level in the domain name hierarchy may transfer authority to lower levels. The chapter finally introduced DNS software, the server and resolver programs that execute the DNS function, including BIND, the most widely used and implemented DNS server software.

Chapter 2 unravels the mysteries of zone files and the most common Resource Records (RRs) used in these files.

CHAPTER 2

∎∎∎

Zone Files and
Resource Records

A zone file describes or translates a domain name into the characteristics, hosts, and services provided by the *domain* in a way that can be used by DNS software. Badly configured zone files can make a domain unreachable, send e-mail to the wrong location, or even redirect customers to a competitor's web site. Obviously, these are serious consequences, but it can get worse. Answers to *queries* from a badly configured DNS may be *cached* (or stored) by other DNS systems for hours, days, or even weeks. It can take a long time for the effects of an error to be rectified—your customers or employees can be left without service or access for prolonged periods. Correctly configured zone files are essential to the running of every service offered by an organization with Internet presence.

This chapter describes the format and layout of zone files and the most common *Resource Records* (RRs) and *directives* that are used in the *forward mapping* of a zone. Forward mapping defines the name-to-IP address relationship used by any hosts (or services) within the zone; for example, it could contain an RR that maps the host `www.example.com` to an IPv4 address such as 192.168.2.3. *Reverse-mapping* zones, which define the IP address-to-host relationship and the unique RRs used in their definition, are described in Chapter 3. A reverse-mapping zone file could, for instance, contain an RR that defines the IPv4 address 192.168.2.3 to have the name `www.example.com`. Because this topic is so central to DNS, zone files and their contents are discussed at length in several other chapters, most notably in Chapter 7, where I'll consider various zone file samples, and Chapter 13, which offers a complete reference on all the RRs and directives.

Zone File Format

Zone files are text files (standardized by RFC 1035) that may be read or edited using any standard editor and can contain three types of entries:

- *Comments*: All comments start with a semicolon (;) and continue to the end of the line. Comments can be added to any other record type and are assumed to terminate the line.

- *Directives*: All directives start with a dollar sign ($) and are used to control processing of the zone files.

- *Resource Records*: Resource Records (RR) are used to define the characteristics, properties, or entities contained within the domain. RRs are contained on a single line with the exception that entries enclosed in parentheses can spread across multiple lines.

- *Field Separators*: The separators between fields in a RR can be either spaces or tabs. In zone files, tabs are traditionally used to make a more attractive layout and to clearly indicate which fields are missing.

The following is a sample zone file fragment that illustrates the preceding points and entry types:

```
; this is a full line comment
$TTL 12h     ; directive - comment terminates the line
$ORIGIN example.com.
; Start of Authority (SOA) record defining the zone (domain)
; illustrates an RR record spread over more than one line
; using the enclosing parentheses
@  IN  SOA  ns1.example.com. hostmaster.example.com. (
              2003080800 ; se = serial number
              3h             ; ref = refresh
              15m            ; ret = update retry
              3w             ; ex = expiry
              2h20m          ; min = minimum
              )
; single line RR
    IN  NS  ns1.example.com.
...
```

The preceding Start of Authority RR could have been written on a single line like so:

```
@  IN  SOA  ns1.example.com. hostmaster.example.com. 2003080800 3h 15m 3w 3h
```

■**Note** Standard RFC 1035 zone files define time periods in seconds, which results in very large numbers. In the preceding fragment, the values 3h, 15m, 3w, and 2h20m use a BIND-specific short form for time-in-seconds values. The case-insensitive short forms allowed are m = minutes, h = hours, d = days, and w = weeks. The standards-compliant time-in-seconds values used previously would be 10800, 900, 1814400, and 8400, respectively. This book uses the BIND short format throughout simply because it is more easily understood. A number of alternative DNS implementations have adopted the BIND format as a de facto standard. If you want to stick to the standard and use seconds, keep a calculator handy.

Zone File Contents

One of the many confusing aspects of zone file definition is that it offers many shortcuts and ways to avoid excessive two-finger typing. In general, there is more than one way to do almost everything in a zone file. In the interests of clarity, this chapter uses a single zone file format to avoid confusion. Where appropriate, shortcuts and alternative formats will be illustrated.

In general, a zone file will typically contain the following RRs and directives, each of which is described in more detail later in the chapter:

- *The* $TTL *directive*: Defines the default *Time to Live* (TTL) value for the zone or domain, which is the time a RR may be *cached* (or saved) by another DNS server. This directive is mandatory.

- *The* $ORIGIN *directive*: The domain name for the zone being defined. This directive is optional.

- *A Start of Authority (SOA) RR*: The SOA RR, which must appear as the first RR in a zone file, describes the global characteristics of the zone or domain. There can be only one SOA RR in a zone file. This RR is mandatory.

- *The Name Server (NS) RR*: Defines name servers that are authoritative for the zone or domain. There must be two or more NS RRs in a zone file. NS RRs may reference servers in this domain or in a *foreign* or *external* domain. These RRs are mandatory.

- *The Mail Exchanger (MX) RR*: Defines the mail servers for the zone. There may be zero or more MX RRs in a zone file. If the domain does not provide e-mail services, there is no need for any MX RRs. An MX RR may reference a mail server in this domain or in a foreign or external domain. This RR is optional.

- *The Address (A) RR*: Used to define the IPv4 address of all the hosts (or services) that exist in this zone and are required to be publicly visible. IPv6 entries are defined using AAAA (called *Quad A*) RRs. There may zero or more A or AAAA RRs in a zone file. This RR is optional.

- *The CNAME RR*: Defines an Alias RR, which allows one host (or service) to be defined as the alias name for another host. There may be zero or more CNAME RRs in a zone file. This RR is optional.

Other RR types and directives exist, some of which will be introduced in later chapters. You'll find a full list of RR types and zone file directives defined in Chapter 13. The preceding RRs and directives allow the definition of a fully functional zone file.

An Example Zone File

The example zone file that appears later in this section illustrates the general format of a zone file and shows how RRs are used to describe the characteristics of the zone. Each directive and RR is described in detail and in the context of this example zone file. In this example, the zone example.com has the following characteristics:

- The zone has two name servers: one hosted in this domain (ns1.example.com), the other externally (ns2.example.net).

- The zone has two mail servers: one hosted in the domain (mail.example.com) and a second (backup) mail server hosted externally (mail.example.net).

- The zone has an internal web service with a name of www.example.com.

- The zone has an FTP server with a name of ftp.example.com (but provided by ftp.example.net).

- The zone has a single publicly visible host called joe.example.com.

The preceding scenario both illustrates some specific features of zone files and defines a zone that will provide some important services even in the event of failures or outages. Figure 2–1 shows the preceding configuration in operation.

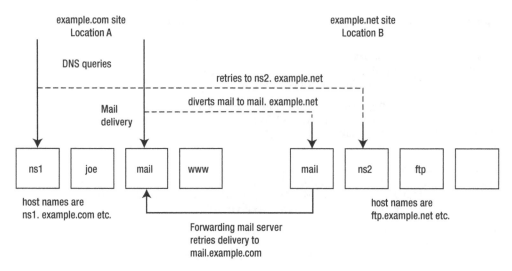

Figure 2–1. Example configuration

The configuration provides some simple resilience and will continue to accept mail even if the site at Location A is offline for some period of time. It achieves resilience using the following strategies:

- There are two name servers located in separate physical locations. In the event ns1.example.com is unreachable, ns2.example.net will continue to provide DNS service for example.com. Failure to provide for geographical separation of name servers led to Microsoft's web sites being offline for over 23 hours in one famous incident in 2001.[1]

- In the event that mail cannot be delivered to mail.example.com, the zone records (the MX RRs described in the "The MX Resource Record" section later in this chapter) will cause redirection to mail.example.net. The server mail.example.net would be configured as a forwarding mail server for the domain example.com. The mail server mail.example.net will retry at periodic intervals to deliver the mail to mail.example.com. No mail will be lost even during extended outages.

Many smaller sites think this kind of resilient configuration is only for large and complex organizations and therefore locate both the alternate name and mail servers on the same site. There is nothing wrong with this kind of configuration, and indeed it's very common, especially in smaller organizations and a surprising number of large ones as well. However, it's also easier than you think to organize peering by simply swapping backups with another friendly or noncompetitive site (that is, you back up for me and I'll back up for you). Both sites gain the same resilience, and no money need change hands because the additional traffic should be negligible at both locations as long as the sites are reasonably similar in traffic volumes.

Clearly, the web site at www.example.com would be non-operational during an outage of location A, but you may already see that by using the name server at ns2.example.net this could be replicated by

---

[1] Declan McCullagh, "How, Why Microsoft Went Down",
www.wired.com/news/technology/0,1282,41412,00.html, January 25, 2001

simply defining an alternate IP address for the host www.example.com in the zone file used by this name server. Chapter 8 describes some additional ways to provide resilience using the DNS features.

The zone file that describes this configuration is shown here:

```
; IPv4 zone file for example.com
$TTL 2d     ; default TTL for zone
$ORIGIN example.com. ; base domain-name
; Start of Authority record defining the key characteristics
; of the zone (domain)
@          IN      SOA   ns1.example.com. hostmaster.example.com. (
                         2003080800 ; se = serial number
                         12h        ; ref = refresh
                         15m        ; ret = refresh retry
                         3w         ; ex = expiry
                         2h         ; nx = nxdomain ttl
                         )
; name servers Resource Records for the domain
           IN      NS      ns1.example.com.
; the second name server is
; external to this zone (domain).
           IN      NS      ns2.example.net.
; mail server Resource Records for the zone (domain)
; value 10 denotes it is the most preferred
    3w     IN      MX  10  mail.example.com.
; the second mail server has lower preference (20) and is
; external to the zone (domain)
           IN      MX  20  mail.example.net.
; domain hosts includes NS and MX records defined previously
; plus any others required
ns1        IN      A       192.168.254.2
mail       IN      A       192.168.254.4
joe        IN      A       192.168.254.6
www        IN      A       192.168.254.7
; aliases ftp (ftp server) to an external location
ftp        IN      CNAME   ftp.example.net.
```

The following sections explain each directive and RR type used in this example zone file.

The $TTL Directive

Every Resource Record may take an optional Time to Live value specified in seconds. The $TTL directive is standardized in RFC 2038 and defines the default TTL value applied to any RR that does not have an explicit TTL defined. TTL in the DNS context defines the time in seconds that a record may be cached by another name server or a *resolver*. Caching is explained in Chapter 4.

The formal syntax for this directive is

```
$TTL time-in-seconds
```

from the example zone file

```
$TTL 2d
```

The preceding $TTL directive uses the *BIND-specific* short form d to indicate days. The RFC 2038 format equivalent is as follows:

```
$TTL 172800
```

The time-in-seconds value may take the value 0, which indicates never cache the record, to a maximum of 2147483647, which is over 68 years! The current best practice recommendation (RFC 1912) proposes a value greater than one day; on RRs that rarely change you should consider multiweek values.

The TTL determines two DNS operational characteristics:

- *Access load*: The lower the TTL, the more rapidly it is removed from resolver caches—forcing more frequent DNS queries to occur and thus raising the operational load on the zone's name server.

- *Change propagation*: The TTL value represents the maximum time that any change will take to propagate from the zone name server to all users.

It's simple to change the zone-wide TTL by altering a single $TTL zone file directive. Many users will set this to a very high value, such as two weeks or more, in normal operational use and thus minimize name server access. When planned changes and upgrades occur that affect the zone records, for example, IP address changes or new service installation, the $TTL will be reduced in advance to a lower value such as 12 hours (12h or 43200). When service has stabilized, the TTL will be restored to the previous high value. The default value 2d used in the example file represents a reasonable balance for stable zones, but the MX RR is assumed to be super-stable and so has an explicit TTL value of 3 weeks (3w or 1814400). Chapter 8 contains a longer discussion on use of the TTL.

The $TTL directive must appear before any RR to which it will be applied, and BIND 9 will now refuse to load a zone that does not have a valid $TTL directive.

Note In older versions of BIND (prior to BIND 9), the default TTL value for the zone was defined in the SOA RR (described in the "The SOA Resource Record" section later in this chapter). RFC 2308 defines both implementation of the $TTL directive and the change to the SOA RR.

The $ORIGIN Directive

The $ORIGIN directive was standardized in RFC 1035; it defines the domain name that will be appended to any incomplete name (sometimes called an *unqualified* name) defined in an RR. This process, whereby a value is appended to names that do not end with a dot, is a major source of confusion, anger, and puzzlement when running DNS systems because the process happens invisibly.

The $ORIGIN Substitution Rule If a name appears in a RR and does *not* end with a dot, then the value of the last or only $ORIGIN directive will be appended to the name. If the name ends with a dot, then it is a *fully qualified domain name* (FQDN) and nothing will be appended. This rule will be illustrated in the following section. The terminating dot in a FQDN is interpreted as the root of the domain tree or hierarchy. As mentioned in Chapter 1, although this dot is normally silent (omitted), it's occasionally VERY important. This rule requires careful attention as to whether the dot is present.

The formal syntax for $ORIGIN is

```
$ORIGIN domain-name
```

returning to the example zone file

```
$ORIGIN example.com.
```

The name of the domain defined by this zone file (example.com.) is defined in the $ORIGIN directive. To avoid confusion the domain-name should be a FQDN as it ends with a dot. $ORIGIN directives can appear anywhere in a zone file and will be used from the point they are defined onwards, like so:

```
$ORIGIN example.com.
; RRs from here will append example.com.
....
...
$ORIGIN us.example.com.
; RRs from here will append us.example.com.
...
```

The $ORIGIN directive is not mandatory. If not present, BIND 9 will create the $ORIGIN value from the zone name defined in its configuration file (the named.conf file described in Chapter 7). BIND 10's loadzone utility requires a command line option (see Chapter 14). This book always uses an $ORIGIN directive in zone files for three reasons:

- A zone file is self-descriptive and self-contained; it requires no reference to any further information.

- The substitution rule (defined previously) is much less confusing. The value to be substituted is immediately apparent (that is, the last $ORIGIN directive).

- Not all software may implement the same assumptions about a missing $ORIGIN directive (as indeed do BIND 9 and BIND 10). Zone files are more portable when the directive is included.

It is always tempting to take shortcuts, but as with all things, there may be consequences.

The SOA Resource Record

The SOA Resource Record defines the key characteristics and attributes for the zone or domain and is standardized in RFC 1035. As befits the most important RR in the zone file, it's among the most complex and takes a significant number of parameters. The formal syntax of the SOA RR is as follows:

```
name  ttl class rr name-server e-mail sn refresh retry expiry min
```

Here is the SOA RR from the example zone file:

```
@           IN      SOA     ns1.example.com. hostmaster.example.com. (
                            2003080800 ; sn = serial number
                            3h         ; refresh time
                            15m        ; retry = refresh retry
                            3w         ; expiry
                            3h         ; nx = nxdomain ttl
                            )
```

The SOA RR illustrates two layout rules previously described:

- It typically uses the standard multiline format where the open parenthesis must appear on the first line; the closing parenthesis can appear on the same or any subsequent line.

- The separators between fields can be either spaces or tabs. In zone files, tabs are traditionally used to make a more attractive layout and to clearly indicate which fields are missing.

Table 2–1 maps the values from the example file to the formal syntax.

Table 2–1. SOA RR Syntax

Syntax	Example Usage	Description
name	@	The @ symbol substitutes the current value of $ORIGIN (in the example file this is example.com.).
ttl		There is no ttl value defined for the RR, so the zone default of 2d (172800 seconds) from the $TTL directive will be used.
class	IN	IN defines the class to be Internet (defaulted if omitted). Other values exist but are rarely used. They are defined in Chapter 13 purely for the sake of completeness.
name-server	ns1.example.com.	Defines the Primary Master name server for the zone and has a special meaning only when used with Dynamic DNS configurations, which are covered in Chapter 3. The name server referenced here also needs to be defined using an NS RR. In DNS specifications, this is called the MNAME field.

Syntax	Example Usage	Description
e-mail	hostmaster. example.com.	Defines an administrative e-mail address for the zone. It is recommended in RFC 2142 that the e-mail address *hostmaster* be used uniquely for this purpose, but any stable and valid e-mail address can be used. While this field uses unusual dot separators (the @ symbol has special significance in a zone as described earlier) to define the e-mail address, in the case of the example file, mail will be sent to hostmaster@example.com. In DNS specifications, this is known as the RNAME field.
sn	2003080800	Defines the serial number currently associated with the zone. The serial number *must* be updated every time any change is made to the domain. Note that sn can take any number in the range of 0 to 4294967295. By convention (but this is only a convention), a date format is used with the form yyyymmddss, where yyyy is the four-digit year number, mm is the month, dd is the day, and ss is the sequence number in case the zone file is updated more than once per day! The value from the example zone file indicates that the last update was on August 8, 2003. This value is used during zone transfer operations (described in Chapter 3) to determine whether the zone file has changed. Recovery from an out-of-sequence sn value is not trivial, as you'll see in Chapter 8. Extreme care should be taken when updating this number. The use of a date convention is designed to minimize errors as well as to provide a simple way to track the date of the last change to the zone but it's not universally implemented.
refresh	12h	When the refresh value is reached, the slave name server (described in Chapter 1) for this zone will try to read the SOA RR from the zone master. If the sn value in the SOA RR is higher than that currently stored by the slave, a zone transfer operation is initiated to update or refresh the slave's copy of the zone records. Depending on how the zone transfers are implemented, the value of this parameter may determine how quickly changes are propagated from the master to the slave. Zone transfers are described in Chapter 3. Typical values are from 3 to 24 hours.
retry	15m	Defines the retry interval in seconds if the slave fails to make contact with the zone master during a refresh cycle. Typical values are from 10 to 60 minutes.
expiry	3w	Defines the time in seconds after which the zone records are assumed to be no longer authoritative. BIND interprets this to mean that the records can no longer be considered valid and consequentially stops responding to queries for the zone. Thus, when the refresh time limit is reached, the slave will try to contact the zone master; in the case of a failure, it will attempt reconnection every retry period. If contact is made, both the refresh and expiry counts are reset. If the slave has failed to make contact when expiry is reached, the slave will stop responding to any queries. The zone is essentially dead at this point. To allow for major outages, expiry is typically set to a very high value such as one to three weeks.

Syntax	Example Usage	Description
nx	3h	nxwas redefined in RFC 2308 to be the period of time that negative responses can be cached by a resolver. Thus, if a request is made for fred.example.com and it can't be resolved (because it doesn't exist), then the resolver will return Name Error (also known as NXDOMAIN). The resolver will continue to return this value until nx expires, at which point it will retry the failing operation. BIND allows an nx value in the range 0 to 10800 (three hours).

To illustrate the use of the $ORIGIN statement and its substitution rule, this zone file fragment shows how it's possible to rewrite the SOA statement:

```
; fragment from example - does not use substitution
$TTL 2d     ; default TTL for zone
$ORIGIN example.com.
; Start of Authority record defining the key characteristics of the zone (domain)
@           IN      SOA   ns1.example.com. hostmaster.example.com. (
                          2003080800 ; sn = serial number
                          12h          ; ref = refresh
                          15m          ; ret = refresh retry
                          3w           ; ex = expiry
                          2h           ; nx = nxdomain ttl
                          )
```

The SOA RR could be rewritten to use the $ORIGIN substitution rule as shown here:

```
; fragment rewritten to use $ORIGIN substitution
$TTL 2d     ; default TTL for zone
$ORIGIN example.com.
; Start of Authority record defining the key characteristics of the zone (domain)
@           IN      SOA   ns1 hostmaster (
                          2003080800 ; sn = serial number
                          12h          ; ref = refresh
                          15m          ; ret = refresh retry
                          3w           ; ex = expiry
                          2h           ; nx = nxdomain ttl
                          )
```

In the preceding fragment, because ns1 and hostmaster are not FQDNs (they do not end with a dot), the value of the $ORIGIN is appended to each name, creating ns1.example.com. and hostmaster.example.com., respectively, as in the initial example file. This format is rarely seen, however, as it can be quite confusing, although it is technically and functionally correct.

■**Note** The name field used in all the RRs (termed in DNS jargon a *label*) was originally defined to allow any letter, digit, or a dash (—); names or labels must start and end with a letter or a number. The specifications were liberalized by RFC 2181 to allow underscores (_). However, there are reputedly still implementations that don't allow them in host names, so it's safest to avoid underscores if possible.

The NS Resource Record

The NS Resource Record is standardized in RFC 1035 and defines the authoritative name servers (there must be at least two) for the domain or zone. The NS RR syntax is as follows:

```
name    ttl    class    rr    name
```

Let's return to the example file:

```
; name servers Resource Records for the domain
            IN    NS    ns1.example.com.
; the second name server is
; external to this zone (domain).
            IN    NS    ns2.example.net.
```

Table 2–2 wraps the formal syntax to the first NS record used in the example zone file, which is internal to the zone.

Table 2–2. NS RR Syntax

Syntax	Example Usage	Description
Name		This field is blank (may be either a space or a tab character) and implicitly substitutes the current value of the name field (in this case, the name field of the SOA RR). You could also write this record as example.com. IN NS ns1.example.com., which may be less confusing. This is an example of how the same result may be achieved in different ways.
ttl		There is no ttl value defined for the RR, so the zone default of 2d from the $TTL directive will be used.
class	IN	IN defines the class to be Internet.
name	ns1.example.com.	Defines a name server that is authoritative for the domain. In this example, an FQDN format has been used, but it could have been written as just ns1 (without the dot) and $ORIGIN substitution would take place. This NS record points to a name server within the domain and therefore MUST have a corresponding A RR for IPv4 (or AAAA RR if IPv6) defined.

The second NS RR from the example file is as follows:

```
            IN    NS    ns2.example.net.
```

This is the classic method of defining a second name server for the domain. In the event that one name server is not available, the alternate server (ideally at a geographically different location) will be used, thus ensuring access to services such as mail even if the main site is not available due to backbone, power, or other system outages.

The second NS RR is defined to be in a foreign or external zone and therefore does not require an A RR if IPv4 (or AAAA RR if IPv6) is defined. In addition, it MUST be defined using an FQDN; in other words, it must terminate with a dot. To illustrate the possible errors that may be caused inadvertently by

$ORIGIN substitution, assume that the terminating dot on this RR was omitted in error, that is, it was written as ns2.example.net (without a terminating dot). DNS software would apply substitution and create a name of ns2.example.net.example.com.—not the desired result!

■**Note** The external name server (ns2.example.net) must contain a zone file and be either a master or a slave for the zone example.com. Failure to do so will result in what is called *lame delegation*. Lame delegation occurs when an NS RR points to a name server that does not answer authoritatively for the zone or domain.

The MX Resource Record

The MX RR is standardized in RFC 1035 and defines the mail servers (or *mail exchangers* in the quaint DNS jargon) for the domain or zone. The formal syntax is as follows:

```
name     ttl    class   rr  preference  name
```

In the example file, the following MX RRs are defined:

```
; mail server Resource Records for the zone (domain)
     3w         IN      MX  10  mail.example.com.
; the second  mail server is
; external to the zone (domain)
                IN      MX  20  mail.example.net.
```

Table 2–3 maps the formal syntax to the first MX record used in the example file, which is internal to the domain.

Table 2–3. MX RR Syntax

Syntax	Example Usage	Description
name		This field is blank and implicitly substitutes the value of the right-hand name field from the previous RR (in the example file, this is example.com.).
ttl	3w	This illustrates the use of an explicit ttl value in a RR that overrides the zone default (defined in the $TTL directive). The value shown (three weeks) is significantly higher than the example zone default, which is two days. Because the domain MX RR is unlikely to change (its corresponding A RR may change more frequently) why not minimize the DNS load on what is normally a very actively used RR type? The ttl can, however, take any value required including omission, in which case the zone default will be used.
class	IN	IN defines the class to be Internet.

Syntax	Example Usage	Description
preference	10	The *preference* field indicates the relative preference or priority of the mail server it defines and can take any value between 0 and 65535. The lower the number, the more preferred the server. Traditionally, the most preferred mail server has the preference value 10. There is absolutely no reason for this other than it allows another MX record with a more preferred value (a lower number) to be added without changing any other record!
name	mail.example.com.	Defines a mail server with the defined preference value for the domain. In this example, an FQDN format has been used, but you could write this as just mail (without the dot) and an $ORIGIN substitution will take place. This MX record points to a mail server within the domain and therefore must have a corresponding A RR for IPv4 (or AAAA for IPv6).

The second MX RR from the example file is as follows:

```
IN      MX   20  mail.example.net.
```

This is the classic method of defining a backup mail server, which has a lower preference value (20 in the example). In the event that the first mail server is not available, the backup mail server (ideally at a geographically different location) would be used. This backup mail server would normally be defined as a simple forwarding mail server for the domain, constantly attempting to pass the mail to the most preferred (or primary) mail server (mail.example.com) when service is happily restored.

The second MX RR is defined to be in a foreign or external domain and therefore does not require an A RR if IPv4 (or an AAAA RR if IPv6) is defined and MUST always be an FQDN (in other words, it must end with a dot).

The A Resource Record

The A RR is standardized in RFC 1035 and defines the IPv4 address of a particular host in the domain or zone. The equivalent RR for IPv6 is the AAAA RR described in Chapter 5. The formal syntax of the Address RR is as follows:

```
name    ttl    class   rr   ipv4
```

In the example file, the following A RRs are defined:

```
ns1           IN      A       192.168.254.2
mail          IN      A       192.168.254.4
joe           IN      A       192.168.254.6
www           IN      A       192.168.254.7
```

Table 2–4 maps the formal syntax to the first A RR used in the example zone file.

Table 2–4. A RR Syntax

Syntax	Example Usage	Description
name	ns1	The name is unqualified, causing $ORIGIN substitution. You could write this as ns1.example.com. (using the FQDN format), which may be more understandable.
ttl		There is no ttl value defined for the RR, so the zone default of 2d from the $TTL directive will be used.
class	IN	IN defines the class to be Internet.
ipv4	192.168.254.2	Defines that the host ns1 has the physical IPv4 address192.168.254.2. Records defined by NS or MX RRs that have names contained within this domain MUST have corresponding A RRs as shown in the example zone file for ns1 and mail. Any other hosts the user wishes to make publicly visible are also defined using A RRs; in the example file, this includes the web service (www) and the host named joe for some reason best known to the owner of the domain.

It is permissible to define the same IP address with multiple names as shown in the following fragment (here the name server and the web server are co-located on the same machine):

```
ns1         IN      A       192.168.254.2
mail        IN      A       192.168.254.4
joe         IN      A       192.168.254.6
; this A RR has the same IPv4 address as ns1 above
www         IN      A       192.168.254.2
```

The same result can be achieved using a CNAME record (see the next section). Multiple IP addresses can also be defined for the same host as in this fragment, where three IPv4 addresses are provided for the host www.example.com:

```
www         IN      A       192.168.254.2
            IN      A       192.168.254.7
            IN      A       192.168.254.8
```

DNS software will supply the defined IP address in a round-robin or random order (defined by configuration directives) to successive queries. This feature may be used to provide load balancing and is further described in Chapter 8. The preceding fragment also illustrates the use of a *null* or *blank* name to inherit the previous name; that is, all the entries with a blank name relate to www (and assuming an $ORIGIN directive of example.com will define www.example.com).

CNAME Resource Record

The CNAME RR is standardized in RFC 1035 and defines an alias for an existing host defined by an A RR. The formal syntax is as follows:

```
name    ttl     class   rr  canonical-name
```

In the example file, the following CNAME RR is defined:

```
ftp          IN     CNAME   ftp.example.net.
```

Table 2–5 maps the formal syntax to the CNAME RR used in the example zone file.

Table 2–5. CNAME RR Syntax

Syntax	Example Usage	Description
name	ftp	The name is unqualified, causing the $ORIGIN directive value to be substituted. You could write this as ftp.example.com. (using the FQDN format), which may be more understandable.
ttl		There is no ttl value defined for the RR, so the zone default of 2d from the $TTL directive will be used.
class	IN	IN defines the class to be Internet.
canonical-name	ftp.example.net.	Defines that the name ftp.example.com is *aliased* to the host ftp.example.net. in a foreign or external domain. In DNS jargon, ftp.example.net. is referred to as the *canonical name*, which simply means the expected or real name.

CNAME RRs are often used when assigning *service* names to existing hosts; for example, if a host is actually called bill but runs an FTP and a web service, then CNAME RRs are frequently used to define these services, as shown in the following fragment:

```
ftp       IN     CNAME      bill
www       IN     CNAME      bill
bill      IN     A          192.168.254.21
```

CNAME RRs have some limitations. It is permissible but considered very bad practice to chain CNAME records.

```
ns1       IN     A          192.168.254.2
mail      IN     A          192.168.254.3
joe       IN     CNAME      www.example.com.
www       IN     CNAME      mail.example.com.
```

CNAME records should not be used with either NS or MX records; thus in the example file, if the mail server and web server were co-located on the same host, the following would be technically invalid but would typically work; this is an approach that is widely used!

```
          IN     MX         mail.example.com.
mail      IN     CNAME      www.example.com.
www       IN     A          192.168.254.7
```

The following fragment is valid and achieves the same result:

```
          IN     MX         mail.example.com.
mail      IN     A          192.168.254.7
www       IN     CNAME      mail.example.com.
```

The rule defining the preceding example (RFC 1034 section 3.6.2) is cautious in regard to use of excessive indirection and says that if a name appears on the right-hand side of an RR (as `mail.example.com` does in the preceding MX RR in the fragment), it should not appear in the left-hand name of a CNAME RR. Many working configurations use this construct routinely. There is always a risk that one day the specification may be tightened and the configuration may not work.

You need to be aware of two other consequences when using CNAME RR. First, CNAME causes the name server to do more work because both the CNAME and the CNAME'd RR must be looked up by the name server. In high-volume name servers, this additional workload may be a consideration. Second, the CNAME RR and the target (CNAME'd) RR record are returned in the answer. When dealing with large answers, this may cause the response to exceed the 512-byte limit of a DNS UDP transaction, thus reducing performance.

When CNAME Records Must Be Used

As noted in the previous section, CNAME RRs are frequently and commonly used to map services such as FTP, web, gopher, and others onto a single host. In these cases, multiple A RRs may also be used to achieve the same result. In general, the only time a CNAME must be used is when the real or canonical host lies in a foreign or external domain, as illustrated in the example file where `ftp.example.com` is aliased to `ftp.example.net`. A CNAME RR is frequently used when the user wishes to address a web site using either `www.example.com` or just `example.com`. In this case, the functionality would typically be implemented using the following fragment:

```
; define an IP that resolves to example.com
            IN    A      192.168.254.7
; alias www.example.com to example.com
www         IN    CNAME      example.com.
```

Here, defining the `www` RR as a simple A RR will achieve exactly the same result. Either form will require a configuration change to your web server, which is fully covered in Chapter 8.

Additional Resource Records

In this chapter, you have seen the main RRs used in constructing zone files. Many more RR types exist; these are documented with examples in Chapter 13. For the sake of completeness, some of the more commonly used additional or specialized RRs are briefly described in the following sections.

PTR Resource Records

Pointer (PTR) RRs are used only for *reverse-mapping* zones and are the corollary of the Address RRs. PTR RRs map an IPv4 address to a name; an A RR *forward-maps* a name to an IPv4 address. Reverse mapping and PTR records are described in Chapter 3. PTR RRs are also used when *reverse mapping* an IPv6 zone, as you'll see in Chapter 5.

TXT Resource Records

Text (TXT) RRs were historically used to define generic text to be associated with a name. The text may be anything the user wishes. The Sender Policy Framework (SPF) and DKIM antispam initiatives both use the TXT RR to carry information. You'll find the SPF and DKIM formats defined in Chapter 8 and the generic TXT RR in Chapter 13.

AAAA Resource Records

The AAAA RR is used to define *forward mapping* of IPv6 hosts, which is covered in Chapter 5.

NSEC, RRSIG, DS, DNSKEY, and KEY Resource Records

These RRs are used in Secure DNS (DNSSEC) configurations as described in Chapters 10 and 11.

SRV Resource Records

Service (SRV) RRs are used to map services onto hosts. Chapter 13 describes the SRV RR, and Chapter 8 contains a discussion of the use of SRV records in load balancing and resilience.

Standard Configuration File Scenarios

Chapter 7 defines further example configurations, including the required zone files for common DNS types such as master, slave, caching, forwarding, and authoritative-only name servers. Chapter 8 contains a number of common configurations that illustrate various aspects of zone files, and Chapter 13 includes a full reference section on zone files and Resource Records.

Summary

This chapter described the format and content of zone files. You learned about the $TTL directive that is used to set the default TTL for the zone. You also encountered the $ORIGIN directive, used to set the base name for the zone, and the $ORIGIN substitution rule, the cause of much DNS aggravation. Using the example zone file as a guide, the text explained the various Resource Record types used to construct basic zone files such as the Start of Authority, Name Server, Mail Exchanger, and Address Resource Records.

Chapter 3 explains DNS operations: the types of DNS queries that may be used; reverse mapping, the process by which an IP address may be mapped to a host name; zone transfers, the method by which zone files are updated from the master to the slave name servers; and finally, a brief overview of the security issues involved in running a DNS service.

CHAPTER 3

■ ■ ■

DNS Operations

This chapter describes the operation of a DNS system. Namely, you'll learn about the following topics:

- *DNS queries*: How does your browser find `www.example.com`? How does your mail software know where to send your outgoing e-mail? Such operations use DNS queries.

- *Reverse mapping*: How does your mail software determine your identity? How do you find out who is hacking your system? These types of operations use a technique known as reverse mapping.

- *Zone maintenance*: How does the address of your new FTP service get propagated across the Internet? How are your customers notified of any change to your e-mail provider? These operations use zone maintenance.

- *DNS security*: How do you prevent your web site from being hijacked? How do you ensure that your e-mail is delivered to you and not someone else? In this chapter, you'll learn key DNS security concepts.

This chapter references configuration directives defined in BIND 9's `named.conf` file, which controls its operational behavior. Chapter 12 describes these directives. A number of zone files containing DNS Resource Records (RRs) are used to illustrate certain points, as discussed in Chapter 2. Chapter 13 contains a complete reference on each record type. The PTR RRs used in reverse mapping of a zone are described in this chapter.

But first let's get some simple DNS protocol details out of the way.

The DNS Protocol

DNS operations for example, queries, and zone maintenance operations by default use port 53. For performance reasons, queries use the UDP protocol with a block-size limit of 512 bytes. TCP can be optionally negotiated on a transaction-by-transaction basis for query operations, but due to the performance overhead incurred with TCP, this is essentially a theoretical capability. Historically, exceeding the 512-byte response size limit was typically avoided at all costs, and indeed the limit of 13 IPv4 root-servers was the maximum that could be returned in a single 512-byte UDP transaction.

Both IPv6, with its significantly longer addresses, and DNSSEC are inexorably increasing the volume of data in DNS transactions. To avoid using TCP when the DNS transaction block size exceeds 512 btyes, a feature called Extended DNS 0 RFC 2671 (EDNS0) is used. EDNS0 (described in more detail in Chapter 17) essentially negotiates an extended UDP block size. BIND 9 and 10 both negotiate a maximum EDNS0 block size of 4096 (4K) bytes by default, though this can be configured. Even when EDNS0 has negotiated this large block size, the majority of nonsecure DNS transactions will still fall under the 512-byte limit. However, implementation of DNSSEC means that block sizes in the range of 1.7K to 2.4K, or even higher, will not be uncommon. At these block sizes, IP fragmentation is required on many communications media including the ubiquitous Ethernet LAN. Although IP fragmentation is a normal transparent part of IP software, the quality of its implementation can vary widely across the various local routers and DSL modems that form the most common parts of today's local communications infrastructure. Zone maintenance operations for reliability reasons use TCP, again by default on port 53.

■**Note** BIND 9 and 10 can be optionally configured to use a port other than 53 for queries or zone maintenance.

DNS Queries

The major task carried out by an authoritative name server is to respond to *queries* (questions) from a local or remote *DNS Resolver* or another name server acting on behalf of a resolver. The PC *resolver* (or more normally the *stub-resolver*) is the software library installed on each PC used to translate a user or application request to a DNS query. For instance, a typical query would be "What is the IP address of www.example.com?" The PC resolver will use a locally configured DNS Resolver, as explained in Chapter 1, "DNS in Action," to perform the queries. Figure 3–1 illustrates this process.

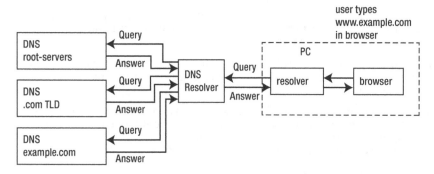

Figure 3–1. DNS queries

■**Note** The list of DNS Resolvers used by the PC resolver (or stub-resolver) is obtained using DHCP, or can be manually configured using Network Properties in Windows systems and /etc/resolv.conf in Linux, BSD, or UNIX systems.

A name server or resolver can have zone files that define it to be authoritative for some (if any) domains and slaves for others; and can be configured to provide caching, forwarding, or other behaviors for other domains or users. Zone files were introduced in Chapter 2.

There are three types of queries defined for DNS systems:

- *Recursive queries*: A recursive query is one in which the receiving name server (resolver) will do all the work necessary to return the complete answer to the question. Answering a query recursively may cause the name server (resolver) to send multiple query transactions to a number of authoritative name servers in the DNS hierarchy in order to fully resolve the requested name. Name servers/resolvers are not required to support recursive queries.

- *Iterative (or nonrecursive) queries*: In an iterative query, if the name server (resolver) has the answer or if it is available in its cache, it will return it. If the name server does not have the answer, it will return any information, generally a *referral* to the next delegation level, that may be useful, but it will not make additional requests to other name server systems. All name servers must support iterative queries.

- *Inverse queries*: The user wants to know the domain name given a RR. Name servers were not required to support inverse queries, and the feature was rarely, if ever, implemented. It finally succumbed to the inevitable when RFC 3425 declared it to be obsolete.

■**Note** The process called *reverse mapping*, which returns a host name given an IP address, does not use inverse queries but instead uses recursive and iterative (nonrecursive) queries using the special domain name `IN-ADDR.ARPA` (described later in this chapter). Historically, reverse IPv4 mapping was not mandatory. Many systems—especially mail servers—now use reverse mapping for simple security and authentication checks, so proper implementation and maintenance of reverse mapping is now practically essential.

Next, I'll introduce each type of query in further detail.

Recursive Queries

A *recursive query* is one that the name server or resolver fully answers (or gives an error). Name servers are not required to support recursive queries, and the resolver (or another name server acting recursively on behalf of another resolver) negotiates the use of recursive service using bits in the query headers. There are three possible responses to a recursive query:

- The answer to the query accompanied by any CNAME records (aliases) that may be useful. For example, the response to a query for an A RR will follow any CNAME chain. The response will always indicate whether the data is authoritative or cached (nonauthoritative).

- An error indicating the domain or host does not exist (NXDOMAIN). This response can also contain CNAME records that pointed to the non-existing host.

- A temporary error indication—for instance, it can't access other name servers due to network errors and so on.

In a recursive query, a name server will, on behalf of the client (resolver or stub-resolver), chase the trail of authoritative name servers across the universe to get the real answer to the question. The journey of a simple recursive query such as "What is the IP address of `www.example.com`?" to a name server that supports recursive queries but is not *authoritative* for example.com (it is not the master or slave for example.com zone) will look something like this:

1. A user types the URL http://www.example.com into a browser.

2. The browser sends a request for the IP address of www.example.com to its local resolver (stub-resolver).

3. The stub-resolver queries the locally configured DNS Resolver for the IP address of www.example.com.

4. The DNS Resolver looks up www.example.com in local tables (its *cache*), but it isn't found.

5. The DNS Resolver sends a query to a root-server for the IP (the A RR) of www.example.com.

6. The root-server only supports iterative (nonrecursive) queries (see the upcoming section "Iterative (Nonrecursive) Queries") and answers with a list of name servers that are authoritative for the next level in the domain name hierarchy, which in this case is the gTLD .com (this is called a *referral*).

7. The DNS Resolver selects one of the authoritative gTLD servers received in the previous referral and sends it a query for the IP of www.example.com.

8. The gTLD name server only supports *iterative* queries and answers with the authoritative name servers for the Second-Level Domain (SLD) example.com (a referral).

9. The DNS Resolver selects one of the authoritative DNS servers for example.com from the previous referral and sends it a query for the IP (the A RR) of www.example.com.

10. The zone file for example.com defines www.example.com as a CNAME record (an alias) for joe.example.com. The authoritative name server answers with the www.example.com CNAME RR and, in this case, the A RR for joe.example.com, which we will assume is 192.168.254.2.

11. The DNS Resolver sends the response joe.example.com=192.168.254.2 (together with the CNAME RR www=joe) to the original client stub-resolver.

12. The stub-resolver sends www.example.com=192.168.254.2 to the user's browser.

13. The browser sends a request to 192.168.254.2 for the web page.

Figure 3–2 illustrates a recursive query in action.

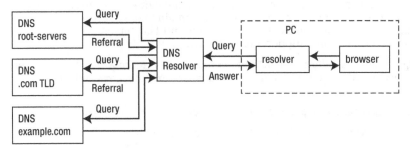

Figure 3–2. *Recursive query*

The stub-resolver on the user's PC always sends a recursive query (a query that requests the receiver to act recursively and return the complete answer). The DNS Resolver accepts the recursive query and starts the process of sending multiple queries throughout the DNS hierarchy to fully resolve the requested name. The DNS Resolver also typically sends a query requesting recursive service to all the authoritative servers. The authoritative root-servers, gTLD servers never support recursion so in this case they simply return a referral to the next level in the hierarchy. The authoritative domain name server should also be configured never to support recursion (but in too many instances is misconfigured, as discussed in Chapter 7). In this case, happily, the final answer is returned.

Which Name Server Is Used

In the case where multiple name servers are available, as is the case with the root-servers or gTLD servers in the preceding explanation, which one should the local DNS use? Most name servers use some algorithm to spread the load and therefore ensure the fastest possible result. In the case of BIND, it maintains a metric called the *round-trip time (RTT)*, in which it tracks the response time to queries from each name server. When a list of name servers is initially supplied in a referral, each name server has an RTT of zero (there is no RTT). In this case, BIND will access each name server once in a round-robin, at the end of which an RTT metric is available for each name server. Thereafter BIND will select the name server with the lowest RTT and continue to use it until its RTT exceeds the RTT of one of the other name servers, at which time that name server becomes the preferred choice.

Iterative (Nonrecursive) Queries

An *iterative* (or *nonrecursive*) query is one where the name server may provide a partial answer to the query (or give an error). Name servers must support nonrecursive queries.

There are four possible responses to a nonrecursive query:

- The answer to the query accompanied by any CNAME records (aliases) that were used in defining the name. The response will indicate whether the data is authoritative or cached (nonauthoritative).

- An error indicating the domain or host does not exist (NXDOMAIN). This response may also contain CNAME records that pointed to the non-existing host.

- A temporary error indication (for example, can't access other DNSs due to network error, and so on).

- A referral (a list of two or more name servers and IP addresses that are closer the next level down in the name hierarchy to the requested domain name). They may or may not be the authoritative name servers for the final domain in the query. A referral is the normal response method used by root-servers and TLD servers because both name server types only support iterative queries.

The journey of a simple query such as "What is the IP address of www.example.com?" to a name server supporting iterative (nonrecursive) queries but that is not authoritative for example.com would look something like this:

1. A user types the URL http://www.example.com into a browser.

2. The browser sends a request for the IP address of www.example.com to its resolver.

3. The resolver on a host sends an iterative query "What is the IP address of www.example.com?" to its locally configured DNS Resolver.

4. The DNS Resolver looks up www.example.com in local tables (its cache), but it isn't found. Because this query is iterative (it does not request recursion), the DNS Resolver responds with a referral containing the list of root-servers.

5. The resolver selects one of the root-servers from the previous referral and directly sends a query to it for the IP (the A RR) of www.example.com.

6. The root-server answers with a list of name servers that are authoritative for the gTLD .com (another referral).

7. The resolver selects one of the authoritative gTLD servers returned in the referral and directly sends it a query for the IP of www.example.com directly to that name server—not the locally configured DNS.

8. The gTLD name server answers the resolver with the authoritative name servers for the SLD example.com.

9. The resolver selects one of the authoritative SLD name servers returned in the referral and directly sends it a query for the IP of www.example.com.

10. The zone file for example.com defines www.example.com as a CNAME record (an alias) to joe.example.com. The authoritative name server answers with the www CNAME RR and, in this case, the A RR for joe.example.com, which we will assume is 192.168.254.2.

11. The resolver sends www.example.com=192.168.254.2 to the browser.

12. The browser sends a request to 192.168.254.2 for the web page.

Figure 3–3 illustrates an iterative query.

The preceding sequence is very artificial and designed only to illustrate how iterative queries operate. A resolver technically must be capable of following referrals. The resolver that is installed on most common systems—this includes Windows, Linux, BSD, and UNIX systems—is in fact a stub-resolver. A stub-resolver, which is defined in the standard, is a minimal resolver that cannot follow referrals. In general, DNS Resolvers used by PCs or workstations *must* support recursive queries to avoid returning referrals to the stub-resolver.

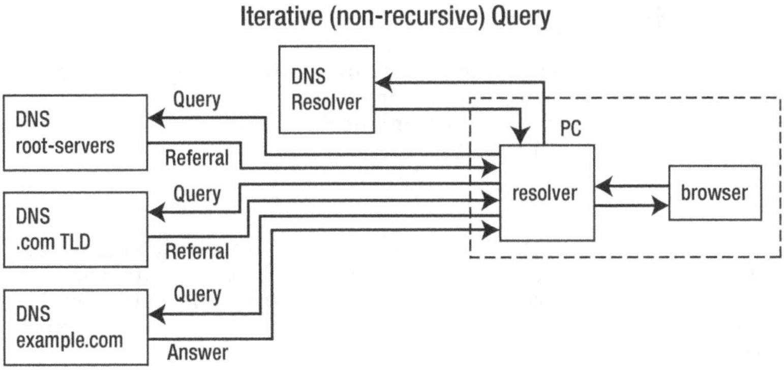

Figure 3–3. Iterative query

■**Note** Most modern platforms have what is called a *caching resolver* (more correctly, a *caching stub-resolver*). It is a stub-resolver—it cannot follow referrals—with a simple cache to increase performance and reduce network traffic.

Inverse Queries

An *inverse query* maps an RR to a domain. An example inverse query would be "What is the domain name for this MX record?" Inverse query support was always defined to be an optional service within the DNS specifications, and it was permitted for name servers to return a response of "Not implemented" (NOTIMP), which they almost invariably did! Consequently, inverse queries were not widely used and were quietly put to rest when they were made obsolete by RFC 3425.

At first blush it may seem obvious that inverse queries are used to find a host name given an IP address. This not the case. The IP-to-host-query process is called *reverse mapping* or *reverse lookup* and uses normal recursive and iterative (nonrecursive) queries with the special domain IN-ADDR.ARPA. Reverse mapping is introduced in the next section.

DNS Reverse Mapping

Given a domain name, a normal DNS query tries to determine its IP address. At times, however, you'll find it useful to be able to determine the name of the host given a particular IP address. Although sometimes this is required for diagnostic purposes, more frequently these days it is used for security reasons to trace a hacker or spammer; indeed, most modern mailing systems use reverse mapping to provide simple authentication by using DNS lookup policies (for instance, IP-to-name and name-to-IP) to confirm that the specified IP address does represent the indicated host.

In order to perform reverse mapping using normal recursive and iterative queries, the DNS designers defined a special (reserved) domain name called IN-ADDR.ARPA. The next section describes how this special domain is constructed and used.

IN-ADDR.ARPA Reverse-Mapping Domain

Reverse mapping can look very complicated. It is, however, an elegant and simple concept and uses a minor variation of the domain name hierarchy introduced in Chapter 1.

The normal domain name structure is hierarchical, starting from the root. A domain name is written left to right, but the hierarchical structure is written right to left.

```
domain name = www.example.com
```

The highest node in the DNS hierarchy (or tree) is the root, defined by the normally silent (omitted) dot, as in the preceding case. This is followed by .com, the Top-Level Domain (TLD); the next (lower) is .example, the Second-Level Domain; and finally the lowest is www, which is the host name and, as you recall from Chapter 2, is always defined in a zone file. To enable an IPv4 address to be used in a normal query operation, it must be converted into a domain name, as described next.

An IPv4 address is written as follows:

```
192.168.254.17
```

This IPv4 address defines a host address of 17 in the Class C address range 192.168.254.x (see the sidebar "IPv4 Addresses and CIDR"). In this case, the most important part (the highest node) is on the left (192), not the right. This is a tad awkward and would make it impossible to construct a sensible tree structure that could be searched in a single lifetime.

The solution is elegantly simple: to create the domain name, reverse the order of the address and build the hierarchy under the special domain name IN-ADDR.ARPA (the SLD is IN-ADDR, the TLD is ARPA).

Note IN-ADDR.ARPA can also be written as in-addr.arpa, which is perfectly acceptable because domains are case insensitive; but the standards state that case *should* be preserved between queries and answers, so this book will continue to use IN-ADDR.ARPA.

Finally, the last part of the IPv4 address (17) is the host address and hosts, as you may recall from Chapter 2, are always defined inside a zone file. The result of the preceding manipulation is as follows:

```
IPv4 address =192.168.254.17
Class C base = 192.168.254 ; omits the host address = 17
Reversed Class C base = 254.168.192
Added to IN-ADDR.ARPA domain = 254.168.192.IN-ADDR.ARPA
```

The organization of the IN-ADDR.ARPA domain is shown in Figure 3–4.

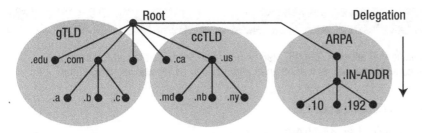

Figure 3–4. IN-ADDR.ARPA reverse mapping

Finally, a zone file is constructed to describe all the hosts in the reverse-mapped zone using the special PTR RR, which is described in the next section. The resulting zone file will look something like this:

```
; simple reverse mapping zone file for example.com
$TTL 2d    ; default TTL for zone
$ORIGIN 254.168.192.IN-ADDR.ARPA.
; Start of Authority record defining the key characteristics of the zone (domain)
@        IN     SOA   ns1.example.com. hostmaster.example.com. (
                      2003080800 ; sn = serial number
                      12h        ; refresh
                      15m        ; retry
                      3w         ; expiry
                      2h         ; nxdomain ttl
                      )
; name servers Resource Records for the domain
         IN     NS    ns1.example.com.
; the second name server is
; external to this zone (domain).
         IN     NS    ns2.example.net.
; PTR RR maps an IPv4 address to a host name
2        IN     PTR   ns1.example.com.
.....
4        IN     PTR   mail.example.com.
.....
16       IN     PTR   joe.example.com.
17       IN     PTR   www.example.com.
....
```

■**Note** The PTR RRs in the preceding zone file use Fully Qualified Domain Names (FQDN) ending with a dot because of the $ORIGIN substitution rule, which was described in Chapter 2.

IPV4 ADDRESSES AND CIDR

An IPv4 address is a 32-bit value that allows 4,294,967,296 unique addresses. It's difficult to remember numbers of this size, so the conventional way of writing an IP address is in *dotted decimal* format (for example, 192.168.23.17).

A dotted decimal IP address is constructed as follows:

1. A 32-bit address contains four 8-bit bytes (or octets).

2. Each 8-bit byte (octet) may represent 256 (0–255) values. The internal (machine) representation of the byte (octet) is known as *hexadecimal* and may contain the hexadecimal values 00 to FF.

3. Dotted decimal simply converts the 8-bit value for each byte (octet) to its decimal value (which is always in the range 0–255) and separates each value with a dot to make it more readable.

Each IPv4 address has two components: a *network address* and a *host address*. The boundary between, or the number of bits in, the network address part and the host address part is determined by the *address class* and the *netmask* or the *subnetmask*.

Before the advent of *Classless Inter-Domain Routing* (CIDR), the world was a simple place—we had four classes of IPv4 addresses: A, B, C, and D (there is also a class E, but for all practical purposes it is not used). The IP address Class is defined by the setting of the top (leftmost) 4 bits of the IP address (or bits 0–3 using the IETF's notation). The IP class provides the separation between the host and the network part of the IP address, as shown in the following table:

Class	Example	Bits 28–31	Network Bits	Host Bits	Netmask
A	126.0.0.0	0xxx	8	24	255.0.0.0
B	172.16.0.0	10xx	16	16	255.255.0.0
C	192.22.22.0	110x	24	8	255.255.255.0
D	224.0.0.0	1110			

The following notes explain and expand on some of the points in the preceding table:

1. x = Don't care.

2. Class D addresses are used for multicasting protocols exclusively; for example, OSPF, IGMP, and so on.

3. Classes A, B, C, and D are routed IPs. (The IPv4 address ranges 10.x.x.x, 172.16.xx to 172.31.xx, and 192.168.x.x are reserved for private use and should be routed only inside a user's private network. They should not be routed across the Internet.)

4. The term *netmask* refers to the standard mask for the address class. You will see later that different masks may be used with any IP class.

5. The terms *netmask* and *subnetmask* are subtly different, but they will be used here as if they were synonymous.

Classless Inter-Domain Routing (CIDR)

CIDR essentially removes the idea of class from IPv4 addresses and allows administrations to allocate and route any valid subnet from any convenient base IP class. The idea is that if you want a group of 32 IP addresses, whether you take them from an IP Class C address or from an IP Class B address, is *not* important. You simply want 32 IP addresses. The following table shows two 32-address subnets, one from a nominal Class B range; the other from a nominal Class C range—spot the difference!

Class	Network	Netmask
B	172.28.227.192	255.255.255.224
C	192.168.15.64	255.255.255.224

In short, the key factors in a CIDR world become the network (base) IP address and the netmask.

IP Prefix or Slash Notation

It is common practice to combine IP addresses and their netmask into a single notation called the *IP prefix*, or more commonly *slash notation*. In the preceding example, the IP address 172.28.227.192 with a subnet mask of 255.255.255.224 would be written in the slash or IP prefix notation as 172.28.227.192/27. The IP address to the left of the slash (/) is the network (base) IP address, and the number (1 to 32) to the right of the slash is the number of contiguous bits in the netmask. The following table illustrates this notation:

Slash Form	Network IP	Netmask	No. of IPs
192.168.32.0/19	192.168.32.0	255.255.224.0	8192
172.28.127.64/27	172.28.127.64	255.255.255.224	32
172.28.127.0/24	172.28.127.0	255.255.255.0	256

In the preceding examples, you will see that multiple Class C addresses have been extracted from a Class C IP address, and subclass C addresses have been subnetted from a Class B address just to illustrate the flexibility of CIDR.

The PTR Resource Record

The PTR RR is standardized in RFC 1035 and maps an IPv4 address to a particular host in the domain or zone as opposed to an A RR, which maps a name to an IPv4 address or an AAAA RR which maps a name to an IPv6 address. The formal syntax is as follows:

```
name     ttl     class   rr   name
```

In the example file, the following PTR RRs are defined:

```
2        IN      PTR     ns1.example.com.
.....
4        IN      PTR     mail.example.com.
.....
16       IN      PTR     joe.example.com.
17       IN      PTR     www.example.com.
```

As you may recall from Chapter 2, the separators between fields can be either spaces or tabs. Table 3–1 maps the formal syntax to the first PTR RR used in the example zone file.

Table 3–1. PTR RR Syntax

Syntax	Example Usage	Description
name	2	Although this looks like a number, it is in fact treated as a name. The name is unqualified, causing the $ORIGIN directive value to be substituted. You could have written this as 2.254.168.192. IN-ADDR.ARPA. (using the FQDN format).
ttl		There is no ttl value defined for the RR, so the zone default of 2d from the $TTL directive will be used.
class	IN	IN defines the class to be Internet.
name	ns1.example.com.	Defines that a query for 192.168.254.2 will return ns1.example.com. This name *must* be written in the FQDN notation (it must end with a dot). If the dot were omitted in error, then $ORIGIN substitution would create ns1.example.com.254.168.192.IN-ADDR.ARPA..

One IPv4 address may be mapped to one or more host names using PTR RRs. Where multiple A RRs or CNAME RRs can be used to define the same IPv4 address, they can all be mapped to the same IPv4 (or IPv6) address in the IN-ADDR.ARPA zone file. A set of PTR RRs mapping the same IP address to different hosts is called a PTR RRset in the DNS jargon.

> **■ Caution** During the writing of this book, the author conducted a series of tests using a multiple host to single IPv4 PTR RRset (the last one in the RRset was the name of a mail server) in the reverse mapped zone file with a number of widely used mail systems. Some of the mail systems correctly extracted the required name from the RRset and therefore permitted mail to be delivered; some did not, resulting in mail being rejected. In these latter cases, when a single IP address to host name PTR was used, the mail was always accepted. Thus, although PTR RRs may be used (as with almost all other RR types) to form an RRset, and indeed there are many cases in which this is very useful (especially when mail is concerned) it may be wise to use only a single IP address to host name PTR RR. The text and examples that follow illustrate this approach.

In the zone fragment that follows, either ns1 or www could appear in the IN-ADDR.ARPA zone:

```
ns1             IN      A       192.168.254.2
; this A RR has the same IPv4 address as ns1 above
www             IN      A       192.168.254.2
```

Here's the same definition using a CNAME RR:

```
ns1             IN      A       192.168.254.2
www             IN      CNAME   ns1.example.com.
```

Reverse-map lookups are used extensively by e-mail software. If two names are defined for a host, using either A or CNAME RRs, that provides e-mail (SMTP) services, then the mail server name should always be defined in the IN-ADDR.ARPA zone file. Failure to do this will result in mail being rejected by any mail server that implements reverse lookup as part of an authentication (antispam) process. The zone fragment that follows shows the same host being defined using two A RRs:

```
mail            IN      A       192.168.254.4
; this A RR has the same IPv4 address as mail above
www             IN      A       192.168.254.4
```

Here's the same definition using a CNAME RR:

```
mail            IN      A       192.168.254.4
www             IN      CNAME   mail.example.com.
```

The IN-ADDR.ARPA zone should define the mail host to enable reverse-lookup checks by, say, e-mail software:

```
; the IN-ADDR.ARPA zone file defines mail not www
4               IN      PTR     mail.example.com.
```

The reverse map may reference a host defined in the forward-map zone file using either an A or a CNAME RR as shown here:

```
www             IN      A       192.168.254.4
ftp             IN      CNAME   mail.example.com.
```

The reverse map defines the host forward-mapped with a CNAME:

```
4          IN     PTR     ftp.example.com.
```

IPv6 also uses the PTR RR for reverse mapping in the domain IP6.ARPA and is described in Chapter 5.

Reverse-Map Queries

Reverse-map queries use normal *recursive* or *iterative* queries, as described previously, under the special domain IN-ADDR.ARPA. The .ARPA (now renamed the Address and Routing Parameter Area) domain is structured hierarchically with ICANN/IANA (www.icann.org) at the root as normal and is administered jointly by ICANN/IANA and the IETF/IAB (RFC 3172). Unlike *forward domains*, which use the gTLD or ccTLD servers as the next level of delegation, IPv4 addresses are delegated through the Regional Internet Registries (RIRs), which are shown in Table 3–2.

Table 3–2. Regional Internet Registries

RIR Name	Coverage	Web
APNIC	Asia Pacific	www.apnic.net
ARIN	North America, parts of the Caribbean	www.arin.net
LACNIC	South America, parts of the Caribbean	www.lacnic.net
RIPE NCC	Europe, Middle East, parts of Asia	www.ripe.net
AFRINIC	Africa	www.afrinic.net

RIRs operate under the procedures defined in RFC 2050. IPv4 addresses are allocated in *netblocks* by the RIRs to either a Local Internet Registry (LIR), typically an ISP, or to a National Internet Registry (NIR), which in turn will allocate to an LIR. Each Internet Registry level is delegated the responsibility for reverse mapping the addresses it has been assigned. The LIR *may* delegate the responsibility for reverse mapping to the end user if static IPv4 addresses are involved. However, the organization of reverse mapping is based on each dot-separated value in an IP address, as shown in Figure 3–4. If the last part of the IPv4 address assigned to an end user is a subnet (fewer than 256 addresses), then a problem arises because any entity, a domain name or an address block, in the domain hierarchy can be delegated *once and only once*. In the case of a subnet, the same netblock would require to be delegated to each subnet user. To illustrate this point, assume the netblock 192.168.254.0 is to be allocated to four users, each of whom will have 64 addresses (a subnet of 64 addresses). They will be allocated as shown here in slash or IP prefix notation (see the sidebar "IPv4 addresses and CIDR"):

```
First User - 192.168.254.0/26 (same as netmask of 255.255.255.192)
Second User - 192.168.254.64/26 (same as netmask of 255.255.255.192)
Third User - 192.168.254.128/26 (same as netmask of 255.255.255.192)
Fourth User - 192.168.254.192/26 (same as netmask of 255.255.255.192)
```

When the netblock for this group is reverse mapped, the host part is omitted as defined previously, giving 192.168.254, and then reversed to the IN-ADDR.ARPA domain, giving the following:

```
254.168.192.IN-ADDDR.ARPA
```

Each of our four users would require delegation of this domain in order to provide the reverse mapping of their own assigned address range. This contravenes the single delegation principle defined previously.

In order to overcome this limitation, the construction of reverse maps for the delegation of subnets uses a very specialized *reverse-map name* construct that essentially creates an additional namespace and is described in Chapter 8. Reverse mapping of IPv4 subnets is very uncommon because few organizations are aware of the special techniques involved.

A reverse-map inquiry using a recursive query is shown in Figure 3–5 for the IPv4 address 192.168.250.15, which is assumed to have been reverse-map delegated all the way to the end user.

Recursive Query for 15.250.168..192.IN-ADDR.ARPA

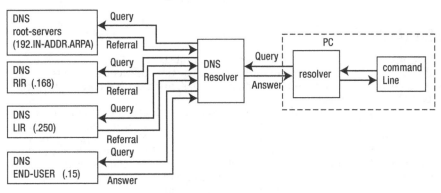

Figure 3–5. Reverse-mapping query

The examples appearing in this reverse-map section use, in the interest of promoting good netizenship, a private IPv4 address (from the set defined in RFC 1918), which in Figure 3–5 is 192.168.250.15. This is shown as interrogating the root-servers for the purpose of illustration only. These IPv4 addresses are private and are meaningless as far as the public network is concerned, yet studies suggest that up to 7% of all queries received at some root-servers comprise reverse-map queries for private IPv4 addresses, which are caused as a result of badly configured name servers. If the local configuration contains private IP addresses in any zone files, then a reverse–mapped zone file for the private IP range must be included in the name server configuration to prevent these meaningless queries being forwarded to the public root-servers. In Chapter 7, the section "Reverse-Map Zone Files" shows an example of such a configuration.

Zone Maintenance

In order to simplify the operation of multiple name servers, it is useful if a single source can update multiple servers. This process—*zone maintenance*—can involve transfer of zone files from one DNS server to another—between a master and slave DNS for the zone—using features of the DNS protocol.

The time between transferring zone file changes is a major determinant of the speed with which changes to the zone information are propagated throughout the Internet. The initial design of DNS allowed for changes to be propagated using full zone transfer (AXFR) operations, but the world of the Internet was simpler and more sedate in those days (1987). The desire to speed up the process of zone update propagation, while minimizing use of resources, has resulted in a number of changes to this aspect of DNS design and implementation from simple—but effective—tinkering such as *incremental zone transfer* (IXFR) and NOTIFY messages to the more complex concept of *dynamic update (DDNS)*.

■**Warning** While zone transfers are generally essential for the efficient operation of DNS systems, they are also a major source of threat. A slave DNS can become *poisoned* if it accepts zone updates from a malicious source. Care should be taken during DNS configuration to ensure that, as a minimum, the slave DNS will accept transfers from only known and trusted sources. The example configurations provided in later chapters implement these minimum precautions.

Full Zone Transfer (AXFR)

The original DNS specifications (RFC 1034 and RFC 1035) envisaged that slave (or Secondary) name servers for the zone would poll the master name server for the zone. The time between polling is determined by the *refresh* value of the domain's SOA RR, which was described in Chapter 2. In a typical zone file, this value will be 12 hours or more.

The DNS polling process is accomplished by the slave name server sending a query to the zone master requesting the SOA RR. If the SOA RR's serial number is greater than the current one maintained by the slave name server, a full zone transfer (AXFR) is requested by the slave DNS. This is the reason it is vital to be disciplined about updating the SOA serial number every time anything changes in any of the zone records. The following example demonstrates updating the serial number using the recommended date number format of *yyyymmddss*, where *yyyy* is a four-digit year number, *mm* is a two-digit month number, *dd* is a two-digit day number, and *ss* is a sequence number so that the zone can be updated more than once per day. Assume an SOA RR as shown here:

```
@        IN      SOA     ns1.example.com. hostmaster.example.com. (
                         2003080803 ; sn = serial number
                         3h         ; refresh time
                         15m        ; retry = refresh retry
                         3w         ; expiry
                         3h         ; nx = nxdomain ttl
                         )
```

Using the date format, this shows that this zone file was last updated four times (ss = 03) on August 8, 2003. If we assume that today's date is September 7, 2003, then the serial number should be set to the value shown here:

```
@        IN      SOA     ns1.example.com. hostmaster.example.com. (
                         2003090700 ; sn = serial number
                         3h         ; refresh time
                         15m        ; retry = refresh retry
                         3w         ; expiry
                         3h         ; nx = nxdomain ttl
                         )
```

The sequence number has also been reset to 00 to ensure we have plenty of space for fixing errors! If the month and date of the preceding example were to be swapped in error, then the serial number would be

```
2003070900 ; sn = serial number
```

This number is not greater than the previous number, so the slave would not request a zone transfer and the updates would not be propagated. The fix in this case is simple because the error is back in time. The following example shows the serial number being incorrectly placed forward in time:

```
2005090700 ; sn = serial number
```

To restore this serial number to the correct date is much more complex, and you would want to do it only once in your life. The procedure is documented in Chapter 8. Remember that the date format is a widely used and recommended *convention*; BIND does not validate the number for correct ranges, that is, the following is accepted quite happily by BIND, which is the 45th day of the 14th month of 2003!:

```
2003144500 ; sn = serial number
```

In this case, a zone transfer will take place because the number is greater than our initial value. Zone transfer (AXFR) operations use TCP on port 53.

Warning Not updating the serial number field of the SOA RR when any change is made to the zone file is one of the most common causes of head scratching, screaming, and other more seriously aberrant behavior when dealing with DNS systems. Always update the SOA RR serial number when you make any changes to a zone file.

Incremental Zone Transfer (IXFR)

Transferring very large zone files can take a long time and waste bandwidth and other resources. It is especially wasteful if only a single record has been changed! RFC 1995 introduced the *incremental zone transfer* (IXFR), which (as the name suggests) allows the slave name server and master name server to transfer only those records that have changed.

The process works as for AXFR. The slave name server sends a query for the domain's SOA RR to the zone master every refresh interval. If the serial number of the SOA RR is greater than the one currently stored by the slave, the name server requests a zone transfer and indicates whether or not it is capable of accepting an IXFR. If both master and slave name servers support the feature, an IXFR takes place; otherwise, an AXFR takes place. IXFRs use TCP on port 53.

The default mode for BIND when acting as a slave name server is to request IXFR unless it has been configured not to by use of the request-ixfr statement in the server or options clause of the named.conf file (see Chapter 12 for details).

The default mode for BIND when acting as a master name server is to use IXFR only when the zone is dynamic. The use of IXFR is controlled through the provide-ixfr statement in the server or options clause of the named.conf file (see Chapter 12 for details).

IXFRs affect only the volume of data that is transferred; they have no impact on the time it takes to propagate zone file changes.

Notify (`NOTIFY`)

RFC 1912 recommends an interval of 2 to 12 hours or higher on the refresh interval for the SOA RR. This means that changes to the zone master may not be visible to the zone slave for up to 12 hours or whatever this value is set to. In the fast-moving world of the Internet, this may be unacceptable.

RFC 1996 introduced a scheme whereby an authoritative zone name server (either master or slave) will send a `NOTIFY` message to the zone name servers (defined by the NS RRs for the zone) whenever the zone is loaded or updated. This message indicates that a change *may* have occurred in the domain records. The name server on receipt of the `NOTIFY` message will request the SOA RR from the zone master, and if the serial number is greater than the one currently stored, will attempt a zone transfer using either an AXFR or an IXFR.

BIND's default behavior is to send `NOTIFY` messages to name servers that are defined in the NS RRs for the zone. `NOTIFY` behavior in BIND is controlled by `notify`, `also-notify`, and `notify-source` statements in the `zone` or `options` clauses of the `named.conf` file (see Chapter 12 for details).

`NOTIFY` can considerably reduce the time to propagate zone changes to servers.

Dynamic Update

The classic method of updating zone RRs is to manually edit the zone file and then stop and start the name server to read the zone files and propagate the changes. When the volume of changes reaches a certain level, this can become operationally unacceptable—especially considering that in organizations that handle large numbers of zone files, such as service providers, BIND can take a long time to restart because it initializes very large numbers of zone files.

Many larger users of DNS seek a method to rapidly change the zone records while the name server continues to respond to user queries. There are two architectural approaches to solving this problem:

- Allow runtime updating of the zone RRs from an external source or application.

- Directly feed the zone RRs from a database, which can be dynamically updated.

RFC 2136 takes the first approach and defines a process, called *Dynamic DNS (DDNS)*, whereby zone records can be updated from one or more external sources. The key limitation in this specification is that a new domain or zone cannot be added or deleted dynamically. All records within an existing zone can be added, changed, or deleted—with the exception that the SOA RR cannot be added or deleted because this would essentially add or remove the zone.

As part of RFC 2136, the term *primary master* was introduced to describe the name server defined in the SOA RR for the zone. When dynamically updating zone RRs, it is essential to update only one server, even though there may be multiple master servers for the zone. In order to solve this problem, a *boss* server must be selected. The boss server, the primary master, has no special characteristics other than it is defined as the name server in the SOA RR and may appear in an `allow-update` statement of BIND's `named.conf` configuration file to control the dynamic update process (see Chapter 12 for details).

DDNS is normally described in conjunction with Secure DNS features—specifically, TSIG (RFC 2845) and TKEY (RFC 2930). DDNS, however, does not require or rely on TSIG/TKEY features.

The reason why the two features are tightly coupled is that by enabling Dynamic DNS, zone files may be opened up to the possibility of corruption or poisoning by malicious sources. Simple IP address protection can be configured into BIND (using BIND's `allow-update` statement described in Chapter 12), but this provides limited protection. System architecture can further remove risk by positioning both the target name server and all the hosts that are allowed to update it behind secure perimeters. The real power, however, of DDNS is that remote and distributed users are able to semiautonomously update and control their domain configurations. Under these circumstances, serious users of Dynamic DNS will always use TSIG/TKEY procedures, described in Chapter 10, to authenticate incoming requests.

BIND's default DDNS behavior is to *deny from all hosts*. Control of dynamic update is provided by the BIND `named.conf` statements `allow-update` (usable with and without TSIG/TKEY) and `update-policy` (usable only with TSIG/TKEY) in the zone or options clauses. The statements and clauses mentioned are described in Chapter 12.

There are a number of Open Source tools that will initiate DDNS updates; they include nsupdate, which is one of the utilities distributed with BIND (and described in Chapter 9).

Alternative Dynamic DNS Approaches

As noted earlier, the major limitation in DDNS (RFC 2136) is that new domains cannot be created dynamically. Alternative approaches to this problem do exist.

BIND-DLZ (code base integrated into BIND since release 9.4) takes a much more radical approach and replaces all zone files with a single zone file that simply describes a database. BIND-DLZ supports the major Open Source databases including MySQL, PostgreSQL, BDB, and LDAP. All incoming DNS queries are first directed to the database access routines so that new, modified, or deleted zone data is immediately reflected in the name server's responses. As with all things in life, there is a trade-off. Depending on the selected database, performance can drop precipitously. BIND-DLZ database drivers are included in the /contrib directory of a BIND release (since 9.4). For BIND-DLZ configuration information, the latest database drivers and performance data use the BIND-DLZ web site (bind-dlz.sourgeforge.net).

PowerDNS (www.powerdns.com) is an authoritative-only name server that takes a similar approach with its own (non-BIND) code base by referring all queries to the database back-end and thereby allowing new domains to be added dynamically.

BIND 10 (described in Chapter 14) supports full dynamic creation and deletion of zones using a database back-end (the default is SQLite). Standard text zone files may be loaded into the database using the new loadzone utility.

■ **Caution** The use of real-time changes to DNS records without the proper safeguards can result in trivial errors being immediately propagated throughout the Internet with potentially catastrophic consequences. Because DNS caches will typically hold such records for 12 or more hours (determined by either the $TTL for the zone file or the TTL value for the specific RR), such errors can take a long time to correct.

Security Overview

DNS operation, the simple act of running a DNS, opens up potential security threats. This is true of any publicly accessible service; for example, a web site or FTP site. Somehow it is easier to forget that DNS is a publicly accessible service.

This security overview steps back from the detail of DNS security configuration minutiae—Chapters 10 and 11 cover DNS security configuration—to try and provide a clear and dispassionate overview of the topic. There is nothing more annoying, on finding oneself in deep trouble halfway up a mountain, that one really didn't need to climb this particular mountain.

The critical point in defining security policies and procedures is to understand what needs to be secured—or rather what threat levels need to be secured against and what threats are acceptable. The answers to these two points will be very different if the DNS is running as a root-server versus running a modest in-house DNS serving a couple of low-volume web sites.

The term *DNSSEC* is thrown around as a blanket term to cover DNS security. This is not quite correct. There are at least three forms of DNS security, two of which are (relatively) painless and a full-blooded DNSSEC implementation that is (relatively) painful.

Security Threats

In order to be able to assess both the potential threats and the possible countermeasures, it is first and foremost necessary to understand the normal data flow in a DNS system. Figure 3–6 shows this flow.

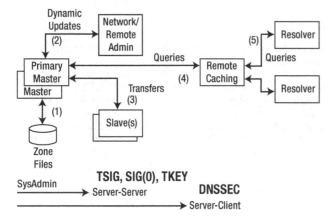

Figure 3–6. *DNS data flow*

Every part of this data flow—each numbered line in Figure 3–6—is a *potential* source of threat. Table 3–3 defines the potential outcomes of compromise at each point and the possible solutions.

Table 3–3. *DNS Security Threats*

Number	Area	Threat	Classification	Solution
1	Zone files	File corruption (malicious or accidental)	Local	System Administration
2	Dynamic updates	Unauthorized updates, IP address spoofing (impersonating update source)	Server-Server	Network architecture, TSIG, SIG(0), or disable
3	Zone transfers	IP address spoofing (impersonating update source)	Server-Server	Network architecture, TSIG, TKEY, or disable
4	Remote queries	Cache poisoning by IP spoofing, data interception, or a subverted master or slave	Server-Client	DNSSEC
5	Resolver queries	Data interception, poisoned cache, subverted master or slave, local IP spoofing	Remote Client–Client	DNSSEC, SSL/TLS

The first phase of any security review is to audit what threats are applicable and how seriously they are rated in the particular organizational circumstances. As an example, if dynamic updates are not supported—BIND's default mode—there is no dynamic update threat!

It can be easier to disable a process than to secure it. While alternate processes may be required, they may be far simpler to secure. As an example, for organizational reasons it may be easier to manually update zone records on each name server than to secure or limit zone transfers. In this case, simply disabling all zone transfers is the securest solution. This is sometimes referred to as *security by obscurity*.

Finally, a note of caution: *the farther you go from the zone master, the more complicated the solution and implementation*. Unless there is a very good reason for not doing so, it is recommended that you always start from the zone master and work outward. It would be a tad frustrating to have completed a successful implementation of a complex DNSSEC solution only to discover that the installation's zone files were world readable and writable.

Security Classification

The security classification is simply a means to allow selection of the appropriate remedies and strategies for avoiding the implied risk. All the methods described next are discussed in detail in Chapters 10 and 11. The numbering used in the following list relates to Figure 3–6.

- *Local threats (1)*: Local threats are usually the simplest to prevent, typically requiring good system administration polices. Zone files and any DNS configuration files—named.conf contains lots of interesting data—should be secure; that is, have limited read and write access and be securely backed up. Stealth (or Split) name servers can be used to minimize public access (described in Chapter 7), and BIND can be run in a *chroot jail* (described in Chapter 10).

- *Server-Server (2)*: If an organization runs slave name servers, it will do zone transfers. It is possible to run multiple master name servers rather than master-slave servers. Alternative methods are required to distribute zone files, but these methods may be easier to secure than zone transfers, depending on the organization's requirements and procedures. If zone transfers are required, BIND offers multiple configuration parameters that can be used to minimize the inherent risks in the process (described in Chapter 12), and TSIG and TKEY offer secure methods for transmission of zone files (described in Chapter 10).

- *Server-Server (3)*: The BIND default is to *deny* dynamic zone updates. If an organization requires this feature, then BIND provides a number of configuration parameters to minimize risk (described in Chapter 12). Network architecture design—all systems involved within a trusted perimeter—can further reduce the exposure. TSIG and SIG(0) can be used to secure the transactions (described in Chapter 10).

- *Server-Client (4)*: Remote caches can become poisoned—their contents can become corrupted to point at competitors' web sites—by IP spoofing, data interception, and other hacks. Although modest web sites probably have little to fear from this form of attack, if the site is high profile, high volume, open to competitive threat, or a high revenue earner, then the costs and complexity of implementing a full-scale DNSSEC solution are worthwhile. DNSSEC implementation is described in Chapter 11.

- *Client-Client (5)*: The DNSSEC protocol allows for a concept called the *security-aware resolver* whereby the security chain can be propagated from the authoritative name server to the client resolver. Additionally, BIND allows SSL/TLS to be used to secure the transmission path between the client resolver's host and the local name server.

Summary

This chapter described the various operations and services provided by the DNS protocol. These operations include queries, recursive and interactive (nonrecursive); zone transfers; and dynamic update. I described the process known as reverse mapping, in which a normal query is used to obtain the name of a host given its IP address, and illustrated it with some examples. The chapter concluded with a brief overview of the security implications that necessarily arise from running any DNS service.

Chapter 4 describes a number of name server (DNS) types while recognizing that the majority of name servers are required to provide multiple functions.

CHAPTER 4

■■■

DNS Types

DNS servers play a wide variety of roles—a single name server may be a master for some zones, a slave for others, and provide caching or forwarding services for still others. Indeed, much of BIND 9's power comes from allowing fine-grained control over operational functionality.

The role of the name server is controlled by its configuration file, which in the case of BIND 9 is called named.conf. The combination of global parameters in the named.conf file (defined in an options clause) and the zones being serviced (defined in one or more zone clauses) determine the complete functionality of the name server. Depending on the requirements, such configurations can become very complex. In order to provide an approachable starting point to what can become a task of daunting complexity, this chapter breaks down configuration of the name server into a number of basic types such as a *master server type* and an *authoritative-only server type*. I describe their characteristics and properties in isolation in order to create a series of building blocks from which progressively more complex configurations can be constructed. In some cases, the basic types may themselves be sufficient to create the required name server such as a *caching-only server type* (a resolver) or a *forwarding server type*; in other cases, the required name server may consist of, for example, many master server types, many slave server types, and a caching server type. Indeed, in later chapters of this book, you will meet many examples that combine a number of these basic types to create unique solutions.

In order to most effectively introduce the characteristics of each basic name server type, some BIND 9 configuration file (named.conf) fragments are used where appropriate. The term *clause* is used to describe a group of related statements that can appear in the named.conf file. This terminology is applied rigorously throughout this book in the interests of consistency and ease of understanding rather than the myriad terms used in other documentation on this subject. The full format and layout of the named.conf file is described in Chapter 12, but the following identifies some important clauses and statements used in this file and which appear in the upcoming fragments:

- *The options clause* groups together statements that control the global behavior of the name server. In some cases, the global statements may be overridden in specific clauses, such as the zone clause.

- *The zone clause* groups statements that relate to specific zones within the configuration—the zone clause for example.com will define all the characteristics or properties of the zone.

- *The type statement* is used within a zone clause and defines how the name server will act for the specific zone (for example, it may act as a master or as a slave for the zone).

- *The recursion statement* controls whether recursive queries are supported or not. Caching is an artifact of recursion; therefore, this statement effectively controls the provision of caching services in the name server. This statement may appear either in a global options clause or a view clause. By default, BIND 9 will support recursive queries and hence provides caching.

- *The file statement* is used to define the physical location of the zone file and appears in a zone clause.

BIND 10 (covered in an online chapter of this book) has chosen a radically different method to control configuration. Later versions of BIND 10 are planned to parse and accept a named.conf file for compatibility and conversion purposes. However, BIND 10's normal control and configuration method consists of run-time commands that are saved in a configuration file and can, therefore, be reloaded in the event of a restart. While the user can edit the BIND 10 saved configuration information, this is discouraged. BIND 9 may thus be characterized as a *batch system* whereas BIND 10 is optimized to run continuously and to react to real-time stimuli such as configuration (behavior) changes, added or deleted zones, or modified zone data.

Master (Primary) Name Servers

A *master* DNS configuration, also known as a *zone master* configuration, contains one or more zone files for which this DNS is authoritative and that it reads from a local file system. The term *master* is related to the location of the zone file rather than any other operational characteristics. A master may be requested to transfer zone files—using zone transfer operations (described in Chapter 3)—to one or more *slave* servers whenever the zone file changes.

■**Note** The term *master* was introduced in BIND 8.x releases and replaced the slightly confusing term *primary*.

Zone master status for a zone is defined in BIND 9 by including type master in the zone clause of the named.conf file as shown in the following fragment:

```
// example.com fragment from named.conf
// defines this server as a zone master for example.com
zone "example.com" in{
    type master;
    file "master.example.com";
};
```

In this fragment, zone "example.com" defines the zone to which the following statements apply, type master defines this DNS to be the zone master for example.com, and file "master.example.com" defines the name of the zone file on the filesystem containing the resource records (RRs) for example.com.

Figure 4–1 illustrates a zone master DNS.

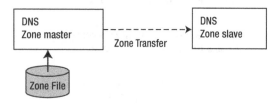

Figure 4–1. Master and slave servers

Note The terms *primary* and *secondary* name servers are widely used in two contexts. In the context of zone transfer, *primary* may be used to describe what this book calls the zone *master* and *secondary* describes the zone *slave*. Unfortunately, the terms *primary* and *secondary* are also frequently used when describing the order of name servers when registering a domain name and also in many PCs when defining the order of DNS used in the network properties on Windows systems especially. BIND 8 introduced the terms *master* and *slave* to reduce the confusion caused by the conflicting use of primary and secondary. This book uses the terms *master* and *slave* throughout when describing name servers used in zone transfer operations; purely in this context the term *primary* means master and the term *secondary* means slave. Just to further confuse things, the term *primary master* has crept into the jargon; it has a special meaning only in the context of dynamic DNS (DDNS) updates and is defined to be the name server that appears in the SOA resource record (discussed in Chapter 2).

A zone master obtains the zone data from a local zone file as opposed to a zone slave, which obtains its zone data via a zone transfer operation from the zone master. This seemingly trivial point means that it is possible to have any number of zone masters for any zone if that makes operational sense. Zone file changes need to be synchronized between zone masters by a manual or automated process. This may be easier to manage than securing the zone transfer operations inherent in a master-slave configuration.

A master name server can indicate (using NOTIFY messages) zone changes to slave servers. This ensures that zone changes are rapidly propagated to the slaves rather than simply waiting for the slave to poll for changes at each SOA RR refresh interval. The BIND default is to automatically NOTIFY all the name servers defined in NS records for the zone.

NOTIFY messages may be disabled by use of the configuration statement notify no in BIND's named.conf file in the zone clause for the domain.

When a DNS server that is a master for one or more zones receives a query for a zone for which it is not a master or a slave, it will act as configured. In BIND 9, this behavior is defined in the named.conf file as such:

1. If caching behavior is permitted and recursive queries are allowed (described in Chapter 3), the server will completely answer the request or return an error.

2. If caching behavior is permitted and iterative (nonrecursive) queries only are allowed, the server can respond with the complete answer if it is already in the cache because of another request, a referral, or return an error.

3. If caching behavior is not permitted (an authoritative-only DNS server), the server will return a referral or an error.

Tip Example configuration files for all of the server variations in this chapter are provided in Chapter 7.

Slave (Secondary) Name Servers

The critical nature of DNS—no Internet services can work without it—requires that there be at least two name servers to support each domain or zone; larger or more active domains may rely on many more. For instance, examination of the NS resource records using the dig tool (see Chapter 9) shows a typical range from 4 to 9 name servers for a number of high-profile zones. It is possible to run multiple master name servers, but any changed zone files must be copied to all masters. Apart from the obvious problem of synchronization when multiple masters are used, each master must be reloaded to use the new zone files, thus taking the name server out of service for a short period of time. With larger sites being hit hundreds of times per second, even modest out-of-service times can lose thousands of DNS transactions—effectively making the site unreachable or slowing down access. To resolve this problem, the DNS specifications provide a feature—zone transfer—whereby one name server, the slave, can be updated from a zone master while continuing to provide responses to queries for the zone.

A slave name server obtains its zone information from a zone master, but it will respond as authoritative for those zones for which it is defined to be a slave and for which it has valid zone records (the zone records have not expired). The act of transferring the zone may be viewed as having delegated authority for the zone to the slave for the time period defined in the expiry value of the SOA record (described in Chapter 2) and thus enables the slave to respond authoritatively to queries.

■ **Note** There is no visible difference to other name servers (resolvers) between the response from a zone master and the response from a zone slave.

Slave status is defined in BIND by including type slave in the zone clause of the named.conf file, as shown:

```
// example.com fragment from named.conf
// defines this server as a zone slave
zone "example.com" in{
    type slave;
    file "slave.example.com";
    masters {192.168.23.17;};
};
```

Here, zone "example.com" defines the zone for which the following statements apply, and type slave; indicates that this name server will act as a slave for example.com. The statement file "slave.example.com"; is optional and allows the zone data to be saved to the specified file. If the name server is reloaded, it can read the zone data from this file rather than forcing a new zone transfer from the master, as would be the case if no file statement were present. The file statement can save considerable time and resources. The statement masters {192.168.23.17}; defines the IP address of the name server(s) that hold the master zone file for this zone. One or more IP addresses may be present. There can be *more than one master DNS for any zone.*

A slave server attempts to update the zone records when the refresh parameter of the SOA RR is reached. If a failure occurs, the slave will periodically try to reach the zone master(s) every retry period. If a slave has still not reached the master DNS when the expiry time of the SOA RR for the zone has been reached, it will stop responding to queries for the zone. The slave will not use time-expired data.

Slave (Secondary) DNS Behavior

As previously mentioned, slave servers will respond as authoritative to queries for the domain as long as they hold valid zone records. This feature provides the user with a lot of flexibility when registering name servers for a given domain. When registering such name servers, the only requirement is that the servers listed will respond as authoritative to queries for the domain or zone. It is not necessary to define the zone master as one of these name servers; two or more slave servers will satisfy the requirement. This flexibility allows the zone master to be hidden from public access if required (a.k.a. *a hidden master*). To illustrate why such a strategy may be useful, consider the following scenario: if a slave zone file becomes corrupted through a malicious attack, it can be quickly restored from the master by a zone transfer. If the master zone file were to become similarly corrupted, the zone files may have to be restored from backup media, which could take some time. One way to prevent such a problem is simply to avoid it by not making the master publicly visible. It is visible to the slave only using the masters parameter of BIND's named.conf but would not appear in any NS RR for the zone. Every name server, master, or slave that the user wishes to make visible must be defined using an NS RR in the zone.

Figure 4–2 illustrates a typical master and single slave configuration, and Figure 4–3 illustrates a slave server when used with a hidden master.

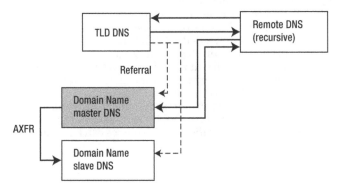

Figure 4–2. *Typical master-slave configuration*

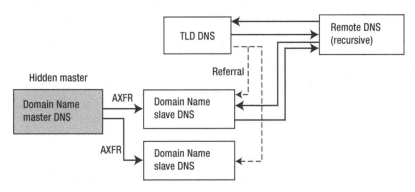

Figure 4–3. *Hidden master-slave configuration*

67

Slave vs. Cache

A zone slave obtains *all the zone data* for which it is acting as a slave via zone transfer operations. This process should not be confused with a cache. The slave server uses the refresh and expiry values from the SOA RR to time-out its zone data and then retransfers all the zone data. A cache, on the other hand, contains individual RRs obtained in response to a specific query originating from a resolver or another name server acting on behalf of a resolver and discards each RR when its TTL is reached. In addition, a slave server always responds authoritatively to requests for information about its zone. A cache will only respond authoritatively with zone data the first time it obtains the data (directly from the zone's master or slave). Thereafter, when reading from its cache, the data is not marked as authoritative. Failure to understand the difference between slave servers and caching can lead to *lame delegation*. Only zone master or slave authoritative servers can appear in any NS RRs for the zone since only these server types can answer authoritatively for the zone.

Change Propagation Using NOTIFY

The slave will periodically poll the zone master for changes at a time interval defined by the refresh parameter of the zone's SOA RR. In this scenario, the refresh parameter, which typically may be 12 hours or longer, controls the time taken to propagate zone changes. If NOTIFY behavior is enabled in the zone master—BIND's default—then every time the zone is loaded or reloaded, a NOTIFY message is sent to all the slave servers defined in the NS RRs of the zone file. On receipt of a NOTIFY message, the slave will request a copy of the zone's SOA RR. If the serial number of the current zone data is lower than the serial number of the newly requested SOA RR, the slave initiates a zone transfer to completely update its zone data. There can be zero, one, or more slave name servers for any given zone.

The NOTIFY message—and its subsequent zone transfer operation—presents a potential security threat. To minimize this threat, BIND's default behavior is to only accept NOTIFY messages from the zone master (name servers listed in the masters statement). Other acceptable NOTIFY sources can be defined using the allow-notify statement in the named.conf file.

Caching Name Servers

A caching name server (a.k.a. caching resolver, DNS cache, or, most commonly, resolver) obtains specific information in the form of one or more resource records about a domain by querying a zone's authoritative name server (master or slave) in order to answer a host/client query and subsequently saves (caches) the data locally. On a subsequent request for the same data, the caching server will respond with its locally stored data from the cache. This process will continue until the Time to Live (TTL) value of the RR expires, at which time the RR will be discarded from the cache. The next request for this RR will result in the resolver again querying an authoritative name server for the zone. Caches considerably increase DNS performance for local PCs or hosts and can also significantly reduce network loads by obtaining a single copy of frequently accessed data and making it available many times with no additional overhead. Consider the example zone file in which the mail server was defined using the following RR:

```
3w      IN      MX 10   mail.example.com.
```

The effect of caching in this case is that every request for the mail server for example.com for the next *three weeks* will be satisfied from the cache and will require no further—possibly slow—network access. If a caching name server (a resolver) is reloaded or restarted, then caches are usually erased and the process begins again. It is worth emphasizing at this point that the only way RR data is removed from a cache is by either its TTL expiring or the resolver being reloaded. This means that changes to the preceding MX record will take up to three weeks to propagate throughout the Internet and thus only stable RRs, such as mail servers, would typically have such very long TTL values.

If the resolver obtains its data directly from an authoritative DNS, then it too will respond as authoritative. Otherwise, if the data is supplied from its cache, the response is nonauthoritative.

By default, BIND 9 will cache resource records. This behavior is defined using the recursion parameter—the default is recursion yes;—in BIND 9's named.conf file. This may seem a little strange at first, but caching is essentially an artifact of recursive query behavior.

Note There are many configuration examples that show caching behavior being controlled using a *type hint* statement in the zone declaration section of BIND's named.conf file. These configurations confuse two distinct but related functions. If a server provides caching services, then it *must* support recursive queries, and recursive queries need access to the root-servers. Root-server access is provided using the *type hint* statement in a special root-server zone. The root-server zone definition is described in Chapter 7.

A BIND 9 caching server (resolver) will have a named.conf file that includes the following fragment:

```
// options clause fragment of named.conf
// recursion yes is the default and may be omitted
options {
        recursion yes;
        allow-recursion {10.2/16;192.168.2/24;}; // limits (closes) recursion
};
// zone clause
....
// the DOT indicates the root domain = all domains
zone "." IN {
   type hint;
   file "root.servers";
};
```

The options clause indicates the following statements apply to all zones in the configuration unless explicitly overridden with another statement; recursion yes; turns on caching behavior, which is the BIND default and could be omitted. The allow-recursion {10.2/16;192.168.2/24;}; statement defines those IP addresses that are allowed to issue recursive queries. If this statement were not present, this would be an OPEN caching name server and as such could be used by malicious third parties in DDoS attacks. Indeed, so serious is this problem that since BIND 9.4+ failure to provide any limits on recursion will cause the configuration to default to accepting recursive queries *only* from locally connected hosts. For more information see the "Resolver (Caching-Only)" section in Chapter 7 and Chapter 12 for allow-recursion, allow-recursion-on, allow-query-cache, and allow-query-cache-on statements.

The zone "."; clause defines the normally silent root domain and is used to access any zone that is not defined in the remainder of the configuration; type hint; simply indicates the zone references the root domain and is only ever used in conjunction with a zone "."; clause. The statement file "root.servers"; locates the zone file that contains the Address (A) RRs of the root-servers.

Tip The root.servers zone file, which may be called named.ca or named.root, is normally supplied with BIND 9 distributions. Chapter 7 illustrates an example root.servers zone file.

Caching Implications

To cache or not to cache is a crucial question in the world of DNS, since it incurs substantial performance overheads. Also, because it interfaces with the external network, you run the risk of cache poisoning or corruption through malicious attacks. This downside must be offset against the significant performance gains that are obtained when using a resolver. The most common uses of DNS caching configurations are as follows:

- As a name server acting as master or slave for one or more zones (domains) and as a caching server for all other queries. A general-purpose name server.

- As a caching-only name server (resolver)—typically used to support standard PC-based resolvers (stub resolvers), which as you may recall from Chapter 1, require recursive query support that is only provided by a caching name server. One or more caching-only servers are typically present in networks such as ISPs or large organization networks. The term *area resolver* is frequently used to describe caching-only name servers in larger networks since they tend to be provisioned on a geographic basic.

However, if a general-purpose name server is being hit thousands of times per second in support of a high-volume site, performance becomes a major factor; in this case, caching would typically be disabled. Furthermore, there are many DNS administrators who, due to the cache-related dangers described previously, will never allow caching behavior on a name server that has any master or slave zones. BIND 9 provides only limited controls to disable caching behavior, principally by including the statement recursion no; in the named.conf file, but many caching overheads remain. As previously noted, there is an increasing trend for DNS systems to become more specialized. BIND 9 continues to provide general purpose functionality but the BIND 10 family has opted for a model that separates the functionality of master/slave and caching. In addition, there are now a number of open source and commercial DNS offerings that provide only master/slave name server functionality (authoritative-only name servers) or caching-only name server (resolver) functionality.

Forwarding (Proxy) Name Servers

A forwarding (a.k.a. proxy, client, or remote) DNS server is one that forwards all queries to another DNS and caches the results. On its face, this looks to be a pretty pointless exercise. However, a forwarding name server can pay off in the following ways when access to an external network is slow, expensive, or heavily congested:

1. The name server to which queries are forwarded will provide recursive query support resulting in a single query-answer DNS transaction. If the local name server were a caching-only server and did not forward queries, multiple transactions would occur, thus increasing network load and time delays.

2. The local or on-site forwarding DNS server will cache results and thereby provide both faster responses for frequently accessed information and eliminate unnecessary (and potentially risky) external traffic.

Forwarding name servers can also be used tactically to ease the burden of local administration. Each PC may be defined to use a local forwarding name server, which in turn is defined to pass all queries to an external server. If the external DNS server changes when the user changes ISP, for example, a single configuration change to the local name server's named.conf file is all that is required, instead of having to change all the local PC configurations. The same result can be accomplished using DHCP, but that's not always convenient.

Forwarding may also be used as part of a stealth (or split) server configuration, which is described in the next section, for perimeter defense.

Figure 4–4 illustrates the use of forwarding DNS.

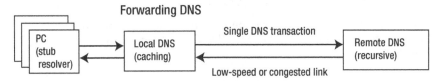

Figure 4–4. *Forwarding DNS server*

BIND 9 allows configuration of forwarding using the `forward` and `forwarders` statements either at a global level (in an `options` clause) or on a per-zone basis (in a zone clause) of the `named.conf` file. Both configurations are shown in the following examples.

The following `named.conf` fragment causes global forwarding of all queries received by the name server:

```
// options clause fragment of named.conf
// forwarders can have multiple choices
options {
                forwarders {10.0.0.1; 10.0.0.2;};
                forward only;
};
// zone clauses
....
```

By defining the `forwarders` statement in the `options` clause, it applies to the whole configuration unless overridden in a subsequent zone clause. The `forwarders` and `forward` statements are always used in conjunction with each other. The `forwarders {10.0.0.1; 10.0.0.2;};` statement contains two IP addresses that are used in rotation; one, two, or more IP addresses may be used. The `forward only;` statement forces *all* queries to be forwarded. The next fragment provides forwarding for the specific zone only:

```
// zone clause fragment of named.conf
zone "example.com" IN {
                type forward;
                forwarders {10.0.0.1; 10.0.0.2;};
                forward only;
};
```

Where dial-up links are used with forwarding name servers, BIND 9's general-purpose nature and strict standards adherence may not make it an optimal solution. A number of alternative DNS solutions specifically target support for such links. BIND 9 defines two parameters, `dialup` and `heartbeat-interval` (see Chapter 12), whose objective is to minimize network connection time.

Stealth (DMZ or Split) Name Server

A *stealth server* is defined as a name server that does not appear in any publicly visible NS RRs for the domain. Stealth servers are used in configurations that are sometimes called *demilitarized zones* (DMZs) or *split servers* and can be defined as having the following characteristics:

- The organization needs to expose DNS servers to provide access to its public services such as web sites, e-mail, FTP sites, and so forth.

- The organization does not want the world to see any of its internal hosts either by interrogation (query or zone transfer) or in the event the DNS service or external servers are compromised.

Note The term *hidden master* is sometimes used to describe this configuration. This book reserves the term *hidden master* to describe a name server whose function is limited to necessary zone transfers only but which, in the normal course of events, never answers queries from either internal or external sources and can thus be made highly secure. A hidden master may be used within a stealth or split configuration to provide additional security

---

A stealth or split server architecture is illustrated in Figure 4–5.

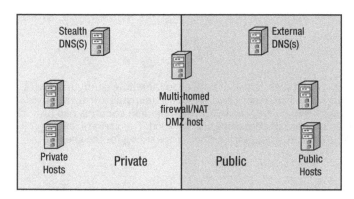

Figure 4–5. Stealth or split server architecture

The external or public servers are configured to provide authoritative-only responses and no caching services—recursive queries are not accepted. In this case, caching is both wasteful in terms of performance and a possible source of pollution or corruption, both of which can lead to system compromise. The zone file used by these public servers is a public subset of the zone file data and will contain only those systems or services that the user needs to make externally visible, for example, an SOA RR (required), NS RRs for the public (not stealth) name servers, MX RRs for mail servers, and A RRs for, say, www.example.com and ftp.example.com for the public web and FTP services.

Zone transfers can be allowed between the public name servers as required, but they should not transfer to or accept transfers from the stealth server. This clear separation between the private and public side of the network is necessary because if the public name server is compromised, then simple inspection of the named.conf file or zone files must not yield information that describes any part of the hidden network. BIND 9's named.conf directives such master, allow-notify, allow-transfer, and others, if present, will provide information that allows an attacker to penetrate the veil of privacy.

Stealth Servers and the View Clause

BIND 9 provides a view clause that may be used to provide similar functionality using a single server, but this does not address the problem of the name server host system being compromised, thereby revealing additional data about the organization via a simple inspection of the named.conf file and any zone files. Careful consideration of the likelihood of file system compromises on publicly visible servers and the design of the view statements must be undertaken before using view in a stealth DNS configuration. BIND's view statement can, however, be used to augment the functionality of the public and private parts of a stealth configuration; this is described further in Chapter 7.

Stealth Server Configuration

A simple public master zone file containing only those hosts and services that are required to support public or external access for the organization is shown here. This zone file does not contain any hosts or services used in the internal network:

```
; public zone master file
; provides minimal public visibility of external services
example.com. IN      SOA    ns1.example.com. hostmaster.example.com. (
                            2010121500 ; sn = serial number
                            12h        ; ref = refresh
                            15m        ; retry = refresh retry
                            3w         ; expiry
                            3h       ; nx = nxdomain ttl
                            )
            IN      NS     ns1.example.com.
            IN      NS     ns2.example.com.
            IN      MX  10 mail.example.com.
            IN      MX  20 mail.example.net.
ns1         IN      A      192.168.254.1
ns1         IN      A      192.168.254.2
mail        IN      A      192.168.254.3
www         IN      A      192.168.254.4
ftp         IN      A      192.168.254.5
```

The internal name server—the stealth server—zone file will make visible internal and external hosts, provide recursive queries, and all manner of other services. For instance, this name server would use a private zone master file that could look like this:

```
; private zone master file used by Stealth server(s)
; provides public and private services and hosts
example.com. IN      SOA    ns3.example.com. hostmaster.example.com. (
                            2010121500 ; sn = serial number
                            12h        ; ref = refresh
                            15m        ; retry = refresh retry
                            3w         ; expiry
                            3h         ; nx = nxdomain ttl
                            )
            IN      NS     ns3.example.com.
            IN      NS     ns4.example.com.
            IN      NS  10 mail.example.com.
            IN      MX  20 mail.example.net.
; public hosts
```

```
mail            IN      A       192.168.254.3
www             IN      A       192.168.254.4
ftp             IN      A       192.168.254.5
; private hosts
joe             IN      A       192.168.254.6
bill            IN      A       192.168.254.7
fred            IN      A       192.168.254.8
ns3             IN      A       192.168.254.9
ns4             IN      A       192.168.254.10
....
accounting      IN      A       192.168.254.28
payroll         IN      A       192.168.254.29
```

Clearly, the internal users must cross the perimeter at some point to access external services, including DNS services. There are two possible solutions to this problem:

1. The classic firewall solution in which the internal systems, including the DNS server, are permitted on a transaction-by-transaction basis to send and receive data externally.

2. BIND 9's view clause may be used to provide support for caching and recursive query services for the internal network on the public DNS server. The view clause can be used to provide these services while continuing to deny them to external users and without exposing the structure of the internal network. The relevant configuration files and a further explanation of this style of operation is provided in Chapter 7. This solution does not eliminate the need for a firewall for non-DNS traffic.

Figure 4–6 illustrates the traffic flows for firewall-based and BIND view-based solutions.

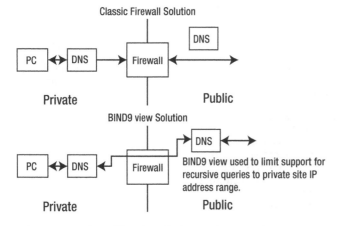

Figure 4–6. Firewall and DNS view perimeter solutions

■**Note** There is a third possibility, which is to define the internal network as using exclusively private IP addresses and to use a NAT gateway as the means of securing the internal network and limiting access to the external world. The world of the Internet has many conceptual disagreements. The argument between those who view NAT as a perfect solution that kept the Internet alive when it was in danger of running out of IPv4 addresses and those who see NAT as inherently evil is one of the more contentious. This book will stay gracefully agnostic on the topic of NAT, other than to point out that, increasingly, services that are delivered to desktops, such as VoIP, do require network visibility of end-user systems.

Example configuration files for a stealth DNS configuration are provided in Chapter 7.

Authoritative-only Name Server

The term *authoritative-only name server* is normally used to describe two related properties of a DNS server:

1.   The name server will deliver authoritative answers; it is a zone master or slave for one or more domains.

2.   The name server does not cache.

Authoritative-only servers are typically used in two distinct configurations:

1.   As public or external servers in a stealth DNS configuration used to provide perimeter security.

2.   As high-performance name servers, for example, root-servers, TLD servers, or name servers for high-volume sites.

Authoritative-only servers typically have high performance requirements. For many years, BIND was the only DNS software used by the root-servers and many of the TLD servers, which also have serious performance requirements, since it provides a high quality, highly functional, and stable platform. However, general-purpose DNS software, such as BIND 9, provides an excellent solution but is not optimized for use in high-performance authoritative-only servers. There are now a number of open source and commercial alternatives that specialize in high-performance authoritative-only DNS solutions, as discussed in Chapter 1. Indeed, the first member of the new BIND 10 family of DNS products is an authoritative-only name server (a first look at BIND 10 is available as an online chapter of this book).

It is not possible to directly control caching behavior in BIND 9, but the recursion statement effectively inhibits caching, as shown in the following BIND named.conf file fragment:

```
// options clause fragment of named.conf
// recursion no = effectively inhibits caching
options {
        recursion no;
};
// zone clauses
....
```

BIND 9 provides three more parameters to control caching: `max-cache-size` (limits the size of the cache on the file system) and `max-cache-ttl` (defines the maximum time RRs may live in the cache and overrides all RR TTL values), neither of which will have much effect on performance in the particular case just discussed, and `allow-recursion` (provides a list of hosts that are permitted to use recursion—all others are not).

Summary

This chapter described a number of commonly used DNS configurations and characteristics. Name servers, especially in smaller organizations, rarely perform a single function. They are almost by their nature schizophrenic. Indeed, the strength of general-purpose DNS software, especially BIND 9, is that it can be used to precisely configure multifaceted solutions. However, DNS software is undergoing significant change—driven by increasing complexity (notably but not exclusively, DNSSEC), increased demand for robustness and reliability, data-source flexibility, and superior performance. The increasing trend is to specialized DNS software, which is reflected in the significant number of both open source and commercial products that are providing either authoritative-only functionally (master or slave) or caching-only (resolver) functionality. The BIND 10 family (available as an online chapter of this book) is part of this trend. You also learned about the behavior of zone masters, zone slaves, caching servers, forwarding servers, and authoritative-only servers. You saw the configuration of stealth (or split) servers used in perimeter defense employing both classic configurations and BIND 9's `view` clause.

In Chapter 5, you'll look at the world of IPv6 and its implications for DNS.

CHAPTER 5

■ ■ ■

DNS and IPv6

While IPv6 provides many improvements in network management, one of the major driving forces behind its design was to greatly increase address space. An IPv4 address uses 32 bits whereas an IPv6 address uses 128 bits. Thus, IPv6 is theoretically capable of providing many millions of IP addresses for every human on the planet!

The original IETF specifications for IPv6 date from 1995 but the Classless Inter-Domain Routing and Network Address Translation (see the "IPv4 Addresses and CIDR" sidebar in Chapter 3) initiatives of the mid-90s effectively postponed the urgent need for additional address space. IPv6 usage until 2006 was largely confined to experimental networks such as the IETF's 6bone (www.6bone.net) and large-scale deployment was limited to academic institutions.

There are a number of significant developments that have given urgent impetus to IPv6 and have significantly increased its deployment:

- *Mobile communications*: The emerging 4G standards (primarily LTE and WiMax) will use packet switching (IP) technologies for all communications (voice and data), thus requiring every mobile device to have an IP address at all times. The 3rd Generation Partnership Project (www.3gpp.org), consisting of mobile wireless equipment suppliers and operators, has proposed standards that allow for both IPv4 and IPv6 but Release 8 (March 2009) defined a new, more efficient, dual-stack mechanism (IPv4v6). Since 4G networks will likely be deployed at a time when IPv4 address depletion (see below) will be reaching critical levels, it's reasonable to assume that IPv6 will be the preferred, if not the only viable, IP address technology for 4G networks. The first IPv6 mobile usage was publicly demonstrated in late 2004.

- *DNS support*: IPv6 addresses are already published by 8 of the 13 root-servers.

- *Address allocation*: IPv6 address block assignments may be obtained from all the regional Internet registries (RIRs), which comprise ARIN (www.arin.net covering North America and Southern Africa), RIPE (www.ripe.net covering Europe, North Africa, and the Middle East), APNIC (www.apnic.net covering Asia Pacific), LACNIC (www.lacnic.net covering South America), and AFRINIC (www.afrinic.net covering Africa).

- *Software availability*: IPv6 stacks and dual (IPv6/IPv4) stacks are provided with Windows (from Server 2003 and XP), Linux, UNIX, and the BSDs (FreeBSD, NetBSD, and OpenBSD).

- *Mainstream technology*: The IETF wrapped up its 6bone experimental and test-bed network and transferred its special IPv6 addresses range to IANA in June 2006. In essence, this endorsed the production-ready status of IPv6.

- *IPv4 address depletion*: Increasingly dire warnings are being heard from all the RIRs that the remaining IPv4 address stock will, for all practical purposes, be exhausted shortly—perhaps even as soon as the end of 2011.

Probably the most significant push for IPv6, however, is coming from the changing nature of Internet-based applications. Classic Internet applications such as those providing web access, e-mail, and FTP use a traditional client-server model and can handle mapping private addresses to a limited range of IPv4 public IP addresses using network address translation (NAT) strategies with some help from application-level gateways (ALGs). However, the new generation of Internet applications—such as Instant Messaging (IM) and Voice over IP (VoIP) among others—use a peer-to-peer model and increasingly require *always-on* capabilities (permanent connection to the Internet) and need end-user address transparency (any given user's equipment IP address must be publicly visible and fixed (*static*) over a reasonable period of time). The current IPv4 address scheme is incapable of providing all peer-to-peer users with end-user address transparency; there simply are not enough addresses. Figure 5–1 illustrates the difference between the client-server model with NAT and peer-to-peer applications.

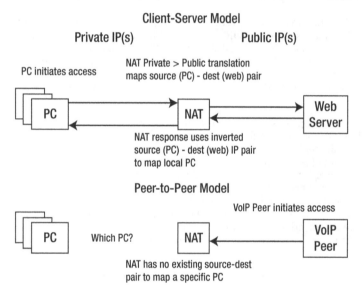

Figure 5–1. *IP Address Transparency*

The huge investment in IPv4 together with the size of the current installed base means IPv4 will not disappear overnight. IPv6 and IPv4 will have to coexist for some considerable period of time, and serious attention has been paid to IPv4 transition and interworking schemes in the various IPv6 RFCs. There are significant implications for DNS in both IPv6 and mixed IPv6/IPv4 environments.

Now that you have a better general understanding for why IPv6 will soon become a particularly important part of the network environment, let's take a moment to introduce IPv6 before delving into the implications it will have on DNS implementations.

IPv6

IPv6 is a big and complex protocol providing many new features for the efficient operation and management of dynamic networks, including the following:

- Significantly expanded address space using 128 bits (IPv4 uses a 32-bit address).

- Scoped addresses—IPv6 addresses can be limited to the local LAN or a private network, or they can be globally unique.

- Security is defined as part of the protocol.

- Autoconfiguration—stateless or stateful (DHCP enhancements).

- Mobile IPv6 (MIPv6) is significantly more powerful than its IPv4 counterpart.

This section is not designed to fully describe the IPv6 protocol but rather to familiarize you with the addressing features of IPv6 as they affect the DNS system.

Each IPv6 network interface, such as a LAN card on a PC or a mobile phone, may have more than one IPv6 address—that is, IPv6 is naturally *multihomed*. An IPv6 address has a *scope*: it can be restricted to a single LAN, a private network, or be globally unique. Table 5–1 defines the types of IPv6 addresses that are supported and contrasts them with the closest IPv4 functional equivalent.

Table 5–1. Comparison of IPv6 and IPv4 Functionality

IPv6 Name	Scope/Description	IPv4 Equivalent	Notes
Link-Local	Local LAN only. Automatically assigned based on MAC. Can't be routed outside local LAN.	No real equivalent. Assigned IPv4 over ARP'd MAC.	Automatically configured by most stacks from the LAN Media Access Control (MAC) address of the network interface. Scoped address concept new to IPv6.
Site-Local	Optional. Local site only. Cannot be routed over the Internet. Assigned by user.	Private network address (RFC 1918) with multihomed interface is closest equivalent.	Work is ongoing by the IETF to clarify the use of the Site-Local address and support has currently been withdrawn.
Global Unicast	Globally unique. Fully routable. Assigned by IANA/aggregators/Internet registries (IRs).	Global IP address.	IPv6 and IPv4 similar but IPv6 can have *other* scoped addresses.

IPv6 Name	Scope/Description	IPv4 Equivalent	Notes
Multicast	One-to-many. Hierarchy of multicasting.	Similar to IPv4 Class D.	Significantly more powerful than IPv4 version. No broadcast in IPv6, replaced by Multicast.
Anycast	One-to-nearest. Uses Global Unicast addresses. Routers only. Discovery uses.	Unique protocols in IPv4, for example, IGMP.	Some *Anycast* addresses reserved for special functions. Since *anycasting* is transparent and is supported only by routers it can be used in IPv4 networks.
Loopback	Local interface scope.	Same as IPv4 127.0.0.1.	Same function.

IPv6 Address Notation

An IPv6 address consists of 128 bits, whereas an IPv4 address consists of 32 bits. An IPv6 address is written as a series of eight hexadecimal strings separated by colons. Each string represents 16 bits and consists of four hexadecimal characters (0 – 9, A - F), thus each hexadecimal character represents 4 bits. The following are IPv6 address examples:

```
# all the following refer to the same address
2001:0DB8:0234:C1AB:0000:00A0:AABC:003F
# leading zeros can always be omitted
2001:DB8:234:C1AB:0:A0:AABC:3F
# not case sensitive - any mixture allowed
2001:db8:234:C1ab:0:A0:aabc:3F
```

Complete zero entries can be omitted entirely but only once in an address, like so:

```
# full ipv6 address
2001:db8:234:C1AB:0000:00A0:0000:003F
# address with single 0 dropped
2001:db8:234:C1ab:0:A0::003F
# alternate form using single 0 dropped
2001:db8:234:C1ab::A0:0:003F
# but the following is invalid
2001:db8:0234:C1ab::A0::003F
```

Multiple zero entries can be omitted entirely but only once in an address, like so:

```
# omitting multiple zeros in address
2001:db8:0:0:0:0:0:3F
# can be written as
2001:db8::3F
# lots of zeros (loopback address)
0:0:0:0:0:0:0:1
```

```
# can be written as
::1
# all zeros (unspecified, a.k.a unassigned IP)
0:0:0:0:0:0:0:0
# can be written as
::
# but this address
2001:db8:0:1:0:0:0:3F
# cannot be reduced to this
2001:db8::1::3F  # INVALID
# instead it can only be reduced to
2001:db8::1:0:0:0:3F
# or
2001:db8:0:1::3F
```

A hybrid format may be used when dealing with IPv6-IPv4 addresses where the normal IPv4 dotted decimal notation may be used after the first six 16-bit address elements, like so:

```
# generic IPv6-IPv4 format x.x.x.x.x.x.d.d.d.d
# example of an IPv4 mapped IPv6 address
# with an IPv4 number of 192.168.0.5
2001:db8:0:0:0:FFFF:192.168.0.5
# or using zero ommission
2001:db8::FFFF:192.168.0.5
```

Prefix or Slash Notation

IPv6 addresses use the IP prefix or slash notation in a similar manner to IPv4 to indicate the number of contiguous bits in the netmask, like so:

```
# a single IP address - 128 bit netmask for loopback
::1/128
# /128 is a netmask of FFFF:FFFF:FFFF:FFFF:FFFF:FFFF:FFFF:FFFF
# equivalent of IPv4 127.0.0.1/32
# values only required to cover the prefix
# Link-Local address mask (see below)
FE8::/10
# or top 3 bits only with fixed value 001 (binary)
2::/3
# example end user site prefix routing mask
2001:db8:222::/48
# example end user subnet routing mask
2001:db8:222:1::/64
```

See the "IPv4 Addresses and CIDR" sidebar in Chapter 3 for more information.

IPv6 Address Types

The type of IP address is defined by a variable number of the top bits of its address—the bits are collectively known as the *binary prefix* (BP). Only as many bits as required are used to identify the address type, which is defined in RFC 4291. Table 5–2 describes the types.

Table 5–2. IPv6 Address Types

Use	Binary Prefix	IP Prefix	Description/Notes
Unspecified	00...0	::/128	IPv6 address = 0:0:0:0:0:0:0:0 (or ::). Used before an address allocated by DHCP (equivalent of IPv4 0.0.0.0).
Loopback	00...1	::1/128	IPv6 address = 0:0:0:0:0:0:0:1 (or ::1). Local PC Loopback address (equivalent of IPv4 127.0.0.1).
Multicast	1111 1111	FF00::/8	IPv6 Multicast replaces both multicast and broadcast in IPv4.
Link-Local Unicast	1111 1110 10	FE80::/1	Local LAN scope. Lower bits assigned by user.
Reserved Unicast	1111 1110 11	FEC0::/10	Was the Site-Local address range. This address range is currently reserved by IANA while the IETF considers the status of the Site-Local features of IPv6.
Global Unicast	All other values		Assigned by IANA and aggregators. IANA assigns address netblocks to aggregators (RIRs) as defined at www.iana.org/assignments/ipv6-unicast-address-assignments/. The Global Unicast address format is defined in the "Global Unicast IPv6 Address Allocation" Section.

■**Note** The generic term *aggregator* is used to describe various Internet registries (RIRs and ISPs) that are responsible for the allocation of IPv6 addresses and for IPv6 reverse-map delegation.

Global Unicast IPv6 Address Allocation

The IPv6 Global Unicast address is hierarchical and is divided into what was historically called a *site prefix* but has now been renamed a *global routing prefix*, a subnet ID and interface ID address parts. Various agencies or Internet registries—called *aggregators* in IPv6 terminology—assign the global routing prefix as defined in Figure 5–2.

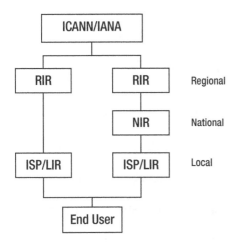

Figure 5–2. *IPv6 hierarchical address allocation*

IP address allocation follows similar rules as those for domain name delegation in that each level delegates control to the next level in the hierarchy. Thus, Figure 5–2 allows the RIRs (APNIC, AFRINIC, ARIN, RIPE, and LACNIC) to assign either directly to ISPs/LIRs (local Internet registries) or via an NIR (national Internet registry). As an illustration, APNIC assigns directly to LIRs in certain countries whereas in a number of other countries (for example China) assignments are made to the NIR (in this case CNNIC at www.cnnic.cn), which then assigns to its national LIRs or end users.

RFC 3177 defines the current IETF/IAB policy for end-user IPv6 address allocation. It is important to note that this RFC has only informational status and RIRs/NIRs/LIRs can, and do, adopt varying allocation policies. According to RFC 3177 end users may be allocated one of three IPv6 address ranges:

1. *Normal end user*: An end user is normally allocated a full 80 bits of address space (see Table 5–4 in the next section for a description of the format). The allocated address space may be assigned in any way required by the end user. This *normal* end-user address range allocation is greater than the whole of the current IPv4 Internet. This allocation is written as /48 in the slash or IP prefix notation.

2. *Single subnet*: Where it is known that only a single subnet (site) will be used, the end user may be allocated only 64 bits of address space. This allocation is written as /64 in the slash or IP prefix notation.

3. *Single device*: Where it is known that only one device will be used, a single IPv6 address may be allocated. This allocation is written as /128 in the slash or IP prefix notation.

Internet registries may, however, allocate much larger IPv6 address blocks to groups of users such as governments.

IPv6 Global Unicast Address Format

The generic format of an IPv6 Global Unicast address is shown in Table 5–3.

Table 5–3. *Generic IPv6 Global Unicast Address Format*

Name	Size	Description/Notes
Global routing prefix	Variable	Assigned by IANA/Aggregators/RIRs/NIRs
Subnet ID	Variable	Used for subnet routing. Assigned by RIRs/NIRs/ISPs/LIRs
Interface ID	64 bits	Equivalent of the host address in IPv4. May also be referred to as either IID or EUI-64.

In the original, now obsolete, IPv6 RFCs a Global Routing Prefix consisting of 48 bits was subdivided into a strict hierarchy of fixed length bit fields, each of which was assigned by an aggregator. In addition, the Subnet ID was a fixed 16 bits in length and assigned to the end user as described above. The current IPv6 addressing standard (RFC 4291) has opted for a more flexible structure which retains a fixed 64 bit Interface ID but defines the Global Routing Prefix and Subnet ID as being of variable length within the remaining 64 bits of the IPv6 address. The net effect of this change is two-fold. First, ICANN/IANA and the RIRs, as well as any NIRs/ISPs/LIRs, can tactically allocate from the combined 64 bit space based on local requirements and agreements. IANA publishes its current IPv6 allocations, which typically vary from /12 to /23 netblocks (www.iana.org/assignments/ipv6-unicast-address-assignments); RIRs do not publish their allocations. Second, the Subnet ID may be 16 bits (a /48, as in the original IAB recommendation), 8 bits (a /56), or even lower if conditions require it. A request by an end user for an IPv6 address block should be directed to the Local LIR, which is normally, but not always, an ISP. Lists of LIRs may be obtained from each RIR, as defined in Table 5–4.

Table 5–4. *Regional Internet Registries*

RIR Name	Coverage	Web
APNIC	Asia Pacific	www.apnic.net
ARIN	North America, Southern Africa, parts of the Caribbean	www.arin.net
LACNIC	South America, parts of the Caribbean	www.apnic.net
RIPE	Europe, Middle East, Northern Africa, parts of Asia	www.ripe.net
AFRINIC	Africa	www.afrinic.net

■**Note** Every ISP or Internet registry that assigns IPv6 address blocks also has the responsibility to provide reverse-map delegation. IPv6 is designed to provide complete reverse-map coverage down to every host or end device.

Status of IPv6 DNS Support

The DNS has included support for IPv6 from its earliest definition in 1995. During that time, the IPv6 standard has evolved—indeed, it's still evolving—and the DNS specifications have evolved in parallel. The essence of any such evolution is the need to experiment to solve new problems and to provide new functionality. Not all experiments are successful—were this not true, it's doubtful if any real progress could be made. The following sections describe the current DNS features and functionality that support IPv6 in its current stage of evolution.

The AAAA vs. A6 Resource Record

DNS IPv6 support is still the subject of some confusion and requires some historical perspective. As previously stated, DNS has supported IPv6 since 1995 (RFC 1886). This RFC specifies that IPv6 forward mapping will use an AAAA (QUAD A) RR. Reverse mapping (described in Chapter 3) was defined to use an extended version of the PTR RR under the domain name IP6.INT.

RFC 2673 (1999) and RFC 2874 (2000) introduced new DNS capabilities to more efficiently support IPv6 services—specifically network renumbering—using new *bit labels* and two new RRs. The A6 RR was designed to be used for forward mapping, and the DNAME RR was designed to enhance support for reverse mapping. These new RRs were defined to deprecate the use of the AAAA RRs in IPv6 and mixed IPv6/IPv4 networks.

However, after considerable debate and amid much controversy, the IETF issued RFC 3363 (2002) that changed RFC 2673 (bit labels) and RFC 2874 (A6 RR) to EXPERIMENTAL status—effectively removing the A6 RR from operational use (DNAME is still operational). The current IETF recommendation is contained in RFC 3596 (largely a reissue of RFC 1886) and has DRAFT STANDARD status as summarized here:

- Forward mapping of IPv6 addresses will use the AAAA (Quad A) RR (same as RFC 1886).

- Reverse mapping will use the IP6.ARPA domain (change from RFC 1886).

- Reverse mapping will use the PTR RR (same as RFC 1886).

The AAAA and PTR RRs are used exclusively in all the examples since they constitute the current IETF recommendation. For the sake of completeness, the A6 and DNAME RRs are described in Chapter 13.

Mixed IPv6 and IPv4 Network Support

A DNS system must support both IPv6 and IPv4 networks during what may be a long transitional period. BIND provides two features for supporting this capability:

- Forward mapping of IPv4 addresses (using A RRs as described in Chapter 2) and IPv6 addresses (using AAAA RRs described in this chapter) may appear in the same zone file.

- BIND 9 and 10 support both IPv4 and IPv6 native protocol DNS queries. Previous versions, while supporting IPv6 AAAA and PTR RRs, only supported IPv4 protocol queries. Thus, it's possible to query a BIND 9 or 10 DNS using IPv4 and obtain an IPv6 AAAA RR and/or an A RR and conversely to query a DNS using IPv6 and obtain an A RR and/or an AAAA RR.

The reverse-mapping files, however, can't be mixed since IPv4 reverse maps under the domain IN-ADDR.ARPA while IPv6 uses IP6.ARPA.

IPv6 Resource Records

As previously mentioned, the current IETF recommendation defined in RFC 3596 mandates the use of the AAAA (colloquially referred to as *Quad A*) RR for forward mapping of IPv6 address records and PTR RRs for the reverse mapping of IPv6 addresses. To illustrate the use of the two RRs, the standard IPv4 zone file introduced in Chapter 1 is enhanced to provide support for both IPv4 and IPv6. It is assumed that all the defined systems will provide dual stack support; that is, each host is capable of responding to both IPv4 and IPv6 protocol requests. This is one of a number of techniques that may be used during IPv4-to-IPv6 transition and is embraced by all mainstream platforms, including Microsoft Windows, Linux, UNIX, and BSD platforms.

The following is a standard IPv4 version of the example zone file:

```
; IPv4 zone file for example.com
$TTL 2d    ; default TTL for zone
$ORIGIN example.com.
; Start of Authority RR defining the key characteristics of the zone (domain)
@         IN     SOA   ns1.example.com. hostmaster.example.com. (
                       2010121500 ; sn = serial number
                       12h        ; refresh
                       15m        ; retry = refresh retry
                       3w         ; expiry
                       2h         ; nx = nxdomain ttl
                       )
; name server RRs for the domain
          IN     NS    ns1.example.com.
; the second name server is
; external to this zone (domain).
          IN     NS    ns2.example.net.
; mail server RRs for the zone (domain)
     3w   IN     MX  10 mail.example.com.
; the second  mail server is
; external to the zone (domain)
          IN     MX  20 mail.example.net.
; domain hosts includes NS and MX records defined earlier
; plus any others required
ns1       IN     A     192.168.254.2
mail      IN     A     192.168.254.4
joe       IN     A     192.168.254.6
www       IN     A     192.168.254.7
; aliases ftp (ftp server) to an external location
ftp       IN     CNAME ftp.example.net
```

The IPv6 user configuration used throughout the following sections is as follows:

1. Example, Inc. has been allocated a normal end user IPv6 address range of 2001:db8::/48. This allocation provides addresses in the range 2001:db8:0:0:0:0:0:0 (or 2001:db8::) to 2001:db8:0:FFFF:FFFF:FFFF:FFFF:FFFF, which may be assigned and used at the discretion of Example, Inc. The global routing prefix is 2001:db8:0::, which is assumed to be allocated by IANA and the various aggregators (the regional and local Internet registries).

2. Example, Inc. will have two IPv6 subnets: the first contains the hosts ns1.example.com and mail.example.com and the second contains joe.example.com and www.example.com.

3. IPv6 addresses in the first subnet will be in the range 2001:db8:0:1::/64 and the second in 2001:db8:0:2::/64.

4. Each host supports dual stack operation—it has both an IPv4 address and an IPv6 address.

5. IPv6 reverse-map delegation is automatically provided by the aggregators that allocated the IPv6 address range, and Example, Inc. is required to provide reverse-mapping support for its locally assigned addresses using the IP6.ARPA domain.

When this configuration is upgraded to support IPv6 and IPv4, the modified zone file becomes the following:

```
; transitional IPv6/IPv4 zone file for example.com
$TTL 2d     ; default TTL for zone
$ORIGIN example.com.
; Start of Authority RR defining the key characteristics of the zone (domain)
@          IN      SOA    ns1.example.com. hostmaster.example.com. (
                          2010121500 ; sn = serial number
                          12h        ; refresh
                          15m        ; retry = refresh retry
                          3w         ; expiry
                          2h         ; nx = nxdomain ttl
                          )
; name server RRs for the domain
           IN      NS     ns1.example.com.
; the second name server is
; external to this zone (domain).
           IN      NS     ns2.example.net.
; mail server RRs for the zone (domain)
      3w   IN      MX  10 mail.example.com.
; the second mail server is
; external to the zone (domain)
           IN      MX  20 mail.example.net.
; domain hosts includes NS and MX records defined above
; plus any others required
; the following hosts are in IPv6 subnet 1
ns1        IN      A         192.168.254.2
ns1        IN      AAAA 2001:db8:0:1::1
mail       IN      A         192.168.254.4
mail       IN      AAAA 2001:db8:0:1::2
; these hosts are defined to be in the IPv6 subnet 2
```

```
joe          IN     A       192.168.254.6
joe          IN     AAAA 2001:db8:0:2::1
www          IN     A       192.168.254.7
www          IN     AAAA 2001:db8:0:2::2
; aliases ftp (ftp server) to an external location
ftp          IN     CNAME   ftp.example.net
```

For the purposes of clarity only, this zone file has repeated the name of each host in the AAAA RR. Using blank label substitution, these names could have been omitted as shown in the following fragment for the www.example.com RR:

```
www          IN     A       192.168.254.7
             IN     AAAA 2001:db8:0:2::2 ; = www
```

Forward mapping of the IPv6 address is accomplished using the AAAA (Quad A) RR, which is described in the next section.

■**Note** The address range 2001:db8::/32 is nonroutable and specifically reserved by RFC 3849 for use in documentation.

The AAAA Resource Record

The AAAA (Quad A) RR is the current IETF recommendation for defining forward mapping of IPv6 addresses and is defined in RFC 3596. It is equivalent to the A RR used for IPv4 forward mapping. The formal syntax is as follows:

name   ttl   class   rr   ipv6

In the enhanced IPv6/IPv4 example file shown previously, the following AAAA RR is defined:

ns1   IN   AAAA 2001:db8:0:1::1

The separators between fields can be either spaces or tabs. In zone files, tabs are traditionally used to make a more attractive layout and to clearly indicate which fields are missing.

Table 5–5 maps the formal syntax to the AAAA RR used in the example zone file.

Recall that IPv6 provides scoped addresses. Your hosts will have Link-Local IPv6 addresses as well as the Global Unicast addresses. When software on the host wishes to access a local host, it doesn't use a name server to look up the address; instead, it uses a local Multicast group to find all such local hosts. Only Global Unicast addresses need appear in the zone file.

Table 5–5. AAAA RR Syntax

Syntax	Example Usage	Description
name	ns1	The name is unqualified, causing the $ORIGIN directive value to be substituted. This could be written as ns1.example.com. (using the FQDN format), which may be more understandable.
ttl		There is no ttl value defined for the RR, so the zone default of 2d from the $TTL directive will be used.
class	IN	IN defines the class to be Internet.
ipv6	2001:db8:0:1::1	This is a Global Unicast address and takes the format defined in Table 5–3. The address shown uses the zero elimination feature of IPv6 and could have been written as 2001:db8:0:1:0:0:0:1. The value 2001:db8:0 is the global routing prefix assigned by IANA and the aggregators (the Internet registries). The first 1 is the subnet and the value ::1 is the locally assigned (end user) Interface ID (EUI-64).

Reverse IPv6 Mapping

Like its IPv4 cousin it is now a policy matter for the IPv6 address assignor (RIR or ISP) to decide whether to delegate IPv6 reverse mapping to the end user. There is no current consensus on the matter. The end user may therefore be responsible for creation of reverse-mapping zone files using the IP6.ARPA domain for the address range they have been assigned. The IP6.ARPA domain is similar to the IN-ADDR.ARPA domain used for reverse mapping of IPv4 addresses (described in Chapter 3). From the zone files defined previously, you can see that the Global Unicast address range allocated to the end user Example, Inc. is:

2001:db8:0::/48

Example, Inc. is responsible for reverse mapping the 80-bit addresses in this range (see Table 5–3). IPv6 reverse mapping uses the normal principle of reversing the address and placing the result under the domain IP6.ARPA. The key difference from the IN-ADDR.ARPA domain is that a *nibble* is the unit of delegation. A nibble is one of those glorious terms that have survived to enter the jargon. Each byte (or octet) is comprised of 8 bits; a nibble is part of a byte and consists of 4 bits. So a nibble is a small byte! In the context of reverse mapping, each character in the IPv6 address string constitutes a nibble. To illustrate how this works, you must write each character—with no zero elimination—of the Example, Inc. assigned addresses range, like so:

2001:0db8:0000::/48

Each character is reversed and separated with the normal dot notation to give a reverse-map domain name, as shown here:

0.0.0.0.8.b.d.0.1.0.0.2.IP6.ARPA

Finally, you construct a zone file to contain the definitions, like so:

```
; reverse IPV6 zone file for example.com
$TTL 2d    ; default TTL for zone
```

```
$ORIGIN 0.0.0.0.8.b.d.0.1.0.0.2.IP6.ARPA.
; Start of Authority RR defining the key characteristics of the zone (domain)
@          IN     SOA   ns1.example.com. hostmaster.example.com. (
                        2010121500 ; sn = serial number
                        12h        ; refresh = refresh
                        15m        ; retry = refresh retry
                        3w         ; expiry = expiry
                        2h         ; nx = nxdomain ttl
                        )
; name server RRs for the domain
           IN     NS    ns1.example.com.
; the second name server is
; external to this zone (domain).
           IN     NS    ns2.example.net.
; PTR RR maps a IPv6 address to a host name
; hosts in subnet ID 1
1.0.0.0.0.0.0.0.0.0.0.0.0.0.0.0.1.0.0.0         IN     PTR   ns1.example.com.
2.0.0.0.0.0.0.0.0.0.0.0.0.0.0.0.1.0.0.0         IN     PTR   mail.example.com.
; hosts in subnet ID 2
1.0.0.0.0.0.0.0.0.0.0.0.0.0.0.0.2.0.0.0         IN     PTR   joe.example.com.
2.0.0.0.0.0.0.0.0.0.0.0.0.0.0.0.2.0.0.0         IN     PTR   www.example.com.
```

The individual PTR address labels can become brutally long. The constructed domain name, however, doesn't have to reflect the address segmentation between the global routing prefix and the end-user part of the address as shown in the preceding example. If you assume that Example, Inc. will only ever have a maximum of 65,535 hosts in each subnet (using only the right-most 16 bits of the Interface ID), then you can move some of the end user address into the zone domain name (which is written once) to reduce the address part in each PTR line (which may be written many hundreds of times). Thus, the IPv6 address splits in Table 5–6 achieve the same result.

Table 5–6. *IPv6 Alternative Reverse Mappings*

Zone Name	PTR Part	Note
0.0.0.0.8.b.d.0.1.0.0.2.IP6.ARPA.	1.0.0.0.0.0.0.0.0.0.0.↪ 0.0.0.0.0.1.0.0.0	Uses a split based on the global routing prefix.
0.0.0.0.0.0.0.0.0.0.0.0.1.0.0.0.0.0. ↪ 0.0.8.b.d.0.1.0.0.2.IP6.ARPA.	1.0.0.0	Uses a split based on user convenience to reduce the size of each PTR RR. Because the subnet ID appears in the zone name, a second zone file is required in this scenario to describe subnet 2.

The two zone files to implement this alternate structure are shown next. Here's the zone file for subnet ID 1:

```
; reverse IPV6 zone file for example.com subnet ID 1
$TTL 2d    ; default TTL for zone
$ORIGIN .0.0.0.0.0.0.0.0.0.0.0.0.1.0.0.0.0.0.0.0.8.b.d.0.1.0.0.2.IP6.ARPA.
; Start of Authority RR defining the key characteristics of the zone (domain)
@          IN     SOA   ns1.example.com. hostmaster.example.com. (
                        2010121500 ; sn = serial number
```

```
                12h            ; refresh = refresh
                15m            ; retry = refresh retry
                3w             ; expiry = expiry
                2h             ; nx = nxdomain ttl
                )
; name server RRs for the domain
        IN     NS     ns1.example.com.
; the second name server is
; external to this zone (domain).
        IN     NS     ns2.example.net.
; PTR RR maps a IPv6 address to the hostnames in subnet ID 1
1.0.0.0        IN     PTR     ns1.example.com.
2.0.0.0        IN     PTR     mail.example.com.
```

And the zone file for subnet ID 2 is:

```
; reverse IPV6 zone file for example.com subnet ID 2
$TTL 2d    ; default TTL for zone
$ORIGIN .0.0.0.0.0.0.0.0.0.0.0.0.2.0.0.0.0.0.0.0.8.b.d.0.1.0.0.2.IP6.ARPA.
; Start of Authority RR defining the key characteristics of the zone (domain)
@         IN     SOA    ns1.example.com. hostmaster.example.com. (
                2010121500 ; sn = serial number
                12h            ; refresh = refresh
                15m            ; retry = refresh retry
                3w             ; expiry = expiry
                2h             ; nx = nxdomain ttl
                )
; name server's RRs for the domain
        IN     NS     ns1.example.com.
; the second name server is
; external to this zone (domain).
        IN     NS     ns2.example.net.
; PTR RR maps a IPv6 address to the hostnames in subnet ID 2
1.0.0.0.         IN     PTR     joe.example.com.
2.0.0.0          IN     PTR     www.example.com.
```

The PTR RR that is used in IPv6 is described in the next section.

■**Note** An earlier version of the IPv6 specification used the reverse-map domain IP6.INT. This domain has been superseded in RFC 3596 with IP6.ARPA to make it consistent with IPv4's IN-ADDR.ARPA domain.

IPv6 Reverse Map Issues

In the case of an IPv6 end-user delegation, the normal expectation of IPv6 is that any address that is forward mapped using an AAAA RR is also reverse mapped using a PTR RR. Specifically, RFC 1912 (an INFORMATIONAL RFC) says "PTR records must point back to a valid A record" and that administrators should "Make sure your PTR and A records match." For the following reasons this may not be as simple as it sounds:

1. In most cases IPv6 addresses are configured using SLAAC (StateLess Address Auto Configuration) or DHCPv6 and therefore may not be known other than by manual inspection. Both methods may be configured to provide Dynamic DNS (DDNS) updates to the forward and reverse-mapped zones though in the case of very large networks even this can be problematic due to the potentially large number of hosts involved.

2. Some modern OS platforms can optionally generate essentially random IPv6 addresses for each session to provide some level of end-user/host privacy. These changes can only be mapped using DDNS since they are, by nature, both dynamic and transient.

This topic is currently the subject of considerable on-going discussion. It is worth noting however, that, as with the equivalent IPv4 addresses, the only current applications which are known to use reverse mapping consistently are mail systems. Thus, steps should be taken to ensure that, at least, mail server hosts have a valid IPv6 reverse-map.

The IPv6 PTR Resource Record

The PTR RR is standardized in RFC 1035 and maps an IPv6 address to a particular interface ID (*host* in IPv4 terminology) in the domain or zone as opposed to an AAAA RR, which maps a name to an IPv6 address. The formal syntax is as follows:

name   ttl   class   rr   name

In the first reverse-map example zone file, the first PTR RR is defined as follows:

1.0.0.0.0.0.0.0.0.0.0.0.0.0.0.0.1.0.0.0   IN   PTR   ns1.example.com.

Table 5–7 maps the formal syntax to the first PTR RR used in the example zone file.

Table 5–7. PTR RR Syntax

Syntax	Example Usage	Description
name	1.0.0.0.0.0.0.0.0.0.↪ 0.0.0.0.0.0.1.0.0.0	This is the subnet ID and interface ID parts of the IPv6 address written in reverse nibble format. While this looks like a number, it is treated as a name. The name is unqualified, causing the $ORIGIN directive value to be substituted. This could be written as 1.0.0.0.0.0.0.0.0.0.0.0.0.0.0.0.1.0.0.0.0.0.0.↪ 8.b.d.0.1.0.0.2.IP6.ARPA. (using the dot-terminated FQDN format) if that is more understandable.
ttl		There is no ttl value defined for the RR, so the zone default of 2d from the $TTL directive will be used.
class	IN	IN defines the class to be Internet.
name	ns1.example.com.	Defines that a query for 2001:db8::1 will return ns1.example.com.

Summary

This chapter described the use and implementation of IPv6 as it relates to the DNS. The chapter describing the long history of IPv6, starting in 1995, and suggested that a number of factors are currently causing a rapid increase in its the spread and deployment. A brief tutorial on IPv6 address notation was provided to help you become familiar with its format and usage.

There has been some confusion created by the withdrawal of support for bit labels and the A6 RR by the IETF in RFC 3363, so I provided an update on the status of DNS support. The current IETF IPv6 DNS recommendation specifies that forward mapping of IPv6 addresses will use the AAAA (Quad A) RR, and reverse mapping will use the PTR RR under the domain IP6.ARPA.

In Chapter 6, you move from theory to practice by looking at the installation of BIND on Linux, BSD (FreeBSD), and Windows platforms.

## PART II

Get Something Running

CHAPTER 6

■ ■ ■

Installing BIND

BIND (Berkeley Internet Name Domain) is an open source implementation of the Domain Name System (DNS) protocols and was originally developed by the University of California, Berkeley. BIND is generally viewed as the reference implementation of the Internet's DNS, the standard against which all other implementations are compared. Due to its stability and high quality, BIND is the most widely deployed DNS software, servicing most of the root and gTLD name servers as well as innumerable ISPs, commercial organizations, and, because of its incomparable cost advantage (freely available under the BSD license), even very small sites and individual PCs. In 1994, the responsibility for BIND development moved to Internet Systems Consortium, Inc. (ISC), a US-based nonprofit company that is also, among other things, the operator of the f.root-servers.net (one of the 13 root-servers). ISC funding comes from a wide variety of corporate sponsors for whom the availability of high-quality DNS software is vital to their commercial interests. BIND, reflecting its widespread deployment, is available on a bewildering number of OS platforms.

BIND has gone through a number of iterations over years from the original BIND 4 (deprecated in 2001) through BIND 8 (deprecated in 2007) to the first version of BIND 9 (a complete rewrite of the codebase) starting in 2000. BIND 9 remains the production release family and is being actively developed and maintained (and will be for some years to come) but BIND 10 (first release April 2010) represents a new and significant architectural departure from previous releases, so much so that its description, including installation, is separately addressed in an online chapter available with this book.

This chapter describes the installation of BIND 9.7.2-P2—the stable version at the time these tests were run—on a variety of widely deployed OS platforms using their packaged formats where available:

- *Ubuntu Server 10.04*: A representative Linux platform. Ubuntu (www.ubuntu.com) is a community-supported open source OS project backed by Canonical Group Limited. (See www.canonical.com for more information.) Ubuntu is layered on top of Debian (www.debian.org) and uses the same apt-get command line update manager (though different package repositories are involved).

- *FreeBSD 8.1*: A representative OS from the BSD/Unix family that comprises FreeBSD, NetBSD, OpenBSD, and DragonflyBSD. (See www.freebsd.org for more information.)

- *Windows*: ISC supplies a binary packaged version of BIND 9 for Windows Server 2003 and XP. BIND was also installed on Windows 7, which, while not officially supported by ISC, was a relatively trouble-free operation.

■**Note** BIND 9.7.2-P2 was the current version when all the *nix tests in this chapter were undertaken (Ubuntu and FreeBSD). However, readers are advised to always obtain the latest stable version of BIND software. The latest versions may always be found at `www.isc.org/software/bind` but only in source tarball or Windows binary format. OS suppliers (such as FreeBSD and Ubuntu in this case) will periodically update their package repositories from the ISC base. If your OS or distribution does not have the latest version available, you have three choices; wait until it does (how long is a piece of string?); install your current OS/distribution version (you might want to check what bugs are outstanding before you do this); or build it from the ISC source tarball.

Many of BIND's security features (including DNSSEC) require OpenSSL. Both FreeBSD and Ubuntu 10.04 install this package by default, and no special action is required. The Windows binary version of BIND uses standard Windows services and libraries, and again no special action is required. In the event that a packaged version of software is not available, the chapter describes building BIND from a source *tarball*—the widely used term that describes the file (that typically ends with `tar.tz`) containing the source and makefiles necessary to build the software and packaged using the `tar` (archive) and `compress` utilities. In all cases, BIND was configured and tested as a simple caching server using the files described in Chapter 7 in the "Caching-only DNS Server" section.

It is increasingly common that default installations of BIND are either configured to run in a *sandbox* or *chroot jail* (FreeBSD and Fedora) or offer an optional package to do so (bind-chroot RPM on Fedora). This method of running BIND is described in Chapter 10.

The installation procedures make no attempt to secure the various files before running BIND. This was deliberately done to avoid complication. Various methods of securing a BIND installation are described in Chapter 10; once you're thoroughly familiar with the initial installation and configuration, you are urged to read this chapter before running a live or operational server.

Let's start by looking at installation of BIND 9.7.2-P2 on Ubuntu Server 10.04 as a representative example of a Linux installation—it could just as easily have used Fedora Core, Debian, Mandriva, Gentoo, SUSE, or one of the many other Linux distributions.

■**Note** BIND runs as a *daemon* on Linux, Unix, and BSD systems and as a *service* on Windows OSes. When running as a daemon or service, it is called `named` not BIND. This book uses the term *BIND* to describe the package and `named` to describe the running or operational software.

Ubuntu Server 10.04 Installation

This section describes the installation, configuration, and testing of BIND 9.7.2-P2 on a clean Ubuntu Server 10.04 system. The Ubuntu Server software is freely available for download at `www.ubuntu.com/server` or as a multi-CD set at no cost (but users are warned that delivery could take up 10 weeks). In the case below, a single iso image was downloaded (Server version 10.04.1) and burned to a CD. Ubuntu (in common with many other systems) offers a USB memory stick installation method that can be created under Windows (XP/Vista/7), MAC, or Ubuntu. The installed Ubuntu Server 10.04 configuration used the following features:

1. Ubuntu offers a modest textual interface for the server install.

2. Manual partitioning was selected. This was not a perverse desire by the author to incur needless pain—simply that all the automatic (*guided* in Ubuntu terminology) methods assumed that the whole disc would be used. Since this machine was to be multi-boot, there was no alternative choice but to grind through the manual process.

3. A single partition containing the root (/) using the default ext4 filesystem and a single swap partition were created. It may be worth noting in passing that Ubuntu servers offers RAID and LVM configurations as well as normal file systems during the partitioning process.

4. No options were noticed during the install to select any graphical windows packages, for example GNOME or KDE, and thus a command line-only system resulted, which is entirely in keeping with the author's view of minimal software installation for a server. Alternatively, the lack of such an offer could have been down to the author's myopia not good design.

5. Ubuntu Server install offered a variety of software update methods. While this can be an extremely powerful feature, it can also do things at entirely inappropriate times. It is a matter of personal taste. No auto updates were selected, meaning that all software updating would be manual.

6. The installer offers a selection of software to be loaded and installed. Both DNS and OpenSSH were selected. Impressively, the installer checked for the latest versions of software (using apt-get) before installing anything, meaning that software was not frozen at the moment of release.

7. Installation of Ubuntu Server took less than 30 minutes and was very uneventful on a 2GHz PC.

Note One of the idiosyncrasies of the Ubuntu Server install is that it does not request a root password (meaning you can't log into the root account); rather, it has elected to use a user account (it prompts for the name and password of this account). The net effect is that many commands must use be preceded by sudo. If you feel naked without having access to a root account or detest unnecessary typing, simply issue sudo passwd root and at the next three prompts enter your normal account password, then the new root password, finally re-enter your new root password. You can then login as root and rejoice in a *sudoless* existence. All the commands in the following section assume a login as root but can all be run as a normal admin account (set up during the install process) by simply prepending *sudo*.

Post Ubuntu Server Installation

Selecting DNS during the Ubuntu Server install process causes the packages bind9, bind9utils, bind9-host to be added, which in turn trigger a number of dependent packages. This resulted in a default installation of BIND 9.7.0-P1-1, as shown:

```
# dpkg -l |grep bind
1:9.7.0.dfsg.P1-1
```

All the files necessary to run a viable default configuration were installed in /etc/bind and consisted of named.conf, various files included from **named.conf**, **db.root** (root servers hints file—what this book calls *root.servers*), localhost IPv4 reverse mapping zone file (**db.127**), a localhost forward IPv4 and IPv6 mapping zone file (**db.local**), and an empty zone file (**db.empty**). A startup script was installed as /etc/init.d/bind9 and this script was linked to start from runlevel startup directories for rc2.d – rc5.d (the server installation defaults to use runlevel 2). Both a user and group account called bind were set up to allow running of BIND 9 and a default set of flags (-u bind) were written to the file /etc/default/bind9. Curiously, no reverse localhost for IPv6 was present—though current versions of BIND include this as default empty zone (see Chapter 12).

To start the service with its default configuration, simply enter:

```
# /etc/init.d/bind9 start
```

The default configuration loaded under these circumstances is an *open resolver* (a.k.a. an *open caching name server*) meaning it will answer queries from any IP address arriving at port 53 and could thus be used in DDoS attacks and for other nefarious purposes. While one can argue that no one in their right minds would run a DNS server without at least checking its configuration, the inclusion of DNS in the startup process means that any reboot (a highly likely event during installation) would result— perhaps inadvertently—in an open resolver loose on the Internet—never a desirable goal. The simple inclusion of a listen-on {127.0.01;}; statement, with an appropriate descriptive comment, in the file /etc/bind/named.conf.options would have resulted in a safe, closed resolver configuration by limiting the scope of any DNS operations to the local system only.

■**Note** Since BIND 9.5+ the open status of this configuration has been prevented by defaulting the named.conf statement allow-query-cache {localnets;}; (see Chapter 12). However, this requires in-depth knowledge of the default values of BIND configuration on behalf of any user. It would have been significantly safer to have added a simple configuration parameter such as listen-on, allow-recursion, or allow-query-cache with appropriate comments to draw the users attention to the dangers of open resolvers.

The resulting Ubuntu configuration was tested using various dig commands and performed flawlessly.

Version Upgrade

The installation objective was to install BIND 9.7.2-P2—the then current and stable version of BIND 9— and thus required an upgrade to the default installation. There are two potential methods for checking updates to the Ubuntu system. The first method uses the excellent apt-get utility (aptitude is an alternative utility):

```
# apt-get update
```

This command simply updates the local package lists from the host services defined in the file /etc/apt/sources.list but does not change the installed state of any package. It is a necessary precursor to the next step but unfortunately doesn't list the updated packages. To find what packages have been updated, issue:

```
# apt-get upgrade
```

This command lists all the packages that will be upgraded and allows the user to make the choice as to whether to proceed with the upgrade or not. Only a single blanket choice is offered, not on a package-by-package basis. In the case of BIND 9, there was no upgrade; the upgrade was allowed to continue as matter of routine maintenance though it could have been safely abandoned at that stage.

The second method is to simply look for changes at the Ubuntu package site (packages.ubuntu.com). This method clearly requires a web browser and most likely a second PC on site since the server install does not provide a GUI, which may limit its usefulness. Select the relevant release (lucid 10.04 LTS, in the example case) at the web site, then select the Network group and scan for BIND9. Repeat the exercise by selecting "lucid updates" and again search under Network group. In neither case was BIND 9.7.2-P2 available. The reason for the apparent lack of an upgrade requires some understanding of the Ubuntu and Debian release philosophy.

Ubuntu and Debian

Ubuntu is based on Debian. The project aims may be different, and the relationship between the Ubuntu and Debian groups may at times be rocky, but they do share a firm technical base of which the Debian packaging system is a crucial part. Debian packages are listed at the web site packages.debian.org. Available packages are listed under Stable, Testing, and Unstable—this latter category is not for the faint hearted and was therefore avoided completely. However, BIND 9 version 9.7.2-P2 was found under the Testing category (the Debian Stable category listed BIND 9.6).

Any packaging system (Debian packages, RPMs, FreeBSD ports, etc) is designed to handle all the package dependency problems. That, together with saving the sanity of countless thousands of system administrators, is the good news. The bad news is that they do that by essentially freezing into the packaging process the various versions of the dependent software of the system on which they were built. This an oversimplification since some dependencies are expressed as > version x rather than specific version numbers but is essentially correct. While it would have been entirely possible to install the Debian Testing version of BIND 9.7.2-P2, the risk would be that all its associated dependencies would have in turn destabilized or even conflicted with other packages on the Ubuntu Server system. Short of manually inspecting all the dependency version numbers—a daunting and error prone task—the risks were simply judged to be both too high and contrary to the Ubuntu philosophy to use the Debian sourced package.

Ubuntu Summary

In summary, in the case of Ubuntu Server 10.04, the lesser risk by which BIND 9.7.2-P2 could be safely installed was judged to be building from a source tarball (see the "Building BING From Source" section later in this chapter).

Finally, the default Ubuntu BIND 9 install does not configure a chroot jail (see Chapter 10) unlike many other distributions (but does automatically configure BIND to run under a user account using the –u bind argument) and no standard packages were discovered that would provide this capability.

FreeBSD 8.1 Installation

FreeBSD is available for download from www.freebsd.org/where.html (in CD and DVD .iso format and in memory stick .img format since 8.1); for a modest cost you can also purchase a CD or DVD from a number of vendors.

A clean install of FreeBSD 8.1 was done using a downloaded CD (disk1) .iso image and a CD created locally. The following notes apply to the basic install process:

1. A single BSD slice (a.k.a. primary partition) was created and formatted on what would become a multi-boot PC.

2. Manual partitioning was selected since the author believes that FreeBSD's automatic partitioning system is excessively mean in its allocation or a /var partition (entirely a matter of taste).

3. Manual configuration of the local network was performed rather than use the default DHCP (an artifact of the test configuration).

4. IPv6 was selected.

5. FreeBSD offers a number of canned install profiles to simplify the process. The basic User profile was selected, essentially installing minimal sources and documentation.

6. The ports collection was not installed from the CD. This significantly speeds up the install process at the expense of the post-install tasks (see the "Post Install Tasks" section below) and download performance. However, if your download speed is anywhere from modest to pathetic you may want to install the ports from the CD.

7. The installation took around 15 minutes on a modestly powered 2GHz Intel Celeron (i686) powered PC and was entirely uneventful.

Post Install Tasks

The ports collection was not selected during the initial installation; this was a tactical decision to avoid a CD install and then an immediate update. To install the latest versions of the ports collection using the superb (post 6.x) **portsnap** utility, login as root and issue:

```
# portsnap fetch extract
```

Alternatively, if you had previously installed the ports collection during the install process then simply issue:

```
# portsnap fetch update
```

■**Tip** In the above case, using the extract form of the command a whopping 63M was downloaded. Careful editing of /etc/portsnap.conf (preferably before issuing the **portsnap** command!) and the REFUSE parameters to avoid port categories you will never use can save considerable download volume. Ports may alternatively be managed using csup, which is also part of the base installation. The venerable cvsup-without-gui is still available but needs to be installed from the net ports category.

Before installing any operational ports, it was found essential to install the gccmakedep port from the devel collection; otherwise, port dependencies will not be handled:

```
# cd /usr/ports/devel/gccmakedep
# make install clean
```

You may also want to install the useful **portupgrade** utility which, in spite of its name also installs **portinstall**, **portversion**, and **portsdb** among others. It also has, in this author's opinion, the delightful side effect of installing Ruby. To install portupgrade, simply issue:

```
# cd /usr/ports/ports-mgmt/portupgrade
# make install clean
```

Installing BIND 9

FreeBSD differentiates between a base DNS install and a normal (nonbase) DNS install. This differentiation allows two versions of BIND to be installed completely independently of each other—they use separate named.conf files and program locations. It is thus possible to test a new DNS release by installing as the nonbase system, changing only the /etc/rc.conf file or using the command line to run the tests. Reversion to the previous version is trivial since it has not been removed during the testing process. Once testing is complete, a base system install can be used to update the operational version. The base version of named is installed in /usr/sbin and the tools in /usr/bin (with some in /usr/sbin), whereas a normal (nonbase) installation is made to /usr/local/sbin and the tools to /usr/local/bin (with some also in /usr/local/sbin). The base version of named assumes the named.conf file is located in /etc/namedb/named.conf, whereas a nonbase install assumes /usr/local/etc/named.conf. FreeBSD creates the user account bind (as opposed to named for Linux) for use with BIND installations and installs, in all cases, a startup script as /etc/rc.d/named.

In all the cases that follow, BIND 9.7.2-P2 was installed unless otherwise specified. By default, FreeBSD installs BIND to run in a sandbox or chroot jail (use of chroot jails is described in Chapter 10). If a chroot jail is not required, it may be removed (see the "FreeBSD Considerations" section).

BIND 9 Nonbase Install

Assuming you have updated the ports-dns collection (using either csup or even cvsup) or used portsnap fetch update to get the latest versions, issue the following commands:

```
# cd /usr/ports/dns/bind97
# make rmconfig
# make install clean
```

■**Tip** The use of the make rmconfig is precautionary and deletes any previously selected configure options and thus ensures that the configure screen of Figure 6–1 is displayed. The configure options are not reset by make clean. However, if you are changing from a base to nonbase install (or vice versa), make rmconfig is essential.

BIND 9.7 offers a gruesome range of configure/compile time options. FreeBSD has for sometime used a configure selection window in the ports system to save a lot of command line typing. In the normal (nonbase) installation of BIND 9.7.2-P2, the configure window and the options that were selected are shown in Figure 6–1.

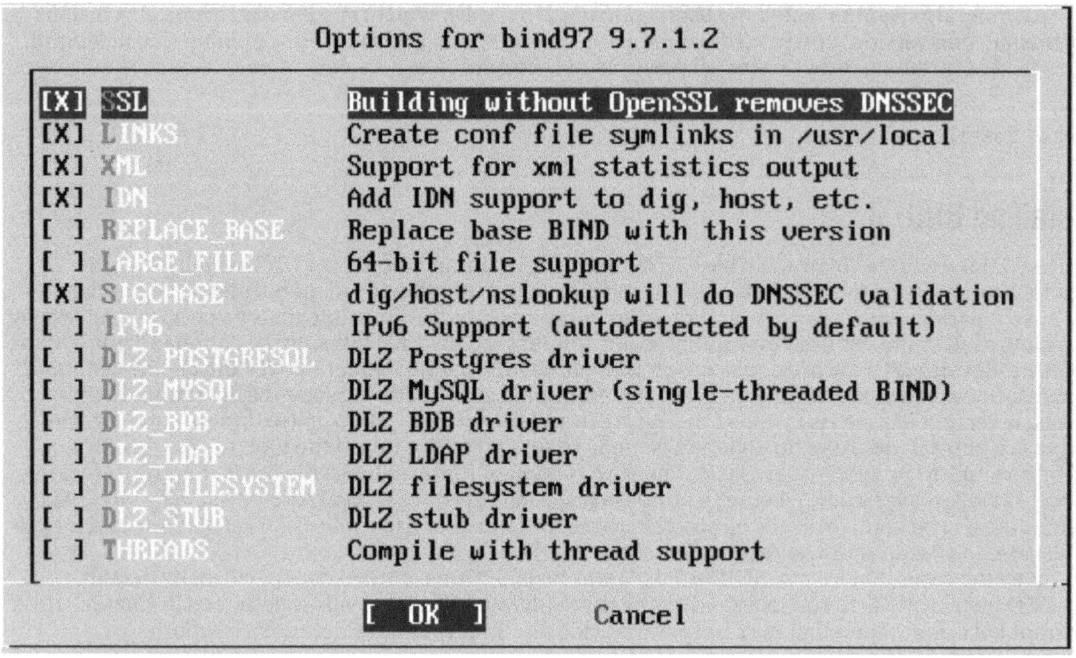

```
                    Options for bind97 9.7.1.2

 [X] SSL              Building without OpenSSL removes DNSSEC
 [X] LINKS            Create conf file symlinks in /usr/local
 [X] XML              Support for xml statistics output
 [X] IDN              Add IDN support to dig, host, etc.
 [ ] REPLACE_BASE     Replace base BIND with this version
 [ ] LARGE_FILE       64-bit file support
 [X] SIGCHASE         dig/host/nslookup will do DNSSEC validation
 [ ] IPV6             IPv6 Support (autodetected by default)
 [ ] DLZ_POSTGRESQL   DLZ Postgres driver
 [ ] DLZ_MYSQL        DLZ MySQL driver (single-threaded BIND)
 [ ] DLZ_BDB          DLZ BDB driver
 [ ] DLZ_LDAP         DLZ LDAP driver
 [ ] DLZ_FILESYSTEM   DLZ filesystem driver
 [ ] DLZ_STUB         DLZ stub driver
 [ ] THREADS          Compile with thread support


                [   OK   ]        Cancel
```

Figure 6–1. FreeBSD normal (nonbase) configure options

The above selection allows a validating DNSSEC (see Chapter 11) capable tool set (SIGCHASE option). DNSSEC is supported (SSL option) and installs symbolic links from /usr/local/etc/named.conf to /etc/namedb/named.conf (LINKS option). If you plan to use a separate named.conf for the nonbase install, uncheck this option. The XML option allows server statistics to be displayed as a XML page using a web browser connected to **named**. The various DLZ Options are discussed in the "BIND Configure Choices" section later in the chapter.

The preceding sequence installs BIND 9 in /usr/local/sbin and the tools in /usr/local/bin and /usr/local/sbin and assumes the named.conf file is in /usr/local/etc. To run BIND 9 at startup from this location, edit /etc/rc.conf as follows:

```
# add following line if not present
named_enable="YES"
# the line below must replace the line named_program="/usr/sbin/named' if present
# otherwise add it
named_program="/usr/local/sbin/named"
```

If you want to use an operational named.conf, either copy it from /etc/namedb to /usr/local/etc before starting BIND 9 (via the named daemon) or modify the default version of the file in this directory. To use the BIND 9 tools installed earlier, the command must be preceded with the BIND 9 tool directory path as shown:

```
# /usr/local/bin/dig @127.0.0.1 example.com any
```

Use of @127.0.0.1 will force use of the local DNS irrespective of the state of the /etc/resolv.conf file.

Prior to running BIND for the first time and assuming rndc (see Chapter 9) will be used, the following command should be issued to generate default keys:

```
# /usr/local/sbin/rndc-confgen -a
```

Assuming that /etc/rc.conf has been verified and edited appropriately as defined above, BIND 9 may be started using:

```
/etc/rc.d/named start
```

BIND 9 Base Install

This section assumes you either want to run the latest version of BIND as the base system—replacing any existing BIND—or a new install with Bind 9 as the base system. Assuming you have updated the ports-dns collection, issue the following commands:

```
# cd /usr/ports/dns/bind97
# make rmconfig
# make install clean
```

In the base installation of BIND 9.7.2-P2, the configure window and the options that were selected are shown in Figure 6–2.

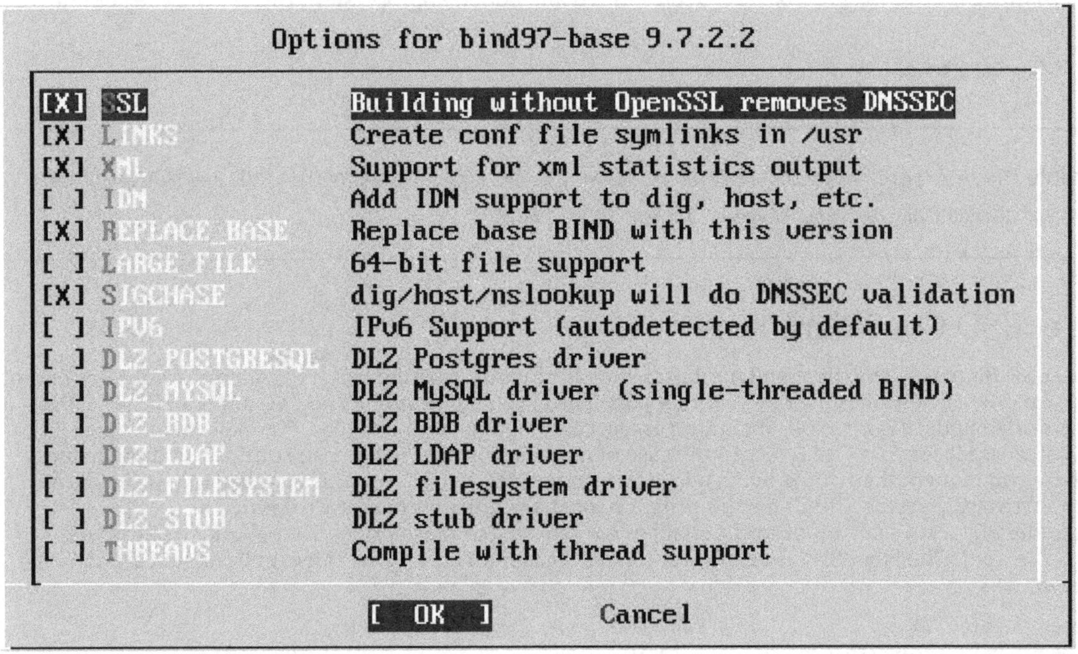

```
┌──────────────────────────────────────────────────────────────┐
│              Options for bind97-base 9.7.2.2                   │
│  ┌─────────────────────────────────────────────────────────┐  │
│  │ [X] SSL         Building without OpenSSL removes DNSSEC  │  │
│  │ [X] LINKS       Create conf file symlinks in /usr        │  │
│  │ [X] XML         Support for xml statistics output        │  │
│  │ [ ] IDN         Add IDN support to dig, host, etc.       │  │
│  │ [X] REPLACE_BASE  Replace base BIND with this version    │  │
│  │ [ ] LARGE_FILE  64-bit file support                      │  │
│  │ [X] SIGCHASE    dig/host/nslookup will do DNSSEC validation │
│  │ [ ] IPV6        IPv6 Support (autodetected by default)   │  │
│  │ [ ] DLZ_POSTGRESQL  DLZ Postgres driver                  │  │
│  │ [ ] DLZ_MYSQL   DLZ MySQL driver (single-threaded BIND)  │  │
│  │ [ ] DLZ_BDB     DLZ BDB driver                           │  │
│  │ [ ] DLZ_LDAP    DLZ LDAP driver                          │  │
│  │ [ ] DLZ_FILESYSTEM  DLZ filesystem driver                │  │
│  │ [ ] DLZ_STUB    DLZ stub driver                          │  │
│  │ [ ] THREADS     Compile with thread support              │  │
│  └─────────────────────────────────────────────────────────┘  │
│              [  OK  ]          Cancel                          │
└──────────────────────────────────────────────────────────────┘
```

Figure 6–2. FreeBSD base configure options

The above selection allows a validating DNSSEC (see Chapter 11) capable tool set (SIGCHASE option). The REPLACE_BASE option does what it says. The XML option allows server statistics to be displayed as a XML page using a web browser connected to **named**. The various DLZ options are discussed in the "BIND Configure Choices" section later in the chapter. The selection of the THREADS option (defaulted) may be historically regarded by some as living too close to the edge but default packages now routinely use this feature; it's a question of taste.

The preceding sequence installs BIND 9 in /usr/sbin and the tools in /usr/bin and /usr/sbin, and assumes the configuration file is /etc/namedb/named.conf. To run BIND 9 at startup or from a command line, /etc/rc.conf may need to be edited as shown in the following fragment:

```
# add the following line if not present
named_enable="YES"
# add the following line if not present
named_program="/usr/sbin/named"
```

No special action is required to run BIND 9 tools: The following command will run the base BIND 9 tool dig (from /usr/bin):

```
# dig @127.0.0.1 example.com
```

Use of @127.0.0.1 will force use of the local server irrespective of the state of the /etc/resolv.conf file.

Prior to running any (base or nonbase) BIND 9 for the first time, and assuming rndc (see Chapter 9) will be used, the following command should be issued to generate default keys:

```
# rndc-confgen -a
```

Assuming that /etc/rc.conf has been verified and edited appropriately, BIND 9 may be started using:

```
/etc/rc.d/named start
```

Note The /etc/rc.d/named script referenced above will check that the appropriate rndc key files are present and will automatically run rndc-keygen -a if you forgot do this.

FreeBSD Considerations

FreeBSD Bind 9 installs (base and nonbase) and automatically configures it to run in a sandbox or chroot jail. Chapter 10 describes the use of chroot jails. The chroot jail configuration assumes all BIND's files are located under /var/named—including named.conf, log files, and PID files. FreeBSD installs hard links in /etc/namedb (or /usr/local/etc in the case of nonbase installs) so you can continue to find the files where you thought they would be. In all cases, a script (/etc/rc.d/named) is installed that will be used by the init startup system. BIND default program locations and arguments are defined in /etc/defaults/rc.conf; as always, if changes are required to these values, they should be made to /etc/rc.conf. The FreeBSD 8.1 default values in /etc/defaults/rc.conf relevant to named are shown below:

```
named_enable="NO"              # Run named, the DNS server (or NO).
named_program="/usr/sbin/named" # Path to named, if you want a different one.
named_conf="/etc/namedb/named.conf"    # Path to the configuration file
#named_flags=""                # Use this for flags OTHER than -u and -c
named_pidfile="/var/run/named/pid" # Must set this in named.conf as well
named_uid="bind"               # User to run named as
named_chrootdir="/var/named"   # Chroot directory (or "" not to auto-chroot it)
```

```
named_chroot_autoupdate="YES"      # Automatically install/update chrooted
                                   # components of named. See /etc/rc.d/named.
named_symlink_enable="YES"         # Symlink the chrooted pid file
named_wait="NO"                    # Wait for working name service before exiting
named_wait_host="localhost"        # Hostname to check if named_wait is enabled
named_auto_forward="NO"            # Set up forwarders from /etc/resolv.conf
named_auto_forward_only="NO"       # Do "forward only" instead of "forward first"
```

As an example of how to change the default configuration, to disable the sandbox or chroot jail, add to /etc/rc.conf the following line(s):

```
named_chrootdir=""                   # disables jail/sandbox
named_pidfile="/var/run/named/pid"   # Must set this in named.conf as well
named_chroot_autoupdate="NO"         # Automatically install/update chrooted
                                     # components of named. See /etc/rc.d/named.
named_symlink_enable="NO"            # Symlink the chrooted pid file
```

The FreeBSD BIND 9 installation (either base or nonbase) adds a named.conf (in either /etc/namedb or depending on selected options in /usr/local/etc), standards hints file (named.root—what this book calls root.servers) in /etc/namedb and forward and reverse mapping files for localhost (IPv4 and IPv6) in respectively /etc/namedb/master/localhost-forward.db and /etc/namedb/master/localhost-reverse.db. Assuming no changes, the default named.conf file will provide a *closed* resolver; that is, a caching name server that will only support requests from the local machine (accomplished using a listen-on {127.0.0.1}; statement). This is a very safe default configuration. In addition, the named.conf file will prevent significant numbers of unnecessary queries from being forwarded to the root servers (see Chapter 12). Careful perusal of this named.conf file will amply reward the time spent.

Finally, in spite of the FreeBSD configure screens (Figures 6–1 and 6–2 above), there are additional options that the user may wish to invoke (see the "BIND 9 Configure Options" section later in this chapter). If these options are required, you must build from source.

Building BIND from Source

This section describes building BIND from a source tarball. In general, there are only three reasons to build BIND using this method:

1. There is no available package or RPM either for the particular host or OS or with the required version number.

2. Unique features are required that are not satisfied by the standard packages or RPMs. The unique features may include, for example, not wishing to update dependant libraries that are included with a standard package.

3. You like to control everything yourself and have a high tolerance for pain.

While most OS distributions do a remarkable job in keeping packages current—especially considering many involve only volunteer effort—there can be unforeseen or unfortunate delays. While compiling software from source may seem to many an arcane and anachronistic process, if you want to keep your DNS software constantly updated with minimal delays, you really have no other option that to build it–perhaps only in exceptional conditions–from the source tarball. Practice the process before trying it for the first time under non-optimal circumstances—avoid 3 AM panic.

Life is not all simple, however, and if building from tarballs, the advantages of any packaged system (for instance, RPMs) are not available. Any dependencies on other software will have to be manually identified—perhaps even discovered at run time!

The test build was run under the Ubuntu Server installation described earlier but the process is similar for FreeBSD and notes are included where necessary. The objective of this procedure was to update the existing Ubuntu BIND installation using software built from the tarball. Prior to starting the process, you must install the following two packages (either login as root or precede all commands with *sudo*):

```
# apt-get install build-essential
# apt-get install libssl-dev
```

The first installs the required tools and compilers and the second installs essential openssl library files.

Note If BIND is already installed from a package then the configure and build options used to create it may be obtained using the command named -V. In general, the package builders and maintainers for any distribution will have selected the most sensible options; this provides a useful starting point for custom tweaking.

To build BIND 9 from the source tarball, follow these steps (you must be either logged in as root or precede all commands with *sudo*):

1. Download the source tarball from www.isc.org (bind-9.7.1-P2.tar.tz) or one of its mirrors into /usr/src. You can use any suitable location, but /usr/src is a general convention. The reader is reminded again to always obtain the latest stable version of the software. The tarball is signed using various algorithms (SHA1, SHA256, SHA512) and the signatures may be downloaded from the same web site. To verify the signature file, you will also need to download ISC's OpenPGP key obtained from www.isc.org/about/openpgp. The following sequence will verify the downloaded tarball (both *wget* and *gnupg* are installed with the base Ubuntu Server; both need to be installed from the ports collection in FreeBSD):

```
# cd /usr/src
# wget http://ftp.isc.org/isc/bind9/9.7.2-P2/bind-9.7.2-P2.tar.gz
# wget http://ftp.isc.org/isc/bind9/9.7.2-P2/bind-9.7.2-P2.tar.gz.sha256.asc
# wget https://www.isc.org/files/pgpkey2009.txt
# gpg -import pgpkey2009.txt
# gpg -verify bind-9.7.2-P2.tar.gz.sha256.asc bind-9.7.2-P2.tar.gz
```

The last command, assuming all is well, will indicate a good signature but with a warning message to indicate the ISC key is not certified with a verifiable trust signature. This is simply an artifact of the command sequence used.

2. Unzip the tarball using the following commands:

```
# cd /usr/src
# tar xzf bind-9.7.2-P2.tar.gz
```

3. When this operation is complete, it will have created a new directory named bind-9.7.2-P2. Move to this directory:

```
# cd bind-9.7.2-P2
```

4. The software must now be configured. The following command (the line has been split for formatting reasons only using \ and should be entered as a single line) represents the standard package configure and build options used for BIND under Debian/Ubuntu:

```
# ./configure --prefix=/usr --mandir=/usr/share/man --infodir=/usr/share/info \
--sysconfdir=/etc/bind --localstatedir=/var --enable-threads --enable-largefile \
--with-libtool --enable-shared --enable-static --with-openssl=/usr --with-gnu-ld \
--enable-ipv6 'CFLAGS=-fno-strict-aliasing -DDIG_SIGCHASE -O2' \
'LDFLAGS=-Wl,-Bsymbolic-functions' 'CPPFLAGS='
```

The equivalent configure line for FreeBSD, based on the selected options under BIND 9 Base Install earlier in the chapter, is:

```
# ./configure --localstatedir=/var --disable-linux-caps --disable-symtable \
--with-randomdev=/dev/random --with-openssl=/usr --with-libxml2=/usr/local \
--without-idn --enable-threads --sysconfdir=/etc/namedb --prefix=/usr \
--mandir=/usr/share/man --infodir=/usr/share/info/ --build=i386-portbld-freebsd8.1 \
'build_alias=i386-portbld-freebsd8.1' CC='cc' CFLAGS='-O2 -pipe -fno-strict-aliasing -
DDIG_SIGCHASE' LDFLAGS='-rpath=/usr/lib:/usr/local/lib' CPP='cpp' CXX='c++' \
CXXFLAGS='-O2 -pipe -fno-strict-aliasing'
```

The major configure arguments used in this line are

- --prefix: Indicates that named will be installed to /usr/sbin and the tools to /usr/bin

- --sysconfdir: Tells named to look for named.conf in /etc/bind/named.conf (for Ubuntu) and /etc/namedb for FreeBSD

- --localstatedir: Tells named to write the PID file to /var/run/named.pid

- --enable-threads: The standard option on both systems since BIND 9.6

- --with-openssl: Indicates that DNSSEC services will be built (requires **libssl** to be installed)

When building for FreeBSD, the arguments --disable-linux-caps and --with-randomdev=/ dev/random are also used. If the BIND XML statistics option is required by Ubuntu (the required XML2 dependency is installed by default), then add --with-libxml2=/usr.

■**Caution** The preceding step configures BIND such that after issuing `make install` (see step 6) it will overwrite any currently installed BIND package. If the software built is incorrect or fails, you will have a nonoperational DNS system. It may be wiser to use a technique such as described in the "FreeBSD" section and use `--prefix=/usr/local`. This will have the effect of installing `named` to `/usr/local/sbin` and the tools to `/user/local/bin` and provide two copies of BIND. The newly built system can then be tested (any currently running version will have to be stopped first) and—only when you are completely satisfied—rebuilt using the preceding parameters. If anything goes wrong during testing of the new software, DNS service can be restored by simply restarting the previous BIND version from `/usr/sbin/named` or `(in Ubuntu) /etc/init.d/bind9 start` or `(FreeBSD) /etc/rc.d/named start`.

5. If anything goes wrong with the `configure` sequence, check the entered line carefully and inspect the file `config.log`, which contains the output of the configure session including error messages. When the `configure` process is finished (less than five minutes on a 1GHz PC), BIND should now be built using the following single command:

```
# make
```

6. The `make` command outputs voluminous data and took roughly 10 minutes on a 2GHz PC. On successful completion, issue the following command:

```
# make install
```

This will install all the various files generated by the build—well over 200. Running this command with the `./configure` arguments defined earlier will replace any existing installed version of BIND—please read the earlier Caution.

■**Note** In the event that an error occurs during any of the `configure`, `make`, or `make install` procedures, before rerunning, issue the command `make distclean` to remove any previous data before starting the sequence. As noted previously, the `configure` command logs its output to `config.log`. In the case of `make` and `make install`, the commands may be run with data being logged to a file, for instance, `make >make.log`.

BIND 9 Configure Options

BIND 9.7 contains a huge number of compile time options. Historically, the majority were concerned with the location of programs and configuration files. Increasingly, however, basic functionality is being determined by the configure options. To list all the available options use (as root or precede with *sudo*):

```
# cd /to/bind/source/directory
# make --help
```

To list only the user options, use:

```
# ./configure --help=short
```

An edited list of the full options for BIND 9.7.2-P2 is shown below:

```
`configure' configures this package to adapt to many kinds of systems.

Usage: ./configure [OPTION]... [VAR=VALUE]...
```

Defaults for the options are specified in brackets.

```
Installation directories:
  --prefix=PREFIX         Install architecture-independent files in PREFIX
                          [/usr/local]
  --exec-prefix=EPREFIX   Install architecture-dependent files in EPREFIX
                          [PREFIX]

By default, `make install' will install all the files in
`/usr/local/bin', `/usr/local/lib' etc.  You can specify
an installation prefix other than `/usr/local' using `--prefix',
for instance `--prefix=$HOME'.
```

For better control, use the options below.
Fine tuning of the installation directories:

```
  --bindir=DIR            User executables [EPREFIX/bin]
  --sbindir=DIR           System admin executables [EPREFIX/sbin]
  --libexecdir=DIR        Program executables [EPREFIX/libexec]
  --sysconfdir=DIR        Read-only single-machine data [PREFIX/etc]
  --sharedstatedir=DIR    Modifiable architecture-independent data [PREFIX/com]
  --localstatedir=DIR     Modifiable single-machine data [PREFIX/var]
  --libdir=DIR            Object code libraries [EPREFIX/lib]
  --includedir=DIR        C header files [PREFIX/include]
  --oldincludedir=DIR     C header files for non-gcc [/usr/include]
  --datarootdir=DIR       Read-only arch.-independent data root [PREFIX/share]
  --datadir=DIR           Read-only architecture-independent data [DATAROOTDIR]
  --infodir=DIR           Info documentation [DATAROOTDIR/info]
  --localedir=DIR         Locale-dependent data [DATAROOTDIR/locale]
  --mandir=DIR            Man documentation [DATAROOTDIR/man]
  --docdir=DIR            Documentation root [DATAROOTDIR/doc/PACKAGE]
  --htmldir=DIR           HTML documentation [DOCDIR]
  --dvidir=DIR            Dvi documentation [DOCDIR]
  --pdfdir=DIR            Pdf documentation [DOCDIR]
  --psdir=DIR             Ps documentation [DOCDIR]
```

System types:

```
  --build=BUILD    Configure for building on BUILD [guessed]
  --host=HOST      Cross-compile to build programs to run on HOST [BUILD]
```

Optional Features:

```
  --disable-option-checking  Ignore unrecognized --enable/--with options
  --disable-FEATURE       Do not include FEATURE (same as --enable-FEATURE=no)
  --enable-FEATURE[=ARG]  Include FEATURE [ARG=yes]
  --enable-shared[=PKGS]  Build shared libraries [default=yes]
  --enable-static[=PKGS]  Build static libraries [default=yes]
  --enable-fast-install[=PKGS]
                          Optimize for fast installation [default=yes]
  --disable-libtool-lock  Avoid locking (might break parallel builds)
  --enable-libbind        Deprecated
  --enable-kqueue         Use BSD kqueue when available [default=yes]
  --enable-epoll          Use Linux epoll when available [default=auto]
  --enable-devpoll        Use /dev/poll when available [default=yes]
  --enable-openssl-version-check
                          Check OpenSSL Version [default=yes]
  --enable-openssl-hash   Use OpenSSL for hash functions [default=no]
  --enable-threads        Enable multithreading
  --enable-largefile      64-bit file support
  --enable-backtrace      Log stack backtrace on abort [default=yes]
  --enable-symtable       Use internal symbol table for backtrace
                          [all|minimal(default)|none]
  --enable-exportlib      Build exportable library (GNU make required)
                          [default=no]
  --enable-ipv6           Use IPv6 default=autodetect
  --enable-getifaddrs     Enable the use of getifaddrs() [yes|no].
  --disable-isc-spnego    Use SPNEGO from GSSAPI library
  --disable-chroot        Disable chroot
  --disable-linux-caps    Disable linux capabilities
  --enable-atomic         Enable machine specific atomic operations
                          [default=autodetect]
  --enable-fixed-rrset    Enable fixed rrset ordering
                          [default=no]
  --enable-filter-aaaa    Enable filtering of AAAA records over IPv4
                          [default=no]
```

Optional Packages:

```
  --with-PACKAGE[=ARG]    Use PACKAGE [ARG=yes]
  --without-PACKAGE       Do not use PACKAGE (same as --with-PACKAGE=no)
  --with-gnu-ld           Assume the C compiler uses GNU ld [default=no]
  --with-pic              Try to use only PIC/non-PIC objects [default=use
                          both]
  --with-tags[=TAGS]      Include additional configurations [automatic]
  --with-openssl=PATH     Build with OpenSSL yes|no|path.
                          (Required for DNSSEC)
  --with-pkcs11=PATH      Build with PKCS11 support yes|no|path
                          (PATH is for the PKCS11 provider)
  --with-gssapi=PATH      Specify path for system-supplied GSSAPI
  --with-randomdev=PATH   Specify path for random device
  --with-ptl2             on NetBSD, use the ptl2 thread library (experimental)
  --with-libxml2=PATH     Build with libxml2 library yes|no|path
  --with-purify=PATH      Use Rational purify
  --with-libtool          Use GNU libtool
  --with-export-libdir=PATH
```

```
                        installation directory for the export library
                        [EPREFIX/lib/bind9]
  --with-export-includedir=PATH
                        Installation directory for the header files of the
                        export library [PREFIX/include/bind9]
  --with-kame=PATH          Use Kame IPv6 default path /usr/local/v6
  --with-docbook-xsl=PATH Specify path for Docbook-XSL stylesheets
  --with-idn=MPREFIX        Enable IDN support using idnkit default PREFIX
  --with-libiconv=IPREFIX GNU libiconv are in IPREFIX default PREFIX
  --with-iconv=LIBSPEC    Specify iconv library default -liconv
  --with-idnlib=ARG        Specify libidnkit
  --with-dlz-postgres=PATH   Build with Postgres DLZ driver yes|no|path.
                        (Required to use Postgres with DLZ)
  --with-dlz-mysql=PATH    Build with MySQL DLZ driver yes|no|path.
                        (Required to use MySQL with DLZ)
  --with-dlz-bdb=PATH     Build with Berkeley DB DLZ driver yes|no|path.
                        (Required to use Berkeley DB with DLZ)
  --with-dlz-filesystem=PATH    Build with filesystem DLZ driver yes|no.
                        (Required to use file system driver with DLZ)
  --with-dlz-ldap=PATH    Build with LDAP DLZ driver yes|no|path.
                        (Required to use LDAP with DLZ)
  --with-dlz-odbc=PATH    Build with ODBC DLZ driver yes|no|path.
                        (Required to use ODBC with DLZ)
  --with-dlz-stub=PATH    Build with stub DLZ driver yes|no.
                        (Required to use stub driver with DLZ)
  --with-make-clean       Run "make clean" at end of configure [yes|no].
```

Some of the above are self-evident; many are highly exotic and should be used with extreme caution and even then only if you known what you are doing. The lines starting with --with-dlz all refer to the use of BIND-DLZ, which since BIND 9.4.x has been included in the BIND code base. BIND-DLZ allows zone files to be read from a variety of source locations including transactional databases (such as MySQL, Postgres, and BDB), LDAP, and other sources. For full information on configuring and using BIND-DLZ, see the website (bind-dlz.sourgeforge.net). The option --with-fixed-rrset is used to enable the fixed option within the **rrset-order** statement (see Chapter 12); without this option (which is not defaulted in either Ubuntu or FreeBSD standard packages), only random and cyclic ordering is supported. In these systems, if you want to support fixed rrset ordering you will need to build from the source tarball.

Due in part to the increase in available options, when **named** (BIND) is loaded, it now helpfully outputs its configure options to the log file and it can be interrogated at any time using the command named -V.

Windows Installation

A packaged binary version of BIND that will install on either Windows 2003 Server or Windows XP is available from the ISC site (www.isc.org). The package also includes standard uninstall functions. The basic procedure for installing BIND 9 on all Windows platforms is similar. This section describes installation of BIND 9.7.2-P2 under Windows 7 Home Premium (64 bit) on a modestly powered laptop using the standard binary package. Windows 7 is not currently supported by ISC; however, after being in daily use for some time (> 2 months), it has yielded no operational problems. It is presented here in the hope that it will encourage readers to explore BIND 9 in what is becoming an increasingly popular environment—especially since some of the changes in procedure illustrated reflect current Windows architectural changes (especially in the area of security practices) and therefore are likely to more useful over time. The officially supported platforms (Server 2003 and XP) have minor differences that are noted as appropriate. The installation process was found to be fast and relatively simple.

■**Note** Many people—especially those who like to experiment—lose patience with the User Account Control (UAC) features of modern Windows platforms (Vista, Server 2008, and 7) and turn it off completely. This is entirely a matter of choice and taste. The system used to illustrate the installation uses an unmodified Windows 7 UAC. There is no need to sacrifice UAC capabilities in order to install and use BIND 9. Windows 7 has many features to allow customization of displays and menus. Consequently, some of the screens displayed may not look exactly like those on another system. Notes are supplied where there is a high likelihood this may be the case, perhaps reflecting the author's attempts to make all Windows systems look like his much-missed frozen-in-time Windows NT 4.0 system wherever possible.

---

1. Download Bind 9.7.2-P2.zip from the ISC site (www.isc.org) and unzip it into any suitable temporary location, such as c:\temp\bind. As always, readers are advised to get the latest stable release of BIND 9.

2. There is a file called readme1st.txt with the distribution that provides some useful information about the installation. In particular, it mentions that BIND (or named.exe) will run as a *service* on Windows and will require a user account called named with specific permissions. The install process will create the required account and basic permissions.

3. In the temporary directory (c:\temp\bind), find and right-click BindInstall.exe. This will display the screen shown in Figure 6-3.

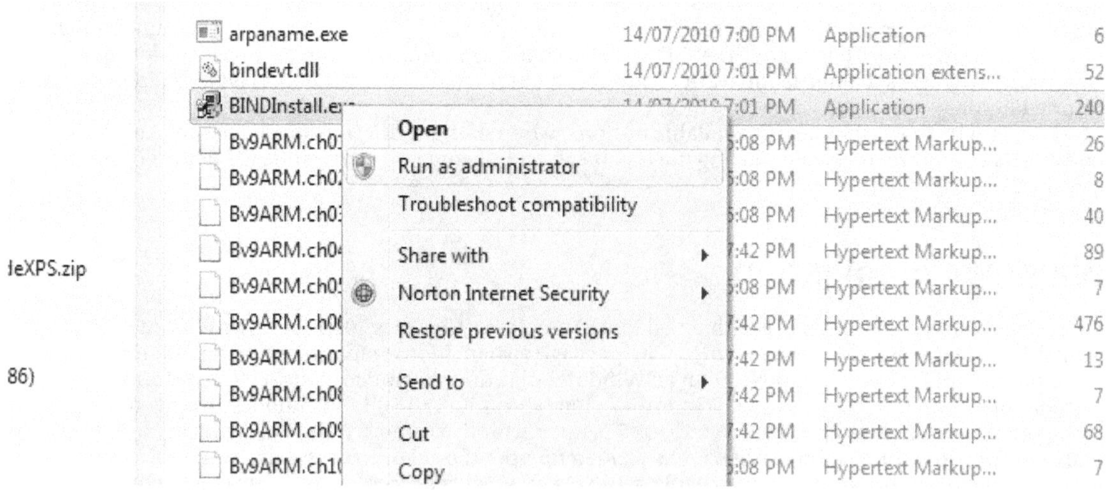

Figure 6-3. Run BIND install

4. From the popup window, select Run as administrator to provide the right permissions required for the installation.

5. BIND 9 install will display the screen shown in Figure 6–4.

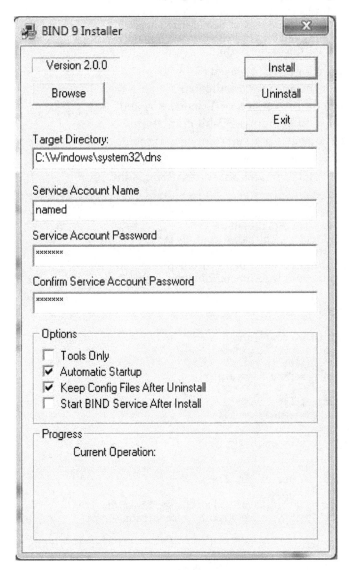

Figure 6–4. BIND 9 install screen

6. The password entry is mandatory with the default named account name. The readme1st.txt file contains descriptions of other accounts that may not require a password if you wish to experiment. The test installation used the default Service Account Name, as shown in Figure 6–4. The default install directory is c:\Windows\system32\dns (or %SystemRoot%\system32\dns in Windows terms). Do *not* check the box labeled Start BIND Service after Install. The Tools Only box works as advertised; leave it unchecked for this install, unless you only want the tools and not the DNS server. Click the Install button.

7. Use Windows Explorer to navigate to the directory called c:\Windows\sysWOW64\dns\etc. The install screen indicated c:\Windows\system32\dns this is a 64-bit version of Windows 7, and BIND 9 is a 32-bit application. The Windows 32-bit emulation system intercepts all runtime requests for c:\Windows\system32 and replaces them with c:\Windows\sysWOW64 (Windows on Windows 64). In the case of a 32-bit Windows system, c:\Windows\system32\dns is the location for all installed files and all subsequent paths should be modified appropriately. Place or create the master.localhost, localhost.rev, named.conf, and root.servers files in the c:\Windows\sysWOW64\dns\etc subdirectory. The named.conf file is the standard example file used in the "Caching-only DNS Server" section in Chapter 7; it's been modified to reflect the Windows path values in the installation and shown below. BIND will accept either Windows or Unix line termination conventions.

```
// generated by ME
        // CACHING NAME SERVER for WINDOWS
        //   Oct 2010
        //   a. changed directory statement to windows format
        //   b. changed location of log file to named\log\named.log
        //    c. changed location of all zone files to named\zones
        //    d. added pid-file directive in named\run\named.pid
        options {
          directory "C:\Windows\system32\dns\etc";
          // version added for security, otherwise may be able
                // to exploit known weaknesses
          version "not currently available";
          pid-file "named.pid";
          recursion yes;
          // the following statement closed the server but limits
          // limits queries to the location PC only
          // alternatively use allow-recursion {192.188.2/24;}; (change IP as required)
          // or allow-recursion {"localnets"}; if your netmask is appropriate
          listen-on {127.0.0.1;};
        };

        // log to named.log events from info UP in severity (no debug)
        // defaults to use 3 files in rotation
        // failure messages up to this point are in the event log
          logging{
          channel my_log{
            file "named.log" versions 3 size 250k;
```

```
      severity info;
    };
    category default{
      my_log;
    };
  };
  zone "." {
    type hint;
    file "root.servers";
  };

  zone "localhost" in{
    type master;
    file "master.localhost";
    allow-update{none;};
  };
  zone "0.0.127.in-addr.arpa" in{
    type master;
    file "localhost.rev";
    allow-update{none;};
};
```

8. Windows 7 uses the NTFS filesystem; assuming the PID and log files are written to the installed directories, no further permissions need to be set. Writing PID and log files into the /etc subdirectory may offend the aesthetic values of certain readers, but it has the merit of requiring the minimal work—always an important consideration. If the reader is still offended by this gross breach of normal *nix practice, then appropriately named subdirectories may be created—but permissions will need to be added to allow the named account to write to these locations. The broad principle of setting permissions is shown in the next section.

9. If the UAC system denies you access to the Windows sysWOW64 or other required directories for adding or modifying files, you will need to change permission. One method of doing this is illustrated. Select the required directory (directory, right-click, and click Properties from the pop-up menu. This will display a tabbed window from which the Security tab should be selected. Select the Users account (secondary description will reflect the name of the user's PC) and confirm that Full Control (or Write as a minimum) is enabled, as shown in Figure 6–5.

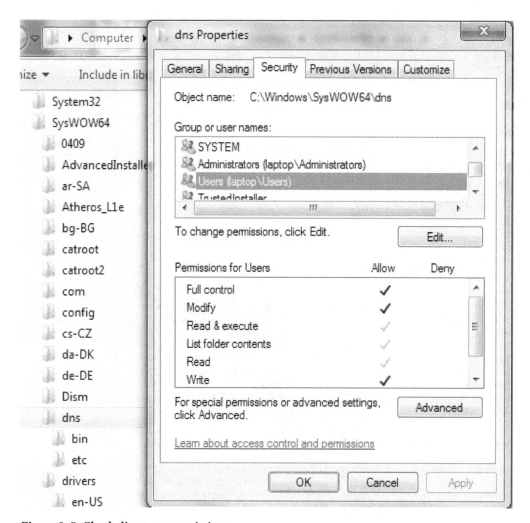

Figure 6–5. Check directory permissions

10. If the required permissions are not available, click the Edit button, again select the Users account, and then add the required permissions (see Figure 6–6). Finally, click OK. Windows will prompt with a warning along the lines that the sun will fall out of the sky if you continue, but in spite of that just click OK.

Figure 6–6. Add permissions

11. BIND installs its software to a nonstandard location (%SystemRoot%\
    system32\dns\bin or c:\Windows\sysWOW64\dns\bin). To use diagnostic tools
    such as dig and other command-line tools, the full path will be required or the
    Windows path environment variable can be changed to include the BIND
    installation directory. You can then forget where the BIND tools are installed!
    The path variable can be set using the following procedure. Click the Start icon,
    then right-click Computer, and select Properties (the Computer entry on the
    Start menu is controlled by its properties, which may be modified by right-
    clicking the Start icon and selecting Properties then the Customize button on
    the Start Menu tab). Alternatively, if you have a My Computer icon, right-click
    that and select Properties. In the resulting window, select the advanced tab and
    click Environmental Variables (see Figure 6–7). If you enjoy typing long paths at
    the command prompt, you can ignore this item.

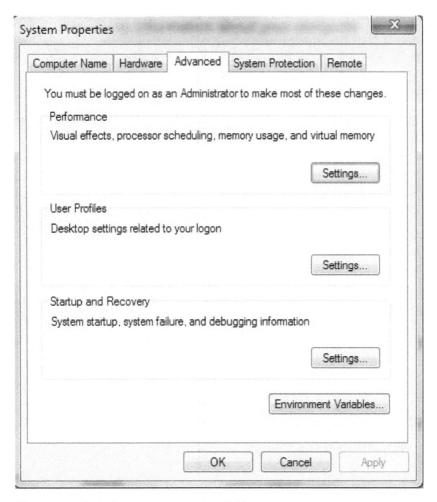

Figure 6–7. Changing environmental variables

12. On the resulting screen select the path variable in the lower widow and click
    Edit. At the end of the line add the following ;%SystemRoot%\sysWOW64\dns\bin
    (or ;%SystemRoot%\system32\dns\bin for 32-bit systems) and click OK. See
    Figure 6–8.

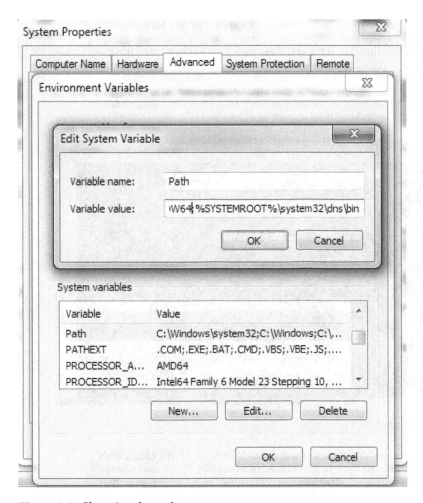

Figure 6–8. Changing the path

■**Note** The path separator on Windows is a semicolon, not a colon as in the Unix world. Setting the path has the effect of automatically locating, say, dig or nsupdate. However, there is a Windows version of nslookup that will be found first. Using the BIND version of nslookup either requires a full path command, such as c:\Windows\sysWOW64\dns\bin\nslookup.exe (or c:\Windows\system32\dns\bin\nslookup.exe for 32-bit systems) when running it from the command line, or the preceding path directive must be placed first in the list—which, in turn, has the disadvantage that it will add an extra check for all other program loading operations that use normal Windows locations.

13. As both a test of the success of the path change operation and in order to add the required rndc key file prior to starting BIND, run rndc-confgen from a command prompt. Click the Start icon and then click the Run button (if the run button is not present, it may be added by right-clicking the Start icon, selecting Properties, and then Customize from the Start Menu tab—all kinds of interesting goodies are also available using this procedure). At the run prompt, type cmd and OK. At the resulting command prompt (aka DOS Box), enter rndc-confgen -a to write the rndc.key file as shown in Figure 6–9.

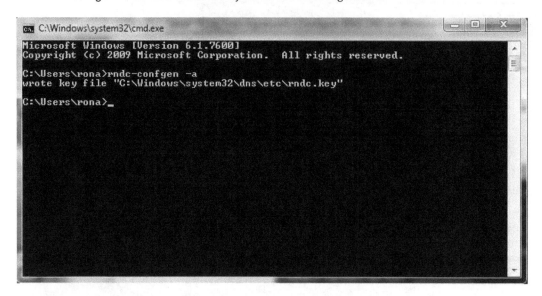

Figure 6–9. Run BIND 9 commands

14. Now the installation is ready to replace the normal Windows 7 DNS Client with the BIND 9 version. Click the Start icon, click Administrative Tools, and select Services. At the resulting screen, find and right-click the DNS Client entry, then click Properties. The screen shown in Figure 6–10 will be displayed.

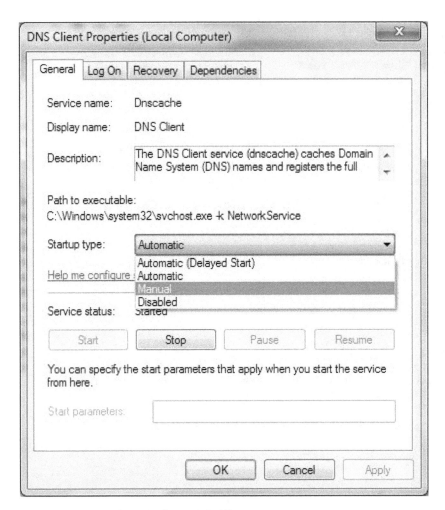

Figure 6–10. Stopping Windows DNS Client

15. Select Manual (or Disabled) from the drop down box, then click the Stop button. Finally, click OK to close the window. At this point, the PC has no DNS service and any applications that depend on it will fail temporarily until you start the BIND 9 replacement service.

16. Find and select the service named ISC BIND, right-click, and click the Start menu item, as shown in Figure 6–11.

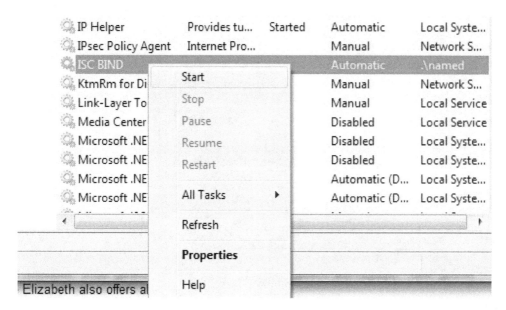

Figure 6–11. Start BIND 9

17. Finally, the PC may need to be configured to use the local DNS service other than one which may have been allocated by DHCP or a similar service. Click the Start icon and click Control Panel. Click Network and Sharing Center, then from the resulting window select Local Area Network, and click Properties. See Figure 6–12.

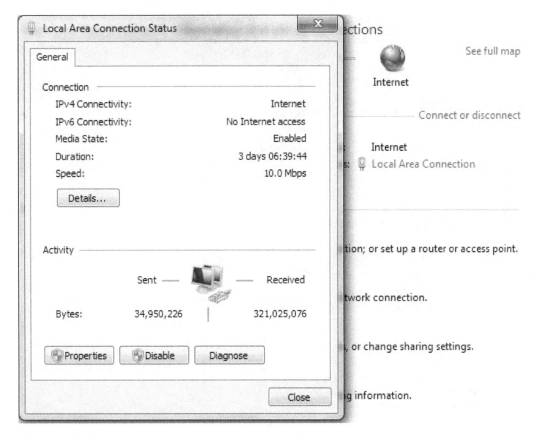

Figure 6–12. Network properties

18.   From the properties screen, select Internet Protocol Version 4 (TCP/IPv4), then
      click Properties. See Figure 6–13.

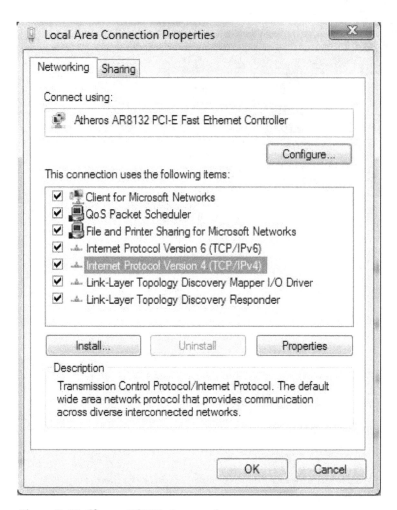

Figure 6–13. Change TCP/IPv4 properties

In the TCP/IPv4 Properties window, click the radio button for Use the following DNS server addresses, then enter the IPv4 address of the PC or more simply, as shown, its loopback or local address 127.0.01 (see Figure 6–14). Click OK to dismiss all previous windows. You are now fully operational using a BIND 9 caching resolver (assuming use of the named.conf file shown previously—though any configuration shown in Chapter 7 can be used depending on local needs).

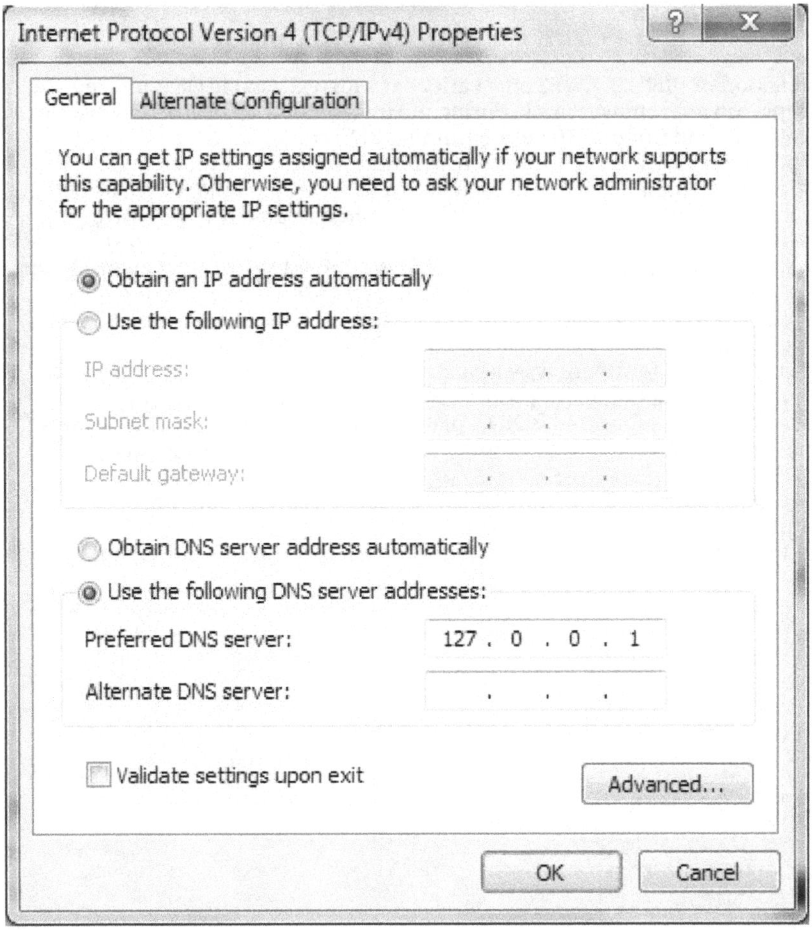

Figure 6–14. Change DNS location

19. To fully test the server, it's necessary to reboot. When the server has rebooted, use Event Viewer to check the Applications log for failure messages, and then use Task Manager to check that the ISC BIND service started up (it loads as named.exe).

Installing BIND on Windows 2003 Server, Windows XP, or the (currently) unsupported Windows 7 is a simple task requiring little user intervention. The entire process takes less than 10 minutes. If you need or want consistency of DNS for maintenance and other purposes across mixed Windows, Unix, Linux, or BSD environments, using BIND is the only solution. As a happy side benefit, you also get dig, nsupdate, rndc, nsupdate, and other tools, meaning that you can diagnose, update, and control BIND installations on other OS platforms from a Windows desktop, laptop, or server.

Summary

This chapter covered the installation of BIND 9.7.2-P2 on a variety of widely available OS platforms. In order to keep installations simple, no attempt was made during the installations to secure the various files used by BIND. You are urged to read Chapter 10 before running BIND operationally.

BIND was installed on Ubuntu Server 10.04 LTS as a representative of the Linux range of OS platforms. The BIND installation using standard Ubuntu/Debian packages was simple, but in its default install state resulted in a potentially dangerous open resolver that required relatively trivial corrective action.

BIND was installed on FreeBSD 8.1 as representative of the BSDs (FreeBSD, NetBSD, OpenBSD, and DragonflyBSD) and Unix OS platforms. The powerful ports collection was used to perform the installation. No problems were encountered during this installation which, in its default state, resulted in a chrooted, closed caching resolver.

The packaged binary version of BIND for Windows was installed on a Windows 7 and a full set of tests was run to ensure that it was fully functional. No problems were encountered during this installation. Windows 7 is not an officially supported BIND 9 platform (official support is only for Server 2003 and XP) but no problems were encountered both during the initial install and throughout prolonged (> 2 months) operation.

To cover those situations where a packaged version is not available, BIND was built on the Ubuntu Server 10.04 and FreeBSD 8.1 platforms from a source tarball.

The next chapter looks at the detailed configuration of BIND necessary to run the DNS types defined in Chapter 4.

CHAPTER 7

■ ■ ■

BIND Type Samples

This chapter presents sample BIND configurations and accompanying descriptions for each of the DNS types described in Chapter 4. But before jumping into these configurations, let's take a moment to quickly review these types:

- *Zone master*: A name server that responds authoritatively for the zone, reads the zone file from a local file system, and is capable of transferring the zone file to one or more slave servers.

- *Zone slave*: A name server that responds authoritatively for the zone, obtains its zone file by a zone transfer from a zone master, and is capable of transferring the zone file to one or more slave servers.

- *Resolver (or caching name server)*: A name server that provides recursive query support to clients and saves the results in a cache.

- *Forwarding server*: A name server that passes all queries for which it has no cached results to a resolver.

- *Stealth or split server*: A name server configuration typically used in perimeter defense, which separates the services provided to external and internal users

- *Authoritative-only server*: A name server that only provides responses for zones for which it is either a zone master or a zone slave; it does not support recursive queries.

Most name server configurations are schizophrenic in nature—they may be masters for some zones, slaves for others, forward others, and provide caching services for all comers. Each configuration type described next represents a building block and may be used in a stand-alone configuration or combined with other types to provide more complex configurations.

Caution: The standard security recommendation is that a DNS server provide only the minimum necessary functionality and ideally only support a single function. Thus, a name server should be, for example, either a master (or slave) zone server or a forwarding name server, never both. In many cases, especially for smaller sites, this is not practical or cost-effective, so hybrid configurations are frequently used at the cost of some modest increase in risk. Chapter 10 discusses DNS security in detail.

Before You Start

In order to make sense of the samples used in this chapter, the following sections cover some background information and formatting issues.

Configuration Layout

A BIND system consists of the following items:

- A `named.conf` file that describes the server characteristics and the zone files used. The entries in this file are described in Chapter 12. The `named.conf` file is normally located in `/etc` for most Linux distributions, `%SystemRoot%\system32\dns\etc` for Windows, and in either `/etc/namedb` or `/usr/local/etc` for BSD-based systems.

- Depending on the configuration, the name server may use one or more zone files describing the domains being managed. The entries in zone files are described in Chapter 2; Chapter 13 provides a complete reference. By convention, the zone files are normally located in `/var/named` for Linux and most Unix-based systems, but this location can be controlled by BIND configuration parameters (using the `directory` statement).

- Depending on the services being provided by the name server, it may require additional zone files describing the localhost environment, and reverse maps for local IP addresses and root-servers.

All the configuration files are deliberately kept simple; references are provided to various chapters that describe more advanced parameters as appropriate. Comments are included in the files to describe functionality; in general, the files are complete and can be copied directly to a name server configuration with some simple editing to change local name values, IP addresses, and file names.

Configuration Conventions

For reasons of consistency, the configuration scenario used throughout this chapter adheres to these characteristics:

- The domain name is `example.com`.

- The zone has two name servers. One is hosted within `example.com` (in-zone), the other in an external (out-of-zone) domain.

- The IP addresses used assume the private Class C address 192.168.254.0/24—a slightly artificial case (for information on address classes and the / (IP Prefix) notation, see the "IPv4 Addresses and CIDR" sidebar in Chapter 3).

- The zone consists of the following servers:

- *Two mail servers*: One is hosted within `example.com` (in-zone) and a second (backup) mail server hosted in an external (out-of-zone) domain.

- A web server that is hosted internally and accessed as `www.example.com`.

- An FTP server that is hosted externally (out-of-zone) and accessed as `ftp.example.com`.

- An additional host called `joe.example.com` for some reason best known to the domain owner.

■**Note** Some readers may think using `example.com` as the default domain name in sample configurations is about as exciting as reviewing a Hello World coding snippet. However, the dilemma is that most of the really bizarre or interesting domain names that would be descriptive or just plain fun to use have already been registered! It would seem a little unfair if the domain name owner were suddenly bombarded with strange diagnostic commands or other artifacts while readers experiment with features. RFC 2606 identifies that IANA (`www.iana.org`) in its infinite wisdom has reserved the domain names `example.com`, `example.org`, and `example.net` purely for the purposes of experimentation and documentation. In the interests of being a good netizen, this book generally uses `example.com` throughout, but just to spice things up a bit, it occasionally uses `example.net`.

Zone File Naming Convention

If your particular situation calls for just one or two zone files, it may not matter how you title them. However, as the number of zone files increase, this can quickly become a management problem, so establishing a standard file naming convention is key in order to quickly locate a particular file. These days it seems everyone has their own ideas regarding an ideal naming convention, and thus something that is supposed to be useful can become contentious. This book uses the following convention throughout:

- `/var/named/`: This base directory contains all the housekeeping zone files (for example, localhost zone files, reverse-mapping zone files, `root.servers` zone file, etc.) with a subdirectory structure used as follows:

- `/var/named/master`: This directory contains the master zone files.

- `/var/named/slave`: This directory contains the slave zone files.

- `/var/named/view`: This directory contains the view zone files.

- Master zone files are named `master.example.com` (`master.example.net` etc.); if it is a subdomain, it will be `master.sub-domain.example.com`.

- Slave zone files are named `slave.example.com` (or `slave.example.fr`, etc.); if it is a subdomain, it will be `slave.sub-domain.example.com`, etc.

- The root server zone file is called `root.servers` (typically called `named.ca` or `named.root` in BIND distributions).

- The reverse-mapping file name uses the IP address in its correct or normal order with `.rev` appended to it. For example, if the zone is `23.168.192.IN-ADDR.ARPA`, then the reverse-mapping zone file is called `192.168.23.rev`. There is no reason for the zone file name to be as confusing as the reverse-mapped zone file contents!

- The `localhost` zone file is called `master.localhost` (typically called `localhost.zone` when supplied with BIND distributions). The reverse-mapping file is called `localhost.rev` (typically called `named.local` when supplied with many BIND distributions).

■ **Note** For most Linux and BSD BIND distributions, there is a small overhead after installation to rename the standard distribution files, but the equation *"meaningless file names + 2 AM panic = serious chance of error"* is one that should be avoided at all costs. There are plenty of things in the DNS world that need to be remembered; meaningless file names are not one of them.

Keep in mind this is just a convention, and it doesn't affect the behavior of BIND. You are not bound to following this convention; however, it's crucial that you do establish some sort of convention in order to lessen the possibility of administration gaffes.

Required Zone Files

Depending on operational requirements, BIND may need a number of zone files to allow it to provide the required functionality; these are in addition to any zone files that explicitly describe master or slave zones.

root.servers

This file (called named.ca or named.root in many distributions but renamed root.servers in this book) is a standard zone file containing A (and increasingly AAAA) RRs for the root-servers (A.ROOT-SERVERS.NET—M.ROOT-SERVERS.NET). When BIND is initially loaded, it uses this zone file to query the root zone to obtain a complete list of the current authoritative root-servers and subsequently uses the obtained list rather than the root.servers zone file. When a name server can't resolve a query from its local zone files or its cache, it uses the name servers obtained via this query to return a referral (if an iterative query) or to find an answer (if a recursive query). The root.servers file is defined using a normal zone clause with a type hint statement as in the following example:

```
// BIND named.conf fragment
zone "." {
  type hint;
  file "root.servers";
};
```

The zone "." declaration is short for the root zone (the normally silent dot at the end of an FQDN). A query to this zone will return a list of the root-servers, which is then used by the name server as a starting point for any domain query, for which there is no locally defined zone (slave or master) or a cached answer.

By convention, the hint zone is usually included as the first zone clause in named.conf, but there is no good reason for this. Indeed, it may be placed anywhere suitable. If the configuration is running an internal name service on a closed network, or the name server does not support recursive queries, the root.servers file or hint zone is not required. If the root zone is not defined, but recursive queries are required, BIND has an internal list that it uses so all is not lost.

The root-servers change very infrequently for obvious reasons; nevertheless, the zone file supplied with any distribution will eventually become outdated. A new zone file can be obtained from a number of locations including ICANN/INTERNIC (ftp://ftp.internic.net/domain download file named.root). BIND will log any discrepancies from the current root.servers zone file and the list it obtains on the initial query of the root zone (see earlier), but it will carry on using the retrieved list. The root.servers file should be updated perhaps every 12 months or whenever there are log messages noting discrepancies when BIND loads. A root.servers fragment is shown here:

```
;         This file holds the information on root name servers needed to
;         initialize cache of Internet domain name servers
;         (e.g. reference this file in the "cache  .  "
;         configuration file of BIND domain name servers).
;
;         This file is made available by InterNIC
;         under anonymous FTP as
;             file                 /domain/named.root
;           on server              FTP.INTERNIC.NET
;         -OR-                     RS.INTERNIC.NET
;
;         last update:    Jan 29, 2004
;         related version of root zone:    2004012900
;
;
; formerly NS.INTERNIC.NET
;
.                         3600000  IN  NS    A.ROOT-SERVERS.NET.
A.ROOT-SERVERS.NET.       3600000      A     198.41.0.4
```

The right-hand dot in the NS RR line indicates it is an FQDN and signifies this is a name server for the root domain. In total, there are 13 name servers listed in this zone file, namely a.root-servers.net to m.root-servers.net.

master.localhost

This zone file allows resolution of the name localhost to the loopback address 127.0.0.1 when using the name server. Any query for localhost from any host using the name server will return 127.0.0.1—namely its fixed localhost address. This file is particularly important because localhost is used by many applications and should generally be included in all BIND configurations. The localhost zone is defined as shown here:

```
// BIND named.conf fragment
zone "localhost" in{
  type master;
  file "master.localhost";
  allow-update {none;}; // optional
};
```

In the standard files supplied with many BIND 9 distributions, the zone-specific statement allow-update (none;); is defined, which suppresses any accidental or malicious Dynamic DNS (DDNS) behavior that may corrupt the localhost zone file. Dynamic DDNS is disabled by default in BIND 9, and the statement is not strictly required; its inclusion may be regarded as defensive or paranoid at your discretion. An example master.localhost file (called localhost or localhost.zone in many distributions) is shown here:

```
$TTL 86400 ; 24 hours could have been written as 24h or 1d
$ORIGIN localhost.
@  1D  IN    SOA @ hostmaster (
            2004022401 ; serial
            12h ; refresh
```

```
                 15m ; retry
                 1w ; expiry
                 3h ; minimum
       )
@   1D  IN  NS @ ; localhost is the name server
    1D  IN  A  127.0.0.1 ; always returns the loop-back address
```

The file embodies the true minimalist (and occasionally incomprehensible) tradition of configuration files. Extensive use is made of @, which will force $ORIGIN substitution, as explained in Chapter 2. Every record uses a 24-hour (1D) TTL; in RFC 1035 format, this time value would be 86400. Even recent BIND distributions use a zone e-mail address of root (the historic practice); current practice (RFC 2142) recommends the use of hostmaster for this purpose, and the file has been correspondingly modified.

The following offers an alternate version of the preceding file that may be more understandable:

```
$TTL 1d ;
$ORIGIN localhost.
localhost.    IN    SOA localhost. hostmaster.localhost. (
              2002022401 ; serial
              3H ; refresh
              15M ; retry
              1w ; expire
              3h ; nx
       )
localhost.    IN  NS localhost. ; localhost is the name server
localhost.    IN  A  127.0.0.1 ; the loop-back address
```

■ **Note** The preceding file uses the *BIND only* abbreviations for time periods in an ugly variety of upper and lowercase formats to reinforce the point that they are case-insensitive. The file has also changed the comment on the last numeric parameter of the SOA RR to nx in keeping with this books convention of using a current usage abbreviation (nx = negative (NXDOMAIN) caching time) rather than the obsolete minimum (TTL) value.

IPv6 Localhost

The IPv6 localhost or loopback address is ::1 and is defined using an AAAA RR (a Quad A RR). Recall from Chapter 5 that A and AAAA RRs may be freely mixed in a zone file; this enables the standard master.localhost zone file to be modified, thus requiring no change to the zone file declaration in the named.conf file, as shown here:

```
$TTL 86400 ; 24 hours could have been written as 24h or 1d
$ORIGIN localhost.
@   1D  IN    SOA @ hostmaster (
              2004022401 ; serial
              12h ; refresh
              15m ; retry
              1w ; expiry
              3h ; minimum
       )
@   1D  IN  NS @ ; localhost is the name server
```

```
1D  IN  A     127.0.0.1 ; IPv4 loop-back address
1D  IN  AAAA  ::1 ; IPv6 loop-back address
```

Reverse-Map Zone Files

Reverse mapping describes the process of translating an IP address to a host name. This process uses the reserved domain IN-ADDR.ARPA and, if it is to be supported, requires a corresponding zone file. Reverse-mapping and its zone file format are described in Chapter 3.

Many service providers do not provide delegation of reverse mapping for IPv4 addresses (described in Chapter 8); as a consequence, users can get into the bad habit of not including reverse-map files in their name server configurations. If the name server is behind a firewall/NAT gateway and is using local (RFC 1918) IPv4 addresses (for example, 192.168.0.0/16), it's very important that a reverse-map zone file be included to cover the private IPs being used. Failure to do so will result in queries for these IPs being passed to the public network, thus consuming both resources and slowing up all local traffic while operations timeout. Studies suggest that up to 7% of all traffic hitting certain root-servers comes from badly configured name servers, which generate unnecessary reverse-map queries for local IP addresses. Indeed, the problem has become so acute that BIND 9 now implements a number of zone files automatically. Currently, the reverse map zone files for IPv4 and IPv6 loopback addresses are included in this list. (For a full list of default zone files see Chapter 12).

Note: The default zone files implemented by BIND 9 use what is called an *empty zone*. An empty zone simply contains an SOA RR and a single NS RR; that is, it contains no PTR RRs. If your system is likely to generate reverse map lookups for localhost (for instance, if you have a mail server and a mail client running on the same host), the default zone file will not give an adequate response and an explicit localhost reverse map will be required. In any event, it is always good practice to include such files in case BIND 9 default behavior changes at some point in the future.

0.0.127.IN-ADDR.ARPA

This special zone allows reverse mapping of the loopback address 127.0.0.1 to satisfy applications that do reverse or double lookups. It is sometimes called named.local in Linux distributions but is renamed localhost.rev in this book. Any request for the address 127.0.0.1 using this name server will return the name localhost. The 0.0.127.IN-ADDR.ARPA zone is defined like so:

```
// BIND named.conf fragment
zone "0.0.127.IN-ADDR.ARPA" in{
  type master;
  file "localhost.rev";
  allow-update{none;}; // optional
};
```

In the standard files supplied with many BIND 9 distributions, the zone-specific statement allow-update (none;); is defined, which suppresses Dynamic DNS (DDNS) behavior. This is BIND 9's default mode and is not strictly required; its inclusion may be regarded as defensive, paranoid, or prudent at your discretion. An example localhost.rev file is shown here:

```
$TTL 86400 ; 24 hours
```

```
; could use $ORIGIN 0.0.127.IN-ADDR.ARPA.
@       IN      SOA     localhost. hostmaster.localhost.  (
                        1997022700 ; Serial
                        3h      ; Refresh
                        15      ; Retry
                        1w      ; Expire
                        3h )    ; Minimum
        IN      NS      localhost.
1       IN      PTR     localhost.
```

This file, supplied with most BIND distributions, normally has no $ORIGIN directive (the comment line shows the form the $ORIGIN directive would take if present) and thus serves to illustrate the additional work required when it's missing. In this case, the @ name is taken to mean the value in the zone clause of named.conf, which in the preceding named.conf fragment reads as follows:

```
zone "0.0.127.IN-ADDR.ARPA" in{
```

This name will be used by the $ORIGIN substitution rule within this file. The absence of an $ORIGIN directive means you need to look in two places (the named.conf file and the zone file) to understand exactly what is happening. In the last line of this file, the leading 1 is a name; because it's unqualified (it doesn't end with a dot), $ORIGIN substitution also takes place. This line could have been written as follows:

```
1.0.0.127.in-addr.arpa.    IN   PTR   localhost.
```

IPv6 Localhost Reverse Map

The IPv6 loopback address is written typically as ::1 but its full format is 0:0:0:0:0:0:0:1. Recall from Chapter 5 that reverse mapping for IPv6 uses a reversed nibble format: each 4 bits of the 128-bit address is defined and then placed under the IP6.ARPA domain. The result is this brutally long definition that is comprised of a 1 followed by 31 zeros:

```
1.0.0.0.0.0.0.0.0.0.0.0.0.0.0.0.0.0.0.0.0.0.0.0.0.0.0.0.0.0.0.0.IP6.ARPA.
```

The split between the zone or domain name part and the host part defined inside the zone file is arbitrary. The following definitions use a domain name comprising the global routing prefix (or site prefix) of 48 bits and the remainder defined inside the zone file. The zone clause fragment for named.conf is shown here:

```
// named.conf fragment
....
zone "0.0.0.0.0.0.0.0.0.0.0.0.IP6.ARPA" in{
   type master;
   file "localhost-ipv6.rev";
   allow-update {"none";};
};
```

Here is the zone file localhost-ipv6.rev:

```
$TTL 86400 ; 24 hours
$ORIGIN 0.0.0.0.0.0.0.0.0.0.0.0.0.IP6.ARPA.
@       IN      SOA     localhost. hostmaster.localhost.  (
                        1997022700 ; Serial
                        3h      ; Refresh
                        15      ; Retry
```

```
                        1w      ; Expire
                        3h )    ; Minimum
        IN      NS      localhost.
1.0.0.0.0.0.0.0.0.0.0.0.0.0.0.0.0.0.0.0.0.0.0.0      IN      PTR      localhost.
```

BIND named.conf File Format and Style

The following notes provide a brief overview of some terminology to enable the reader to make sense of the files presented in this chapter, though some reference to Chapter 12 will be necessary if a detailed description of a particular value is required.

BIND's standard documentation uses a confusing number of terms to describe the various elements in the named.conf file. To reduce the confusion that can arise, this book uses only two terms consistently throughout. Individual configuration lines are called *statements*. Each statement is terminated with a semicolon. Statements are defined within clauses. A *clause* starts on new line, and all its statements are enclosed within braces (curly brackets) and terminate with a semicolon. The following fragment illustrates this organization:

```
// zone starts a new clause
zone "example.com" {
  // all clause statements are contained within braces
  // type, file, and masters are statements and terminate with a semicolon
   type slave;
   file "slave.example.com";
   masters {10.0.0.1;};
  // the zone clause is terminated with a closing brace
};
```

BIND named.conf clauses and statements can seem quite complex, and BIND is pretty picky when it comes to syntax: semicolons, braces, and all that wonderful stuff. There are many named.conf layout styles possible, the majority of which are simply designed to minimize syntax errors. The following examples show various layout styles, each of which is handled by BIND:

```
// dense single-line layout style
zone "example.com" {type slave; file "sec.example.com"; masters {10.0.0.1;};};
// multiple-line layout style
zone "example.com" {
   type slave;
   file "slave.example.com";
   masters {10.0.0.1;};
};
// a slightly confusing hybrid layout style
zone "example.com" {
   type slave;
   file "slave.example.com";
   masters {10.0.0.1;}; };
```

Use the layout style that makes the most sense and that will be the least error prone.

Finally, there is the question of quotes or no quotes with names. In the preceding fragment, zone "example.com" could have been written as simply zone example.com. The rule is if a name contains spaces, it must be enclosed in quotes; if not, the enclosing quotes are optional. This book mostly uses enclosing quotes with names, but especially with reserved names such as any and none (or "any" and "none") will occasionally omit the enclosing quotes.

Standard Zone File

The next sections describe the detail configuration of BIND's named.conf and, where appropriate, the zone files for each of the DNS types. Unless otherwise noted, the standard zone files defined earlier for root.servers, master.localhost, and localhost.rev are unchanged. Also, unless otherwise noted, the example.com zone file first introduced in Chapter 2 remains unchanged. However, for convenience it is reproduced here:

```
; simple zone file for example.com
$TTL 2d     ; default TTL for zone
$ORIGIN example.com. ; base domain-name
; Start of Authority RR defining the key characteristics of the zone (domain)
@          IN     SOA   ns1.example.com. hostmaster.example.com. (
                        2003080800 ; se = serial number
                        12h        ; ref = refresh
                        15m        ; ret = update retry
                        3w         ; ex = expiry
                        2h         ; min = minimum
                        )
; name server RR for the domain
           IN     NS      ns1.example.com.
; the second name server is
; external to this zone (domain).
           IN     NS      ns2.example.net.
; mail server RRs for the zone (domain)
    3w     IN     MX   10  mail.example.com.
; the second  mail servers is  external to the zone (domain)
           IN     MX   20  mail.example.net.
; domain hosts includes NS and MX records defined above
; plus any others required
ns1        IN     A      192.168.254.2
mail       IN     A      192.168.254.4
joe        IN     A      192.168.254.6
www        IN     A      192.168.254.7
; aliases ftp (ftp server) to an external domain
ftp        IN     CNAME  ftp.example.net.
```

Common Configuration Elements

The named.conf files used in the example files have a common core containing statements and clauses, which are either required or advisable. This common core is shown here, and each part is briefly described:

```
// Master & Caching Name Server for Example, INC.
// Recommended that you always maintain a change log in this file as shown here
// CHANGELOG:
// 1. 9 july 2005 INITIALS or NAME
//   a. did something
// a. 23 july 2005 INITIALS or NAME
//   a. did something again
//   b. another change
// options clause defining the server-wide properties
options {
```

```
  // all relative paths use this directory as a base
  directory "/var/named";
  // version statement for security to avoid hacking known weaknesses
  // if the real version number is published
  version "not currently available";
};
// logging clause
// log to /var/log/named/example.log all events from info UP in severity (no debug)
// uses 3 files in rotation swaps files when size reaches 250K
// failure messages up to this point are in syslog e.g. /var/log/messages
//
logging {
  channel example_log{
    file "/var/log/named/example.log" versions 3 size 250k;
    severity info;
 };
  category default{
  example_log;
 };
};
```

The file always starts with a gentle reminder that, as with all configuration files, disciplined commenting of all changes is one of the simplest and most powerful diagnostic tools available as well as being plain good sense. The directory statement in the example shown is the normal path but serves as a constant reminder of the base used for any relative file name (those that don't start with a /) such as zone files. The version statement inhibits disclosure of the BIND version number. This is done to prevent advertising that the site is running a version of BIND that may have a known exploit; it just makes any attacker's life a tad more difficult. The logging clause simply streams all messages into a separate file, rotates the log when it reaches 250K in size, and keeps the last three rotated versions. If a logging clause is not present, all logging is done using syslog to /var/log/messages on most systems or the event log on Windows.

Master DNS Server

Recall from the description in Chapter 4 that a zone master will supply authoritative data for the zone. There may be one or more zone masters and zero or more zone slaves for any given domain or zone. The term *master* simply means that the zone file will be read from the local filestore, and the name server will respond to requests for zone transfer from slaves if permitted by named.conf configuration parameters.

Master Name Server Configuration

The BIND configuration samples that follow provide the following functionality:

- The name server is a master for the zone example.com. This characteristic is defined by the zone "example.com" clause containing a type master; statement.

- The name server provides caching services for all other domains. This characteristic is defined by the combination of the recursion yes; statement in the options clause and the zone "." clause (the root zone).

- • The name server provides recursive query services for resolvers or other name servers acting on behalf of resolvers. This characteristic is defined by the recursion yes; statement in the options clause.

Here is the BIND named.conf file:

```
// Master & Caching Name Server for EXAMPLE.COM.
// Recommended that you always maintain a change log in this file as shown here
// CHANGELOG:
// 1. 9 july 2005 INITIALS or NAME
//   a. did something
// a. 23 july 2005 INITIALS or NAME
//   a. did something again
//   b. another change
// options clause defining the server-wide properties
options {
  // all relative paths use this directory as a base
  directory "/var/named";
  // version statement for security to avoid hacking known weaknesses
  // if the real version number is published
  version "not currently available";
  // configuration unique options statements
  // optional - disables zone transfers except for the slave
  // in the example.net domain
  allow-transfer {192.168.1.2;};
  // optional - BIND default behavior is recursion
  recursion yes;
  allow-recursion {10.0/16;}; // prevents Open resolver behavior
};
// logging clause
// log to /var/log/named/example.log all events from info UP in severity (no debug)
// uses 3 files in rotation swaps files when size reaches 250K
// failure messages up to this point are in syslog e.g. /var/log/messages
//
logging {
  channel example_log{
    file "/var/log/named/example.log" versions 3 size 250k;
    severity info;
  };
  category default{
  example_log;
  };
};
// root.servers - required zone for recursive queries
zone "." {
  type hint;
  file "root.servers";
};
// zone clause - master for example.com
zone "example.com" in{
  type master;
  file "master/master.example.com";
  allow-update {none;};
};
```

```
// required local host domain
zone "localhost" in{
  type master;
  file "master.localhost";
  allow-update {none;};
};
// localhost reverse map
zone "0.0.127IN-ADDR.ARPA" in{
  type master;
  file "localhost.rev";
  allow-update {none;};
};
// reverse map for local addresses at example.com
// uses 192.168.254.0 for illustration
zone "254.168.192.IN-ADDR.ARPA" in{
  type master;
  file "192.168.254.rev";
  allow-update {none;};
};
```

The allow-recursion statement limits the range of IP addresses that can issue recursive queries to this name server and prevent it from being what is called an *open resolver*. The IP values should be adjusted to site-specific values. Open resolvers, like open mail relays, are deceiving; at first glance, they may look like a helpful, neighborly act, but they are potentially very dangerous since they can be used in Distributed Denial of Service (DDoS) attacks on other sites. Indeed, so serious is the threat posed by *open resolvers* that in the absence of an allow-recursion statement, BIND 9 .5+ will only allow recursive queries from local LAN connected hosts (localnets). This topic is discussed in detail in the section on resolvers later in the chapter and in Chapter 12 in the sections that cover allow-recursion and allow-query-cache statements.

The allow-transfer statement prohibits any zone transfer except to the defined IP address; in this case, it's the IP address of ns2.example.net (defined in the sample zone file covered earlier). BIND 9's default behavior is to allow zone transfers from any host that requests one. An alternative strategy is to disable all transfers in the options clause and selectively enable them in each zone clause, as shown in this fragment:

```
....
options {
  ....
  allow-transfer {none;};
  ....
}
....
zone "example.com" in {
  ....
  allow-transfer {192.168.1.2;};
  ....
};
```

Additional zone clauses defining either type master or type slave may be added as required in order to create larger configurations.

Slave DNS Server

The functionality of the slave name server was described in Chapter 4. The term *slave* simply indicates that a name server will obtain the zone records using zone transfer operations but will answer authoritatively for the zone for as long as it has valid zone data (defined by the expiry field of the zone's SOA RR). The term *slave* in no sense implies priority of access. As previously described, slave servers will be accessed, in general, just as frequently as any master name server. Slave servers may also transfer their zone files to other slave servers.

Slave Name Server Configuration

The BIND named.conf slave sample configuration provides the following functionality:

- The name server is a slave for the zone example.com. This characteristic is defined by the zone "example.com" clause containing a type slave; statement.

- The name server provides resolver services for all other domains. This characteristic is defined by the combination of the recursion yes; statement in the options clause and the zone "." clause (the root zone).

- The name server provides recursive query services for resolvers or other name servers acting on behalf of resolvers. This characteristic is defined by the recursion yes; statement in the options clause.

The sample configuration file shows that the slave name server is provided in an external or out-of-zone domain called example.net (not example.com) by the following fragment from the standard zone file:

```
; the second name server is
; external to this zone (domain).
            IN      NS      ns2.example.net.
```

This type of configuration is normally used for physical diversity. If the example.com site is offline due to communication or other problems, then example.net, assumed to be at a different physical location, will continue to provide service for the example.com zone or domain. Clearly, this is not always practical, and the second name server could have been defined as ns2.example.com and located on the same site. There is nothing wrong with such a configuration other than the risk associated with a physical outage. The named.conf sample file that follows, based on the standard sample file, would be located at ns2.example.net:

```
// Slave & caching Name Server for EXAMPLE.NET.
// provides slave name server support for example com
// Recommended that you always maintain a change log in this file as shown here
// CHANGELOG:
// 1. 9 july 2005 INITIALS or NAME
// a. did something
// a. 23 july 2005 INITIALS or NAME
// a. did something again
// b. another change
//
options {
  // all relative paths use this directory as a base
  directory "/var/named";
  // version statement for security to avoid hacking known weaknesses
```

```
  // if the real version number is published
  version "not currently available";
  // configuration unique statements
  // disables all zone transfer requests
  allow-transfer {"none";};
  // optional - BIND default behavior is recursion
  recursion yes;
  allow-recursion {172.16.2/24;};
};
//
// log to /var/log/named/examplenet.log all events from info UP
//  in severity
// defaults to use 3 files in rotation
// failure messages up to this point are in (syslog) /var/log/messages
  logging{
  channel examplenet_log{
  file "/var/log/named/examplenet.log" versions 3 size 250k;
  severity info;
 };
  category default{
  examplenet_log;
 };
};
// required zone for recursive queries
zone "." {
  type hint;
  file "root.servers";
};
// assumes this server is also master for example.net
zone "example.net" in{
  type master;
  file "master/master.example.net";
  allow-update {none;};
};
// slave for example.com; see following notes
zone "example.com" in{
  type slave;
  file "slave/slave.example.com";
  masters (192.168.254.2;);
  // allows notify messages only from master
  allow-notify {192.168.254.2;};
};
// required local host domain
zone "localhost" in{
  type master;
  file "master.localhost";
  allow-update{none;};
};
// localhost reverse map
zone "0.0.127.IN-ADDR.ARPA" in{
  type master;
  file "localhost.rev";
  allow-update{none;};
};
```

```
// reverse map for example.net local IPs
// assumed 192.168.1.0 (see notes)
zone "1.168.192.IN-ADDR.ARPA" IN {
  type slave;
  file "slave.192.168.1.rev";
  masters {192.168.1.1;};
};
```

The allow-recursion statement limits the range of IP addresses that can issue recursive queries to this name server and prevent it from being an open resolver.

The example.com slave zone statement file "slave/slave.example.com"; is optional and allows the slave to store the zone records obtained on the last zone transfer. If BIND 9 or the zone is reloaded, the current stored zone file—assuming it is still valid (within the time defined by the SOA RR expiry field)—is used rather than immediately requesting a zone transfer and thus wasting both time and network resources. To create the secondary file initially, just create an empty file with the correct file name (using touch or a similar command); BIND may complain the first time it loads the file but not thereafter.

The zone example.com contains a statement masters {192.168.254.2;}; that has a single IP address referencing ns1.example.com. Any number of IP addresses could appear in the list. There may be one or more zone masters. The allow-notify {192.168.254.2;}; statement disables NOTIFY messages from any host except the zone master to minimize possible malicious action.

The reverse map for the local IP addresses at example.net (zone "1.168.192.IN-ADDR.ARPA") is defined as a slave for administrative convenience; only one copy of this zone file need be maintained. IN-ADDR.ARPA zones provide all the normal zone functionality, including master and slave. This zone could have been defined as a master with a local copy of the reverse-map zone file, which is the more normal, but unnecessary, configuration.

The named.conf file shows ns2.example.net acting as a zone master for its zone or domain (example.net). It could equally well have been a slave for the domain or even contained no zone section or clause for example.net.

Resolver (Caching-only) DNS Server

The *resolver* (or *caching-only name server* or even *recursive name server*) is one that provides caching service to its clients (resolvers or other DNSs acting on behalf of resolvers). When the resolver obtains the answer to a query, it saves the resulting resource records (RRs) to a cache, which may be a local file or, in the case of BIND, to in-memory storage. It will return this saved result to a subsequent query for the same information until the TTL value of the cached RR expires, at which time it will discard the RR. If the resolver is restarted, the current in-memory cache will be discarded.

Note A DNS cache is not the same as a slave's zone data. Zone data consists of all the zone records obtained through zone transfer operations; importantly, this data is timed out using the values in the zone's SOA RR. A cache contains individual RRs obtained as answers to specific queries and timed out according to the TTL value of the specific RR.

Caching-only Name Server Configuration

The BIND named.conf configuration sample provides the following functionality:

- The resolver is assumed to have a name of resolver.example.com. This name will be defined using an A or AAAA RR in the zone file for example.com (not illustrated).

- The name server is neither a master nor slave for any domain. There are no zone clauses for other than the essential zones needed for local operations (master.localhost and localhost.rev) and to support recursive queries (the root zone).

- The name server provides caching services for all domains. This characteristic is defined by the recursion yes; statement in the options clause and the zone "." clause (the root zone).

- The name server provides recursive query services for resolvers or other DNSs acting on behalf of resolvers. This characteristic is defined by the recursion yes; statement in the options clause.

Here is the BIND named.conf:

```
// Caching Name Server for dns.example.com.
// Recommended that you always maintain a change log in this file as shown here
// CHANGELOG:
// 1. 9 july 2005 INITIALS or NAME
//   a. did something
// a. 23 july 2005 INITIALS or NAME
//   a. did something more
//   b. another change
//
options {
  // all relative paths use this directory as a base
  directory "/var/named";
  // version statement for security to avoid hacking known weaknesses
  // if the real version number is published
  version "not currently available";
  // configuration-specific option clause statements
  // disables all zone transfer requests
  allow-transfer{"none"};
  // optional - BIND default behavior is recursion
  recursion yes;
  allow-recursion {10/8; 192.168.5.3; 192.168.7/24}; // prevents Open resolver
};
//
// log to /var/log/example.log all events from info UP in severity (no debug)
// uses 3 files in rotation swaps files when size reaches 250K
// failure messages up to this point are in (syslog) /var/log/messages
//
  logging{
  channel example_log{
   file "/var/log/named/example.log" versions 3 size 250k;
   severity info;
 };
  category default{
```

```
  example_log;
 };
};
// required zone for recursive queries
zone "." {
  type hint;
  file "root.servers";
};
// required local host domain
zone "localhost" in{
  type master;
  file "master.localhost";
  allow-update{none;};
};
// localhost reverse map
zone "0.0.127.IN-ADDR.ARPA" in{
  type master;
  file "localhost.rev";
  allow-update{none;};
};
```

This is a resolver and contains no zones (other than localhost) with master or slave types. Previous samples for master and slave server types included resolver (recursive) behavior combined with one or more master or slave zones.

There are no reverse-map zone files for any user IP addresses since it is assumed that another name server or an ISP, for example, is the zone master for example.com and is therefore also responsible for the reverse map. A reverse-mapping zone could be added if required for local operational reasons.

The allow-recursion statement limits the range of IP addresses that can issue recursive queries to this name server and prevent it from an open resolver. BIND 9.5+ also introduced a new statement allow-query-cache which now, officially, controls access to the cache by external users but this statement, when omitted, defaults to the values defined in an allow-recursion statement when present. It is permitted to use both allow-recursion and allow-query-cache statements but this can be confusing and consequently lead to conflicts, which can be a serious pain to debug. In general, it is best to use one allow-recursion statement type unless very fine-grained cache access control is required. It is always possible to define the IPv4 and/or IPv6 addresses allowed to issue queries even when the ranges are fragmented, as shown in the example. An ACL clause (see Chapter 12) may also be used as an alternative method to define the list of permitted IP addresses; the ACL name is then referenced in the allow-recursion statement. If the list of permitted IP addresses is very fragmented, do *not* be tempted to use the blanket allow-recursion {any;}; which has the effect of making the resolver fully open and lethal. Remember, if everyone were to take the same short cut, one day you could be on the receiving end of the DDoS attack. As always, enlightened self-interest is the best policy. This is not the only possible method to close and open resolver: listen-on and allow-query statements, depending on the context, can also achieve the same results.

Forwarding (a.k.a. Proxy, Client, Remote) DNS Server

The functionality of the forwarding name server was described in Chapter 4 and is used primarily to minimize traffic on congested, slow, or expensive external network connections such as a dial-up network.

Forwarding Name Server Configuration

The BIND named.conf configuration sample provides the following functionality:

- The name of this forwarding server is assumed to be forward.example.com. An A or AAAA RR will appear with this name in the example.com zone file (not illustrated).

- The name server is neither a master nor slave for any domain. There are no zone clauses for other than essential zones needed for local operations (master.localhost and localhost.rev).

- The name server provides caching services for all domains. This characteristic is an artifact of BIND's normal behavior. When the results of queries forwarded to an external name server are returned, they are automatically cached.

- The name server does not provide recursive query support. This characteristic is defined by the recursion no; statement and by the definition of the forward only; statement in the options clause.

- The name server forwards all queries to a remote DNS that must provide recursive query support from all local host (stub-) resolvers (global forwarding). This characteristic is defined by the forward and forwarders statements in the options clause.

Here is the BIND named.conf:

```
// Forwarding & Caching Name Server for forward.example.com.
// Recommended that you always maintain a change log in this file as shown here
// CHANGELOG:
// 1. 9 july 2005 INITIALS or NAME
//   a. did something
// a. 23 july 2005 INITIALS or NAME
//   a. did something more
//   b. another change
//
options {
  // all relative paths use this directory as a base
  directory "/var/named";
  // version statement for security to avoid hacking known weaknesses
  version "not currently available";
  // configuration specific options statements
  forwarders {10.0.0.1; 10.0.0.2;};
  forward only;
  // disables all zone transfer requests
  allow-transfer{"none"};
  // turn off recursion
  recursion no;
  allow-query-cache {localnets;}; //enables access to the  cache for local LAN users
};
// log to /var/log/example.log all events from info UP in severity (no debug)
// uses 3 files in rotation swaps files when size reaches 250K
// failure messages up to this point are in (syslog) /var/log/messages
  logging{
  channel example_log{
   file "/var/log/named/example.log" versions 3 size 250k;
```

```
  severity info;
 };
  category default{
  example_log;
 };
};
// required local host domain
zone "localhost" in{
  type master;
  file "master.localhost";
  allow-update{none;};
};
// localhost reverse map
zone "0.0.127.IN-ADDR.ARPA" in{
  type master;
  file "localhost.rev";
  allow-update{none;};
};
```

The forwarding name server typically contains no zones (other than localhost) with master or slave types.

The allow-query-cache statement is necessary in this case to permit queries to be answered from the local cache if the information is available, thus saving time and resources. In the example, the reserved name localnets (see Chapter 12 - BIND address_match_list Definition) is a quick way to enable all local LAN connected hosts assuming the hosts IP address and *netmask* covers the full range. If this statement were not present then it would default to allow-query-cache {none;}; because of the presence of the recursion no; statement. The net effect of the omission would be that every query would be forwarded, even if exactly the same query had been answered 1 microsecond previously for another user and the data was in the cache. While everything would continue to work, it would not be the fastest, most efficient, or smartest configuration.

No user IP address reverse-map zone is present since it is assumed that another name server or ISP is the zone master for the domain and is therefore also responsible for the reverse map. It could be added if required for local operational reasons.

The forward statement must be used in conjunction with a forwarders statement. The statement forward only overrides local recursive query behavior. All queries are forwarded to a resolver (in the example case, these are assumed to 10.0.0.1 and 10.0.0.2) that will return a complete answer in a single transaction, thus minimizing external network traffic, while local clients see an apparently recursive name server.

Since all queries are forwarded to another name server, the root.servers zone (type hint) is omitted.

Forwarding can also be done on a per-zone basis, in which case the values defined override the global options. The following example shows its use in a zone clause:

```
// BIND named.conf fragment
// use of forward in a zone clause
zone "example.net" in{
  type forward;
  forwarders{10.0.0.3;};
  forward only;
};
```

Here all queries (indicated by forward only) for the domain example.com will be forwarded to the host 10.0.0.3, whereas the global forwarders statement in the main file uses the hosts 10.0.0.1 and

10.0.0.2. If forward first had been used, then the plan would be to forward to host 10.0.0.3; if no response is obtained, only then use the global forwarders 10.0.0.1 and 10.0.0.2.

Stealth (a.k.a. Split or DMZ) DNS Server

The *stealth name server* configuration is typically used to provide perimeter security (see Chapter 4). Figure 7–1 illustrates the conceptual view of a stealth (a.k.a. *split* or *DMZ*) DNS server configuration.

The key concept in a stealth DNS system is that there is a clear line of demarcation, sometimes colloquially referred to as a DMZ (demilitarized zone), between the internal stealth server(s) and the external or public name server(s). The primary difference in configuration is that stealth servers provide a comprehensive set of services to internal users (include caching and recursive queries) and would be configured as a typical zone master, slave, or a resolver; the public server provides limited services and would typically be configured as an authoritative-only server (see the "Authoritative-only DNS Server" section later in this chapter).

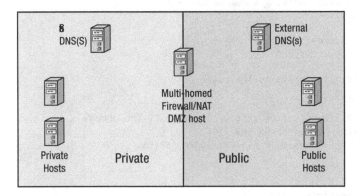

Figure 7–1. *Stealth server configuration*

There are two critical points in a stealth configuration:

1. The zone file for the stealth server may contain both public and private hosts, whereas the public server's zone file will contain only public or publicly visible hosts.

2. To preserve the stealth nature, it is vital that the public named.conf file does not include statements such as master, allow-notify, allow-transfer, etc. with references to the IP(s) of the stealth server. If the stealth server's IP were to appear in the public name server and its file system were to be compromised, the attacker could gain knowledge about the organization. In other words, he could penetrate the *veil of privacy* by simply inspecting the named.conf file.

Stealth Configuration

The samples that follow depict named.conf files for the public and private name servers used in a stealth configuration.

Stealth (Private) Configuration Files

Here is the BIND named.conf file used on the private or stealth name servers:

```
// Master & Caching Name Server for Example, INC. STEALTH SIDE
// Recommended that you always maintain a change log in this file as shown here
// CHANGELOG:
// 1. 9 july 2005 INITIALS or NAME
//   a. did something
// a. 23 july 2005 INITIALS or NAME
//   a. did something again
//   b. another change
//
options {
  // all relative paths use this directory as a base
  directory "/var/named";
  // version statement for security to avoid hacking known weaknesses
  // if the real version number is published
  version "not currently available";
  // configuration-specific options statements
  // optional - BIND default behavior is recursion
  recursion yes;
  allow-recursion {172.18/16;}; // permits access to the cache
};
//
// log to /var/log/named/example.log all events from info UP in severity (no debug)
// uses 3 files in rotation swaps files when size reaches 250K
// failure messages up to this point are in syslog e.g. /var/log/messages
//
  logging{
  channel example_log{
  file "/var/log/named/example.log" versions 3 size 250k;
  severity info;
 };
  category default{
  example_log;
 };
};
// required zone for recursive queries
// transactions will pass through a classic firewall
zone "." {
  type hint;
  file "root.servers";
};
// zone clause - master for example.com
zone "example.com" in{
  type master;
  file "master/master.example.com.internal";
  allow-update{none;};
};
// required local host domain
zone "localhost" in{
  type master;
  file "master.localhost";
```

```
  allow-update {none;};
};
// localhost reverse map
zone "0.0.127IN-ADDR.ARPA" in{
  type master;
  file "localhost.rev";
  allow-update{none;};
};
// reverse map for local address at example.com
// uses 192.168.254.0 for illustration
zone "254.168.192.IN-ADDR.ARPA" in{
  type master;
  file "192.168.254.rev";
};
```

The allow-recursion statement in the options clause is not required to prevent an open resolver. Since this name server is behind a firewall, it's essentially prevented from external recursive query access. However, it or allow-query-cache {172.17/16;}; is still required to enable access to the cache for recursive queries from the internal network. Finally, if recursive query access is required that is within the scope defined by the IP address and netmask of the name server host, both statements may be omitted, since this would default to allow-query-cache {localnets;};, which permits the required operations. Even in this case, however, it would be a wise move to explicitly define the statement; first, because defaults can change; second, because it makes the functionality crystal clear without having to scrabble for a manual—or heaven forbid, this book—to look up default values.

The zone file master.example.com.internal will contain both the public and internal hosts. The standard sample zone file has been modified to add some internal or private hosts.

```
; simple zone file for example.com
$TTL 2d    ; default TTL for zone
$ORIGIN example.com. ; base domain-name
; Start of Authority RR defining the key characteristics of the zone (domain)
@         IN    SOA   ns3.example.com. hostmaster.example.com. (
                       2003080800 ; se = serial number
                       12h        ; ref = refresh
                       15m        ; ret = update retry
                       3w         ; ex = expiry
                       2h         ; min = minimum
                       )
; name server RRs for the domain
            IN    NS    ns3.example.com.
; mail server RRs for the zone (domain)
     3w     IN    MX  10 mail.example.com.
; the second  mail servers is  external to the zone (domain)
            IN    MX  20 mail.example.net.
; domain hosts includes NS and MX records defined previously
; plus any others required
mail        IN    A     192.168.254.4
joe         IN    A     192.168.254.6
www         IN    A     192.168.254.7
; aliases ftp (ftp server) to an external domain
ftp         IN    CNAME ftp.example.net.
; private hosts and services
ns3         IN    A     192.168.254.10
accounts   IN    A     192.168.254.11
```

```
hr              IN      A       192.168.254.12
....
last            IN      A       192.168.254.233
```

The stealth side zone file uses a nonpublicly visible name server, ns3.example.com, to provide local DNS services (mixed resolver and internal master zone server). A single name server is used in this configuration file, but two or more could be used depending on the size of the organization and the requirement for resilience. This file does not reference the public name servers ns1.example.com and ns2.example.com, which are defined in the zone file used by the public server to minimize unnecessary traffic across the firewall. The mail servers referenced are the same as those used in the public server to avoid having to synchronize mail from multiple servers, and it's assumed all access to the mail servers will be via a firewall.

Public Configuration Files

The BIND named.conf file for the public name server is the same as that defined for an authoritative-only name server. The zone file is the standard sample zone file that contains only public hosts and services.

BIND provides a powerful view clause that may be used to provide similar functionality using a single server. The view clause allows different users or clients to gain access to different services. When a view clause is used, the stealth and public zone files are hosted on the same server. If this host's file system is compromised for any reason, then simple inspection of the zone and configuration files will reveal information about the organization. Unless the file system can be guaranteed against compromise, the view clause can't provide a stealth DNS solution in a highly secure environment. The descriptions that follow, however, extend this topic further and present configurations in which the real power of the view clause can be used.

Authoritative-only DNS Server

An *authoritative-only* name server will only provide authoritative answers to queries for zones or domains for which it is either a master or a slave. It will not provide either caching or recursive query support. If security is not the primary requirement, then the view clause may be used to provide authoritative-only services to external users and more comprehensive services to internal users as described previously. An example configuration of this style of operation using a view clause is also shown in the "View-based Authoritative-only DNS Server" section.

Authoritative-only Name Server Configuration

The BIND named.conf configuration sample provides the following functionality:

- The name server is authoritative for example.com. This characteristic is defined by the inclusion of the zone "example.com" clause with type master; but it could also be type slave; since both are authoritative.

- The name server does not provide caching services for any other domains. This is defined by the recursion no; statement in the options clause and the absence of the zone "." clause (root zone). See the Note below.

- The name server does not provide recursive query services for resolvers or other DNSs acting on behalf of resolvers. It supports *only iterative* queries. This characteristic is defined by the recursion no; statement in the options clause.

- The name server is optimized for maximum performance. Any optional but performance-affecting characteristics should be inhibited. In the following sample, the allow-transfer {"none";}; statement is shown for this reason as well as reasons of security.

Note: The non-inclusion of the root zone (.) is not a clear cut case. It depends on a number of factors. The example.com zone file contains three of out-of-zone RRs: the **MX 20 example.net. RR**; the **CNAME ftp.example.net RR**; the **NS ns2.example.net RR**. The final resolution of these RRs will require obtaining the associated A or AAAA RR, which will be done by the resolver issuing separate queries to the example.net zone so the root zone is not required. However, the inclusion of the NS ns2.example.net RR in this case means the server will need the IP of ns2.example.com to send NOTIFY messages, so the root zone is required unless notify no; is used. BIND 9 has a compiled a list of root servers so the example configuration will always work, though on creaky theoretical ground. It has been omitted simply to remind readers that the root zone is not always required. In summary, authoritative only name servers *only* require a root zone if NOTIFY is being used (the default) *and* if one or more of the NS RRs is out-of-zone *and* if this server is not authoritative for the out-of-zone domain name (example.net in this case). All pretty obvious, really!

Here is the BIND named.conf:

```
// Authoritative only Name Server for example. com
// Recommended that you always maintain a change log in this file as shown here
// CHANGELOG:
// 1. 9 july 2005 INITIALS or NAME
//   a. did something
// a. 23 july 2005 INITIALS or NAME
//   a. did something again
//   b. another change
//
options {
  // all relative paths use this directory as a base
  directory "/var/named";
  // version statement for security to avoid hacking known weaknesses
  version "not currently available";
  // configuration specific options statements
  recursion no;
  // disables all zone transfer requests
  // for performance as well as security reasons
  allow-transfer{"none"};
  dnssec-enable no; // zone not signed in this case - see Chapter 11
  minimal-responses yes;  // optional - improved performance
  additional-from-auth no; // optional - improved performance
  additional-from-cache no;  // optional - minimal performance change
};
//
// log to /var/log/zytrax-named all events from info UP in severity (no debug)
```

```
// uses 3 files in rotation swaps files when size reaches 250K
// failure messages up to this point are in (syslog) /var/log/messages
//
  logging{
  channel example_log{
   file "/var/log/named/example.log" versions 3 size 250k;
   severity info;
 };
  category default{
  example_log;
 };
};
zone "example.com" in{
  type master;
  file "master/master.example.com";
  allow-transfer {10.0.0.1;}; // slave server for the domain
  allow-update{none;};
};
// reverse map for local address at example.com
// uses 192.168.254.0 for illustration
zone "254.168.192.IN-ADDR.ARPA" in{
  type master;
  file "192.168.254.rev";
};
// required local host domain
zone "localhost" in{
  type master;
  file "master.localhost";
  allow-update{none;};
};
// localhost reverse map
zone "0.0.127.IN-ADDR.ARPA" in{
  type master;
  file "localhost.rev";
  allow-update{none;};
};
```

The authoritative-only server does not provide services for any domain except those for which it is either a master or a slave; as a consequence the root.servers zone file is not present (zone "."). The recursion no; statement inhibits recursive behavior; the name server will return REFUSED status (BIND 9.7+) if it receives a query for any domain or zone for which it is neither master nor slave.

DNSSEC is turned off using dnssec-enable no; since this zone is not signed (see Chapter 11) and, since BIND 9.5, yes is the BIND 9 default setting. Zone transfers are disabled (allow-transfer {none;};) in the options clause which means you can avoid possible DDoS attacks via zone transfer on the localhost or reverse-map zones as well as the more obvious example.com zone. Zone transfer is allowed to the assumed slave zone at 10.0.0.2 in the zone example.com only (see also Chapter 10 - Securing Zone Transfers). This configuration also assumes that the master file is moved to this server by some out-of-band method such as USB stick, secure FTP, ssh, etc. It is also possible to make this a slave server to a *hidden master*. However, the IP address of this hidden master (because it will appear in the slave's masters statement) is easily compromised if an attacker can simply read the named.conf file; since this external server must be able to communicate with the hidden master (to transfer the zone), so can an attacker—with less benign motives.

The biggest single impact on performance is to reduce the volume of data returned to the bare essentials. The statements minimal-responses, additional-from-auth and additional-from-cache all do that. `minimal-responses` alone, depending on the configuration, can almost double query throughput. This is slightly misleading, however, because some of the data that is omitted is still required by the resolver, and in the case of in-zone data, will immediately result in another query. On balance, however, it can still have a significant effect. Neither of the statements `additional-from-auth no;` nor `additional-from-cache no;` will have any effect on performance with the example configuration. But with some changes they could have. The zone file for `example.com` contains three out-of-zone references to `example.net`: an NS RR to `ns2.example.net`, an MX RR to `mail.example.net` and a CNAME RR to `ftp.example.net`. If `additional-from-auth` was not present (it defaults to yes) *and* this name server was also authoritative (master or slave) for `example.net`, then this name server would add data to the `ADDITIONAL SECTION` (see Chapter 16 - DNS Message Format) in responses to `example.com` queries by following the out-of-zone references to `example.net`. `additional-from-cache` prevents adding any data to the ADDITIONAL SECTION if it happens to be lying around in the cache. Since you turned off recursion completely, there should be nothing in the cache, but it does prevent the cache from even being searched. Prior to BIND 9.7, this statement also controlled returning referrals to a query for a zone this server was not authoritative for. Since BIND 9.7 such queries now result in `REFUSED` status being returned. The effect of `additional-from-cache no;` is probably less than minimal and it could be omitted with little loss of performance.

The reverse-map zone (`zone "254.168.192.IN-ADDR.ARPA"`) is assumed to represent the domain's public addresses (the use of a private IP RFC 1918 address netblock is simply to avoid using a real public IPv4 address range). This reverse-map zone would only be present if the domain owner has the responsibly for reverse mapping. Either because they own the IPv4 netblock or their service provider has delegated the responsibility (see Chapter 8 - Delegate Reverse Subnet Maps). In all cases, because mail servers do reverse-map look-ups, you will need to ensure that your mail server(s) have properly configured reverse maps either by creating and maintain a reverse-map zone or ensuring that your service providers adds the required the reverse map entries. In the case of IPv6, reverse maps are compulsory and will be the user's responsibility. BIND provides three statements to control caching behavior, `max-cache-size` and `max-cache-ttl`, neither of which will have any effect on performance in the preceding case; and `allow-recursion`, which allows a list of hosts that are permitted to use recursion—all others are not (a kind of poor man's `view` clause).

View-based Authoritative-only DNS Server

The functionality of the authoritative-only name server was described in Chapter 4. If high security is not the primary requirement, then the `view` clause may be used to provide authoritative-only services to external users and more comprehensive services, including caching, to internal clients.

View-based Authoritative-only Name Server Configuration

The BIND `named.conf` configuration sample provides the following functionality:

- The name server is the zone master for `example.com`. This characteristic is defined by the inclusion of the zone `"example.com"` clause in both `view` clauses but each referencing a different zone file.

- The name server does not provide caching services for any external users. This is defined by the `recursion no;` statement in the `view "badguys"` clause and the absence of the zone `"."` clause (root zone) within the same `view` clause.

- The name server does not provide recursive query services for any external resolvers or other DNSs acting on behalf of resolvers. It supports only iterative queries. This characteristic is defined by the recursion no; statement in the view "badguys" clause.

- The name server provides caching services for internal users. This is defined by the recursion yes; statement in the view "goodguys" clause and the presence of the zone "." clause (root zone) within the same view clause.

- The name server provides recursive query services for internal users. This is defined by the recursion yes; statement in the view "badguys" clause.

Here is the BIND named.conf:

```
// View-based Authoritative Name Server for EXAMPLE, INC.
// Recommended that you always maintain a change log in this file as shown here
// CHANGELOG:
// 1. 9 july 2005 INITIALS or NAME
//  a. did something
// a. 23 july 2005 INITIALS or NAME
//  a. did something again
//  b. another change
//
// global options
options {
  // all relative paths use this directory as a base
  directory "/var/named";
  // version statement for security to avoid hacking known weaknesses
  version "not currently available";
  dnssec-enable no; // zone not signed in this case - see Chapter 11
};
//
// log to /var/log/example.com all events from info UP in severity (no debug)
// uses 3 files in rotation swaps files when size reaches 250K
// failure messages up to this point are in (syslog) /var/log/messages
//
  logging{
  channel example_log{
   file "/var/log/named/example.log" versions 3 size 250k;
   severity info;
 };
  category default{
  example_log;
 };
};
// provide recursive queries and caching for internal users
view "goodguys" {
  match-clients { 192.168.254/24; }; // the example.com network
  recursion yes;
  allow-recursion { 192.168.254/24;}; // allows cache access for selected IPs
  // required zone for recursive queries
  zone "." {
   type hint;
   file "root.servers";
```

```
 };
 zone "example.com" {
  type master;
  // private zone files including local hosts
  file "view/master.example.com.internal";
  allow-update{none;};
 };
 // required local host domain
 zone "localhost" in{
  type master;
  file "master.localhost";
  allow-update{none;};
 };
 // localhost reverse map
 zone "0.0.127.IN-ADDR.ARPA" in{
  type master;
  file "localhost.rev";
  allow-update{none;};
 };
 // reverse map for local address at example.com
 // uses 192.168.254.0 for illustration
 zone "254.168.192.IN-ADDR.ARPA" in{
 type master;
 file "view/192.168.254.rev.internal";
  allow-update{none;};
};

}; // end view

// external hosts view
view "badguys" {
  match-clients {"any"; }; // all other hosts
  // recursion not supported
  recursion no;
  minimal-responses yes;  // optional - improved performance
  additional-from-auth no; // optional - improved performance
  additional-from-cache no;  // optional - minimal performance change
 zone "example.com" {
   type master;
   // only public hosts
   file "view/master.example.com.external";
   allow-update{none;};
   allow-transfer {10.0.0.1;}; // slave server for the external zone
   };
   // reverse map for local address at example.com
   // uses 192.168.254.0 for illustration
   zone "254.168.192.IN-ADDR.ARPA" in{
     type master;
     file "view/192.168.254.rev.external";
   allow-update{none;};
   };
}; // end view
```

The principle when using view clauses is that each view contains all the zone clauses required within that view and defines how they will behave within that view. The zone example.com appears in each view clause but references a different zone file (in the file statement). The zone file master.example.com.internal will contain both internal and public hosts, whereas the zone file master.example.com.external will have only the publicly visible hosts. The same principle applies to the reverse-mapping files: 192.168.254.rev.internal will contain reverse mapping for all the internal and public hosts, whereas 192.168.254.rev.external will only reverse map externally visible or public hosts.

The view "goodguys" clause provides recursive support and consequentially requires a root.servers zone file (zone "."). The view "badguys" clause doesn't require this zone, since it doesn't support recursive queries and is not present. Similarly, there is no need for the master.localhost and localhost.rev zone files in the view "badguys" clause (all local requests are answered by the view "goodguys" clause and they are not present).

Since BIND 9.5+ the statement allow-recursion {192.168.254/24;}; in the "goodguys" view is essential to permit recursive queries. It could also have been enabled with an allow-query-cache {192.168.254/24;}; as either will work. On balance, the author's prejudice is for allow-recursion since it's unambiguous in its intent. In either case, the purpose is to ensure that the resolver is not Open by limiting the scope of recursive support.

The order in which the view statements are defined is very important. In the view "goodguys" clause, the line match-clients { 192.168.0.0/24; } is used to match the 256 IP addresses from 192.168.254.0 to 192.168.254.255 (the IP prefix format, or slash notation, for defining an IP address range is described in the "IPv4 Addresses and CIDR" sidebar in Chapter 3). Only when this match fails does the process fall through to the view "badguys". In the view "badguys", match-clients {"any"; }; is interpreted to be "any not matched previously." If the order of view clauses were reversed, all IP addresses, including the internal IP addresses (192.168.254.0/24), would match "any", hence no additional services would be provided to internal clients.

Security and the view Section

Both this chapter and Chapter 4 have suggested that there is a weakness in using view clause if the name server's file system is compromised. This is in no sense a reflection on BIND's innate security; quite the contrary. In order to compromise the file system, an attack does not depend upon BIND or BIND's integrity, but rather can focus on any software running in the host with the sole objective of gaining some form of root privilege or even limited (read-only) access to well-known locations. If the zone files master.example.com.internal and 192.168.254.rev.internal could be read, then all the information about the internal organization of the zone could be discovered irrespective of all BIND's attempts to stop it. In short, it is *potentially* dangerous to keep internal zone files or internal reverse-map files on a view based name server.

However, careful inspection of the named.conf file earlier indicates that it contains relatively innocuous data, which would be of very little use to a hacker and indeed the most revealing data, namely the line match-clients { 192.168.254.0/24; };, may be available via a simple whois enquiry!

This characteristic of the view clause means that it can be used irrespective of the state of the underlying file system where it will not expose private information. That is, you can use the views to support resolver behavior mixed with external authoritative server behavior, neither of which requires private (internal) data. The view clause can be used in a stealth configuration to provide access from the internal network, as illustrated in Figure 7–2.

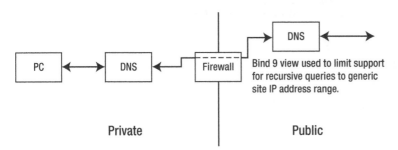

Figure 7–2. *Use of BIND's* `view` *section in a stealth configuration*

This `named.conf` sample file on the public side of this configuration provides the following services:

- The name server does not provide caching services for any external users. This characteristic is defined in the `view` `"badguys"` clause by the `recursion no;` statement in the `options` clause and the lack of a zone `"."` (root zone).

- The name server does not provide recursive query services for any external resolvers or other name servers acting on behalf of resolvers. It supports only iterative queries. This characteristic is defined in the `view` `"badguys"` clause by the `recursion no;` statement in the `options` clause.

- The name server provides caching services for internal users. This characteristic is defined in the `view` `"goodguys"` clause by the `recursion yes;` statement in the `options` clause and the presence of the zone `"."` (root zone).

- The name server provides recursive query services for internal users. This characteristic is defined in the `view` `"goodguys"` clause by the `recursion yes;` statement in the `options` clause.

The BIND `named.conf` file for this configuration is shown here:

```
// View based Authoritative Name Server for EXAMPLE.COM.
// Recommended that you always maintain a change log in this file as shown here
// CHANGELOG:
// 1. 9 july 2005 INITIALS or NAME
//   a. did something
// a. 23 july 2005 INITIALS or NAME
//   a. did something again
//   b. another change
//
// global options
options {
  // all relative paths use this directory as a base
  directory "/var/named";
  // version statement for security to avoid hacking known weaknesses
  version "not currently available";
  dnssec-enable no; // zone not signed in this case - see Chapter 11
};
//
```

```
// log to /var/log/example.com all events from info UP in severity (no debug)
// uses 3 files in rotation swaps files when size reaches 250K
// failure messages up to this point are in (syslog) /var/log/messages
//
  logging{
  channel example_log{
   file "/var/log/named/example.log" versions 3 size 250k;
   severity info;
 };
  category default{
  example_log;
 };
};
// provide recursive queries and caching for our internal users
view "goodguys" {
  match-clients { 192.168.254.0/24; }; // example.com's network
  recursion yes;
  // required zone for recursive queries
  zone "." {
   type hint;
   file "root.servers";
  };
}; // end view

// external hosts view
view "badguys" {
  match-clients {"any"; }; // all other hosts
  // recursion not supported
  recursion no;
  minimal-responses yes;  // optional - improved performance
  additional-from-auth no; // optional - improved performance
  additional-from-cache no;  // optional - minimal performance change zone "example.com" {
   type master;
   // only public hosts
   file "view/master.example.com.external";
  allow-transfer {10.0.0.1;}; // slave server for the domain
  };
  // reverse map for local address at example.com
  // uses 192.168.254.0 for illustration
  zone "254.168.192.IN-ADDR.ARPA" in{
    type master;
    file "view/192.168.254.rev.external";
  };

}; // end view
```

To invoke the service from the Stealth side of the configuration, the zone "." (defined as type hint in the sample file earlier) should be replaced with the following fragment, which forwards all requests for domains other than example.com to ns1.example.com—one of the public name servers:

```
// BIND named.conf fragment
// forwards requests for domains other than example.com
// to the public name server ns1.example.com = 192.168.254.2
zone "." in{
```

```
   type forward;
   forwarders{192.168.254.2;};
   forward only;
};
```

There are no files involved in this configuration that will divulge additional information that is not already publicly available or that could be found out without access to any of the systems or hosts involved in the configuration. The most revealing information is contained in the line `match-clients {` `192.168.254.0/24;`, and it's the IPv4 address range used by the entire configuration. As previously noted, this could probably be obtained with a `whois` enquiry. To further tighten security, communication between the stealth server and the public name server could use a unique port and thus allow port 53 access to be entirely blocked in the firewall configuration. I used this configuration to illustrate the power of the `view` clause and the kind of applications in which it can be used irrespective of the environment in which it is running.

Summary

This chapter introduced a number of configuration samples that reflect widely used DNS types while bearing in mind that many name servers, especially on smaller sites, are multifunctional or hybrid configurations. The objective of the chapter is to acquaint you with the configuration of a set of building blocks, DNS types, from which more complex configurations can be constructed. The text described BIND 9's powerful new `view` clause together with its use in various stealth configurations. This new clause provides many opportunities to reduce physical configurations in secure perimeter defenses, but careful attention to system design and especially `named.conf` file contents may be required to maximize its potential.

Chapter 8 presents some advanced DNS configurations including delegation of subdomains, load balancing, and resilience, among many others.

CHAPTER 8

■ ■ ■

DNS Techniques

This chapter describes a number of common configurations when working with zone files and, in some cases, with BIND. These solutions are presented to assist you in quickly implementing some commonly used features, recovering from errors, and illustrating some of the more subtle uses of the DNS. The following topics are covered:

- How to delegate a subdomain: This configuration allows the domain name owner to pass the responsibility to a subdomain owner (which may be another party or another part of the organization) who will be entirely responsible for the zone files describing the subdomain.

- How to delegate a virtual subdomain: This configuration uses a single zone file to provide subdomain addressing (for instance, www.us.example.com or www.uk.example.com).

- How to configure fail-over mail servers: The configuration allows backup mail servers to support a domain.

- How to reverse-map subnets: This configuration allows the delegation of reverse mapping to subnets of typically less than 256 IPv4 addresses.

- How to load balance with DNS: The configurations describe various ways in which load balancing may be implemented using DNS features. The BIND statements that control the order in which addresses are returned are also covered.

- How to define an SPF record: The Sender Policy Framework (SPF) is an anti-spam measure that allows an e-mail server to verify that the SMTP source is valid for the sending e-mail address. SPF records are currently implemented by Microsoft, Google, and AOL to name but three of the many hundreds of thousands of users.

- How to define a DKIM record: DomainKeys Identified Mail (DKIM) is an anti-spam feature using signed mail and used by several major mail providers such as Google, Yahoo, and others.

- How to support http://example.com: The configuration allows both the URL www.example.com and example.com to directly address a web or other service. The required changes to the Apache server are also covered.

- How to fix an out-of-sequence SOA serial number: The process used to fix various SOA serial number errors is covered.

- How to use DNS wildcards: The DNS RRs support the use of a wildcard (*). The section on wildcards illustrates the use of this error-prone feature.

- Zone file Construction: Zone files can be constructed in a variety of ways to ease configuration.

- Split horizons: Techniques for giving different IP addresses based on query location. A poor man's anycasting.

- DNSBL: DNS blacklists and other alternative uses for DNS.

- TTL values: The TTL value for any resource record can play a significant part in DNS reliability.

The examples shown use a number of BIND's named.conf statements (described in Chapter 12) and standard resource records (defined in Chapter 13). If you are running name server software other than BIND, the zone files will remain the same but the configuration statements may differ.

In the next section, the process of delegation of a subdomain, us.example.com, is described to illustrate the general principle of delegation within an owner's domain name space. The domain owner can delegate everything to the *left* of the domain name in any way that makes sense—or for that matter that doesn't make sense!

Delegate a Subdomain (Subzone)

This technique configures a zone to *fully delegate* the responsibility for a subdomain to another name server. This is not the only possible method of defining subdomains—another technique involves configuring what this book calls a *virtual* or *pseudo* subdomain, which uses a single zone file to provide subdomain addressing structures and is described later in the chapter. Assume a fully delegated subdomain is required with the following addressing structure :

- Zone (domain) name: example.com

- Domain host name: bill.example.com

- Subdomain name: us.example.com

- Subdomain host or service name: ftp.us.example.com

To ease the zone administration load, this technique assumes the responsibility for the subdomain will be fully delegated to the us.example.com zone administrator who will be responsible for the subdomain zone files and their supporting name servers. The zone administrators of the corporate domain for example.com want nothing further to do with us.example.com other than they have generously agreed to act as the slave DNS for the subdomain name servers. When dealing with subdomains, it's important to remember that as far as the Internet registration authorities and the TLD servers are concerned, subdomains do not exist. All queries for anything that ends with example.com will be referred to the name servers for the example.com zone or domain. In turn, these name servers are responsible for referring the query to the subdomain name servers. For the want of any better terminology, the name servers for example.com are called the *domain name servers* and are visible to the gTLD .com servers; the name servers for us.example.com are called the *subdomain name servers* and are visible only to the domain name servers (they are invisible to the gTLD servers).

■**Note** The term *subzone* was originally defined in RFC 1034 to describe what is most commonly called a *subdomain* today. This book uses the term *subdomain* throughout.

Domain Name Server Configuration

The following is a fragment from BIND's named.conf file controlling the example.com domain name servers:

```
// named.conf file fragment

zone "example.com" in{
                type master;
                file "master.example.com";
};
// optional - example.com acts as the slave (secondary) for the delegated subdomain
zone "us.example.com" IN {
                type slave;
                file "slave.us.example.com";
                masters {10.10.0.24;};
};
```

The optional definition of a slave (secondary) name server for your delegated us.example.com subdomain is a good practice but not essential. The subdomain can use any suitable name server including an external (out-of-zone) name server, such as ns1.example.net. The zone file master.example.com will contain the domain configuration supporting two name servers for both the domain and the subdomain (recall that the generous zone administrators volunteered to configure one of their domain name servers to act as a slave subdomain name server). The following zone file fragment shows this configuration:

```
; zone fragment for 'zone name' example.com
$TTL 2d      ; default TTL is 2 days
$ORIGIN example.com.
@         .  IN      SOA   ns1.example.com. hostmaster.example.com. (
                2010121500 ; serial number
                12h         ; refresh =  12 hours
                15m         ; refresh retry = 15 minutes
                3w12h       ; expiry = 3 weeks + 12 hours
                2h20m       ; nx  = 2 hours + 20 minutes
                )
; main domain name servers
                IN      NS      ns1.example.com.
                IN      NS      ns2.example.com.
; mail domain mail servers
                IN      MX      mail.example.com.
; A records for preceding name servers
ns1          IN      A       192.168.0.3
ns2          IN      A       192.168.0.4
; A record for preceding mail server
mail         IN      A       192.168.0.5
....
; subdomain definitions in the same zone file
; $ORIGIN directive simplifies and clarifies definitions
$ORIGIN us.example.com. ; all subsequent RRs use this ORIGIN
; two name servers for the subdomain
@               IN      NS      ns3.us.example.com.
; the preceding record could have been written without the $ORIGIN as
; us.example.com. IN NS ns3.us.example.com.
```

```
; or @          IN    NS ns3
; the second name server points back to preceding ns1
                    IN    NS    ns1.example.com.
; A records for name server ns3 required - the glue record
ns3             IN    A      10.10.0.24 ; glue record
; the preceding record could have been written as
; ns3.us.example.com. A 10.10.0.24 if it's less confusing
```

■ **Note** The somewhat bizarre time values in the SOA RR are to illustrate what is possible using BIND 9. The values are certainly not recommended; unless there is a good reason not to do so, it's always wiser to use a rounded value such as 1d or 15h.

The preceding fragment makes the assumptions that the domain name server ns1.example.com will act as a slave for the us.example.com subdomain. If this is not the case, any other name server can be defined the same way, but if this second name server also lies in the us.example.com domain, it will require an A RR. The A RR for ns3.example.com for the preceding subdomain is the so-called *glue* record (see the "Glue Records in DNS" sidebar). Glue records are necessary to allow a DNS query for the subdomain to return a referral containing both the name of the name server and its IP address. IP addresses are always defined using an A RR (or an AAAA RR if IPv6).

GLUE RECORDS IN DNS

Strictly speaking, glue records (the IP address of the name server defined using an A or AAAA RR) are only required for every name server lying *within* the domain or zone for which it is a name server. The query response—the referral—*must* provide both the name and the IP address of the name servers that lie within the domain being queried. In practice, the top-level domain (TLD) servers provide the IP address for every second-level domain (SLD) name server, whether in the domain or not, in order to minimize the number of query transactions. When a query to a generic top-level domain (gTLD) is issued, this name server provides the glue records for all the SLD domain's name servers. These glue records were defined and captured when the domain was registered. In the preceding configuration, the domain name server is acting in this role and must supply the IP addresses of the name servers in response to subdomain queries. To satisfy this requirement, the A RR for the name server (ns3.us.example.com) is a glue record and must be present. The reason a glue record *must* exist for servers *within* the domain but is required only for performance reasons for those in an external or out-of-zone domain can be illustrated by looking at what would happen if the glue record were not present. If you assume the query to the gTLD server for example.com returned the name but not the IP address of ns1.example.com, then a further query would be required for the A record of ns1.example.com; but since the IP of the SLD name server is not yet known, it must requery the gTLD server, which answers again with the name but not the IP . . . and so on ad infinitum. Name servers for a domain (for instance, example.com) that lie in another domain (for instance, ns1.example.net) only *need* the name, since a normal query for the A RR of ns3.example.net will return the required IP. As noted earlier, to increase performance, the IP addresses of all name servers for a domain, whether the name servers lie in the queried domain or not, are always returned by root and TLD name servers.

Subdomain Name Server Configuration

The BIND `named.conf` file controlling the subdomain name servers will contain statements similar to the following fragment:

```
// named.conf file fragment for the subdomain us.example.com

zone "us.example.com" in{
                type master;
                file "master.us.example.com";
};
```

The file `master.us.example.com` will contain the subdomain (`us.example.com`) configuration and use the two name servers that were defined in the preceding domain fragment. Here is a fragment of the subdomain zone file:

```
; zone file for subdomain us.example.com
$TTL 2d ; zone default of 2 days
$ORIGIN us.example.com.
        IN      SOA   ns3.us.example.com. hostmaster.us.example.com. (
        2010121500 ; serial number
        2h              ; refresh =  2 hours
        15m             ; refresh retry = 15 minutes
        3w12h           ; expiry = 3 weeks + 12 hours
        2h20m           ; nx = 2 hours + 20 minutes
        )
; subdomain name servers
                IN      NS      ns3.us.example.com.
                IN      NS      ns1.example.com. ; see following notes
; subdomain mail server
                IN      MX 10   mail.us.example.com.
; preceding record could have been written as
;               IN      MX 10   mail
; A records for preceding name servers
ns3             IN      A       10.10.0.24
ns1.example.com. IN     A       192.168.0.3 ; 'glue' record
; A record for preceding mail server
mail            IN      A       10.10.0.25
; next record defines our ftp server
ftp             IN      A       10.10.0.28
; the preceding record could have been written as
; ftp.us.example.com. A 10.10.0.24 if it's less confusing
....
; other subdomain records
....
```

The preceding fragment makes the assumption that `ns1.example.com` will act as a slave server for the `us.example.com` subdomain. If this is not the case, other name servers could be defined in a similar manner. The A record for `ns1.example.com` is a glue record and is not strictly necessary because it must already be available in a resolver from a previous query. This point is worth emphasizing further since it illustrates the nature of the DNS hierarchy. To make any query for the subdomain `us.example.com`, the `example.com` domain *must have been queried first*. Since `ns1.example.com` is one of the name servers for `example.com`, its IP address is already known to the resolver that issues the subdomain query. If the second name server for the subdomain lies in an external domain, there is no need for the glue record.

The FTP service host, and any others required, are only defined in the subdomain zone file and are not visible in the domain name-server zone file.

Virtual Subdomains

This technique implements what this book calls a *virtual* or *pseudo* subdomain in which the domain and the subdomain definitions appear in the same zone file. Subdomains may also be fully delegated; this is the subject of a previous technique. The advantage of this configuration is that unlike a fully delegated subdomain, no additional name servers are required while still creating the subdomain style addressing structure. The disadvantage is that all changes to both the domain and the subdomain will require reloading of the main zone file. The addressing structure required is assumed to be the following:

- Zone (domain) name: example.com

- Domain host name: bill.example.com

- Subdomain name: us.example.com

- *Subdomain host name*: ftp.us.example.com

This solution assumes that for operational reasons the owner has decided to maintain all the information for example.com and us.example.com in a single zone file.

Domain Name Server Configuration

The BIND named.conf file will contain statements similar to the following fragment defining the zone example.com as normal:

```
// named.conf file fragment

zone "example.com" in{
            type master;
            file "master.example.com";
};
```

The file master.example.com will contain the domain and subdomain configuration and support two name servers, like so:

```
; zone fragment for example.com
$TTL 2d ; zone TTL default = 2 days
$ORIGIN example.com.
@               IN      SOA     ns1.example.com. root.example.com. (
                2010121500 ; serial number
                2h          ; refresh =  2 hours
                15m         ; refresh retry = 15 minutes
                3w12h       ; expiry = 3 weeks + 12 hours
                2h20m       ; nx = 2 hours + 20 minutes
                )
; main domain name servers
                IN      NS      ns1.example.com.
                IN      NS      ns2.example.com.
; mail servers for main domain
                IN      MX 10   mail.example.com.
; A records for preceding name servers
ns1             IN      A       192.168.0.3
```

```
ns2          IN     A     192.168.0.4
; A record for preceding mail servers
mail         IN     A     192.168.0.5
; other domain-level hosts and services
bill         IN     A     192.168.0.6
....
; subdomain definitions
$ORIGIN us.example.com.
             IN     MX 10  mail
; preceding record could have been written as
; us.example.com.   IN  MX 10 mail.us.example.com.
; A record for subdomain mail server
mail         IN     A     10.10.0.28
; the preceding record could have been written as
; mail.us.example.com. A 10.10.0.28 if it's less confusing
ftp          IN     A     10.10.0.29
; the preceding record could have been written as
; ftp.us.example.com. A 10.10.0.29 if it's less confusing
....
; other subdomain definitions as required
$ORIGIN uk.example.com.
....
```

Additional subdomains could be defined in the same file using the same strategy. For administrative convenience, the standard zone file $INCLUDE directive may be used to include the subdomain RRs as demonstrated in the following fragment:

```
; fragment from zone file showing use of $INCLUDE
....
; other domain-level hosts and services
bill         IN     A     192.168.0.5
....
; subdomain definitions
$INCLUDE sub.us.example.com
; other subdomain definitions as required
```

This solution illustrates that subdomain addressing can be easily accomplished in a single zone file at the possible cost of administrative convenience. This structure, as well as being simpler than a fully delegated subdomain, does not require any additional name servers.

Configure Mail Servers Fail-Over

This technique is provided here for the sake of completeness and uses material already covered in Chapter 2. It configures a DNS server to provide fail-over or alternate mail service when the primary mail service is offline or not accessible for a period of time. It involves use of the preference field of the MX RRs (see Chapter 13) as shown in the following fragment:

```
; zone file fragment
     IN  MX  10 mail.example.com.
     IN  MX  20 mail.example.net.
....
mail IN  A     192.168.0.4
....
```

If the most preferred mail server, the one with the lowest number (in the preceding fragment, it's 10 and `mail.example.com`) is not available, mail will be sent to the second most preferred server, the one with the next highest number, which in the preceding fragment is 20 and `mail.example.net`. The secondary mail server (`mail.example.net`), ideally located at a separate geographic location, would typically be configured as a simple relay (or forwarding) mail server with a very long retry time. In this case, it will accept the mail and try to relay it to the proper destination (`mail.example.com`) over the next six weeks or whatever you configure the retry limit to be.

Delegate Reverse Subnet Maps

This technique describes how to delegate reverse mapping for subnets. Delegation of reverse subnet maps may be used by ISPs or other service providers as a means to enable a user of a static IP range, delegated from the service provider, to be responsible for their own reverse-mapping zone files. In the example shown, a subnet is defined to be less than 256 IPv4 addresses though the solution could be used for any part of an IPv4 address range. Normal reverse mapping is described in Chapter 3 and in the example case is assumed to reverse map down to the third element of an IPv4 address; for instance, if you assume an IPv4 address of 192.168.199.15, then normal reverse mapping will typically cover the 192.168.199 part, which is then reversed and placed under the domain IN-ADDR.ARPA, giving `199.168.192.IN-ADDR.ARPA`. The resulting reverse map will contain the hosts from 192.168.199.0 to 192.168.199.255. You now assume that subnets of 64 addresses are assigned to four separate users (192.168.199.0/26; 192.168.199.64/26; 192.168.199.128/26; 192.168.199.192/26); to minimize work, the assignee wishes to delegate responsibility for reverse mapping to the subnet users (the assignors). The reverse map has been delegated once to the assignee of 192.168.199.0 and can't therefore be delegated again. Your assignee must use a special technique defined in RFC 2317. The technique involves creating additional space in the reverse-map address hierarchy. Both the assignee (a service provider) and the assignor (an end user) are required to implement the technique in their zone files; examples of both zone files are shown later in the chapter.

Assignee Zone File

The following fragment shows the 192.168.199.64/26 subnet as a fragment of a reverse-map zone file located at the assignee (using the example.net domain) of the subnet:

```
; zone file fragment for example.net
$TTL 2d ; zone default TTL = 2 days
$ORIGIN 199.168.192.IN-ADDR.ARPA.
@           IN   SOA   ns1.example.net. hostmaster.example.net. (
                            2010121500 ; serial number
                            2h         ; refresh
                            15m        ; refresh retry
                            2w         ; expiry
                            3h         ; nx
                            )
            IN   NS     ns1.example.net.
            IN   NS     ns2.example.net.
; definition of other IP address 0 - 63
....
; definition of our target 192.168.199.64/26 subnet
; name servers for subnet reverse map
64/26       IN   NS   ns1.example.com.
64/26       IN   NS   ns2.example.com.
```

```
; the preceding could have been written as
; 64/26.199.168.192.IN-ARDDR.ARPA.  IN NS ns2.example.com.
; IPs addresses in the subnet - all need to be defined
; except 64 and 127 since they are the subnets multicast
; and broadcast addresses not hosts/nodes
65              IN  CNAME   65.64/26.199.168.192.IN_ADDR.ARPA. ;qualified
66              IN  CNAME   66.64/26 ;unqualified name
67              IN  CNAME   67.64/26
....
125             IN  CNAME   125.64/26
126             IN  CNAME   126.64/26
; end of 192.168.199.64/26 subnet
.....
; other subnet definitions
```

The method works by forcing the CNAME lookup to use the name servers defined for the subnet; that is, the address 65 will find the CNAME 65.64/26.199.168.192.IN-ADDR.ARPA., which is resolves to the name servers ns1.example.com. and ns2.example.com., both of which are located at the assignor (end user) in this case. The 64/26 name, which makes the additional name space look like a IP prefix or slash notation address, is an artificial but legitimate way of constructing the additional space to allow delegation. The / (slash) relies on a liberal interpretation of the rules for a name or label (allowed by RFC 2181), but it could be replaced with - (dash) such as 64-26 if that makes you more comfortable. Any number of subnets of variable size can be assigned in this manner; that is, the subnet following the one defined previously could be 128/27 (32 IP addresses) or 128/28 (16 addresses) or 128/25 (128 IP addresses). No changes are required to the BIND configuration to support this reverse map.

Assignor (End User) Zone File

The zone file for the reverse map (ns1.example.com in this example) is a conventional reverse map and looks like this:

```
$TTL 2d ; zone default = 2 days
$ORIGIN 64/26.199.168.192.IN-ADDR.ARPA.
@           IN  SOA   ns1.example.com. hostmaster.example.com. (
                            2010121500 ; serial number
                            2h         ; refresh
                            15m        ; refresh retry
                            2w         ; expiry
                            3h         ; nx
                            )
            IN  NS    ns1.example.com.
            IN  NS    ns2.example.com.
; IPs addresses in the subnet - all need to be defined
; except 64 and 127 since they are the subnets multicast
; and broadcast addresses not hosts/nodes
65          IN  PTR   fred.example.com. ;qualified
66          IN  PTR   joe.example.com.
67          IN  PTR   bill.example.com.
....
125         IN  PTR   web.example.com.
126         IN  PTR   ftp.example.com.
; end of 192.168.23.64/26 subnet
```

Finally, the reverse-map zone clause in the named.conf file needs to be changed to reflect the revised zone name. The following example shows the reverse-map zone clause fragment:

```
// named.conf fragment at example.com
// revised reverse-map zone name
zone "64/26.199.168.192.IN-ADDR.ARPA" in{
                type master;
                file "192.168.23.rev";
};
```

Note The technique used in the preceding method is credited to Glen A. Herrmannsfeldt, who is obviously a very creative person. One might conjecture that he had problems persuading his ISP to delegate reverse-mapping responsibility.

DNS Load Balancing

These techniques use the DNS to configure various forms of load balancing. In this context, load balancing is defined as the ability to use standard DNS services to share the load between two or more servers providing the same or similar services. The section covers the following topics:

- Balancing mail

- Balancing other services (for instance, web or FTP)

- Balancing services using the SRV RR

- Controlling the order of RRs

This section ends with a brief discussion of the effectiveness of DNS-based load-balancing strategies.

Balancing Mail

Mail is unique in that two possible strategies may be used. The following fragment shows use of multiple MX records with equal-preference values:

```
; zone file fragment
        IN  MX  10  mail.example.com.
        IN  MX  10  mail1.example.com.
        IN  MX  10  mail2.example.com.
....
mail   IN  A       192.168.0.4
mail1  IN  A       192.168.0.5
mail2  IN  A       192.168.0.6
```

The name sever will deliver the MX RRs in the order defined by the rrset-order statement (covered later in this section and fully in Chapter 12) and which defaults to round robin (or cyclic) order. The requesting SMTP server will then apply its algorithm to select one from the equal preference list that *may* work *against* the BIND rrset-order statement. Currently, sendmail (8.3.13), Exim (4.44), and Postfix

(2.1) all have documented references to indicate that they use a random algorithm for records of equal preference; indeed, Postfix allows control over the behavior using the `smtp_randomize_addresses` parameter (default is yes). In this case, the randomizing algorithm may select the very IP that BIND's `rrset-order` algorithm positioned, say, last in the returned order. Documentation for qmail, courier-mta, and Microsoft (Exchange and IIS SMTP) does not describe what these packages do with equal-preference MX values.

An alternative approach is to use multiple A records with the same name and different IP addresses, as shown in this fragment:

```
; zone file fragment
        IN  MX  10  mail.example.com.
....
mail    IN  A       192.168.0.4
        IN  A       192.168.0.5
        IN  A       192.168.0.6
```

The name server will deliver the A RRs in the order defined by any `rrset-order` statement in BIND's `named.conf` file. In order to satisfy reverse lookup requests used by most mail servers for simple authentication, all the IP addresses listed must be reverse mapped to `mail.example.com`, as shown in the following fragment:

```
; reverse-map file fragment
; for 0.168.192.IN-ADDR.ARPA
....
4           PTR     mail.example.com.
5           PTR     mail.example.com.
6           PTR     mail.example.com.
```

The net effect of the two methods is the same. In the case of equal-preference MX records, the control of the load lies with the SMTP server's algorithm. In the case of multiple A RRs, control lies with the name server, which in the case of BIND provides the `rrset-order` statement to select the order of A RRs (RRsets) as well as other RRsets. In both the preceding cases, each mail server must be capable of synchronizing mailbox delivery by some method or all but one of the servers must be mail relays or forwarders.

Balancing Other Services

This section illustrates load balancing with web and FTP services, but the same principle applies to any service. In this case, the load-balancing solution uses multiple A RRs, as shown in the following fragment:

```
; example.com zone file fragment
....
ftp  IN  A   192.168.0.4
ftp  IN  A   192.168.0.5
ftp  IN  A   192.168.0.6
www  IN  A   192.168.0.7
www  IN  A   192.168.0.8
```

This RR format, which relies on blank name replication, produces exactly the same result:

```
; example.com zone file fragment
....

ftp  IN  A   192.168.0.4
```

```
        IN  A   192.168.0.5
        IN  A   192.168.0.6
www     IN  A   192.168.0.7
        IN  A   192.168.0.8
```

The name server will deliver all the IP addresses defined for the given name in answer to a query for the A RRs; the order of IP addresses in the returned list is defined by the rrset-order statement in BIND's named.conf file. The FTP and web servers must all be exact replicas of each other in this scenario.

■ **Note**: All modern browsers are capable of handling multiple A (or AAAA) RRs and will automatically rollover to the next IP address if they fail to get a response from the first. As well as being a load-balancing strategy, it's also the fastest and most efficient fail-over strategy in this case.

Balancing Services

The SRV record provides load balancing by using both a *priority* field and a *weight* field for fine-grained control as well as providing fail-over capability. The SRV RR description in Chapter 13 contains an example illustrating its use in load balancing. The SRV RR is not yet widely supported at this time with two notable exceptions: Lightweight Directory Access Protocol (LDAP), which was partly responsible for development for the SRV record and is used as a part of the discovery process for LDAP servers, and the Session Initiation Protocol (SIP) used in VoIP.

Controlling the RRset Order

BIND versions after 9.4.x implement the rrset-order statement, which can be used to control the order in which equal RRs, an RRset, of *any* type are returned. The rrset-order statement can take a number of arguments, which are described in Chapter 12, but the following fragment only uses the order keyword, which may take the values fixed (the order the records were defined in the zone file), cyclic (starts with the order defined in the zone file and round-robin for each subsequent query; this is the default), and random (randomly order the responses for every query). The rrset-order statement can only appear in the global options clause for BIND but can take addition arguments that can make it applicable to one or more zones. The following named.conf fragment returns any RRset (a set of equal RRs) in round-robin order:

```
// named.conf fragment
options {
// other options
        rrset-order {order cyclic;};
};
```

Assume a zone file has the following MX records:

```
; zone file fragment for example.com
        MX  10  mail1.example.com.
        MX  10  mail2.example.com.
        MX  10  mail3.example.com.
```

The first query to this zone for MX records will return in the order `mail1.example.com.`, `mail2.example.com.`, `mail3.example.com.` and the second query will return `mail3.example.com.`, `mail1.example.com.`, `mail2.example.com.` and so on in cyclic (or round-robin) order.

■**Note** For bizarre reasons known only to the BIND developers, the support of `fixed` order must be configured in BIND when it is built (see Chapter 6 - BIND 9 Configure Options). Neither Ubuntu (and Debian) nor FreeBSD configures this option in their standard packages.

Effectiveness of DNS Load Balancing

Clearly the effects of caching can significantly distort the effectiveness of any DNS IP address allocation algorithm. A TTL value of 0 may be used to inhibit caching, or the increasingly common very short TTL values (30–60 seconds) could be used to reduce the potentially negative caching effect, but only at the cost of a significant rise in the number of DNS queries. It would be a little unfortunate to achieve excellent load balancing across two or three web servers at the cost of requiring ten more name servers purely for performance reasons. Intuition, without serious experimentation, would suggest that assuming a normal TTL (12 hours or more) and *any* changing IP allocation algorithm (cyclic or random) would result in loads that would be reasonably balanced (measured by request arrivals at an IP) given the following assumptions:

- Traffic is balanced over a number of DNS caches; that is, traffic originates from a number of ISPs or customer locations where DNS caches are maintained. Specifically, there are no pathological patterns where 90% (or some largish number) of the load originates from one particular cache.

- The volume of traffic is reasonably high since pathological patterns are more likely in small traffic volumes.

DNS load balancing can't, however, account for service loading; for instance, certain transactions may generate very high CPU or resource loads. For this type of control only a specialized load balancer—which measures transaction response times from each server—will be effective.

Define an SPF Record

This section defines how to configure a Sender Policy Framework (SPF) record for a domain and its mail servers. SPF is being proposed as an IETF experimental standard to enable validation of legitimate sources of e-mail. The SPF record is defined by RFC 4408.

The design intent of the SPF record is to allow a receiving Message Transfer Agent (MTA) to verify that the originating IP (the source-ip) of an e-mail from a sender is authorized to send mail for the sender's domain. The SPF information may be contained in either a standard TXT RR or an SPF RR (both of which are described in Chapter 13). If an SPF or TXT RR exists and authorizes the source IP address, the mail can be accepted by the MTA. If the SPF or TXT RR does not authorize the IP address, the mail can be bounced—it did not originate from an authorized source for the sender's domain. If the domain does not have an SPF or TXT RR, the situation is no worse than before. Many commercial and open source MTAs have already been modified to use the SPF record, including sendmail, qmail, Postfix, courier, Exim, and Microsoft Exchange to name but a few. Microsoft is advocating a standard called Send ID,[1] which contains SPF as a subset but adds a new Purported Responsible Address (PRA) field to the e-mail to provide additional checking. DomainKeys Identified Mail (DKIM) is an alternative anti-spam cryptographic technique that is described later in this chapter. Additionally, DNS blacklists (DNSBL) may also be used for anti-spam purposes and are also described later in this chapter.

This technique both describes the format of the SPF record and presents a number of example configurations. The following terminology is used to simplify the subsequent descriptions:

- Sender: The full e-mail address of the originator of the mail item (obtained from the return path in the actual SPF checks); for instance, info@example.com.

- Sender-ip: The IP address of the SMTP server trying to send this message; for instance, 192.168.0.2.

- *Sender-domain*: The domain name part of the sender's e-mail address; for instance, if the sender is info@example.com, then the sender-domain is example.com.

The SPF record defines one or more tests to verify the sender. Each test returns a condition code (defined by the pre field shown in the next section). The first test to pass will terminate SPF processing.

SPF RR Format

An SPF RR is functionally identical to a TXT RR containing SPF data. However, since not all DNS software or e-mail validation libraries support the SPF RR type (but all will support the TXT RR type), RFC 4408 recommends that the TXT RR format be used; if the DNS software supports it, an SPF RR containing identical data should be added as well. It's always possible to use only a TXT RR containing SPF data; it's not sensible, however, to use only a SPF RR due to a possible lack of support in validating libraries or resolvers identified previously. BIND from version 9.4.x supports the SPF RR format. The standard TXT and SPF RR formats are defined as follows:

```
name ttl class   TXT     text
name ttl class   SPF     text
```

The SPF data is entirely contained in the text field (a quoted string). SPF defines the contents of the quoted string as shown here:

```
"v=spf1 [pre] type [[pre] type] ... [mod]"
```

SPF records are normally defined for the domain and the mail server(s). The following shows a zone file fragment containing SPF records for the domain and the mail server, which in this case only allows mail for the domain to be sent from the host mail.example.com:

```
; zone file fragment for example.com
            IN  MX 10 mail.example.com.
....
mail        IN  A     192.168.0.4
; SPF records
; domain SPF
example.com.  IN  TXT   "v=spf1 mx -all"
```

---

[1] More information on Send ID can be found at
www.microsoft.com/mscorp/safety/technologies/senderid/default.mspx

```
; AND if supported
example.com.  IN  SPF   "v=spf1 mx -all"
; mail host SPF
mail          IN  TXT   "v=spf1 a -all"
; AND if supported
mail          IN  SPF   "v=spf1 a -all"
```

The following text describes the fields used in an SPF record and references where appropriate the v=spf1 mx -all SPF record from the preceding example fragment:

v=spf1 Field

This field is mandatory and defines the version being used. Currently, the only version supported is spf1.

pre Field

This optional field (defaults to +) defines the code to return when a match occurs. The possible values are + = pass (default), - = fail, ~ = softfail (indeterminate result), ? = neutral. If a test is conclusive, either add + or omit (defaults to +) as in the first test in the example fragment, which could have been written as +mx. If a test might not be conclusive, use ? or ~. Note that - is typically only used with -all to indicate the action if there have been no previous matches as in the terminating test from the same fragment.

type Field

This defines the mechanism type to use for verification of the sender. Multiple type tests may be defined in a single SPF record. In the example fragment, there are two type tests: mx (or +mx) and all (-all). Each of the type values is described in detail in the "SPF Type Values" section.

mod Field

Two optional record modifiers are defined. If present, they should follow the last type directive; that is, after the terminating all. The current values defined are as follows:

redirect=domain Field

This redirects verification to use the SPF record of the defined domain. This format may be used to enable additional processing in the event of a failure or may be used on its own in an SPF to provide a single domain-wide definition. This format is the same as the type include but may be used without the terminating all type.

This SPF allows additional processing using the SPF for example.net if the mail from example.com tests fail, like so:

```
        IN  TXT "v=sfp1 mx ?all redirect=example.net"
; AND if supported
        IN  SPF "v=sfp1 mx ?all redirect=example.net"
```

This SPF redirects all processing for example.com to a standard SPF record in the domain example.net:

```
           IN   TXT "v=spf1 redirect=_spf.example.net"
; AND if supported
           IN   SPF "v=spf1 redirect=_spf.example.net"
```

The zone file for example.net would include the following record:

```
_spf       IN   TXT  "v=spf1 mx -all"
; AND if supported
_spf       IN   SPF  "v=spf1 mx -all"
```

exp=text-rr Field

The exp type, if present, should come last in an SPF record (after the all type, if present). It defines the name of a TXT record, text-rr, whose text may be optionally returned with any failure message. This fragment shows a trivial example where the sender of the mail is informed that they are not authorized to send mail. More complex examples, including the use of macro expansion, can be constructed, referring users to a site that could inform them of the procedure to define SPF records.

```
; domain example.com SPF record
           IN   TXT "v=spf1 mx -all exp=getlost.example.com"
; AND if supported
           IN   SPF "v=spf1 mx -all exp=getlost.example.com"
; the getlost TXT record
getlost  IN   TXT "You are not authorized to send mail for the domain"
```

The text field is allowed to contain macro expansions as described in the "Macro Expansion" section.

SPF type Values

The SPF type parameter defines either the mechanism to be used to verify the sender or to modify the verification sequence as described in the following sections.

Basic Mechanisms

These types do not define a verification mechanism but affect the verification sequence:

- include:domain: Recursive testing using the supplied domain. The SPF record for domain replaces the sender-domain's SPF and processing uses the rules defined in the included SPF. This is the most common form when clients send mail through an ISP's servers.

- all: Terminates a test sequence if no positive results have been found previously.

Sender Mechanisms

These types define a verification mechanism.

Type ip4 Format

This type may take one of the following formats:

```
ip4:ipv4 ip4:ipv4/cidr
```

The ip4 type uses the sender-ip for verification. If the sender-ip is the same as ipv4, the test passes. This may take the additional argument ip4:ipv4/cidr, in which case if the source IPv4 address lies in the range defined by cidr(the IP prefix or slash notation), the test passes. This type uses no additional DNS resources and is therefore the recommended solution for IPv4.

This SPF only allows e-mail for the domain to be sent from 192.168.0.2:

```
        IN  TXT "v=spf1 ip4:192.168.0.2 -all"
; AND if supported
        IN  SPF "v=spf1 ip4:192.168.0.2 -all"
```

This SPF allows mail to be sent from any of the 32 addresses that contain the address 192.168.0.38 (CIDR range is from 192.168.0.32–63):

```
        IN  TXT "v=spf1 ip4:192.168.0.38/27 -all"
; AND if supported
        IN  SPF "v=spf1 ip4:192.168.0.38/27 -all"
```

Type ip6 Format

This type may take one of the following formats:

```
ip6:ipv6 ip6:ipv6/cidr
```

The ip6 type uses the same formats defined for ip4 previously. This type uses no additional DNS resources and is therefore the recommended solution for IPv6.

The following only allows messages for the domain to be sent from the single address 2001:db8:0:0:0:0:0:10:

```
        IN  TXT "v=spf1 ip6:2001:db8::10 -all"
; AND if supported
        IN  SPF "v=spf1 ip6:2001:db8::10 -all"
```

The next example allows mail to be sent from 32 addresses that contain the address 2001:db8:0:0:0:0:0:10 (range is from 2001:db8:0:0:0:0:0:1 to 2001:db8:0:0:0:0:0:1f).

```
        IN  TXT "v=spf1 ip4:2001:db8::10/123 -all"
; AND if supported
        IN  SPF "v=spf1 ip4:2001:db8::10/123 -all"
```

Type a Format

This type may take one of the following formats:

```
a a/cidr a:domain a:domain/cidr
```

The a type uses an A RR for verification. In the basic format with no additional arguments, if the A RR for the sender-domain is the same as the sender-ip, the test passes. The optional form a/cidr will apply the test to the extended range defined by the IP prefix (or slash) notation. The form a:domain will cause the test to be applied to the A RR of domain, and a:domain/cidr will apply the test to the range of IPs defined by the IP prefix (or slash) notation. The domain argument may also use macro expansion, defined later in this section. The a and a/cidr formats require an A RR for the domain, as shown:

```
; zone fragment for example.com
$ORIGIN example.com.
...
@            IN   A      192.168.0.2
             IN   TXT  "v=spf1 a -all"
; AND if supported
             IN   SPF  "v=spf1 a -all"


....
```

This SPF allows only the host smtp.example.net to send mail for the domain example.com:

```
             IN   TXT  "v=spf1 +a:smtp.example.net -all"
; AND if supported
             IN   SPF  "v=spf1 +a:smtp.example.net -all"
```

The advantage of using the preceding construct is that if the IP address of smtp.example.com changes, the preceding SPF record doesn't change. The cost, however, is one more DNS transaction for every SPF check.

Type mx Format

This type may take one of the following formats:

```
mx mx/cidr mx:domain mx:domain/cidr
```

The mx type uses the MX RRs and the mail server A RRs for verification. Remember, this type uses the MX RR for the domain, which may not be the same as the SMTP server for the domain. In the basic format with no additional arguments, the MX record for the sender-domain and the A RRs for the defined mail host(s) are obtained; if the IP address of the sender-ip matches any of the mail host IPs, the test passes. The format mx:/cidr applies the address range defined by cidr (IP prefix or slash notation) to the match. The format mx:domain uses the MX and A RRs for domain instead of the sender-domain, and the format mx:domain/cidr extends the IP address check to the cidr (IP prefix or slash notation) range of IP addresses. The domain argument may also use macro expansion defined later in this section. Use of the mx format involves at least two DNS lookups per SPF verification operation.

This SPF allows mail from the domain example.com to be sent from any mail server defined in an MX RR for the domain example.net:

```
             IN   TXT  "v=spf1 mx:example.net -all"
; AND if supported
             IN   SPF  "v=spf1 mx:example.net -all"
```

This SPF allows mail to be sent from any of the 16 IP addresses containing each of the mail servers defined in MX records for the sending domain:

```
             IN   TXT  "v=spf1 mx/28-
all"
; AND if supported
             IN   SPF  "v=spf1 mx/28-all"
```

Type ptr Format

This type may take one of the following formats:

ptr ptr:domain

The ptr type uses PTR RRs of the sender-ip for verification. In the basic format with no additional arguments, the sender-ip is used to query for the host name using the reverse map. The A or AAAA RR for the resulting host is then obtained. If this IP matches the sender-ip and the sender-domain is the same as the domain name of the host obtained from the PTR RR, then the test passes. The form ptr:domain replaces the sender-domain with domain in the final check for a valid domain name. The domain argument may also use macro expansion (defined later in this section). The PTR record is the least preferred solution since it places a load on the IN-ADDR.ARPA (IPv4) or IP6.ARPA (IPv6) reverse-map domains, which generally have less capacity than the gTLD and ccTLD domains.

This SPF would allow any host in the domain example.com that is reversed mapped to send mail for the domain:

```
        IN  TXT "v=spf1 ptr -all"
; AND if supported
        IN  SPF "v=spf1 ptr -all"
```

Type exists Format

This type may take one of the following formats:

exists exists:domain

The exists type tests for existence of the sender-domain using an A RR query. In the basic format with no arguments, an A RR query is issued using the sender-domain and if any result is obtained, the test passes. The form exists:domain applies the same test but for domain. The domain argument may also use macro expansion. The exists form requires an A RR for the domain, as shown:

```
; zone fragment for example.com
$ORIGIN example.com.
...
@             IN   A       192.168.0.2
              IN   TXT "v=spf1 +exists -all"
; AND if supported
              IN   SPF "v=spf1 +exists -all"
....
```

Macro Expansion

The SPF record allows macro expansion features using a %{x} format where % indicates a macro and x is a character defining the macro type, as defined in Table 8–1.

Table 8–1. *SPF Macro Expansion Arguments*

Macro	Function
%{c}	Only allowed in TXT records referenced by the exp field. The IP of the receiving MTA.
%{d}	The current domain, normally the sender-domain %(o), but replaced by the value of any domain argument in the type field.
%{h}	The domain name supplied on HELO or EHLO; normally the host name of the sending SMTP server.
%{I}	The sender-ip value. The IP of the SMTP server sending mail for user info@example.com.
%{l}	Replace with local part of sender. For instance, if the sender is info@example.com, the local part is info.
%{o}	The sender-domain value. For instance, if the e-mail address is info@example.com, the sender-domain is example.com.
%{p}	The validated domain name. The name obtained using the PTR RR of the sender-ip. Use of this macro will require an additional query unless a ptr type is used.
%{r}	Only allowed in TXT records referenced by the exp field. The name of the host performing the SPF check. Normally the same as the receiving MTA.
%{t}	Only allowed in TXT records referenced by the exp field. Defines the current timestamp.
%{s}	Replace with sender e-mail address; for instance, info@example.com.
%{v}	Replaced with in-addr if sender-ip is an IPv4 address and ip6 if an IPv6 address. Used to construct reverse-map strings.

The preceding macros may take one or more additional arguments as follows:

- r: Indicates a reverse of the order of the field. For instance, %{or} would display example.com as com.example, and %{ir} would display 192.168.0.2 as 2.0.168.192. The default splitting point for reversing the order uses . (dot) as the separator but any other separator may be used; for instance, %{sr@} splits info@example.com at the @ separator and when reversed displays example.com.info (when fields are rejoined they will always use a dot).

- Digit: The presence of a digit (range 1 to 128) controls the number of rightmost names or labels displayed. For instance, %{d1} uses the d part to extract the current domain (assume it's example.com) as defined previously, and the qualifying digit (1) displays only one rightmost label from the name (in this case com); but %{d5} would display five right-hand names or labels up to the maximum available (which, in this example, would display example.com).

SPF Record Examples

The following examples are designed to illustrate various uses of the SPF record. The SPF macro expansion features in particular can lead to complex definitions; further examples may be discovered by interrogating such domains as microsoft.com, aol.com, and google.com, all of whom are among the many domains that currently publish SPF records. A dig command (introduced in Chapter 9) such as shown here will yield an SPF record if published

```
# dig example.com txt
```

or, if supported

```
# dig example.com spf
```

Substitute your favorite domain in the preceding example to verify the existence of an SPF record.

Single Domain Mail Server

This example assumes a single mail server that both sends and receives mail for the domain:

```
; zone file fragment for example.com
$ORIGIN example.com.
....
          IN  MX 10 mail.example.com.
....
mail      IN  A      192.168.0.4
; SPF records
; domain SPF
@         IN  TXT    "v=spf1 mx -all"
; AND if supported
@         IN  SPF    "v=spf1 mx -all"
; mail host SPF
mail      IN  TXT    "v=spf1 a -all"
; AND if supported
mail      IN  SPF    "v=spf1 a -all"
```

The domain SPF is returned from a sender-domain query using the sender e-mail address; for instance, the sender is info@example.com, and the sender-domain is example.com. The SPF record only allows the MX host(s) to send for the domain. The mail host SPF is present *in case* the receiving MTA uses a reverse query to obtain the sender-ip host name and then does a query for the SPF record of that host. The SPF record states that the A record of mail.example.com is permitted to send mail for the domain. If the domain contains multiple MX servers, the domain SPF would stay the same, but each mail host should have an SPF record.

SMTP Server Offsite

This example assumes the domain example.com will send mail through an off-site mail server in example.net, for instance, an ISP:

```
; zone file fragment for example.com
$ORIGIN example.com.
....
          IN  MX 10  mail.example.net.
```

```
....
; SPF records
; domain SPF
@               IN  TXT     "v=spf1 include:example.net -all"
; AND if supported
@               IN  SPF     "v=spf1 include:example.net -all"

; WARNING: example.net MUST have a valid SPF definition
```

This format should be used if and only if it is known that example.net has a valid SPF record. The include recurses (restarts) verification using the SPF records for example.net. Mail configuration changes are localized at example.net, which may simplify administration. The include could have been replaced with redirect as shown here:

```
@               IN  TXT     "v=spf1 redirect=example.com"
; AND if supported
@               IN  TXT     "v=spf1 redirect=example.com"
```

Virtual Mail Host

This example assumes example.net is the host for a large number of virtual mail domains and supplies SMTP services for others. The zone file fragment that follows describes one of the virtual mail domains example.org:

```
; zone file fragment for example.org
$ORIGIN example.org.
....
                IN  MX 10 mail.example.net.
....
; SPF records
; domain SPF
@               IN  TXT     "v=spf1 include:example.net -all"
; AND if supported
@               IN  TXT     "v=spf1 include:example.net -all"
```

The domain SPF is returned from a sender-domain query using the sender e-mail address; for instance, the sender is info@example.org, and the sender-domain is example.org. The SPF record recurses to the domain name example.net for verification.

Here is the zone file for example.net:

```
; zone file fragment for example.net
$ORIGIN example.net.
....
                IN  MX 10   mail.example.net.
....
mail        IN  A       192.168.0.37
; SPF records
; domain SPF - any host from
; 192.168.0.32 to 192.168.0.63 can send mail
; and any MX host
@               IN  TXT     "v=spf1 ip4:192.168.0.37/27 mx -all"
; AND if supported
@               IN  SPF     "v=spf1 ip4:192.168.0.37/27 mx -all"
; mail SPF
```

```
mail        IN  TXT    "v=spf1 a -all"
; AND if supported
mail        IN  SPF    "v=spf1 a -all"
```

The domain SPF is returned from a sender-domain query using the sender e-mail address; for instance, the sender is info@example.net, and the sender-domain is example.net or the include:example.net if the mail originated from the example.org zone. The SPF record allows any host in the 32 address subnet that contains 192.168.0.37 to send mail for this domain (example.net) and any hosted virtual domain (example.org) in the preceding example. The SPF also allows any host defined in an MX RR as an alternative if the first test fails and allows for a future reconfiguration of the network that may move the host mail.example.net IP address outside the defined ip4 range. The scenario could have used a slightly shorter version:

```
@           IN  TXT    "v=spf1 mx/27 -all"
; AND if supported
@           IN  SPF    "v=spf1 mx/27 -all"
```

This record has the same effect as a:192.168.0.37/27 but will cost a further DNS lookup operation, whereas the IP is already available. The scenario relies on the fact that customers will only send mail via the domain example.net; that is, they will *not* send mail via another ISP when at home or when traveling. If you are not sure if this is the case, the sequence can be terminated with ?all, which indicates that the results may not be definite; it allows the mail to pass, perhaps after logging the incident to capture statistics. If the domain contains multiple MX servers, the domain SPF would stay the same but each mail host would have an SPF record.

No Mail Domain

This example assumes that the domain example.org *never* sends mail from any location—ever. Typically, this would be done to prevent bogus mail using this domain for everyone else—it is a supreme act of self-sacrifice!

```
; zone file fragment for example.org
; zone does NOT contain MX record(s)
$ORIGIN example.org.
...
; SPF records
; domain SPF
@           IN  TXT    "v=spf1 -all"
; AND if supported
@           IN  SPF    "v=spf1 -all"
```

This SPF test will always fail since the only condition it tests is the -all, which, because of the - (minus), results in a fail.

Using Macro Expansion

This example uses macro expansion in the SPF and the polite message is sent to users to indicate that the sender may be being impersonated. The zone file fragment is as follows:

```
; zone file fragment for example.com
$ORIGIN example.com.
....
            IN  MX 10 mail.example.com.
```

```
....
; SPF records
; domain SPF
@           IN  TXT   "v=spf1 exists:%(d) -all ext=badguy.example.com"
; AND if supported
@           IN  SPF   "v=spf1 exists:%(d) -all ext=badguy.example.com"
badguy      IN  TXT "The email from %{s} using SMTP server at %{I} was rejected \
    by %{c} (%{r}) at %{t} \
    because it failed the SPF records check for the domain %{p}. \
    Please visit http://abuse.example.com/badguys.html for more information"
```

The badguy TXT RR is split across multiple lines (each ending with a \) for presentation reasons only and should appear on a single line in the zone file. The `exists:%{d}` tests for the existence of the sender-domain, which is the default value for the `exists` test but is used to illustrate use of macros in expressions.

Define a DKIM Record

DKIM allows a receiving mail handler to authenticate one or more entities that have signed the mail item. It is significantly more complex that SPF but also provides significantly more functionality.

In DKIM, any sending or handling mail agent—either an MTA (Mail Transfer Agent) or a MUA (Mail User Agent)—can cryptographically sign mail by adding a DKIM-Signature mail header to the mail item. The DKIM-Signature header contains a number of fields of which the most important are:

- *Signer* identifies the mail signing source—either the originator of the mail or a delegated third party acting on their behalf.

- *Coverage* describes what parts of the mail item are covered, such as nominated mail headers, the mail body, or specific parts of the mail body.

- *Scope* defines the mail signer's scope; for example, a single e-mail address, mail for the whole domain, or some subset of the domain.

The DKIM-Signature header is protected and authorized by the mail signer's digital signature (see Chapter 10). Any DKIM-compliant receiving (or intermediate) mail handler will read a DKIM-Signature header (there may be more than one), extract the fields describing the signing source, and construct a domain name. A DNS query is used to read the DKIM TXT RR, containing, among other fields, a public key at the constructed domain name. The public key obtained is then used to validate both the integrity of the DKIM-Signature and authenticate the mail signer. The mail handler, if an intermediate (or relay), can simply pass the message on, add another DKIM-Signature header, and/or add an Authenticated-Results header (defined in RFC 5451). In the case of a final delivery mail handler, the mail can be accepted or even rejected based on the trustworthiness of the mail signer.

DKIM mail signing uses public-key (or asymmetric) cryptography to create the DKIM-Signature digital signatures. The public keys used in signature verification (stored in DKIM TXT RRs) are generated by the mail signer using, for example, OpenSSL, and thus do not *require* the purchase of third party SSL (X.509) certificates.

In addition to a DKIM TXT RR, the DKIM specifications allows the domain owner to define an Author Domain Signing Policies (ADSP) TXT RR which essentially provides advice to the validating mail receiver about what to do if a mail item is not signed.

DKIM is defined by a series of RFCs: RFC 4871 and RFC 5672 define the DNS DKIM TXT RR format (as well as the added mail headers), RFC 5617 defines DNS Author Domain Signing Policies (ADSP) TXT RR formats for indicating signing practices, and RFC 5585 describes how it all works.

Only that part of DKIM concerned with the DNS is described here. It is beyond the scope of this section to detail all the functionality offered by DKIM; readers are advised to consult the various listed RFCs for all the grubby details.

Clearly, bad guys could equally use DKIM to sign their e-mail. The various DKIM RFCs emphasize that DKIM only authenticates the mail signer and needs to be used in conjunction with, say, a whitelist or other reputation system such as Vouch By Reference (RFC 5518) to allow decisions to be made about accepting or rejecting DKIM signed mail.

Many of the values in the DKIM TXT RR will depend on those used by the mail signer software. While creating and testing this documentation, OpenDKIM (`www.opendkim.org`), which supports (currently) sendmail and postfix through the milter (`www.milter.org`) interface, was used as a reference source. Many other DKIM implementations exist; you are advised to carefully read your mail system's DKIM documentation.

A number of major email organizations have already implemented DKIM including, perhaps most notably, Google's Gmail.

As noted previously, DKIM provides significant functionality and flexibility and is consequently a complex standard. As with all complex standards, it's easy to get lost in the mass of detail. However, to avoid getting lost irretrievably, the reader is advised to quickly skim the detailed content of the DNS TXT RRs with the objective of getting an overall feeling for their content, then study the examples. With a heavy heart, and suitably fortified with a stimulating beverage of choice, there may be little alternative at this stage but to return to the gory details of the DKIM TXT RRs to tie up all the loose ends.

■ **Note** While not specifically relevant to the DNS DKIM implementation, it's worth remembering that DKIM uses cryptographically signed mail that has time limits. Therefore, accurate clock synchronization is essential using, say, Network Time Protocol (NTP).

DKIM DNS TXT RR Format

DKIM uses a TXT RR to contain all the DNS stored data. There may be one or more DKIM TXT RRs for any domain. The format of the TXT and DKIM TXT RR, defined by RFC 4817 and 5672, is:

```
; Generic TXT RR format
name ttl class   TXT      text
;DKIM TXT RR format is
selector._domainkey.domain-name. ttl class TXT DKIM-specific-text
```

The content of the DKIM-specific text field is defined in detail below but its principal role is to supply the public key to be used to authenticate arriving mail for the originating domain or some selected sub-set of the domain. The validating e-mail receiver constructs the *name* of a DKIM TXT RR by extracting values contained in the DKIM-Signature mail header field (present in all DKIM signed mail), specifically the selector field (s= tag-value, defined in RFC 4871 Section 3.1 and 3.5), which is essentially a unique but arbitrary tag value appending the fixed subdomain name _domainkey and finally appending the extracted domain-name field (d= tag-value, defined in RFC 4871 Section 3.5). Thus, if the selector field contains the value all-mail and the domain-name field is example.net then a DNS TXT query is issued for all-mail._domainkey.example.net.

In part, the relative complexity of DKIM relates to the designers' objective to allow mail from a domain to be handled, and possibly signed, by various parties. For example, while **user@example.com** may normally send mail through a company mail service (MTA), the same user using the same e-mail address may also wish to send mail from home via an ISP's MTA. Equally, bulk mailing for **example.com** may be delegated to an external third party. Other scenarios may be imagined. DKIM's architecture allows for the domain owner, or one or more trusted third parties, to sign some or all of the mail from a given domain name. It is up to the receiving MTA to decide whether to trust the mail signer.

To illustrate this process, assume that mail with an address of **user@example.com** when originated from the office is sent from and signed by the **example.com** MTA, which maintains a single private/public key pair for this purpose. The example.com domain publishes the public key in its DNS in a DKIM TXT RR under the name onlyone._domainkey.example.com. The DKIM-Signature mail header from mail originating from the example.com MTA will therefore contain (among others) an s=onlyone (selector) field and a d=example.com (domain-name) field from which any validating mail server can construct the DKIM TXT RR name and authenticate the e-mail. Now assume that **user@example.com** will also send mail from home via an ISP's MTA whose domain name is example.net and which publishes its DKIM public key under the name publicmail._domainkey.example.net. In this case, the DKIM-Signature mail header covering mail sent from the mail address **user@example.com** (and perhaps all other mail originating from this MTA) will contain an s=publicmail (selector) field and a d=example.net (domain-name) field from which, again, the receiving or validating mail server can construct the DKIM TXT RR name as defined above and authenticate the e-mail.

This is a relatively trivial illustration and a number of additional examples are provided.

DNS RR DKIM-Specific-Text

The text part of the DKIM TXT RR can contain a number of semi-colon (;) separated tag=value fields (defined in RFC 4871 Section 3.6.1). Table 8–2 documents the allowed tags and values; a number of examples are provided to show scenario specific RR values.

Note DKIM uses a tag=value notation to define fields in both the DKIM-Signature header and the DNS TXT RR text field. Somewhat confusingly, in some cases, the tag name part, such as v= or s=, will take the same value for both the DKIM-Signature mail header and the DNS TXT RR. In other cases, the meaning will be the same but the valid values may be different. In yet other cases, the meaning of the tag is different for each entity. Readers are advised to consult the correct section of the specification. Specifically, for DKIM-Signature mail header tag=value pairs, use RFC 4871 Section 3.5 (updated by RFC 5672); for DNS TXT RR tag=value pairs, use RFC 4871 Section 3.6.1.

Table 8–2. Allowed Tags and Values for DKIM TXT RRs

Tag	Description
v= (version)	Optional. Defines the DKIM version number and may only (at this time) take the (defaulted) value DKIM1. While it may be safely omitted, it's good practice to include it. `v=DKIM1;`

g= (granularity)	Optional. Defines the user (local) part of the email address—everything to the left-hand side of the @) to which this DKIM TXT RR applies. A single wild card (*) value may be used anywhere in the field. Defaults to g=*(all user - local - part addresses match). This value, after any wildcard processing, must exactly match the address in the *From:* header's user (local) part.
	
	`# single email address form`
	`# only joe@example.com covered`
	`g=joe;`
	`# partial wildcard- any local part adress ending with -maillist`
	`# joe-maillist@example.com or fred-maillist@example.com etc.`
	`g=*-maillist;`
	`# default form - everything`
	`# joe@example.com or fred@example.com etc.`
	`g=*;`

h= (hash algorithm)	Optional. Defines one or more colon (:) separated hash (digest) algorithms that will be used for the purpose of creating digital signatures (in conjunction with k=) covering either or both of the defined mail headers or the mail body (including, optionally, MIME attachments). Allowable values are from the set *sha1* and *sha256*. Default is h=* (all). Since all implementations of DKIM are mandated to support both sha1 and sha256 hash (digest) algorithms, it may be safely omitted.
	
	`h=sha1:sha256;`
	`h=*;`

k= (key algorithm)	Optional. Defines the public key algorithm being used. Defaults to k=rsa. Since rsa is the only algorithm currently supported, it may be safely omitted. `k=rsa;`
n= (notes)	Optional. Defines human readable text that may be used by validating receiver administrators. Unless this imparts significant (perhaps world-stopping) knowledge, it may be safely omitted. `n=trust us;`

Tag	Description
p= (public key)	Mandatory. Defines the public key (in base64, RFC 4648, format) for the algorithm defined by the k= tag whose private key was used to digitally sign user defined parts of the mail item. The data for the public key may be created by OpenSSL using the following command sequence (taken from RFC 4871 Appendix C and reproduced here only for convenience):
	Create the RSA public private key pair in dkim.private with a key length of 1024 bits.
	`# openssl genrsa -out dkim.private 1024`
	Extract the public key to file dkim.public in PEM (Privacy Enhanced Mail) format.
	`# openssl rsa -in dkim.private -out dkim.public -pubout -outform PEM`
	The PEM key uses base 64 encoding and looks something like this:

	<pre>-----BEGIN PUBLIC KEY-----
	MIGfMA0GCSqGSIb3DQEBAQUAA4GNADCBiQKBgQDwIRP/UC3SBsEmGqZ9ZJW3/DkM
	oGeLnQg1fWn7/zYtIxN2SnFCjxOCKG9v3b4jYfcTNh5ijSsq631uBItLa7od+v/R
	tdC2UzJ1lWT947qR+Rcac2gbto/NMqJOfzfVjH4OuKhitdY9tf6mcwGjaNBcWToI
	MmPSPDdQPNUYckcQ2QIDAQAB
	-----END PUBLIC KEY-----</pre>

	Remove the lines beginning with "-" and edit the remaining text in any of the following formats (most key material replaces with "…" for brevity):

	<pre>; single line format
	name._domainkey IN TXT "v=DKIM1;p=MIGfMA0G ... cQ2QIDAQAB"</pre>

	<pre>; multi-line format
	name._domainkey IN TXT ("v=DKIM1"
	                       "p=MIGfMA0G ... "
	                       "oGeLnQg ... "
	                       "tdC2UzJ1lW ... "
	                       "MmPSPDdQPNUYckcQ2QIDAQAB")</pre>

	See TXT RR for additional information on layout and formatting of text.
	If a key is to be revoked (declared invalid), then setting the p= tag to a null value will achieve this:
	`p=;`
s= (service type)	Optional. Defines the service type to which DKIM is applied. At this time the only valid value is **email** but clearly the designers had their sights set on greater goals. The default is s=* (all). Since email is the only DKIM currently supported service, it may be safely omitted.

	<pre>s=email;
	s=*;</pre>

Tag	Description
t= (flags)	Optional. Defaults to no flags set. A colon (:) separated list of flags to be used by the validator. Two flags are currently defined:
	y
	Indicates test mode. If set, it may (and hopefully does) generate additional diagnostic messages from the validating receiver, but still permit the validator to treat the mail normally; that is, a validation failure must still be treated as a failure. No validation leniency is implied by setting this flag.
	s
	If defined, this flag indicates that this key is *not* valid for subdomains of the domain name (defined in the d= tag of the DKIM-Signature). If subdomains are never used in domain e-mail addresses, then this flag should be set as a further safeguard.
	t=y:s;

ADSP TXT RR Format

The Author Domain Signing Practices (ADSP) TXT RR allows a domain to indicate its mail signing policies. The ADSP TXT RR is optional but the ADSP policies may be used to assist a validating receiving MTA in determining how to handle mail that is not signed. The format of the ADSP TXT RR, defined by RFC 5617, is:

```
; Generic TXT RR format
name  ttl  class   TXT      text
;ADSP TXT RR format is
_adsp._domainkey.domain-name. ttl class TXT ADSP-specific-text
```

Only one ADSP TXT RR per domain may be defined; however, each subdomain may also have its own ADSP TXT RR.

Note While trusted third parties may sign some or all of a domain's mail (and therefore the DKIM TXT RR containing the public key will appear in the signers domain zone file) an ADSP TXT RR, if present, can only appear in the mail originator's zone file. Thus, if mail with the name user@example.com is signed by example.net, then the DKIM TXT RR containing the signer's public key will appear in the example.net zone, but any DKIM ADSP TXT RR containing the sender's signing policy can only appear in the example.com zone.

ADSP TXT RR Format - Text

The ADSP TXT RR text field uses the same tag=value format used throughout DKIM. The allowed tags and their corresponding values are:

Tag	Values
dkim=	A single value from the following set of permissible values is allowed:

unknown

The domain as it appears in the e-mail address may or may not sign all mail. This is the most common setting during testing, but if used in a production environment will essentially nullify the use of DKIM since a receiving MTA will have no idea what to do with unsigned mail.

all

The domain as it appears in the e-mail address signs all mail. This setting leaves the validating receiver free to carry out its own policies if it receives unsigned mail.

discardable

The domain as it appears in the e-mail address signs all mail. This setting also advises the validating receiver that unsigned mail can be discarded. This is the sleepless-nights-for-mail-administrators setting.

dkim=discardable;

Examples

The public key material is denoted by *blah...blah* for simplicity and brevity.

All Mail Signed - One MTA, No Subdomains

The tightest and simplest scenario assumes that all mail for the domain is sent using a single mail signer—typically an in-house MTA. No subdomains are used in e-mail addresses. All the mail is signed and users working from home or remotely will use, say, a webmail interface to the in-house MTA. E-mail from any other source is deemed to be invalid and may be discarded. A single selector called *mail* will be used in this instance, whose choice—as is true for any selector—is arbitrary but unique. In this case, its value, while perfectly valid, may be said to demonstrate a singular lack of imagination:

```
; zone example.com fragment
$ORIGIN example.com.
...
; DKIM TXT RR
mail._domainkey  IN TXT "v=DKIM1;t=s;p=blah....blah;"
; ADSP TXT RR
_adsp._domainkey IN TXT "dkim=discardable;"
; OR, if you like typing you could have written
mail._domainkey.example.com.  IN TXT "v=DKIM1;t=s;p=blah....blah;"
_adsp._domainkey.example.com. IN TXT "dkim=discardable;"
```

```
; OR, using an $ORIGIN
$ORIGIN _domainkey
mail  IN TXT "v=DKIM1;t=s;p=blah....blah;"
_adsp IN TXT "dkim=discardable;"
; if RRs appear below, $ORIGIN may have to be set to a new value
```

Note The $ORIGIN _domainkey directive is deliberately used for illustration without a trailing dot and is therefore additive. In the above example it will create, using the origin substitution rule, a value of _domainkey.example.com.

The DKIM TXT RR contains the version number v=DKIM1 (not essential but good practice), t=s; that indicates subdomain e-mail addresses of the form **joe@us.example.com** are not allowed and p=blah....blah contains the public key that will authenticate the DKIM-Signature. All other fields are defaulted, specifically g=*; which means that any e-mail address of the form **bill@example.com** or **sheila@example.com** is covered by this DKIM TXT RR. The ADSP TXT RR dkim=discardable; indicates to a receiving mail handler that any unsigned mail from this domain may be discarded. This is the macho setting; more cautious administrators may choose to opt for dkim=all;. The DKIM-Signature mail header (created by the in-house MTA) will contain, among other fields, a selector field of s=mail and a domain-name field of d=example.com that enables the mail handler to find the DKIM TXT RR and the optional ADSP TXT RR.

Loose DKIM Signing

This is for use during testing or by those organizations not entirely sure what their mail users actually do—including whether or not they use subdomains in their mail addresses. It is assumed that any mail the domain can be bothered to sign will be done by an in-house MTA at example.com.

```
; zone example.com fragment
$ORIGIN example.com.
...
;DKIM TXT RR
hope._domainkey  IN TXT "v=DKIM1;t=y;p=blah....blah;"
; ADSP TXT RR
_adsp._domainkey IN TXT "dkim=unknown;"
; OR, if you like typing you could have written
hope._domainkey.example.com.  IN TXT "v=DKIM1;t=y;p=blah....blah;"
_adsp._domainkey.example.com. IN TXT "dkim=unknown;"
; OR, using an $ORIGIN
$ORIGIN _domainkey
hope  IN TXT "v=DKIM1;t=y;p=blah....blah;"
_adsp IN TXT "dkim=unknown;"
; if RRs appear below, $ORIGIN may have to be set to a new value
```

The absence of an s flag field (t=y;) indicates that mail addresses of the form **user@example.com** and **user@sub.example.com** are covered by this DKIM TXT RR. The DKIM-Signature mail header (created by the in-house MTA) will contain, among many other fields, a selector field of s=hope and a domain-name field of d=example.com that enables the mail handler to find the DKIM TXT RR and the optional ADSP TXT RR.

Multiple Subdomain DKIM Signing

Assume the domain example.com sends mail from the domain with a format of **user@example.com** and two subdomains, secure.example.com with a format of **user@secure.example.com** and maillist.example.com with a format of **newsletter@maillist.example.com**. Mail from example.com and secure.example.com is signed by the in-house MTA but mail from the subdomain maillist.example.com is delegated to and signed by the domain example.net. We always sign mail from the subdomains but not always the main domain.

```
; zone example.com fragment
$ORIGIN example.com.
...
; DKIM TXT RR
; DKIM and ADSP TXT RR for main domain
domain._domainkey  IN TXT "v=DKIM1;t=s;p=blah....blah;"
; ADSP TXT RR
_adsp.domainkey IN TXT "dkim=unknown;"
....
; DKIM and ADSP for secure subdomain
; DKIM TXT RR
internal._domainkey.secure  IN TXT "v=DKIM1;t=s;p=blah....blah;"
; ADSP TXT RR
_adsp._domainkey.secure   IN TXT "dkim=discardable;"
; OR, using an $ORIGIN
$ORIGIN _domainkey.secure
internal  IN TXT "v=DKIM1;t=s;p=blah....blah;"
_adsp   IN TXT "dkim=discardable;"
; if RRs appear below, $ORIGIN may have to be set to anew value
....
; ADSP for maillist subdomain
; ADSP TXT RR
_adsp._domainkey.maillist   IN TXT "dkim=discardable;"
; OR, using an $ORIGIN
$ORIGIN _domainkey.maillist
_adsp    IN TXT "dkim=discardable;"
; if other RRs appear below, $ORIGIN may have to be set to a new value
```

This shows the DKIM TXT RR definitions for the subdomains secure and maillist within the example.com zone using what this book calls a virtual (or pseudo) subdomain structure. Alternatively, if the domains are fully delegated, the definitions would appear within the delegated subdomains' zone file. The DKIM TXT RR for the domain example.com and the subdomain secure.example.com both use the s flag (t=s;) since each RR has its own scope. Thus, the DKIM-Signature mail header for mail with addresses of the form **user@secure.example.com** will have a selector field of s=secure and domain-name field d=secure.example.com, whereas mail with addresses of the form **user@example.com** will have a selector field of s=domain and a domain-name field d=example.com.

The subdomain maillist does not have a DKIM TXT RR in the zone example.com. This is because mail for this subdomain is signed by an external third party (assumed to be example.net). DKIM-Signature mail headers will be authenticated by the public key published in a DKIM TXT RR in the DNS of the signing domain. Thus, if the external signing third party has a domain name of example.net and uses an arbitrary selector value for example.com's mail , say, of example-com-maillist, then the DKIM-Signature mail headers will contain a selector field s=example-com-maillist and a domain-name field d=example.net and will publish a DKIM TXT RR in its zone file at the name example-com-maillist_domainkey.example.net even though the mail being signed may have addresses such as **newsletter@maillist.example.com**. The ADSP TXT RR is always defined in the zone file of the mail originator (in this case **maillist.example.com**) and therefore the validating mail receiver can construct a DNS address of _adsp._domainkey.maillist.example.com. Because mail from the subdomains is always signed, the ADSP RRs both have the value dkim=discardable; (or dkim=all; for those of a less aggressive persuasion), whereas you need to use dkim=unknown; for the base mail since it may not be signed.

Supporting http://example.com

This technique configures a name server to allow URLs of the form http://www.example.com and http://example.com—both URLs will address (or resolve to) the same web server. Seems it's the cool thing to do these days. To make this feature work also requires a change to the web server. The required change to Apache when using virtual hosts is also provided.

```
; zone fragment for example.com
$TTL 2d ; zone ttl default = 2 days
$ORIGIN example.com.
....
; SOA NS MX and other records

; define an IP that will resolve example.com
@               IN      A      192.168.0.3
; you could also write the preceding line as
; example.com.  IN      A      192.168.0.3
www             IN      CNAME  example.com. ; dot essential
; aliases www.example.com to example.com
; OR define another A record for www using same host
; this is the least number of changes and saves a CNAME
www             IN      A      192.168.0.3
```

This will also work for any other host name as long as different ports are in use; for instance, ftp://example.com will work if the FTP server was appropriately configured and on the same host, which in the preceding case is 192.168.0.3.

Apache Configuration

This configuration assumes the use of virtual hosts on an Apache (1.3.x or 2.x) server. Apache's httpd.conf configuration file containing the VirtualHost section for example.com would look something like the following fragment:

```
<VirtualHost 10.10.0.23>
    ServerAdmin webmaster@example.com
    DocumentRoot /path/to/web/root
    ServerName www.example.com
    ErrorLog logs/www.example.err
    CustomLog logs/www.example.log common
</VirtualHost>
```

A second VirtualHost definition is added with ServerName modified to reflect the example.com change as follows:

```
<VirtualHost 10.10.0.23>
    ServerAdmin webmaster@example.com
    DocumentRoot /path/to/web/root
    ServerName example.com
```

```
    ErrorLog logs/example.err
    CustomLog logs/example.log common
</VirtualHost>
```

In the preceding example, a second log and error file is used to avoid possible corruption. An alternate method is to use a single `VirtualHost` definition with the `ServerAlias` directive as shown here and that only requires single log and error files:

```
<VirtualHost 10.10.0.23>
    ServerAdmin webmaster@example.com
    DocumentRoot /path/to/web/root
    ServerName www.example.com
    ServerAlias example.com
    ErrorLog logs/example.err
    CustomLog logs/example.log common
</VirtualHost>
```

In many cases, when example.com is entered, your ever-helpful browser will auto-complete (or guess) that what you really meant was www.example.com and add the www automatically. So after all that hard work in many browsers, example.com would have worked even if you had done nothing!

■**Caution** If you are using MS FrontPage extensions with a single `VirtualHost` definition, then the `ServerName` must be the name that is used to log in to FP. In the preceding example, the FrontPage login name used would be www.example.com.

Out-of-Sequence Serial Numbers

The `serial number` field of the SOA RR (described in Chapter 2) by convention uses a date format defined to be yyyymmddss where yyyy is the four-digit year number, mm is the two-digit month number, dd is the two-digit day within month number, and ss is a two-digit sequence number within the day. Since this is only a convention, BIND and most other DNS software does not validate the format of this field; it is very easy to introduce errors into this number and get out of sequence. Zone transfer to zone slave will, in the event of zone file changes, occur only if the serial number of the SOA RR is greater than the previous one. So the dreaded day has come and while pondering the meaning of life during a zone file update, the serial number is changed, BIND has been restarted, and only with something approaching shock and awe, you discover the SOA serial number is incorrect. Apart from ritual suicide, what can be done?

To illustrate the fixes possible, it's assumed that today's date is 28 February 2010 (serial number 2010022800). If the erroneous serial number entered is less than today, that is, 2010022700, the fix is trivial: simply correct the serial number and restart BIND or reload the zone with rndc (see Chapter 9). If the number is too high, it depends on how high the number is and how frequently the zone file is changed. Assume the changed serial number was set to 2010022900, which as we all know does not exist because 2010 is not a leap year; however, BIND does not know that and a zone transfer will have taken place, 29 being greater than 28. The simple fix is to increment the date again to 2010030100 and keep using the sequence number until the correct date is reached (tomorrow in this case). This works unless you will need to make more than 99 changes until the erroneous date is reached.

If all the quick solutions are not acceptable (for instance, the serial number is 2016022800), then it's time to get out the calculator or do some serious mental arithmetic. The SOA serial number is an unsigned 32-bit field with a maximum value of $2^{32}-1$ which gives a range of 0 to 4294967295 (zero may have special significance in DNS and should always be avoided), but the maximum increment to such a number is $2^{31} - 1$ or 2147483647, since incrementing the number by the maximum would give the same number. Using the maximum increment, the serial number fix is a two-step process. First, add 2147483647 to the erroneous value (for example, 2016022800 + 2147483647 = 4163504447), restart BIND or reload the zone, and make *absolutely* sure the zone has transferred to all the slave servers. Second, set the SOA serial number for the zone to the correct value and restart BIND or reload the zone again. The zone will transfer to the slave because the serial number has wrapped through zero and is greater than the previous value of 4163504447!

This method works perfectly unless the sum of the current serial number and 2147483647 exceeds 4294967295; in this case, simply set the serial number to 4294967295, perform the first zone transfer as described above, and then set the number to the desired/correct one and restart or reload the zone again. Observant readers will have noted that this method will actually work under all conditions, thus saving the computational effort described previously. However, as a service to calculator manufacturers everywhere and in the interest of promoting mental arithmetic, the first method is retained since it, perhaps, describes the fix theory more completely.

RFC 1982 contains all the gruesome details of serial number comparison algorithms if you are curious about such things.

Use of Wildcards in Zone Files

The standard wildcard character * (asterisk) can be used as a name with any RR. Wildcards can have unintended consequences and should only be used with considerable caution. RFC 4952 was written to clarify wildcard behavior in an attempt to avoid at least some of the intended consequences.

Note The Internet Architecture Board (IAB) has even published a paper on the subject of wildcard usage after the infamous use of wildcard A RRs by a gTLD operator to redirect users to a default page when any domain was not found (www.iab.org/documents/docs/2003-09-20-dns-wildcards.html).

Wildcards can be very confusing in the DNS specifications. Normally, wildcards are used in search expressions to find items with imprecisely known information. For example, the command ls |grep $*.html will list all files in the given directory ending with .html; in this case, the * means any character any number of times.

In the case of zone files, the DNS wildcard *creates* or *synthesizes* records of the RR type they appear in such that any query for a particular RR type and for which an explicit RR does *not* exist will be answered with the wildcard RR data as if it *did* exist—that is, no query for the given RR of that type will fail. This may not be the intended result. The DNS wildcard symbol * can only appear in a left-hand (or owner) name. It must also be the only character in the label.

```
*.example.com.     TXT "some text" ; valid wildcard
*joe.example.com. MX 10 mail.example.com. ; invalid wildcard
example.com.       MX 10 *.example.com. ; invalid wildcard
```

While wildcards may be used with any RR type, they are most commonly used with MX records, as shown:

```
; zone file for example.com
$TTL 2d ; zone default = 2 days
$ORIGIN example.com.
```

```
@                      IN   MX   10   mail.example.com.
*                      IN   MX   10   mail.example.com.
```

Here, an MX query for bill.example.com, joe.example.com, and everythingelse.example.com will return the host mail.example.com. The following example shows how an existing RR will block the operation of the wildcard:

```
; zone file for example.com
$TTL 2d ; zone default = 2 days
$ORIGIN example.com.
@                      IN   MX   10   mail.example.com.
*                      IN   MX   10   mail.example.com.
subdomain     IN   MX   10   mail.example.net.
```

As before, MX queries will return mail.example.com except queries for subdomain.example.com, which will return mail.example.net, and any undefined names below subdomain such as bill.subdomain.example.com will return NXDOMAIN (no name).

The wildcard examples shown are terminal wildcards—the * is on the extreme left of the left-hand (owner) name. Non-terminal wildcards are legal, but usually the result of imprecise understanding of wildcard functionality. A non-terminal wildcard is where the * is not on the extreme left of the left-hand name; for example, joe.*.example.com is a non-terminal wildcard. BIND provides the check-wildcard (see Chapter 12) statement to check and warn of fail on non-terminal wildcards.

A wildcard can't do anything that can't be done by one or more (perhaps many more) RRs. There is no *essential* reason to use wildcards other than to reduce the amount of data that may otherwise have to be defined. Whether this reduction in administrative effort is worth the potentially confusing effect of using wildcards in RRs is a matter for local decision.

Zone File Construction

This book takes a very formal approach to the design and construction of zone files. Some readers may even consider it excessively pedantic at times. This approach is adopted for reasons of safety. It is always good practice to add $ORIGIN directives, use FQDNs where sensible, and be long-winded rather that use cryptically short forms. This is partly because it makes sense to become thoroughly familiar with a subject before indulging in some of the more esoteric forms possible and partly because someone may have to try to understand a hieroglyphic zone file at 3 AM with a dark zone and a senior manager breathing down their neck. That someone may be you.

However, it's also fun to kick over the traces, break the rules, let your hair down, and rejoice in the vanity of incomprehensibility. Good judgment should be used to decide when this is practical, possible, or even desirable.

As an example, this book insists in Chapter 7 that IPv4 and IPv6 loopback reverse maps should use distinct zone files. However, rules can be broken. The following single zone file may used to reverse map both the IPv4 and IPv6 loopback address:

```
$TTL 86400 ; 24 hours
@ IN SOA @ hostmaster (2010020800 12h 15m 1w 3h)
@ IN NS localhost.
1.0.0 IN PTR localhost.
```

Since there is no $ORIGIN statement, it is synthesized as the zone name that appears in the named.conf file. For this file to work, the zone clauses for the IPv4 and IPv6 reverse-mapped loopback must be:

```
// named.conf fragment
...
zone "127.IN-ADDR.ARPA" in{ // IPv4 reverse loopback
   ...
}
zone "0.0.0.0.0.0.0.0.0.0.0.0.0.0.0.0.0.0.0.0.0.0.0.0.0.0.0.0.0.0.0.0.IP6.ARPA" in{ // IPv6 reverse
loopback
   ...
}
```

This example is presented to give the reader who is comfortable with the basics of zone files some feel for the possibilities (or abuses) of zone file construction. Is it worth the saving of one file and perhaps six lines of additional definition? Probably not. Is it fun? Definitely.

Split Horizon DNS

BIND 9's view clause was introduced in Chapter 7 as an alternative method of providing a stealth server. It has many other usages and this section introduces one more example to illustrate its potential power.

The term *split horizon* is normally used to describe a name server that will give different responses (IP addresses) based on the source address or some other characteristic of the query. While it has similar configuration properties to the stealth server, it can be used in a variety of unique situations such as:

- *Geographic mapping:* If, for example, a web service is replicated in a number of locations (for either performance or access latency reasons), then a specific IP address may be returned based on the source address of the query to ensure the shortest possible path from the user to the service. For those familiar with anycast this could be considered a poor man's anycast service.

- *Naming Consistency:* Assume a corporate in-house LDAP service where highly secure data is maintained on one server that is only accessible to certain individuals or organizational sections, each of which have unique or identifiable IP addresses or address ranges; all other users can access another server containing only insecure data. For reasons of consistency (scripts, configuration files, etc.), it's required that both secure and insecure LDAP services be named, say, ldap.example.com.

Other possibilities may strike imaginative readers. The unifying element is that some characteristic of the incoming query will cause the DNS to generate a query-dependent result.

The BIND configuration provides the following functionality:

1. Assume you want geographic users to get the lowest possible latency from a web service with a name of www.example.com.

2. Assume you have a single worldwide e-mail server called mail.example.com.

3. Assume addresses 172.16.x.x originate in Mordor and you want them to be serviced by a local web server (172.1.1.1) we have installed in the vicinity.

4. Assume addresses 172.15.x.x and 172.14.x.x originate in Gondor and you want them to be serviced by a local web server (17.2.1.1) we have installed in the vicinity.

5. All other originations will default to a **www.example.com** at 192.168.1.2.

6. For simplicity, assume an authoritative-only server is being configured.

The BIND 'named.conf' fragment is:

```
// View based geographic name server for EXAMPLE, INC.
// global options
options {
  ...
  recursion no;          // authoritative only
};
...
// map service to geographic origination
view "gondor" {
 match-clients { 172.15/16; 172.14/16; }; // originate in gondor
  zone "example.com" {
    type master;
    // zone file will return www.example.com = 172.2.1.1
    file "view/gondor.example.com";
    ...
  };
}; // end view

view "mordor" {
 match-clients { 172.16/16; }; // originate in mordor
  zone "example.com" {
    type master;
    // zone file will return www.example.com = 172.1.1.1
    file "view/mordor.example.com ";
    ...
  };
}; // end view

// default for everything else lies outside views
 zone "example.com" {
    type master;
          // zone file will return www.example.com = 192.168.1.2
    file "view/master.example.com";
    ...
  };
```

All the required zones must be declared in each view and for simplicity of configuration an authoritative-only server is assumed, which does not require root.servers, localhost or reverse mapping files.

Queries that do not satisfy the match-clients statements fall through to use the default (outside view clause) zone file. If it is more understandable, the default zone could have been wrapped in a view clause with a name of, say, "default" using a **match-clients { any; };** statement, as shown:

```
// default for everything else lies in a default view
view "default"
 match-clients { "any"; }; // must be in the last clause
 zone "example.com" {
    type master;
    // zone file will return www.example.= 192.168.1.2
    file "view/master.example.com.default";
  };
};
```

The configuration uses the only the `match-clients` statement. Two other statements, `match-destination` and `match-recursive-only` (neither of which is applicable in the example) may also be used to select which view is used.

DNSBL (DNS Blacklists)

DNS software simply translates a name to an address. That apparently simple fact has caused DNS software and specially constructed zone files to be used for a variety of non-DNS purposes, the most frequently used example of which is e-mail blacklists. Other exotic applications are discussed later in the section.

DNS blacklists (DNSBL) are used in the context of e-mail (and chat or other IM services) to define the IP addresses or netblocks of *well known* sources of SPAM. DNSBL describes a method of using standard DNS zone files to store such IP addresses. Standard DNS A (IPv4) or AAAA (IPv6) RR queries are used to interrogate the blacklist that is organized as a conventional reverse mapping zone file (see Chapter 3). Assuming the blacklist is held at the domain name `blacklist.example.com`, the process works as follows:

1. The receiving SMTP Agent extracts the IP address of the sending SMTP Agent; for example 192.168.2.135.

2. The address is reversed to create a label series; in our example, it becomes 135.2.168.192.

3. The reversed label series is prepended to the DNSRBL name to give a domain name of `135.2.168.192.blacklist.example.com`

4. A DNS A RR query is issued to the domain name of `135.2.168.192.blacklist.example.com`

5. The responding name server either returns a valid A RRset (confirming the IP address is in the blacklist) or an NXDOMAIN error (the IP address is not in the blacklist).

6. For those IP addresses which appear in the blacklist, the DNSBL may optionally store a standard TXT RR at the same name giving some explanation for the blacklisting.

7. The fact that an A RRset is returned confirms that the queried IP address does appear in the specific blacklist. One or more A RRs may be returned, each of which will, by convention, lie in the IPv4 loopback range of 127/8 (127.0.0.1 - 127.0.0.255). Each A RR address may have a specific meaning; it may be used as a return code and a representative example is shown later in this section.

8. IPv6 addresses may also be interrogated using such blacklists via the standard IPv6 reversed nibble process (see Chapter 5) and may be mixed in the same file as IPv4 addresses but will yield a brutally long name, as is illustrated in the example blacklist file below. Even when used with IPv6 addresses, an A query is still used to interrogate the DNSBL.

DNSBL usage has now been defined in RFC 5782 which has INFORMATIONAL status.

Example blacklist zone file

The following shows a blacklist zone file fragment:

```
$TTL 2d # default RR TTL
$ORIGIN blacklist.example.com
              IN     SOA    ns1.example.com. hostmaster.example.com.(
                            2010080800 ; sn = serial number
                            3h         ; refresh
                            15m        ; retry = refresh retry
                            3w         ; expiry
                            3h         ; nx= nxdomain ttl
                            )
              IN     NS     ns1.example.com.
              IN     NS     ns2.example.com.
# black list records - using origin substitution rule
# order not important other than for local usage reasons
# by convention this address should be listed to allow for external testing
2.0.0.127      IN     A                      127.0.0.2
# black list RRs
135.2.168.192  IN  A    127.0.0.2 # presence result
                        IN   A    127.0.0.5 # optional reason/result code
                        IN   TXT "Optional - Some explanation for black listing"
# the above entries expand to 135.2.168.192.blacklist.example.com
...
135.17.168.192 IN       A        127.0.0.2 # presence result
...
# IPv6 addresses may be mixed with IPv4 addresses in the same zone file
1.0.0.0.0.0.0.0.0.0.0.0.0.0.0.0.0.0.0.0.0.0.0.0.0.0.0.0.8.b.d.0.1.0.0.2 IN  A 127.0.0.2 # presence
result
# Maps IPv6 address 2001:0db8:0000::1
```

Here the reversed IPv6 address is mapped to an A (not AAAA) RR and returns an IPv4 value. There is no inconsistency in this; the returned address is simply a result value or code not a meaningful address.

Note: An A RR for the address 127.0.0.2, by convention and RFC 5782, should always be present in any DNSBL system to allow for external testing and confirmation of operation. Bear in mind that spammers may also use this knowledge to mount DoS attacks on the DNSBL.

Blacklist Return Addresses

Many blacklist sites wish to provide some granularity in the results they return—specifically, one or more reasons why the IP address is in the DNSBL. There are two ways to do this. First, the IP address returned may be used to indicate the reason. If the IP is listed for more than one reason, multiple A RRs each with a different IP address can be used. Second, subdomains can be used to stream lists. Thus, the reversed IP address may be appended to a domain name open.blacklist.example.com to check for, say, an open SMTP relay or appended to, say, spam.blacklist.example.com to check for the presence of a known spam source. While the later method may appear to require more queries, typically the context of the query will limit the actual number. Thus, in this example if a receiving MTA wishes to check for a known spam source, only one query is actually required. Indeed, some DNSBL providers even combine both approaches by using a specific address as a result code but place all entries in all subdomains. In this case, the validating MTA must carefully process or filter the results or use them in some form of weighting system.

There is no standard, or even consensus, on usage of either subdomain names or the address(es) returned by the DNS A RR query other that it lies in the netblock 127/8 (127.0.0.0 - 127.255.255.255) and must exclude 127.0.0.1 (to avoid confusion with the *real* loopback address). In most cases, e-mail software that uses DNSBL access will return a failing code if any address is returned (the IP is in the list). When reviewing a number of DNSBL web sites to obtain the value of return addresses, there were no obvious patterns and RFC 5782 is silent on the issue.

The following is the meaning of the returned address(es) when using the SORBS blacklist (www.au.sorbs.net/using.shtml) and is presented only as an illustrative example:

```
127.0.0.2  - Open HTTP Proxy Server (http.dnsbl.sorbs.net)
127.0.0.3  - Open SOCKS Proxy Server (socks.dnsbl.sorbs.net)
127.0.0.4  - Open Proxy Server not listed in the SOCKS or
                  HTTP lists. (misc.dnsbl.sorbs.net)
127.0.0.5  - Open SMTP relay server (smtp.dnsbl.sorbs.net)
127.0.0.6  - Hosts sending spam/UCE/UBE to SORBS, netblocks
                  of spam supporting service providers (list.spam.dnsbl.sorbs.net)
127.0.0.7  - Web servers email vulnerabilities (e.g. FormMail scripts)
                  (web.dnsbl.sorbs.net)
127.0.0.8  - Hosts demanding not to be tested by SORBS (block.dnsbl.sorbs.net)
127.0.0.9  - Networks hijacked from original owners (zombie.dnsbl.sorbs.net)
127.0.0.10 - Dynamic IP Address ranges (dul.dnsbl.sorbs.net)
127.0.0.11 - Domain names with bad A or MX RRs (badconf.rhsbl.sorbs.net)
127.0.0.12 - Domain names with no emai originating (nomail.rhsbl.sorbs.net)
```

In this list, the name associated with each IP address (for example, block.dnsbl.sorbs.net) refers to a subdomain to which the target IP address may be appended and which will yield the corresponding IPv4 address code.

Since DNSBLs are zone files, they may be transferred using normal zone transfer methods (AXFR/IXFR – see Chapter), assuming the provider enables such a service. This offers a relatively simple method of distributing updates and reducing loads. Thus, to slave a local copy of a DNSBL from blacklist.example.com at IP address 192.168.2.23 would simply require a slave zone to be incorporated into the local named.conf file:

```
// local named.conf
...
zone "blacklist.example.com"{
  type slave;
  file "slave/blacklist.example.com"
  masters {192.168.2.23;};
  notify no; // inhibits notify propagation
}
...
```

Additional Usage

While the terminology—DNSBL—defines the above to be a blacklist, there's nothing to stop such a zone file being used as, say, a *whitelist* to speed up handling of incoming mail by using the SMTP Agent's IP addresses. Always assuming your favorite mail software will support such a concept and format. Furthermore, by prepending domain names or full e-mail addresses, such a *whitelist* may be even more useful. For example, assume the following zone file fragment for whitelist.example.com:

```
$TTL 2d # default RR TTL
$ORIGIN whitelist.example.com
...
# whitelist records - using origin substitution rule
# order not important other than for local usage reasons

# normal whitelist RRs

# by convention this address should be listed to allow for external testing
2.0.0.127       IN      A                       127.0.0.2
# white list RRs
135.2.168.192  IN      A       127.0.0.2 # or some specific result code address
                IN      TXT     "Optional - Some explanation for white listing"
# the above entries expand to 135.2.168.192.blacklist.example.com
...
135.17.168.192 IN      A       127.0.0.2 # generic list
...
# name based RRs for white listing
friend.com      IN      A       127.0.0.1 # all domain email addresses
# expands to friend.com.whitelist.example.com
joe.bigbank.my      IN      A       127.0.0.2 # single address
# expands to joe.bigbank.my.whitelist.example.com
...
```

In this file, the e-mail address joe@bigbank.com replaces @ with a dot before issuing an A query in a manner similar to that used in the SOA RR **email** field. Thus, the resulting A query will be for joe.bigbank.my.whitelist.example.com.

No known implementations of such a whitelist system exist. It is presented simply to provide imaginative readers with possible addition uses of DNS. Vouch By Reference (RFC 5518) outlines a scheme using TXT RRs, rather than the A RRs described here, to provide reputation information for a variety of named entities. Those of a curious disposition may find this RFC yields some more interesting ideas.

DNS TTLs and Time Values

The DNS TTL field on each RRset is used exclusively by resolvers (recursive or caching name servers) to discard expired records from their caches. DNS TTL values reflect a balance between three issues:

1. *DNS load:* The lower the TTL, the more frequently the authoritative name server (and possibly the DNS hierarchy) is accessed. If the TTL is not carefully chosen, DNS reliability may become more important than the reliability of, say, the corporate web server—not a particularly desirable outcome.

2. *DNS Changes:* The lower the TTL, the quicker changes will propagate through various external caches. Conversely, the longer the TTL, the longer invalid records may be maintained in external caches.

3. *Cache poisoning:* Every query from a resolver to the authoritative name server also offers a DNS poisoning possibility. Simply stated, the longer the TTL, the less frequently an RRset is read and the lower the possibility the cache may be poisoned.

These are competing and mutually exclusive requirements, thus any TTL value is always a trade-off.

While the $TTL directive is very convenient for creating a zone-wide TTL value, it's not always appropriate. To paraphrase George Orwell, all RRs are equal but some RRs are more equal than others. The group of RRs at the zone apex (or root)—SOA, NS, and MX RRs—are frequently and collectively referred to as the *infrastructure* RRs. These RRs have different properties than those of address RRs—such as A/AAAA RRs—in that they involve multiple DNS queries. The first query will read, say, the MX RRset and subsequent queries will return the A (or AAAA) RR(s) of the names pointed to in the MX RRset, similarly with NS RRs.

How frequently does the *name* of the infrastructure servers, such as name servers or mail servers, change? The server's IP address(es) (the A or AAAA RRs) will likely change—perhaps even very frequently—but their names? Thus, the MX RRs could run with a TTL of multiple weeks while the A/AAAA RR(s) may run with only hours. The net effect of even this trivial strategy would be to reduce the load on authoritative name servers significantly.

Note DNS simply translates a name to an IP address. It does not know, or care, what is returned by the hostname command for the host at that IP address. Thus, if an authoritative name server for the domain example.com is hosted at 192.168.2.1, it can be defined as, say, ns1.example.com in an NS RR even if its hostname is, say, superfast.example.com. The A RRs for ns1.example.com and, if required, superfast.example.com, will both point to the same IP. If this double A RR definition offends, then a dreaded CNAME RR could be used to achieve the same goal. The point is that NS RRs can stay stable while only the corresponding A RRs change.

It is inappropriate to think of a single domain TTL; rather, think in terms of an appropriate TTL value for the major RRs and RR groups. Table 8–3 discusses both TTLs and other DNS time values.

Table 8–3. TTLs and Other DNS Time Values

SOA RR	The only value in the SOA that normally changes is the serial number. However, the resolver does not use this value. It is used exclusively by slave servers. Thus, if a cached copy of the zone's SOA has an incorrect serial number there are no negative implications. If DDNS is being used, the primary master referenced in the SOA is used to confirm which DNS to update, and if this *name* is likely to change, the TTL value may need to be lower than would otherwise be desirable. TTL values of 2-7 days (or perhaps significantly longer) may be appropriate for this RR.

SOA Refresh

The refresh parameter of the SOA RR defines when the slave will read the master's SOA and compare its current serial number with that received from the master. If it can't reach the master, the slave will continue to service the domain until the expiry value is reached. If NOTIFY is being used, there is little merit in setting refresh to anything but 12-24 hours, perhaps even longer, since its only real use is in cases where the NOTIFY was lost or blocked. If NOTIFY is not being used, then this value will determine the rate at which zone changes are propagated and should be set to, perhaps, 1 to 6 hours.

SOA Expiry

The expiry parameter of the SOA RR defines when the slave will stop responding to zone requests if it cannot reach the master and has a significant effect on overall DNS availability. Setting this to a very high value (2+ weeks) will ensure that even if the master name server is out for an extended period, DNS service will continue for the zone using the zone slave copies.

NS RR

NS RRsets simply point to the name of the authoritative servers for the domain and thus can be made very stable. If the host of a name server changes, this will require a change in the corresponding A/AAAA RR not the NS RR. NS RR TTLs in the range of 2-7 days, perhaps even weeks, are appropriate. In the event that an NS change is required (for example, changing to an external DNS supplier), this would typically be a planned activity and thus changing the TTL to a lower value (hours) during the transition period would probably be a wise move before restoring to a very high value after the change.

MX RR

The MX RR is similar to the NS RR in that it simply provides the name of the mail server and can be made stable using the same techniques used for NS RRs. There is no advantage in having anything but long TTLs (typically weeks) for MX RRs. The preference parameter of the MX RR provides for resilience, not the TTL. Again, if mail servers are to be changed (as opposed to their A/AAAA RRs), this will typically be a planned activity and changing the TTL to a lower value (hours) during the transition would probably be a wise move before restoring to a high value after the change.

A/AAAA RR

The use of very low TTLs (sub-one minute) is a generally misguided if not a fundamentally flawed strategy and indeed may just break the name server through increased load. The most charitable explanation for low TTLs may be for fast fail-over in the event of catastrophic server failure. This needs some examination. Both NS and MX RRs provide for alternative forms of resilience and can be discounted. In the case where TCP services are provided by hosts (for example, FTP or HTTP), then TCP error recovery, which typically takes around 1 minute 30 seconds or longer, will be invoked before a client is even aware of the problem. Multiple A/AAAA RRs can result in a very fast automatic roll-over and is completely independent of the TTL value. Not all software supports the use of multiple A/AAAA RRs but all the major web browsers and many tested FTP clients do. In cases where a single IP address may need to be replaced quickly, a TTL value of 900-1800 (15-30 minutes) is really the lowest sensible value imaginable. Otherwise, the TTL should be set to the acceptable propagation delay, say, 2-12 hours or higher.

SRV/NAPTR RR	These two RRs are similar in characteristic to infrastructure RRs in that they define a name (or label) which requires a further DNS A/AAAA query. Again, long TTLs (2-7 days) are appropriate.
TXT/SPF RR	The SPF RR may contain a mixture of names and IP addresses. If using explicit IP addresses within the record definition, it has properties similar to the A/AAAA RR above. If only names are used, the properties are those of the infrastructure RRs (NS, MX, SOA).
TXT/DKIM RR	The DKIM TXT RR contains the public key used to authenticate incoming mail. Such public keys may be compromised or rolled over (replaced) periodically. The safest approach is to change the DKIM selector value and create a new DKIM TXT RR at this new name with the new public key (see the DKIM section earlier in this chapter). In this case, the TTL value is not significant and can be set to a high value of 12 hours or even longer. If changing the selector value is not practical, then the TTL needs to be set to an acceptable value during which invalid mail may be accepted as valid mail. Google's Gmail, as an example, uses a TTL value of 300 (5 minutes) on its DKIM TXT RR.
DNSSEC RRs	The TTL values used with DNSKEY RRs particularly are significant in the context of key maintenance for DNSSEC. This is discussed in-depth in Chapter 11.

RFC 1912 also provides useful advice on the above issues, as well as others, and is well worth the reader's time investment. Finally, since there are usually more A (or AAAA) RRs in a zone and they are most likely to change frequently, default all these to the $TTL value for the zone and use explicit overrides on all other RR types. Minimum typing, maximum flexibility—can life get any better?

Summary

This chapter covered a number of common name server configurations and also illustrated some more subtle uses of the DNS system. The next chapter describes the use of various DNS diagnostic tools and techniques to cover the situations when head-scratching fails to yield the required results.

## CHAPTER 9

DNS Diagnostics and Tools

Diagnosing DNS problems can be complex, made so by its interaction with other DNS systems. A DNS problem may originate locally or anywhere in the chain of name servers that provide the response to a query. Finding the location of the problem is, depending on your outlook, either the bane or the challenge of a DNS administrator's life. This chapter is divided into two parts. The first describes a number of tools that may be used to verify, support, or interrogate DNS systems—DNS utilities. The second part looks at diagnosing DNS systems, in some cases using the tools described and in other cases using methods such as log inspection and invoking debug levels to increase reporting.

DNS Utilities

There are a number of DNS utilities, some of which are specific to BIND distributions and some of which are available on a variety of platforms. The author maintains reference material about this book on his site, www.netwidget.net/books/apress/dns; there you will find listed additional DNS utilities—including web-based and Windows utilities—not covered in this book. The following utilities are introduced in this chapter:

- nslookup: Utility for interrogating DNS servers. Widely available on multiple platforms, including Windows.

- dig: Utility for interrogating DNS servers. Typically only available on BIND-supported platforms.

- rndc: Remote maintenance tool for BIND.

- rndc-confgen: Utility to generate keys and rndc.conf files for use with the rndc utility, including a trivial default configuration.

- nsupdate: Utility for dynamically updating zone files.

- named-compilezone: Utility for verifying zone and converting to a raw (binary) format for faster loading.

- named-checkconf: Utility for checking the syntax of the named.conf file.

- named-checkzone: Utility for verifying zone files.

- dnssec-revoke: Utility to set the REVOKE flag on DNSKEY RRs.

- dnssec-settime: Utility for manipulating timing metadata (TMD) for use with BIND's Smart signing and RFC 5011 compliant systems.

- dnssec-signzone: Utility for cryptographically signing zones for use with DNSSEC. Chapter 11 makes significant reference to this utility.

- dnssec-keygen: Utility for generating keys used in various secure DNS transactions. Chapters 10 and 11 make significant reference to this utility.

The descriptions typically take the form of a quick usage example followed by a detailed description of the various options and parameters available, in some cases followed by further advanced examples. This chapter omits the host utility, yet another DNS interrogation utility similar in function to nslookup and dig but having neither the batch service of dig nor the interactive format of nslookup. For information on this utility, use man host or host -h at a command-line prompt.

Every DNS administrator should be thoroughly familiar with either nslookup or dig for troubleshooting and diagnostic work. If a choice needs to be made, it will depend on circumstance. If you are working on a variety of platforms, nslookup is available on Linux, BSD, and Windows platforms and may be the best choice. If DNSSEC (Secure DNS) is being implemented or is in the short-term plan, there is no choice: dig is DNSSEC aware, nslookup is not.

The following sections all use the ubiquitous example.com domain in conjunction with private IPv4 addresses to illustrate the various commands. This is done purely in the interests of being a good netizen. If you run the dig and nslookup examples on the public network, some will work, many will not; the actual commands and results were all carried out using a private configuration and are intended to illustrate techniques and formats rather than be taken literally. However, example.com does in fact exist on the public network and resolves to an IPv4 address of 192.0.34.166, which is on a reserved IANA netblock. It is not a very interesting domain for experimentation, however, since it has only a limited number of hosts; for instance, there is a www.example.com RR, but it does not have MX RRs or an FTP site or anything really exciting. Indeed, its only reason for existence is to minimize the load on the DNS hierarchy of badly configured DNS systems.

Instead, either build your own name server using one or more of the example configurations in Chapter 7 and use it as the basis of experimentation or get onto the public network and select a domain that you either know well or are curious about, replace the example.com in the various examples with your chosen domain name, and explore it using the commands as a starting point. You may be astonished at some of the results you get. Other interesting tasks: look for the more exotic RR types (a full list is defined in Chapter 13) such as LOC RRs (geographic location RRs); discover who publishes SPF records (in TXT/SPF RRs); and find how many MX or NS RRs some of the more high-profile domains have and whether they are all on the same subnet. An endless world of fun is at your fingertips.

■ **Note** One of the happy side effects of installing BIND on Windows (Server 2003, 2008, XP, Vista or 7), even if it's not planned to be used as a name server, is that all the diagnostic tools are also installed, including dig, rndc, and nsupdate (see Chapter 6 for how to install BIND on Windows). Recent versions of the standard BIND 9 Windows installer even provide a "tools only" installation option. For portable use on, say, a USB stick simply unpack the normal BIND windows distribution zip file and copy dig.exe (and any other required tools, such as rndc.exe), libbind9.dll, libdns.dll, libisc.dll, libisccfg.dll and liblwres.dll onto the USB stick.

The *nslookup* Utility

The nslookup utility was once officially deprecated in favor of dig, but with the current BIND releases it has received a new lease on life. The major advantage of nslookup is its almost universal availability, specifically on Windows systems where dig is still pretty exotic. Therefore, if you work in a mixed environment, you are more likely to come across nslookup than dig. nslookup provides both command-line and interactive formats. It can look relatively trivial at first glance, but its configuration parameters (in .nslookuprc in the user's home directory or by default from /etc/resolv.conf or Windows Network Properties), which may be modified in interactive mode, adds tremendous power to the utility. The default configuration parameters can be displayed using the -all option (or set all option in interactive mode).

■ **Tip** The Windows version of the nslookup command is documented in the Microsoft Knowledge Base article number 200525 (http://support.microsoft.com/default.aspx?scid=kb;en-us;200525).

---

nslookup Command Format

nslookup has four generic command formats:

- *Format 1*: Lookup target using the default name server:
- nslookup [-opt] target
- *Format 2*: Lookup target using the specific name server:
- nslookup [-opt] target dns
- *Format 3*: Enter interactive mode using the default name server:
- nslookup [-opt]
- *Format 4*: Enter interactive mode using the specific name server:
- nslookup [-opt] - dns

Format 4 does not work in the native Windows version of nslookup but does on any BIND version including the BIND version installed on Windows. To achieve the same effect on the native Windows version requires use of the server command after entering interactive mode using Format 3.

Quick Examples

The following examples are provided for readers who prefer to experiment before reading about the multiple options that can affect the behavior of the nslookup command. They are designed to illustrate techniques and should not be taken literally; just replace example.com with your favorite domain name and experiment with various formats. The nslookup command is available on Linux, Unix, BSD, and Windows systems.

Format 1: Use the command-line mode with the default name server to perform a simple host lookup:

```
# nslookup www.example.com
Server: ns1.example.com
Address: 192.168.2.53

Name: www.example.com
Address: 192.168.2.80
```

This returns the A record for www.example.com using the default name server—in this case ns1.example.com, which is defined in Windows Network Properties or /etc/resolv.conf in Linux and BSD systems.

Format 1: Use the command-line mode with the default name server to perform a simple reverse map IP lookup:

```
# nslookup 192.168.2.80
Server: ns1.example.com
Address: 192.168.2.53

Name: www.example.com
Address: 192.168.2.80
```

This returns the PTR record for 192.168.2.80 using the IN-ADDR.ARPA domain hierarchy.

Format 2: Use the command-line mode with a specific name server to perform a simple host lookup:

```
# nslookup www.example.com 192.168.255.53
Server: ns1.example.net
Address: 192.168.255.53

Name: www.example.com
Address: 192.168.2.80
```

This returns the A record for www.example.com using the name server at 192.168.255.53. The command format allows either an IP or a name for the specified name server, so the preceding command could have been written as follows:

```
# nslookup www.example.com ns1.example.net
```

Interactive Format

nslookup's interactive format (Formats 3 and 4) provides a single prompt (>) and allows any directive that follows to be entered. To terminate interactive mode, use Ctrl+C (for Windows and for Linux and BSD if no command is currently active), Ctrl+D (Linux and BSD only), or the command exit (Windows, Linux, and BSD). In Linux or BSD, Ctrl+C will terminate a currently active interactive command or will terminate nslookup if no command is active.

```
# nslookup -all
// list all records in the domain - needs axfr to be enabled
> ls example.com
// list all text records in domain
> ls -t TXT example.com
// set the base domain to be used for subsequent commands
> set domain=example.org
// find host
> mail
// returns mail.example.org
```

```
// exit interactive mode
> exit
```

Options

nslookup provides a dizzying number of options that vary its processing. Some of these options are only available in interactive mode. The Windows version adds a couple of unique commands. Multiple options can be specified on a single command line.

The set of options defined in Table 9–1 will only work in interactive mode.

Table 9–1. nslookup Interactive Commands

Option	Parameters	OS[1]	Mode[2]	Processing
ls	[opt] domain	W	I	Lists all the information for the target domain. This command uses AXFR to transfer the zone file. If AXFR is disabled on the target domain, the ls command will fail with an appropriately obscure error. It takes the standard redirection commands > or >> file name to output or append to a file for subsequent processing. The options supported are:
				-a: Lists aliases (CNAME) in the domain (synonym for -t CNAME). -d: The default behavior. Lists all records in the domain (synonym for -t ANY). -h: Lists all information records in the domain (synonym for -t HINFO). -s: Lists all well-known service records in the domain (synonym for -t WKS). -t: Lists the specific record type in the domain; for instance, -t A.
lserver	Dns server	A	I	Sets the name server for subsequent commands. May be either a name or an IP address. The name is looked up using the original default name server (before any server or lserver commands are issued). The default server is defined in /etc/resolv.conf or in the .nslookuprc file in the user's home directory for Linux and BSD systems and in Network Properties for Windows systems.
root	root-dns	A	I	Changes the root server used for certain operations and can be specified as a name, such as k.root-servers.net, or an IP address.

[1]*OS Column Key: **W** = Windows only. **A** = Windows, Linux, BSD. **U** = Linux, BSD*

[2]*Mode Column Key: **B** = Interactive and command-line format. **I** = Interactive only. **C** = Command-line only*

The options defined in Table 9–2 may be used in interactive mode if preceded with the keyword set or on the command line if preceded with - (hyphen or minus). When used on the command line, the option only affects the single command (it's not saved). When used with set in interactive mode, the option will persist until set by another similar option command. In interactive mode, the command set all will list the default settings (the equivalent command-line version would be nslookup -all). In a number of cases a short form is also provided.

Table 9–2. nslookup *Options*

Option	Parameters	OS[1]	Mode[2]	Processing
all		A	B	Displays a list of the default values used by nslookup, including the current name server.
class=	class	A	B	Allows the class value to be set for all subsequent commands and may take the case-insensitive values of IN (Internet—the default), ANY, CH (CHAOS), and HS (HESIOD).
domain=	domain-name	A	B	Allows a base to be set for all subsequent searches when used in interactive mode. The default domain is defined in /etc/resolv.conf for Linux or BSD systems and Network Properties for Windows systems. Setting domain= will reset any previously defined srchlist.
[no]debug [no]deb		A	I	Allows control over the debugging information; debug (short form deb) turns it on, nodebug (or nodeb) turns it off. The default is nodebug.
[no]d2		A	I	Enables/disables debugging information; d2 turns it on, nod2 turns it off. The default is nod2.
[no]defname [no]def		A	I	Controls whether a domain name (in either domain or srchlist) is added to a target, which does not end with a dot, that is, it is not an FQDN. See also the entry for search for full behavior description.
[no]ignoretc		A	I	Controls whether packet truncation errors are ignored (ignoretc) or whether they cause termination (noignoretc—the default).
[no]msxfer		W	I	Controls use of MS fast zone transfer. msxfer turns it on, nomsxfer (the default) turns it off.
[no]recurse [no[rec]		A	B	Controls recursive behavior. recurse (the default) turns it on, and norecurse turns it off.
[no]vc		A	I	Controls whether to use TCP (vc) or UDP (novc); the default is novc.
[no]search [no]sea		A	I	This parameter controls how the srchlist= value is used. search and defname are interrelated based on the matrix shown in Table 9–3 for targets that are not FQDNs.
port=	port-no.	A	B	Changes the default port from the default (53) to that specified by port-no.

Option	Parameters	OS[1]	Mode[2]	Processing
type= querytype=	rr-type	A	B	May take most case-insensitive RR type values, including the meta RRs ANY, IXFR, and AXFR. The default value is type=A. type=ANY with a domain root name will return any RR with a blank name (label) entry; these include SOA, NS, and MX RRs if directed at an authoritative server for the domain. Thus it provides a quick way to get useful domain info.
retry=	number	A	B	Controls the number of retries that will be attempted. The default is 4.
root=	dns	A	B	Controls the name server used when querying the root-servers. The default is typically f.root-server.net. (on Linux and BSD) and a.root-servers.net on Windows.
srchlist=	dom1/dom2	A	I	Allows setting of a search list (up to six names are allowed separated by a forward slash).

[1]*OS Column Key: **W** = Windows only. **A** = Windows, Linux, BSD. **U** = Linux, BSD*

[2]*Mode Column Key: **B** = Interactive and command-line format. **I** = Interactive only. **C** = Command-line only*

Table 9–3 shows the relationship between the search and defname options when used with srchlist.

*Table 9–3. Effect of the **search** and **defname** Options*

search	defname	**Result**
search	defname	Adds domain names from srchlist or until answer is found.
nosearch	defname	Adds domain name from domain.
nosearch	nodefname	Must be an FQDN.
search	nodefname	Must be an FQDN.

In all cases, the first good result will terminate the command; srchlist cannot be used to look up multiple targets. In general, the srchlist is most useful with subdomains but can be used with different domains.

Examples: Command Line

Use this command to get mail records for a domain:

```
nslookup -type=MX example.com
```

215

The following lists all the options being used and gets the host address for mail.example.com:

```
nslookup -all mail.example.com
```

The next command gets the SOA record using a specific DNS:

```
nslookup -type=SOA example.com 192.168.23.53
```

This one gets all records without labels (the zone apex or root) for the domain (gets SOA, NS, and MX and others if defined) if pointed at an authoritative server for the domain; otherwise, it returns only NS RRs:

```
# nslookup -type=any example.com ns1.example.com
```

Finally, the following gets all domain records if zone transfer (AXFR) is not inhibited for the domain (will return BAD ERROR VALUE if inhibited using an allow-transfer statement (see Chapter 12) or similar):

```
# nslookup -type=axfr example.com
```

Example: Interactive Mode

Enter interactive mode and list the default options—this test was run on a Windows system to illustrate the default superset offered by the Windows native version of nslookup. The items noted as Windows only will not be present on a BIND nslookup utility. Lines beginning with // are intended as comments to describe the function of the following line and should not be entered; only those beginning with the prompt (# or >) should be entered:

```
# nslookup -all
Default Server:  ns1.example.com
Address:  192.168.2.53
Set options:
  nodebug
  defname
  search
  recurse
  nod2
  novc
  noignoretc
  port=53
  type=A
  class=IN
  timeout=2
  retry=1
  root=A.ROOT-SERVERS.NET.
  domain=example.com
  MSxfr [note: Windows only MS fast zone xfer]
  IXFRversion=1 [note: Windows only incremental zone xfer]
  srchlist=example.com
// list all records in the domain - needs axfr to be enabled
> ls example.com
// list all text records in domain
> ls -t TXT example.com
// set the base domain to be used for subsequent commands
> set domain=example.org
// find host
```

```
> mail
// returns mail.example.org
// but will handle full format also
> mail.example.org
// return mail.example.org as expected
>set type=any
> example.com
// list apex records for the domain example.com
// and override the domain= value set previously
> set type=mx
// type=mx is persistent
> example.com
// this works as expected for the domain root
> www.example.com
// fails because there is no MX RR for www.example.com!
> set type=a
> www.example.com
// works as expected to give IP
>set type=any
// this is much more useful because it will get all RRs with given name
> www.example.com
// will return ALL RRs with this name.
// exit interactive mode
> exit
```

Tip The nslookup default is type=a (an A RR only will be returned). It is far better, as illustrated in the preceding sequence, to change this to ANY (set type=ANY), since it will get *all* records with a particular name, which would include an A RR if present. You get a lot more bang for the buck with type=ANY!

BIND *dig* Utility

dig (Domain Information Groper) is the current DNS diagnostic tool of preference, but as noted earlier, it is not always widely available and rarely on Windows systems. dig has both a command line and a batch mode (but no interactive mode like nslookup). In general, the command line of dig is more powerful than nslookup—even allowing multiple queries in a single line—and the batch mode makes running check files a breeze. dig offers a daunting array of options, but the following section provides simple examples. dig will support Internationalized Domain Names for Applications (IDNA; see Chapter 12) if built using the --with-idn configure option. This is not standard for Ubuntu/Debian packages but is an optional selection for FreeBSD ports users.

Quick Examples

The following examples are offered for those readers who wish to experiment before reading about the huge number of options that are available with the dig command. They are designed to illustrate that a lot can be done with a limited set of options. They should not be taken literally; instead, replace `example.com` and the various IP addresses with your favorite domain name and start exploring. More examples, together with an explanation of the results, are provided at the end of this section.

The following returns any RRs without a label. It will provide the SOA, NS, and MX RR at the domain apex if pointed at an authoritative server for the domain; otherwise, it returns only the domain NS RRs:

```
dig example.com any
```

This returns only the MX record for the domain:

```
dig example.com mx
```

The next command returns the A record for the `www.example.com` using a specific name server indicated by the @ argument; either a name or an IP address may be used:

```
dig @ns2.example.com www.example.com
```

Using the following command will always generate much more interesting results because the pseudo RR type ANY is slightly misleading and actually means *all* RRs with the given name, so any hidden RRs, such as AAAA, TXT, RP, or KEY RR types with the same name, will be displayed as well as the A RR:

```
dig @ns2.example.com www.example.com any
```

To return all domain records using zone transfer (if allowed), try this command:

```
dig example.com axfr
```

This command returns the PTR RR for the IP address:

```
dig -x 192.168.23.23
```

dig Syntax

```
dig [@dns] [-q] domain [[-c ]q-type] [[-t ]q-class] [+q-opt] [-arguments] [%comment]
```

■ **Note** The `dig` command uses a mixture of positional/contextual arguments and identified options (that is, identified with an option value @, -, or +) to keep simple queries simple! There are times when it is necessary to disambiguate the `q-type` and `q-class` options described later; in such times, both can be specified in an identified option format. The examples illustrate this usage.

---

dig Options

Table 9–4 defines the options available with the `dig` command. The `dig` command may be controlled using a file (`.digrc`) in the user's home directory to set defaults that will override the `/etc/resolv.conf` file.

Table 9–4. dig Options

Parameter	Value	Description
@dns		Defines the optional name or IP address (IPv4 or IPv6 format) of the name server to be used for the query. The default is defined in /etc/resolv.conf for Linux and BSD systems and Network Properties for BIND's dig on Windows. If present, it must be preceded by @; for example, dig @192.168.2.53 www.example.com.
domain		Defines the name to be used in the query. Unlike nslookup, if this is an IP address, it must be preceded with the -x option (see arguments parameter entry). It can always be preceded with -q to disambiguate, though this is rarely necessary.
q-type	RR	Query Type. Defines the type of record to return and may take any valid, case-insensitive RR type, including ANY, IXFR, and AXFR. If omitted, the value A is assumed. This parameter may appear following the domain name or may be optionally preceded with -t in the identified option format. The following two commands will obtain only the TXT RR at the specified host if present: dig www.example.com txt dig -t txt www.example.com
		To get a full listing of the domain records, use the AXFR option. The AXFR feature may be disallowed by the allow-transfer statement in named.conf, in which case the command will fail with a "Connection refused" message. When using the IXFR type, it takes the form IXFR=sn, where sn indicates display all changes since the serial number sn on the SOA RR. The value ANY will list all available records at domain; so to get a listing of the SOA, NS, and MX records, as well as any others at the domain apex, use dig @ns1.example.com example.com any
		If the dig is directed at a nonauthoritative server, it will return only the domain NS RRs, which can then be used to issue the above query.
q-class	IN ANY HESIOD CHAOS	Query Class. The default is IN. May be optionally preceded with -c in the identified option format. The value ANY is a valid option for both q-type and q-class; to ensure the correct value is used (to *disambiguate*, in the - jargon), always specify both q-type and q-class when using this value, as shown here (the lines beginning with // are comments and should not be entered):

		// this will get any record for class IN only
		dig example.com any
		// this will get any record for any class
		dig example.com any any

		Alternatively, you can use an identified option format with -c for q-class and -t for q- type. When the identified option format is used, the parameter order is not important, as shown here: dig -c any -t any example.com See the entry for argument for the identified option format.

Parameter	Value	Description
q-opt		Query Options. The following query options are preceded with a plus (+) and control how the resulting DNS query operates. Multiple values may appear in a single command.
	bufsize=bytes	Defines the number of bytes to be advertised in an EDNS0 OPT meta (or pseudo) RR. May be set to any value in range 0 to 65535. Only used with the dnssec option. The default is 4096.
	domain=name	Replaces the default domain name (found in resolv.conf).
	edns=version	Defines the EDNS version to be used in the outgoing query. Default is edns=0. Using +noedns will reset any previously defined value to the default.
	ndots=num	Defines the minimum number of dots that must appear in a domain name before it is used as a qualified name. Domain names with a lower number of dots will have any default domain name (from resolv.conf) added before the query is issued. The default is 1.
	[no]aaonly	Controls whether to use authoritative query only. The default is noaaonly.
	[no]aaflag	Synonym for [no]aaonly.
	[no]additional	Controls whether to print the ADDITIONAL SECTION. The default is additional.
	[no]adflag	Controls setting the AD flag in the query. Setting this flag (adflag) will cause the resolver to return an AD=1 flag if the zone was signed and is fully validated. The default is noadflag. Not relevant if query sent to an authoritative server.
	[no]all	Sets or unsets all flags that control printed values, such as additional or comments. The default is all.
	[no]answer	Controls whether to the print ANSWER SECTION. The default is answer.
	[no]authority	Controls whether to print the AUTHORITY SECTION. The default is authority.
	[no]besteffort	Controls whether dig will attempt to print malformed responses. The default is nobesteffort.
	[no]comments	Controls whether to print comments. The default is comments.
	[no]cdflag	Sets the CD (Checking Disabled) bit, which inhibits a security-aware resolver from performing DNSSEC validation on signed zones; it must be used with the dnssec option. The default is nocdflag.

Parameter Value	Description
[no]cl	Controls whether to print class information. The default is cl.
[no]cmd	Controls whether to echo valid dig command-line arguments. The default is cmd.
[no]defname	Synonym for [no]search.
[no]dnssec	Controls whether to set the DNSSEC OK (DO) bit in the OPT pseudo header, thus requesting a security-aware resolver to provide security information. The default is nodnssec.
[no]fail	Controls whether dig will stop processing if it receives a SERVFAIL message to one of the default name servers listed in resolv.conf. The default is fail.
[no]identify	Only valid with short option and suppresses or prints the name server identity. The default for the short option is noidentify.
[no]ignore	Controls whether to ignore truncation errors rather than retry using TCP. The default is noignore; that is, TCP retry is used.
[no]multiline	Displays long RRs in standard parentheses format for multiple-line display. The default is nomultiline.
[no]nsid	Include an NSID request (OPCODE = 3; see Chapter 15) when sending a query. Useful if sending queries to an anycasted server. The default is nonsid.
[no]nssearch	If set, dig will attempt to obtain the SOA RRs for each authoritative name server for the domain name being queried. The default is nossearch.
[no]question	Controls whether to print QUESTION SECTION. The default is question.
[no]qr	Controls whether to print the outgoing query used to obtain the results. The default is noqr.
[no]recurse	Controls recursive query behavior. Recursion is automatically inhibited when nssearch and trace are invoked. The default is recurse.
[no]search	Controls whether to use any domain or searchlist parameters in resolv.conf. The default is nosearch.
[no]short	Controls whether to display only the answers to the query; for instance, in an A query, short will only display the IP address(es). The default is noshort.
[no]showsearch	Show intermediate results (search) or not (noshowsearch). The default is noshowsearch. Only applicable if +search option being used.

Parameter	Value	Description
	[no]sigchase	Controls whether signature chains (chains of trust) will be followed or not for signed zones. This option is not enabled by default and requires dig to be built with DDIG_SIGCHASE (standard on Ubuntu/Debian packages, optional with FreeBSD). The default is nosigchase.
	[no]stats	Controls whether to display dig statistics. The default is stats.
	[no]tcp	Controls whether to use TCP (tcp) or UDP (notcp) for queries. The default is notcp unless AXFR or IXFR is used.
	[no]topdown	Controls whether signature validation is carried out top-down. Not enabled by default and requires dig to be built with DDIG_SIGCHASE (standard on Ubuntu/Debian packages, optional with FreeBSD). The default is notopdown.
	[no]trace	Using the trace option causes dig to inhibit its default recursion and issue queries for the requested name to the root-servers and follow (and print) all referrals until an authoritative name server for the domain name is reached. The default is notrace.
	[no]ttlid	Controls whether to print TTL. The default is ttlid.
	[no]vc	Synonym for [no]tcp.
	retry=num	Controls the number of query retries to each server. The default is 2.
	time=seconds	Controls the query timeout period in seconds. The default is 4 seconds.
	tries=number	Controls the number of tries to each server. The default is 3.
	trusted-key=key	Defines the base64 material to be used as a trusted key when chasing signatures. Not enabled by default and requires dig to be built with DDIG_SIGCHASE (standard on Ubuntu/Debian packages, optional with FreeBSD).
arguments		The following arguments control how dig operates and are preceded with a minus (-). Multiple options may appear in a single command line.
	-4	Use IPv4. Only valid for dual-stack (IPv4/IPv6) servers.
	-6	Use IPv6. Only valid for dual-stack (IPv4/IPv6) servers.
	-b	Defines the IP address to be used in the outgoing dig (query) message. Only required on a multihomed server.

Parameter Value	Description
-c	Indicates that a q-class argument follows (this is the identified option format) and can be used as a convenience or to disambiguate from the same q-type options.
-f filename	Specifies a file containing batch commands. Any options specified on the command line will be in effect during the batch run; that is, they are global. Lines beginning with ; or # or \n in the batch file are ignored and may be used as comment or whitespace lines. Each line in the batch file will represent a single command-line query.
-k dir:key	Signs the message with TSIG using the key file in dir.
-h	Displays a short list of the dig options available and exits.
-q	Indicates that the domain argument follows (identified argument format)
-p port	Changes the port used for queries to port. The default is 53.
-t	Indicates a q-type (RR type) argument follows (this is the identified argument format).
-v	Displays the dig version number and exits.

-x	Specifies that inverse notation is being used as shown here:
	 `// this will fail NXDOMAIN (not found)`
	 `dig 192.168.2.53`
	 `// instead use`
	 `dig -x 192.168.2.53`
	 `// OR if you are a masochist!`
	 `dig 53.2.168.192.in-addr.arpa ptr`

-y key	Allows the user to enter the base64 shared secret to be used in a TSIG transaction. This both a long process and extremely dangerous. Use only if desperate and the -k option is not viable.

dig Examples

The following examples are designed to illustrate techniques and should not be taken literally; rather, use them as a starting point for experimentation and exploration on a domain of your choice.

dig Host Query

Here is a simple host lookup that defaults to an A RR:

```
# dig www.example.com
```

The preceding command could have been written as follows (uses a positional argument so the order is important):

```
# dig www.example.com a
```

This is the same command but with the identified option format, so order isn't important:

```
# dig -t a www.example.com
```

Contrast the previous output with the short response by using this command:

```
# dig -t a www.example.com +short
```

As noted previously, type always defaults to type A. Using type ANY will always obtain more interesting results by providing all RR types with any given name; for example, it will get TXT, DKIM or SPF RR for mail servers if present; TXT, LOC or even RP RRs for A RRs; and both A and AAAA RRs for any address RR type. Finally, with the increasing use of DNSSEC, it's also a trivial way to show if the zone is signed or not.

The following shows a real example (however, the names have been changed, as usual, to www.example.com to protect the innocent) of the results (ANSWER SECTION only) when used without and with ANY:

```
# dig www.example.com
;; ANSWER SECTION:
www.example.com.        84778 IN  A      192.168.129.35

# dig www.example.com any
;; ANSWER SECTION:
www.example.com.        84799 IN  RRSIG A 5 3 86400 20110202103357 20110103103357 31662
example.com. j3LjAMHXos1lWTL1xyivarEeqexhb5y4bySWDuV1h8PvBElyeI9zrgfb
zpYtt2EHUKGydoJOl5veowkML1AXvbHRxIox18snuT/n9OMCPxLIWENR
12pnLNQ9Jr2zDZGy93V3ydLpXsqjdLfyTxUiLm6iLq6V6MvwDrGTqsSl KPU=
www.example.com.        84799 IN  A      192.168.129.35
```

This command forces use of the name server at 192.168.2.224 for the query:

```
# dig @192.168.2.224 www.example.com a
```

To force use of the named server at ns1.example.com for the query, use the following:

```
# dig @ns1.example.com www.example.com a
```

The next command is a reverse-map query that returns a PTR RR:

```
# dig -x 192.168.2.224
```

dig Domain Query

Here is a quick domain lookup that returns all RRs without labels, the domain apex or root, and typically gets SOA, NS, MX, and others. If a nonauthoritative server is used, it returns only the NS RRs:

```
# dig @ns1.example.com example.com any
```

This is the same query using the identified option format, so order isn't important:

```
# dig @ns1.example.com -t any example.com
```

The next command forces use of the name server at 192.168.2.224 for the query:

```
# dig @192.168.2.224 example.com any
```

This forces use of the name server at ns1.example.net for the query:

```
dig @ns1.example.net example.com a
```

dig Multiple Queries

dig will accept multiple queries per command line—as long as each query is clearly identified (or disambiguated). This multiple domain lookup returns nonlabel RRs (at domain apex) for both domains:

```
# dig example.com any example.net any
```

The following multiple domain lookup returns A RRs for the first domain and domain apex RRs for the second domain:

```
# dig www.example.com example.net any
```

This multiple domain lookup returns apex RRs for the first domain and an A RR for the second:

```
# dig example.com any example.net
```

If a command line starts with one format, it must be consistent. This fails on the second query:

```
# dig example.com -t any example.net any
```

But this format works for both:

```
# dig example.com -t any example.net -t any
```

And this really does work—though how useful it would be is questionable!

```
# dig example.com any example.net any example.org any
```

This works, too:

```
# dig www.example.com www.example.net fred.example.net
```

dig Output

The following shows the output from a simple dig command to the sample example.com zone using one of the authoritative name servers for the zone. Chapter 11 shows the output from a dig command issued to a DNSSEC signed zone, and Chapter 15 contains the output from a dig command to the root-servers.

```
# dig @ns1.example.com www.example.com
; <<>> DiG 9.3.0 <<>> @ns1.example.com www.example.com
;; global options:  printcmd
;; Got answer:
;; ->>HEADER<<- opcode: QUERY, status: NOERROR, id: 826
;; flags: qr aa rd ra; QUERY: 1, ANSWER: 4, AUTHORITY: 2, ADDITIONAL: 2

;; QUESTION SECTION:
;www.example.com.  IN  A

;; ANSWER SECTION:
www.example.com.  86400  IN  A  10.1.2.1
```

```
www.example.com.   86400   IN   A   192.168.254.3
www.example.com.   86400   IN   A   172.16.2.1
www.example.com.   86400   IN   A   192.168.2.5

;; AUTHORITY SECTION:
example.com.   86400   IN   NS   ns1.example.com.
example.com.   86400   IN   NS   ns2.example.com.

;; ADDITIONAL SECTION:
ns1.example.com.   86400   IN   A   192.168.2.6
ns2.example.com.   86400   IN   A   192.168.23.23

;; Query time: 31 msec
;; SERVER: 192.168.2.3#53(ns1.example.com)
;; WHEN: Tue May 31 20:16:25 2005
;; MSG SIZE  rcvd: 165
```

The output from a dig command is a formatted version of the binary, or *wire format*, message response to the query formed from the dig command parameters (unless the +short option is used). The detailed layout of the message is described in Chapter 15. The preceding response reflects a typical positive response to a dig command and includes the following items:

- The >>HEADER<< is an interpreted version of the message header. The flags and values of the status fields are defined in the next section, "dig Response Values."

- The QUESTION SECTION reflects the original query that is being answered; in this case, it's a query for the A RR of www.example.com.

- The ANSWER SECTION provides the four A RRs for www.example.com that fully answer the question in this case. If the ANSWER SECTION is present but contains no entries, then the query was not successful; the status field in the HEADER typically provides the reason unless the response was a referral, in which case the status field will be NOERR (see Chapter 15 for a referral dig response).

- The AUTHORITY SECTION provides the NS RRs of the servers that are authoritative for the domain example.com.

- The ADDITIONAL SECTION provides information that may be useful to the server; in this case, it is the A RRs of the name servers.

dig Response Values

This section describes the various fields that are present in the >>HEADER<< output to a dig command.

DNS Flags

The values of the flags in the dig command >>HEADER<< are an interpretation of various bits set in the message header, which are described in Chapter 15, Table 15–2.

qr: Query Response. This flag is set in the preceding dig response. It simply means that this is a response to a query and will always be set in a dig response.

aa: Authoritative Answer. This flag is set in the preceding dig response. It means that either the response came from an authoritative name server for the domain, which is true for the preceding case, or this was the first time the data was read from an authoritative name server into a caching name server. In the latter case, if the dig command is immediately reissued, the aa bit will not be set because it will have been read from the cache, in which case the aa bit is never set.

rd: Recursion Desired. This flag is set in the preceding dig response. This flag is copied from the query request (the dig command) and means that the incoming query (the dig message) requested recursive support.

ra: Recursion Available. This flag is set in the preceding dig response. This flag means that the responding name server (ns1.example.com) supports recursive queries.

ad: Authenticated Data. This flag is not set in the preceding dig response. This flag is only valid with DNSSEC (the +dnssec option was set in the dig command) and indicates the target name server is security aware (the dnssec-enable yes; statement is present in the named.conf file), the query response came from a signed zone, and the data was fully authenticated.

cd: Checking Disabled. This flag is not set in the preceding dig response. This flag is only valid with DNSSEC and indicates that the issuing query wishes to bypass any DNSSEC validation sequence performed by the name server when accessing a signed zone. This flag will only be set in the response to a dig command if the +cdflag option is used.

do: DNSSEC OK. This flag is not set in the preceding dig response. This flag is only valid with DNSSEC and is set in the extended OPT PSEUDOSECTION that is always present in DNSSEC transactions (see Chapter 11). It will only be set in a dig response if the +dnssec option is used and the target name server is security aware (a dnssec-enable yes; statement is present in its named.conf).

DNS Status

The values of the status field in a dig response are an interpretation of the RCODE field of the message header and are described in Chapter 15, but reproduced here for convenience:

NOERR: No error condition.

FORMERR: Format error—the name server was unable to interpret the query.

SERVFAIL: Server failure—the name server was unable to process this query due to either a problem with the name server or a requested feature that can't be satisfied due to configuration problems.

NXDOMAIN: Name error—meaningful only for responses from an authoritative name server, this code signifies that the domain name referenced in the query does not exist.

NOTIMP: Not implemented (versions of BIND prior to 9.3 would respond with NOTIMPL)—the name server does not support the requested operation.

REFUSED: The name server refuses to perform the specified operation for policy reasons. For example, a name server may not wish to provide the information to the particular requester or a name server may not wish to perform a particular operation such as a zone transfer (AXFR).

YXDomain: Name exists when it should not (RFC 2136).

YXRRSet: RRset exists when it should not (RFC 2136).

NXRRSet: RRset that should exist does not (RFC 2136).

NotAuth: Server not authoritative for zone (RFC 2136).

NotZone: Name not contained in zone (RFC 2136).

BIND *named-compilezone* Utility

The named-compilezone utility translates a normal text zone file into a raw (binary) format that may be loaded by BIND using the named.conf masterfile-format statement (see Chapter 12). When a number of text zones are being loaded, BIND's startup time can be considerable. Having zone files in raw format can save significant time during the load or reload cycle. Dynamic DNS (DDNS) will work with either text or raw zone files. BIND typically performs significant checks when text zones are loaded but is unable to perform such checks when raw format is used. In order to compensate, the utility named-compilezone performs the normal load checks (and others) when the raw file is created. Thus, any raw file may be assumed to have undergone at least the same checks—and typically more—as a normal text file when loaded by BIND. The arguments used by named-compilezone are the same as those used for named-checkzone, with the single exception of the utility name and are therefore documented (with both named-checkzone and named-compilezone usage examples) under the "BIND named-checkzone/named-compilezone Utility" section later in the chapter.

BIND *named-checkconf* Utility

The named-checkconf utility verifies the syntax of the named.conf file that controls BIND's operation. Whenever changes are made to the named.conf file, this utility should be run before restarting BIND. If you don't do this and you do have a problem, your name server will be offline while you scramble around making changes under pressure. If the named.conf file has no errors, the utility provides silent confirmation—it outputs nothing. No news in this case is indeed good news.

named-checkconf Syntax

```
named-checkconf [-h] [-j] [-p] [-t directory] [-v] [-z] [filename]
```

named-checkconf Options

Table 9–5 describes the options available with the named-checkconf command.

Table 9–5. named-checkconf Options

Argument	Meaning
-h	Outputs a summary of the named-checkzone/named-compilezone arguments and exits.
-j	Relevant only with the -z option when checking zone files that are dynamically updated and causes the utility to check any journal files (zonefile.jnl).
-p	Prints to stdout (but may be redirected (>) to a suitable file). Removes all comments and expands include statements. This a clean copy of the operational named.conf file. Any failure will inhibit the print action, thus ensuring that only operationally ready files are displayed.
-t directory	Chroots to directory when running the check to ensure the correct permissions are available for include statements when run in a similar chrooted environment; that is, the -t directory argument is the same as would be used on the BIND command line when running in a chroot jail or sandbox.
-v	Prints the named-checkconf version number and exits.
-z	Causes named-checkconf to load and verify the master zone files specified in named.conf. The utility displays the zone file name and the SOA serial number for each zone found.
filename	Optional. The name of the configuration file to be checked. If not specified, it defaults to /etc/named.conf on Linux or /etc/namedb/named.conf on BSD systems and %SystemRoot\system32\dns\etc\named.conf on Windows.

BIND *named-checkzone/named-compilezone* Utility

The named-checkzone utility verifies the nominated zone file and provides a useful method to ensure correctness of a zone file before loading into a live name server. When BIND loads any zone at run-time, it also runs a number of the checks that are performed by this utility. However, named-checkzone provides (by default) a significant number of additional tests. In particular, it will follow and verify out-of-zone names when used with MX, NS, SRV and other RRs. It is recommended that named-checkzone always be run on zone file prior to its use with BIND.

The utility named-compilezone was summarized earlier in the chapter and translates standard text zone files into raw (binary) format zone files that may be loaded by BIND using the masterfile-format statement (see Chapter 12). The command line arguments for both utilities are the same, with the sole exception of the utility name. Operationally, the utility name may change the default value of certain arguments; these are noted in the following descriptions. Normal usage examples of both utilities are included.

named-checkzone/named-compilezone Syntax

```
named-checkzone/named-compilezone [-c class] [-D] [-d]  [-F format] [-f format] [-h]
    [-i mode] [-j] [-k mode]
    [-M mode] [-m mode] [-n mode] [-o filename]
    [-q] [-r mode] [-S mode] [-s style] [-t directory] [-v] [-W mode] [-w directory]↵
zonename filename
```

named-checkzone/named-compilezone Arguments

Table 9–6 describes the options available with the named-checkzone/ named-compilezone commands.

Table 9–6. BIND named-checkzone/named-compilezone Arguments

Options	Parameter	Meaning and Use
-c	class	Zone class. The default is IN. May take values CH (CHAOS) or HS (HESIOD).
-D		Writes zone file in canonical (alphabetic by host name) order to stdout (console). If used with the -o argument, this option will write output to a file.
-d		Turns on debugging.
-F	format	Defines the format of the output file (-o argument). Takes the values text (default) and raw when used with named-compilezone.
-f	format	Defines the format of the input zone file. Takes the values raw (output from named-compilezone) or text (default).
-h		Outputs a summary of the named-checkzone/named-compilezone arguments and exits.
-i	mode	Defines the integrity checks to be performed. May take the following values:
		full (default): Checks that NS, SRV, and MX RRs point to a valid in-zone or out-of-zone A or AAAA RR. For delegations (NS RRs), it checks that glue records are present and correspond to those used by the child zone.
		local: Performs the same checks as full but will only verify in-zone names and will not check child zones for compatible glue records.
		full-sibling: Performs the same checks as full (in-zone and out-of-zone) but inhibits the check on child zones. This would be used typically when the child zone has not yet been published.
		local-sibling: Performs the same checks as local (in-zone only) and also inhibits the check on child zones.
		none: Disables all zone checks.

Options	Parameter	Meaning and Use
-j		If using DDNS, this option will read any journal file when checking the zone.
-k	mode	Performs check-name functions (see the check-name statement in Chapter 12) to verify that host names are in compliance with RFC 952 and RFC 1123 formats. The value of mode may be fail, warn, or ignore, which indicates the action to be taken if the check fails. Many modern RRs (notably SRV) will fail these checks. Defaults to warn for named-checkzone and fail for named-compilezone.
-M	mode	Check for MX RRs pointing to CNAME RRs. A technically illegal but common configuration which usually works. Make take the values fail, warn (default), ignore.
-m	mode	Check for MX RRs pointing to A or AAAA RRs. Make take the values fail, warn (default), ignore. Check also performed by -i full (default).
-n	mode	Causes all NS RRs to be verified for a corresponding A RR (a so-called glue record). The mode value indicates the action if the check fails and may take one of the values fail, warn, or ignore. Check also performed by -i full (default).
-o	filename	Defines an output file name. Required for named-compilezone; optional when used with -D for named-checkzone.
-q		Quiet mode. Displays no error messages, just the termination code.
-r	mode	Only relevant to DNSSEC signed zones. Checks for RRs that are the same for non-DNSSEC but are treated as different for DNSSEC. Make take the values fail, warn (default), ignore.
-S	mode	Checks if a SRV RR points to a CNAME. Make take the values fail, warn (default), ignore.
-s	style	Only relevant for text output (-F default). May take the value relative (normal human zone file format) or full (format suitable for scripts and confusing for humans).
-t	directory	Chroots to directory when running the check to ensure the correct permissions are available for include statements when run in a similar chrooted environment; that is, the -t directory argument is the same as would be used on the BIND command line when running in a chroot jail or sandbox.
-W	mode	Checks for non-terminal wildcards (names where the * is not on the extreme left of the name). Make take the values warn (default), ignore.
-w	directory	Defines a directory that will be used for relative addressing in $INCLUDE directives. The default is /var/named.
-v		Displays the version number of named-checkzone and exits.
zonename		The domain name of the zone being checked.
filename		The name of the zone file to be checked.

named-checkzone/named-compilezone Examples

Simple zone verification with full zone checks of the text zone file master.example.com:

```
named-checkzone example.com master.example.com
```

Validation of zone file, including subdomain delegations that are not currently published (-i full-sibling):

```
named-checkzone -i full-sibling example.com master.example.com
```

Validation of the master.example.com zone file and outputs (-o) a sorted (-D) file in human readable (-s) format:

```
named-checkzone -D -o sorted.example.com -s relative example.com master.example.com
```

Creates (-o) a raw (-F) format zone file after performing all checks from master.example.com:

```
named-compilezone -F raw -o raw.example.com example.com master.example.com
```

rndc

The rndc utility controls the name server and may, depending on the value of the controls clause in the named.conf file, be run from one or more local or remote locations, including Windows (Server 2003 and 2008, XP and 7). BIND defaults to enable rndc access from localhost (127.0.0.1) whether required or not. If rndc will not be used, it must be explicitly disabled using a blank controls clause; that is, controls {};.

The rndc utility uses TCP to access the name server on port 953 by default and requires a shared secret to provide TSIG-like authentication on each transaction. The various features supported by the utility are defined in a configuration file called rndc.conf. However, to make initial setup a trivial process, rndc will operate without an rndc.conf file and with a default shared secret. The required default secret is created by running the following command:

```
rndc-keygen -a
```

This command generates two files in the directory in which named.conf resides: rndc.key contains a default key clause used by both rndc and BIND, and rndc.conf.sample, which may be edited to provide additional control of rndc operation. This default configuration is sufficient to support a localhost service but should be enhanced if remote access is required.

The rndc command-line options are described next, followed by the format of the rndc.conf file. The commands available when using rndc are then documented, and finally a worked example is shown that supports access to multiple name servers from a remote host.

■ **Note** The default shared secret name is nominally defined to be "rndc-key"; the Fedora Core and some other Linux distributions, however, seem to use "rndckey". The rndc.key file should be inspected to verify the key clause name used by any specific distribution.

---

rndc Syntax

```
rndc [-b source-ip] [-c config-file] [-k key-file] [-p port] [-s server] [-V] [-y key-id]
command
```

rndc Options

Table 9–7 describes the command-line options available with rndc.

Table 9–7. rndc Options

Option	Parameter	Meaning and Use
-b	source-ip	Use source-ip as the source IP address rather the default value, which would typically be localhost (127.0.0.1). Multiple values are allowed to provide for both IPv4 and IPv6 options.
-c	config-file	By default, the configuration file is called rndc.conf, but may be changed using this option.
-k	key-file	If this option is not used, the key is assumed to be in the rndc.conf file. If an rndc.conf file is not present, the default rndc.key file created by the rndc-confgen -a command is used. The key-file defines a shared secret (HMAC-MD5 algorithm), which was generated by the rndc-confgen utility.
-p	port	The default port used by rndc is 953. This option may be used to change the port number and must be supported by an equivalent inet statement in the controls clause of BIND's named.conf file to change the port number.
-s	server	The server to be accessed, which may be defined as either a name or an IP address (IPv4 or IPv6). If none is specified, the default value from the rndc.conf file is used. If neither is present (the default configuration), localhost is assumed.
-V		If used, this turns on verbose logging.
-y	key-name	Uses the key-name when connecting to the server and must be defined in a key clause in the rndc.conf file. If none is specified, a key statement will be looked for in the server clause for the server specified in the -s option. If this isn't present, the default-key statement in the options clause is checked, and if this isn't present (the default configuration), "rndc-key" is used from the rndc.key file created by the rndc-confgen -a command.
command		The rndc command to be executed; for instance, halt.

rndc.conf Clauses and Statements

The rndc.conf file controls the connection and authentication of the rndc utility to one or more name servers. This file has a similar structure and syntax to named.conf, but with a significantly reduced number of clause types and a limited number of statements.

■ **Note** To provide consistent terminology, this book uses the term *clause* to describe an entity that starts with the name of the clause, which is enclosed in braces and terminated by a semicolon and may contain a number of *statements*. The rationale for this policy is contained in Chapter 12.

The rndc.conf file may contain comments that are exactly the same as those used in the named.conf file: multiline C style (/* */), single line C++ style (//), or single-line UNIX style (#). The rndc.conf file may take a single options clause, one or more server clauses, and one or more key clauses.

The *options* Clause

A single options clause may be defined in the rndc.conf. The options clause defines the default server, authentication key, and port that will be used if not overridden on the command line. It may contain three statements. The first is the default-server statement, which defines the name or IP address of the server that will be used unless overridden by the -s option. If no default-server is specified, localhost is assumed. The second is the default-key statement, which defines the default key-name as a quoted string. It is used if the -y option is not supplied on the command line. If no default-key is defined, the default "rndc-key" is used from the rndc.key file created by rndc-confgen -a. The third is the default-port statement, which, in the absence of a -p option, will define the port number to be used for connection to the server. In the absence of either, port 953 is used. The following example shows an options clause:

```
// rndc.conf fragment
options {
    default-server 127.0.0.1;
    default-key "my-key";
    default-port 3346;
};
```

In the preceding case, a corresponding inet statement in the controls clause of named.conf will be required to specify port 3346 and reference "my-key".

The *server* Clause

One or more server clauses may exist. The server clause defines a specific name server (either a name or an IP address) that rndc may connect to. It may take two statements. The first is the key statement, which defines the specific key to be used to connect to the server. If not present, the default-key statement is used. The second, the port statement, defines the port number to be used with the specific server. If not present, the default-port statement from the options clause is used; otherwise the rndc default of 953 is used. The example that follows illustrates a typical server clause:

```
// rndc.conf fragment
server "ns1.example.net" {
    key "ns1.example.net";
    port 953;
};
```

The *key* Clause

One or more key clauses may be defined. The key clause defines the name of a shared secret key that may be used by one of the servers being accessed. The key clause may take two statements. The algorithm statement identifies the encryption algorithm and *must* take the case-insensitive value hmac-md5. This is followed by the secret statement, which contains the base64 encoding of the key enclosed in quotes. The example that follows illustrates a key clause:

```
// rndc.conf file fragment
key "ns1.example.net" {
    algorithm hmac-md5;
    secret "c3Ryb25nIGVub3VnaCBmb3IgYSBtYW4gYnVoIG1hZGUgZm9yIGEgd29tYW4K";
};
```

There are two ways to generate the keys clause: either using the rndc-confgen utility (see the section that follows), which creates a complete key clause that may be edited into the rndc.conf file without change, or using the dnssec-keygen command (see the "dnssec-keygen Utility" section later in the chapter), in which case some editing will be required. There must also be a corresponding key clause in the named.conf for the name server being accessed. The key clause in the named.conf and rndc.conf files are exactly the same, and as with named.conf, key clauses must appear before being used.

rndc Configuration Examples

Setting up a default configuration—one in which rndc access is only allowed from localhost—requires no modifications to the named.conf file. The default authentication key file (rndc.key) is set up using the following command:

```
rndc-confgen -a
```

The following example shows the configuration of rndc.conf on the host bill.example.com (192.168.2.15) to allow access to two name servers with names of ns1.example.com (IP 192.168.2.3, which uses a port number of 3396) and ns2.example.com (IP 192.168.2.4, which uses the default port 953). Each server will use a separate key for security. There are many ways to create the rndc.conf; the method shown here keeps typing and editing to a minimum.

The key for use with ns1.example.com is generated using the following command (see the "rndc-confgen" section for details):

```
rndc-confgen -k ns1.example.com -p 3396 -s 192.168.2.3 > rndc.conf
```

The command creates a 128-bit HMAC-MD5 shared secret (the rndc-confgen default) with a name of ns1.example.com (the -k option). The -p option is used to create the default-port statement, and the -s option defines the IP address used in the default-server statement. The rndc.conf file as shown here is created:

```
# Start of rndc.conf
key "ns1.example.com" {
    algorithm hmac-md5;
    secret "tRNNxQ240B7Gwc/XhS+VLQ==";
};

options {
    default-key "ns1.example.com";
    default-server 192.168.2.3;
    default-port 3396;
};
```

```
# End of rndc.conf

# Use with the following in named.conf, adjusting the allow list as needed:
# key "ns1.example.com" {
#     algorithm hmac-md5;
#     secret "tRNNxQ240B7Gwc/XhS+VLQ==";
# };
#
# controls {
#     inet 192.168.2.3 port 3396
#     allow { 192.168.2.3; } keys { "ns1.example.com"; };
# };
# End of named.conf
```

The rndc-confgen utility helpfully outputs comments to indicate the required changes to the named.conf file for the name servers being accessed, which, since they are comments, you can leave in the file; if they offend you, delete them. This file will work for ns1.example.com, but to allow the same rndc.conf file to be used for ns2.example.com, you create another key again using rndc-confgen (though you could use dnssec-keygen and some trivial editing):

```
rndc-confgen -k ns2.example.com -s 192.168.2.4 >>rndc.conf
```

This command again creates a 128-bit shared secret using the HMAC-MD5 algorithm (the rndc-confgen default) with a name of ns2.example.com. It also creates an additional options clause that will be removed. The resulting output is appended to the rndc.conf file created by the first rndc-confgen command as shown next (the comment line containing "// start of second (appended) rndc.conf file" was added to indicate the split and would not be present). The presence of multiple comment lines may appear confusing, but it's an artifact of the super-friendly rndc-confgen's willingness to help the user. The output has been left intact, since this reflects the real output from this sequence of commands:

```
# Start of rndc.conf
key "ns1.example.com" {
    algorithm hmac-md5;
    secret "tRNNxQ240B7Gwc/XhS+VLQ==";
};

options {
    default-key "ns1.example.com";
    default-server 192.168.2.3;
    default-port 3396;
};
# End of rndc.conf

# Use with the following in named.conf, adjusting the allow list as needed:
# key "ns1.example.com" {
#     algorithm hmac-md5;
#     secret "tRNNxQ240B7Gwc/XhS+VLQ==";
# };
#
# controls {
#     inet 192.168.2.3 port 3396
#     allow { 192.168.2.3; } keys { "ns1.example.com"; };
# };
# End of named.conf
```

```
// start of second (appended) rndc.conf file
# Start of rndc.conf
key "ns2.example.com" {
   algorithm hmac-md5;
   secret "oSbqEQ7KVw3PZlisH+g/XQ==";
};
options {
   default-key "ns2.example.com";
   default-server 192.168.2.4;
   default-port 953;
};
# End of rndc.conf

# Use with the following in named.conf, adjusting the allow list as needed:
# key "ns2.example.com" {
#    algorithm hmac-md5;
#    secret "oSbqEQ7KVw3PZlisH+g/XQ==";
# };
#
# controls {
#    inet 192.168.2.4 port 953
#    allow { 192.168.2.4; } keys { "ns2.example.com"; };
# };
# End of named.conf
```

To create the final rndc.conf file, three edits must be performed using your favorite editor:

1. Move the key clause for ns2.example.com to just below the key clause for ns1.example.com (key clauses must always appear before they are referenced).

2. Add a server clause for ns2.example.com.

3. Delete the second options clause that was generated by the last rndc-confgen file, which is not required.

The various comment fields from both rndc-confgen commands will be retained because they provide some useful information. The final rndc.conf file will look as shown here (comments beginning with // have been inserted to show the edits described earlier):

```
# Start of rndc.conf
key "ns1.example.com" {
   algorithm hmac-md5;
   secret "tRNNxQ240B7Gwc/XhS+VLQ==";
};
// moved ns2.example.com key clause
key "ns2.example.com" {
   algorithm hmac-md5;
   secret "oSbqEQ7KVw3PZlisH+g/XQ==";
};

options {
   default-key "ns1.example.com";
   default-server 192.168.2.3;
   default-port 3396;
};
```

```
server ns2.example.com { // create server clause
   key ns2.example.com;
   port 953; // required because of default-port in options clause
};
# End of rndc.conf

# Use with the following in named.conf, adjusting the allow list as needed:
# key "ns1.example.com" {
#    algorithm hmac-md5;
#    secret "tRNNxQ240B7Gwc/XhS+VLQ==";
# };
#
# controls {
#    inet 192.168.2.3 port 3396
#    allow { 192.168.2.3; } keys { "ns1.example.com"; };
# };
# End of named.conf

// start of second (appended) rndc.conf file
# Start of rndc.conf
// deleted second options clause
# End of rndc.conf

# Use with the following in named.conf, adjusting the allow list as needed:
# key "ns2.example.com" {
#    algorithm hmac-md5;
#    secret "oSbqEQ7KVw3PZlisH+g/XQ==";
# };
#
# controls {
#    inet 192.168.2.4 port 953
#    allow { 192.168.2.4; } keys { "ns2.example.com"; };
# };
# End of named.conf
```

The two key clauses and controls clause must be made available in the named.conf file for the respective name servers, ns1.example.com and ns2.example.com, as shown in the comment lines. The key clauses used in both rndc.conf and named.conf are identical, so it's also possible to use the actual key clause, not the commented versions, which will save some editing. To run rndc to connect to ns1.example.com (the default in the rndc.conf file), the following command would be used:

```
rndc stop
```

This form of the command uses the defaults defined in the options clause to connect to ns1.example.com and therefore requires no options. To run rndc with ns2.example.com, the following command would be used:

```
rndc -s ns2s.example.com stop
```

This form uses the values defined in the server clause for ns2.example.com.

■ **Note** The `rndc.conf` file contains extremely sensitive shared-secret information and should be read protected from nonessential users. The `key` clauses that will be added to the `named.conf` files for the servers `ns1.example.com` and `ns2.example.com` should use the normal technique of placing them in a separate file and including them in the `named.conf` file. The included files should then be read protected from nonessential users.

The next section describes the commands that may be used with `rndc`.

rndc Commands

The `rndc` utility provides a number of commands to control the operation of the name server; these are shown in Table 9–8.

Table 9–8. rndc Commands

Command	Options	Meaning or Use
addzone	zone [class [view]] clause	Adds a new zone dynamically and is only effective if allow-new-zones yes; is set for the appropriate scope (options or view clause). The clause parameter is the exact zone clause (a quoted string) that would be used if the zone was defined normally in named.conf. For illustration, rndc addzone example.com in "goodguys" '{ type master; file "master/master.example.com"; allow-transfer {10.2.2.1;}; };'. **Note:** the single quotes are necessary to escape the double quotes of the file statement. Added zone file configurations are written to a file with a suffix of .nzf (in the location defined by the directory statement or its default) and are therefore persistent between named restarts or reloads. Added zones can be deleted using the delzone command. If the zone is subsequently manually added to the named.conf file after using the addzone command, the .nzf file must be deleted before reloading/restarting named.
delzone	zone [class [view]]	Deletes zones added with an addzone command, optionally in a view within class.
dumpdb	[-all | -cache | -zone] [view]	By default, or using the -cache option, dumps the cache for all views to the default named_dump.db file in the location defined by a directory statement (or the location and file name defined by the dump-file statement of named.conf). Optionally, a specific view may be selected. Zone files may also be dumped using -all (zone files and cache) or -zone (zone files only), again within an optional view.
flush	[view]	Without the optional view, flushes (clears) all current caches. If view is used, it will only flush the cache for the specified view name.

Command	Options	Meaning or Use
flushname	name	Cause the specified name to be flushed from all the server's caches.
freeze	[zone [class [view]]]	Stops all dynamic updates on the zone and updates the zone file with any outstanding entries in the .jnl file. The dynamic update is reenabled with a thaw zone command. A view within class may be optionally selected. If no zone is specified all updates on the server will be stopped.
halt	[-p]	Causes the name server to be immediately halted. The name server can't be restarted using an rndc command. The optional -p parameter causes named's Process ID (PID) to be returned for use by scripts or applications.
loadkeys	zone [class [view]]	Authoritative DNSSEC servers only. This command is only effective if auto-dnssec is set to auto, maintain, or create (see Chapter 12 for the "auto-dnssec" section) in the target zone clause *and* DDNS is enabled for the zone. Similar to sign but incrementally signs the zone over a period of time. See description of the sign command for details.
notify	zone [class [view]]	Send NOTIFY commands for the given zone (or view within class).
notrace		Sets debug level to 0.
querylog		Toggles logging of all queries to the relevant log file.
reconfig		Reloads the named.conf file and any new zones only. Current zones are not reloaded even if they have changed.
recursing		Dump to the location defined for dumpdb a list of all the recursive queries named is working on.
refresh	zone [class [view]]	Schedules a zone transfer of a nominated slave zone. May optionally define the class and view to be transferred.
reload	[zone [class [view]]]	Reloads named.conf and all zone files but retains all cache entries. If the optional zone parameter is used, it will only reload the nominated zone, and the class and view may be additionally selected.
retransfer	zone [class [view]]	Forces a zone transfer of a nominated slave zone. May optionally define the class and view to be transferred.
secroots	[view]	Dumps the security roots (contents of the trusted-keys or managed-keys clauses) optionally for the specific view. By default they are dumped to the file named.secroots but this can be overriden by the secroots-file statement.

Command	Options	Meaning or Use
sign	zone [class [view]]	Authoritative DNSSEC servers only. This command is only effective if auto-dnssec is set to auto, maintain or create in the target zone clause *and* DDNS is enabled for the zone. This command initiates what BIND calls online smart signing. The timing metadata (TMD; see the "dnssec-keygen TMD" section later in the chapter) of the zone's keys (defined by a managed-keys-directory statement or its default) are inspected and DNSKEY RRs added or deleted as defined by the TMD data. If any change to the DNSKEY RRset occurs after this inspection, the zone is immediately re-signed (in the case of the loadkeys command, it's incrementally re-signed). Optionally, a specific view within class may be used.
stats		Dumps current zone statistics to the default /var/ named/ named.stats file (or the name defined in the statistics-file statement of named.conf). Only valid if the zone-statistics yes; statement appears in the named.conf file.
status		Displays information about the name server, including the current status of query logging.
stop	[-p]	Causes a graceful stop of the name server, allowing any dynamic update and zone transfers to complete. The name server can't be restarted by an rndc command. The optional -p parameter causes named's Process ID (PID) to be returned for use by scripts or applications.
thaw	[zone [class [view]]]	Enables dynamic updates to the specified zone optionally for a specific view within class. This is issued after a freeze zone command. unfreeze is a synonym for thaw. If no zone is specified, dynamic updates are enabled for all zones on this server.
trace	[level]	If issued without the optional level parameter, this will increment the current debug level by one. The level parameter explicitly sets the debug level.
validation	on | off [view]	Valid for resolvers only. Turns on or off (optionally per view) DNSSEC validation, thus overriding the value of any dnssec-validation statement (whose default is yes since BIND 9.5). Only effective if dnssec-enable yes; is set or not present (the default is yes since BIND 9.5). For validation to be effective a trusted-keys or managed-keys clause with appropriate scope must be configured in named.conf.

rndc-confgen Utility

The rndc-confgen utility is used to generate HMAC-MD5 shared-secret (symmetric) keys and a shell rndc.conf configuration file for use with rndc. When the -a option is used, it creates a default configuration (rndc.key file) for use with localhost access only. When used without the -a option, rndc-confgen writes all output to stdout, which must be captured to a file using a redirection command. The output file contains comments describing the format of the inet statement required in the controls clause of named.conf.

rndc-confgen Syntax

```
rndc-confgen [-a] [-b keysize] [-c key-file] [-h] [-k keyname] [-p port]
    [-r randomdev] [-s address] [-t chrootdir] [-u user] [>outfile]
```

rndc-confgen Options

Table 9–9 describes the options available for use with the rndc-confgen utility.

Table 9–9. rndc-confgen Options

Option	Parameter	Meaning or Use
-a		This option creates a configuration for use with rndc in its default mode of operation (with localhost only). The file rndc.key is written into the same directory as named.conf (and is read by both named and rndc) and an rndc.conf.sample file, which may be edited for subsequent configuration of rndc.
-b	keysize	Defines the key size for use with the HMAC-MD5 MAC algorithm. May take a value in the range 1 to 512 and defaults to 128 if not defined.
-c	key-file	When used with the -a option, it defines an alternative file name (replaces the default rndc.key). If this option is used, the key-file name must be included in the named.conf file, since BIND only looks by default for rndc.key.
-h		Displays a list of the options and exits.
-k	key-name	The key-name to be used when creating the key clause. The default is "rndc-key", though some distributions change this to "rndckey".
-p	port	The port number to be used for rndc connections. The default is 953. This option overrides the default-port statement in the rndc.conf file.

Option	Parameter	Meaning or Use
-r	randomdev keyboard	Defines the source of randomness used to generate keys. The default is to use /dev/random, in which the OS captures randomness (entropy) from various system events. If significant key generation is being done, this source may become depleted and the utility will apparently freeze, waiting for entropy. Typing any characters on the keyboard will allow the system to capture randomness from the typing intervals. Many systems also provide /dev/urandom, which is faster but significantly less random, leading to less secure keys. If neither device is present, the value keyboard may be used to force use of the keyboard technique described earlier.
-s	address	The IP address (IPv4 or IPv6) to which connection will be made. The value overrides the default-server statement of the options clause in the rndc.conf file.
-t	chrootdir	Only valid with the -a option and defines the directory in which BIND will be run chrooted; that is, directory will be the same value as used with BIND's -t command-line option for defining a chroot base directory. A copy of the rndc.key file is placed in this directory.
-u	user	Defines the user (UID) name whose permission will be applied to the rndc.key file. If used in conjunction with the -a option, only the copy in the -t directory will be allocated the defined user (UID) permission.
>outfile		If used without the -a option, output from rndc-confgen is written to stdout, and therefore the standard redirection command will capture the data to the outfile name.

BIND *nsupdate* Utility

The nsupdate utility allows dynamic updating of the zone files for which the name server is the primary master—the name server that appears on the SOA RR for the zone. nsupdate typically accepts commands from the console but may optionally be used to read commands from a batch file. Zones may not be added or deleted using nsupdate, but a zone's SOA RR may be edited. Zones being dynamically updated should not normally be manually edited. Should manual editing be required, the server should be stopped, the manual edit carried out, the .jnl files for the zone deleted, and the server restarted; alternatively, you could use the rndc freeze zone command, edit the zone, delete any .jnl files for the zone, and then use rndc thaw/unfreeze zone to enable dynamic updates for the zone. nsupdate may be secured using either TSIG or SIG(0) transaction security—both methods, including illustrative examples, are described in Chapter 10. The keys used in both TSIG and SIG(0) are generated using the dnssec-keygen utility but a new utility ddns-confgen provides a simplified method of generating suitable TSIG keys as well as the configuration details necessary to add the resulting key to named.conf and to invoke the key from nsupdate. ddns-confgen is not described in this book; use man ddns-confgen for more information. Dynamic updates are controlled by the allow-update or update-policy statements in view, options, or zone clauses of the named.conf file (see Chapter 12). The update-policy local; statement (see Chapter 12) automatically generates a suitable TSIG key that may be used when nsupdate and the name server are run on the same host. That is, nsupdate scope is limited to localhost only when using this feature. Dynamic updates can be performed on both normal and signed (DNSSEC) zones, as described in Chapter 11 with some additional notes in this section.

nsupdate Syntax

```
nsupdate [-D] [-d] [-g] [-l] [-k key-file | -y keyname:secret ] [-o] [-R randev] [-r
udpretries] [-t timeout]
     [-u interval] [-v] [filename]
```

nsupdate Options

Table 9–10 defines the options available with the nsupdate utility.

Table 9–10. nsupdate Options

Option	Parameter	Meaning or Use
-D		Turns on additional debugging in addition to -d.
-d		Turns on debug mode.
-g		Turns on standard GSS-TSIG support. Needs to be specially built to support this feature. Standard Ubuntu and FreeBSD packages do not support this feature.
-k	key-file	Defines the name of the key-file output when the dnssec-keygen program that created the key was run. This option must have the .private suffix appended on the command line, but both the .key and .private files must be available in the same directory.
-l		Indicates that nsupdate will operate only using the default values created by BIND when an update-policy local; statement appears in a master zone clause of named.conf.
-o		Turns on Windows compliant GSS-TSIG. Needs to be specially built to support this feature. Standard Ubuntu and FreeBSD packages do not support this feature.
-R	randev	Defines the source of randomness used to generate keys. The default is to use /dev/random, in which the OS captures randomness (entropy) from various system events. If significant key generation is being done, this source may become depleted and nsupdate will apparently freeze, waiting for entropy. Typing any characters on the keyboard will allow the system to capture randomness from the typing intervals. Many systems also provide /dev/urandom, which is faster but significantly less random, leading to less secure keys. If neither device is present, the value keyboard may be used to force use of the keyboard technique described earlier.
-r	udpretries	Defines the number of retries for a dynamic update. The default is 3. The value of 0 means no retries are attempted.

Option	Parameter	Meaning or Use
-t	timeout	Defines the time in seconds before the update is regarded as having failed. The default is 300. The value 0 will disable timeout checking.
-u	interval	If an update fails, this option may be used to define the time in seconds between retries. The default is 3.
-v		By default, nsupdate will use UDP unless the block size is greater than 512 bytes, in which case TCP will be used. This option forces use of TCP for all updates.
-y	keyname:secret	Allows a shared secret to be entered on the command line. This is a dangerous option and should only be used if there is no alternative. The keyname field is the name as it appears in the receiving server's key clause, and secret is the base64 material that comprises the secret key!
	filename	The optional filename may be used to supply update commands from a nominated file. The default is to accept commands from stdin (the console).

nsupdate Command Format

nsupdate commands define the environment, the RRs to be deleted or added, and any required conditions (prerequisites) for the updates to take place. The prerequisites are optional and allow checks to be performed before the update is executed. Commands are built locally and only sent using either the send command or a blank line. Any number of RRs (and the required prerequisites) may be added or deleted in a single send operation, or individual RRs may be added or deleted in a single send operation.

The command formats are defined in Table 9–11.

Table 9–11. nsupdate Commands

Command	Parameter	Meaning or Use
answer		Displays the results of the last send operation.
Class	IN | CH |HS	The zone class. The default is IN.
Debug		Turns on debugging.
gsstsig		The GSS-TSIG feature is not described in this book. Equivalent to specifying the -g argument when nsupdate was loaded.
Local	address [port]	If not specified, the nsupdate utility sends updates using a random port number on the configured IP address for the host. This option may be used to define a specific IP and optionally a port number.

Command	Parameter	Meaning or Use
Key	name secret	Has the same meaning and overrides the value of the -y option on the nsupdate command line.
oldgsstsig		The GSS-TSIG feature is not described in this book. Equivalent to specifying the -o argument when nsupdate was loaded.
prereq nxdomain	name	The following update add or update delete commands will only be executed if the defined name does not exist in the zone.
prereq yxdomain	name	The following update add or update delete commands will only be executed if the defined name does exist in the zone.
prereq nxrrset	name [class] type	The following update add or update delete commands will only be executed if the defined name and RR type do not exist in the zone. class is optional and, if not present, defaults to IN.
prereq yxrrset	name [ttl] type	The following update add or update delete commands will only be executed if the defined name and RR type do exist in the zone. class is optional and, if not present, defaults to IN.
prereq yxrrset	name [ttl] type data	The following update add or update delete commands will only be executed if the defined name, RR type, and data do exist in the zone.
Quit		Terminates the nsupdate utility.
realm	[realm-name]	Used with GSS-TSIG and Kerberos 5. If specified, realm-name overrides the default realm name (defined in krb5.conf). If no realm-name is defined, it resets to use that defined in krb5.conf.
send		Sends the current command or commands, equivalent to a blank line being entered.
server	server-name [port]	Defines the name server to which the updates will be sent until the next server command is issued. The optional port parameter may be used to override the default port (53). If not specified, nsupdate will send updates to the primary master name server for the zone.
show		Displays the last send operation.
ttl	seconds	Defines the default TTL to be applied to all added RRs (using update) when TTL is not explicitly defined. The keyword none may be used to clear a previously defined value.

Command	Parameter	Meaning or Use
update add	name [ttl] [class] type data	The RR to be added as it will appear in the zone file; for instance, update add fred 8600 IN A 192.168.2.3.
update delete	name [ttl] [class] type data	The RR that should be deleted; for instance, update delete fred A 192.168.2.3.
zone	zone-name	Defines the name of the zone that will be used for subsequent updates until another zone command is issued. If not supplied, nsupdate will attempt to guess the required zone from the update add and update delete commands.

nsupdate Example

The following sequence is used to add an MX record and its corresponding A RR for the domain example.com and is secured using SIG(0):

```
cd /var/named/dynamic
# nsupdate -k Kexample.com.+001+00706.private
> server ns1.example.com
> zone example.com
> update add example.com. 36000 IN MX 10 mail2.example.com.
> send
> show
Outgoing update query:
;; ->>HEADER<<- opcode: UPDATE, status: NOERR id: 0
;; flags: ; ZONE: 0, PREREQ: 0, UPDATE: 0, ADDITIONAL: 0
> update add mail2 36000 IN A 192.168.2.5
> send
> show
Outgoing update query:
;; ->>HEADER<<- opcode: UPDATE, status: NOERR id: 0
;; flags: ; ZONE: 0, PREREQ: 0, UPDATE: 0, ADDITIONAL: 0
> quit
```

nsupdate and DNSSEC Signed Zones

When nsupdate is used with DNSSEC signed zones, the following points should be noted:

- *Online Private Keys*: Any changes made to a signed zone require that the zone be re-signed. When using nsupdate, zone re-signing will be initiated automatically, requiring that the private keys be constantly available online. This requires extreme care: it may or may not present unique security problems for the user. Using a dynamically updated DNSSEC signed zone on a publically visible name server without a hardware security module (HSM) is an extremely risky, if not suicidal, configuration. Even with a HSM in place, many users would feel distinctly queasy at even the thought. DNSSEC DDNS servers should be well hidden behind firewalls.

- *Adding DNSKEY RRs*: DNSKEY RRs can be added like any other RR type. If a zone is not currently signed, it will be signed automatically as a consequence of adding DNSKEY RRs. Depending on the flag field (see the "DNSKEY Record" section in Chapter 13) they will trigger the required level of signing/re-signing: for KSKs, the DNSKEY RRset only; for ZSKs, all zone RRsets (subject to the setting of dnssec-dnskey-kskonly statement).

- *NSEC3/NSEC*: If a zone is already signed using either NSEC or NSEC3, no special action is required; any resigning operation will automatically use the current (NSEC or NSEC3) method.

- *NSEC to NSEC3*: If a zone currently signed with NSEC RRs is to be converted to use NSEC3, then a valid NSEC3PARAM RR (see the "NSEC3PARAM Record" section in Chapter 13) must be added at the zone apex. If Opt-Out is to be used, the Opt-Out flag must be set in the added NSEC3PARAM RR. Zone re-signing with NSEC3 will be automatically initiated when the NSEC3PARAM is added.

- *NSEC3 to NSEC*: If a zone currently signed with NSEC3 RRs is required to be converted to use NSEC RRs, the NSEC3PARAM RR at the zone apex must be deleted. Resigning with NSEC will be initiated automatically using NSEC when the NSEC3PARAM RR is deleted.

- *Signed to Unsigned*: If a signed zone is to be converted to an unsigned zone, deleting all the DNSKEY RRs at the zone apex will automatically initiate this. The DS RRs at the parent must have been deleted at least one TTL of the DNSKEY RRset prior to deleting the DNSKEY RRs in the zone; otherwise the zone *may* return bogus (invalid) status to end users.

dnssec-keygen Utility

The dnssec-keygen utility is a general-purpose cryptographic key generation utility that generates keys for use with TSIG, SIG(0), TKEY, and DNSSEC operations (see Chapters 10 and 11) as well as generic KEY or DNSKEY RRs. When the utility is run, it outputs a key-file reference. The key-file is used subsequently in dnssec-signzone and other commands; it references two files (frequently referred to as a *keyset*) created in either the current working directory (the directory from which the command was run) or a nominated directory (using the -K argument) with the following names

```
Khostname.+algorithm+key-tag.private
Khostname.+algorithm+key-tag.key
```

where K is a fixed identifier, hostname is the host name value in FQDN format (terminated with a dot) from the dnssec-keygen command line (see the "dnssec-keygen Options" section later in this chapter), and + is a fixed separator. algorithm is a three-digit number identifying the key algorithm specified in the command line and takes the following values:

> 001 = RSAMD5
>
> 002 = DH (Diffie-Hellman)
>
> 003 = DSA
>
> 005 = RSASHA1
>
> 006 = NSEC3DSA
>
> 007 = NSEC3RSASHA1

008 = RSASHA256

010 = RSASHA512

157 = HMAC-MD5

161 = HMAC-SHA1

162 = HMAC-SHA224

163 = HMAC-SHA256

164 = HMAC-SHA384

165 = HMAC-SHA512

The next + is a fixed separator, key-tag is a five-digit value (generated with a modified one's complement algorithm) used to identify this key from others that may have the same hostname. The key-tag is used explicitly, implicitly in other places, in the Delegated Signer (DS) RR of DNSSEC (see Chapter 11).

The .private file contains the private key of a public key (asymmetric) algorithm, such as RSA-SHA-1, or the shared secret in a symmetric algorithm, such as HMAC-MD5. The .key file contains a formatted KEY or DNSKEY RR, depending on the -T and -n arguments that follow such that the file may be directly included where appropriate in a zone file using the $INCLUDE directive (see Chapter 13).

■ **Caution** The dnssec-keygen utility always generates .private and .key files. When used with a shared-secret (symmetric) algorithm such as HMAC-MD5 for use in TSIG operations to secure DDNS or zone transfers, the .key file will contain a KEY RR with the shared secret! This is a potentially dangerous file and *must not* be included in any zone file; instead, it should be deleted immediately unless there is a very good reason to retain it, in which case it must be secured.

The .private file of any public key system contains highly sensitive information. When it has been used for, say, zone signing, should be taken offline, which may mean physically removing it from the system or moving to another location and securing with appropriate privileges. When using dynamic update with signed zone files, however, the .private file of the ZSK must be online at all times and should be secured with minimal read permissions.

When generating keys for use with DNSSEC systems, dnssec-keygen (as well as dnssec-settime and dnssec-keyfromlabel) will create or manipulate time and date metadata (-A, -D, -I, -P, and -R arguments or their default values) for use with zone-signing software. The metadata is used to enable and simplify key management processes defined in RFC 5011 (see Chapter 11's "Key Handling Automation" section) and its presence is indicated by use of a v1.3 header in the *private* file of the keyset. The -C argument inhibits writing of this information (indicated by a v1.2 header) either in cases where it is not required, such as for TSIG or SIG(0) keys, or where non-RFC 5011 compliant zone-signing software is being used. See also "Timing Metadata" later in the chapter.

BIND HSM Support (cryptoki)

By default, BIND 9 is built to use the cryptographic library features of OpenSSL (standard packages on Ubuntu, Fedora, BSD, and Windows). Alternatively, dnssec-keygen (as well as dnssec-signzone and named) may be configured to use a HSM when generating and using keys for asymmetric cryptographic algorithms (see Chapter 10) such as SIG(0) and DNSSEC. An HSM will generate keys without disclosing the private part of the key (and may also provide crypto-hardware acceleration) and is frequently used with highly secure or high-value sites. BIND 9 supports a limited set of HSMs at this time and has to be specially built (see Chapter 6's "Building BIND from Source" section) to include a pkcs11 (cryptoki) library typically supplied by the HSM vendor. When built this way, the -E argument can be used to toggle between pkcs11(cryptoki) and OpenSSL.Further discussion is beyond the scope of this book; interested users should consult the BIND ARM Section 4.11 and the various BIND mailing lists for more information.

dnssec-keygen Syntax

```
dnssec-keygen  [-3] [-A date] -a algorithm -b keysize [-C][ -c class ] [-D date]↲
[-E engine] [ -e ]
       [ -f flag ] [ -g generator ] [ -h ]  [-I date] [-I interval] [-K directory]↲
-n nametype [-P date]
       [ -p protocol ][-q] [-R date] [ -r randomdev ] [-S key-file] [ -s strength ]↲
[-T rrtype] [ -t type ]
       [ -v level ] [-z] hostname
```

dnssec-keygen Arguments

Table 9–12 shows the various arguments available with the dnssec-keygen utility.

Table 9–12. dnssec-keygen Arguments

Option	Parameter	Meaning and Use
-3	-	If present, it indicates that a NSEC3 compatible algorithm (-a) must be used. If no algorithm is defined (no -a argument), it will default to NSEC3RSASHA1 when -3 is present.
-A	date	Only relevant for DNSSEC (not TSIG/SIG(0)) keys. Defines the key activation date—the date at which the key may be included and used to sign a zone file. If the argument is not present, the key may be included and used to sign the zone immediately. If -A is present without -P, both are set to the *same* time value. See "Timing Metadata" below.

Option	Parameter	Meaning and Use
-a	algorithm	Defines the cryptographic algorithm for which the key is being generated and implicitly determines both usage and the RR type (KEY or DNSKEY) generated. The implicit value may be overridden with the -T option. May take one of the following case-insensitive values based on required usage: TSIG/TKEY: DH, HMAC-MD5, HMAC-SHA1, HMAC-SHA224, HMAC-SHA256, HMAC-SHA384, or HMAC-SHA512. Creates a KEY RR unless -T option used. DNSSEC/SIG(0): RSAMD5, RSASHA1, DSA, NSEC3RSASHA1, NSEC3DSA, RSASHA256 or RSASHA512. Creates a DNSKEY RR by default. Use -T KEY for SIG(0) use. Only NSEC3RSASHA1, NSEC3DSA, RSASHA256 and RSASHA512 will generate a key suitable for use with NSEC3. If -a is omitted, the default is RSASHA1 unless -3 is present in which case it will default to NSEC3RSASHA1.
-b	keysize	Specifies the number of bits to be used in the key and depends on the algorithm being used: RSAMD5, RSASHA1, RSASHA256, and NSEC3. RSASHA1 range is 512 - 4096 (current RSA recommendation is 1024 but this changes over time); RSASHA512 range is 1024- 4096 (current RSA recommendation is 1024 but this changes over time); DSA range is 512-1024 (must be a multiple of 64); DH range is 128-4096; HMAC-MD5 range is 1-512; HMAC-SHA1 range is 1-160; HMAC-SHA224 range is 1-224; HMAC-SHA256 range is 1-256; HMAC-SHA384 range is 1-384; HMAC-SHA512 range is 1-512. If -a is omitted then -b will default to 1024 for a ZSK and 2048 for a KSK (-f KSK). However, if -a is present then -b must also be present.
-C		When present, it writes the *private* file without including timing metadata (indicated by use of a v1.2 header in the resulting keyset files). Use -C when generating TSIG/SIG(0) keys; omit when generating DNSSEC keys.
-c	class	Defines the class of the KEY or DNSKEY RR generated. The default is IN. May take the case-insensitive value IN (Internet), CH (CHAOS), or HS (HESIOD).
-D	date	DNSSEC keys only. Defines the date at which the key may be deleted from the zone file. See "Timing Metadata" below.
-E	engine	Only applicable if BIND built to support pkcs11 (cryptoki). Not available with standard Ubuntu, FreeBSD, or Windows distributions.
-e		Valid only with RSA algorithm types (-a option) —and specifies use of a large exponent when generating the key. Some cryptographic papers have suggested that use of a large exponent is more secure but significantly increases computational resources required. The default is to use a normal exponent.

Option	Parameter	Meaning and Use
-f	flag	Only relevant to DNSSEC keys (not TSIG/TKEY/SIG(0) keys). May take the case-insensitive values KSK, which defines for DNSSEC operations that this a Key Signing Key or REVOKE(see Chapter 11). Both -f KSK and -f REVOKE may be used. Short forms for keyboard-challenged users may take the form -fk (equivalent to -f KSK) or −fr (eqivalent to -f REVOKE).
-G		Writes an enhanced v1.3 meta header to the keyset files but does not write any metadata. The resulting keyset can't be used in smart dnssec-signzone or by any other software that uses RFC 5011 procedures. Not valid when used with the A, -D, -I, -P, or -R arguments.
-g	generator	Used only for the Diffie-Hellman algorithm (-a DH). Value may be either 2 or 5 and defines the generator of the prime number used in the algorithm. The default is to use the values defined in RFC 2539, but if not possible, to use the value 2.
-h		Outputs a summary of the dnssec-keygen options and exits.
-I	date	Only relevant for DNSSEC keys. Defines the date at which the key will be made inactive (or retired); it will remain in the zone file but will not be used to sign zones. See "Timing Metadata" below.
-i	interval	Only valid when used with -S argument. Defines the period, relative to the replacement key's activation date, when it can be published. interval may terminate with mo (month), w (week), d (day), h (hour), or mi (minute); otherwise seconds will be assumed. Defaults to 30 days. For usage, see -S argument.
-K	directory	Defines a directory in which the key files are maintained. Default assumes the current working directory.
-k		Deprecated (use -T)
-n	nametype	Mandatory for TSIG/TKEY/SIG(0) and may be omitted for DNSSEC keys. May take the value host, entity, user, other, or zone. When generating keys for TSIG, use -n host; for SIG(0), use -n user (or -n host) with -T KEY; for DNSSEC, use -n zone (optionally with -f KSK/REVOKE) or omit. Ignore all other values.
-P	date	Only relevant with DNSSEC keys. Defines the date at which the key may be published in the zone file but will not be used to sign the zone. The date at which the key may be used to sign the zone is defined by the -A option. See "Timing Metadata" below.
-p	protocol	Defines the value of the proto field used in the KEY and DNSKEY RRs (see Chapter 13). This is currently restricted to the value 3, which is the default. This field had a historic usage in the KEY RR that was limited to the value 3 by RFC 3445.
-q		Suppresses console output when running with manual input (-r keyboard).

Option	Parameter	Meaning and Use
-R	date	Only relevant to DNSSEC keys and defines the date at which a key will be revoked (the REVOKE bit is set in the DNSKEY flags field). When the REVOKE flag is set, the key is still included and *must* sign the DNSKEY RRset. See "Timing Metadata" below.
-r	randomdev keyboard	Defines the source of randomness used to generate keys. The default is to use /dev/random, in which the OS captures randomness (entropy) from various system events. If significant key generation is being done, this source may become depleted and dnssec-keygen will apparently freeze, waiting for entropy. Typing any characters on the keyboard will allow the system to capture randomness from the typing intervals. Many systems also provide /dev/urandom, which is faster but significantly less random, leading to less secure keys. If neither device is present, the value keyboard may be used to force use of the keyboard technique described earlier. The default is to use /dev/random if it exists.
-S	key-file	If keys are being managed strictly in accordance with RFC 5011 procedures (see Chapter 11's "Key Handling Automation" section), the -S argument may be used to generate a replacement key for key-file which must have a valid retrial/inactive date (set by -I argument to dnssec-settime or the -I argument to dnssec-keygen when the key was originally generated). Thus -S Kexample.com.+005+18181 will generate a new key with the same algorithm, key size, and DNSKEY RR with the same flags as that defined by Kexample.com.+005+18181. The activation date and time meta data of the replacement key will be set to the retrial/inactive time of the key it will replace. The publication date and time metadata of the new key will be set to a default value of 30 days before the activation date and time (assuming a standard 30-day rollover cycle). However, the publication date and time may be modified by use of the -i argument, in which case the time specified will be subtracted from the activation date of the new key. Thus -i 2d will create a publication date and time 2 days prior to the activation date and time of the replacement key.
-s	strength	Not currently used. Defines the strength of the generated key and may take the value 0 to 15.
-T	rrtype	Optional. May take the values KEY or DNSKEY (case-insensitive). If not present the algorithm argument (-a) and type argument (-n) determines the key RR. When generating SIG(0) keys, -T KEY must be used.
-t	type	Optional. No known current use (historically was used to set bits in the KEY RR flags field). The default is AUTHCONF (authenticate and encrypt). May take the values AUTHCONF, AUTH, CONF, NOAUTH, and NOCONF NOAUTHCONF.
-v	level	Defines the debugging level and may take the values 0 to 3.

Option	Parameter	Meaning and Use
hostname		Defines the name of the KEY or DNSKEY RR that will be generated. For ZSKs and KSKs used in DNSSEC operations, this will be the zone apex; for example, if the zone name is subdomain.example.com, the hostname will be subdomain.example.com. In TSIG applications, the name used is defined in the key clauses of the peers and may be hostname or any other suitable value such as, transfer-key, to indicate key usage.

Timing Metadata (TMD)

dnssec-keygen will write date and time metadata to the .private files created by the utility (indicated and contained in a v1.3 header). This metadata is only applicable to DNSSEC keys and may be optionally suppressed for all other key types by using either the -C or -G arguments. The metadata is used by dnssec-signzone (-S argument) to implement RFC 5011 procedures (see Chapter 11's "Key Handling Automation" section) and may be manipulated by the dnssec-revoke and dnssec-settime utilities.

The timing metadata values are set by the arguments -A, -D, -I, -P, or -R (or their default values) as appropriate. The arguments have the same values, format, and meaning when used in dnssec-keygen, dnssec-revoke, and dnssec-settime. The arguments take a date format that may be either an absolute value or a relative offset from the present time. Absolute time values may be either YYYYMMDDHHMMSS or YYYYMMDD (HHMMSS is defaulted to 000000). Relative offsets must start with either + or - (minus) and are respectively added or subtracted to the time the utility is run and when written to the .private file are normalized to *Universal Coordinated Time* (UCT; also known as GMT). Relative values are numeric but may terminate with y (year; assumes 365 days, no leap years), mo (month; assumes 30 days), w (week), h (hours) or mi (minutes). If no terminating alpha-character is present, seconds are assumed. The keyword now may be used to indicate the runtime of the utility. The meaning and use of the metadata are defined in detail in the "Key Handling Automation" section of Chapter 11 but for convenience their usage by dnssec-signzone (-S) is described here:

> *Publication Date (-P):* When a key reaches its publication date, its DNSKEY RR will be included in the signed zone but it will not be used to sign any RRsets.

> *Activation Date (-A):* When a key reaches its activation date, its DNSKEY RR will be included in the signed zone and it will be used to sign RRsets as either a KSK or a ZSK as defined by its flags.

> *Retrial/Inactivation Date (-I):* When this set is set and in the past, the key will remain in the output signed zone but will not be used to sign RRsets.

> *Revocation Date (-R):* This date and time may only be effectively set by the dnssec-revoke utility since it will also set the REVOKE flag on the DNSKEY RR. The -R argument should not be used with dnssec-keygen, dnssec-settime or dnssec-signzone.

> *Deletion Date (-D):* When this date is set and in the past, the DNSKEY RR will be removed from the zone file (and obviously will not be used to sign any RRsets!).

In addition to the above values, a creation data meta record is set to UCT of the dnssec-keygen run used to create the key. Its use is informative, not operational.

dnssec-keygen Examples

The following command will generate a shared secret for use with TSIG operations (when -a hmac-md5 is used, a KEY RR is *always* generated, so the -T key argument is not required). The -C argument inhibits writing of unnecessary, in this case, time and date metadata:

```
# dnssec-keygen -a hmac-md5 -b 128 -C -n user example.com
Kexample.com.+157+23417
```

The following command will generate a public/private key pair using the DSA algorithm for use, say, as a KSK in DNSSEC. It creates a DNSKEY RR with a flags field of 257:

```
# dnssec-keygen -a dsa -b 2048 -f KSK -n zone example.com
Kexample.com.+003+03733
```

The following command will generate a public/private key KEY RR for use with, say, SIG(0) dynamic update (DDNS) security using the RSA-SHA-1 algorithm:

```
# dnssec-keygen -a rsasha1 -b 1024 -T KEY -n user bill.example.com
Kexample.com.+005+03733
```

The following example will generate a public/private key pair suitable for signing with NSEC3 (-3). The key will not be activated for 3 days -A) but the key may be published immediately (default -P argument). The algorithm used will be NSEC3RSASHA1 (007), which is the default when no -a argument is present but -3 is present:

```
# dnssec-keygen -b 2048 -3 -A +3d example.com
Kexample.com.+007+04262
```

The following example, using every default known to mankind, will generate a KSK (for use with DNSSEC) using the algorithm RSASHA1 and with a keysize of 2048 bits suitable for use with the zone *example.com* and with a DNSKEY RR flags field of 257:

```
dnssec-keygen -fk example.com
Kexample.com.+005+13934
```

Next, you generate a replacement key for the key generated in the previous example with a publication date 4 days prior to its activation. The retrial/inactive date and time for the key must have been set for the key as shown in the dnssec-settime command (see dnssec-setttime for details) prior to issuing this dnssec-keygen command. The activation date of the new key will be exactly the same as the retrial/inactivation date and time of the key being replaced. All other characteristics of the key are the same as those defined above including algorithm, key size and DNSKEY flags.

```
dnssec-keygen -i 4d -S Kexample.com.+005+13934
Kexample.com.+005+07345
```

dnssec-revoke Utility

dnssec-revoke is used when RFC 5011 procedures are being used (see Chapter 11's "Key Automation" section). The utility changes the Revoke date and time metadata, adds the REVOKE flag to the DNSKEY RR, and changes the keytag associated with the key. As a consequence of the keytag change it writes a new set of key files.

dnssec-revoke Syntax

```
dnssec-revoke [-f] [-h] [-E engine] [-K directory] [-r] [-v level] keyfile
```

dnssec-revoke Arguments

Table 9–13 shows the various arguments available with the dnssec-revoke utility.

Table 9–13. dnssec-revoke Arguments

Option	Parameter	Meaning and Use
-f		Overwrites existing files with the same name. This argument should used with extreme caution since it may imply a more serious problem.
-h		Outputs a summary of the dnssec-keygen options and exits.
-E	engine	Only applicable if BIND built to support pkcs11 (cryptoki). Not available with standard Ubuntu, FreeBSD, or Windows distributions.
-K		Defines a directory in which the key files are maintained. Default assumes the current working directory.
-r		After creating the new keyset files, this removes the original files.
-v	level	Defines the debugging level and may take the values 0 to 3.
keyfile		The name of the keyset of the key that should be revoked (any suffix will be ignored).

dnssec-revoke Example

The following example shows the normal usage of dnssec-revoke. Arguments are rarely required.

```
dnssec-revoke Kexample.com.+005+18181
Kexample.com.+005+18309
```

This shows that the new keytag for the revoked keyset file is 128 higher than the old one, which is the normal result.

dnssec-settime Utility

The dnssec-settime utility manipulates metadata maintained in the .private file of a key (or keyset) and is indicated by the presence of a v1.3 format header. While this utility allows manipulation of the Revoke metadata (-R argument) it does not add the REVOKE flag to the DNSKEY RR required for correct operation using RFC 5011 procedures (see Chapter 11's "Key Automation" section). Instead, the dnssec-revoke utility should be used to revoke a key when using RFC 5011 procedures.

dnssec-settime Syntax

```
dnssec-settime [-A date] [-D date] [-E engine] [-f] [-h] [-I date]
     [-K directory] [-P date] [-p field] [-R date] [-u] [-v debug] keyfile
```

dnssec-settime Arguments

Table 9–14 shows the various arguments available with the dnssec-settime utility.

Table 9–14. dnssec-settime Arguments

Option	Parameter	Meaning and Use
-A	date	Activation time. For usage and meaning, see "Timing Metadata" under dnssec-keygen.
-D	date	Delete time. For usage and meaning, see "Timing Metadata" under dnssec-keygen.
-E	engine	Only applicable if BIND built to support pkcs11 (cryptoki). Not available with standard Ubuntu, FreeBSD, or Windows distributions.
-f		Used to create a v1.3 header containing date and time metadata on a keyset that does not have this information (indicated by a v1.2 header). When metadata is created, it is initially populated with a creation date set to the UCT runtime of the utility, a publish date (set to now in the absence of any -P argument), and an activation date (set to now in the absence of any -A argument). Additional metadata fields are only added if the appropriate argument is present (-D, -I or -R). If used with a keyset that already contains metadata, it has no effect.
-h		Outputs a summary of the dnssec-keygen options and exits.
-I	date	Retrial/inactive time. For usage and meaning, see "Timing Metadata" under dnssec-keygen.
-K	directory	Defines the absolute or relative path to a directory in which the keyset-name exists. If not defined the current directory is assumed.
-P	date	Publish time. For usage and meaning, see "Timing Metadata" under dnssec-keygen.
-p	field	Causes output of the field date and time meta data to be displayed. field may take the case-insensitive value A (activation time), D (deletion time), I (retrial/inactivation time), P (publish time), R (revoke time) or all (A/D/I/P/R). Times displayed are in UCT unless the -u argument is used.
-R	date	Revoke time. For usage and meaning, see "Timing Metadata" under dnssec-keygen.

Option	Parameter	Meaning and Use
-u		Only valid with -p and causes the time and date metadata to be output in seconds from midnight January 1, 1970 (UNIX epoch).
-v	debug	May take the value 1 to 10 for various levels of debugging.
keyset-name		The name of the keyset associated with the key being manipulated without any file suffix; for example, Kexample.com.+005+12732. The keyset will contain files with .private and .key suffixes.

dnssec-signzone Utility

The dnssec-signzone utility secures a zone file by cryptographically signing it using a public key (asymmetric) algorithm for use in DNSSEC to create a signed zone (see Chapter 11). Zones are signed using one or more ZSKs and optionally one or more KSKs. Use of separate ZSKs and KSKs is the currently IETF recommended best practice (RFC 4641). The utility performs the following tasks:

1. Sorts the RRs into canonical order (alphabetic based on name).

2. Adds an NSEC RR for each name in the zone file such that it is possible to **chain** through the list of all valid names. Alternatively, NSEC3 RRs (-3 argument) may be generated used hashed next names. This process provides *proof of nonexistence* of any name.

3. If an unsigned zone file is used as input, it signs each RRset in the zone file by adding an RRSIG RR (a digital signature), including the NSEC/NSEC3 RRs added in Step 2, using one or more ZSKs.

4. If a signed zone file is used as input, it signs the DNSKEY RRset comprising the ZSK(s) and KSK(s) at the zone apex or root with the KSK(s) if requested.

5. Optionally creates (through the -g argument) files containing the DS RR and the KSK for use by the parent zone to create a chain of trust.

6. Writes a signed zone file. The default is to append .signed to the zone file name.

The RRSIG RRs that sign each RRset (in Step 3) have a start time value (when they become valid) and an end time value (when they expire). By default, time dnssec-signzone uses the UTC value of the local run time minus 1 hour (for clock skew) as the start time; the end time is set to the start time plus 30 days. If nothing else is done to the signed zone file, it will become invalid after this period. Both start and end values can be changed by arguments described in Table 9–15. The input zone file, the zone file to be signed or re-signed, may be an unsigned zone file or it can be a signed zone file. If it is a signed file, existing signatures may be renewed, depending on their remaining period of validity. The default behavior is that any signature that has less than one quarter of its time remaining will be renewed to either the default (30 days) or a user-defined value. Thus if the original signature period was 30 days, only RRSIG RRs with less than 7.5 days remaining will be renewed.

If the ZSK and KSK values to be used in the signing process are not defined explicitly, the dnssec-signzone command will use any DNSKEY value in the zone file for which it can find a corresponding private key in the current directory to sign the file. While leading to much shorter command lines (and the dnssec-signzone command line can get pretty big), it is always better to explicitly define the ZSK and KSK values in the command line to ensure that the results are as expected. This is especially true when key rollovers are being processed (see the "Secure Zone Maintenance" section in Chapter 11) when inactive DNSKEY RRs may be present in the zone file.

All time values used in dnssec-signzone operations are relative to UTC (historically known as GMT or Greenwich Mean Time), so it is vital that both the name server clock is correctly synchronized to a suitable time source; for instance, using NTP or the ntpdate command *and* that the time zone is correctly configured on the system.

■ **Note** If a signed file, say, master.example.com.signed, is input to a dnssec-signzone command, the output file will, unless changed by the -f option described in Table 9–14, be master.example.com. signed. signed—perhaps not the desired result.

---

dnssec-signzone Syntax

```
dnssec-signzone [-3 salt] [-A] [ -a ] [ -c class ] [ -d directory ] [-E engine] [↵
 -e end-time ]
    [ -f output-file ] [ -g ] [-H iterations] [ -h ] [ -i interval ] [-K directory]↵
[ -k ksk-key-file ]
    [ -l domain   ] [-I input-format] [-i  interval] [-j jitter] [ -N soa-serial] [-n threads]
    [-O output-format] [ -o origin ] [-P] [ -p ] [ -r randomdev ] [-S][ -s start-time ]
    [-T ttl] [ -t ] [-u] [ -v level ] [-x]  [ -z ]  zonefile [ zsk-key-file]
```

dnssec-signzone Arguments

Table 9–15 describes the options available with the dnssec-signzone utility.

Table 9–15. dnssec-signzone Arguments

Option	Parameter	Meaning and Use
-3	salt	Indicates the zone will be signed using NSEC3 RRs. If omitted, the zone will be signed using NSEC RRs. salt is pairs of hex characters (0-9, A-F) that will be appended to each name before hashing when generating NSEC3 RRs (see Chapter 13's "NSEC3PARAM" section). If no salt is required, use a single - (dash/minus).
-A		Only relevant when either the -3 or -u argument is used. -A indicates that the OPTOUT flag will be set on all NSEC3 RRs and that only secure delegations will be signed (see Chapter 11's "Opt-Out" section). -AA indicates that the OPT-OUT flag will be unset for all NSEC3 RR and may be used when rebuilding the chains with the -u argument.
-a		Verifies the generated signatures. A new zone file is not written.
-c	class	The default is IN, but this may take the standard optional values of CH (CHAOS) or HS (HESIOD).

Option	Parameter	Meaning and Use
-d	directory	Looks for key-files in the defined directory as opposed to the current working directory.
-E	engine	Only applicable if BIND built to support pkcs11 (cryptoki). Not available with standard Ubuntu, FreeBSD, or Windows distributions.
-e	end-time	Defines the time the RRSIG RRs will expire; defaults to 30 days, but may be overridden with this option. May take the format YYYYMMDDHHMMSS or +secs (seconds from -s start-time) or now+secs (seconds from current run time).
-f	output-file	Defines the file name of the signed zone file to be created. The default output file name is the zone file name with .signed appended to it; for instance, if the zone file name is master.example.com, the default output file name is master.example.com.signed. When signing (or re-signing) a signed zone, this value should be the same as the input file name to avoid changes to the named.conf file.
-g		If present, generates files containing the DS RR and the DNSKEY RR to be used by the parent zone when creating a chain of trust. The files are named dsset-domain. and keyset-domain. (both files names terminate with a dot) where domain is the value of the -o domain option.
-H	iterations	Only relevant to when -3 or -u arguments are used. Indicates the number of iterations that will be used when hashing the names used in NSEC3 RRs. The value iterations will appear in all NSEC3 RRs and the NSEC3PARAM RR.
-h		Displays a short description of each option available and terminates.
-i	interval	Defines the time in seconds after which RRSIG RRs will be retained; otherwise they will be renewed. The default is to take one quarter of the time from the RRSIG start to its expiry. Thus if the default difference of 30 days is being used, any record having more than 7.5 days remaining will be retained; otherwise it will be re-signed for another 30 days or the value defined by the -s and -e options. The -i option may be used to explicitly change the time at which records are re-signed, thus -i 3600 will retain (not re-sign) any RRSIG that has more than 1 hour remaining, and -i 2419200 will only retain RRSIG RRs that have more than 28 days remaining. All others will be re-signed.
-K	directory	Defines a directory (absolute or relative to the current directory) where the DNSSEC keys used to sign the zone may be found. If not defined, the current directory will be used.

Option	Parameter	Meaning and Use
-k	ksk-key-file	Defines the key to be used as the KSK (ignores the value of the flags field in its DNSKEY RR) where key-file is the name of the key generated by the dnssec-keygen utility. This key will be used to sign the DNSKEY RRset at the zone apex and to generate any required DS RRs for use in a chain of trust (if the -g option is used). The -k option may appear more than once if a zone is *double-signed* (see Chapter 11). The key-file name is used *without* either the .key or .private suffix (see examples that follow). If this option is not present, dnssec-signzone will attempt to guess the key by inspecting the flags field of the DNSKEY RRs in the zone, but it is much safer to control the behavior using this option at the expense of longer command lines.
-l	domain	Generates a DNSSEC lookaside validation (DLV) record set in a file named dlvset-domainname. DLV is an experimental RR type that replaces the normal DS RR with a DLV RR (similar in every respect), which is added to a unique zone controlled by use of the dnssec-lookaside statement in the named.conf file. The domain value is appended to the zone name for all KSK keys in the zone file; that is, if the zone name is example.com and, say, -l dlv.example.net is used, then the DLV RR name is example.com.dlv.example.net. (DLV is described in Chapter 11.)
-I	input-format	Optional. May take the value text (default) or raw. Use -I raw when signing a zone that is being dynamically updated (using DDNS) to indicate the input is in non-text (.jnl compatible) format.
-i	interval	Optional. When a zone is signed (or re-signed), all signatures (RRSIG RRs) generated during the signing will expire at the same time. This argument indicates that a random number of seconds, up to a maximum of interval seconds, will be added to each expiry time.
-N	soa-serial	Optional. Defines how the SOA serial number (sn) field will be handled during zone signing. May take the value keep (default; SOA serial number is unchanged), increment or incr (SOA is incremented by 1), or unixtime (SOA set to UNIX epoch time; seconds from January 1, 1970).
-n	threads	By default, a single thread is started for each CPU detected. This can be overridden using the threads value.
-O	output-format	Optional. May take the value text (default) or raw. raw indicates the zone is being dynamically updated (using DDNS) and the output in non-text (.jnl compatible) format.
-o	origin	Defines the name of the zone apex. If not specified, the name of the zone file is assumed to be the zone origin.
-P		Optional. Disable post-signing verification tests. Normal post-signing verification checks for at least one non-revoked self-signed KSK in zone, that all revoked keys are self-signed, and that all RRs are signed with the ZSK(s) algorithm(s).

Option	Parameter	Meaning and Use
-p		Uses pseudo random data; while faster, this is significantly less secure and in general should only be used if a suitable, ample supply of entropy is not available to the server on which the dnssec-signzone is being executed.
-r	randomdev keyboard	Defines the source of randomness. The default is to use /dev/random, in which the OS captures randomness (entropy) from various system events. If this source becomes depleted, the utility will apparently freeze, waiting for more entropy. If this happens, typing any characters on the keyboard will allow capturing of randomness from the typing intervals. Many systems also provide /dev/urandom, which is faster but significantly less secure. If neither device is present, the value keyboard may be used to force use of the keyboard technique described earlier. The default is to use /dev/random if it exists.
-S		Optional. Indicates that smart signing will be used, in which case the -k argument and the zsk-key-file arguments should be omitted. Instead, the key file directory (-K) will be searched for suitable KSK and ZSK keys and the zone signed with all suitable keys. If there is no -K argument, the current directory will be searched. The DNSKEY RRs for all suitable keys are automatically included in the output zone file (the input file, if different, is not updated). Suitable keys are defined by their metadata fields according to the rules previously described under "dnssec-keygen Timing Metadata."
-s	start-time	Defines the time the RRSIG RRs will become valid. The default is UTC minus 1 hour for clock skew, but it may be set explicitly using this option. May take the format YYYYMMDDHHMMSS or +secs (seconds from current run time).
-T		Optional. Only valid when the -S argument is used. Defines the TTL that will apply to all imported DNSKEY RRs unless a DNSKEY RR is already present in which case its TTL will be applied to all imported DNSKEY RRs. If -T is not present and no DNSKEY RR(s) are present, the default TTL for the zone is applied. The time may use the standard BIND shortforms (w, d, m, or h; case insensitive) and if none is present, seconds are assumed.
-t		Prints statistics on completion of the zone signing.
-u		Optional. Only used when a previously signed zone is used as input. When present, it will rebuild the NSEC/NSEC3 chains. It must always be used when changing from NSEC to NSEC3; from NSEC3 to NSEC or when changing the value of salt (-3); iterations (-H); when changing the OPTOUT zone status (using either -A or -AA); and when any DS RR is added to the file. If -u is not specified and the input zone is already signed, the previous values of the NSEC/NSEC3 RRs will be unchanged.
-v	level	May take the value 1 to 10 for various levels of debugging.

Option	Parameter	Meaning and Use
-z		Ignores KSK (SEP) flag on keys found in DNSKEY RRs. Setting this option allows a KSK to be used as a ZSK, but by ignoring the SEP flag, it does not perform the KSK signing function even if a -k option is defined. To avoid problems, DNSKEY RRs should always have the correct flags set, which is controlled by the dnssec-keygen utility options.
-x		Optional. If present, only sign the DNSKEY RRset at the zone apex using the KSK. If omitted, the DNSKEY RRset will be signed using both the KSK and the ZSK.
zonefile		The name of the zone file containing the records to be signed. May be an unsigned or a signed zone file. This file name may be the same as that used on the -f option if required. If signing a signed zone file, it may be convenient to retain the same zone file name on the output file to save changing the named.conf file.
zsk-key-file		Not required if -S argument used. Defines the key-file name (generated by the dnssec-keygen utility) to be used as the ZSK. Multiple zsk-key-file values may be used to allow signing with multiple keys.

dnssec-signzone Examples

The following examples illustrate the use of the dnssec-signzone utility (there are a number of other examples throughout Chapter 11). The first example signs the zone file master.example.com using a separate KSK and ZSK, both of which are in the current working directory using the default 30-day signature period:

```
# dnssec-signzone -k Kexample.com.+003+12456 -o example.com \
 -t master.example.com Kexample.com.+005+03556
master.example.com.signed
Signatures generated:                        20
Signatures retained:                          0
Signatures dropped:                           0
Signatures successfully verified:             0
Signatures unsuccessfully verified:           0
Runtime in seconds:                       0.357
Signatures per second:                   53.079
```

The \ in this example splits the line for presentation purposes only. The command should appear as a single line to the OS. In this example, the –t option shows the typical statistics output by the utility.

The next example shows use of the end time option to provide a 90-day validity period; separate ZSKs and KSKs are used:

```
# dnssec-signzone -k Kexample.com.+003+12456 -o example.com \
-e 7776000 -t master.example.com Kexample.com.+005+03555
```

The -e option could have been specified as, say, 20050614110523 (using the date format) if that is more convenient; however, assuming the zone signing policy is fixed (that is, it's always 90 days), the time in seconds is calculated only once rather than adding 90 days to the current date on every run!

The next example shows signing the zone with two KSKs and two ZSKs. The example also requests a DS keyset (the -g option) for sending to the parent. The resulting dsset-example.com. file will contain two DS RRs, one for each of the KSKs:

```
# dnssec-signzone -k Kexample.com.+003+12456 -k Kexample.com.+005+33789 \
 -g -o example.com -t master.example.com Kexample.com.+005+03556 \
 Kexample.com.+005+44776
```

In this example, the DNSKEY RRset at the zone apex will be signed four times, and all other RRsets signed twice for use in double-signing key-rollover strategies, which are described in Chapter 11.

When used in what BIND calls smart signing mode, a significant number of parameters may be omitted. In the following example, all the zone keys are assumed to be present in the directory /var/named/keys:

```
dnssec-signzone -t -o example.com -K /var/named/keys master.example.com
```

More examples of smart signing, plus examples covering the creation and maintenance of zone keys, are provided in section 3 of Chapter 11.

Diagnosing DNS Problems

DNS problems can come in many shapes and sizes—no single method fits all. Instead, this section approaches DNS diagnosis in two ways:

- *What to do before the problem happens*: This covers both fault prevention and having the necessary tools and information available before a problem occurs.

- *What to do when a problem occurs*: Some techniques that may help isolate the problem will be presented.

Finally, the section looks at a relatively nasty problem that may happen increasingly in the future—in this case, a secure zone's signature has expired—and shows how it is also simple to interpret information incorrectly.

Before the Problem Happens

A number of sensible precautions can be taken before any problem happens that may allow you to avoid, or at the very least minimize, the headless-chicken act that can occur if you are told that your domain is unreachable.

Log All Changes

Comment features are available in zone files, named.conf, and all other files that may be used in DNS configurations. Keep a log in the file of each change made to the file. Using the file rather than, or in addition to, a paper record means the information (usually) can't be lost or mislaid! As a minimum, the change should contain the date, the name or initials of the person who made the change, and what changes, no matter how trivial, were made to the file. The majority of problems in relatively stable systems arise from a simple change—they are always simple—that had an unintended side effect. Close examination of the change logs may be the fastest way to resolve the problem. Dynamic update can present a problem, but there are strategies available to help here also (see "Logging").

Back Up Files

While it might sound trivial, regular backup of all the major configuration and zone files is essential. A good versioning system or a conventional backup program can be used for this process.

Logging

Design and configure your logs to ensure you have enough data to let you diagnose any problem that may have occurred without—and there will always be exceptions to this—having to reconfigure your logs, and then try to reproduce the problems. BIND's logging features are extremely powerful, particularly the ability to control the number and size of the files produced if you are short on disk space. As a general rule, keep at least three days of logs and log as much information as practical (severity info; or lower in the channel statement). Stream the logs if that makes operational sense. Many administrators don't like doing this—they would rather an overall picture of what is happening from a single log rather than having to look at multiple logs and synchronize times. As a minimum, use the print-category yes;, print-severity yes;, and print-time yes; features of the channel statement. If dynamic updates are being used, it is seriously worth considering streaming this log using a category update statement, as shown here:

```
logging {
    ....
    channel example-update {
    file "/var/log/named/update.log" versions 3 size 1m;
    severity info;
    print-time yes;
    print-severity yes;
    print-category yes;
    };
    category update{
    example-update;
    };
};
```

Understand what a normal log looks like. Take some time to review a log file for a normal operational period. If the first time you look at a BIND log is when a problem has been reported, you have no real basis for spotting abnormalities.

Tools

Always run named-checkconf after any named.conf changes. It won't find everything, but it will pick up those trivial errors. The alternative is to let the BIND reload find the single missing semicolon in your 200-item change and take your name server offline while you are thrashing around in the bowels of vi (or your favorite editor) trying to fix it before anyone really notices.

Take the time to get thoroughly familiar with either dig or nslookup before you need to use them—the one you select is a matter of preference and may be a function of what systems you have available or need to work with. nslookup is typically available on Windows and dig is not. If you only work on Linux, Unix, or BSD and are using DNSSEC, you have no choice: dig is the only utility that supports DNNSEC.

External Sources

Always keep a list of two or three recursive name servers handy at all times that you can use as an alternative source for dig commands (for instance, dig @ns2.example.net www.example.com) to diagnose your own domain. With the push to remove open resolvers such recursive servers are getting increasingly rare (try Google's public DNS servers at the IPv4 addresses 8.8.8.8 and 8.8.4.4) but they can help you triangulate where a problem may be coming from or which users it may be affecting.

Similarly, make sure you keep the names of a couple of whois servers (your favorite domain registration web site should also provide such a service) so that you can verify the domain has not expired—yes, it does happen, especially where you may not be the responsible authority.

When the Problem Occurs

So the fateful day arrives and you get the dreaded call—your domain is unreachable. After the panic attack, what should you do? Unfortunately, there is no single solution. While there is usually a tendency to jump into action, always resist it. Too many administrators confuse the word "action" with "progress." Remember the old doctor's adage, "Do no harm." Unless you know what you are doing and why you are doing it, you may make the problem worse than it was! Instead, the following sections list in rough priority what you can do to locate the cause.

Make No Assumptions

Take nothing for granted. Verify immediately that everything is operational—name servers, web sites, mail servers, backbone links, routers, firewalls, etc.

Describe the Problem

Establish the precise nature of the problem: Does it happen all the time? When did it start to happen? What software was being used (for instance, a browser)? Can users still access e-mail or use some other domain-based services? What is their local DNS configuration and addresses? If they bypass the DNS, can they still access, say, the web site using an explicit IP address format URL such as http://192.168.2.3? All this is designed to get a precise picture of what is happening.

Scope the Problem

Establishing the scope of affected users is a vital step. Is it all users everywhere or just a single group of users? Is there a common DNS involved (which may be poisoned), or does it affect everyone? Is it a single zone or all zones on a single name server?

Once you know where to start looking, you can decide whether log inspection and/or DNS inspection are the most appropriate techniques to use next.

Check Your Logs

Assuming that yours is a disciplined operation, check for recent changes in configuration; for instance, check the change logs in the zone and named.conf files, or whatever process you use for change control. Now it's time to take a look at the BIND logs.

The first step is to verify your logs for around the time you think the problem started and work forward. In the first instance, this should probably just be a rudimentary check for any obvious error messages and failures. BIND logs are reasonably good; they output lengthy text messages describing the problem—it may not always describe the actual problem, but it will at least give you an indication of where to start looking. The following log fragment may serve to illustrate:

```
updating zone 'example.com/IN': adding an RR at 'www.example.com' A
updating zone 'example.com/IN': could not get zone keys for secure dynamic update
updating zone 'example.com/IN': RRSIG/NSEC update failed: permission denied
```

This example (the date and time have been removed for brevity) occurred when using secure dynamic update with a DNSSEC signed zone. The actual error is described by the second log entry; the third log entry merely describes the effect of the error. In the preceding case, the zone key being requested was indeed present and in the correct directory. At first blush, the log message was incorrect; however, further examination of the file containing the zone key showed that its permissions were incorrect. The log message was correct in that it described the effect of the error—BIND could not read the key in this case because it was denied permission. Sure, it would have been nice if the message had said "Permission denied," but we can't have everything in life.

Start Digging

Either dig or nslookup are the next tools if nothing obvious has turned up in the log. Start by using a dig (or nslookup) at all the authoritative name servers for the domain for both the domain apex and the particular RR that may be having a problem, say www.example.com. The following commands assume the ubiquitous example.com domain with name servers of ns1.example.com (IP 192.168.2.3) and ns2.example.com (IP 192.168.54.3). The following two commands will give you a quick picture:

```
# dig @ns1.example.com example.com any
# dig @ns2.example.com example.com any
```

The first thing to note in the dig output is whether the IP address associated with ns1.example.com and ns2.example.com resolve to the actual IPs for the two servers, which indicates the local name server is working correctly. If the name format is used, dig will use your locally configured name server to perform the lookup of ns1.example.com and ns2.example.com. If your domain has been hijacked or corrupted, these may not resolve correctly, and your first pointer may be already visible. Check that the SOA serial number, the A RRs for the name servers, and any other RRs such as MX are all correct and as expected. Finally, check that the aa (Authoritative Answer) flag in the >>HEADER<< section is present. Repeat using the IP address of the name servers:

```
# dig @192.168.2.3 example.com any
# dig @192.168.54.3 example.com any
```

Confirm that the data is the same for the two sets of outputs. If all is correct so far, verify any failing record, such as www.example.com, using the following two commands:

```
# dig @192.168.2.3 www.example.com any
# dig @192.168.54.3 www.example.com any
```

While it is possible to either omit ANY from the preceding command (it defaults to a) or use the value a, it is always better to use the value ANY, which will return all RRs with the preceding name and can occasionally yield very interesting results. Confirm that the values are the same in both responses and correct and that again the aa flag is set.

The preceding process has essentially eliminated the authoritative name servers from the problem, so it's time to start looking further afield. Locate one or more name servers that are being used by any affected users—you can get this information from their /etc/resolv.conf on Linux, Unix, or BSD systems, or through Network Properties or using the ipconfig command on most Windows systems. Use the following dig commands with the IP address of this particular name server, assumed in this case to be 192.168.254.1:

```
# dig @192.168.254.1 example.com any
# dig @192.168.254.1 example.com soa
# dig @192.168.254.1 www.example.com any
```

Again, with the move to remove open resolvers, this may be increasingly difficult to do from a location outside the scope server by the particular resolver. You may have to get the end user to issue the command—with all the problems that may entail. Confirm that the data is the same as that provided from the authoritative name server. It should be exactly the same with the exception that the aa flag would not be typically set; if it is set, immediately repeat the dig command and it should disappear. The reason it may be set is that when a caching name server supplies any RR that it obtains directly from an authoritative server, the aa flag is set; if it is supplied from its cache, it will not be set. Thus, if set on the first dig, the cached RR may have timed out and been reread from the authoritative servers, whereas the second dig must have obtained it from the cache, and therefore the aa flag will not be set. While authoritative name servers will provide SOA RRs using the ANY query type when accessing a caching server, they will typically only provide the NS RRs, and all others, the SOA in this particular case, will have to be explicitly requested.

Diagnosing the Problem

This brief example illustrates diagnosis of a particular problem—in this case, a DNS security-related problem. While this may seem a little obscure for many users, it does illustrate a number of points of general interest when diagnosing DNS-related problems. The first is to make no assumptions. The second is that, with the increasing use of DNSSEC, there are two separate worlds: a *security-aware* world and a *security-oblivious* world. They coexist and may not even be aware of each other until it really matters.

The scenario is that a client is having a problem reaching a particular web site, www.example.com, and the problem started happening about two hours ago. We do not own the domain example.com and know nothing about it, but since we know something about name servers, we have been asked to help. The client is using a caching name server with an address of 192.168.2.3. We checked the web site from our location and we can get the web site perfectly. We use dig to check the address as normal:

```
dig www.example.com
; <<>> DiG 9.7.2-P2 <<>> www.example.com
;; global options:  printcmd
;; Got answer:
;; ->>HEADER<<- opcode: QUERY, status: NOERROR, id: 1957
;; flags: qr aa rd ra; QUERY: 1, ANSWER: 4, AUTHORITY: 2, ADDITIONAL: 2

;; QUESTION SECTION:
;www.example.com. IN A

;; ANSWER SECTION:
www.example.com. 86400 IN A 10.1.2.1
www.example.com. 86400 IN A 172.16.2.1
www.example.com. 86400 IN A 192.168.2.5
www.example.com. 86400 IN A 192.168.254.3

;; AUTHORITY SECTION:
example.com.  86400 IN NS ns1.example.com.
example.com.  86400 IN NS ns2.example.com.
```

```
;; ADDITIONAL SECTION:
ns1.example.com.  86400 IN A 192.168.2.6
ns2.example.com.  86400 IN A 192.168.23.23

;; Query time: 15 msec
;; SERVER: 192.168.254.2#53(ns1.example.net)
;; WHEN: Thu Jun 02 17:20:36 2005
;; MSG SIZE  rcvd: 165
```

Note that we just made two mistakes with this command: the first is we did not use the name server of our client (using dig @192.168.2.3 www.example.com)—though in this case it would have made no difference to our results—and the second mistake was we made the *assumption* that the A record was the only important one. By simply changing the dig command we issue to use ANY, not the default (A), this is the output we get:

```
dig www.example.com any
;; Truncated, retrying in TCP mode.

; <<>> DiG 9.7.2-P2 <<>> www.example.com any
;; global options:  printcmd
;; Got answer:
;; ->>HEADER<<- opcode: QUERY, status: NOERROR, id: 1725
;; flags: qr aa rd ra; QUERY: 1, ANSWER: 8, AUTHORITY: 2, ADDITIONAL: 2

;; QUESTION SECTION:
;www.example.com.  IN ANY

;; ANSWER SECTION:
www.example.com.  86400 IN A 10.1.2.1
www.example.com.  86400 IN A 172.16.2.1
www.example.com.  86400 IN A 192.168.2.5
www.example.com.  86400 IN A 192.168.254.3
www.example.com.  86400 IN RRSIG A 5 3 86400
   20050629162118 (Y43c= )
www.example.com.  3600 IN  NSEC example.com. A RRSIG NSEC
www.example.com.  3600 IN  RRSIG NSEC 5 3 3600 20050629161227 (
   20050530151227 3977 example.com.
   SnZJ96ZkmDaB6q4v9PHAMpZuPOKDshlj7loPXL4= )
www.example.com.  3600 IN  RRSIG NSEC 5 3 3600 20050629161227 (
   20050530151227 12513 example.com.
   s9GMC2J+1LVLOiwWST7yDgD8JC2IzzPEsj+dijE= )

;; AUTHORITY SECTION:
example.com.  86400 IN NS ns1.example.com.
example.com.  86400 IN NS ns2.example.com.

;; ADDITIONAL SECTION:
ns1.example.com.  86400 IN A 192.168.2.6
ns2.example.com.  86400 IN A 192.168.23.23

;; Query time: 31 msec
;; SERVER: 192.168.254.2#53(ns1.example.net)
;; WHEN: Thu Jun 02 17:21:14 2005
```

```
;; MSG SIZE  rcvd: 711
```

A considerable amount of material was cut from this output purely for the sake of brevity. The point, however, is already clear: we have a significant indication as to the probable error. The various additional RRs in this output, RRSIG and NSEC, are related to DNSSEC security. The example.com zone is signed—and further diagnostic work will show us that the signatures have expired, rendering the domain invisible to security-aware name servers but still available to security-oblivious name servers and other diagnostic tools. We did not see the additional output on the first dig because the basic dig command is not security aware. We can get results with no indication of any security context—that is the way the standards are supposed to work. If we do not ask for it, we do not get it. Had we set the +dnssec option, we would have received additional data and an indication of the problem. We were able to reach the web site because our local name server is also not security aware (it does not use a dnssec-enable yes; statement or the default). This situation will become increasingly common over the next few years. At the risk of sounding trite, it will be increasingly necessary to dig below the surface.

■ **Note** As previously noted, the drive to remove open resolvers from the Internet, for extremely laudable reasons, means it is becoming increasingly difficult to emulate a user's behavior from outside the coverage of their normal resolver by using dig @.... There is no real answer to this problem, other than to have the user try nslookup/dig from their PC, use VNC or a similar tool to get access to their desktop, or have the service provider give you specific access within their allow-recursion ACL—a pretty unlikely event for all but the heaviest of hitters.

Summary

This chapter covered a number of utilities for diagnosing, maintaining, and verifying the DNS system. The chapter covered the nslookup utility used to diagnose name servers, which is generally available on Linux, BSD, and Windows platforms. The nslookup utility provides both command-line and interactive formats and uses a default configuration file to add significant power to the interactive format. The dig utility provides similar functionality to nslookup but is typically available only on systems on which BIND is installed. It is the recommended utility for diagnosing BIND name servers and provides support for the latest DNS features such as DNSSEC. The dig utility has both a command line and batch mode format but no interactive format. The named-checkconf and named-checkzone utilities are used to verify the named.conf and zone files, respectively, before being run on a live name server.

The rndc utility may be used to control the name server operation locally or remotely. Operation of this utility is enabled by use of the controls clause in the named.conf file. rndc mandates secure authentication (using a shared secret) but provides a default mode where the minimal required files are provided using the rndc-confgen utility with the -a option. The rndc utility uses an rndc.conf file to control server access and the keys to be used. An example is shown that allows remote access to more than one name server, each with a separate key. The nsupdate utility allows dynamic updates to the primary master zone file. The nsupdate utility transactions may be secured using either TSIG or SIG(0) security and are enabled by the allow-update or update-policy statements in the named.conf file.

The dnssec-keygen utility is used to generate cryptographic keys used in TSIG, SIG(0), DNSSEC, or for other purposes. The dnssec-signzone utility is used to cryptographically sign a zone file for use in DNSSEC operations.

The next chapter introduces the topic of DNS security, with is divided into the categories of administrative security, zone transfer security, dynamic update (DDNS) security, and, in Chapter 11, DNSSEC. Each security category uses different techniques and has a different level of complexity.

PART III

■ ■ ■

DNS Security

CHAPTER 10

■■■

DNS Secure Configurations

At the macro level, the DNS service is essential to the operation of the Internet. At the micro or local level, the DNS service could be essential to the operation of an enterprise or a humble but much-loved family web site. In all cases, the appropriate investment in security must be made to ensure the effectiveness and safety of the DNS system. The DNS is by its nature a public system and acts like a honeypot for the bad bees of the Internet world. This chapter and Chapter 11 introduce DNS security with the intent of allowing the reader to select the appropriate techniques for the perceived level of threat.

Unfortunately, the term *DNSSEC* has a bad reputation because of its perceived complexity and is frequently used to cover the whole topic of DNS security. There are many facets to DNS security, ranging from relatively simple to implement to brutally complex. This chapter divides security into four topics:

- *Administrative security*: This part of the chapter covers the use of file permissions, server configuration, BIND configuration, and sandboxes (or chroot jails). All of these techniques are relatively simple to implement; they can (and should) be applied to stand-alone DNS servers or to servers that run DNS as one of a number of services. Administrative security is a baseline topic. All the fancy cryptographic techniques in the world are useless if the base system is unstable or has world read-and-write privileges on all of the interesting files.

- *Zone transfers*: Unless a multimaster configuration system is being used, zone transfers are essential to normal operation. Limiting and controlling both the source and destinations of zone transfer operations using physical security, BIND parameters, or external firewalls is always prudent. Secure authentication of the source and destinations of zone transfer operations may or may not be worth the effort.

- *Dynamic updates*: Dynamic updates expose a master zone file to possible corruption, destruction, or poisoning. Not taking sensible precautions to limit access through good system design, BIND parameters, firewalls, or authentication probably constitutes a misplaced reliance on the essential goodness of mankind.

- *Zone integrity*: If it's essential that the zone data used by either another DNS or an end host be correct (that is, query responses have not been tampered with and the returned data could only have come from the zone owner), then DNSSEC is required. DNSSEC is a big and perhaps a vital topic for the long term safety of the Internet and is described in Chapter 11.

Because it is so critical, the DNS system is the subject of many myths, including the "great bug myth." This myth purports that BIND is so full of bugs that we must go to any lengths to protect our systems from its self-destructive ways. Although this may have been true in the bad old days of early version 4 and version 8 releases of BIND, it is no longer the case. DNS systems need to be protected from external sources and attacks, but not from BIND itself. The emphasis in the following sections is primarily on outward-facing security, not inward-facing security.

Security Overview and Audit

Figure 10–1 was introduced in Chapter 3 and is reproduced here as a reminder of the possible sources of threat that form the basis of any security audit. Every data path is a potential source of threat.

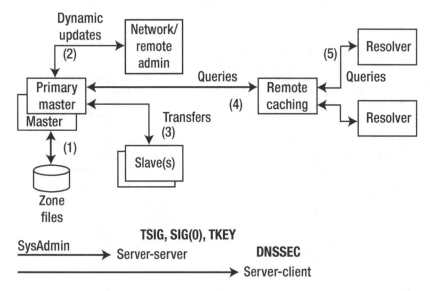

Figure 10–1. Security overview

The critical point in defining security policies and procedures is to understand what needs to be secured—or rather what threat levels need to be secured against and what threats are acceptable. The answers to these two questions will be different if the DNS is running as a root-server versus running as a modest in-house DNS serving a couple of low-volume web sites. There are no specific rules; defining your policy is a matter of blending paranoia with judgment.

DNS Normal Data Flow

Every data flow—that is, each numbered line in Figure 10–1—is a potential source of threat. Table 10–1 defines the potential outcomes of compromise at each point and the possible solutions.

Table 10–1. *DNS Security Threats*

Number	Area	Threat	Classification	Solutions
1	Zone files	File corruption (malicious or accidental)	Local	System administration
2	Dynamic updates	Unauthorized updates, IP address spoofing (impersonating update source)	Server-to-server	Network architecture, Transaction Signatures (TSIG), SIG(0), or disable
3	Zone transfers	IP address spoofing (impersonating update source)	Server-to-server	Network architecture, TSIG, or disable
4	Remote cache	Cache poisoning by IP spoofing, data interception, or a subverted master or slave	Server–client	DNSSEC
5	Resolver queries	Data interception, poisoned cache, subverted master or slave, local IP spoofing	Remote cache–client	DNSSEC

The first phase of any security review is to audit which threats are applicable and how seriously they are rated in the particular organizational circumstances. As an example, if dynamic updates are not supported (BIND's default mode), there will be no dynamic update threat.

It can be easier to disable a process than to secure it. For example, consider zone transfers. If a classic master–slave configuration is being used, then zone transfers will be inevitable and the configuration's security implications must be evaluated. However, it's possible to replace such a configuration with a multiple-master one in which each name server obtains its zone files locally. Thus, zone transfers may be globally disabled. In this environment, synchronization of master zone files must be done by some out-of-band process such as secure FTP or secure e-mail. However, these out-of-band processes may be simpler to organize or already exist. Using such alternative procedures is sometimes referred to as *security by obscurity*. It can be a useful tactical fix but is not always a strategic solution. However, as a matter of principle, it's always more efficient and effective to design-out or remove sources of problems than to attempt to secure poor or unnecessary operational procedures.

Finally, a note of caution: there is a single master to secure; in zone transfers there may be one or two slaves to secure; in dynamic updates there may be tens of update sources to secure; and there may be many hundreds or thousands of remote caches to consider in DNSSEC solutions. In general, the further you go from the master, the more systems you have to consider; consequently, the solutions are more complicated. Unless there is a good reason for not doing so, it's always smart to start from the zone master and work out. It would be a tad embarrassing to have completed a successful implementation of a complex DNSSEC solution, only to discover that anyone in the world could dynamically update your zone files.

Security Classification

Using security classificationis a means to allow selection of the appropriate remedies and strategies for avoiding the implied risk. Many of the following methods are described in detail in this chapter and Chapter 11. The following numbering relates to Figure 10–1.

- *Local threats (1)*: Local threats are usually the simplest to prevent and are typically implemented simply by maintaining sound system-administration policies. All zone files and DNS configuration files should have appropriate read and write access, and they should be securely backed up or maintained in a CVS repository. Stealth DNS servers can be used to minimize public access, and BIND can be run in a *sandbox* or a *chroot jail* (described in the "BIND in a Chroot Jail" section later in the chapter).

- *Server–server (2)*: If an organization runs slave DNS servers, it needs to execute zone transfers. As noted earlier, it's possible to run multiple-master DNS servers rather than master–slave servers, and thus avoid any associated problems. If zone transfers are required, BIND offers multiple configuration parameters that can be used to minimize the inherent risks in the process. TSIG and Transaction KEY (TKEY) also offer cryptographically secure methods for authenticating requesting sources and destinations. Both methods are described in detail in the "Securing Zone Transfers" section later in the chapter. The physical transfers can be secured using Secure Sockets Layer (SSL) or Transport Layer Security (TLS).

- *Server–server (3)*: The BIND default is to deny Dynamic DNS (DDNS) from all sources. If an organization requires this feature, BIND provides a number of configuration parameters to minimize the associated risk; these are described in detail later in this chapter. Network architecture design—that is, all systems involved are within a trusted perimeter—can further reduce the exposure. TSIG and SIG(0) can be used to cryptographically secure the transactions from external sources. Configuration of stealth servers was described in Chapters 4 and 7, and TSIG and SIG(0) security are described in the "Securing Dynamic Updates" section of this chapter.

- *Server–client (4)*: The possibility of remote cache poisoning due to IP spoofing, data interception, and other hacks is likely quite low with modest web sites. However, if the site is high profile, high volume, contains sensitive data, is open to competitive threat, or is a high revenue earner, then a full-scale DNSSEC solution may be essential. Significant effort is being invested by software developers, Registry Operators, Registrars, the RIRs, root-server operators, and others into DNSSEC. Indeed, since the DNS root was signed in July 2010, a number or observers are suggesting that DNSSEC will become the default state for all zones within a reasonable period of time. The definition of reasonable in this context will entirely depend on whether you are of an optimistic or pessimistic disposition.

- *Client–client (5)*: DNSSEC standards define the concept of a *security aware resolver*—a currently mythical entity—that can elect to handle all security validation directly, with the area resolver acting as a relatively passive DNS gateway.

Administrative Security

Administrative security in the context of this book is concerned with the selection and configuration of the DNS software and the server or servers on which it runs. The items in the following section are listed in approximate order of priority, defined in this case as a combination of return for effort expended and its effect on overall security. Clearly, the order is not rigid, nor is it meant to suggest that if you only keep software up to date, the DNS installation will be secure. However, a fully chrooted installation with a known root exploit bug can still create pretty serious havoc. Judgment and local circumstance always override any tactical list, such as the one in the following section. The following sections are presented in the form of checklists with some limited explanations where appropriate.

Up-to-Date Software

Although it may seem trite, keeping software up to date is a vital security component. Upgrading mature, stable software may be an evil, but it is a necessary—and essential—evil for the health and security of an installation. The longer the task is postponed, the worse it gets. The following is offered as a generic upgrade policy:

1. *BIND Announce Mailing List*: The ISC (BIND's author) provides a relatively low volume mailing list for the announcement of BIND releases and BIND specific security issues. You can subscribe to this list at https://lists.isc.org/mailman/listinfo/bind-announce.

2. *Known security exploit*: Subscribe to one of the advisory services provided by SANS (www.sans.org), CERT (www.cert.org), or another organization to take action on BIND and related technology alerts. Depending on the severity of the alert, this can demand an immediate upgrade followed by a quick test before a fast system-wide replacement. It's better in this case to risk a new problem than a known exploit.

3. *Required new feature*: If a new feature is required, time is not generally of the essence. Upgrading should be done slowly, with serious testing of limited initial deployment before a final upgrade of all operational systems.

4. *Time*: Every 12–18 months, the author upgrades operational systems even if items 1, 2, or 3 have required an upgrade recently, and even if it means some serious work. The reasoning here is that the longer this task is put off, the greater the pain of upgrade. Upgrade is slow and includes limited initial deployment before system-wide replacement.

The following additional points may be useful or just plain sensible:

*   *Maintain an upgrade checklist*: This should include, at a minimum, the order of upgrades, previous problems, specific items to verify (such as log messages, dig test scripts, and results), AXFR block tests, and anything else you deem useful. In a busy environment, your own memory is not a useful planning tool, especially if the frequency of upgrade is low. Add to the list after each upgrade. Keep it readily available on a secure intranet, in the configuration file as comments, or in some other suitable location. It must be a living document to be useful.

- *Block communication of the BIND software version*: All the sample `named.conf` configuration files (see Chapter 7) use the `version` statement in an `options` clause to hide the current version of BIND being run. If the version number is not blocked, it is simple to use `dig version.bind txt ch` to discover what version is being used at any particular location. In the event of a known exploit, why boast that you are vulnerable?

Limit Functionality

The best way to limit vulnerabilities is to avoid using exploitable operations, if practical. As an example, by using multiple masters it's possible to run an operational system without doing DNS zone transfers, in which case `allow-transfer` and `notify` statements can be set to "none" in the global options clause. Take some time to ponder alternate strategies and the relative efforts and returns involved in the operations, rather than just opting to use a BIND feature because it exists. Hackers love that way of thinking—it gives them plenty of targets.

Defensive Configuration

A defensive configuration is one in which all the major, especially security-related, features are explicitly identified as enabled or disabled. Such a configuration ignores any default setting and values. It takes as its starting point the site's needs and defines each requirement, positive or negative, using the appropriate configuration statements or other parameters. Defaults are great for us lazy folks, but they can also be dangerous if they change. As an example, the current version of BIND disables DDNS by default. However, many DNS administrators like to add the statement `allow-update {"none";};` explicitly in a global `options` clause, both as clear indication that the feature is not being used and as a protection against a future release that may change the default. A defensive configuration file that identifies all the requirements explicitly is also self-defining; that is, by inspecting the file—without needing to find a manual or reference documentation—the functionality is self-evident. When pandemonium does occur, such self-defining files may be a useful side-effect.

Deny All, Allow Selectively

Even when operations are permitted (for example, in `NOTIFY` or zone transfers), it may be worth globally denying the operation and selectively enabling it, as in the following fragment:

```
options {
....
    allow-transfer {none;}; // no transfer by default
....
};
....
zone "example.com in{
....
    allow-transfer {10.0.1.2;}; // this host only
....
};
```

Although the preceding configuration requires additional typing, it also requires a minor act of thought—always a good thing—before adding the line in the zone clause.

Remote Access

BIND releases come with an administration tool called rndc (described in Chapter 9) that may be used locally or remotely. rndc is a useful tool; however, if you can get access, so can a less friendly person. The BIND default is to enable rndc from the loopback address only (127.0.0.1). If rndc will not be used, it should be explicitly disabled using a null controls clause, as shown here:

```
// named.conf fragment
controls {};
....
```

If rndc is used, then it is recommended that an explicit controls clause be used, even if access is only allowed from localhost, as shown here:

```
// named.conf fragment
controls {
   inet 127.0.0.1 allow {localhost;} keys {"rndc-key"};
};
```

In the preceding fragment, the default key name of rndc-key is shown (generated by the command rndc-confgen -a), and should be replaced with whatever name was allocated to the key being used to control rndc access. The rndc.conf file and those files containing keys such as rndc.key must be protected with limited permissions as described in the following section, "Limit Permissions." BIND thoughtfully provides a simple method to create a default key configuration (rndc-confgen -a) for use with rndc, which for loopback-only (127.0.0.1) use may be adequate to get you started. However, it is neither advisable nor sensible for remote use. Take the few minutes required to learn how to generate your own rndc keys. Change them every 30 to 90 days without fail.

Limit Permissions

The theory behind limiting permissions has two distinct parts that must not be confused and that may have separate implementation issues and strategies:

- *Confidentiality*: This involves limiting access to confidential files used by BIND or the DNS application to ensure that another application or user can't read or write to them.

- *Containment*: This prevents BIND from reading or writing to other locations if it's compromised.

As discussed earlier, this book places more emphasis on protecting the name server from external attack, such as cache poisoning or accessing confidential information, than from damage inflicted by BIND itself being compromised. In this context, the files that BIND uses and their access permissions are of considerable importance. The following list describes seven files or file groups BIND may use and their protection requirements:

- named.conf: This file should be treated as confidential because it contains information about the style of your configuration that may assist an attacker; it frequently contains other interesting information, such as IP addresses, that may be used to launch spoofing and other attacks. The named.conf file should *never* contain key clauses as a matter of policy, including those used for rndc access. Instead, key clauses should be maintained in separate files in a separate directory and included in the named.conf file (using an include statement). If view clauses are being used, then as a minimum those containing private information for use by a stealth configuration (see Chapter 4) should also be contained within separate files and included in the named.conf file. If the organizational policy allows zone clauses or parts of the named.conf file to be controlled or edited by end users or more than one user, then these parts should be saved as separate files in separate directories. In this way, appropriate permissions can be applied and then the files can be included in the final named.conf file. It is worth noting here that trusted-keys clauses contain only public keys, which are not sensitive information, unlike key clauses, which contain shared secrets and are extremely sensitive. The requirement for trusted-keys clauses is to prevent write corruption rather than to prevent unauthorized reading, as is the case for key clauses.

- *Included files*: Each file included in the named.conf file can have different permissions applied to it. The policy should be to categorize the type of file and the required access, and then separate the files into directories whereby directory-level permissions can be applied, rather than fooling around with individual files. Thus, included files containing keys could be saved in a directory called /var/named/keys and private views in a directory called /var/named/views. Any private zone clauses could be saved in, say, /var/named/zone-private. Generally editable zone clauses could be saved in the home directory of the user who is allowed to edit it. Each such directory can be assigned appropriate permissions.

- *Zone files*: Zone files typically contain public information, so there seems little point in protecting them (other than from global write permission). However, if a view clause-based stealth system is being used, then the zone files on the private side of the configuration will contain sensitive data and thus will require separate treatment. Again, it is prudent to separate private zone files into a separate directory such as /var/named/master/private. Zone files that may be edited by users can be placed in the respective home directories with appropriate user permissions, or you can place them in a /var/named/master/ddns directory and allow dynamic updates. Finally, slave zones in, say, /var/named/slave require write permission for BIND.

- *PID file*: This is normally written to /var/run/named.pid or /var/run/named/named.pid. Although it contains sensitive information (the Process Identifier of the named daemon), the information can only be used by root. If you're faced with a root exploit, the PID files are among the last items to be concerned about. The PID file requires write access for BIND and read access for scripts (start, stop, restart, and so on) that make use of it.

- *Log files*: This book configures the logs to be written to the /var/log/named directory mostly for convenience rather than security. In general, the log does not contain sensitive information and does not require special handling. However, if a view clause is being used in a stealth configuration, the log—depending on options—may contain sensitive information relating to private IPs and should be protected.

- *rndc files*: If using rndc, keep in mind that the rndc.conf file (see Chapter 9) and especially any files containing keys, including the default rndc.key file, contain extremely sensitive information and need to be protected.

- *Journal files*: A zone file is normally a read-only file from BIND's perspective. If Dynamic Update (DDNS) is being used, then updates are written to a binary .jnl file for each zone and only periodically written to the zone file. For public zone files, such information is not sensitive; for private zone files, appropriate permissions are required. Once DDNS is invoked for a zone, special procedures are generally required to edit the zone files manually. Therefore, permissions can be made tight. To reflect these permissions, zone files that will use DDNS could be placed in a directory such as /var/named/master/ddns.

Before building a permission strategy, let's look at how BIND is run. BIND 9 can run in three possible ways:

- *Run BIND as* root: This is a dangerous thing to do. It normally requires additional work to override the options defined in most packaged BIND installations. This method of running BIND 9 is not recommended and will not be discussed further.

- *Run BIND under a unique (nonroot) UID (Linux, Unix, or BSD) or user account (Windows)*: This method uses the -u command line argument of BIND (see Chapter 12) and is the standard method used by most packaged installations on Linux, BSD, and Windows (including the Ubuntu 10.04 Server installation described in Chapter 6). The User ID (UID) is typically named for Linux/UNIX, bind if you are running FreeBSD, and the user account is named for Windows.

- *Run BIND in a sandbox or chroot jail*: FreeBSD 8.x default installations use this mode of operation which uses the -t command line argument of BIND (see Chapter 12). Many Linux distributions provide a bind-chroot RPM that can be applied after BIND has been installed to add the necessary directories and scripts to apply the appropriate permissions. With Ubuntu 10.04 Server no explicit chroot package exists and the process is entirely manual though schroot (apt-get install schroot) could be used for this purpose.

The last two methods are described in detail in the "Running BIND 9 as Nonroot" Section. Table 10–2 shows the permissions that lock down the various files to their minimum requirements. Before considering the required file permissions, it's necessary to understand the various stages BIND adopts during its initialization sequence. When BIND 9 is loaded, it runs as user root because it requires certain privileges—notably the ability to allocate and bind to its normal-but-privileged port number of 53, and if rndc is permitted, also to port 953. During this phase, BIND 9 reads all configuration (and include) files as well as zone files (and $INCLUDE files) and logs any failures to syslogd. On completion of this process, it then issues a suid() call (change user name) to the user name defined in the -u command line argument. Only then does it proceed to write the PID file, log, and any other required files. This structure lends itself perfectly to tailoring precise file permissions, because read-only files (from BIND's perspective) can be set to permissions based on their editing requirements. BIND 9, because it running as root during its read phase, can read these files in all cases. Table 10–2 illustrates the kind of structure and flexibility that may be created. This structure may look complex, but it shows the possibilities; also, once established, it requires little maintenance.

■**Note** The preceding sequence is slightly different when running in a chroot jail, which is described in the "BIND 9 in a Chroot Jail" section.

Table 10–2 assumes that BIND 9 runs with a UID of named, editing of secure (but not secret) files is done under a nonroot user with a user name of dnsadmin and a group of root /wheel (to allow su commands if necessary), and editing of multiuser access files (for example, public zone files and zone clauses) is done under a group called dnsusers. The files containing secrets can only be read by BIND and edited by root. Files are placed in the directories named under each file type described earlier. The home directory of dnsadmin is assumed to be /var/named; for dnsusers, it's /home/username or similar. In Table 10–2, the Permissions column shows the directory permission first, separated from the file permissions with a colon (":"). A question mark ("?") indicates that this value may be determined by other system requirements. The setting of limited permissions on Windows systems is described in Chapter 6.

Table 10–2. Directory and File Permissions

File/Group	Typical Location	user:group	Permissions	Notes
named.conf	/etc	dnsadmin:root	? : 0660	Read-only BIND file. dnsadmin can edit.
Included public named.conf	username home directory	username: dnsusers	0770 : 0660	Read-only BIND files. Permissions allow dnsusers group to edit.
Included key files	/var/named/keys	named:named	0400 : 0400	Read-only BIND file. Only root can edit or view.
Included private views	/var/named/views	dnsadmin:root	0770 : 0660	Read-only BIND file. dnsadmin can edit.
Private zone files—no DDNS	/var/named/masters / private	dnsadmin:root	0770 : 0660	Read-only BIND file. dnsadmin can edit.
Private zone files with DDNS	/var/named/masters / ddns	named:root	0770 :0660	Read/write for BIND. dnsadmin can edit.
Slave zone files	/var/named/slaves	named:root	0770 : 0660	Read/write for BIND. dnsadmin can edit if required.
Public zone files	username home directory	username: dnsusers	0770 : 0660	Allows dnsusers group to edit. These files can't be dynamically updated.

File/Group	Typical Location	user:group	Permissions	Notes
`named.pid`	`/var/run/named`	named:named	? : 0664	Allows access by BIND tools/ scripts and root.
`named.log`	`/var/log/named`	named:root	0770 : 0640	Write access for BIND, dnsadmin can read. If not using views, wider permissions can be set depending on local policy.
`rndc.conf`	`/var/named/rndc`	dnsadmin:root	0770 : 0660	Allows access by dnsadmin group.
`rndc.key`	`/var/named/rndc/ke ys`	named:named	0400 : 0400	Only root can edit.

In Table 10–2, FreeBSD users should replace the group root with wheel and named with bind. If the local policy is to allow only BIND administrators to touch any BIND-related material, then some of the preceding configuration will be unnecessary.

The named.conf file fragment that would reflect such a strategy could look something like the following:

```
// named.conf fragment
include "/var/named/rndc/keys/key.clause"; // single file containing rndc keys
include "/var/named/keys/key.clauses"; // single file containing keys
controls {
    inet 127.0.0.1 allow {localhost;} keys {"rndc-key"};
};
options {
    ....
};
include "/var/named/views/private-view.clause"; // hidden private view
view "public-view" {
    include "/home/firstuser/zone.clause";
    zone "example.com" in {
    type master;
    file "var/named/masters/ddns/example.net";
    // key clause referenced below will be in
    // /var/named/keys/keys.clause above
    allow-update {key "example.net";};
    };
};
```

> ■**Note** In Table 10–2 keys are shown in /var/named/keys. When more than one zone is present and especially when used with DNSSEC, an alternative method is to maintain zone specific keys using a structure such as /var/named/zone-name/keys; see Chapter 11 for more details. Directory and file permissions would stay the same in this case.

Running BIND 9 As Nonroot

Most packaged BIND systems, for instance RPMs, Ubuntu/Debian packages, and FreeBSD ports, install BIND to run with a unique (nonroot) UID—typically named on Linux and Windows and bind on FreeBSD. This section describes how to configure your system if BIND is not installed and configured to run with a unique UID and how to set permissions to lock down the files. Even if your BIND system has been installed to run under a unique UID, you may still want to look at and set appropriate file permissions, especially on the more sensitive files. If BIND is running on your system, its status can be interrogated by issuing the following command:

```
# ps aux |grep named
```

It returns something like the following:

```
named  36120  0.0  0.9  5372 4376  ??  Is    1:02PM   0:00.11 named -u named
```

This output shows that the daemon named is running under the UID named (the first named in the line), which is initiated by the -u argument at the end of the line. If the output looks like the following, named is running as root indicated by the first root in the line and the absence of a -u argument:

```
root  36120  0.0  0.9  5372 4376  ??  Is    1:02PM   0:00.11 named
```

Action should be taken immediately to change this state, as described in the following section.

Setting the Run Time UID of BIND

To run BIND under its own UID, you need to create a user and group for the named daemon. By convention this is normally named (or bind under FreeBSD). This book uses named throughout, but you can change it to any appropriate value (for example, dns) if you wish. First, confirm that you do not already have an existing account by using the following command:

```
# id named
uid=255(named) guid=25(named) groups=25(named)
```

The preceding response indicates the UID already exists. If the user account does not exist, the following response is returned:

```
id: named: no such user
```

Try again with id bind, and if there is still no valid user, then create a unique user and group as follows:

```
# groupadd -r named
```

This command adds the group named with the first free system account group (the -r argument). The presence of the group can be confirmed with the command vigr, which displays and allows editing of the list of groups in the system (use :q! to exit vigr without making changes).

Now add the system account named using the following command:

```
# useradd -c 'Bind daemon' -d /var/named -s /sbin/nologin -g named -r named
```

If the -c argument (a comment) contains a space, it must be enclosed in quotes as shown. The -d /var/named is the default directory at login and is required but isn't used because this is a system account without a login or password. The -s /sbin/nologin argument is the Linux/BSD default for a no-shell account, The -g named argument defines the initial group to be used by the account and references the named group you just created. useradd requires that the group named exists, so always define groups before users. The -r argument defines this to be a system account (typically with a UID < 500 for Linux and < 1000 for FreeBSD) with an account name of named.

Setting Permissions for the UID

You now set up and create the permissions for the various essential files. Assume that the user account dnsadmin has already been established as a normal login user account using your favorite tool and is a member of the root group to allow su commands to be issued if required.

■**Note** Some of the following permissions differ from those defined in Table 10–2 because they are applied to a directory and are typically intended to allow inspection of file properties. Specific files within the directory may be set to the values defined in Table 10–2.

To create and set permissions for run time write files (log and PID), use the following commands:

```
# cd /var/log
# mkdir named
# touch named/example.log
# chown named:dnsadmin named/*
# chmod 0660 named/*
# cd /var/run
# mkdir named
# touch named/named.pid
# chown named:named/*
# chmod 0664 named/*
```

The following commands all assume that the various directories have been created. If this is not the case, then a preceding mkdir dirname command should be issued, as shown in the preceding command sequence. Set permissions on any keys directory, as shown in the following commands:

```
# cd /var/named
# chown named:named keys/*
# chmod 04000 keys/*
```

Set permissions on any private zone files:

```
# cd /var/named
# chown -R dnsadmin:root master/private/*
```

```
# chmod -R 0660 master/private/*
```

Set permissions on any DDNS zone files:

```
# cd /var/named
# chown -R named:root masters/ddns/*
# chmod -R 0660 masters/ddns
```

Set permissions on any private-view include files:

```
cd /var/named
chown -R dnsadmin:root views/*
chmod -R 0660 views/*
```

Secure any rndc key files:

```
# cd /var/named
# chown -R named:named rndc/*
# chown -R 0660 rndc/*
```

Secure the named.conf and rndc.conf files:

```
# cd /etc
# chown dnsadmin:root named.conf
# chmod 0660 named.conf
# chown dnsadmin:root rndc.conf
# chmod 0660 rndc.conf
```

Finally, to run BIND, use the following command:

```
# /usr/sbin/named -u named
```

Now verify that BIND is loaded and running using the following command:

```
# ps aux |grep named
```

If it isn't loaded and running, inspect syslog using the following command:

```
vi + /var/log/messages
```

Alternatively, you can use a command such as tail /var/log/messages to display the last ten lines of the file if there isn't much syslog traffic. Then, verify that BIND has loaded the various zones by inspecting the BIND log file:

```
# cat /var/log/named/named.log
zone 0.0.127.in-addr.arpa/IN: loaded serial 1997022700
zone example.com/IN: loaded serial 2010121500
zone localhost/IN: loaded serial 2002022401
running
zone example.com/IN: sending notifies (serial 2010121500)
```

To ensure that BIND starts at boot time, you need to create a script that you have chosen to call named in the startup directory (for Linux, normally /etc/rc.d/init.d, or /etc/rc.d for FreeBSD). Such a script would look like the following code, which is a simplified version of the current scripts being used on Fedora Core. It provides start, stop, and restart services only:

```
#!/bin/sh
#
# named          This shell script takes care of starting and stopping
#                named under its own (non-root) UID.
```

```
#

# Source function library.
. /etc/rc.d/init.d/functions

# Source networking configuration.
. /etc/sysconfig/network

# Check that networking is up.
[ ${NETWORKING} = "no" ] && exit 0

[ -f /usr/sbin/named ] || exit 0

# See how we were called.
case "$1" in
  start)
        # Start daemons.
        echo -n "Starting named: "
        daemon /usr/sbin/named -u named
        echo
        ;;
  stop)
        # Stop daemons.
        echo -n "Shutting down named: "
        killproc named
        echo
        ;;
  restart)
        $0 stop
        $0 start
        exit $?
        ;;
  *)
        echo "Usage: named {start|stop|restart}"
        exit 1
esac

exit 0
```

This script must then be linked to the normal run level(s) used, such as run level 3 (non-X11) and 5 (X11). The default run level is normally defined in /etc/inittab by a line that looks something like this:

```
id:3:initdefault:
```

For the preceding example, you would link the script to the appropriate rc.d run level initialization sequence, which for run level 3 would be as follows:

```
# ln /etc/rc.d/init.d/named /etc/rc.d/rc3.d/S68named
# ln /etc/rc.d/init.d/named /etc/rc.d/rc3.d/K68named
```

To test this process, a command such as the following should be executed:

```
# /etc/rc.d/init.d/named restart
```

The equivalent startup process for FreeBSD users requires adding the following lines to the /etc/rc.conf file:

```
named_enable="YES"  # Run named, the DNS server (or NO).
named_program="/usr/sbin/named"  # assumes a base installation.
named_flags="-u bind"  # Flags for named
```

To be absolutely certain that everything is working while it is still fresh in your mind, the server ideally should be rebooted and named confirmed to be running successfully with a command such as this:

```
# ps aux|grep named
named 36120 0.0 0.9 5372 4376 ?? Is    1:02PM   0:00.11 named -u named
```

Although the preceding process may appear to involve a number of steps, it offers the flexibility of being able to control precisely and flexibly the editing permissions of the various files and file groups used in the operation of a BIND-based DNS system. Running BIND in a chroot jail (or sandbox) offers an alternate strategy and is described in the following section.

BIND 9 in a Chroot Jail

The terms *chroot jail* or *chroot cage* (now frequently referred to as a *sandbox*) are named from the system call chroot("/base/directory");, which takes a base directory argument and doesn't let the application read or write outside the base directory. All referenced files and paths within the chrooted application are appended to the base directory. Thus, if the chroot base directory is /var/named/chroot and the application accesses a file called /etc/named.conf, then the full path is translated to be /var/named/chroot/etc/named.conf. When running BIND, the -t /base/directory command line argument indicates that BIND should run chrooted and defines the base directory to be used. In a chroot environment, both the -t and -u (BIND UID) arguments must be present to provide a secure environment.

Most OS distributions provide a packaged method of running BIND in a chroot jail. The following sections define using such a package for both Linux (Fedora Core) and FreeBSD 8.x. Ubuntu Server 10.04 does not provide a chroot package though BIND9 packages may be run in a schroot system. In the case of Ubuntu, and any other distribution which does not provide a standard package, chroot jails must be manually configured as described below.

Fedora Core bind-chroot Package

DNS may be run in a chroot jail on Fedora Core in one of two ways:

- Selecting the DNS software option during the install process causes a chrooted caching name server installation by default.

- Installing the bind-chroot RPM (for FC 13 this was bind-chroot-9.7.2-1.P2.fc13.i686.rpm).

In the preceding cases, the process is the same because the install process also runs the bind-chroot RPM. The chroot RPM does the following:

- It creates the chroot base directory as /var/named/chroot.

- The following directories are added under /var/named/chroot: etc, var/named, var/run/named, and /dev (containing only null and random).

- Relevant files are copied from the corresponding directories. For instance, /etc/named.conf is copied to /var/named/chroot/etc/named.conf, and ownership of the chroot directories is set to root:named with permissions of 0640.

- The startup script (in /etc/rc.d/init.d/named) is modified to add the argument -t /var/named/chroot to invoke the chroot feature.

The Fedora Core default configuration uses syslogd. If a log file is required, then an appropriate directory must be created. For instance, assume you're creating a log file using the following fragment:

```
logging{
    channel normal_log {
    file "/var/log/named/normal.log" versions 3 size 2m;
    severity error;
    print-time yes;
    print-severity yes;
    print-category yes;
    };
....
```

In this case, a directory /var/named/chroot/var/log/named is required with write permission for the named UID.

FreeBSD 8.x

The installation of DNS on FreeBSD 8.x creates a chroot installation by default with a chroot base of /var/named. The installation performs the following tasks:

- Creates the directory /var/named/etc/namedb and links it to /etc/namedb (by default, FreeBSD organizes all its files, including zone files, under this base directory). Thus, going to the normal location for these files (etc/namedb) follows the link to the chroot location.

- Additionally, the following directories are created under /var/named: var/dump, var/stats, var/run/named, and var/log (with a default file name of named.security.log). Ownership is bind:bind for the directories, and world read permissions are set on all files.

- The file /etc/defaults/rc.conf contains the defaults, as shown in the following fragment:

```
#
# named.  It may be possible to run named in a sandbox, man security for
# details.
#
named_enable="YES"  # Run named, the DNS server (or NO).
named_program="/usr/sbin/named"  # path to named, if you want a different one.
named_flags="-u bind"   # Flags for named
named_pidfile="/var/run/named/pid" # Must set this in named.conf as well
named_chrootdir="/var/named" # Chroot directory (or "" not to auto-chroot it)
named_chroot_autoupdate="YES" # Automatically install/update chrooted
    # components of named. See /etc/rc.d/named.
named_symlink_enable="YES" # Symlink the chrooted pid file
```

- As always, if changes are required to this file, they should be made to /etc/rc.conf, which overrides the equivalent value in /etc/defaults/rc.conf.

- The script (/etc/rc.d/named) processes the parameters in rc.conf to create or update the configuration during startup. This startup script creates a default rndc configuration by running the command rndc-confgen -a (see Chapter 9), which allows rndc access from localhost only (assuming the default controls clause).

Manual Configuration of Chroot Jail

This section identifies the manual setup of a chroot jail or sandbox. Why manual? Perhaps you enjoy doing this kind of thing and like to keep in practice; perhaps because there isn't an available RPM to install the chroot option; perhaps things went wrong with a chroot install. The configuration has been tested on Linux (Ubuntu 10.04) and FreeBSD (both are documented separately). It assumes a chroot base directory of /chroot/named. The configuration could have used the more normal location of /var/named/chroot or /var/named/ for FreeBSD, but using /chroot/named means you can create a clean chroot environment and avoid any partial results from default installations. It is further assumed that the user named and group named accounts have been set up (FreeBSD users would normally use bind:bind). If these accounts are not present, the process is described in the "Setting the Run Time UID of BIND" section. The standard caching name server named.conf file (from the "Caching-only DNS Server" section in Chapter 7) is used as the target configuration and is reproduced here:

```
// Caching Name Server for Example.com.
// We recommend that you always maintain a change log in this file as shown below
// CHANGELOG:
// 1. 9 july 2010 INITIALS or NAME
//  a. did something
// a. 23 july 2010 INITIALS or NAME
//  a. did something more
//  b. another change
//
options {
  // all relative paths use this directory as a base
  directory "/var/named";
  // version statement for security to avoid hacking known weaknesses
  // if the real version number is published
  version "not currently available";
  // configuration specific option clause statements
  // disables all zone transfer requests
  allow-transfer{"none"};
  // optional - BIND default behavior is recursion
  recursion yes;
};
//
// log to /var/log/example.log all events from info UP in severity (no debug)
// defaults to use 3 files in rotation
// failure messages up to this point are in (syslog) /var/log/messages
//
  logging{
  channel example_log{
   file "/var/log/named/example.log" versions 3 size 250k;
   severity info;
  };
  category default{
  example_log;
  };
```

```
};
// required zone for recursive queries
zone "." {
  type hint;
  file "root.servers";
};
// required local host domain
zone "localhost" in{
  type master;
  file "master.localhost";
  allow-update{none;};
};
// localhost reverse map
zone "0.0.127.in-addr.arpa" in{
  type master;
  file "localhost.rev";
  allow-update{none;};
};
```

Finally, it is assumed that a default rndc configuration was established using the command rndc-confgen -a so that a default /etc/rndc.key file is present.

Linux (Ubuntu Server 10.04) Chroot

This configuration builds a chroot environment in a unique location to show the entire process involved. The following series of commands creates the required directories and moves the basic files required. Lines beginning with // are comments and should not be entered; all others assume a root account or if root is not available (the default install) simple prepend *sudo* to each command line:

```
# cd /
# mkdir chroot
# mkdir chroot/named
# mkdir chroot/named/var
# mkdir chroot/named/var/named
# mkdir chroot/named/var/run
# mkdir chroot/named/var/run/named
// create empty default pid file
# touch chroot/named/var/run/named/named.pid
# mkdir chroot/named/var/log
# mkdir chroot/named/var/log/named
// create empty log file
# touch chroot/named/var/log/named/example.log
# mkdir chroot/named/dev
// create chroot/named/dev/null and /dev/random
# mknod chroot/named/dev/null c 1 3
# mknod chroot/named/dev/random c 1 8
// copy required files
# cp /etc/named.conf chroot/named/etc/named.conf
# cp /etc/localtime chroot/named/etc/localtime
# cp /var/named/localhost.rev chroot/named/var/named/localhost.rev
# cp /var/named/master.localhost chroot/named/var/named/master.localhost
# cp /var/named/root.servers chroot/named/var/named/root.servers
// rndc default key file (if not disabled)
```

```
# cp /etc/rndc.key chroot/named/etc/rndc.key
// set permissions and ownerships
# chown -R named:named chroot/named/*
# chmod -R 0660 chroot/named/*
# chmod 0666 chroot/named/dev/null
# chmod 0644 chroot/named/dev/random
# chmod 0664 chroot/named/var/run/named/named.pid
```

If the name server has additional zone files (for instance, if it is a zone slave or master), additional directories and file copies are required for the relevant files. If a default rndc configuration has been created (using rndc-confgen -a), the key file needs to be copied as shown. If rndc has been disabled with an empty controls clause (control {};), this file is not required. If a custom rndc configuration has been built, /etc/rndc.conf needs to be copied together with any specific .key file. Although Linux device types tend to remain stable, it may be worth verifying that the major and minor device numbers are as shown in the mknod commands by issuing the following command:

```
# ls -l /dev/null
crw-rw-rw- 1 root root 1,3 Feb 23 2004 /dev/null
# ls -l /dev/random
crw-r—r— 1 root root 1,8 Feb 23 2004 /dev/random
```

Finally, named may be started using the following command:

```
# named -u named -t /chroot/named
```

Assuming named must be started at system boot time, the startup script (/etc/rc.d/init.d/named) needs to be edited to add the -t /chroot/named argument.

The preceding configuration is a simplified version using a minimum of commands to show the process involved. If more complex configurations are required, then the procedures and techniques described in the "Limit Permissions" section may be applied.

FreeBSD 8.1 Chroot

FreeBSD users have two options. The first method assumes that all files will use the standard (default) FreeBSD locations; it simply involves adding the following three lines to /etc/rc.conf:

```
named_chrootdir="/chroot/named" # Chroot directory (or "" not to auto-chroot it)
named_chroot_autoupdate="YES" # Automatically install/update chrooted
named_symlink_enable="YES" # Symlink the chrooted pid file
```

This code overrides any values in /etc/defaults/rc.conf and automatically configures the required values including directory creation according to the FreeBSD standard (all files are stored under the etc/namedb directory) at the next system boot.

The second method should be used if non-FreeBSD default locations are being used for any files. This method uses the same command sequence as defined for Linux in the preceding section, with the exception that /dev/null and /dev/random are not created using the mknod commands and are replaced with:

```
# mount -t devfs devfs /chroot/named/dev
devfs -m /chroot/named/dev rule apply hide
devfs -m /chroot/named/dev rule apply path null unhide
devfs -m /chroot/named/dev rule apply path random unhide
```

Finally, the following lines need to be added to /etc/rc.conf if not already present:

```
named_enable="YES"  # Run named, the DNS server (or NO).
```

```
named_program="/usr/sbin/named"  # path to named, if you want a different one.
named_flags="-u bind -t /chroot/named"   # Flags for named
named_chrootdir="" # Chroot directory (or "" not to auto-chroot it)
```

The second method bypasses the default chroot initialization process and allows much tighter control over configuration—at the expense of the user doing all the work.

Dedicated Server

The ultimate in permission limitation or the ultimate sandbox is a dedicated server either running as part of a stealth server configuration (see Chapter 4) or as a stand-alone server. Such a server relies on minimalism to reduce the possibility of subversion and would typically look something like the following:

- No GUI (X-Windows, Gnome or KDE) to reduce software complexity.

- No compilers or other development tools.

- Firewall (packet filter) to inhibit access to all ports other than port 53.

- No remote access to system—Secure Shell (SSH) or BIND (rndc). Some users may wish the additional convenience that comes with either or both of these tools at the expense of the additional security risks involved.

- No Network File System (NFS) or Samba connections.

- Removal of all unnecessary utilities; for example, Telnet, FTP, and so on.

- BIND or NSD software running in a sandbox and typically configured as an authoritative-only server.

Stream the Log

If security is a significant concern, then monitoring for security violations using intrusion-detection software such as Snort (www.snort.org) is important, but such tools lie outside the scope of this book. However, BIND's logging features can assist in this process by streaming security messages into a separate log file to minimize the work content of scanning logs manually, and hence the likelihood of missing key events. The following named.conf fragment streams the security events into a separate log:

```
// named.conf fragment
logging{
    channel normal_log {
    file "/var/log/named/normal.log" versions 3 size 2m;
    severity error;
    print-time yes;
    print-severity yes;
    print-category yes;
    };
    channel security_log { // streamed security log
    file "/var/log/named/security.log" versions 3 size 500k;
    severity info;
    print-time yes;
    print-severity yes;
    print-category yes;
```

```
    };
    category default{
    normal_log;
    };
    category security{
    security_log;
    };
};
....
```

The severity setting (see Chapter 12) can be experimented with to find the most acceptable value to balance volume and information. BIND's server clause with a bogus yes; statement or the blackhole statement can be used to inhibit service completely to a persistent security offender.

Software Diversity

Significant effort has been spent by many of the root-server operators to minimize exploitable risks by running BIND on multiple host operating systems (for example, Linux, Solaris, FreeBSD, and so on), to reduce exposure to a single weakness. The theory is that if an exploit is discovered in one OS, it is unlikely to be present in all OSes at the same time. Therefore, the vulnerable systems can be retired immediately while service continues. The NSD package (www.nlnetlabs.nl/nsd), an open source authoritative-only name server, has been running in the RIPE operated root-server (k.root-servers.net) since 2003; it now also runs in h.root-servers.net and l.root-servers.net, and fully supports DNSSEC features. If the thought of a single BIND exploit taking all your systems off the air at the same time keeps you awake at night, the possibly significant additional effort of maintaining a second version of DNS software may be worthwhile.

A Cryptographic Overview

The next sections and Chapter 11 include techniques that make extensive use of modern cryptographic processes. This section is designed to give the reader a brief overview of the terminology plus the functionality and limitations associated with each technique. For the faint-hearted, the mathematical processes used in cryptography are treated as automagical ("stuff happens") and are not described at all. For a cryptanalyst, such a statement is pure heresy. However, understanding how the math works in the actual algorithmic processes is not necessary to understand the security concepts. Additional resources are provided at www.netwidget.net/books/apress/dns for those readers who revel in the gruesome mathematical details.

However, before ignoring the mathematics entirely, it is important to understand a couple of points. Cryptographic techniques are not provably secure. Instead, they are exposed to attacks by dedicated researchers and specialists. Only after having weathered such attacks are the techniques made available for operational use. Research is ongoing to keep ahead of the bad guys; occasionally it discovers new weaknesses in techniques and algorithms that have been used for considerable periods of time. Finally, all cryptographic techniques are based on a concept known as *computationally infeasible*. This means either it would cost too much to assemble the computing power necessary to find the key or it would take too long. This concept is relative, not absolute, and thus it changes over time; so a key size that may be computationally infeasible today may not be so 5 or 10 years hence. When selecting key sizes, bear in mind the duration of effectiveness of the protection.

Cryptology can be used for three purposes:

- *Confidentiality*: Only the parties to the communication can understand the messages sent between the parties.

- *Authentication*: The data could only have come from a known source.

- *Data integrity*: The data that is received by one party is the data that was sent by the other party.

In the context of DNS standards, only authentication and data integrity are of interest. Where confidentiality is required, it is assumed to be provided by a communications process such as SSL or its successor TLS; it's not defined within the DNS standards. BIND 9 does support TLS.

Most of us have been cryptographers at some stage in our lives. The secret codes and methods we invented to send notes to our school friends reflect the earliest cryptographic processes whereby the "secret" was contained in the process (or algorithm). For example, we could shift the letters two positions in the alphabet to encode the message. The disadvantage with this method was that once the process was discovered, the algorithm was useless; it had to be discarded and a new one invented. By contrast, modern cryptography assumes that the algorithm used—the method of encryption—is known to everyone, including the bad guys, and indeed can only be proven to be secure by repeated attack. The secret part of the process lies with a unique key or keys. If a key is compromised, it is simply discarded and a new one created. An attacker must start again with no greater knowledge than before, even though the basic algorithm or process stays the same. There are two classes of key-based cryptographic algorithms in modern usage: symmetric and asymmetric.

Symmetric Cryptography

Symmetric encryption algorithms (also called *single-key*, *shared-secret*, or even, confusingly, *private-key* systems) use a single key to encrypt and decrypt the data. This single key—the shared secret—must be securely exchanged between the parties that will use it prior to the commencement of secure communication. The limitations of shared-secret systems are twofold. First, the key must be distributed securely using a process called key management, which itself is not trivial. Second, the method of securing the key once distributed lies with all the parties to the communication: "I trust myself but do I trust all the other parties to keep the key secret?" Examples of common symmetric key algorithms are DES, AES, IDEA, and RC4; typical key sizes are 64, 128, or 192 bits. Figure 10–2 shows the operational use of a shared secret for classic confidential communications.

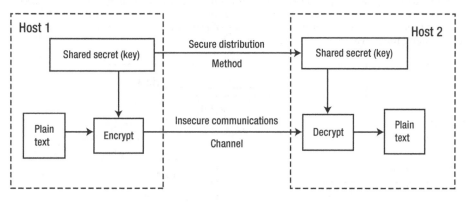

Figure 10–2. Symmetric, or shared-secret, cryptography

■ **Note** The term *shared secret*, which describes a single key used or shared by both ends of the communication, should not be confused with *secret sharing*, which describes a process whereby the shared or single secret key is broken up into parts and shared between multiple persons to make it more secure.

Shared-secret algorithms are used in the DNS in TSIG operations. The problem of distributing the keys (key management) is not defined in the DNS standards and can be anything that works for the user; for instance, telephone, fax, secure e-mail, or carrier pigeon. The shared-secret key(s) used by DNS software must be constantly available (known as *online* in the jargon) to allow their use when validating transactions. However, the keys require minimum visibility; thus, it is impossible to store them in the zone file. Instead, such keys are stored in one or more key clauses within BIND's named.conf file. Due to their extremely sensitive content (a shared secret), they are normally stored as separate files with limited read permissions and included (using the include statement) into the named.conf file.

Asymmetric Cryptography

Asymmetric encryption algorithms use a pair of keys and are generally referred to as *public-key cryptographic systems* or sometimes as *nonsecret encryption* (a slight oxymoron). In these systems, data (called *plain-text* in the jargon) that is encrypted with one key can only be decrypted with the paired key. Given one key, it is *computationally infeasible* to derive the paired key. The system works by making one key, called the public key, widely available while maintaining the other key, called the private key, a secret. This process has an interesting side effect. If a message is encrypted with a private key and can be decrypted with its paired public key, then only the owner of the private key could have done it. This property is used in digital signatures and is described further in the "Digital Signatures" section. The most widely used public-key encryption systems are RSA (after the inventors Rivest, Shamir, and Adelman) and elliptic curves. Typical key sizes for public-key systems are 1024 bits, 2048 bits, or higher. The public keys of a private/public key pair can be safely stored in a public service such as DNS, while the private key must be maintained securely in a private location or a hardware security module (HSM). Figure 10–3 illustrates the use of public-key cryptography for classic confidential communications in which data to be sent to a host is encrypted using the public key of the receiving host, thus ensuring that it can only be decrypted using the private key of the receiver.

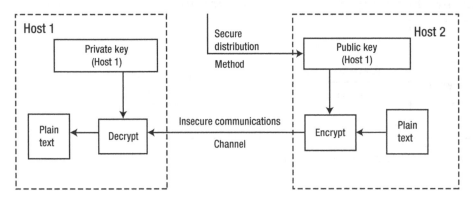

Figure 10–3. Asymmetric or public-key cryptography

Public-key systems have one significant limitation: they rely on knowing or trusting that the public key that will be used in communications with a person or organization really is the public key of the person or organization and has not been spoofed by a malicious third party. The method by which this is usually accomplished is sometimes called a Public Key Infrastructure (PKI), in which a trusted third party securely manages public keys. If the third party is requested to provide the public key of X, they are trusted to provide the correct key. The third party is trusted to have satisfied themselves by some process—attestation, notarization, and so on—that X is the one and only, or globally unique, X.

Message Digests

As stated previously, DNS systems require authentication and data integrity, not confidentiality. To provide data integrity, the message could be simply encrypted. Thus, only the possessor of the single key (in symmetric systems) or the private key (in asymmetric systems) could decrypt it; therefore, tampering is eliminated. However, encryption systems use complex mathematical functions, making them big users of CPU resources. Encrypting all messages would create unacceptably high overheads. Fortunately, other techniques can be used to reduce this load. The most common is a lightweight procedure called a *one-way hash*, or more commonly a *message digest*. The hash or digest creates a unique and relatively small fixed-size block of data (irrespective of the original message length) that can't be reversed. The messages being sent typically include both the plain text (unencrypted) and a digest of the message. The hash algorithm is applied to the received plain text; if the result matches the transmitted message digest, this means the received data was not altered. The message digest is, in some senses, similar in concept to a checksum but has significantly different mathematical properties. The most common forms of message digest are MD5, SHA-1, and increasingly SHA-2 (SHA-224, SHA-256, SHA-384, SHA- SHA-512). Figure 10–4 shows the message digest in action.

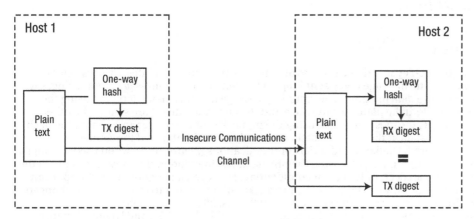

Figure 10–4. Message digests

Message Authentication Codes

Two possible solutions exist for authenticating the sender and ensuring integrity. In the case of symmetric, shared-secret systems, a message authentication code (MAC) is created that combines the message digest with a shared key. The message is hashed to create a digest which is then encrypted using the symmetric key. The key part authenticates the sender, and the hash part ensures data integrity. The process is repeated at the receiver and the MACs are compared. The most common forms of MACs are HMAC-MD5, HMAC-SHA-1, and increasingly HMAC-SHA-256. MACs are used for TSIG secure operations in DNS. Figure 10–5 shows how the MAC is used.

Note For the insatiably curious, HMAC simply means hashed message authentication code.

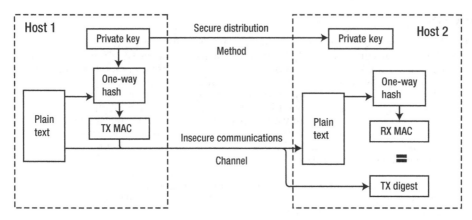

Figure 10–5. How a MAC is used

Digital Signatures

In the asymmetric or public-key world, the process of authentication and data integrity uses what is called a *digital signature*. The message being sent is again hashed to create a message digest using, say, SHA-1 or SHA-256 to ensure data integrity. The resulting message digest is then encrypted using the private key of the sender. Both the plain-text message and the encrypted digest are sent to the other party. The receiver decrypts the message digest using the public key of the sender and applies the hash algorithm to the plain-text data; if the results match, then both the authenticity of the sender and the integrity of the data is assured. Unlike confidential communications (Figure 10–3), when used as a digital signature the data (plain text) is encrypted using the private key of the sender, thus any receiver with the corresponding public key can decrypt it (it's not confidential). However, a naughty eaves-dropper can't tamper with the message since it would require the private key of the sender to re-encrypt the changed digest. Typical key sizes for digital signature systems are 1024 bits, 2048 bits, or higher. The most common digital signature algorithms are RSA-MD5, RSA-SHA-1, RSA-SHA-256, and Digital Signature Architecture (DSA; a US government standard). Digital signatures are used in the DNS for SIG(0) secure transactions and for all DNSSEC transactions described in Chapter 11. Figure 10–6 shows how the digital signature is used.

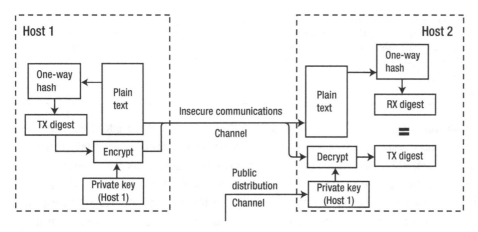

Figure 10–6. *Digital signatures*

■**Note** The MD5 hash algorithm (and by implication any algorithm that uses it, such as RSA-MD5) has been moved to a Not Recommended status in most IETF documents due to some theoretical weaknesses published in early 2005. These weaknesses do not invalidate the use of the algorithm.

DNS Cryptographic Use

The DNS standards that cover security—generically and confusingly referred to as DNSSEC—use cryptographic security in two distinct ways. Transaction security, such as that used in zone transfer and dynamic updates, uses a point-to-point security model in which both parties in the transaction are assumed to trust each other. The parties exchange information, including security information, that authenticates the source and data integrity and is relevant only for that transaction. TSIG (shared-secret) and SIG(0) (public key) methods are used to perform the validation. Both methods are described with examples later in this chapter.

Client-server security, now known simply as DNSSEC, allows the receiving DNS to validate the source and integrity of data received in response to any query from a suitably configured *resolver* (called a *validating resolver* or a *security aware resolver*). For such a system to work, it relies critically on an assurance that the source of the data is what it says it is. This problem, described in the preceding section, normally relies on the presence of a PKI, whereby a trusted third party verifies that some information, normally a public key, belongs to *X*, and that *X* is truly the one and only *X*. DNSSEC security does not rely on a PKI, but instead creates a hierarchy or *chain of trust* based on the delegation of DNS names. A trusted party forms the root or the Secure Entry Point (SEP) of the chain of trust, in which certain RRs at the point of delegation are cryptographically signed (using a digital signature) by the parent zone. This creates a secure link to the next domain in the chain, which in turn signs the delegation records and so on, until the end point has been reached. The authenticity of each link in the chain, with the exception of the starting point, is verified by the previous or parent domain. DNSSEC security is described in Chapter 11.

The nature of secure systems is that they must safeguard against many forms of attack. One attack form is called a replay attack, in which a transaction is captured and replayed at a later time. To avoid such forms of attack, all systems involved in cryptographic security must be time synchronized. The protocols typically allow a fudge factor of 300 seconds (5 minutes) or longer, but the implementation of Network Time Protocol (NTP) is essential in systems that use cryptographic techniques. Implementation of NTP lies outside the scope of this book, but open source implementations are available for most major OSes and their distributions. Further information may be obtained from www.ntp.org, including a list of public time servers.

Caution Time synchronization for all hosts involved in cryptographic exchanges is crucial. BIND failure messages do not always indicate clearly that time is the source of a failure in authentication, when 90% of the time that is indeed the problem. NTP uses an incremental approach to synchronizing clocks, and it can take a considerable period to adjust the clocks on any host system. If you are not running NTP software and wish to experiment with the techniques described throughout this chapter and Chapter 11, each host that will participate should synchronize its clocks to Internet time by issuing an ntpdate name.of.time.server command. In this command, name.of.time.server should be replaced with some accessible time server; a list of publicly available time servers can be found at www.ntp.org. Note that ntpdate is a one-time update, and the accuracy of the local clock determines how long its effect will last. Operational systems that participate in DNSSEC must implement NTP.

Securing Zone Transfers

In most DNS configurations, zone transfers are essential. If you are of a security-conscious frame of mind, zone transfers may be viewed as a necessary evil. The default option in BIND is to allow zone transfers to any requesting host. Although this may look like a remarkably friendly act, it's based on the simple premise that a public DNS contains public data. Everything that is transferred can be discovered by exhaustive queries, even if zone transfers are completely banned. If data should not be public, it should not be in the zone file on a public server. Simply securing zone transfers is not a solution to hiding data. Nevertheless, there are cases where it is necessary as part of a security-in-depth configuration to restrict zone transfers—for example, on the private side of a stealth server configuration (see Chapter 4). The simplest way to secure zone transfers is through the use of IP addresses in BIND's named.conf file. The following named.conf fragment limits transfers to named hosts based on the zone name:

```
// named.conf fragment
logging{
    channel normal_log {
    file "/var/log/named/normal.log" versions 3 size 2m;
    severity error;
    print-time yes;
    print-severity yes;
    print-category yes;
    };
    channel security_log { // streamed security log
    file "/var/log/named/security.log" versions 3 size 2m;
    severity info;
    print-time yes;
    print-severity yes;
```

```
        print-category yes;
        };
        category default{
        normal_log;
        };
        category security{
        security_log;
        };
};
options {
....
    allow-transfer {none;}; // none by default
....
};
....
zone "example.com in{
....
    allow-transfer {10.1.2.5;}; // this zone only
....
};
```

This configuration fragment denies all zone transfer requests and selectively permits the allowable hosts on a per-zone basis. For instance, the single IP address 10.1.2.5 is allowed to perform zone transfers for the zone example.com. The log is streamed for security events because it is assumed that as part of this defensive strategy it is of interest to see where transfer requests are coming from. If necessary, after log inspection a server clause with bogus yes; or a blackhole statement could be used to stop service completely to a persistently inquisitive host.

Given the right circumstances, IP addresses can be spoofed, which can result in *man-in-the-middle* attacks where a third party may pretend to be the zone master. When requested to transfer a zone, this third party could transfer counterfeit data resulting in, say, a web site being hijacked by providing alternate IP addresses in the resource records (RRs). To prevent such a possibility, zone transfers can be secured through the use of cryptographic techniques to ensure both authentication (the master and slave are who they say they are) and data integrity (the data received by the slave was the same as the data sent by the master).

Authentication and Integrity of Zone Transfers

The bad news is that of the three methods for cryptographically securing zone transfers, only one is suitable, as may be seen from the following list:

- *TSIG*: TSIG was defined in RFC 2845 and uses a single shared secret between the master and slave servers as part of a MAC. The key must be distributed to the slave locations by some secure process, such as fax, mail, courier, or secure e-mail, and it must be maintained securely at all the sites. Shared secrets, because they rely on a single key maintained at two or more locations, should be changed frequently (perhaps every 30 to 60 days) though it is common, if risky, practice to see the same shared secret key used for extended periods. If there is more than one slave server, either separate shared secrets may be used for each master-slave pair or a single shared secret may be used for all slaves. The latter policy is significantly riskier because any subversion or discovery of the key at a single site invalidates all slave transfers, whereas if separate secrets are used, the subverted slave can be temporarily disabled until the key is replaced. There is no change to the operational zone files when using the TSIG method; only the named.conf file is modified.

- *SIG(0)*: SIG(0) was defined in RFC 2931 and uses a public-key system to generate a digital signature that both authenticates and ensures the integrity of the data involved in each transaction that includes zone transfers. However, there are no tools available with current BIND 9 releases to support SIG(0) for zone transfers. SIG(0) may be used with DDNS; see the "Securing Dynamic Updates" section.

- *TKEY*: The TKEY provides a method of securely exchanging shared-secret keys so that the poor carrier pigeons (or whatever other method you use to securely distribute shared keys) can have a rest. The method is defined to support both the Diffie-Hellman algorithm and the Generic Security Services API (GSSAPI). However, the standard (RFC 2930) mandates that the exchange must be authenticated with either TSIG or SIG(0) methods. Consequently, it appears not to be widely implemented; it's not covered further in this book.

For practical purposes, the only method available to secure zone transfers is TSIG. The detailed configuration required to support this service is covered in the following section.

TSIG Configuration

Transaction signatures (TSIG) use a MAC with a shared secret both to authenticate and ensure the data integrity of every transaction involved in zone transfers between the nominated slave and its master. It is vital to keep in mind that shared-secret data is never placed in the DNS zone files. Instead, the shared secret is used by the two servers when exchanging data, such as a zone transfer. Figure 10–7 illustrates how shared secrets are used in securing transactions.

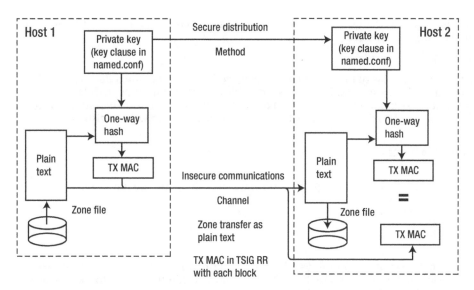

Figure 10–7. Shared-secret TSIG

The shared secret is generated using the dnssec-keygen utility, which is the general-purpose cryptographic utility provided with BIND and is described in Chapter 9. The TSIG standard (RFC 2845) defined the HMAC-MD5 (mandatory) algorithm, RFC 3645 extended this to include GSS-TSIG, and RFC 4635 added HMAC-SHA1, HMAC-224, HMAC-256, HMAC-384, and HMAC-512. All are supported by the current version of the dnssec-keygen utility; the list is maintained at www.iana.org/assignments/tsig-algorithm-names. The shared-secret key is assumed to be generated in a directory called /var/named/keys using a command similar to the following:

```
# cd /var/named/keys
# dnssec-keygen -a hmac-md5 -b 128 -C -n host example.com
```

This command generates a 128-bit key (the -b argument) suitable for use with the HMAC-MD5 MAC algorithm (HMAC-MD5 allows keys from 1 to 512 bits). The -n host argument indicates that a host KEY RR is generated with a name of example.com. The -C inhibits writing of timing metadata information not required for TSIG. This KEY RR is not used in TSIG transactions for reasons explained later in this section. However, the dnssec-keygen utility treats the -n argument as mandatory, so it must be present.

■**Note** The HMAC-MD5 algorithm has been selected since it remains the only one whose support is mandatory for any TSIG-compliant DNS implementation, making it safe to use even in cases where the TSIG algorithm support of the peer DNS is unknown. Where it is known that peer DNS software can support additional algorithms, one of the mutually supported set may be used instead. If TSIG keys were generated prior to BIND 9.7.0 using any HMAC-SHA algorithm, such keys may not work with BIND 9.7.0+. These keys should be regenerated using dnssec-keygen from BIND 9.7.0+. Alternatively, the utility isc-hmac-fixup can be used to modify the keys for use with 9.7.0+.

The command writes two files to the current directory, and when complete, outputs a short message to identify the created files, as shown here:

```
Kexample.com.+157+31313
```

The preceding file name consists of the fixed value K, followed by the host name reflected from the dnssec-keygen command (in this case, example.com). 157 identifies the algorithm (HMAC-MD5). The 31313 is called the key-tag; it's generated using a variant of the "one's complement" checksum algorithm to uniquely identify this key set. Looking in the directory in which the files were written displays two files:

```
Kexample.com.+157+31313.private
Kexample.com.+157+31313.key
```

Viewing the file Kexample.com.+157+31313.private displays something like the following data:

```
Private-key-format: v1.2
Algorithm: 157 (HMAC_MD5)
Key: JuxDyYXIJhAia5WQe9oqUA==
Bits: AAA=
```

The preceding information contains four lines. The line beginning with the text Key: is the base64 (RFC 4648) encoded version of the shared-secret key. The next step is to edit this data into a key clause that will be used in the named.conf file, as shown here:

```
key "example.com" (
    algorithm hmac-md5;
    secret JuxDyYXIJhAia5WQe9oqUA==;
};
```

The key name example.com (which can be a quoted string and contain spaces, or unquoted if there are no spaces) is normally the name used as the hostname in the dnssec-keygen command, as in the preceding case. Depending on the application, it can be any useful string, as long as the same key clause name is used by both parties in the transaction. In the example case, both parties (master and slave) contain a key clause with the name example.com, as shown in the configuration fragments that follow. The name of the key clause could have been "transfer-key" if that was more meaningful; again, the same key clause name must be used by both parties. For a TSIG transaction, there is no required relationship between the name used when running the dnssec-keygen utility and the name of the key clause. The name defined in the key clause is sent in the TSIG meta (or pseudo) RR with each secure transaction to identify the shared secret being used. If the key clause name is not the same in each party, the transaction will fail with a BADNAME error.

The algorithm line of the key clause identifies the algorithm being used (hmac-md5 as defined in the dnssec-keygen command). The data following secret is a copy of the data from the Key line of the Kexample.com.+157+31313.private file, terminated with a semicolon. This key clause should be saved as separate file—let's call it example.com.key—and placed in a directory called /var/named/keys and included in the named.conf file. This file containing the shared-secret key clause must now be made available by some secure process (such as SFTP, secure e-mail, or other secure service) to the slave server or servers. Because this file contains highly sensitive data, it should be immediately secured on the master and slaves such that it can only be read with the UID of BIND. The commands to secure the file look something like this:

```
chown named:named /var/named/keys/example.com.key
chmod 0400 /var/named/keys/example.com.key
```

These commands assume that BIND is being run with the -u named argument (as described earlier in this chapter) and allow BIND's UID read access to the file. However, the root user can both read and write as normal if subsequent modification is required. Alternatively, you can use a chmod setting of 0600 and allow all editing to be done under the BIND UID if you have a deep-seated objection to using root for anything nonessential.

Viewing the file Kexample.com.+157+31313.key shows the following text:

```
example.com. IN KEY 512 3 157 JuxDyYXIJhAia5WQe9oqUA==
```

This is a DNS-ready KEY RR containing the shared-secret key! It is generated as an artifact of the dnssec-keygen standard processing; unfortunately, there is no way to inhibit it. The KEY RR is *never* used with any shared-secret algorithms and *must not under any circumstances* be added to the zone file. Instead, only the named.conf file key clause contains the shared-secret key that is used independently by both ends during the communication, as illustrated in Figure 10–7. Once the key clause is established on both the master and slaves, either secure Kexample.com.+157+31313.key and Kexample.com.+157+31313.private, or better still, delete these files completely—they will not be used again and represent an additional security headache.

The named.conf file at the master will look something like the following fragment:

```
// named.conf example.com master fragment
logging{
    channel normal_log {
    file "/var/log/named/normal.log" versions 3 size 2m;
    severity error;
    print-time yes;
    print-severity yes;
    print-category yes;
    };
    channel dnssec_log { // streamed dnssec log
    file "/var/log/named/dnssec.log" versions 3 size 2m;
    severity debug 3;
    print-time yes;
    print-severity yes;
    print-category yes;
    };
    category default{
    normal_log;
    };
    category dnssec{
    dnssec_log;
    };
};
options {
    ....
    directory "/var/named";
    dnssec-enable yes;  // default and could be omitted
    ....
};
// include the key clause for example.com key name
```

```
include "keys/example.com.key"; // include the key clause
// server clause references the key clause included above
server 10.1.2.3 {
    keys {"example.com";}; // name used in key clause
};
....
zone "example.com" in{
    type master;
    file "master.example.com";
    // allow transfer only if key (TSIG) present
    allow-transfer {key "example.com";};
};
....
```

To assist in testing and experimentation, the log has been streamed to log DNSSEC events separately, as shown in the preceding fragment. The severity debug 3; line generates copious amounts of logging and should be used during testing only. In a production environment, this value can be set to severity info; or higher. Since BIND 9.5+, DNSSEC is turned on by default. The dnssec-enable yes; statement is placed in the global options clause both as a reminder and to illustrate defensive configuration described earlier in the chapter. The key clause contained in the file keys/example.com.key must appear before it's referenced in the server clause, as shown in the preceding fragment. The server clause defines the IPv4 address of the slave server for example.com, and the keys statement in this clause references the key clause containing the secret key to be used. The allow-transfer statement in the zone clause for example.com is an address-match-list construction using the key option (see the "BIND address_match_list Definition" section in Chapter 12) and provides the linkage to validate incoming TSIG messages. The corresponding slave server named.conf file looks something like that shown here:

```
// named.conf example.com slave fragment
options {
    ....
    directory "/var/named";
    dnssec-enable yes;
    ....
};
include "keys/example.com.key"; // include the key clause
server 10.1.2.5 {
    keys {"example.com";}; // name used in key clause
};
....
zone "example.com" in{
    type slave;
    file "slave.example.com";
    masters {10.1.2.5;};
};
```

The key clause again is included from the file keys/example.com.key (remember both sides are sharing this key) and must appear before it is referenced in the server clause, which in this case is the IPv4 address of the zone master for example.com. The masters statement in the zone clause for example.com contains an IPv4 address to link it to the server clause. This triggers the initiation of the authentication sequence using the defined keys statement. Although the masters statement can contain a key option in this case, because the slave initiates the request for zone transfer, it must know where to send it so it uses an IP address. The corresponding allow-transfer statement in the zone master fragment can use the key format because it is *responding* to the request.

For those with insatiable curiosity, it may be worthwhile to look at the resulting zone transfer with a suitable sniffer application (see Chapter 15). A meta (or pseudo) RR called TSIG, containing the MAC for each transaction and with a name of the shared-secret key clause, is placed in the ADDITIONAL SECTION of the query and its response (see Chapter 13 for an explanation of meta RRs). In this case, the response is the zone transfer (AXFR). These TSIG RRs are discarded once the message has been verified; that is, they are not saved as part of the zone transfer data.

■**Caution** The KEY RR generated as part of the dnssec-keygen process (contained in the .key file) is used in public-key systems only. When using shared-secret techniques such as TSIG, the KEY RR is an annoying and dangerous artifact; it must not be placed in the DNS zone file. Unless there are good reasons not to, it should be deleted immediately.

Securing Dynamic Updates

Defined in RFCs 3007 and 2136, Dynamic DNS (DDNS) describes a process whereby RRs for a zone can be added, deleted, and modified by a third party. However, zones can't be deleted or added using this process. To ensure consistency of zone data, the dynamic updates are only carried out on the primary master server, which is defined as the name server that appears in the SOA RR for the zone (the name-server or, officially, MNAME field). The BIND default is to disallow dynamic updates from all IP addresses. Dynamic updating is a powerful capability, and many sites use it extensively to enable customers to edit their zone data directly; they also use it in some cases to synchronize Dynamic Host Control Protocol (DHCP) with both forward and reverse mapping files automatically. As with all positives, there is an accompanying negative: unscrupulous access by malicious third parties can corrupt or poison the zone file. As previously stated, not securing DDNS unless it occurs behind a secure perimeter and between consenting adults constitutes an over-reliance on the essential goodness of mankind. It is imperative to secure DDNS. The simplest way to secure DDNS is through the use of IP-based restrictions. The following fragment uses BIND's allow-update statement to limit access:

```
// named.conf fragment
logging{
    channel normal_log {
    file "/var/log/named/normal.log" versions 3 size 2m;
    severity error;
    print-time yes;
    print-severity yes;
    print-category yes;
    };
    channel security_log { // streamed security log
    file "/var/log/named/security.log" versions 3 size 2m;
    severity info;
    print-time yes;
    print-severity yes;
    print-category yes;
    };
    category default{
    normal_log;
    };
```

```
        category security{
        security_log;
        };
};
options {
....
};
....
zone "example.com in{
....
    allow-update {10.1.2.5;}; // this zone only
....
};
```

This configuration fragment denies all dynamic updates and selectively permits the allowable hosts on a per-zone basis. For example, the single IP address 10.1.2.5 is allowed to perform updates for the zone example.com. The log is streamed for security events because it is assumed that as part of this defensive strategy, it is of interest to see where update requests are coming from. If necessary, after inspection of the security.log file, a server clause with bogus yes; or a blackhole statement could be used to stop service completely to a persistent unauthorized host.

Given the right circumstances, IP addresses can be spoofed, which can result in the bad guys doing naughty things to the master zone file. To prevent such a possibility, dynamic updates can be secured through the use of cryptographic techniques to ensure both authentication (the master and slave are who they say they are) and data integrity (the data received by the master being updated was the same as the data sent by the client performing the update).

Both TSIG and SIG(0) methods are supported by the nsupdate utility provided with BIND releases and described in Chapter 9. Implementation of both TSIG and SIG(0) methods is described in the following sections.

TSIG DDNS Configuration

TSIGs use a MAC with a shared secret both to authenticate and ensure the data integrity of every transaction involved in dynamic updates between the primary master and the update source. The method of generating the shared secret is exactly the same as that defined for the earlier "TSIG Configuration" section and is not repeated here. The shared secret is not shared with another name server in this case, but with the source of the dynamic updates; for instance, the nsupdate utility. Again, it's vital that the KEY RRs generated as part of the dnssec-keygen process *must not* be added to the zone file. When using a shared-secret algorithm such as TSIG, the key clause or clauses in the named.conf file—which is assumed not to be a public file—store the secret keys.

■ **Note** It's possible to use the same shared-secret key to perform both dynamic update and zone transfer authorization, especially if the same host is being used for both operations. However, in general, a separate shared secret should be used for every host pair because this minimizes exposure to compromised keys.

The named.conf file fragment to support the dynamic update is shown in the following code, using both the allow-update and the update-policy statements:

```
// named.conf example.com master fragment
```

```
logging{
    channel normal_log {
    file "/var/log/named/normal.log" versions 3 size 2m;
    severity error;
    print-time yes;
    print-severity yes;
    print-category yes;
    };
    channel dnssec_log { // streamed dnssec log
    file "/var/log/named/dnssec.log" versions 3 size 2m;
    severity debug 3;
    print-time yes;
    print-severity yes;
    print-category yes;
    };
    category default{
    normal_log;
    };
    category dnssec{
    dnssec_log;
    };
};
options {
    ....
    directory "/var/named";
    dnssec-enable yes;  // BIND default - could be omitted
    ....
};
include "keys/example.com.key"; // include the key clause
server 10.1.2.3 {
    keys {"example.com";}; // name used in key clause
};
....
zone "example.com" in{
    type master;
    file "master.example.com";
    allow-update {key "example.com";};
};
....
zone "example.net" in{
    type master;
    file "master.example.net";
    update-policy { grant example.com subdomain example.net ANY;};
    update-policy { grant * self * A;};
    update-policy { grant update-mx name example.net MX;};
};
....
```

The allow-update statement in the zone clause for example.com uses the key option of the address_match_list to permit any updates to the example.com zone file. The zone clause for example.net uses update-policy statements to provide tight control over what can be done and by whom. The first update-policy statement allows a TSIG transaction with the name example.com to update any record in the zone file example.net. The keyword subdomain means that the following parameter (in this case, example.net) is treated as a base name. Any name that includes or terminates with example.net matches;

for example, joe.example.net terminates with example.net and therefore it matches, as would the MX RR for the domain. The second update-policy statement allows any TSIG transaction with a key name of, say, bill.example.net and for which there is a key clause with the same name (bill.example.net) to update only an A RR with a name of bill.example.net. The additional key clauses are not shown in the example, but this construct would require a key clause and a unique shared secret for every possible A RR that could be updated. The final update-policy statement says that a TSIG transaction with a name of update-mx (and for which there must be a key clause with the name update-mx) is allowed to update only the MX RR(s) for the domain example.net.

To reinforce the process of key generation for shared-secret applications, the following sequence shows creation of the shared secret for update-mx. This shared secret is used in the last update-policy statement in the zone clause for example.net in the preceding fragment. Use the following command to generate the key:

```
dnssec-keygen -a hmac-md5 -b 128 -n host -C update-mx
```

When complete, the command responds with a file identifier such as the following:

```
Kupdate-mx.+157+32713
```

Create a new key clause with a name of update-mx using the data from the Key: line of the file called Kupdate-mx.+157+32713.private, as shown here:

```
key "update-mx" (
     algorithm hmac-md5;
     secret 7aBDy3XIJhA775WQ4FoqUA==;
};
```

Add this key clause to the existing file example.com.key, which contains the original key clause you created, or create a new file and add a new include statement in named.conf. Finally, if the data is added to the existing file or a new file is created, remember to check that the file permissions only allow read access for the BIND UID. To illustrate the dynamic update process in action, the example uses the nsupdate utility supplied with all BIND releases. In this case, you use the example.com key, which can update both the example.com and example.net zone files. Before invoking the nsupdate utility, the files Kexample.com.+157+31313.private and Kexample.com.+157+31313.key need to be moved by a secure process into a suitable working directory on the host that will run the nsupdate utility. In this case, assume the directory is /var/named/dynamic.

■**Note** Recall from earlier that when using shared secrets, the file containing the KEY RR (in the preceding case Kexample.com.+157+32713.key), which is generated automatically by the dnssec-keygen utility, must not be added to the zone file. However, this file is required by the nsupdate utility for operational reasons. Once securely transferred to that host or hosts, it should be deleted from the primary master host.

The following sequence adds a new A RR to the zones example.com and example.net:

```
# cd /var/named/dynamic
# nsupdate -k Kexample.com.+157+31313.private
> server ns1.example.com
> zone example.com
> update add new 36000 IN A 192.168.5.4
> send
```

```
> show
Outgoing update query:
;; ->>HEADER<<- opcode: UPDATE, status: NOERR id: 0
;; flags: ; ZONE: 0, PREREQ: 0, UPDATE: 0, ADDITIONAL: 0
> zone example.net
> update add another.example.net.  36000 IN A 192.168.7.15
> send
> quit
```

This example shows adding an A RR to each of the domains example.com and example.net. The key file used with the nsupdate utility has a name of example.com, which has permission to update both example.com (via the allow-update statement in the example named.conf fragment) and example.net (through the first update-policy statement). A dig command can be used to verify that the new RRs are available, as shown here:

```
# dig @192.168.5.12 new.example.com A
; <<>> DiG 9.7.2-P2 <<>> @192.168.5.12 new.example.com A
;; global options:  printcmd
;; Got answer:
;; ->>HEADER<<- opcode: QUERY, status: NOERROR, id: 1082
;; flags: qr aa rd ra; QUERY: 1, ANSWER: 1, AUTHORITY: 2, ADDITIONAL: 2

;; QUESTION SECTION:
;new.example.com.        IN  A

;; ANSWER SECTION:
new.example.com. 36000 IN  A  192.168.5.4

;; AUTHORITY SECTION:
example.com.        86400  IN  NS  ns1.example.com.
example.com.        86400  IN  NS  ns2.example.com.

;; ADDITIONAL SECTION:
ns1.example.com.  86400  IN  A  192.168.5.12
ns2.example.com.  86400  IN  A  192.168.5.11

;; Query time: 15 msec
;; SERVER: 192.168.5.12#53(192.168.5.12)
;; WHEN: Thu Apr 07 21:59:48 2010
;; MSG SIZE  rcvd: 124
```

This output confirms that the update to the example.com domain was successful and is immediately available at the primary master. The update process automatically adds 1 to the sequence number field of the SOA RR. Unless disabled by a named.conf statement, a NOTIFY is sent to the slave servers for the zone, and the update is cascaded to all the slave servers within minutes.

■**Note** It is worth reminding readers that once a dynamic update is invoked, the zone file should not be manually edited because updates are initially written to a journal file (`zone.file.name.jnl`), and the zone file is only periodically updated. If manual editing is required, either stop BIND and perform the edit, or use the `rndc` command `flush`, followed by `freeze zone.name`; perform the manual edit; and then `thaw zone.name`. In either case, the zone's `.jnl` file should be deleted before either restarting BIND or issuing the `rndc thaw` command to ensure subsequent consistency.

SIG(0) Configuration

The `nsupdate` utility also supports SIG(0) authentication and data integrity checking through the use of digital signatures, which are based on public-key technology. Public-key technology has the advantage that no special action is required to distribute the public keys. They are simply placed as KEY RRs in the zone file, and may be read by anyone because without the matching private key they are useless. In an update sequence, the zone master uses the public key. The client performing the update uses the private key to generate the signature, which is verified by the receiving zone primary master. If an encrypted response is required, the server uses the public key to sign the response, which in turn is verified using the private key of the updating client. The downside of public-key technology is that it uses significantly more CPU resources than shared-secret technology. If any significant volume of updates is likely on a busy server, then the use of SIG(0) may warrant careful consideration. As long as the key distribution and management problem associated with shared secrets can be handled, TSIG may be a better option in this case. The term SIG(0) can be a little confusing, because there was a SIG RR type that performed a function similar to the current RRSIG RRs (see Chapter 11) used in historic DNSSEC specifications. However, the SIG(0) RR used to secure transactions is a meta (or pseudo) RR type that is dynamically created by the sending application or server and added to the `ADDITIONAL SECTION` of the transaction (see Chapter 15). The SIG(0) RR is discarded immediately after verification. Specifically, it's not cached or added to the zone file. This form of the SIG RR is uniquely identified by having a type 0 in its `type` field (see the "SIG RR" section in Chapter 13) and is referred to as SIG(0).

The private and public keys for the SIG(0) transaction are created using the `dnssec-keygen` utility (see Chapter 9). Because the client that updates the zone uses the private key, key generation should be done on this host. If this is not possible, the generated files have to be moved to the client machine using a secure process. These commands generate a public/private key pair in the directory /var/named/keys:

```
# cd /var/named/keys
# dnssec-keygen -a rsasha1 -b 1024 -T KEY -n host -C update.example.com
```

In the preceding `dnssec-keygen` command, `-a rsasha1` generates a digital signature using the RSA algorithm with the SHA-1 message digest (the `dnssec-keygen` utility supports the DSA, RSA-SHA-1, RSA-SHA256, RSA-SHA512, and RSA-MD5 public-key methods). The `-b 1024` argument indicates the key will be 512 bits long. An RSA-SHA-1 key may be from 512 to 4,096 bits. The higher the number, the greater cryptographic strength of the key; however, more CPU is used in encryption/decryption. The `-T` argument indicates that a KEY RR type is required (not a DNSKEY RR, which would be the default). The `-n host` indicates a host KEY RR will be created with a name of update.example.com. The `-C` argument inhibits writing of timing metadata not used by SIG(0). When complete, the command will output a message similar to this:

```
Kupdate.example.com.+005+00706
```

K is a fixed value, update.example.com. is the name from the dnssec-keygen command, 005 indicates the algorithm (RSA-SHA-1), and 00706 is the key-tag that is algorithmically generated and uniquely identifies this key pair. Inspection of the directory /var/named/keys shows two files:

```
Kupdate.example.com.+005+00706.private
Kupdate.example.com.+005+00706.key
```

The file Kupdate.example.com.+005+00706.key contains a single KEY RR and looks something like the following:

```
update.example.com. IN KEY 512 3 5 (AQPL1jlhf70f9l1P/h
  PFNMxU55IpkMX1O7EzvDk5OrhOeM7xF+YQdQKD
  brvR1rf6J8oTPFM2MM26sK98aj5MAsJX)
```

The preceding data has been edited to enclose the key material in parentheses (allowing it to be split across several lines for presentation reasons only), but it appears as a single line in the file. This is the public key associated with the public/private key pair, and it may be sent via any suitable method for inclusion in the master zone file for example.com, either by cutting and pasting, or by using the $INCLUDE directive. The Kupdate.example.com.+005+00706.key file containing the KEY RR is public data and requires no special handling. The following example shows the use of the $INCLUDE directive in the zone file for example.com. It assumes the .key file is placed in the directory /var/named/keys on the host of the zone master for example.com:

```
; example.com zone file fragment
$TTL 2d ; zone TTL default of 2 days
$ORIGIN example.com.
....
$INCLUDE keys/Kupdate.example.com.+005+00706.key ;DDNS key
....
```

The named.conf file on the primary master server must now be modified to allow the zone to be updated using an update-policy statement (an allow-update statement could also be used) in the zone clause, as shown in the following example:

```
// named.conf fragment
logging{
    channel normal_log {
    file "/var/log/named/normal.log" versions 3 size 2m;
    severity error;
    print-time yes;
    print-severity yes;
    print-category yes;
    };
    channel dnssec_log { // streamed dnssec log
    file "/var/log/named/dnssec.log" versions 3 size 2m;
    severity debug 3;
    print-time yes;
    print-severity yes;
    print-category yes;
    };
    category default{
    normal_log;
    };
    category dnssec{
    dnssec_log;
    };
```

```
};
options {
   ....
   directory "/var/named";
   dnssec-enable yes; // BIND default - may be omitted
   ....
};
....
zone "example.com" IN{
   type master;
   file master.example.com;
   update-policy {grant update.example.com subdomain example.com ANY};
};
```

Note To assist in testing, the log has been streamed to provide additional information about DNSSEC events using severity debug 3;. This value should not be used in a production environment unless you like large log files. A setting of severity info; or higher should be used. The dnssec-enable yes; statement in the global options clause is the default since BIND 9.5. It is included to illustrate defensive configuration described earlier in the chapter.

This update-policy allows the KEY RR with the name update.example.com to update any RR in the domain example.com. The following update-policy statement only allows update.example.com to modify NS records for the domain:

```
update-policy {grant update.example.com subdomain example.com NS};
```

By careful selection of the host name when generating keys, fine-grained controls can be created at the cost of multiple key RRs. The following example illustrates how to use this process to allow individual users to modify only their own host records. The target zone file fragment is shown here:

```
; example.com zone file fragment
$TTL 2d ; zone TTL default of 2 days
$ORIGIN example.com.
....
bill    IN  A    192.168.2.3
        IN  TXT  "one fine day"
        IN  RP   bill.example.com.
fred    IN  A    192.168.2.4
        IN  RP   fred.example.com.
        IN  AAAA 2001:db8::15
....
```

To control the process, two public/private key pairs with the preceding host names are generated, as shown here:

```
# dnssec-keygen -a rsasha1 -b 1024 -T key -n host bill.example.com
Kbill.example.com.+005+77325
# dnssec-keygen -a rsasha1 -b 1024 -T key -n host fred.example.com
Kfred.example.com.+005+08634
```

It is assumed that these keys are generated on the respective hosts bill.example.com and fred.example.com. The public KEY RRs are included in the zone file, as shown here:

```
; example.com zone file fragment
$TTL 2d ; zone TTL default of 2 days
$ORIGIN example.com.
....
bill    IN  A   192.168.2.3
        IN  TXT "one fine day"
        IN  RP  bill.example.com. .
$INCLUDE keys/Kbill.example.com.+005+77325.key ; bill KEY RR
fred    IN  A   192.168.2.4
        IN  RP  fred.example.com. .
        IN  AAAA 2001:db8::15
$INCLUDE keys/Kfred.example.com.+005+08634.key ; fred KEY RR
....
```

The following named.conf update-policy ensures that the appropriate key can update only its own A, TXT, AAAA, and RP records:

```
update-policy {grant * self * A AAAA TXT RP};
```

The first * says that a reference to any KEY RR with the same name (self) as the host record (the second *) is allowed (grant) to update the A, AAAA, TXT, and RP RRs only with the same host name. Thus, an incoming update with the name bill.example.com (references the KEY RR of bill.example.com) is only allowed to update or add any A, AAAA, RP, or TXT RRs with a host name of bill.example.com. Similarly, if the update uses the name fred.example.com, it can only update the defined RR types that have a host name of fred.example.com.

Having digressed to cover the use of update-policy, it is time to return to the original public-key example. The file Kupdate.example.com.+001+00706.private, which is located on the client that updates the zone file, looks something like this:

```
Private-key-format: v1.2
Algorithm: 1 (RSA)
Modulus: y9Y5YX+9H/ZdT/4TxTTMVOeSKZDF9TuxM7w5OdK4dHjO8RfmEH
UCg2670da3+ifKEzxTNjDNurCvfGo+TALCVw==
PublicExponent: Aw==
PrivateExponent: h+QmQP/TaqQ+NVQNLiMy4OUMG7XZTifLd9L
QOTclovoCO/y4wq3QNg4jNa5kb4Y4UQfx/2HcK84HrM/T66fzew==
Prime1: /sRMFcz/OnBnuueuvvQi4SCKlKSCi1loWgPTHsmKLZO=
Prime2: zNLQux9xD8HxzBmiYl67lHklO5KbeB+TSfVfYaD8p4M=
Exponent1: qdgyuTNUOaBFJOUfKfgXQMBcYxhXB5DwPAKMvzEGyRM=
Exponent2: iIyLJ2pLX9ahMrvBlunSYvtujQxnpWpiMU4/lmtTGlc=
Coefficient: S5di+sst/DCqT5MSNaiNLPNODJWRjxivgkiifB7DPl4=
```

A number of the preceding lines have been split across more than one line for presentation reasons only. This file contains the private key of the public/private key pair and is only used by the nsupdate utility. It should be immediately secured for read-only permission under the UID of the user who will perform the dynamic update. For the purposes of illustration, it is assumed that the user name that will perform the update is updater, with a group name of users. The following commands secure the .private and .key files in /var/named/dynamic:

```
# chown -R updater:users /var/named/dynamic/*
# chmod -R 0400 /var/named/dynamic/*
```

To invoke and test the SIG(0) dynamic update process, the nsupdate utility is invoked and the following sequence is used to add an MX record and its corresponding A RR for the domain example.com:

```
# cd /var/named/dynamic
# nsupdate -k Kexample.com.+001+00706.private
> server ns1.example.com
> zone example.com
> update add example.com. 36000 IN MX 10 mail2.example.com.
> send
> show
Outgoing update query:
;; ->>HEADER<<- opcode: UPDATE, status: NOERR id: 0
;; flags: ; ZONE: 0, PREREQ: 0, UPDATE: 0, ADDITIONAL: 0
> update add mail2 36000 IN A 192.168.2.5
> send
> show
Outgoing update query:
;; ->>HEADER<<- opcode: UPDATE, status: NOERR id: 0
;; flags: ; ZONE: 0, PREREQ: 0, UPDATE: 0, ADDITIONAL: 0
> quit
```

As with the TSIG example, a dig command can be issued to verify that the MX and A RRs are available at the primary master. By pointing the dig command at the slave servers, the cascaded update, initiated by a NOTIFY message, can also be verified.

It is possible to mix TSIG and SIG(0) dynamic update clients if that makes operational sense. It is also possible to support TSIG for zone transfers and SIG(0) for dynamic update operations, or any such combination.

Summary

This chapter introduced DNS security by categorizing the topic into administrative security, zone transfers, dynamic updates, and zone integrity. The first three topics are covered in this chapter; zone integrity using DNSSEC is described in Chapter 11.

The administrative security discussion covered the selection and configuration of DNS servers as well as software updating, limiting functionality, limiting permissions (including sandboxes or chroot jails), log streaming, and the use of multiple sources of both OS and DNS software to reduce the risks involved in running DNS systems. The packaged installation of a chroot jail on Linux Fedora Core 13 and FreeBSD was described, as well as the manual installation of a chroot jail (on Ubuntu Server 10.04 and FreeBSD) in the absence of an available package.

The chapter described the use of cryptographic techniques to secure various transactions. The various techniques were described in outline for readers unfamiliar with general cryptographic processes, including symmetric (shared-secret) systems, asymmetric (public-key) systems, message digests, message authentication codes (MACs, a.k.a. hashed message authentication codes or HMACs), and digital signatures.

The use of simple BIND statements to secure zone transfers using IP addresses and the use of TSIG (shared-secret) transactions to secure zone transfers was described and illustrated with example files and command sequences.

The chapter also described, with examples, the use of BIND commands to secure dynamic updates using IP addresses. Both SIG(0) using public-key or asymmetric cryptographic techniques and TSIG (shared-secret) methods to secure dynamic updates were described and illustrated with example files and configurations.

The next chapter describes the design intent and implementation of DNSSEC to ensure the source and integrity of zone data during normal query operations.

CHAPTER 11

■■■

DNSSEC

When a name server receives the response to a query for, say, the A record of a web site, for instance, `www.example.com`, it can only hope that the data is correct. It has no way of *proving* that this is the case. In fact, it could have been duped or spoofed in a variety of ways, such as the query response may have been supplied from a poisoned zone file, or the query may have been intercepted and bad data substituted in the response. Another possibility is the query may have been redirected by a poisoned resolver cache to a bogus server for the domain in question, or the response could be perfectly valid, containing good data from the correct source. In a situation where revenues, reputation, or security (commercial or national) are at stake, such uncertainty may be unacceptable. DNSSEC, originally defined in RFC 2535, was designed to eliminate the doubt involved in DNS query operations by providing verifiable certainty to suitably configured name servers. Significant efforts were expended over many years by multiple organizations, notably ISC (`www.isc.org`), Nlnetlabs (`www.nlnetlabs.nl`), some of the root-server operators (`www.root-servers.org`), and regional Internet registries (`www.nro.net`), to build and test secure DNS systems such that they can be scaled and deployed in operational environments. This Herculean effort led to what became known colloquially as DNSSEC.bis, but is now simply known as DNSSEC (defined by RFCs 4033, 4034, and 4035 and augmented by 4470, 4509, 5011, and 5155) and constitutes a substantial enhancement to the original specifications.

■ **Note** When the original book was published, it was no exaggeration to say that the paint was still drying on the DNSSEC standards. A few short years later, we have a DNSSEC signed root (July 2010) and over 60 signed TLDs (a mixture of gTLDs and ccTLDs) with many more undergoing testing at various stages—a truly monumental achievement.

This chapter is organized into three sections. The first, "Base DNSSEC Theory," contains both descriptive and practical material regarding the DNSSEC basic standards. It remains entirely possible to implement DNSSEC using only the material contained in this section. This section continues to be very important because certain tools, rightly designed to decrease some of the complexities of DNSSEC, can also disguise some of the fundamental principles of DNSSEC design. The second section, "DNSSEC Enhancements," describes the major developments of DNSSEC; some are essentially tactical, such as NSEC3 and Opt-Out while some have significant implications such as Trust Anchor Automation (RFC 5011). Again, it's a mixture of descriptive and practical material. The third and final section, "DNSSEC Implementation," addresses choice, issues, and implementation in a DNSSEC operational environment. If you have neither a great need nor desire to understand the theoretical environment, this section alone may be enough to satisfy your needs. Another approach is to skim the first two sections and when curiosity or questions arise, as they inevitably will, grid your loins and plunge back into the depths of the first two sections.

Base DNSSEC Theory

DNSSEC defines a process whereby a suitably configured name server can verify the authenticity and integrity of query results from a signed zone. Public key (or asymmetric) cryptography and a special set of resource records (RRs), specifically resource record signatures (RRSIGs), DNSKEY, and Next Secure (NSEC) RRs, are used by DNSSEC to enable a security-aware resolver (increasingly called a *validating* resolver) to do the following:

- Authenticate that the data received could only have originated from the requested zone.

- Verify the integrity of the data. The data that was received at the querying resolver was the data that was sent from the queried named server. The data content is protected, not the communication channel.

- Verify that if a negative response (NXDOMAIN) was received to a host query, that the target record does not exist (called *proof of nonexistence (PNE)* and occasionally *denial of existence*).

The first item to note here is that to support DNSSEC, both the authoritative zone source (master or slave) and the querying resolver must be configured to support DNSSEC. The zone file must be cryptographically signed and becomes, in the jargon, a *secure entry point (SEP)*, and the querying resolver must be configured to support DNSSEC and is said in the jargon to be *security aware* and thus becomes a validating resolver; that is, it is capable of authenticating or validating cryptographically the responses received from an authoritative server. When a zone is cryptographically signed, the public key is added to the zone using a DNSKEY RR. Each RRset is digitally signed (see Chapter 10) by adding an RRSIG RR. Finally, all the records are chained together using an NSEC RR such that we can prove there are no missing names and thus provide PNE.

Islands of Security

It is unreasonable to suppose that every name server in the world will overnight be configured to support DNSSEC nor that every zone in the world will be secured. Figure 11–1 shows the possible configurations that could exist and that the DNSSEC standards have to handle.

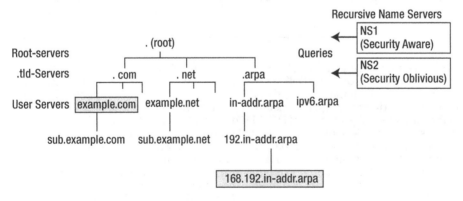

Figure 11–1. Isolated islands of security

Figure 11–1 assumes that the colored domains are secure. The validating (security-aware) resolver (NS1) must continue to provide query results for all domains including the secure domains of example.com and 168.192.in-addr.arpa, and this includes passing through the secure domain of example.com to obtain results for the insecure subdomain of sub.example.com. Equally, the security-oblivious resolver (NS2 is a resolver not configured for DNSSEC security) must continue to obtain transparent results for all the domains, both secure and insecure. NS1 is configured to become security aware by the dnssec-enable yes; and dnssec-validation yes; statements in a global options clause, which causes the name server to advertise its security awareness by including an OPT meta (or pseudo) RR in the additional section of any query with the DNSSEC OK (DO) bit set (see Chapter 15 for details). Conversely, any query without both of these characteristics is said to be security oblivious. If the authoritative server (master or slave) for example.com receives a query that indicates the sender is security aware (NS1 in the Figure 11–1 scenario), it responds with additional security information such as RRSIG RRs that enable the requested RRs to be authenticated. If the name server receives a query from a security-oblivious name server (NS2 in the Figure 11–1scenario), it responds without security information. In the latter case, the query results will be exactly the same as would have been supplied if neither server were security-aware (that is, security is invisible).

■ **Caution** Prior to BIND 9.5, the default for all DNSSEC options in BIND was to turn off security; specifically, the default setting for all name servers was enable-dnssec no;. From BIND 9.5 onward, the default is to turn on DNSSEC security; specifically, the default setting for all name servers is now enable-dnssec yes; and dnssec-validation yes; for recursive servers (resolvers).

Public key cryptography relies on a public and private key pair (see Chapter 10 for a description of public key crytography). The zone at example.com is cryptographically signed using the zone's private key. The receiving name server must have access to the zone's public key in order to perform the required security verification. This gives rise to the classic asymmetric cryptography problem—how to obtain the public key (in the preceding case, for example.com) in a manner that ensures it could only have come from example.com. There are two possible solutions:

- Publish the public key using a DNSKEY RR in the zone file. This method is vulnerable to two problems. If you use a secure query to get the key, validating the response requires the public key that you are requesting but don't yet have, so the security validation will fail—a chicken-and-egg situation. If a nonsecure query is used, then the response could have been spoofed, since it has all the weaknesses of a standard insecure query discussed earlier.

- Obtain the key using an out-of-band process such as secure e-mail, telephone, or some other acceptable process. This is the method adopted by DNSSEC; in BIND the public key, called a *trusted anchor* for reasons that will be clear later, is configured using the trusted-keys clause of named.conf. Figure 11–2 shows this process with NS1 having the trusted-keys clause for example.com.

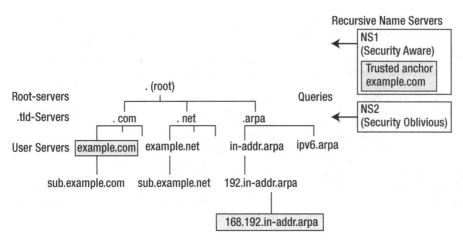

Figure 11–2. *Trusted anchors*

In Figure 11–2, NS2 will continue to operate transparently as before, but NS1 has been configured with a trusted anchor for the domain example.com such that all queries for this domain can be securely authenticated—indicated by setting the Authenticated Data (AD) bit in the message header response (see Chapter 15 for details). It does not, however, have a trusted anchor for the domain 168.192.in-addr.arpa, and in this case, responses from this zone will continue to behave as if they were not secure. Theoretically, NS1, a validating resolver, is able to determine the following states from the responses from any name server:

- *Secure*: A trusted anchor is present for the zone and has been used to validate the received data successfully. In Figure 11–2, only example.com will generate such response states indicated by the Authenticated Data (AD) bit being set.

- *Insecure*: A trusted anchor is present and information allows the name server to prove that at a delegation point there is no secure link to the zone. In Figure 11–2, sub.example.com is the only domain that will generate such a response state.

- *Bogus*: A trusted anchor exists, but the data failed to authenticate at the receiving name server using the trusted anchor. An attempt to spoof or corrupt any response from the domain example.com will generate this state.

- *Indeterminate*: There is no trusted anchor for the domain. This will be the response state for all domains in Figure 11–2 (including 168.192.in-addr.arpa) except example.com and sub.example.com.

Clearly, it's not practical for every name server to have a trusted anchor for every secure domain on the Internet. If this were the only part of DNSSEC, it would simply not scale for Internet-wide deployment. However, before looking at the next set of features, it is worth noting that communities of interest that have finite membership, such as affinity groups, and enterprise networks could implement DNSSEC—even with the relatively limited features described so far—and gain *immediate* access to secured capabilities within the interest groups while continuing to provide transparent service to the wider security-oblivious community.

Chains of Trust

Figure 11–3 shows that any single island of security can be joined to another secure (signed) domain through its delegation point—the NS RRs that point from the parent domain or zone to the child domain or zone—and can be authenticated using the final RR in the DNSSEC set called a Delegated Signer (DS) RR.

In Figure 11–3, a chain of trust is shown from example.com to sub.example.com. Three points flow from this process:

- The child zone, sub.example.com in Figure 11–3, must be secure before secure delegation can occur. Securing the zone is an essential prerequisite to creating chains of trust.

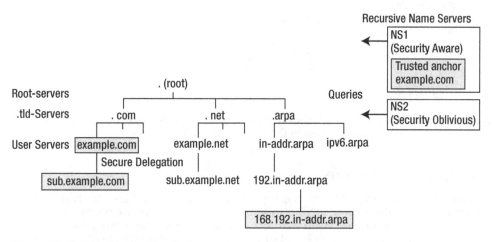

Figure 11–3. Creating chains of trust

- The trusted anchor for example.com covers the secure zones that are delegated from it. In the case of Figure 11–3, the trusted anchor for example.com covers the child zone sub.example.com. The delegation can be securely tracked from example.com (the parent that is covered by the trusted anchor) to sub.example.com (the child) using a chain of trust provided by the DS RR. Any number of levels can be covered using this chain of trust concept.

- Delegation chains can be built both upward as well as downward. Thus, if the gTLD domain .com were secured, the existing secure domain example.com can immediately join the chain, while unsecured domains can continue to operate unchanged (that is, they will not enjoy the benefits of security until action is taken to secure them). The NS1 validating resolver (a security-aware resolver) would require a new trusted anchor to cover the secured .com domain, but this single trusted anchor would cover the *whole* .com domain, including example.com, as shown in Figure 11–4.

As previously noted, the root zone was signed in July 2010. In addition, at the date of publication, over 60 gTLD and ccTLD zones were also signed and had placed DS RRs in the root zone. It is thus possible, using a single root-key as a trusted anchor (in a trusted-keys clause), for a validating resolver to cryptographically validate queries to any signed zone (domain name) under one of these signed TLDs by following the chain through the DS RR(s) from the root.

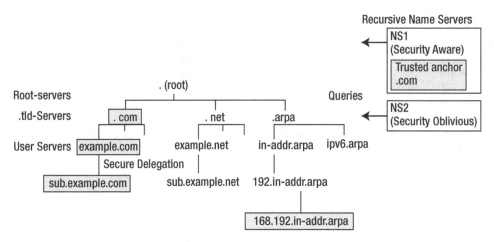

Figure 11–4. Joining chains of trust

Having described the DNSSEC process, it's time to start looking at the details of how it all works starting with securing the zone file—the first step in the implementation sequence.

Securing or Signing the Zone

The first step in implementation of DNSSEC is to cryptographically sign the zone files. This is done using the dnssec-signzone utility provided with all BIND distributions. However, before we get anywhere near the details of running this utility, it's necessary to step back and understand what is being done.

Zones are digitally signed using the private key of a public key (asymmetric) encryption technology. DNSSEC allows for the use of RSA-SHA-1, RSA-SHA256, RSA-SHA512, DSA-SHA-1, and RSA-MD5 digital signatures. The public key corresponding to the private key used to sign the zone is published using a DNSKEY RR and will appear at the apex or root of the zone file; for example, if the zone being signed is example.com, then a DNSKEY RR with a name of example.com will appear in the zone file.

■ **Note** The private key of the signing algorithm is only required to be available during the signing process—all verification at security-aware name servers is accomplished using the public key only. Thus, following signing, it's a common practice to take the public key offline, which may involve physically removing the key from the server or moving it to a more secure part of the server. In the case of Dynamic DNS (DDNS), taking the private key offline may not be possible—see the "Dynamic DNS and DNSSEC" section later in this chapter. Further discussion of this topic is also included in "DNSSEC Implementation."

Two types of keys are identified for use in zone signing operations. The first type is called a *Zone Signing Key (ZSK)*, and the second type is called a *Key Signing Key (KSK)*. The ZSK is used to sign the RRsets within the zone, and this includes signing the ZSK itself. The public key of this ZSK uses a DNSKEY RR at the apex or root of the zone; that is, if the zone being signed is example.com, the ZSK's public key will be defined by a DNSKEY RR, which has a name of example.com.

The KSK is used to sign the keys at the apex or root of the zone, which includes the ZSK and the KSK; it may also be used or referenced outside the zone either as the trusted anchor in a validating resolver or as part of the chain of trust (from the DS RRs) by a parent name server. The KSK is also defined in a DNSKEY RR at the root or apex of the zone; that is, if the zone is called example.com, then the name of the DNSKEY RR of the KSK will also be example.com. The difference between the ZSK and the KSK is therefore one of usage not definition, and it is a matter of local operational choice whether a single DNSKEY RR is used as both the ZSK and the KSK or whether separate DNSKEY RRs are used as the ZSK and KSK. The DNSSEC standards allow both methods. This book will use separate keys for the ZSF and the KSK throughout this section to clearly separate the functionality. The RFC on DNSSEC Operational Practices also recommends the use of separate keys (RFC 4641). Both ZSKs and KSK use a DNSKEY RR; a ZSK DNSKEY RR has a flags field of 256 (see Chapter 13 DNSKEY Record), whereas a KSK is indicated by a flags field value of 257.

■ **Note** The flags field in a DNSKEY RR is a decimal representation of a bit-significant field; thus the decimal value 256 represents bit 7 of the 16-bit flags field (bits numbered from the left starting from 0) and indicates a ZSK. The decimal value 257 represents both bit 7 (ZSK) and bit 15, the Secure Entry Point (SEP) bit. The SEP bit is used to indicate, solely for administrative purposes, that this DNSKEY RR is used as a KSK, and indeed this bit is becoming increasingly known as the KSK bit. This bit is not required and plays no role in the secure validation process or the protocol. While all of the following examples use this feature, specifically trusted anchors and DS RRs point to DNSKEY RRs with the SEP bit set (flags value of 257), they could just as easily have pointed to DNSKEY RRs with only the ZSK bit set (flags value of 256). The SEP bit is, in modern jargon, pure *sugar*. Its job in life is to make matters more pleasant! All that being said, the current recommended best practice is to use separate keys, which means the SEP bit will be set on the KSK.

Figure 11–5 shows the usage of the two key types.

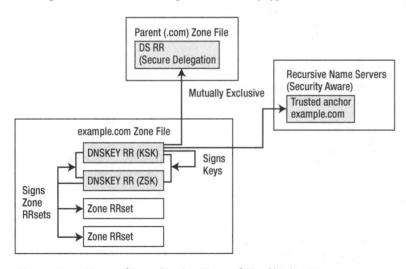

Figure 11–5. Usage of Zone Signing Key and Key Signing Key

When a zone is signed, the ZSK and the KSK (remember they could also be one and the same key) are generated using the normal `dnssec-keygen` utility (described in Chapter 9) with the name of the zone. The detail process including the parameters used will be illustrated later in the various operational examples. The resulting DNSKEY RRs are either added to the zone file directly or by using an $INCLUDE directive (see Chapter 13) as shown in the following example.com zone file:

```
$TTL 86400 ; 1 day
$ORIGIN example.com.
@            IN SOA ns1.example.com. hostmaster.example.com. (
                        2010121500 ; serial
                        43200      ; refresh (12 hours)
                        600        ; retry (10 minutes)
                        604800     ; expire (1 week)
                        10800      ; nx (3 hours)
                        )
             IN  NS ns1.example.com.
             IN  NS ns2.example.com.
             IN  MX 10 mail.example.com.
             IN  MX 10 mail1.example.com.
_ldap._tcp   IN  SRV 5 2 235 www
ns1          IN  A  192.168.2.6
ns2          IN  A  192.168.23.23
www          IN  A  10.1.2.1
             IN  A  172.16.2.1
ftp          IN CNAME ftp.example.net.
mail         IN  A  192.168.2.3
mail1        IN  A  192.168.2.4
$ORIGIN sub.example.com.
@            IN  NS ns3.sub.example.com.
             IN  NS ns4.sub.example.com.
ns3          IN  A  10.2.3.4 ; glue RR
ns4          IN  A  10.2.3.5 ; glue RR
; This is a key-signing key, keyid 34957, for example.com.
; Created: 20101216115248 (Thu Dec 16 06:52:48 2010)
; Publish: 20101216115248 (Thu Dec 16 06:52:48 2010)
; Activate: 20101216115248 (Thu Dec 16 06:52:48 2010)
example.com. IN DNSKEY 257 3 8 (AwEAAcdPX24uAsa2b2dfBG
                                b+GfC2kkEpaDCEXcS2oMmsL
                                mxfUiOjw4+5FlEB74AmvNTY
                                ovJKhcekPlJGUqULnpohbcB
                                qgtGKGPtOy43taTl3kCoH B
                                T+8IE1RzCGnDmG7HNWB6Bjk
                                Qqp1gk/R5Jq6Dp+JyHNO3OH
                                qgHv2KrRu vUOXV+8l)
; This is a zone-signing key, keyid 27228, for example.com.
; Created: 20101216115101 (Thu Dec 16 06:51:01 2010)
; Publish: 20101216115101 (Thu Dec 16 06:51:01 2010)
; Activate: 20101216115101 (Thu Dec 16 06:51:01 2010)
example.com. IN DNSKEY 256 3 8 (AwEAAe9cQz4kHCCaocjIlSB
                                547QVSUZ9xYBPqTXPX2oTXr
                                zyHqfgPPnM ZFvvPwGDZtZT
                                q1K9kkEFXJ9FpwvlslKZTOW
                                emnIci4qH8uWmoY8n7/n/ b
                                wLGAuyE6R1FMWTpDSy8sDSj
```

```
               PKaqqXXf8R77exTNyWDfORf
               dHvQXCjnx Gls1o4Y5)
```

The first DNSKEY RR is the KSK indicated by the flags value of 257; the second DNSKEY RR, the ZSK, has a flags value of 256 (for details see Chapter 13). The zone is now ready for signing, which is done using the dnssec-signzone utility—details of running this utility are fully illustrated later in the example. When a zone is signed, the dnssec-signzone utility does a number of automagical things:

- It sorts the RRs into a canonical order (essentially alphabetic based on host name).

- It adds an NSEC RR after each RR to chain together the valid host names appearing in the zone file. The last NSEC RR will point back to the zone apex or root.

- It uses the ZSK to sign each RRset by creating an RRSIG RR. This includes both the DNSKEY RRs and the newly added NSEC RRs from step 2.

- It uses the KSK to sign (create an RRSIG RR) for the DNSKEY RRset at the zone apex.

The resulting file—which by default has .signed appended to the name of the master zone file—after running the dnssec-signzone utility will look like that shown here:

```
; File written on Sat Dec 18 21:31:01 2010
; dnssec_signzone version 9.7.2-P2
example.com.  86400 IN SOA ns1.example.com. hostmaster.example.com. (
                    2010121500 ; serial
                    43200      ; refresh (12 hours)
                    600        ; retry (10 minutes)
                    604800     ; expire (1 week)
                    10800      ; minimum (3 hours)
                    )
            86400   RRSIG  SOA 8 2 86400 20110118013101 (
                    20101219013101 27228 example.com.
                    Mnm5RaKEFAW4V5dRhP7OxLtGAFMb/Zsej2vH
                    mK5O7zHL+U2Hbx+arMMoA/aOxtp6JxpOFWM3
                    67VHclTjjGX9xf++6qvA65JHRNvKoZgXGtXI
                    VGG6ve8A8J9LRePtCKwo3WfhtLEMFsd1KI6o
                    JTViPzs3UDEqgAvy8rgtvwr80a8= )
            86400   NS             ns1.example.com.
            86400   NS             ns2.example.com.
            86400   RRSIG    NS 8 2 86400 20110118013101 (
                    20101219013101 27228 example.com.
                    ubbRJV+DiNmgQITtncLOCjIw4cfB4qnC+DX8
                    ....
                    S78T5Fxh5SbLBPTBKmlKvKxcx6k= )
            86400   MX       10 mail.example.com.
            86400   MX       10 mail1.example.com.
            86400   RRSIG    MX 8 2 86400 20110118013101 (
                    20101219013101 27228 example.com.
                    K5CVLZDZ/p8KeVVJ/2kxMjN8QaYLZRmvcbiO
                    ....
                    T8a4tw5E+Sv/BX+x1QqksFics64= )
            10800   NSEC     _ldap._tcp.example.com. NS SOA MX RRSIG NSEC DNSKEY
            10800   RRSIG    NSEC 8 2 10800 20110118013101 (
                    20101219013101 27228 example.com.
```

```
                              UO8drM7WOwyaF6FXqFuybQpUUGvhRr58xM2S
                              ....
                              PFnee80+vXd4sgN6+SfY6AyQV2M= )
            86400    DNSKEY   256 3 8 (
                              AwEAAe9cQz4kHCCaocjIlSB547QVSUZ9xYBP
                              qTXPX2oTXrzyHqfgPPnMZFvvPwGDZtZTq1K9
                              kkEFXJ9FpwvlslKZTOWemnIci4qH8uWmoY8n
                              7/n/bwLGAuyE6R1FMWTpDSy8sDSjPKaqqXXf
                              8R77exTNyWDfORfdHvQXCjnxGls1o4Y5
                              ) ; key id = 27228
            86400    DNSKEY   257 3 8 (
                              AwEAAcdPX24uAsa2b2dfBGb+GfC2kkEpaDCE
                              ....
                              5Jq6Dp+JyHNO3OHqgHv2KrRuvUOXV+8l
                              ) ; key id = 34957
            86400    RRSIG    DNSKEY 8 2 86400 20110118013101 (
                              20101219013101 27228 example.com.
                              rRjX4FpgIhRiZgwE1G8pOKH8Uhz2JksbJsif
                              ....
                              apROsSPuroSFcRYyxcfLG3HdIS4= )
            86400    RRSIG    DNSKEY 8 2 86400 20110118013101 (
                              20101219013101 34957 example.com.
                              rGqGH632fMqKC5G5yhLZiTUL3liMzu+CTiC1
                              ....
                              j3d5igODKdRHEZKWnvaPZfVWKXo= )
_ldap._tcp.example.com. 86400 IN SRV 5 2 235 www.example.com.
            86400    RRSIG    SRV 8 4 86400 20110118013101 (
                              20101219013101 27228 example.com.
                              HvjoUq/sQKZb/DnGyWthxNQyeFs62CRtU43a
                              ....
                              oYmF3EUjBdIgBAJiqdTR/2pqBus= )
            10800    NSEC     ftp.example.com. SRV RRSIG NSEC
            10800    RRSIG    NSEC 8 4 10800 20110118013101 (
                              20101219013101 27228 example.com.
                              fYNrf2jm73jltGDC7aF6DlSTvcyCpZ+cHSiT
                              ....
                              ZALrIjznKyH8pl66qE989YCIneY= )
ftp.example.com. 86400 IN CNAME ftp.example.net.
            86400    RRSIG    CNAME 8 3 86400 20110118013101 (
                              20101219013101 27228 example.com.
                              hjChA2GkSRZeQMFY7+LJTlIHDVEL7ZQ3zmyU
                              ....
                              2pOU1junt22N21bYHT7mF6SZsec= )
            10800    NSEC     mail.example.com. CNAME RRSIG NSEC
            10800    RRSIG    NSEC 8 3 10800 20110118013101 (
                              20101219013101 27228 example.com.
                              Odn+xpgWlx7TRJufHlhkfAxo9wMSCG5O25kb
                              ....
                              9NE+9NMhbqDhIiofQ8GEb/b2t4M= )
mail1.example.com. 86400          IN A 192.168.2.4
            86400    RRSIG    A 8 3 86400 20110118013101 (
                              20101219013101 27228 example.com.
                              bMWvyVmoNcBcq/T4zVABdramRz60thZGITcz
                              ....
```

```
                           kojE4FfJRdWjCB6F/lpt1pL72nE= )
              10800    NSEC    ns1.example.com. A RRSIG NSEC
              10800    RRSIG   NSEC 8 3 10800 20110118013101 (
                               20101219013101 27228 example.com.
                               B1oytuMOqcslrDTDnquEKEvO6UVvgxeOROxZ
                               ....
                               7D6lMBbDxLcrab4kQY63PjKjFtw= )
ns1.example.com. 86400 IN A    192.168.2.6
              86400    RRSIG   A 8 3 86400 20110118013101 (
                               20101219013101 27228 example.com.
                               yV3AwrksW8s54jMZdDFsicAVXcdkfvP7jgNo
                               ....
                               i88/ViKCIREhX3Jl33uOzwv4720= )
              10800    NSEC    ns2.example.com. A RRSIG NSEC
              10800    RRSIG   NSEC 8 3 10800 20110118013101 (
                               20101219013101 27228 example.com.
                               R6NF/W2J59eRnaBSQCvpLtjvHXcsV8g1OEUb
                               ....
                               1kjsIkAoSJ6mMnxKhxj7o+CYxJ4= )
ns2.example.com. 86400 IN A    192.168.23.23
              86400    RRSIG   A 8 3 86400 20110118013101 (
                               20101219013101 27228 example.com.
                               juzbAhNyGevhrrpKqoY82EXVStLTZk42/vPt
                               ....
                               7ahKR9HNA9mg2go+H+QLQVYQ18I= )
              10800    NSEC    sub.example.com. A RRSIG NSEC
              10800    RRSIG   NSEC 8 3 10800 20110118013101 (
                               20101219013101 27228 example.com.
                               a63Sf4DP1UEbqdZKRO5I6vMmbNmy9vo7YgS2
                               ....
                               aCRIk45rOr2aSVGe19kCZQc+fFO= )
mail.example.com. 86400 IN A   192.168.2.3
              86400    RRSIG   A 8 3 86400 20110118013101 (
                               20101219013101 27228 example.com.
                               hpArsBJoHqi9+9Ys4o46WZogwd8Li4Zn3FkQ
                               ....
                               MTnI6ULQvwcFfVVifO7zs5xBa8U= )
              10800    NSEC    mail1.example.com. A RRSIG NSEC
              10800    RRSIG   NSEC 8 3 10800 20110118013101 (
                               20101219013101 27228 example.com.
                               TJ+EDteAhUV1KNPG+tbDbGzOjjKjqdHkIoZd
                               ....
                               qtAtFhFysMH7JFvnKZEOeRec2TO= )
sub.example.com. 86400 IN NS   ns3.sub.example.com.
              86400 IN NS      ns4.sub.example.com.
              10800    NSEC    www.example.com. NS RRSIG NSEC
              10800    RRSIG   NSEC 8 3 10800 20110118013101 (
                               20101219013101 27228 example.com.
                               UxsUTlFZ9HIIOelqkHPFpoA7HcB/o/oZchdD
                               ....
                               NbjZ42hmv5kBMq8RKXOZql4hUsc= )
ns3.sub.example.com. 86400 IN A 10.2.3.4
ns4.sub.example.com. 86400 IN A 10.2.3.5
www.example.com. 86400     IN A 10.1.2.1
```

```
86400 IN A      172.16.2.1
86400    RRSIG   A 8 3 86400 20110118013101 (
            20101219013101 27228 example.com.
            wtBArhmhUS76gzkjQR4ounOHMSpeI7UngTFO
            ....
            FVejigwrKPOx+DGGsj6t9qetfmE= )
10800    NSEC    example.com. A RRSIG NSEC
10800    RRSIG   NSEC 8 3 10800 20110118013101 (
            20101219013101 27228 example.com.
            k95zDrRq4UmJAAea+m2Ag2mVtqnMgSGMqHCR
            ....
            NFQ9D+/Tvo/Te6ha7OPvs2JGN3Y= )
```

■ **Note** The first RRSIG RR and the first DNSKEY RR in this file contain a complete copy of the signature and the key material for reference. The lines containing …. in the subsequent RRSIG RRs indicate that lines have been removed, since the base64 material adds no further insight for the human reader—other than the fact that the output would be even bigger than shown. For the insatiably curious, the size of the zone file after signing was 7,965 bytes; before signing, it was 1,833 bytes—a ratio of roughly 4:1. Depending on the content of the zone file, this ratio can be as high as 7:1.

Once you get over the initial feelings of relief that the process is automated, you should note the following points:

- The records have been reordered; specifically, the DNSKEY RRs have been moved to the top or apex of the signed file and the A RRs for ns1, ns2, and www have been sorted into their expected (canonical) order.

- NSEC RRs have been added (the first one is after the last MX RR for the zone) such that it is possible to chain using these records through the zone file and thus prove that any particular host name does not exist (recall that NSEC RRs are used as proof of nonexistence). The last NSEC RR for the A RRs for www.example.com points back to the domain root (example.com), indicating there are no additional records in the zone file..

- Every RRset has been signed with an RRSIG RR. There are four multiple RRsets (the DNSKEY RRs, the NS RRs, the MX RRs, and the www.example.com A RRs); all the other RRsets comprise single RRs—which are still RRsets!

- The DNSKEY RRs have been signed twice (there are two RRSIG RRs). The first signature uses the KSK and is an artifact of the use of a separate ZSK and KSK. The second signature uses the ZSK and is an artifact of the rule that says that all RRsets are signed by the ZSK. If a single DNSKEY RR was used for both the ZSK and KSK functions as allowed by the standards, there would be only one RRSIG RR.

- All comments and zone file directives ($TTL, $ORIGIN) have been removed and all names have been expanded to FQDNs.

- The sub.example.com. NS RRs for the zone are not signed with an RRSIG RR because these RRs (this is the parent) are not authoritative; they will only be authoritative when they appear in the child zone. Only authoritative RRs are signed. However, they have an NSEC RR that is signed. The NSEC RRs are present because the name sub.example.com. is part of the name space of this zone and thus must provide PNE.

- Each zone RR has a TTL value of 86400, which was defined by the $TTL value on the original zone file. However, the TTL value for each NSEC RR (and its associated RRSIG RR) is defined by the nx value of the SOA RR in the original zone file because NSEC RRs are only used with negative (NXDOMAIN) responses, therefore the negative caching value applies.

- The glue AA RRs for the subdomain (ns3.sub.example.com and ns4.sub.example.com) have neither a RRSIG RR nor a NSEC RR because they are neither authoritative (for the same reason as the NS RRs for sub.example.com) nor do they form part of the name space of this zone and therefore require no PNE (which is generated by NSEC RRs).

Finally, every RRSIG RR has a start time (the time after which it is regarded as being valid) that begins at the Universal Coordinated Time (UTC) minus 1 hour (to allow for clock skew) corresponding to the local run time of the dnssec-signzone utility and will expire 30 days after its start time—these are the dnssec-signzone utility defaults. The utility run time (UCT) is always included as a comment on the first line of the file; the expiry and start times are respectively the fourth and fifth parameters after the RRSIG type value (see also Chapter 13). If the zone file is not re-signed before the value defined by the expiry time is reached (in this case 20110118013101, or 18th January 2011 at 1:31:01 a.m. UCT), a validating resolver will discard any data from the zone as being bogus (invalid); paradoxically, a security oblivious name server will continue to receive the data successfully. Signing a zone always introduces an element of time that is not present in an unsigned zone file and requires periodic maintenance of the zone file. The next section will look at the implications of re-signing as well as other aspects of secure zone maintenance, including the essential topic of changing keys by what is called in the jargon *key rollover*.

■ **Note** It is worth pointing out that NSEC RRs are the subject of some controversy since, as a side effect of their purpose, they have the capability of "walking" or enumerating the zone file. By simply following the NSEC chain for any zone, a user can find all the entries in that zone. Some users find this behavior unacceptable, since it speeds up a process that would otherwise require exhaustive search of the zone. An alternative form of NSEC RR, called NSEC3, avoids this problem and is described in the "DNSSEC Enhancements" section later in the chapter.

Secure Zone Maintenance

Re-signing a zone involves simply rerunning the original dnssec-signzone utility using either the original zone file or the currently signed version of it. Secure zone files need to be re-signed for three reasons:

- *When any change is made to the zone records*: In the insecure world, changes were indicated simply by updating the SOA RR serial number; in the world of DNSSEC, whenever a change is made to the zone file, the SOA serial number needs to be updated and the zone needs to be re-signed. The issue of dynamic update (DDNS) and re-signing is discussed later in the chapter.

- *When the signatures expire*: As shown in the example signed zone file earlier, each RRSIG RR will expire by default every 30 days. This time period can be controlled by parameters to the dnssec-signzone utility; nevertheless, periodic zone re-signing will always be required to avoid signature expiry.

- *When one or more of the ZSK or KSK needs to be changed*: This process, called key rollover, may be required either as part of a regular maintenance process or an emergency—the key is either known to be or suspected of having been compromised.

The first two processes use the existing DNSKEY RRs and have no impact on external name servers. The process involving key rollover has significant implications for any external name server that has a DS RR (the parent) referencing the KSK, a trusted anchor that references the current KSK (a trusted-keys clause in BIND), or cached DNSKEY RRs for either the KSK or ZSK.

Cryptographic keys must be periodically changed, from 30 days to multiple years depending on their strength, for three reasons:

- Over a period of time it may be possible for an attacker to accumulate enough plaintext and encrypted material to perform an analysis of the key.

- A brute-force attack will take some period of time. If the key is changed prior to that interval, the attacker will have to start again.

- If a key is silently compromised (unknown to the user or operator), it is unlikely the attacker will boast about it. Instead, he will continue quietly decrypting the material or subverting the zone. Changing the key will limit any damage that may result from this and force the attacker to start again.

When a key is changed, it may, depending on whether it is a ZSK or a KSK, impact one or more of the following processes, which most likely will be controlled by entities other than the zone administrator who initiates the change:

- *Updating of the DS record at the parent (KSK only)*: If the parent zone at which the DS RR must be changed is not controlled by the same owner as the child zone, synchronization of the DS RR change with the KSK change is impossible without a level of automation that is not currently available. The time difference may be considerable and may even involve multiple days.

- *Updating of the trusted anchors at security-aware name servers (KSK only)*: This process will depend on the method being used, but the worst case may involve users manually updating name servers, which could easily take many days. If the update is not performed, a likely event if a manual update is involved, then the zone data will be rejected as bogus by any validating resolver that has not updated the trusted anchor, thus rendering the zone unavailable. With a signed root-zone now in place, at first glance this may look superfluous. However, suppose it is the root-zone KSK that is being changed--every validating resolver will have to change. Also, there may always be islands of security for unique and compelling reasons.

- *RRSIG RR and DNSKEY RR caching in validating resolvers (ZSK and KSK):* Since the RRSIG RR used to sign any RRset and the DNSKEY RRs used to validate them may be acquired at different times, they could expire from any validating resolver cache at different times, even if all zone TTLs are the same. Therefore, if a zone is re-signed with a new ZSK or KSK, it's possible for an old RRSIG RR (an RRSIG RR created with the old ZSK or KSK) and a new DNSKEY RR to be in the same cache; the reverse situation can also occur. In both cases, because compatible DNSKEY and RRSIG RRs were not available in the cache queries for the associated RRs, data will not validate and will therefore will cause a bogus response.

It may be seen from the preceding that there can be no single point in time at which a zone can change from one key to another key, no matter whether it is a ZSK or a KSK. The standards, however, allow for multiple keys to exist (in multiple DNSKEY RRs) at the zone apex and mandate that all available keys should be tried before the zone data is marked as bogus. This feature allows a signed zone to operate for a period of time with old and new keys until the various entities can be guaranteed to have acquired the new key material, at which point old key(s) can be retired. There are two methods by which a zone may operate with multiple keys—the prepublish method and the double-signing method.

The Prepublish Method

The *prepublish* method allows one or more new keys to be simply introduced into the DNSKEY RRset at the zone apex before they are used. Their inclusion in the zone prior to use ensures that the appropriate keys will eventually be available in the cache of all validating resolvers when the key is finally rolled; that is, the zone is re-signed with the new ZSK and/or KSK while leaving the old key(s) at the zone apex, even though they are apparently performing no function. To illustrate this process, it is assumed that all TTLs for a signed zone are for 24 hours (86400 seconds).

1. At least two days (2 x TTL) before the zone signatures expires (it could be any time prior to that if required), a new ZSK or KSK would be added to the DNSKEY RRset at the zone apex. The zone is re-signed using the current, not the new, key(s). The new DNSKEY RR is not used to sign the zone in any way—it is merely present (or published) in the DNSKEY RRset.

2. After 24 hours (1 x TTL), it can be guaranteed that all caches in validating resolvers will have the new DNSKEY RRset containing both the current and the new keys. The RRSIG records for any RR types in these caches will have been signed with the current, not the new, keys.

3. At this point, the zone may be re-signed using the new key or keys. The old key is retained in the DNSKEY RRset.

4. From this point and for the next 24 hours, the RRSIG RRs associated with any requested RR, say the A RR for www.example.com, may be signed with either the old key, if the RR is already in the cache, or the new key, if it has expired from the cache or was not available in the cache and had to be obtained from the authoritative server. Recall that the standards mandate that all available keys should be tried before rejecting any data as being bogus. In either case, a DNSKEY RR that will successfully validate the requested RR data will be present in the cache, or if the DNSKEY RRset has expired or is not present, it can be requested from the authoritative server.

5. After 24 hours (1 x TTL) from re-signing the zone file with the new key(s), the caches can all be guaranteed to contain only RRSIGs signed with the new key. The old key, sometimes called the *stale key*, may be removed at any subsequently convenient time from the DNSKEY RRset at the zone apex and the zone again re-signed only with the new key. It does no harm to leave this stale key in the zone file for an extended period of time.

The Double-Signing Method

As its name suggests, the *double-signing* method involves the use of more than one key to sign the zone if a ZSK, or the DNSKEY RRset at the zone apex if a KSK. For example, imagine that you are using double-signing to roll-over a ZSK. In this instance, there will be two active ZSK DNSKEY RRs in the zone file. Since RRsets are signed with all available keys, double signing ensures that *any* DNSKEY RR contained in the cache at a validating resolver will authenticate (validate) any requested RRset. Similarly with KSK, double-signing *any* DS RR or trusted anchor will point to at least one of the signing keys. Unlike the prepublish method, there are no cache timing implications. When all users of the ZSK have migrated to the new key (after the TTL expiry time), or, in the case of a KSK, the DS RRs have been updated at the parent zone or the trusted anchors have been replaced, the old key can be deleted from the zone file at any convenient time and the zone re-signed only with the new key.

Key Rollover Summary

The method used is largely a matter of operational decision, but to minimize the volume of records involved, especially in larger zone files, the prepublish method is more suited to changing ZSKs and the double-signing method to changing KSKs. The reasoning here is that ZSKs sign each RRset in the zone file, of which there will typically be many. Double signing each RRset will significantly increase the amount of data in the zone file as well as the volume of data sent on each query response. On the other hand, KSKs only sign a single RRset, the DNSKEY RRset at the zone apex, and double signing this RRset will therefore incur a relatively modest overhead.

The process of key rollover involves a number of steps, some of which may involve third parties and some of which lend themselves to automation. Each step itself is not complex, but the totality of the process, coupled with the fact that a zone could become inaccessible (by being treated as bogus) if any step fails, suggests a number of observations:

- The key-rollover process must be thoroughly planned and subject to continuously evolving refinement.

- The process must be automated wherever practical.

- The key rollover process must be exercised on a reasonably frequent and periodic basis. Practice makes perfect. While it's possible, even now, to create keys that could be valid for many years, such attempts to postpone the agony of creating an efficient and streamlined key-rollover process by making it an infrequent event probably exacerbate the problem simply because they ignore the point that, due to a crucial key compromise, any key-rollover process (especially a creaky one) may have to be carried out in short order. The prospect of many thousands of DNS administrators giving great imitations of headless chickens while desperately trying to figure out what they did three years ago, coupled with the signature expiry clock inexorably ticking down, does not leave one with a warm and fuzzy feeling.

- KSKs and ZSKs should be separated and rolled at different intervals. The KSK change is clearly the most significant and, by using a larger key size for increased security, can be rolled perhaps every 12 - 24 months versus a ZSK interval of perhaps 1 to 6 months. The larger the key size, the more CPU load placed on the server. However, since the KSK is used very infrequently relative to the ZSK, having a larger key size for the KSK should present only a modest additional load on the validating resolver.

Some of the above issues have been addressed by the RFC 5011, which is fully described in the "Key Handling Automation" section later in this chapter.

Secure Delegation

Once a zone is secured, it can then be added to an existing chain of trust or can be used to secure delegation to a subdomain. In both cases, this is accomplished using a Delegated Signer (DS) RR. The DS RR is placed in the parent of the zone that will be securely delegated and validates the next key in the chain of trust. The DS RR contains a hash (or digest) of the KSK, defined using a DNSKEY RR, at the apex or the root of the child domain. Thus, if the subdomain sub.example.com is to be securely delegated (joins the chain of trust), a DS RR containing a digest of the DNSKEY RR with a name of sub.example.com and having a flags field value of 257 will be added to the domain example.com at the point of delegation (the NS RRs pointing to the subdomain sub.example.com, in this case). Secure delegation can only occur if the parent and child zones are secure; that is, they both are *signed*. Figure 11–6 illustrates this process.

The dnssec-signzone utility can generate a DS RR during the signing process for the child zone using the -g argument. Depending on the policies in place, the DS RR and perhaps a copy of the KSK (a DNSKEY RR) for the zone may be sent to the owner of the parent domain for inclusion in the zone file, which must then be re-signed. Increasingly, registrars are allowing DS RRs to be added to the domain name registration information using a secure web interface. The child zone is said to join the chain of trust and is authenticated by virtue of the authentication of the parent zone and its secure link (the DS RR) to the child zone. A validating resolver receiving RRs from a secure domain can track the delegation route for sub.example.com back through one or more DS RRs in signed zones to one for which the validating resolver has a trusted anchor.

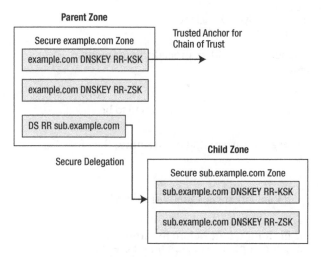

Figure 11–6. Secure delegation in DNSSEC

■ **Caution** A DS RR is simply a hash of the KSK DNSKEY RR (with a flags value of 257). The DS RR could therefore be synthesized or created directly from a child zone's DNSKEY RRset by, for example, the parent domain. Indeed, BIND provides the utility dnssec-dsfromkey that provides this precise functionality. However, if performed remotely when trying to establish the *initial* DS RR(s), this is an insecure and potentially dangerous operation because, until there is a secure delegation, there can be no guarantee that the real zone is being read. The DNSKEY RRset query responses from the child to the parent could have been spoofed. They are not provably secure. Once the initial DS RR(s) have been established, it would perfectly possible to securely read the DNSKEY RRset from the child zone and update the DS RRs at the parent since the established DS RR provides a provably correct link.

Dynamic DNS and DNSSEC

Dynamic DNS can be used with signed zones. The server will automatically update any required NSEC RRs and will re-sign the RRset. The following points, however, apply when working with dynamic updates and signed zones:

- Either TSIG or SIG(0) security can be used to secure the updates as described in Chapter 10. If SIG(0) (public key) security is used, it requires a KEY RR (not a DNSKEY RR as used in DNSSEC) that must be included or added to the zone file.

- The .private file of the ZSK *must* be available (online) in either the directory defined by the directory statement or uniquely defined using the key-directory statement (in a global, view, or zone clause) of named.conf during any update. If this file is not available, then any update attempt will fail with the following log message:

```
'example.com/IN': adding an RR at 'www.example.com' A
'example.com/IN': could not get zone keys for secure dynamic update
'example.com/IN': RRSIG/NSEC update failed: permission denied
```

- When dynamically updated zones are signed, the modified procedures for manual editing of the zone file must be followed:

  1. Stop BIND or use rndc freeze zone.

  2. Bring the KSK .private key online (the ZSK .private file is assumed to be online, as noted previously)

  3. Re-sign the signed zone since it contains the current updates (requires the -f option)

  4. Delete the .jnl file

  5. Take the KSK .private file offline, and then either start BIND or rndc thaw zone.

- In particular, it is vital to delete the .jnl file for the zone before restarting or reloading the zone file after the re-signing is complete to ensure that there is no playback of stale values from this file.

If you are currently using secured dynamic updates, adding DNSSEC to the zones is a transparent process. Care must be taken when signing zones that are dynamically updated to observe the additional steps required.

DNSSEC and Performance

When an authoritative name server (either master or slave) answers queries for a signed zone, it merely has to provide the additional RRs, such as RRSIG RRs, when requested to do so by a validating resolver. This increased traffic will incur a relatively modest performance overhead. However, no cryptographic processing is involved in this process which, being processor intensive, would have caused more significant performance overheads.

When signing is performed using dnssec-signzone, it may be performed on a separate server and the signed zone files simply exported to the operational name servers either using a hidden master configuration with zone transfer, or alternatively using some other secure file transfer method. Since the .private key files are *only* required during signing operations, they can be taken offline when not in use or otherwise secured, using say a hardware security module (HSM), on a signing-only host.

When DDNS is being used, as noted above, the .private key file must be constantly available on the DDNS host, and significant performance overheads will be incurred during the signing process.

■ **Note** Some of the processes described previously can be automated. Indeed a number of such tools already exist, some of which are identified at www.netwidget.net/books/apress/dns.

DNSSEC Base Examples

In order to illustrate the basic DNSSEC operational process, the following procedures will be described with examples:

- Securing the zone example.com using a separate ZSK and KSK.

- Establishing a trusted anchor for example.com in a name server at ns1.example.net

- Securing the zone sub.example.com

- Adding the DS RR for sub.example.com to the zone example.com to create secure delegation within the chain of trust.

- Rolling the ZSK and KSK for example.com

The examples are based on Figures 11–1 through 11–3, presented earlier in the chapter.

Securing the example.com Zone

The zone example.com, which will be signed during this process, is an *island of security* and has a zone file shown here:

```
$TTL 86400 ; 1 day
$ORIGIN example.com.
@          IN SOA ns1.example.com. hostmaster.example.com. (
```

```
                        2010121500 ; serial
                        43200      ; refresh (12 hours)
                        600        ; retry (10 minutes)
                        604800     ; expire (1 week)
                        10800      ; nx (3 hours)
                        )
               IN  NS ns1.example.com.
               IN  NS ns2.example.com.
               IN  MX 10 mail.example.com.
               IN  MX 10 mail1.example.com.
_ldap._tcp     IN  SRV 5 2 235 www
ns1            IN  A  192.168.2.6
ns2            IN  A  192.168.23.23
www            IN  A  10.1.2.1
               IN  A  172.16.2.1
ftp            IN CNAME ftp.example.net.
mail           IN  A  192.168.2.3
mail1          IN  A  192.168.2.4
$ORIGIN sub.example.com.
@              IN  NS ns3.sub.example.com.
               IN  NS ns4.sub.example.com.
ns3            IN  A  10.2.3.4 ; glue RR
ns4            IN  A  10.2.3.5 ; glue RR
```

The zone file contains delegation to a subdomain called sub.example.com, which is assumed at this point to be insecure (as shown in Figure 11–1).

To secure the example.com zone will require a ZSK and a KSK, which, again, may be a single key or two separate keys. For the purposes of clarity and because the processes are significantly different, the examples use the recommended method of using separate keys for each of the ZSK and KSK functions. Both keys are generated by the dnssec-keygen utility. The examples assume that these operations will be carried out in the directory /var/named/keys. To generate the ZSK, the dnssec-keygen utility (see Chapter 9) is run with the following command:

```
# dnssec-keygen -a rsasha256 -b 2048 -n zone example.com
Kexample.com.+008+27228
```

This generates a key pair for the RSA-SHA-256 digital signature algorithm with a key length of 2048 bits and a zone record with the name of the zone apex, which in this case is example.com. The command response of Kexample.com.+008+27228 indicates that the file Kexample.com.+008+27228.key contains the DNSKEY RR with the public key of the key pair, which will be added to the zone file, and the file Kexample.com.+008+27228.private contains the private key used in subsequent signing operations. The value 27228 is the key-tag that uniquely identifies this key. Next, the KSK, is generated using the following command:

```
 # dnssec-keygen -a rsasha256 -b 2048 -f KSK -n zone example.com
Kexample.com.+008+34957
```

This generates a key pair for the RSA-SHA-256 digital signature algorithm with a key length of 2048 bits and a zone DNSKEY RR with the name of the zone apex, which in this case is example.com. The -f KSK argument signifies that this will generate a KSK DNSKEY RR, indicated by the flags field having a value of 257 (the SEP bit is set). Full details of the DNSKEY RR are defined in Chapter 13.

■ **Note** The US National Institute for Science and Technology (NIST) currently recommend 1024 bit keys for use until 2010 and 2048 bits for keys until 2030 (FIP PUBS 800-57 Part 1 Rev 2, Table 4, available from csrc.nist.gov/publications/PubsSPs.html). See a further discussion of this topic in "DNSSEC Implementation." By default, dnssec-keygen uses /dev/random as a source of randomness when generating keys. When running dnssec-keygen under Ubuntu (on a very lightly loaded system), the utility persistently hung due to a lack of entropy. Using -r /dev/urandom will fix the problem but generated keys are less secure, which is acceptable for testing; however, in a production environment, the default /dev/random should always be used.

The command response of Kexample.com.+008+34957 indicates that a file with the name Kexample.com.+008+34957.key contains the DNSKEY RR with the public key of the key pair, which will be added to the zone file, and the file Kexample.com.+008+34957.private contains the private key used in subsequent signing operations. The value 34957 is the key-tag that uniquely identifies this key. The DNSKEY RRs generated by the previous operations are contained in the files Kexample.com.+008+34957.key (KSK) and Kexample.com.+008+27228.key. These may be edited into the zone file (as shown in the "Securing or Signing the Zone" section earlier in the chapter) or included as shown here:

```
$TTL 86400 ; 1 day
$ORIGIN example.com.
@           IN SOA ns1.example.com. hostmaster.example.com. (
                    2010121500 ; serial
                    43200      ; refresh (12 hours)
                    600        ; retry (10 minutes)
                    604800     ; expire (1 week)
                    10800      ; nx (3 hours)
                    )
            IN  NS ns1.example.com.
            IN  NS ns2.example.com.
            IN  MX 10 mail.example.com.
            IN  MX 10 mail1.example.com.
_ldap._tcp  IN  SRV 5 2 235 www
ns1         IN  A   192.168.2.6
ns2         IN  A   192.168.23.23
www         IN  A   10.1.2.1
            IN  A   172.16.2.1
mail        IN  A   192.168.2.3
mail1       IN  A   192.168.2.4
$ORIGIN sub.example.com.
@           IN  NS ns3.sub.example.com.
            IN  NS ns4.sub.example.com.
ns3         IN  A   10.2.3.4 ; glue RR
ns4         IN  A   10.2.3.5 ; glue RR
$INCLUDE keys/Kexample.com.+008+34957.key ; KSK
$INCLUDE keys/Kexample.com.+008+27228.key ; ZSK
```

An alternative way to add the DNSKEY RR directly to the preceding file would be to use the following commands:

```
# cat keys/Kexample.com.+008+34957.key >> master.example.com
# cat keys/Kexample.com.+008+27228.key >> master.example.com
```

Since the DNSKEY RR is a public key, there are no security requirements—either method is perfectly acceptable.

The zone is now ready for signing using the dnssec-signzone command (see Chapter 9), as shown here:

```
# dnssec-signzone -o example.com -t -k Kexample.com.+008+34957 \
master.example.com Kexample.com.+008+27228
Verifying the zone using the following alogoriths: RSASHA256
Algorithm: RSASHA256 KSKs: 1 active, 0 stand-by, 0 revoked
                     ZSKs: 1 active, 0 stand-by, 0 revoked
master.example.com.signed
Signatures generated:                   21
Signatures retained:                     0
Signatures dropped:                      0
Signatures successfully verified:        0
Signatures unsuccessfully verified:      0
Runtime in seconds:                  0.227
Signatures per second:              92.327n
```

▪ **Tip** When signing a zone with a single ZSK, rather than separate the KSK and the ZSK as shown in the example, just omit the -k argument.

The \ in the preceding example indicates that the line has been split for presentation reasons only, meaning the first and second lines actually appear as a single line to the operating system. The -o example.com arguments indicate the name of the domain being signed. The -t argument displays some statistics, which are shown on the following lines. -k Kexample.com.+008+34957 indicates that Kexample.com.+008+34957.private contains the private key that should be used as the KSK. master.example.com is the name of the zone file to be signed, and Kexample.com.+008+27228 indicates that Kexample.com.+008+27228.private contains the private key that will be used as the ZSK. The first line of the resulting output is master.example.com.signed, which is the default file name (input zone file name with .signed appended) allocated if the -f option is not used.

The resulting file is shown here:

```
; File written on Sat Dec 18 21:31:01 2010
; dnssec_signzone version 9.7.2-P2
example.com.  86400 IN SOA ns1.example.com. hostmaster.example.com. (
         2010121500 ; serial
         43200       ; refresh (12 hours)
         600         ; retry (10 minutes)
         604800      ; expire (1 week)
         10800       ; minimum (3 hours)
         )
         86400    RRSIG     SOA 8 2 86400 20110118013101 (
                   20101219013101 27228 example.com.
                   JTViPzs3UDEqgAvy8rgtvwr80a8= )
         86400    NS            ns1.example.com.
         86400    NS            ns2.example.com.
```

```
          86400    RRSIG    NS 8 2 86400 20110118013101 (
                            20101219013101 27228 example.com.
                            S78T5Fxh5SbLBPTBKmlKvKxcx6k= )
          86400    MX       10 mail.example.com.
          86400    MX       10 mail1.example.com.
          86400    RRSIG    MX 8 2 86400 20110118013101 (
                            20101219013101 27228 example.com.
                            T8a4tw5E+Sv/BX+x1QqksFics64= )
          10800    NSEC     _ldap._tcp.example.com. NS SOA MX RRSIG NSEC DNSKEY
          10800    RRSIG    NSEC 8 2 10800 20110118013101 (
                            20101219013101 27228 example.com.
                            PFnee80+vXd4sgN6+SfY6AyQV2M= )
          86400    DNSKEY   256 3 8 (
                            8R77exTNyWDfORfdHvQXCjnxGls1o4Y5
                            ) ; key id = 27228
          86400    DNSKEY   257 3 8 (
                            5Jq6Dp+JyHNO3OHqgHv2KrRuvUOXV+8l
                            ) ; key id = 34957
          86400    RRSIG    DNSKEY 8 2 86400 20110118013101 (
                            20101219013101 27228 example.com.
                            apROsSPuroSFcRYyxcfLG3HdIS4= )
          86400    RRSIG    DNSKEY 8 2 86400 20110118013101 (
                            20101219013101 34957 example.com.
                            j3d5igODKdRHEZKWnvaPZfVWKXo= )
_ldap._tcp.example.com. 86400 IN SRV 5 2 235 www.example.com.
          86400    RRSIG    SRV 8 4 86400 20110118013101 (
                            20101219013101 27228 example.com.
                            oYmF3EUjBdIgBAJiqdTR/2pqBus= )
          10800    NSEC     ftp.example.com. SRV RRSIG NSEC
          10800    RRSIG    NSEC 8 4 10800 20110118013101 (
                            20101219013101 27228 example.com.
                            ZALrIjznKyH8pl66qE989YCIneY= )
ftp.example.com. 86400 IN CNAME ftp.example.net.
          86400    RRSIG    CNAME 8 3 86400 20110118013101 (
                            20101219013101 27228 example.com.
                            2pOU1junt22N21bYHT7mF6SZsec= )
          10800    NSEC     mail.example.com. CNAME RRSIG NSEC
          10800    RRSIG    NSEC 8 3 10800 20110118013101 (
                            20101219013101 27228 example.com.
                            9NE+9NMhbqDhIi0fQ8GEb/b2t4M= )
mail1.example.com. 86400       IN A 192.168.2.4
          86400    RRSIG    A 8 3 86400 20110118013101 (
                            20101219013101 27228 example.com.
                            kojE4FfJRdWjCB6F/lpt1pL72nE= )
          10800    NSEC     ns1.example.com. A RRSIG NSEC
          10800    RRSIG    NSEC 8 3 10800 20110118013101 (
                            20101219013101 27228 example.com.
                            7D6lMBbDxLcrab4kQY63PjKjFtw= )
ns1.example.com. 86400 IN A    192.168.2.6
          86400    RRSIG    A 8 3 86400 20110118013101 (
                            20101219013101 27228 example.com.
                            i88/ViKCIREhX3Jl33uOzwv4720= )
          10800    NSEC     ns2.example.com. A RRSIG NSEC
          10800    RRSIG    NSEC 8 3 10800 20110118013101 (
```

```
                              20101219013101 27228 example.com.
                              1kjsIkAoSJ6mMnxKhxj7o+CYxJ4= )
ns2.example.com. 86400 IN A     192.168.23.23
             86400     RRSIG    A 8 3 86400 20110118013101 (
                              20101219013101 27228 example.com.
                              7ahKR9HNA9mg2go+H+QLQVYQ18I= )
          10800     NSEC     sub.example.com. A RRSIG NSEC
          10800     RRSIG    NSEC 8 3 10800 20110118013101 (
                              20101219013101 27228 example.com.
                              aCRIk45rOr2aSVGe19kCZQc+fFO= )
mail.example.com. 86400 IN A     192.168.2.3
             86400     RRSIG    A 8 3 86400 20110118013101 (
                              20101219013101 27228 example.com.
                              MTnI6ULQvwcFfVVifO7zs5xBa8U= )
          10800     NSEC     mail1.example.com. A RRSIG NSEC
          10800     RRSIG    NSEC 8 3 10800 20110118013101 (
                              20101219013101 27228 example.com.
                              qtAtFhFysMH7JFvnKZEOeRec2TO= )
sub.example.com. 86400 IN NS   ns3.sub.example.com.
             86400 IN NS   ns4.sub.example.com.
          10800     NSEC     www.example.com. NS RRSIG NSEC
          10800     RRSIG    NSEC 8 3 10800 20110118013101 (
                              20101219013101 27228 example.com.
                              NbjZ42hmv5kBMq8RKXOZql4hUsc= )
ns3.sub.example.com. 86400 IN A 10.2.3.4
ns4.sub.example.com. 86400 IN A 10.2.3.5
www.example.com. 86400       IN A 10.1.2.1
             86400 IN A       172.16.2.1
             86400     RRSIG    A 8 3 86400 20110118013101 (
                              20101219013101 27228 example.com.
                              FVejigwrKPOx+DGGsj6t9qetfmE= )
          10800     NSEC     example.com. A RRSIG NSEC
          10800     RRSIG    NSEC 8 3 10800 20110118013101 (
                              20101219013101 27228 example.com.
                              NFQ9D+/Tvo/Te6ha7oPvs2JGN3Y= )
```

In the interest of brevity and because it adds no value to the human reader, most of the base64 material in the DNSKEY and RRSIG RRs has been removed. A full description of all the changes that take place in signed zones using an identical file is contained under the "Securing or Signing the Zone" section earlier in the chapter.

The signed zone file is ready to become operational in ns1.example.com, the primary master for the zone, using a named.conf fragment such as defined here:

```
// named.cong fragment for ns1.example.com
logging{
    channel normal_log {
    file "/var/log/named/normal.log" versions 3 size 2m;
    severity error;
    print-time yes;
    print-severity yes;
    print-category yes;
    };
    channel dnssec_log { // streamed dnssec log
    file "/var/log/named/dnssec.log" versions 3 size 2m;
```

```
        severity debug 3;
        print-time yes;
        print-severity yes;
        print-category yes;
        };
        category default{
        normal_log;
        };
        category dnssec{
        dnssec_log;
        };
};
options {
    ....
    directory "/var/named";
    dnssec-enable yes; // default - could be omitted
    allow-transfer {"none";}};
    ....
};
....
zone "example.com" in{
    type master;
    file "master.example.com.signed";
    allow-transfer {192.168.23.23;}}; // ns2.example.com
    allow-update {"none";}};
};
....
```

The log has been streamed for dnssec events to assist in any test debugging. A sample log output is shown later in the "DNSSEC Logging" section. The severity debug 3; statement should not be used for production because it will generate huge amounts of log data; instead severity info; or higher should be used. The zone file in the example.com zone clause references the signed file created by the zone signing process earlier. No special treatment is required on the slave server (ns2.example.com) whose named.conf would look like so:

```
// named.conf fragment for ns2.example.com
logging{
    channel normal_log {
    file "/var/log/named/normal.log" versions 3 size 2m;
    severity error;
    print-time yes;
    print-severity yes;
    print-category yes;
    };
    channel dnssec_log { // streamed dnssec log
    file "/var/log/named/dnssec.log" versions 3 size 2m;
    severity debug 3;
    print-time yes;
    print-severity yes;
    print-category yes;
    };
    category default{
    normal_log;
    };
```

```
        category dnssec{
        dnssec_log;
        };
};
options {
    ....
    directory "/var/named";
    dnssec-enable yes; // default - could be omitted
    allow-transfer {"none";};
    ....
};
....
zone "example.com" in{
    type slave;
    file "slave.example.com.signed";
    masters {192.168.2.6;}; // ns1.example.com
    allow-update {"none";};
};
....
```

Verifying the Signed Zone

To confirm the zone is working successfully, use a dig command to verify the results. If a normal dig command is issued, it will emulate the behavior of a security-oblivious name server; therefore no security information will be displayed. If the +dnssec option is added, it will respond with the security information as shown in the following example, which has been issued to ns1.example.com, an authoritative name server for the example.com zone:

```
dig @192.168.2.6 www.example.com +dnssec +multiline
; <<>> DiG 9.7.2-P2 <<>> www.example.com +dnssec +multiline
;; global options: +cmd
;; Got answer:
;; ->>HEADER<<- opcode: QUERY, status: NOERROR, id: 38927
;; flags: qr aa rd ra; QUERY: 1, ANSWER: 3, AUTHORITY: 3, ADDITIONAL: 5

;; OPT PSEUDOSECTION:
; EDNS: version: 0, flags: do; udp: 4096
;; QUESTION SECTION:
;www.example.com.        IN A

;; ANSWER SECTION:
www.example.com.        86400 IN A 172.16.2.1
www.example.com.        86400 IN A 10.1.2.1
www.example.com.        86400 IN RRSIG A 8 3 86400 20110118042253 (
                                20101219042253 27228 example.com.
                                3G4VSCGK+YO91uKJoq7pvzBrbAfWa12KfH7B+6o= )

;; AUTHORITY SECTION:
example.com.            86400 IN NS ns2.example.com.
example.com.            86400 IN NS ns1.example.com.
example.com.            86400 IN RRSIG NS 8 2 86400 20110118042253 (
                                20101219042253 27228 example.com.
                                NX7KK6pON/OFRQMiEOUX+C8DvhQ2ULDjv9WkPnI= )
```

```
;; ADDITIONAL SECTION:
ns1.example.com.          86400 IN A 192.168.2.6
ns2.example.com.          86400 IN A 192.168.23.23
ns1.example.com.          86400 IN RRSIG A 8 3 86400 20110118042253 (
                                20101219042253 27228 example.com.
                                1mqk6XgMmVmg7bTpK5mmDLKsfa/SJa6wR23pNj8= )
ns2.example.com.          86400 IN RRSIG A 8 3 86400 20110118042253 (
                                20101219042253 27228 example.com.
                                KLxqPPouowqgBua5OgcjmHNAc/Vq7MzwPxqp/qU= )

;; Query time: 2 msec
;; SERVER: 192.168.2.6#53(192.168.2.6)
;; WHEN: Mon Dec 20 16:59:24 2010
;; MSG SIZE  rcvd: 828
```

Again, in the interest of brevity, most of the base64 material has been eliminated, since it is of no interest to the human reader. The following points should be noted:

- The +multiline option simply adds parentheses to each long RR to create a slightly more readable output format.

- The OPT PSEUDOSECTION shows that EDNS0 features are in use and that a UDP block size of 4096 bytes has been negotiated for use in the much bigger responses from DNSSEC transactions. The OPT meta (or pseudo) RR is actually placed in the ADDITIONAL SECTION, but dig chooses to display and format it separately (see Chapter 15).

- The ANSWER SECTION includes the RRSIG to cover the A RRs returned with the query and can thus be used to authenticate the RRset.

- The AUTHORITY SECTION also includes the RRSIG RR to cover the NS RRs returned and allow verification of this section as well.

- The ADDITIONAL SECTION contains, as expected, the A RRs for the authoritative name servers and its covering RRSIG RR.

- The DNSKEY RRs are not present in this response; a validating resolver would have to separately request them using a DNSKEY RR to the zone apex if they are not already in its cache.

- The HEADER flags do not include the ad (Authenticated Data) flag (see Chapter 15) because this dig was issued to one of the authoritative name servers for the signed zone. The authoritative name server's job is to supply the information, the various RRSIGs, by which a validating resolver can perform the authentication. If, however, the dig had been issued to a validating resolver that was not authoritative for the zone example.com, then that name server *would have performed the authentication* and, assuming it was successful, the ad flag would have been set. This process is illustrated later in the chapter.

PNE with Signed Zones

Proof of nonexistence (PNE) occurs when a signed zone receives a request for a name that does not exist. In this case, the authoritative server returns a query status of NXDOMAIN (name error) and in the

ADDITIONAL SECTION the SOA RR as normal (with its NSEC and RRSIG RRs) plus an NSEC RR (and its RRSIG RR) that spans the requested name as shown in this dig command and response:

```
# dig +dnssec +multiline smtp.example.com
; <<>> DiG 9.7.2-P2 <<>> +dnssec +multiline smtp.example.com
;; global options: +cmd
;; Got answer:
;; ->>HEADER<<- opcode: QUERY, status: NXDOMAIN, id: 40641
;; flags: qr aa rd ra; QUERY: 1, ANSWER: 0, AUTHORITY: 6, ADDITIONAL: 1

;; OPT PSEUDOSECTION:
; EDNS: version: 0, flags: do; udp: 4096
;; QUESTION SECTION:
;smtp.example.com.        IN A

;; AUTHORITY SECTION:
example.com.        10800 IN SOA ns1.example.com. hostmaster.example.com. (
                          2010121500 ; serial
                          43200      ; refresh (12 hours)
                          600        ; retry (10 minutes)
                          604800     ; expire (1 week)
                          10800      ; minimum (3 hours)
                          )
example.com.        10800 IN RRSIG SOA 8 2 86400 20110119230454 (
                          20101220230454 10476 example.com.
                          ….
                          dmZE26/MhBwTa1aEtTmJgk5DGCY42nm3L/JJsnc= )
example.com.        10800 IN NSEC _ldap._tcp.example.com. NS SOA MX RRSIG NSEC DNSKEY
example.com.        10800 IN RRSIG NSEC 8 2 10800 20110119230454 (
                          20101220230454 10476 example.com.
                          ….
                          B9zZ+E9jlH3oqNdJihYij8Tk3W1+vJkie9qeUsk= )
ns2.example.com.    10800 IN NSEC sub.example.com. A RRSIG NSEC
ns2.example.com.    10800 IN RRSIG NSEC 8 3 10800 20110119230454 (
                          20101220230454 10476 example.com.
                          ….
                          VNd/j+7ta+eBRVoVmZCq5LH51BxtNNn3f5YzOis= )

;; Query time: 2 msec
;; SERVER: 192.168.2.21#53(192.168.2.21)
;; WHEN: Sat Jan  8 01:15:57 2011
;; MSG SIZE  rcvd: 695
```

In the above case the ns2.example.com. NSEC sub.example.com. RR spans the name space where smtp.example.com lies and thus provides PNE.

Establishing a Trusted Anchor

The example assumes that a security-aware name server at ns1.example.net wishes to authenticate the data from example.com. This name server needs to establish a trusted anchor for the domain example.com. The administrator of ns1.example.net obtains by some secure process the DNSKEY RR for the KSK of the domain example.com. While the DNSKEY RR itself is not sensitive information (it contains a public key), the administrator must be able to authenticate the source of the key, and therefore a secure distribution process such as secure e-mail or secure FTP must be used to obtain the trusted anchor. This DNSKEY RR is available from the signed example.com zone file shown earlier and is identified as having a flags field value of 257 (which includes the SEP or KSK bit):

```
86400 DNSKEY 257 3 8 (
            5Jq6Dp+JyHNo3OHqgHv2KrRuvUOXV+81

            ) ; key id = 34957
```

The reader should note that much of the base64 material has been eliminated in the interest of brevity and that a real DNSKEY RR would be considerably larger. The trusted anchor is created by editing this DNSKEY RR into a trusted-keys clause for the named.conf file at the server ns1.example.net, as shown in the following fragment:

```
// named.conf fragment for ns1.example.net
logging{
    channel normal_log {
    file "/var/log/named/normal.log" versions 3 size 2m;
    severity error;
    print-time yes;
    print-severity yes;
    print-category yes;
    };
    channel dnssec_log { // streamed dnssec log
    file "/var/log/named/dnssec.log" versions 3 size 2m;
    severity debug 3;
    print-time yes;
    print-severity yes;
    print-category yes;
    };
    category default{
    normal_log;
    };
    category dnssec{
    dnssec_log;
    };
};
options {
    ....
    directory "/var/named";
    dnssec-enable yes;
    dnssec-validation yes;
        allow-recursion {10.2/16; 192.168.2/24;}; // recursion limits - closes resolver
    ....
};
trusted-keys{
    "example.com" 257 3 8 "5Jq6Dp+JyHNo3OHqgHv2KrRuvUOXV+81
";
};
....
```

■ **Caution** The `allow-recursion` statement is required to ensure this is not an open resolver. There are other statements that may also be used to perform this function. See a fuller discussion of this topic in the "Resolver (Caching Name Server)" section of Chapter 7.

The `trusted-keys` clause contains the trusted anchor for example.com and is an edited version of the DNSKEY RR created by removing the TTL and DNSKEY, and adding the domain name in quotes (a quoted string that can be an FQDN, but will work quite happily without the trailing dot); the `flags`, `proto`, and `algorithm` fields are left intact, and the base64 public key material (key-data) is enclosed in quotes and terminated with a semicolon. For the full format and layout of the trusted anchor layout within the trusted-keys clause, see Chapter 12. The `dnssec-enable yes;` and `dnssec-validation yes;` statements are the BIND 9.5+ default values and can be omitted though it is good practice to include them as constant reminder of functionality. The log is again streamed and the `severity debug 3;` is used to generate information that may be useful during debugging (but should not be used in production unless the reader likes managing large logs). Instead, `severity info;` or a higher value should be used based on comfort and experience.

■ **Note** BIND currently uses a DNSKEY format for its trusted-keys clause. Other DNS software, notably Unbound, use a DS RR format for the same purpose. Indeed, there is some ongoing discussion to make the DS RR format the preferred option due to it shorter size.

Using a Trusted Anchor

The following shows a `dig` command issued to the recursive server ns1.example.net that is neither the zone master nor the zone slave for example.com, but has been configured to be security aware (using a dnssec-enable yes; statement) and has a trusted anchor for the zone example.com (in a trusted-keys clause):

```
dig @ns1.example.net www.example.com +dnssec +multiline
; <<>> DiG 9.7.2-P2 <<>> @ns1.example.net www.example.com +dnssec +multiline
;; global options:  printcmd
;; Got answer:
;; ->>HEADER<<- opcode: QUERY, status: NOERROR, id: 60711
;; flags: qr rd ra ad; QUERY: 1, ANSWER: 3, AUTHORITY: 0, ADDITIONAL: 1

;; OPT PSEUDOSECTION:
; EDNS: version: 0, flags: do; udp: 4096
;; QUESTION SECTION:
;www.example.com.  IN  A

;; ANSWER SECTION:
www.example.com.  86061  IN  A  172.16.2.1
www.example.com.  86061  IN  A  10.1.2.1
www.example.com.      86400 IN RRSIG A 8 3 86400 20110118042253 (
                            20101219042253 27228 example.com.
```

3G4VSCGK+YO91uKJoq7pvzBrbAfWa12KfH7B+60=)

```
;; Query time: 1 msec
;; SERVER: 192.168.254.23#53(ns1.example.net)
;; WHEN: Mon Dec 20 17:10:13 2010;; MSG SIZE  rcvd: 327
```

Again, in the interest of brevity, most of the base64 material has been eliminated. In this case, the response is significantly shorter than that shown when the authoritative server was queried directly (shown in the preceding section, "Verifying Signed Zones"). The reason is simply that the name server 192.168.254.23, because it is security aware, has verified the various signatures on your behalf, and confirmed this action by setting the ad (Authenticated Data) flag in the HEADER. Therefore only the query results are supplied to the dig command. The next section shows the security log at the name server to confirm that it has indeed performed this validation.

DNSSEC Logging

The following shows typical log output using the streamed security logging configured as shown in the named.conf fragment example; this is the resulting output from the preceding dig command:

```
dnssec: validating www.example.com A: starting
dnssec: validating www.example.com A: attempting positive response validation
dnssec: validating example.com DNSKEY: starting
dnssec: validating example.com DNSKEY: attempting positive response validation
dnssec: validating example.com DNSKEY: verify rdataset: success
dnssec: validating example.com DNSKEY: signed by trusted key; marking as secure
dnssec: validator @0x8257800: dns_validator_destroy
dnssec: validating www.example.com A: in fetch_callback_validator
dnssec: validating www.example.com A: keyset with trust 7
dnssec: validating www.example.com A: resuming validate
validating www.example.com A: verify rdataset: success
dnssec: validating www.example.com A: marking as secure
dnssec: validator @0x81ab000: dns_validator_destroy
```

For the sake of brevity, the date and time have been removed from this log output, which shows both A RRs being validated and being marked as secure.

Signing the sub.example.com Zone

The process for signing a subdomain is essentially similar to that defined for signing a zone with one single difference. The zone sub.example.com is the child of the secure zone example.com, or, if you prefer, example.com is the secure parent of sub.example.com. A Delegated Signer (DS) RR can be added to the example.com zone file to create secure delegation. The zone sub.example.com will join the chain of trust whose current secure entry point is example.com. For clarity and ease of key rollover, separate KSK and ZSK RR will be used.

You generate the ZSK for sub.example.com like so:

```
# dnssec-keygen -a rsasha256 -b 2048 -n zone sub.example.com
Ksub.example.com.+008+60366
```

You generate the KSK for sub.example.com like so:

```
# dnssec-keygen -a rsasha256 -b 2048 -f KSK -n zone example.com
Ksub.example.com.+008+23110
```

To include the keys in the sub.example.com zone file, do this:

```
$TTL 86400 ; 1 day
$ORIGIN sub.example.com.
@               IN SOA ns1.sub.example.com. hostmaster.example.com. (
                        2010122000 ; serial
                        10800      ; refresh (3 hours)
                        15         ; retry (15 seconds)
                        604800     ; expire (1 week)
                        10800      ; nx (3 hours)
                        )
                IN NS ns3.example.com.
                IN NS ns4.example.com.
                IN MX 10 mail.example.com.
ns3             IN A 10.2.3.4
ns4             IN A 10.2.3.5
fred            IN A 10.1.2.1
$INCLUDE Ksub.example.com.+008+60366.key ; ZSK
$INCLUDE Ksub.example.com.+008+23110.key ; KSK
```

Here's how to sign the zone sub.example.com:

```
# dnssec-signzone -o sub.example.com -t -g -k Ksub.example.com.+008+23110 \
master.sub.example.com  Ksub.example.com.+008+60366
master.sub.example.com.signed
Signatures generated:                   12
Signatures retained:                     0
Signatures dropped:                      0
Signatures successfully verified:        0
Signatures unsuccessfully verified:      0
Runtime in seconds:                  0.137
Signatures per second:              87.469
```

This command line is the same as that for the zone example.com using the revised keys and zone file names, with the exception that the -g argument is used to generate the file dsset-sub.example.com. (containing the DS RRs for the parent). This file may, depending on policy, be sent to the parent DNS administrator by any suitable, but secure, process including, increasingly, via a registrar's secure web interface to enable secure delegation, the creation of a chain of trust, which is described in the next section. While the file does not contain secure information (it contains normal RR data), it is vital that the recipient be able to authenticate the sender and hence create the appropriate level of trust. The named.conf file for the master and slave servers for this subdomain are the same as those used for example.com and require no special treatment. Because sub.example.com is authenticated via the zone example.com, no action is required at the name server ns1.example.net—its trusted-keys clause with a trusted anchor for example.com will cover sub.example.com as well through the chain of trust.

■ **Note** Inspection of the file dsset-sub.example.com. will, in this case, show two DS RRs. The first is using a digest algorithm of SHA1 (value 1, mandatory) that must be supported by all validating resolvers and the second using the algorithm SHA256 (value 2), a more secure digest which may not be supported by all validating resolvers. See also the "DS Record" section in Chapter 13 for details.

Creating the Chain of Trust

When the parent administrator receives the dsset-sub.example.com. it's placed in a suitable directory. The dsset-sub.example.com. file is included in the original example.com zone as shown here (the location in the zone file is not important, but note that the file name always ends with a dot):

```
$TTL 86400 ; 1 day
$ORIGIN example.com.
@            IN SOA ns1.example.com. hostmaster.example.com. (
                         2010122000 ; serial
                         10800      ; refresh (3 hours)
                         15         ; retry (15 seconds)
                         604800     ; expire (1 week)
                         10800      ; nx (3 hours)
                         )
             IN  NS ns1.example.com.
             IN  NS ns2.example.com.
             IN  MX 10 mail.example.com.
             IN  MX 10 mail1.example.com.
_ldap._tcp   IN  SRV 5 2 235 www
ns1          IN  A   192.168.2.6
ns2          IN  A   192.168.23.23
www          IN  A   10.1.2.1
             IN  A   172.16.2.1
mail         IN  A   192.168.2.3
mail1        IN  A   192.168.2.4
$ORIGIN sub.example.com.
@            IN  NS ns3.sub.example.com.
             IN  NS ns4.sub.example.com.
ns3          IN  A   10.2.3.4 ; glue RR
ns4          IN  A   10.2.3.5 ; glue RR
$INCLUDE keys/Kexample.com.+008+27228.key ; KSK
$INCLUDE keys/Kexample.com.+008+34957.key ; ZSK
$INCLUDE dsset-sub.example.com. ; DS RR
```

Re-sign the zone by executing the dnssec-signzone command exactly as before:

```
# dnssec-signzone -o example.com -t -k Kexample.com.+008+34957 \
master.example.com Kexample.com.+008+27228
master.example.com.signed
Signatures generated:                    22
Signatures retained:                      0
Signatures dropped:                       0
Signatures successfully verified:         0
Signatures unsuccessfully verified:       0
Runtime in seconds:                   0.607
Signatures per second:               36.120
```

The only thing that has changed is that the Signatures generated line has gone from 21 in the first version to 22 in this version because of the additional DS RRset, which has now been signed. The resulting zone file is exactly the same as the first signed zone but with an updated signature expiry, and the additional DS RR has been added and signed as shown in the following fragment:

```
sub.example.com. 86400 IN NS    ns3.sub.example.com.
                 86400 IN  NS   ns4.sub.example.com.
```

```
       86400        DS    23110 8 1 (
                          9D9A1E894BEE23B85FD8807A629D3236C2E9
                          9B7E )
       86400        DS    23110 8 2 (
                          12264712A245E1EEB81E077870FB72B19F01
                          E740F9FAA71F9C2A921AC61C35B6 )
       86400        RRSIG DS 8 3 86400 20110119221601 (
                          20101220221601 27228 example.com.
                          EEnwSuLJjm36aJsFm3RWfOG8T6k= )
       10800        NSEC www.example.com. NS DS RRSIG NSEC
       10800        RRSIG NSEC 8 3 10800 20110119221601 (
                          20101220221601 27228 example.com.
                          fFOyyxzJaHqVK/IotrYo4/5CSK8= )
```

BIND will need to be reloaded or rndc (freeze/thaw) used to pick up the new zone file. Because sub.example.com gets its authentication through the delegation point in example.com, the trusted anchor configured at ns1.example.net also covers sub.example.com, and no additional configuration is required.

Key Rollover

As described earlier, the ZSK and the KSK are required to be periodically changed, or *rolled over*, using either a prepublish or double-signing strategy. In general, prepublish is best used for ZSKs and double signing is best for KSKs. The process of key rollover is messy but not difficult, and it lends itself to a level of script or other automation, such as running from cron.

■ **Note** When performing any zone re-signing, for key rollover or normal zone signing maintenance procedures, on zones that are dynamically updated, the additional procedures documented in the "Dynamic DNS and DNSSEC" section earlier in this chapter should be followed.

Prepublish ZSK Rollover

The objective in the prepublish strategy is to get the current and new DNSKEY RRs into the caches of all security-aware name servers. This is done by first adding a new ZSK to the zone file. This example will assume that the signed zone file for example.com created previously with a current ZSK key-tag of 27228 and a current KSK key-tag of 34957 will have only the ZSK (key-tag of 27228) rolled. By looking at the zone file, the longest TTL is 24 hours (86400 seconds). At least two days (2 x TTL) before the zone signatures expire or before the new ZSK is required, a new ZSK is created using the following command:

```
# dnssec-keygen -a rsasha256 -b 2048 -n zone example.com
Kexample.com.+008+10476
```

The new ZSK is included in the zone file, like so:

```
$TTL 86400 ; 1 day
$ORIGIN example.com.
@            IN SOA ns1.example.com. hostmaster.example.com. (
                        2010121500 ; serial
                        10800      ; refresh (3 hours)
```

```
                        15          ; retry (15 seconds)
                        604800      ; expire (1 week)
                        10800       ; nx (3 hours)
                        )
              IN  NS ns1.example.com.
              IN  NS ns2.example.com.
              IN  MX 10 mail.example.com.
              IN  MX 10 mail1.example.com.
_ldap._tcp   IN  SRV 5 2 235 www
ns1          IN  A   192.168.2.6
ns2          IN  A   192.168.23.23
www          IN  A   10.1.2.1
             IN  A   172.16.2.1
mail         IN  A   192.168.2.3
mail1        IN  A   192.168.2.4
$ORIGIN sub.example.com.
@            IN  NS ns3.sub.example.com.
             IN  NS ns4.sub.example.com.
ns3          IN  A   10.2.3.4 ; glue RR
ns4          IN  A   10.2.3.5 ; glue RR
$INCLUDE keys/Kexample.com.+008+34957.key ; KSK
$INCLUDE keys/Kexample.com.+008+27228.key ; current ZSK
$INCLUDE dsset-sub.example.com. ; DS RR
$INCLUDE keys/Kexample.com.+008+10476.key ; new ZSK
```

The zone is signed using the *current* ZSK and KSK—there are no changes to the command used in the previous section:

```
# dnssec-signzone -o example.com -t -k Kexample.com.+008+34957 \
master.example.com Kexample.com.+008+27228
master.example.com.signed
Signatures generated:                   22
Signatures retained:                     0
Signatures dropped:                      0
Signatures successfully verified:        0
Signatures unsuccessfully verified:      0
Runtime in seconds:                   0.234
Signatures per second:               93.621
```

When the file is signed, BIND is either reloaded or rndc (freeze/thaw) commands used to refresh the zone file. The DNSKEY RRset at the zone apex looks like this:

```
        86400      DNSKEY    256 3 8 (
                      kzenp/JaUHd6+VUjLiMGrQ3keBID0clv
                   ) ; key id = 10476
        86400      DNSKEY    256 3 8 (
                      8R77exTNyWDfORfdHvQXCjnxGls1o4Y5
                   ) ; key id = 27228
        86400      DNSKEY    257 3 8 (
                      5Jq6Dp+JyHNO3OHqgHv2KrRuvUOXV+8l
                   ) ; key id = 34957
        86400      RRSIG     DNSKEY 8 2 86400 20110119224405 (
                      20101220224405 27228 example.com.
                      4MNN1+EdmsJuiKsT+9ccBZTsxuE= )
        86400      RRSIG     DNSKEY 8 2 86400 20110119224405 (
```

```
                    20101220224405 34957 example.com.
                    +XyQZnoPOdvdrxCfDlWrhzGZUkw= )
_ldap._tcp.example.com. 86400 IN SRV 5 2 235 www.example.com.
```

The new DNSKEY RR (the second DNSKEY RR shown previously) is now available in the DNSKEY RRset at the zone apex where it can be used by validating resolvers to verify the signatures. At this point, all such attempts will fail because no RRSIG records use this key. Recall, however, that resolvers are mandated to try all available DNSKEY RRs, so the current ZSK will also be used and the RRSIGs will be validated. After 24 hours (1 x TTL) from the zone being reloaded, all security-aware name servers using the example.com zone will be guaranteed to either have the new DNSKEY RRset in the cache or have timed out the old version, which only has the current KSK and current ZSK.

After the 24 hours cache propagation period has passed, the zone is again re-signed using the KSK as before and the new ZSK (key-tag of 10476) using the following command:

```
# dnssec-signzone -o example.com -t -k Kexample.com.+008+34957 \
master.example.com Kexample.com.+008+10476
master.example.com.signed
Signatures generated:                    22
Signatures retained:                      0
Signatures dropped:                       0
Signatures successfully verified:         0
Signatures unsuccessfully verified:       0
Runtime in seconds:                   0.235
Signatures per second:               93.237
```

All the RRSIG RRs have now been signed with the new ZSK. Again, BIND is reloaded or rndc used to refresh the zone. After a further 24-hour period, all security-aware name servers that use the example.com zone will have the new DNSKEY RRset either cached or have timed out the old DNSKEY RRset. Any time after this, the zone file may be modified to delete the previous ZSK (key-tag is 27228) and the zone re-signed—using the new ZSK (key-tag is 10476) as in the preceding command—and then reloaded. There is no particular urgency to delete the old key and to minimize re-signing operations; this can be postponed until either the next scheduled zone re-signing or the next scheduled key rollover.

Double-signing KSK Rollover

Recall that the KSK only signs the DNSKEY RRset at the zone apex. The double-signing strategy uses two KSKs to sign this RRset. Again, the example file created previously and now signed with the new ZSK will be used as a starting point for the KSK rollover. Create a new KSK using the following command:

```
# dnssec-keygen -a rsasha256 -b 2048 -f KSK -n zone example.com
Kexample.com.+008+32647
```

This new DNSKEY is included in the master.example.com zone file:

```
$TTL 86400 ; 1 day
$ORIGIN example.com.
@            IN SOA ns1.example.com. hostmaster.example.com. (
                   2010121500 ; serial
                   10800      ; refresh (3 hours)
                   15         ; retry (15 seconds)
                   604800     ; expire (1 week)
                   10800      ; nx (3 hours)
                   )
          IN  NS ns1.example.com.
          IN  NS ns2.example.com.
```

```
            IN  MX 10 mail.example.com.
            IN  MX 10 mail1.example.com.
_ldap._tcp  IN  SRV 5 2 235 www
ns1         IN  A  192.168.2.6
ns2         IN  A  192.168.23.23
www         IN  A  10.1.2.1
            IN  A  172.16.2.1
mail        IN  A  192.168.2.3
mail1       IN  A  192.168.2.4
$ORIGIN sub.example.com.
@           IN  NS ns3.sub.example.com.
            IN  NS ns4.sub.example.com.
ns3         IN  A  10.2.3.4 ; glue RR
ns4         IN  A  10.2.3.5 ; glue RR
$INCLUDE keys/Kexample.com.+008+34957.key ; current KSK
$INCLUDE keys/Kexample.com.+008+32647.key ; new KSK
$INCLUDE dsset-sub.example.com. ; DS RR
$INCLUDE keys/Kexample.com.+008+10476.key ; new ZSK
```

The zone is signed with the following command:

```
# dnssec-signzone -o example.com -t -k Kexample.com.+008+34957 \
-k Kexample.com.+008+32647 master.example.com Kexample.com.+008+10476
master.example.com.signed
Signatures generated:                    23
Signatures retained:                      0
Signatures dropped:                       0
Signatures successfully verified:         0
Signatures unsuccessfully verified:       0
Runtime in seconds:                   0.265
Signatures per second:               86.686
```

The command has two -k arguments, indicating the DNSKEY RRset will be signed three times, once each with the current and new KSK and once with the ZSK. Note also that the Signatures generated line has increased to 23 to confirm this. BIND should now be reloaded or rndc (freeze/thaw) commands used to refresh the zone. The DNSKEY RRset zone file fragments looks as shown here with three RRSIG RRs covering the DNSKEY RRset:

```
86400     DNSKEY    256 3 8 (
               kzenp/JaUHd6+VUjLiMGrQ3keBIDOclv
               ) ; key id = 10476
86400     DNSKEY    257 3 8 (
               WcArjB35mSEVw+ZWGnmQujc=
               ) ; key id = 32647
86400     DNSKEY    257 3 8 (
               5Jq6Dp+JyHNO3OHqgHv2KrRuvUOXV+8l
               ) ; key id = 34957
86400     RRSIG     DNSKEY 8 2 86400 20110119230454 (
               20101220230454 10476 example.com.
               eqLnidIMy7jO+MYlsNoWfpX+XtE= )
86400     RRSIG     DNSKEY 8 2 86400 20110119230454 (
               20101220230454 32647 example.com.
               X+ZOKqjBKy8hLFYtzg== )
86400     RRSIG     DNSKEY 8 2 86400 20110119230454 (
               20101220230454 34957 example.com.
```

```
cLOrfsoYSui3nskUi9A6h43B1AA= )
```

Again, in the interest of brevity, most of the base64 key material has been omitted. Recall that the KSK is identified by having a flags field of value 257 (see Chapter 13). The DNSKEY RRset is signed three times, once each with the current KSK (key-tag is 34957), the new KSK (key-tag is 32647), and the current ZSK (key-tag is 10476). The file Kexample.com.+008+32647.key can be used to create a trusted-keys clause that needs to be made available to all validating resolver administrators that have a trusted anchor configured for the zone example.com. While this file does not contain sensitive information, it contains a public key; it is important that the recipient be able to authenticate the sender in order to establish the right level of trust, so a secure process such as secure e-mail, HTTPS, or secure FTP should be used.

There are two possible strategies for distribution of a new trusted anchor:

- Delay 24 hours (or whatever TTL is being used) from the time of re-signing before distributing or notifying users of the availability of the new anchor. This ensures that all security-aware name servers will have cached the new DNSKEY RRset or timed out the old (single KSK) DNSKEY RRset, in which case, they will query and obtain the new DNSKEY RRset. At this point, the existing trusted anchor may be *replaced* in the trusted-keys clause.

- Distribute or notify immediately users of the zone's trusted anchor when the zone is re-signed, in which case the trusted anchor must be *added* to the server's trusted-keys clause to allow for cache delays. The example shown uses this procedure for no very good reason.

Only when positive confirmation is received that the new trusted anchor has been *added* or *replaced* in the trusted-keys clause, as shown in the following example, can the current KSK be removed from the zone file and the zone file be re-signed using the new KSK (key-tag is 10476) and the current ZSK (key-tag is 32647). The new DNSKEY RR for the KSK is as follows:

```
86400     DNSKEY    257 3 8 (
                    WcArjB35mSEVw+ZWGnmQujc=
                    ) ; key id = 32647
```

It is added as a trusted anchor to the current trusted-keys clause in all affected name servers such as ns1.example.net, as shown here:

```
trusted-keys{
    "example.com." 257 3 8 "5Jq6Dp+JyHNo3OHqgHv2KrRuvUOXV+81
"; // old KSK
    "example.com." 257 3 8 " WcArjB35mSEVw+ZWGnmQujc="; // new KSK
};
```

Using the delayed notification process described previously, the new trusted anchor could also have replaced the previous one. When the old KSK (key-tag is 34957) is removed from the zone file and the zone re-signed, all users of the stale trusted anchor can be informed so they can remove the trusted anchor from the trusted-keys clause at some suitable time. There is no pressing need to do this, so it can be scheduled as part of a regular DNS maintenance session or even postponed until the next key rollover.

Any security-aware name server that does not upgrade, by adding or replacing, to the new trusted anchor will suddenly start generating bogus data responses to zone data, so it's vital that a reliable process is in place to get feedback. The consequences of re-signing too early with only the new KSK are also severe; again, unless there is a pressing reason such as KSK compromise with active damage occurring, it's better to wait.

■ **Note** A DNSSEC Enhancement (RFC 5011) defines a set of procedures that automate the updating of `trusted-keys` clauses in validating resolvers and is described in the next section under "Key Handling Automation."

DNSSEC Enhancements

The base DNSSEC standards are both viable and have been used operationally for a significant number of years. However, as noted, there are certain weaknesses and complexities involved and DNSSEC standards have evolved to address them. Specifically:

Zone enumeration: As noted previously, in a signed zone that contains NSEC RRs, these may be queried like any other RR type. While it is impossible to hide zone information in any public zone file (it can always be discovered either accidentally or by exhaustive search), the NSEC RR makes the process of zone enumeration trivial by letting a nosy or malicious third party simply follow the chain of NSEC RRs. Thus, all the names and RR types may be discovered for any given signed zone. RFC 5155 defines the NSEC3 RR that continues to provide PNE without disclosing the next name as happens with the NSEC RR type. The functionality and usage of NSEC3 RRs is described later in this section.

Trust Anchor Automation: As described previously, keys must be rolled over periodically for security reasons. When keys are used externally as trusted-anchors (KSKs) this presents significant problems and is almost guaranteed to fail if it is left entirely to we frail humans. RFC 5011 addresses this problem and, almost as a side-benefit, brings a significant amount of rigor and terminology to the handling of keys. It is described under "Key Handling Automation" later in this section.

Zone size: For most domain owners, even those with large zone files, the growth in size of between 4:1 and 7:1 when a zone is signed is not usually significant. However, for very large zone files, such as those of TLD operators (gTLDs and ccTLDs) whose zone files can consist of millions or even hundreds of millions of entries, the problem of zone file growth can be very significant. In the TLD case, almost all the zone file records consist of delegations (NS and A/AAAA RRs). While NS RRs in parents are not signed (they are not authoritative) the NSEC/NSEC3 overhead for unsigned zones (the overwhelming majority in early roll-out) is unwarranted. RFC 4470 (and RFC 4956) defined a method called Opt-In to avoid this overhead, whereas RFC 5155 defines another method, somewhat confusingly called Opt-Out, as a part of the NSEC3 specification. Opt-In is not described further; Opt-Out is described as part of NSEC3 later in this section.

Alternative Validation Sources: The process called Domain Lookaside Validation (DLV) is defined by RFC 4431 which has INFORMAL status and is fully supported by BIND. It provides a method by which alternative DNSSEC validation may be invoked. ISC (BIND's author) provides an operational DLV service that allowed DNSSEC validation prior to root-zone signing. At first glance it may now seem a redundant technique. It is described later in this section because it continues to be relevant as an operational testbed methodology, for use with new algorithms, new delegation methods, etc., and because it offers the prospects of DNSSEC customization for private networks and other such uses.

New Algorithms: Cryptography uses the concept of *computationally infeasible* as its benchmark (see Chapter 10). This is a relative, not an absolute, measure. As computational resources increase and analytical methods improve, weaknesses in specific algorithms, either theoretical or operational, can emerge. In general, the world is moving from the SHA1 digest to the SHA2 family (SHA224, 256, 384, and 512). Additionally, country-specific standards, such as Russia's GOST, are becoming important. The non-trivial problem of algorithm rollover is now clearly established and is discussed further in "DNSSEC Implementation" later in this chapter.

In all cases, the above enhancements sit on top of those discussed in "Base DNSSEC Standards." The procedures and examples already described continue to provide a DNSSEC operational solution. The enhancements are designed to make DNSSEC implementation simpler, more efficient, or, as in the case of NSEC3, more operationally acceptable.

NSEC3/Opt-Out

When NSEC RRs are used, simply by following these RRs, zone-enumeration becomes trivial. In the case of user domains, all RRs must, by their nature, be public. NSEC RRs under these conditions are a perfectly acceptable solution. Nevertheless, under certain circumstances especially, but not exclusively, with TLDs where issues of privacy may be involved, NSEC may be unacceptable. To handle the case where the domain owner does not wish to divulge the real names in their domain, the NSEC3 RR is defined by RFC 5155 and has been available since BIND 9.7+.

In a conventional NSEC RR, the left hand name is the next lowest name to the missing name and the right hand name contains the next highest name. In NSEC3, the left-hand name of the NSEC3 RR is a hash of the next lowest name and the right-hand name contains a hash of the next highest name and thus obscures the name chain while still providing PNE (see also the "NSEC3 Record" section in Chapter 13 for full details). To make it even more difficult for a determined attacker or an excessively nosy observer, NSEC3 adds two more name-obscuring techniques. First, it can optionally add a variable length of salt to the name before hashing. Salt simply means that a defined, but secret string, is added to the name. Thus, as an example, it may be reasonably guessed by an external observer that the label www in the zone example.com probably exists. If the hash algorithm is known or guessed (the possible values are defined in the public RFC), the hashed name could be computed. However, if you add the secret value ABCDEF (a hexadecimal string that may be up 256 octets long) as salt, you get the name x'abcdef + www; this name is hashed and then you append the zone name example.com., which creates a slightly less obvious name. Second, the hash may be applied multiple times, thus you hash the salted name and then hash the hashed salted name…and so on as defined by the number of iterations defined in the NSEC3 RR (BIND defaults to 10 iterations). In the end, everyone is suitably confused. In order to read any NSEC3 RR, an attacker would need to guess its name. Between the salt and hashing iterations, this is a pretty unlikely event.

So far, NSEC3 has been all good news. However, there is a significant negative side to NSEC3. A publically visible DNSSEC authoritative name server using NSEC RRs performs no crytographic functions. The DNSSEC performance impact is limited to the additional RRs (RRSIG etc.) it has to send. Recall also that when a zone is signed, it is sorted into canonical (alphanumeric) name order. In the case of NSEC3, when a name error (NXDOMAIN) status is returned, the authoritative name server has to find the right NSEC3 RR to return. It has to compute the name by adding the salt (stored in a NSEC3PARAM RR; see Chapter 13's "NSEC3PARAM Record" section) and run through the hash the defined number of iterations (stored in each NSEC3 RR) to calculate a lower and higher NSEC3 name. Hashing is not a trivial calculation and will consume serious processor resources, thus reducing name server throughput depending on how many times PNE occurs and, especially, how many hash iterations are defined for each operation. Further, without some form of intrusion detection system (IDS), NSEC3 may also make the authoritative server prone to a relatively simple DoS attack vector, it being normally easier to guess what names are not present and therefore cause the server to have to compute many PNE responses. The pros and cons of NSEC3 need to be carefully considered before implementation.

Opt-Out is normally only relevant when a zone has a significant number of delegations (frequently called a *delegation-centric* zone in the jargon) and inhibits generation of NSEC3 RRs when an unsigned delegation occurs. An unsigned delegation has NS and glue A or AAAA RRs but no DS RR(s). Such a relatively modest step can have a huge impact on zone file size especially, but again not exclusively, for TLD (gTLDs or ccTLD) zones. In general, Opt-Out is not normally of interest to user domains or zones.

Both Opt-Out and NSEC3 are invoked using specific arguments to a zone signing tool or in the case of DDNS by adding a NSEC3PARAM RR manually. The following shows a case where the zone file used in the "Creating a Chain of Trust" section of this chapter is signed with both NSEC3 and Opt-Out with DS RRs present at the point of delegation (the KSK with tag-value 34957 is already present in the zone file). First, you generate a ZSK key of 2048 bits suitable for use with NSEC3:

```
dnssec-keygen -a nsec3rsasha1 -b 2048 -n zone example.com
Kexample.com.+007+16838
```

The -a nsec3rsasha1 (and nsec3dsa) values are unique to NSEC3 and indicate to the validating resolver to apply NSEC3 techniques.

Next, you add the DNSKEY RR to the zone:

```
cat Kexample.com.+007+16838.key >> master.example.com
```

Now you sign the zone to use NSEC3

```
dnssec-signzone -o example.com -3 AABBCC -A -u -P -H 10 -t -k \
Kexample.com.+008+34957 master.example.com Kexample.com.+007+16838
```

where the -3 AABBCC indicates you are using NSEC3 signing and a salt string of AABBCC is added to every label before hashing starts (if salt is not required use - (dash)); -A indicates you want to use Opt-Out; -u indicates the NSEC3 chains should be re-built (it is not strictly necessary in this instance but does no harm);=, -P disables certain checks that cause the zone signing to fail on its first run (it should be omitted on subsequent re-signings); -H 10 defines 10 hashing iterations (this is the BIND default and could be omitted). All other values are as previously described (or see Chapter 9's "dnssec-signzone Utility" section). When dnssec-signzone is run, it generates 24 signatures, one more than the previous (NSEC) run to cover the RRSIG on the NSEC3PARAM RR.

The following zone fragment shows the NSEC3PARAM RR added to the zone apex and that NSEC3 RR are present at the delegation point to cover the DS RRs:

```
; File written on Tue Dec 21 03:13:21 2010
; dnssec_signzone version 9.7.2-P2
example.com.    86400 IN  SOA  ns1.example.com. hostmaster.example.com. (
                              2010121500 ; serial
                              43200            ; refresh (12 hours)
                              600               ; retry (10 minutes)
                              604800          ; expire (1 week)
                              10800           ; minimum (3 hours)
```

```
                    )
....
              86400    DNSKEY    256 3 7 (
                               SPBVL9uYNbrBj309L1hxcMD1kQnuOmLR
                               ) ; key id = 16838
              86400    DNSKEY    257 3 8 (
                               5Jq6Dp+JyHNO3OHqgHv2KrRuvUOXV+8l
                               ) ; key id = 34957
              86400    RRSIG     DNSKEY 7 2 86400 20110120071321 (
                               20101221071321 16838 example.com.
                               /7bC+AQYqmAQyJPhJaiqPF/PC2Y= )
              86400    RRSIG DNSKEY 8 2 86400 20110120071321 (
                               20101221071321 34957 example.com.
                               GHr4w2/GsPDelTzP1k219U7U4Xc= )
              0        NSEC3PARAM  1 0 10 AABBCC
              0        RRSIG     NSEC3PARAM 7 2 0 20110120071321 (
                               20101221071321 16838 example.com.
                               c57tEhTOHeXWl2AgCUMHDvkAOEY= )
....
_ldap._tcp.example.com. 86400 IN SRV   5 2 235 www.example.com.
....
sub.example.com. 86400 IN NS  ns3.sub.example.com.
              86400 IN NS  ns4.sub.example.com.
              86400    DS    23110 8 1 (
                               9D9A1E894BEE23B85FD8807A629D3236C2E9
                               9B7E )
              86400    DS    23110 8 2 (
                               12264712A245E1EEB81E077870FB72B19F01
                               E740F9FAA71F9C2A921AC61C35B6 )
              86400    RRSIG DS 7 3 86400 20110120071321 (
                               20101221071321 16838 example.com.
                               yBwBYM61lazsKL+F8jziFTIoaVQ= )
V36U9R2LNLRI8TUNBBVOSKM9KS2408RK.example.com. 10800 IN NSEC3 1 1 10 AABBCC (
                               2CL01NHSOHH7VPUEFGDGB49TA4CEE44F NS DS RRSIG )
              10800    RRSIG NSEC3 7 3 10800 20110120071321 (
                               20101221071321 16838 example.com.
                               cuXglAMx2OcCUt6kuKNnb7OGW2E= )
VO912EJB1PK7B5BHTVQTEALJGG6OMGD9.example.com. 10800 IN NSEC3 1 1 10 AABBCC (
                               V36U9R2LNLRI8TUNBBVOSKM9KS2408RK SRV RRSIG )
              10800    RRSIG NSEC3 7 3 10800 20110120071321 (
                               20101221071321 16838 example.com.
                               Pi8Zm1yBvVCIYWQxyJnk6/9/2UI= )
```

Many intervening RRs and most of the base64 material has been omitted for the sake of brevity. The following items should be noted:

- There is a NSEC3PARAM RR at the zone apex (see Chapter 13's "NSEC3PARAM Record" section for detail layout) and its corresponding RRSIG RR. The unique TTL value of 0 in this case indicates that these RRs should not be cached by a validating resolver.

- The second and fourth last RRs are NSEC3 RRs. The brutal looking label on the left-hand name is a hashed name in the domain in both cases! By careful inspection, in this case, the last NSEC3 RR covers the SRV RR and since there is only one in the zone file this covers the name _ldap._tcp.example.com.. The second last NSEC3 RR covers the DS RRset.

- The presence of the DS RRset indicates that even though Opt-Out is set, there will be a NSEC3 RR for these DS RRs.

When the DS RRs are removed from the zone file and dnssec-signzone is re-run with unchanged parameters, it generates 22 signatures, implying that there is no DS RRset and its corresponding NSEC3 RR (thus reducing the signatures by 2) for the delegation. This is shown in this fragment of the signed zone:

```
; File written on Tue Dec 21 01:56:54 2010
; dnssec_signzone version 9.7.2-P2
....
sub.example.com.        86400 IN NS    ns3.sub.example.com.
                        86400 IN NS    ns4.sub.example.com.
ns3.sub.example.com.    86400 IN A     10.2.3.4
ns4.sub.example.com.    86400 IN A     10.2.3.5
2CLO1NHS0HH7VPUEFGDGB49TA4CEE44F.example.com. 10800 IN NSEC3 1 1 10 AABBCC (
                        2K9KAPVCJDF7L2FO8PM4M7T2DSKOGKGR A RRSIG
....
```

The NSEC3 RR shown is applicable to an A RR, but recall that the preceding A RRs (for ns3 and ns4.sub.example.com) are glue records and are neither signed nor have an NSEC/NSEC3 RR. The NSEC3 RR shown (exactly in the order in which they appeared in the signed file) therefore applies to one of the other A RRs in the zone file. Perhaps as a quick exercise in mental arithmetic it would be interesting to.....perhaps not!

Validating Resolvers

So far, most of the discussion has focused on the implications for zone signing and authoritative name servers; little attention has been paid to the most important part of DNSSEC—the resolver. If resolvers are not security-aware—they do not validate DNSSEC responses—then the effect of zone signing is rendered moot. For a resolver to participate in DNSSEC, it must satisfy two criteria; it must be configured to be security-aware and it must have one or more trusted anchors. The resolver, when security-aware, requests and uses the additional information supplied with queries for signed zones (RRSIG RRs) to validate the responses and is thus said to be a *validating resolver*. Unsigned zones continue to be handled as normal and will be regarded as either insecure or indeterminate depending on the coverage of the trust anchor(s) defined in the trusted-keys clause and any DS RRs in the parent zone. The DNSSEC standards allow for validation to occur at either an *area resolver* or at the client (typically a *stub-resolver*) illustrated in Figure 11–7.

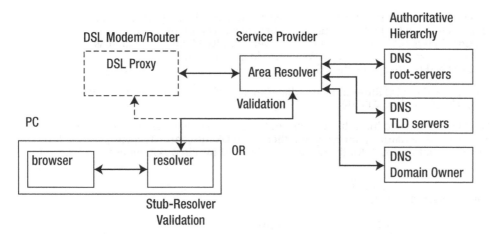

Figure 11–7. Resolver validation

When validation occurs at the area resolver level (typically located at an ISP or within a large network), the client is entirely oblivious to the security status of the responses. The area resolver will either respond to the request, which may imply that the zone was not signed or that it was signed and successfully validated, or it may return a failure, in which case either there was some form of network error or there was a failure to validate a signed zone. The client has no way to differentiate between the various states within the limited responses that it receives. This has positive benefits: the client does not require any changes and is protected more than it was previously by the security umbrella of the area resolver. The downside is that the client can't take special action based on the security status of the response and may actually supply the end user with entirely misleading information. More seriously, messages from the area resolver to the client could be compromised.

The DNSSEC standards, however, allow for the client to be security aware and thus effectively participate in the validation process. Clients can do this by issuing security-aware requests with a special bit set (the CD bit; see Chapter 15). This instructs the area resolver to *not* perform any validation of responses for this client's queries but instead to return in the response both the answer (assuming it received one) and copies of all the RRSIG RRs (or NSEC/NSEC3 RRs if the name does not exist) necessary to validate the response. The client will have to separately obtain and maintain any trusted anchors and DNSKEY RRs necessary to complete the normal validation. Such *validating stub-resolvers* (security-aware stub-resolvers) are the only means to ensure end-to-end security. Unfortunately, they are currently as rare as hens' teeth. It is anticipated over time that this situation will change as security becomes an ever more prevalent requirement at all levels of the Internet.

The common problem for all validating resolvers and validating stub-resolvers is to obtain and maintain trusted anchors. The current solution to this problem is described next.

Key Handling Automation

Figure 11–2 illustrates a trivial set of domains within the total DNS hierarchy. When this process is scaled to cover the entirety of the domain name tree, it begins to resemble a gigantic Swiss cheese with holes (security voids) scattered all over the place. The net effect is that any validating resolver could have to maintain many hundreds, if not thousands, of trust anchors to allow it to bypass the security voids. Additionally, the trust anchors will be rolled-over (changed) from time to time. Further, there will be perhaps millions of validating resolvers that need to reliably update the trust anchor keys. Even in the most optimistic scenario of validating resolvers (and validating stub-resolvers) only requiring and updating a single root-key trusted anchor, the consequences of an error are that signed zones will not validate—they will return a bogus status and, in the jargon, become *dark zones*. For those of a squeamish disposition, this is not a pleasant prospect without some degree of automation, happily provided by RFC 5011 ("Automated Updates of DNS Security (DNSSEC) Trust Anchors").

The objective behind RFC 5011 is to ensure that once reliably established, trust anchors can be automatically updated under well defined conditions. While this is significant, arguably RFC 5011's greatest benefit is to bring rigor to the terminology used when handling DNSSEC keys and their maintenance (roll-over) procedures.

RFC 5011 assumes the initial trusted-anchor at any validating resolver was established using a process that lies outside the definition of both RFC 5011 and DNSSEC. Thus, a manual or, increasingly, a distribution-based approach (similar to the DNS distribution of root-zone hints file and a browser's X.509 root certificates) is used to create the initial trust anchor. RFC 5011 describes when such trust anchors can, or cannot, be reliably updated by automated procedures.

RFC 5011 starts with a premise and a problem. When a key has been established as a trusted anchor, any new DNSKEY in a DNSKEY RRset signed by the established trusted anchor can, at first glance, be trusted. However, if the original key has been compromised, this allows an attacker to immediately gain control of the zone data by introducing new keys that only it controls. Not too healthy. To fix this problem a series of controls are introduced:

1. When a new KSK DNSKEY (officially a DNSKEY RR with the SEP bit set, but colloquially called the KSK bit) is seen for the first time by a validating resolver in a DNSKEY RRset from a zone, the RRset is saved (including a record of the key/keys used to sign the DNSKEY RRset) and an acceptance timer is started. This acceptance timer is defined to be the greater of 30 days or the TTL value of the current trusted-anchor DNSKEY RR(s) for the zone. The new key will not be used to validate any zone RRs until the acceptance timer has successfully expired. The newly introduced key does not have to have signed any zone RRs and is thus defined to be a *stand-by key*. The private key (in the .private file) of a stand-by key, because it does not actively sign zone records, can be maintained more securely at the authoritative zone than active, or current, keys and thus should be less likely to be compromised. In the case of BIND a stand-by key has a PUBLISH date (equal to or greater than the current date) but either does not have an ACTIVE date or the ACTIVE date is some time in the future (see the "dnssec-keygen Timing Metadata" section in Chapter 9).

2. If, before the expiry of the acceptance timer, the validating resolver sees a DNSKEY RRset *without* the *new* KSK DNSKEY RR but signed by the saved signing key or keys, the current acceptance sequence is terminated and any saved DNSKEY RRset discarded. In this case, the signing key is assumed to have been compromised.

3. If the validating resolver continues to see the new KSK DNSKEY RR in the DNSKEY RRset until the acceptance timer expires, then immediately after expiry it may start to use the new DNSKEY RR as a validating key—it's added to the trusted-anchor set. A validating resolver is defined to be able to handle a minimum of five keys as trusted-anchors for any zone.

4. When a validating resolver has an established trusted-anchor, it must refresh (re-query from the authoritative server) the zone's DNSKEY RRset the lesser of 15 days, half the TTL of the DNSKEY RRset, or half the difference between the start and expiration date of the RRSIG RRs for the DNSKEY RRset (see the "RRSIG Record" section in Chapter 12), but no more frequently than once per hour.

5. RFC 5011 allows for DNSKEY RRs to be revoked. The revoked status is indicated by the use of bit 8 of the DNSKEY flags field (see the "DNSKEY Record" section in Chapter 12). Thus a KSK with the REVOKED bit set will have a decimal flags value of 385. If a validating resolver sees a DNSKEY RR in a DNSKEY RRset and, importantly, signed by the DNSKEY RR with the REVOKE bit set (it may be also signed by other DNSKEY RRs) it will *immediately* stop using the key for validation of RRSIGs and remove it from its trusted-anchor list. *Revoke* may be used as both a method to remove stale keys from the validating resolvers trusted-anchor list or as compromise recovery method.

■ **Note** Keys are revoked by using the BIND utility dnssec-revoke (see Chapter 9).

To use RFC 5011 procedures with BIND, see the "DNSSEC Implementation - Key Life-Cycle Examples" section for worked BIND examples. The following is a textual description of the normal method of handling keys:

1. Assume key A has been established as a trusted-anchor (in a trusted-keys clause) in a validating resolver by some secure process.

2. A new key B is generated and introduced into the DNSKEY RRset of the zone but is not used to sign any zone records (key A is used for this purpose). Key B is a stand-by key and its private key (in the .private file) should be kept securely offline to minimize the chances of it being compromised.

3. After 30 days, key B will become a trusted-anchor at any RFC 5011-compliant validating resolver and the zone owner may leave it in this stand-by state for as long as necessary or operationally desirable. Equally, any time after its acceptance as a trusted-anchor, key B may become active and be used to sign zone records, if a ZSK, or sign DNSKEY RRsets if a KSK.

4. Once key B has become an active key and signed zone records, key A can be revoked as soon as sensible (perhaps after the DNSKEY RRset TTL period) and the zone signed by both key A (to confirm the revocation) and B. Additionally, a new stand-by key C can be introduced into the DNSKEY RRset. Key A may be removed at any appropriate time thereafter (after the DNSKEY RRset TTL period) and the zone signed with key B only.

Compromised Key Recovery

Recovery from key compromise when using RFC 5011 is possible according to the following rules:

-   Assume key A is active (a trusted-anchor) and key B is a stand-by key (not yet a trusted-anchor). Now, assume key B is known to have been compromised. Key B is revoked (and the DNSKEY RRset signed by both key A and B). A new stand-by key C is generated (but does not sign the zone, only A does) and introduced into the DNSKEY RRset (with improved safeguards for the private key!). After the acceptance period (typically 30 days) key C becomes a trusted-anchor and can become an active key.

- Assume key A and key B are both trusted-anchors. Assume key A is known to have been compromised. Key A is immediately revoked, a new stand-by key C is introduced, and the zone signed by key A and B. After the acceptance period (typically 30 days), key C becomes a trusted-anchor and can become an active key.

- Assume key A is an active key (a trusted-anchor) and key B is a stand-by key (not a trusted-anchor). Assume key A is known to have been compromised. In this case, no automatic recovery is possible and a manual fall-back process must be used.

Removing a Trusted-Anchor

Finally, to illustrate the complete usage of RFC 5011 procedures, assume that you have established a trusted-anchor in a validating resolver for example.com at some point, say, prior to the signing of the .com zone. Now assume that the .com zone has been signed and you wish to add your DS RR to it (join the chain of trust) and remove the trusted-anchor for example.com in all RFC 5011 compliant validating resolvers:

1. Assume key A is an active key for the zone and is a trusted-anchor in a validating resolver.

2. Create a new key B but do not add it to the DNSKEY RRset. Generate DS RRs for keys A and B (see the "dnssec-dsfromkey Utility" section in Chapter 9) and add all DS RRs to the parent.

3. At least one DNSKEY RRset TTL after the DS RRs have been published by the parent, add key B to the zone's DNSKEY RRset, revoke key A at the same time, and sign the zone with both key A (necessary to confirm its revocation to the validating resolver) and B. Adding the REVOKE flag to A's DNSKEY RR changes its fingerprint, which means the DS RR for A will no longer be valid and it can be removed from the parent when convenient.

4. After a suitable period, the revoked key A may be removed and the zone signed with key B.

Key Handling Summary

The crucial issue in all cases is maintenance of the private key to ensure it is not compromised. While this can be done using normal computer security methods with hidden masters or signing-only configurations, it is increasingly done, especially on high value or vulnerable zones, using hardware security modules (HSMs). The "DNSSEC Implementation - Key Maintenance" section discusses this point further.

DNSSEC Lookaside Validation

The DNSSEC Lookaside Validation (DLV) service is an alternative method by which a chain of trust may be created and verified without the need to sign the parent zone file. The service makes use of a DLV RR, which is currently defined by RFC 4431 (INFORMATIONAL status) and which is fully supported by the current (9.4+) versions of BIND 9. The DLV RR is functionally identical to the DS RR and may be generated by the dnssec-signzone utility by use of the -l domain option (see Chapter 9). A DLV RR is placed in a special signed zone called a *lookaside zone* instead of the DS RR that would normally be added to the parent zone, thus removing the need to sign the parent zone. The DLV service works by providing an alternative method to verify a chain of trust as described next.

Assume that the lookaside domain is called `dlv.example.net` and the name server is trying to verify the chain of trust for the signed zone `example.com`. In a normal sequence, when a validating resolver tries to verify the chain of trust for `example.com`, it will first check for a trusted anchor in its `trusted-keys` clause, and if one is not found, it will issue a query to find a DS RR at the parent `.com` zone. If neither is found, the zone will be marked as insecure. DLV adds an additional step by allowing the name server to query a lookaside zone, for which it must have a trusted anchor, for the DLV RR of the zone being verified. When the validating resolver detects that the lookaside feature is enabled (by a `dnssec-lookaside` statement in `named.conf`), it will issue a DLV query with the domain name `example.com.dlv.example.net`. If found, and assuming the trusted anchor for `dlv.example.net` is present in a `trusted-keys` clause, the `example.com` zone is verified to be secure. Figure 11–8 illustrates the DLV process.

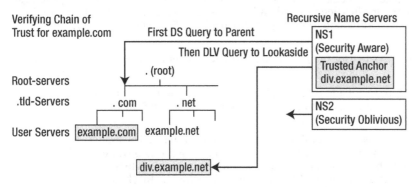

Figure 11–8. *DLV verification procedure*

The initial query will try to find a DS RR for `example.com` at the parent `.com` zone, and only if that fails will the DLV query be issued to the lookaside zone. While the lookaside zone `dlv.example.net` must be signed, the trusted anchor at NS1 means that its parent, `example.net`, does not have to be signed, as is shown in Figure 11–8.

DLV was originally designed as a method to reduce the number of trusted-anchors required by validating resolvers before the root-zone was signed. The root-zone was signed in July 2010 and thus removes the immediate need for DLV technology. However, DLV is included in this book for the following reasons:

DNSSEC Last-step Testing: Assume a user with a number of domain names or a DNS hosting service wishes to implement DNSSEC service across all domains. DNSSEC has associated risks, so a thorough program of testing would naturally be prepared, in which zones would be signed and validating resolvers configured in some captive or test environment while operational processes were being developed. However, this still leaves a relatively big jump from a test environment to a live environment. DLV can offer an *almost live* environment. All operational zones can be signed—this incurs no risk until DS RRs are sent to the parent. However, to fully test DNSSEC, each validating resolver must be configured with a trusted-anchor for each zone under test, which can be very messy and does not reflect the final configuration since only a single root-zone key would be required. Alternatively, a DLV service can be configured in which case only a single trusted-keys (or managed-keys) clause for the local DLV service is required in each validating resolver being used to test the processes. The domain names that will be validated using DLV can be precisely configured (using dnssec-lookaside statements) to only validate the zones under test via DLV; all others can use the normal root-zone process. This is as close to live operation as it is possible to get and may provide a worthwhile, if not essential, reduction in risk for many users.

Private Networks: Private networks, especially larger ones, are not immune from internal attacks. DLV provides a method to secure such networks, using a single trusted-anchor in validating resolvers.

Alternative Validation: For multiple reasons, a user, affinity group, or enterprise network may want DNSSEC benefits without wishing to make public any secure information. This could be for political, cultural, or privacy reasons. DLV offers a relatively simple method of doing this.

■ **Note** BIND 9.7.2-P2 is distributed with a managed-keys clause (a variant of the trusted-keys clause; see the "BIND managed-keys Clause" section in Chapter 12) for the DLV service at dlv.isc.org.

To create DLV, RRs from the KSK Kexample.com.+008+34957.key file created in previously in

```
dnssec-dsfromkey -l dlv.example.net Kexample.com.+008+34957 > dlvkey
```

which creates the following two DLV RRs

```
example.com.dlv.example.net. IN DLV 34957 8 1 592954781DFD76BC8255F03D28FDB0D483537682
example.com.dlv.example.net. IN DLV 34957 8 2 (
                                  E64FAFC9A5CFA883C045FA171608389F8FF
                                  CC4B1652E0DB2F743C000 17A57713)
```

DLV Service

There is nothing magical about a DLV service. A DLV service uses a standard name server with a standard signed zone file and could be created for use by any affinity group as an alternative to multiple trusted anchors for each member of the group. To illustrate creation of a DLV service, assume an affinity group comprised of the domains example.org, example.com, and example.net decide to set up a DLV service that will hosted by dlv.example.net. Each member domain will create a DLV RR by the zone signing process described using a -l dlv.example.net argument. Alternatively, the DLV RRs can be created from a KSK DNSKEY RR using the dnssec-dsfromkey utility (see the "dnssec-dsfromkey Utility" section in Chapter 9).

To create DLV RRs from the KSK Kexample.com.+008+34957.key file created in the "Securing the example.com Zone" section earlier in the chapter, do this:

```
dnssec-dsfromkey -l dlv.example.net Kexample.com.+008+34957 > dlvrrs
```

which creates the following two DLV RRs in the file dlvrrs via the normal shell redirection service (>):

```
example.com.dlv.example.net. IN DLV 34957 8 1 (
                      592954781DFD76BC8255F03D28FDB0D483537682)
example.com.dlv.example.net. IN DLV 34957 8 2 (
                      E64FAFC9A5CFA883C045FA171608389F8FF
                      CC4B1652E0DB2F743C000 17A57713)
```

The DLV RRs have been reformatted using standard RR parentheses notation purely for presentational purposes.

The DLV RRs are sent to the domain administrator for dlv.example.net by a process that will authenticate the sender, such as secure e-mail. A zone file comprising the supplied DLV RRs will be created as shown here:

```
; zone fragment for dlv.example.net
$TTL 1d ; zone default
$ORIGIN dlv.example.com.
@       IN SOA ns1.dlv.example.com. hostmaster.dlv.example.com. (
                    2010121500 ; serial
                    10800      ; refresh (3 hours)
                    15         ; retry (15 seconds)
                    604800     ; expire (1 week)
                    10800      ; nx (3 hours)
                    )
            NS ns1.dlv.example.com.
            NS ns2.dlv.example.com.
ns1     A  192.168.254.2
ns2     A  192.168.254.3
; DLV RRs for affinity group
example.com.dlv.example.net. IN DLV 34957 8 1 (
                      592954781DFD76BC8255F03D28FDB0D483537682 )
example.com.dlv.example.net. IN DLV 34957 8 2 (
                      E64FAFC9A5CFA883C045FA171608389F8FF
                      CC4B1652E0DB2F743C000 17A57713)
example.org.dlv.example.net. IN DLV 42134 5 1 (blah, blah, blah)
example.net.dlv.example.net. IN DLV 02557 5 1 (more blah, blah, blah)
....
```

A ZSK and KSK for the dlv.example.net zone will be created using the dnssec-keygen utility and added to the zone file as described earlier, and the zone will be signed with the dnssec-signzone utility using both KSK and ZSK as normal. The public key of the KSK for dlv.example.net is distributed to be used as a trusted anchor by all validating resolvers of the affinity group; thus a single trusted anchor is used to replace the alternative of three trusted anchors, which would otherwise be required.

The zone dlv.example.net would be delegated from example.net and an authoritative-only name server (see Chapter 7) created to support the service. Finally, each validating resolver would add the trusted anchor for dlv.example.net in a trusted-keys clause in their named.conf file, and to invoke the service each member would further add the following three lines to the options clause in the same named.conf file:

```
dnssec-lookaside "example.com" trusted-anchor "dlv.example.net";
dnssec-lookaside "example.net" trusted-anchor "dlv.example.net";
dnssec-lookaside "example.net" trusted-anchor "dlv.example.net";
```

The specification of dnssec-lookaside says that any domain *at or below* the defined domain name will use the lookaside zone defined in the trusted-anchor option, which means that only domain names ending with example.com, example.org, or example.net will incur a DLV lookup. However, the specification also says that the *deepest* domain name (which actually means the one with the most labels) defined in a dnssec-lookaside will be used for the lookaside query. So if a name server that included the previous three lines also wished to use, say, the ISC DLVservice, it would *add* the following statement to invoke that DLV service:

```
dnsssec-lookaside "." trusted-anchor "dlv.isc.org";
```

The effect of this statement would be that any secure domain that does not end with example.com, example.org, or example.net would incur a DLV lookup to the dlv.isc.org lookaside domain (for which there must also be a trusted-anchor in a trusted-keys clause), whereas only our three target domains, example.com, example.net, and example.org, would query the dlv.example.net lookaside domain. It is therefore possible to support a number of concurrent DLV services, each of which may target specific markets or affinity groups prior to the widespread availability of signed TLDs.

DNSSEC Implementation

This section focuses on DNSSEC implementations issues and provides additional usage examples, specifically on the latest BIND DNSSEC technologies designed make life simpler, as well as some purely tutorial material. There are a bewildering number of BIND options to choose from and innumerable more from both commercial and open source suppliers. Few hard and fast rules are provided; rather, the approach taken is to enumerate the pros and cons of various options from which the reader can select the most appropriate choices suited to their operational environment. While studiously trying to avoid it, the choice of language used can reflect the author's inevitable prejudices. The reader is encouraged to treat all adjectives and adverbs with extreme suspicion and to maintain their natural cynicism at all times.

Why implement DNSSEC?

- It can provide your customers with added confidence, especially if you operate a commercial site. In the short term, this could be leveraged as a commercial advantage. In the medium term, it will be essential simply to keep up with the competition. Lead or follow.

- Many influential commentators and those close to governmental policy makers are indicating they think DNSSEC should be targeted at 100% coverage within a reasonable period of time to ensure ongoing Internet security.

- Necessity. It is possible, perhaps even likely, that to do business in certain sectors, notably with governments, that DNSSEC may become a mandatory requirement.

- Even with the current generation of tools, it really is not difficult. If you know how to run a cron job, you can implement it today (see "DNSSEC Implementation - a Plan").

When should you implement DNSSEC?

- Start the implementation plan, at least the testing phase, as soon as your TLD (gTLD or ccTLD) is signed *and* as soon as your registrar allows addition of DS RRs to your registration information. About 60 TLDs were signed by the end of 2010 (out of about 230 total). Or you could wait for the next appearance of Halley's Comet.

- Seriously, evaluate the technical and business risks sensibly. Then build a test implementation; see "Implementing DNSSEC - A Plan."

DNSSEC Algorithms and Keys

Key Management

The asymmetric cryptographic algorithms used in DNSSEC (RSA, and to a lesser extent DSA) have public and private keys. The integrity, and ultimately therefore the usefulness, of any DNSSEC implementation is about how the private key is controlled and managed.

In most organization, this normally means administrative procedures such as using OS file permissions to limit access; see Chapter 10 for a full discussion. But a lot more can be done, such as:

- When a key is not being actively used, its private key can be physically removed from any server.

- Use a hidden master configuration to avoid exposing any server with private keys to public access.

- Establish a *signing-only* server. If offline signing is being performed, only key generation and zone signing tools need be present on a hardened server. There is no need to run a named daemon. Secure FTP can be used to transfer the resulting files to operational systems or a hidden master. Authoritative name servers that are not using DDNS have no requirement for private keys.

The increasing use of cryptography is reducing the prices of HSMs. While they come in a variety of shapes and sizes, they should all be compliant with either the joint US/Canadian standard FIPS 140-2 Level 3 or Level 4 or its ISO equivalent ISO/IEC 19790:2006 Level 3 or Level 4. The HSM essentially maintains the private key in a separate hardware module that is either tamper-proof or tamper-evident (the HSM knows when its security has been breached). Keys are generated within the unit by command, the public key can be read and formatted for external use, but operations using the private key are only performed within the HSM. Data being encrypted or decrypted is passed to the HSM and the output is returned.

HSMs come in three broad flavors: those that provide only key management functionality, those that provide key management and crytographic hardware acceleration, and those that provide crytographic hardware acceleration only. The latter are particularly useful for validating resolvers, which are required to do all the serious crypto heavy-lifting in DNSSEC.

HSMs typically use a library/driver interface known as pkcs11 or cryptoki (defined by RSA Laboratories and available at www.rsa.com/rsalabs/node.asp?id=2133). By default, BIND is built to use the OpenSSL cryptographic libraries. While outside the scope of this book, BIND can be configured and built from source (see the "Building BIND from Source" section in Chapter 6) to support the pkcs11 interface. Interested readers are pointed to the rudimentary descriptions in the BIND ARM Section 4.11 as a starting point.

Key Sizes and Algorithms

All cryptographic processes are based on the concept of *computational infeasibility*, a relative concept not an absolute one. The general rule is that the bigger the key size and the stronger the algorithm, the better; however, these should be commensurate with the risks involved. It must be remembered that in DNSSEC, the zone owner gets to choose algorithms and key size but it is the poor old validating resolver, on which the zone owner also depends, that has to do all the hard work. The effect of choosing an excessively large key size is relatively trivial for the zone owner—signing the zone file from time to time. But the effect on the validating resolver is increased load, which will impact its performance and throughput and thus affect customer access to the domain. Enlightened self-interest is crucial.

The best formal advice on the topic of key size is contained in NIST (US National Institute of Standards and Technology) Special Publication 800-57 Part 1 Rev2, in particular Table 4 (available from csrc.nist.gov/publications/nistpubs/800-57/sp800-57-Part1-revised2_Mar08-2007.pdf). In summary, it recommends that RSA and DSA key sizes used in the period from 2011 to 2030 should be 2048 bits. Lower key sizes will incur an increased level of risk; higher values will place excessive demand on validating resolvers while incurring no additional benefit.

■ **Note** The referenced NIST publication is well worth the reader's time investment since it provides a good background into cryptographic characteristics and usage.

The algorithms used in DNSSEC's digital signatures (the RRSIG RRs) consist of an asymmetric (public/private) algorithm and a hash algorithm. The only mandatory hash algorithm was SHA1 at the time this book was published; SHA256 and SHA512 were optional. The hash algorithm recommended by NIST in the period from 2011 until 2030 is SHA256 (SP 800-57 Part 1 Rev2, Table 4 Note b) and therefore a decision was taken that the root would be signed using SHA256, an optional standard. It is likely, at some future date, that Elliptic Curve (ECC) asymmetric algorithms will be supported by DNSSEC. The point here is that cryptographic algorithms (asymmetric or hashes) may change over time. It is both expected and natural. Users may want to take advantage of such changes.

However, this can be a problem. There is no way to know the algorithmic support in any, never mind every, validating resolver. It is thus possible for the user to select and use an algorithm not implemented by a *fully DNSSEC-compliant validating resolver*. In these circumstances, the effect will be the zone will be marked as insecure—there is no DNSSEC support. In the case of the root zone, this was simple: if you want to use the root, you need SHA256 support. Few zones have this power! While validating resolvers at larger service providers are usually upgraded regularly and maintained to a high level, this not the case for all validating resolvers. If the user decides to use a new algorithm that is optional within the DNSSEC standards, there is a risk that it may not be supported by all required resolvers. The only solution is to treat such algorithm changes similarly to a key rollover and use two keys, one with the older algorithm and one with the new algorithm for whatever period of time the user thinks is appropriate and then the older one can be retired.

At this time, the safest set to use is RSASHA256, simply because that is the algorithm used by the root, and with a key size of 2048 bits, because that is what NIST recommends. However, if you are using NSEC3, your only hash choice today is SHA1 (the only hash supported by NSEC3), again with a 2048 bit key size.

Key Life Cycle Management

RFC 5011 nominally defines the automation of trusted-anchors. In practice, it's added a rigor, missing from the original standards, over the use and states of keys. While RFC 5011 necessarily focuses on the KSK, the life cycle defined is applicable to both KSK and ZSKs. The BIND utilities dnssec-keygen, dnssec-signzone, dnssec-settime, and dnssec-revoke all either manipulate or can, optionally, make automated decisions based on newly introduced key timing metadata (TMD) maintained in the .private key files and which reflects key states. TMD data is maintained in Universal Coordinated Time (UCT), not local time. While it is possible to use DNSSEC without either manipulating or even being aware of BIND's key states, in the long term this is probably a mistake, so effort expended now could yield big dividends in the future.

Now that the root-zone has been signed (July 2010), it is arguable that as a practical matter only the root-zone will be subject to RFC 5011 life cycle management and thus for the normal domain owner the key life-cycle process is rendered moot. However, understanding the life-cycle will aid in the use of certain BIND tools, bring clarity to key handling, and may, in either unique or emergency situations, be essential. Further, in cases where the zone is part of a secure delegation chain, certain key state transitions will also trigger the need to either add or remove DS RRs from the parent. These events are duly noted in the state descriptions below.

The key states and life cycle are described with appropriate references to RFC 5011 and BIND's definitions:

■ **Note** The following explanations use BIND timing metadata (TMD) terminology, such as publish date, active date, etc. A practical example of generating and manipulating this data is illustrated in the "Key Life-Cycle Examples" section later in the chapter. In the following descriptions the terms *less than* and *greater than current UTC date and time* are used. The term *current UTC date and time* means the time at which any utility (or daemon) that uses the time values is run. To illustrate these terms, assume that the utility dnssec-signzone is run on a server located on the eastern seaboard of North America (EDT, 5 hours after UTC) on January 15, 2011 at 10:23:46. The UCT time will be January 15, 2011 15:23:46. The UTC date and time January 15, 2011 15:22:46 is *less than* and January 15, 2011 15:24:46 is *greater than* the current UTC time and date.

STANDBY state: A key is said to be in the standby state when it appears in a DNSKEY RRset but is not used to sign any zone records (a.k.a. a pre-publish strategy). When the key is a KSK, it will not be accepted as a trusted-anchor by validating resolvers who implement RFC 5011 procedures until 30 days plus ½ the TTL of the DNSKEY RRset after its first appearance in the RRset. Thus, if the TTL is 1 day, it will take 30 ½ days, or for practical purposes 31 days, to be accepted as a trusted-anchor and thus be used for active validation. A standby KSK should not be used to sign zone records (become active) before expiry of this acceptance period, though there is nothing wrong in doing so; it's simply a waste of resources. A standby ZSK can be used to sign zone records (become active) one TTL period after being introduced into the DNSKEY RRset if using the prepublish method, or immediately if double-signing. Keys may remain in the standby state as long as required. The values defined previously constitute minimum thresholds. Other than the overheads of sending the standby DNSKEY RR, there is no penalty. Any number of ZSK or KSK standby keys may exist in a DNSKEY RRset. This is subject only to the limit imposed by RFC 5011-compliant validating resolvers that five accepted KSKs per zone should be supported (this is the minimum figure; individual implementations may accept more). Standby keys, by definition, do not take part in any signing operations, so their private keys can therefore be kept securely offline where they are less likely to be compromised. In the case of a standby KSK for a zone that is securely delegated, no DS RR is required for this key at the parent zone. In BIND, a standby key is one whose publish date and time (in the TMD) is less than the current UTC date and time and whose active date and time is greater than the current UTC date and time.

ACTIVE State: A key is said to be active when it signs resource records either as KSK or a ZSK. Recall that for KSKs there is a minimum period required to accept a new KSK DNSKEY RR as a trusted-anchor (see "STANBY State" above) in RFC 5011-compliant validating resolvers. In the case of a KSK for a securely delegated zone, a DS RR will need to be added to the parent zone. The DS RR should be published *at least* one TTL period (of the DS RRs at the parent) prior to the key entering the active state. In BIND, an active key is one whose active date and time is less than the current UTC date and time.

INACTIVE/RETIRED State: A key, KSK or ZSK, is said to be inactive when it continues to appear in a DNSKEY RRset but no longer signs zone records (in this sense only it is similar to a standby state). If the inactive key is a KSK, it is not removed from the trusted-anchor set at a validating resolver (only REVOKE causes this). An inactive key could be returned to an active state at any time. However, assuming that the reason for making the key inactive was due to normal preventative maintenance, the extended period of use that would result would necessarily increase risk. Other than the increased size of the DNSKEY RRset, a key may remain in the inactive state for any period of time. An inactive key in BIND is one whose inactive time and date is less than the current UTC time and date.

DELETE State: When a key is in the delete state it may be removed from the DNSKEY RRset. If the key is a KSK, it should be put into the revoke state before the delete state (see "REVOKE state" below). In BIND, a delete state is indicated when the delete time and date is less than the current UTC time and date.

REVOKE State: The revoke state is only applicable to KSK keys. When a key is in the revoke state, the REVOKE bit is bit 8 of the flags field of the DNSKEY RR (see Chapter 13's "DNSKEY Record" section). Revoke has two uses. First, it should be used to indicate that a key has been, or is suspected of being, compromised; it immediately stops the use of this key for the purposes of validation at a validating resolver. A key may move from any state (except delete) to the revoke state in an emergency. Second, it should always be used when making a KSK inactive, and certainly before the delete state is reached. This is required because the revoke state is the only way that a validating resolver will remove a trusted-anchor. Failure to do this may cause an RFC 5011-compliant validating resolver to reach its trusted-anchor limit (set to a minimum of 5 by RFC 5011). In the revoke state, the DNSKEY RRset must be signed by the revoked key *even if it was not previously being used to sign any RRsets*; for example it was in the standby state. It will take a minimum of ½ the DNSKEY TTL period for any RFC 5011 compliant validating resolver to see the revoked DNSKEY RR. In BIND, a revoke state is indicated by the revoke time and date being less than the current UTC time and date.

The following set of rules, by no means the only ones possible, are applicable for all keys (ZSK and KSK) and will work whether part of a signed delegation using DS RRs at the parent (increasingly the case) or using RFC 5011-compliant trusted-anchor procedures. Thus, there is no need to modify procedures irrespective of the end use of the keys. They will work equally well in a local test environment and on the public DNSSEC service.

Assuming that the KSK is rolled-over every 2 years and the ZSK every 90 days (longer if desired) with a 5 day overlap (double signing), and that the TTL of the DNSKEY RRset is no more than 2 days, then:

1. Thirty-six days *before* any current key (ZSK or KSK) is to be rolled-over, create a new standby key of the required type and re-sign the zone (without using the new key). If the key is a KSK, generate the DS RRs at this time for simplicity (they are not secure RRs). Take the private key of the new key offline.

2. Thirty-one days later, bring the private key online and activate the key by re-signing the zone (ZSK or KSK). If a KSK and the zone is a signed delegation, add the DS RRs to the parent. If using the KSK as a trusted-anchor, do nothing with the DS RRs.

3. Five days later, make the old key inactive if a ZSK or revoke it if a KSK. Resign the zone. Note that when a key is revoked (KSK), it must sign the DNSKEY RRset, unlike an inactive key. If a KSK *and* a signed delegation, delete the DS RR(s) for the revoked key. If a trusted-anchor (using RFC 5011 procedures), do nothing.

4. Two days later, delete the key (KSK or ZSK) from the DNSKEY RRset and re-sign the zone.

5. Repeat forever.

Some of the above processes are only essential under certain conditions. However, they will cause no problems under *any* conditions. They are a least common denominator set. Careful examination of the above rule set will reveal that it uses both a prepublish strategy (rule 1) and a double-signing strategy (rule 3) during a brief overlap period. This may be viewed as an unnecessary overhead. Its justification is pure simplification and safety. But, as previously noted, there are many other possible strategies that may be devised and that will work.

■ **Caution** In rule 3, the time of five days *must* allow for the total process time of adding, publishing, and cache propagation of the DS RRs via the parent (a TLD in most cases). The cache propagation time has a worst case value of the TTL of the DS RRset of the parent, which for most TLDs cases ranges from a low of 24 hours to a high of 48 hours. Thus, it is assumed that the process of adding the DS RR to the parent (perhaps via secure web interface to the registrar) and the DS RRs appearing in the zone, plus a little wobble time, will take no more than three days. If in doubt, lengthen this time, since other than the overhead of additional data volumes there is no consequence. However, if it's too short, the zone can go dark.

Key Life-Cycle Examples

To illustrate how BIND uses the various timing metadata, a KSK and ZSK will be generated using the rules described in the previous section.

To generate a ZSK, use an RSASHA256 algorithm with a 2048 bit key size, which will be published immediately, will become active 31 days from now, become inactive (or retired) after 90 more days, and be deleted 2 days after that, do the following:

```
dnssec-keygen -a rsasha256 -b 2048 -P now -A +31d -I +121d -D +123d -n zone \
example.com
Kexample.com.+008+48384
```

To display the meta information associated with this key, use this:

```
# dnssec-settime -p all Kexample.com.+008+48384
Created: Thu Dec 23 14:01:38 2010
Publish: Thu Dec 23 14:01:38 2010
Activate: Sun Jan 23 14:01:38 2011
Revoke: UNSET
Inactive: Sat Apr 23 15:01:38 2011
Delete: Mon Apr 25 15:01:38 2011
```

To generate the equivalent KSK, the command is exactly the same but the -f ksk argument is used and you set the -R rather than -I values, this case to two years (assumed 2 x 365 = 730), like so:

```
dnssec-keygen -a rsasha256 -b 2048 -f ksk -P now -A +31d -R +761d -D +763d \
-n zone example.com
Kexample.com.+008+48031
```

To display the meta information associated with this key, use:

```
dnssec-settime -p all Kexample.com.+008+48031
Created: Mon Jan 10 09:22:41 2011
Publish: Mon Jan 10 09:22:41 2011
Activate: Thu Feb 10 09:22:41 2011
Revoke: Sat Feb  9 09:22:41 2013
Inactive: UNSET
Delete: Mon Feb 11 09:22:41 2013
```

To revoke the above key at day 761, the following command must be used:

```
# dnssec-revoke Kexample.com.+008+48031
Kexample.com.+008+48159
```

This shows that a new key-tag (48159) will be generated as a consequence of the additional REVOKE flag. This is normal and expected.

The timing metadata (all times are UCT not local time) plays no role in the DNSSEC standards, but it is used by the various tools, especially dnssec-signzone, to decide what action to take, as may be seen in the next section.

■ **Note** To initially sign a zone, a ZSK and a KSK with an active date of now (the default) must also be generated. The above commands show generation of subsequent maintenance-only keys.

BIND Signing Models

The current BIND releases provide broadly three signing models. Two models are offline; one is online and assumes DDNS. They are:

> *Manual Offline*: The signing process uses dnssec-signzone with explicit definitions of the all parameters as shown in the examples under the "Base DNSSEC Theory" section of this chapter. All keys have to be edited into or included in the zone files and removed appropriately. When zones have been signed, BIND is either restarted or rndc (freeze/thaw) is used to pick up the new zone file; if done on a signing-only server, the files need to be securely transferred to an operational name server and BIND restarted or rndc used. This process makes no use of the timing metadata with the exception that, if using RFC 5011 procedures, the REVOKE bit must be explicitly set using the dnssec-revoke utility. This process has been fully described and is not discussed further other than to note that, given adequate script support, it is viable but perhaps slightly error prone due to the number of operations involved.

> *Smart Offline*: BIND provides the option to use what it calls *smart signing*. In this mode, all zone keys may be placed into a directory and their TMD appropriately set and manipulated. dnssec-signzone is supplied with the location of the directory containing the keys and the name of the zone file. There is no need to explicitly include or delete keys from the zone file. Depending on the TMD data, the appropriate keys are included automatically in the zone file and used to sign the zone if they are in an active state. When zones have been signed, BIND is either restarted or rndc (freeze/thaw) is used to pick up the new zone file; if done on a signing-only server, the files need to be securely transferred to an operational name server and BIND restarted or rndc used. A worked example using this method is shown in the "Implementing DNSSEC" section later in the chapter.

> *Smart Online*: By adding the auto-dnssec statement (it has two possible modes; see the "auto-dnssec" section in Chapter 12) the smart signing process (whereby keys are added or removed as appropriate using their TMD) can be invoked either by using rndc sign zone-name (if auto-dnssec allow;) or automatically (if auto-dnssec maintain;). In either case, the zone must be configured to allow DDNS with either an allow-update or update-policy statement.

The above is not a complete list of the current feature set; for instance, there is a nsupdate based method whereby DNSKEY RRs are manually added or deleted and that triggers a zone-signing process.

This method is described in Chapter's 9 "BIND nsupdate" section. Nevertheless, the above constitutes the major choices available at this time. Which of these methods is most suitable will be determined by the operational characteristics and requirements of any user or organization.

Offline vs. Online

This section briefly discusses the pros and cons of offline (using dnssec-signzone) and online (DDNS) signing.

Offline:

- Pro: Private keys are only required during signing operations and can be offlined when not in active use. If an HSM is being used, this point is moot.

- Pro: A signing-only server can be created. Private keys can be maintained in a hardened environment (again moot if an HSM is being used). Processor loads incurred during signing will have no impact on operational systems. In small zones (< 100 RRs), this is a modest load, but can increase rapidly with zone size, the number of keys being used per zone, and the number of zones being signed.

- Con: Manual intervention is required when zone signing is complete. Either BIND needs to be explicitly restarted or rndc (freeze/thaw) used. This can be scripted but is more difficult in a signing-only server configuration.

Online:

- Con: Private keys need to be constantly available. Moot if an HSM is being used.

- Con: Processor loads will impact operational server performance; even in a hidden master configuration, this can be significant. BIND uses a time-slice technique (a quantum) to minimize the impact.

- Pro: BIND does not need to be restarted.

- Pro: Limited (auto-dnssec allow;) or no (auto-dnssec maintain;) manual intervention is required.

Offline Smart Signing

The following assumes that all zone keys are in a directory /var/named/keys and have been created using the commands shown above; specifically, they are using keys that have appropriate timing metadata. Keys for multiple zones may be present in this directory. An unsigned zone *without* any included DNSKEY RRs is used as the input file (DS RRs must be manually added if required). The following command will create a signed zone file with a default file name of master.example.com.signed:

```
dnssec-signzone -t -o example.com -K /var/named/keys master.example.com
```

The original unsigned zone file (master.example.com) may be used as input every time the zone is resigned (dnssec-signzone is rerun). This zone file may therefore be managed and handled in exactly the same way as it was before it was signed. Keys are simply manipulated in the key directory (using dnssec-settime, dnssec-keygen and dnssec-revoke as required) and the dnssec-signzone command rerun with the same parameters every time.

DNSSEC Implementation - A Plan

There are risks involved with implementing DNSSEC. If things go wrong, the zone could be left unreachable (*dark* in the jargon) when accessed from the increasing number of validating resolvers—recall this is now BIND's default configuration. The consequence is not that DNSSEC should be avoided like the plague but rather that it needs to be tested to both acquire operational experience and confidence. There are, in this author's opinion, two pre-conditions before DNSSEC should be considered on anything but a purely experimental basis. First, the zone parent (gTLD or ccTLD) should be signed or a credible date be available. Check this status with dig +dnssec parent-zone. (the trailing dot is important), which will return an SOA RR plus one or more RRSIG/NSEC/NSEC3 RRs if the TLD is signed. Second, the zone registrar has in place a procedure, or an acceptable date for such a procedure, to enable either direct addition of or acceptance of DS RRs for zones. Alternatively, if DNSSEC is a priority, the zone could be transferred to a registrar that does provide DS RR support. The following outlines an extremely conservative, low-risk plan to implement DNSSEC:

1. Experiment with dnssec-keygen, dnssec-signzone and dnssec-revoke utilities in a captive test environment. Use a copy of an operational zone file with a single validating resolver with a trust-anchor (managed-keys clause) using RFC 5011 procedures configured on (or accessed only from) a tester's desktop. This ensures that at least one person is constantly accessing the signed zone and will therefore detect any errors immediately. Perform at least three cycles of KSK and ZSK roll-overs using shortened key life times (perhaps 10 to 30 days) to test continuous availability of the zone during roll-overs. This is perhaps a one to three month process. If any error occurs, examine and correct the cause and restart the process from the beginning.

2. When the user is confident of the mechanics of DNSSEC, sign one or more operational zones. Do NOT publish DS RRs at the parent. This step incurs no risk—only when DS RRs are published or an external trusted-anchor is established is DNSSEC visible off-site. The zone will have insecure or indeterminate status at external validating resolvers but that will not, in any way, inhibit access—even if signatures expire. Start key maintenance procedures using a 30-day ZSK replacement cycle and a 60-day KSK replacement cycle. Configure internal validating resolver(s) with a managed-keys clause (RFC 5011) for all signed zones. Alternatively, configure an internal DLV service and use a single trusted-anchor (in a managed-keys clause) if many zones are involved. Allow two full KSK replacement cycles to occur with no reported problems (four ZSKs roll-overs will occur during this period). Restart the process if any errors occur.

3. Change the ZSK and KSKs maintenance procedures to use normal operational roll-over values such as 90 days (or longer) for ZSKs and 2 years for KSKs. Allow a single ZSK rollover to occur with no reported problems.

4. DNSSEC is fully operational internally at this point and can remain in this state as long as the user wants. To make the zone externally DNSSEC visible, simply publish the DS RRs to the zones parent, normally the domain registrar.

Summary

This chapter describes the theory and implementation of DNSSEC (historically known as DNSSEC.bis), which represents the second generation of standards used to ensure the authenticity and integrity of data supplied from a suitably configured authoritative name server to a validating resolver. DNSSEC standards use public key (asymmetric) cryptography to ensure that the data supplied in response to a query for, say, www.example.com, could only have come from the domain example.com (authenticity), that data received by the querying name server is the same as the data sent by the queried name server (data integrity), and that in the event www.example.com does not exist, it can be proven that such is the case (proof of nonexistence (PNE) or denial of existence). Transaction security using TSIG or SIG(0), used to secure operations such as DDNS or zone transfer, is covered in Chapter 10.

The chapter began by describing the Base DNSSEC theory, including the establishment of islands of trust whereby single, unconnected zones may be secured, or a group of such isolated islands that are part of an affinity or common interest group, such as an enterprise network, may be secured. In this case, to get security coverage, the zone requires a trusted anchor—the public key used to sign the secured zone—that is obtained by a secure process that authenticates the source and is then configured into all security-aware name servers that wish to validate responses for the zone using a trusted-keys clause. Securing the zone involves the use of a private key to digitally sign all the RRsets in the zone using an RRSIG RR type. Once established, secure zones can be linked together into chains of trust using their delegation points; thus, if example.com is secured, it may be linked to the .com gTLD or it may be securely delegated to sub.example.com. This process is accomplished using the Delegated Signer RR, which is added to the parent domain and secures the delegation to the child domain. The public keys used in signing are defined in the zone file using DNSKEY RRs and are categorized as either a Zone Signing Key, which is used to sign the records within the zone file, or a Key Signing Key, which is used to sign only the DNSKEY RRs used in the signing process and may be used externally as either a trusted anchor or referenced by a DS RR. While the standards allow a single DNSKEY RR to be used for both ZSK and KSK purposes, this not a recommended practice. Proof of nonexistence is provided by the NSEC RRs, which chain together all the RRs within the zone file. Cryptographic keys need to be changed either periodically to minimize risk or immediately in the case where a key is known to be compromised. This process, called key rollover, may use either a prepublish or double-signing strategy, both of which were described. Finally, examples illustrating the implementation of DNSSEC and covering all the preceding points were presented.

"DNSSEC Enhancements" covered new developments to simplify DNSSEC processes or solve tactical and operational problems. These include NSEC3, Trust Anchor Automation, DLV, Opt-Out, and the introduction of new cryptographic algorithms or hash functions.

"DNSSEC Implementation" describes the various issues that need to be considered when planning for DNSSEC operations and includes selection of key sizes, online vs. offline signing, key management including the use of hardware security modules (HSMs) and Key Handling Automation. The section contains a mixture of tutorial material and worked examples.

The next chapter describes, with examples where appropriate, the statements and clauses used in named.conf, the configuration file that controls BIND's operational behavior.

CHAPTER 12

■■■

BIND 9 Configuration Reference

This chapter contains reference information about the daunting list of parameters that control the BIND 9 series of applications. The reference is split into two parts:

- The BIND command-line *arguments* that control the operational environment at load time and *signals* that are accepted by a running daemon.

- The BIND configuration *parameters* defined in the named.conf file that control operational functionality.

While the very number of configuration options may seem initially confusing, only a small subset is required for a typical BIND configuration. The normal set of parameters is illustrated in the examples in Chapter 7. This reference chapter is useful when control over a specific behavior is required, when checking the different forms of certain statements or clauses, and when considering a new design or implementation. The first section deals with command-line arguments and signals and run-time control. It's followed by the section on the named.conf parameter, which this book has separated into *clauses* (listed in Table 12–3) and *statements* (listed in Table 12–5) to provide a simple and more logical basis for the large number of configuration options available.

BIND 9 has undergone significant changes since the first edition of this book. While some of the new clauses and statements relate to feature creep, the perennial disease of all mature and widely-used software, a significant number relate to increased understanding of the operational implementation of DNSSEC and how it can be simplified. Finally, in a number of cases, the functionality of BIND 9 has been changed to reduce theoretical security vulnerabilities and especially to introduce improvements required to combat the increasing, and increasingly innovative, DNS attacks. In a non-trivial number of cases, this means that historic functionality has significantly changed.

BIND 10 uses a completely different architectural approach to BIND 9. Behavioral functionality in BIND 10 is provided interactively using the command line or external tools. The results of these command stimuli are saved into a private configuration file that can be manually edited—but this is not encouraged and is not expected to be used in normal operation. BIND 10 is described separately in an online chapter to reflect its maturing nature.

BIND Command Line

Table 12–1 describes the various command-line options used to control BIND.

Table 12–1. BIND Command-Line Arguments

Argument	Parameter	Description
-4		Use IPv4 even if the host is dual stacked (it has both IPv4 and IPv6 protocol stacks). This is the default in the absence of any -6 or -4 argument on dual stack hosts.
-6		Use IPv6 even if the host is dual stacked (it has both IPv4 and IPv6 protocol stacks).
-c	/path/to/config-file	Absolute path to the BIND configuration file (normally named.conf). This argument allows change of both the location and the name of the configuration file. The default depends on OS (typically, for Linux it's /etc/named.conf; for BSD it's either /etc/namedb/named.conf or /etc/local/etc/named.conf; and for Windows it's c:\winnt\system32\dns\etc\named.conf) and is defined by the -sysconfdir parameter to configure.
-d	#debug	See Table 12–2.
-E	engine	This is only relevant when BIND has been specially built to support a hardware security module (HSM) using a pkcs11 (cryptoki) library. See additional notes in Chapter 10's "dnssec-keygen - HSM Support" section.
-f		Runs in foreground; do not run as daemon. Normally only used for debugging purposes.
-g		Runs in foreground; do not run as daemon and log to stderr (console). Normally only used for debugging purposes.
-m	flag	Turns on memory usage debugging. The values of flag may be usage, trace, record, size, and mctx. See also memstatistics under "BIND Operations Statements."
-n	#cpus	Creates #cpus threads to take advantage of multiple CPUs. If not specified, named will try to determine the number of CPUs present and create one thread per CPU. If it is unable to determine the number of CPUs, a single thread will be created.
-p	port-no	Listens on defined port-no. The default is 53. Normally only used for debugging purposes.
-S	max-socks	Defines the maximum sockets BIND may use. It should typically only be used if normal BIND operation results in socket exhaustion. See also reserved-socket under BIND Operations Statements.

Argument	Parameter	Description
-t	chroot/path	Use of this argument indicates that named will be run in a chroot jail (or sandbox). chroot/path defines the directory path of the chroot base and is conventionally set to /var/named/chroot (Linux) or /var/named (FreeBSD) but can be set to anything required. Must be used in conjunction with the -u argument to provide any meaningful security.
-u	UID	Causes BIND to suid() (change user name) to the defined UID after creating sockets on port 53 (which is in the privileged range of < 1024). If not present, runs as user root. Must be used with chroot options (see the -t entry), but many startup scripts now use a -u named or -u bind argument even if not chrooted, which means that log and PID files will have to have appropriate permissions set.
-v		Displays the BIND version number to stdout (console) and exit.
-V		Displays the BIND version number and build (configure) options to stdout (console) and exit. This information is automatically sent to the log when BIND is loaded.

There are two additional arguments (-s and -x) that should only be used by developers and therefore have been omitted.

BIND Debug Levels

Table 12–2 defines an incomplete list of the various debug levels that may be set using the -d command-line option or the rndc trace log_level option (see Chapter 9). For maximum logging, use 100.

Table 12–2. BIND Debug Log Levels

Debug Level	Coverage
0	No debugging—can also be set using rndc notrace (see Chapter 9).
1	Logs the basic name server operations: zone loading, maintenance (including SOA queries, zone transfers and zone expiration, and cache cleaning), NOTIFY messages, queries received, and high-level tasks dispatched.
2	Logs multicast requests.
3	Logs the low-level task creation, operation, and journal activity, such as when the name server writes a record of a zone change to the zone's journal file (.jnl) or when the name server applies a journal to a zone at startup. This level also logs the operation of the DNSSEC validator and checking of TSIG and SIG(0) signatures.

Debug Level	Coverage
4	Logs when a master name server uses AXFR because the transferred zone's journal is not available.
5	Logs the view used while servicing a particular request.
6	Logs outbound zone transfer messages, including checks of the query that initiated the transfer.
7	Logs the journals added and deleted, and a count of the number of bytes returned by a zone transfer.
8	Logs the following dynamic update messages: prerequisite checks, journal entries, and rollbacks. This level also logs low-level zone transfer messages and the resource records sent in a zone transfer.
10	Logs zone timer activity messages and client errors.
50	Logs internal event tracing.
90	Logs low-level operation of the BIND 9 task dispatcher.

BIND Signals

In general, BIND should be controlled using the rndc utility or the various startup scripts such as /etc/rc.d/init.d/named (for Linux) or /etc/rc.d/named (for BSD). The following signals may be used:

- *SIGHUP (1)*: This signal is documented to reload the server but doesn't; it just terminates the server. To perform a reload or restart, see the upcoming text.

- *SIGINT (2)*: Terminate BIND.

- *SIGTERM (15)*: Terminate BIND.

To terminate BIND from the command line, the following command can be used

killall named

or obtain the named PID using

ps ax|grep named

then issue this command

kill -2 named-pid

To perform a reload of the configuration file (named.conf), either stop and start the server using an rc.d script (such as /etc/rc.d/init.d/named restart on Linix or /etc/init.d/bind9/restart on Ubuntu or /etc/rc.d/name restart on BSD) or issue the following command:

named.reconfig

The command rndc reload will perform the same operation if issued from the control channel (see the section "BIND controls Clause" later in this chapter).

BIND Configuration Overview

BIND uses a single configuration file called named.conf, which can contain a brutally long list of parameters to control its operation. The named.conf file can reside in a variety of places depending on your OS; for most Linux distributions, in /etc/named.conf; for Ubuntu/Debian 10.04, in /etc/bind/named.conf; for 32-bit Windows (Windows Server 2003, XP, and 7), in %SystemRoot%\system32\dns\etc\named.conf (normally c:\Windows\system32\dns\etc\named.conf); for 64-bit Windows in %SystemRoot%\sysWOW64\dns\etc\named.conf (normally c:\Windows\sysWOW64\dns\etc\named.conf); and for FreeBSD, in /etc/namedb/named.conf or /usr/local/etc/named/conf. If BIND is being run in a sandbox (or chroot jail), the typical locations are as defined in Chapter 10.

■ **Note** Older versions of BIND (the 4.x series) used a configuration file called boot.conf, which this book does not describe or mention other than in this note. Unless you are running a 4.x version of BIND version, ignore any references to this file in any documentation.

The named.conf file can contain three types of entries:

- *Comments*: Comments can take one of three formats: C++ style, UNIX shell style, or C style. Comments in the C++ style start with // and occupy a single line. This comment style can appear on its own on a line or can terminate any line. Comments in the UNIX shell style start with # (hash or pound) and have the same single-line or line-terminating properties as the C++ style. Comments in the C style use /* to open a comment and */ to close the comment. C-style comments can occupy a single line or more than one line or even be used within a line. Examples:

```
/* C-style comment format needs opening and closing markers
** but allows multiple lines or */
/* single lines or */
zones /* in-line comment does not terminate line */ in {some zone statements};
// C++-style comments have single line format, no closing required
   some statement; // comment ends this line
# SHELL/PERL-style comments have single lines, no closing required
   some statement; # comment ends this line
```

- *Clauses*: Clauses are used to group sets of statements. Clauses in some documentation are called *statements* or *options* and even *sections*, but this book uses the term *clause* throughout. Table 12–3 lists all the available clauses and their general content and scope.

- *Statements*: Statements appear within clauses and control specific behaviors. Statements may have one or more parameters. Statements are also called *clauses*, *phrases*, and even *options*, but this book uses the term *statement* throughout. Certain statements may appear in multiple clauses or clause types. The scope of the behavior depends on the clause in which the statement appears. Thus, a statement that appears inside a zone clause has a scope for that zone—it affects behavior only for that zone. If the same statement appears inside an options clause, it has global scope across all zones unless explicitly overridden by a statement in a zone clause. Table 12–6 lists the statements and the clauses to which they apply. Table 12–5 lists each available statement with a brief description of its function. BIND releases include a list of the latest statements and clauses supported, which is accessible using man named.conf. Windows users are not so lucky, but the normal *nix main pages are available in html format in the directory from which BIND was installed (see Chapter 6).

BIND provides a serious list of configuration statements, but only a small subset is necessary to create an operational configuration. Chapter 7 includes a number of sample files that use the minimum required statements and clauses.

■ **Note on Terminology** It's easy to get confused when documentation refers to the same entity by more than one term. This book has sought to use common and consistent terminology throughout. Accordingly, this book uses the term *clause* to define a grouping of statements, since Merriam-Webster (www.m-w.com) defines *clause* to be "a separate section of a discourse or writing; *specifically*: a distinct article in a formal document," which is good enough for us. *Statement* has an atomic meaning and is defined by Webster to be "a single declaration or remark."

Layout Styles

BIND is very picky about opening and closing brackets/braces, semicolons, and all the other separators defined in the formal syntaxes in later sections. There are many layout styles that can assist in minimizing errors, as shown in the following examples:

```
// dense single-line style
zone "example.com" in{type slave; file "slave.example.com"; masters {10.0.0.1;};};
//  single-statement-per-line style
zone "example.com" in{
   type slave;
   file "slave.example.com";
   masters {10.0.0.1;};
   };
// spot the difference
zone "example.com" in{
   type slave;
   file "sec.slave.com";
   masters {10.0.0.1;}; };
```

The variations are simply attempts to minimize the chance of errors—they have no other significance. Experiment, and use the method you feel most comfortable with.

named-checkconf Is Your Friend

BIND releases contain a utility called named-checkconf that will do nothing except check your named.conf file and tell you what's wrong. To check any named.conf file for syntax errors, just issue the following command:

named-checkconf

This command will verify the named.conf file in the normal location for the distribution. If you are building a new file in another location or with a test file name, then issue a command something like the following:

named-checkconf /path/to/file.name

To check any master zone files referenced in the named.conf file, just add the -z argument:

named-checkconf /path/to/file.name -z

For a full list of named-checkconf arguments, see Chapter 9.

■ **Note** In the normal minimalist BIND style, if your test named.conf file is correct, named-checkconf will output nothing—not even a courtesy "OK." Silence is indeed golden.

BIND Clauses

The named.conf file can contain a number of clauses. Clauses are used to group together sets of related statements. Table 12–3 defines the clauses available in named.conf with a brief description of their purpose and scope.

Table 12–3. BIND Clause Summary

Clause	Description
acl	Defines one or more access control lists, groups of hosts, or users identified by keys that may be referenced in view and other clauses or statements.
controls	Describes and manages access to the control channel used by the remote administrator when using the rndc utility.
dlz	Defines a dynamically loadable zone (DLZ) and is a placeholder clause for future developments. Not described further.
include	This statement is unique and is documented here solely because it can be used to include clauses, parts of clauses, individual statements, or groups of statements. It obeys none of the normal rules and can appear anywhere in the named.conf file inside and outside of a clause. The include statement allows subsidiary files containing configuration clauses or statements to be included in-line. It is typically used for security or maintenance purposes.

Clause	Description
key	Defines shared-secret keys used to control and authenticate TSIG operations such as zone transfer, Dynamic DNS (DDNS), and the remote control channel (the controls clause). May also be nested within a view clause.
logging	Defines the behavior and formatting of BIND's extensive logging feature.
lwres	Groups statements defining the behavior of BIND in lightweight resolver (lwres) mode.
managed-keys	Defines zones that will be managed by RFC 5011 procedures (see also the "Key Handling Automation" section in Chapter 11).
masters	Defines a named set of masters for use by slave or stub zones to simplify maintenance in cases where multiple zones use common master servers.
options	Groups statements that control generic or global behavior and that have scope for all zones and views unless overridden within a zone, view, or other clause.
server	Defines the properties or behavior this name server will use when accessing or responding to a defined remote name server. May also be nested within a view clause.
statistic-channels	Controls access to BIND 9's statistics feature using a standard XML capable browser.
trusted-keys	Used to contain trusted anchors (an authenticated public key) used in DNSSEC operations (see Chapter 11). May also be nested within a view clause.
view	The view clause allows BIND to respond differently to different hosts, interfaces on the same server, or users. The view clause is unique in that each required zone must be defined within the view, thus allowing the defined zone to have completely different characteristics within any view. Any number of view clauses may be included.
zone	Contains statements defining the behavior for a specific zone. The scope of statements in a zone clause is limited to that zone only. May also appear within a view clause.

The whole named.conf file is parsed for completeness and correctness before use—this is a major change from previous releases of BIND. Prior to the availability of or in the absence of a valid logging clause, failure messages use syslogd and are (depending on your syslog.conf file) typically written to /var/log/messages; thereafter, failures are written according to the logging clause definition. In the case of Windows, pre-logging clause failures are written to the Event Log. There are some modest rules defined for the order of clauses in BIND 9, and these are illustrated next. The general statement layout of a named.conf file is usually as follows:

```
// change log
// 1. changed by M.E. on 24th January
//    a. added something
acl "name" {...
                // acl clauses if present generally come first
                // to avoid forward references
```

```
};
key "name" {...
            // key clauses if present must appear
            // before being referenced
};

logging {
          // requires at least a file
          // statement unless using syslog
          // order not important with BIND 9
};
options {
          // other statements (as required)
};
// zones clauses including 'required' zones
zone {
....
};
zone {
....
};
```

If the view clause is being used, the order changes significantly, as shown here:

```
// change log
// 1. changed by M.E. on 24th January
//    a. added something
acl "name" {...
            // acl clauses if present come first
            // to avoid forward references
};
key "name" {...
            // key clauses if present must appear
            // before being referenced
};
logging {.
          // usually requires at least a file statement
          // unless using the syslog
          // order not important with BIND 9
};
options {
          // global options
          // other statements as required
};
view "first" {
  // view specific statements
  // view specific zone clauses
  // including required zones such as hint or localhost
  zone {
        };
  .....
  zone {
        };
};    // end of view "first"
```

```
view "second" {
 // view specific statements
 // view specific zone clauses
 // including required zones such as hint or localhost
 zone {
      };
 zone {
      };
};   // end of view "second"
```

BIND address_match_list Definition

Many statements and some clauses use the address_match_list construct as a basic and consistent building block from which complex matching conditions may be constructed. It is described here, somewhat out of order, simply because it is referenced and used so frequently. Rather than try and understand it now, you should skim this section and get a general feel for what it contains, and then continue reviewing the clauses and statements until the need to understand this structure in detail becomes inevitable. The full syntax allows multiple variations:

address_match_list = element ; [element; ...]

An address_match_list is comprised of one or more elements, each of which has the following syntax:

element = [!] (ip [/prefix] | key key-name | "acl_name" | { address_match_list })

The following are elements that make up an address_match_list:

- Optional negation (!) of an element.

- An IP address (IPv4 or IPv6).

- An optional IP prefix (in the slash notation); for instance, 10.0.0.0/16 (or 10.0/16).

- A key-name, as defined in a key clause.

- The name of an address_match_list previously defined with an acl clause or one of four predefined names (see Table 12–4).

- A nested address_match_list enclosed in braces.

Table 12–4 shows the four predefined address_match_list names.

Table 12–4. Predefined address_match_list Names

Name	Description
any	Matches all hosts.
none	Matches no hosts.
localhost	Matches the IPv4 and IPv6 addresses of all network interfaces on the server but only when accessed from the server—it doesn't have scope when access is external. For instance, if the server has a single interface with an IP address of 192.168.2.3, then localhost will match 192.168.2.3 and 127.0.0.1 (the loopback address is always present).
localnets	Matches any host on an IPv4 or IPv6 network for which the server has an interface including the loopback address. That is, if the server has a two interfaces, the first with an IP address of 192.168.2.3 and a netmask of 255.255.255.0 (or 192.168.2/24) and the second with an IP address of 10.0.2.2 and a netmask of 255.255.0.0 (or 10.0/16), localnets will match 192.168.2.0 to 192.168.2.255, 10.0.0.0 to 10.0.255.255 and 127.0.0.1 (the loopback address is always assumed to be a single address).

One of the major uses for the address_match_list structure is with IP addresses for access control. When a given IP address is compared to an address_match_list, the list is traversed in order until an element matches, at which point processing stops. The action taken will depend on the context of the statement to which it is being applied, as shown in the following example:

```
options {
    allow-transfer { !192.168.2.7;192.168.2.3/24;};
};
```

If the IP address 192.168.2.47 requests a transfer, it doesn't match the first element but matches the second element and the transfer is permitted. If, however, the IP 192.168.2.7 requests a transfer, it matches the first element that is negated, resulting in the transfer being denied. Because a match stops processing, the match order is significant. If the preceding were rewritten to reverse the order as shown in the following fragment, then 192.168.2.7 would always be permitted to transfer because the first item always matches:

```
options {
    allow-transfer {192.168.2.3/24;  !192.168.2.7;};
};
```

The general rule may be expressed as follows: a non-negated match *permits* the operation and a negated match *denies* the operation; if there is no match, the operation is *denied*.

An address_match_list can contain an acl-name. The following example shows the use of an acl clause to standardize an address_ match_list. By simply changing the contents of the acl, these changes are available to all users of the referenced acl clause:

```
acl "good-guys" {
    !192.169.2.5/28; // denies first 16 IPs
    192.168.2.5/24;  // allows rest of subnet
    localnets;   // allows our network
    2001:db8:0:1::/64; // allows this subnet only
};
```

```
options {
      allow-transfer {"good-guys";};
};
```

The key-name parameter allows the address_match_list to reference a key clause—the match in this case will occur if the incoming key-name in, say, a secure dynamic update transaction matches the key-name in a key clause.

Nesting is generally only used with the topology (not currently implemented in BIND 9); the sortlist statement and the address_match_list behavior is slightly changed. Its use is described in the context of the sortlist statement.

■ **Note** When using names in the named.conf file, such as the address_match_list predefined name "none" shown previously or any user-defined name, they can be written with or without the quotation marks. However, if the name contains a space character, it must be enclosed in quotes. In general, and to avoid errors, this book uses quotes to enclose all names and will typically refer to them as *quoted strings*. While not always necessary, as just explained, it's designed solely to prevent errors of omission.

BIND acl Clause

The acl (access control list) clause allows fine-grained control over which hosts may perform what operations on the name server. The acl clause can be used to hide complexity throughout the named.conf configuration. One or more acl clauses can contain complex sets of conditions, the address_match_list, just once in the named.conf file; thereafter, whenever the same conditions apply, the acl clause is simply referenced by name. The most common use of the acl clause is in conjunction with the view clause, but using it solely for this purpose undervalues the utility of this clause.

acl Clause Syntax

```
acl "acl-name" {
      address_match_list
};
```

The acl clause defines a named structure (acl-name) containing an address_match_list that may then be referenced from one or more statements and view clauses. The acl clause *must* be defined before it is referenced in any other statement or clause. For this reason, acls are usually defined first in the named.conf file. acl-name is an arbitrary, but unique, quoted string defining the specific name by which the address_match_list may be subsequently referenced. Any number of acl clauses may be defined. The following predefined or special acl-name values are built into BIND:

- none: Matches no hosts.

- any: Matches all hosts.

- localhost: Matches all the IP address(es) of the server on which BIND is running.

- localnets: Matches all the IP address(es) and subnet masks of the server on which BIND is running.

The special acl-name values and the full address_match_list structure are described in further detail in the "BIND address_match_list Definition" section earlier. The following examples show acl clauses being created and used, including use of the special or predefined acl-names:

```
//defining acls
// simple ip address acl
acl "someips" {
   10.0.0.1; 192.168.23.1; 192.168.23.15;
};
// ip address acl with '/' format
 acl "moreips" {
   10.0.0.2;
   192.168.23.128/25; // 128 IPs
};
// nested acl
acl "allips" {
   "someips";
   "moreips";
};
// messy acl
acl "complex" {
   "someips";
   10.0.15.0/24;
   !10.0.16.1/24; // negated
   {10.0.17.1;10.0.18.2;}; // nested
 };
view "my stuff" {
    match-clients {"someips";};
    ....
};
// using acls
zone "example.com" in{
  type master;
  file "master.example.com";
  also-notify {"allips";};
};
zone "example.net" in{
  type slave;
  masters {192.168.2.3;192.168.2.4;};
  file "slave.example.net;
  allow-transfer {"none";}; // this is a special acl
};
```

BIND controls Clause

The controls clause is used to define access information when using remote administration services, specifically the rndc utility. The controls clause takes a single inet statement type, though more than one inet statement may be defined in a controls clause. The inet statement is defined in the later section "BIND controls Statements."

```
controls {
   inet inet_spec [inet_spec]  ;
};
```

A controls clause is *always defaulted* and generates a TCP listen operation on port 953 (the default control port) of the loopback address for either or both IPv4 and IPv6 (127.0.0.1 and/or ::1). If remote administration will not be used (that is, the rndc utility will not be used), this control interface can be explicitly disabled by defining an empty controls clause as shown here:

```
controls {};
```

The primary access control method for remote administration, rndc in BIND 9, is via the use of keys defined within the inet statement (see the following example). To retain compatibility with previous versions of BIND or to run without a user-generated key, a default key may be generated using the following command:

```
rndc-confgen -a
```

This command will create a file called rndc.key, which contains a default key clause with the name "rndc-key" (rndckey in Fedora), in the same directory as the named.conf file for the version of BIND being used; this file is used for subsequent access to the control channel. If this command is not executed before BIND is loaded, the following message will appear:

```
named [39248] none:0: open: /path/to/default/rndc.key: file not found
```

BIND will continue to run in this state, but the control channel will not be operable. For full configuration of the inet statement and examples of its use in the controls clause, see the "BIND controls Statements" section later in this chapter.

BIND include Statement

The include statement is unique in that it can appear anywhere in the named.conf file, either inside or outside a clause. It causes the specified file to be read at the point it is encountered and takes the following form:

```
include "file-name";
```

file-name is a quoted string and can be an absolute path such as /var/named/file.name or a relative path such as file.name, in which case it will be assumed to be in the directory previously defined by a directory statement. In the absence of a directory statement, this will be the directory in which named.conf is located (defined by the -sysconfdir configure argument—see Chapter 6), which is normally /etc (or /etc/namedb for FreeBSD).

■ **Note** The include statement is BIND specific and should not be confused with the RFC 1035 standard $INCLUDE directive used in zone files, though it has a similar function.

The include statement is typically used for three purposes:

- *To simplify or distribute administration of* named.conf *file maintenance*: For example, zone clauses may be administered independently by divisions of a company.

- *To isolate and partition changes and updates*: For example, if acl clauses change frequently, it may be desirable to separate them into files that can be included, thus minimizing the need to edit the primary named.conf file.

- *To control permissions*: It may be desirable to limit access using restricted permissions on files containing, for example, key clauses. Conversely, it may be used to loosen permissions on widely edited parts of the file.

The following example shows use of the `include` statement:

```
// include two acl clauses
include "/var/named/acl/private.acl"
include "/var/named/acl/public.acl"
options {
    // relative to named.conf directory
    include "some.options";
    directory "/var/named";
    // relative to 'directory'
    include "other.options"
};
//  using include for zones
...
// zones for chemical division - absolute path
include "/var/named/chemical/zone.files";
// zones for engineering division
include "/var/named/engineering/zone.files";
// these load from the path specified by 'directory' option
include "more-zone.files";
// housekeeping zones explicitly included
zone "64/27.23.168.192.in-addr.arpa" in{
    type master;
    file "192.168.23.rev";
};
```

The included files are simply the clauses or statements that would have been present in the `named.conf` were the `include` statement not present. To illustrate this principle, the included file `/var/named/acl/private.acl` referenced previously could look as shown here:

```
// included acl
 acl "private-acl" {
  10.0.0.1;
  192.168.23.128/25; // 128 IPs
};
```

Similarly, the `other.options` file could contain one or more statements as follows:

```
recursion yes;
allow-transfer {"none";};
```

BIND key Clause

The key clause is only used to contain a shared secret (symmetric) message authentication code (MAC) algorithm used in a TSIG transaction (see Chapter 10) or with the `rndc` utility (see Chapter 9). Any keys used with a public key (asymmetric) algorithm are either stored in the zone file as KEY or DNSKEY RRs or, when used as a *trusted anchor* (DNSSEC), in a `trusted-keys` clause (see Chapter 11). The key clause may also be defined within a `view` clause.

key **Clause Syntax**

```
key key-name {
   algorithm algorithm-name;
   secret "key-data";
};
```

The algorithm and secret statements are described later in the "BIND Security Statements" section. The data for the key clause may be generated by using the dnssec-keygen or the rndc-confgen utilities (see Chapter 9).

The material contained in a key clause is a *shared secret* and therefore represents extremely sensitive information. By convention, the key clause or clauses are always placed in a separate file and the include statement used to embed them into the named.conf file. The included file can therefore have specific permissions applied to ensure limited visibility. The key clause must always appear in the named.conf file before it is referenced. The key-name field may be any suitable name that is used by both ends of the communication transaction; as a result, the same key clause must be used by the peer application. For example, when used for TSIG operations during zone transfer, a key clause with the same key-name must be present in the corresponding slave name server, or if it is being used with the rndc application, a key clause with the same key-name must be present in the rndc.conf file. The key clause used in rndc.conf and named.conf is exactly the same (see Chapter 9 for information on rndc.conf). The examples in Chapter 10 in the "Securing Zone Transfers" section describe how a key clause is constructed from the output of the dnssec-keygen utility.

BIND logging Clause

The logging clause defines the extensive logging services available in BIND. Prior to BIND 9, the logging clause had to appear first in the named.conf file. This is no longer the case, so the logging clause may be placed anywhere convenient. BIND uses syslogd before a valid logging clause is available, so named.conf parse errors and other information will appear in /var/log/messages (depending on syslog.conf) prior to, or in the absence of, a valid logging clause. In the case of Windows, parse errors are written to the Event Log. Only one logging clause can be defined, but multiple channels may be defined to stream logs. The logging clause can be omitted, in which case a default one is assumed—this default is described in the later section "BIND logging Statements" because its functionality requires some understanding of the various statements used in a logging clause.

logging **Clause Syntax**

```
logging {
   [  channel channel_name { channel_spec }; ]
   [ category category_name { channel_name ; [ channel_name ; ... ] };
};
```

This example shows a minimal logging configuration that will work and generate modest log volumes:

```
// named.conf fragment
logging{
    channel single_log {
    file "/var/log/named/bind.log" versions 3 size 2m;
    severity info;
    print-time yes;
    print-severity yes;
```

```
    print-category yes;
    };
    category default{
    single_log;
    };
};
```

Further examples are shown in the "category Statement" section later in this chapter.

BIND `lwres` Clause

BIND provides two methods of running a resolver (called a *lightweight resolver* in the BIND jargon) that uses a simplified and nonstandard (BIND-only) UDP-based protocol. The first method uses a separate daemon called lwresd, which is not described further, and the second uses the lwres clause within a normal BIND named.conf file. Using the latter method means that a single instance of BIND can provide both normal DNS processing and lightweight resolver support.

`lwres` Clause Syntax

```
lwres {
    // lwres clause statements
};
```

By default, the lightweight resolver provides service on port 921. The lwres clause can include the listen-on, view, search, and ndots statements, which are described in the "BIND Resolver Statements" section.

BIND `managed-keys` Clause

managed-keys clauses are used by validating resolvers and define trusted anchors that will be managed automatically by BIND using RFC 5011 procedures (see Chapter 11's "Key Handling Automation" section) unlike the similar trusted-keys clause in which case all management of trusted anchors must be done either manually or using a third party tool. BIND 9 distributes a managed-keys clause for the ISC (BIND's author) DLV service (dlv.isc.org; see also DVL in Chapter 11) in a file called bind.keys. This file is not installed by default by either FreeBSD or Ubuntu Server, causing named to log a reminder message every time it is loaded. Only one managed-keys clause may appear in named.conf.

`managed-keys` Clause Syntax

```
managed-keys {
    domain-name initialize flags proto algorithm "key-data";
};
```

The meaning and value of the flags, proto, and algorithm fields are as defined for the corresponding DNSKEY RR (see Chapter 13's "DNSKEY Record" section). The domain-name field is the name value from the DNSKEY RR, optionally enclosed in quotation marks (a quoted string), and must be the name of the domain that it will be used to verify. The key-data field is copied from the key-data field of the corresponding DNSKEY RR and is the base64 (RFC 4648) representation of the public key enclosed in quotation marks and terminated with the ubiquitous semicolon. initialize describes how the key will be used and currently can only take the value initial-key. Its use is described below.

The following shows the standard managed-keys clause in the file bind.keys distributed with BIND 9.7.2-P2:

```
/* $Id: bind.keys,v 1.5.42.1 2010/06/20 07:32:24 marka Exp $ */
managed-keys {
        # NOTE: This key is current as of October 2009.
        # If it fails to initialize correctly, it may have expired;
        # see https://www.isc.org/solutions/dlv for a replacement.
        dlv.isc.org. initial-key 257 3 5
"BEAAAAPHMu/5onzrEE7z1egmhg/WPOO+juoZrW3euWEn4MxDCE1+lLy2
brhQv5rN32RKtMzX6Mj70jdzeND4XknW58dnJNPCxn8+jAGl2FZLK8t+
1uq4W+nnA3qO2+DL+k6BD4mewMLbIYFweOPG73Te9fZ2kJb56dhgMde5
ymX4BI/oQ+cAK50/xvJvOOFrf8kw6ucMTwFlgPe+jnGxPPEmHAte/URk
Y62ZfkLoBAADLHQ9IrS2tryAe7mbBZVcOwIeU/Rw/mRx/vwwMCTgNboM
QKtUdvNXDrYJDSHZws3xiRXF1Rf+al9UmZfSav/4NWLKjHzpT59k/VSt TDNOYUuWrBNh";
};
```

A managed-keys clause can be trivially created from its corresponding DNSKEY RR. The above managed-keys clause was created from the corresponding DNSKEY RR taken from the dlv.isc.org site and shown below:

```
dlv.isc.org.    7168    IN    DNSKEY    257 3 5 (
    BEAAAAPHMu/5onzrEE7z1egmhg/WPOO+juoZrW3euWEn4MxDCE1+lLy2
    brhQv5rN32RKtMzX6Mj70jdzeND4XknW58dnJNPCxn8+jAGl2FZLK8t+
    1uq4W+nnA3qO2+DL+k6BD4mewMLbIYFweOPG73Te9fZ2kJb56dhgMde5
    ymX4BI/oQ+cAK50/xvJvOOFrf8kw6ucMTwFlgPe+jnGxPPEmHAte/URk
    Y62ZfkLoBAADLHQ9IrS2tryAe7mbBZVcOwIeU/Rw/mRx/vwwMCTgNboM
    QKtUdvNXDrYJDSHZws3xiRXF1Rf+al9UmZfSav/4NWLKjHzpT59k/VSt TDNOYUuWrBNh)
```

When BIND finds either a new managed-keys clause or a new domain-name record in an existing managed-keys clause, it reads the DNSKEY RRset at domain-name and confirms that a *non-revoked* DNSKEY RR with the same key-data and key-tag as that supplied in the managed-keys clause exists. While this process is necessarily insecure, the presence of the managed-keys clause data (obtained by a trusted process) ensures integrity. Assuming the corresponding DNSKEY is found, BIND 9 then creates (on initial load) or updates a DDNS zone file called managed-keys.bind (and a corresponding DDNS journal file managed-keys.bind.jnl) in either the directory pointed to by directory or managed-keys-directory statements. As a minimum, this directory must have read and write permission for user bind (or named for FreeBSD). From this point onward the domain-name is managed by RFC 5011 procedures, and the contents of the domain-name record in the managed-keys clause is no longer used (the actively managed data being in the managed-keys.bind zone file).

To stop any domain-name from being managed automatically using RFC 5011 procedures, simply delete either the managed-keys clause (assuming only the single domain-name entry) or the relevant domain-name entry from a managed-keys clause and reload BIND. Unless a trusted-keys clause with the appropriate key is added (in which case it will have to be maintained manually), domain-name will no longer be validated by the reloaded server. The following shows the managed-keys.bind file (the DDNS zone) resulting from use of the bind.keys file shown above:

```
$ORIGIN .
$TTL 0  ; 0 seconds
@               IN      SOA     (
                                        5       ; serial
                                        0       ; refresh (0 seconds)
                                        0       ; retry (0 seconds)
                                        0       ; expire (0 seconds)
                                        0       ; minimum (0 seconds)
```

```
                                       )
dlv.isc.org  KEYDATA  20101130030914 20101129230908 19700101000000 257 3 5 (
                                    BEAAAAPHMu/5onzrEE7z1egmhg/WPOO+juoZrW3euWEn
                                    4MxDCE1+lLy2brhQv5rN32RKtMzX6Mj7OjdzeND4XknW
                                    58dnJNPCxn8+jAGl2FZLK8t+1uq4W+nnA3qO2+DL+k6B
                                    D4mewMLbIYFweOPG73Te9fZ2kJb56dhgMde5ymX4BI/o
                                    Q+cAK50/xvJvOOFrf8kw6ucMTwFlgPe+jnGxPPEmHAte
                                    /URkY62ZfkLoBAADLHQ9IrS2tryAe7mbBZVcOwIeU/Rw
                                    /mRx/vwwMCTgNboMQKtUdvNXDrYJDSHZws3xiRXF1Rf+
                                    al9UmZfSav/4NWLKjHzpT59k/VStTDNOYUuWrBNh
                                    ) ; key id = 19297
```

The KEYDATA RR is not currently standardized by any RFC and must therefore be regarded, currently, as proprietary to BIND (see also the `sig-signing-type` statement under the "BIND Security Statements" section later in the chapter).

The DNS root zone has been signed and managed by RFC 5011 procedures since in July 2010. While the current `bind.keys` file contains a `managed-keys` clause for the DLV service operated at `dlv.isc.org`, it's anticipated that at some future time this will be changed to use the signed root zone. In the meantime, the "DNSSEC Implementation" section in Chapter 11 describes how the root key may be obtained and configured into BIND for use by a validating resolver.

■ **Caution** If recursion is enabled (BIND 9 default) and the file `bind.keys` is present (in `directory`, `managed-keys-directory`, or their defaults), BIND 9 will automatically become a validating resolver and will attempt to verify every signed zone against the DLV service at `dlv.isco.org`. This may not be the desired behavior, in which case setting `dnssec-enable no;` will disable all DNSSEC services and `dnssec-validation no;` will disable only DNSSEC validation. Alternatively, delete the `bind.keys` file, the `managed-keys.bind` (and `managed-keys.bind.jnl` file), and reload BIND to just disable use of the ISC DLV service.

BIND masters Clause

The `masters` clause is a *named list* of zone masters that may be referenced from a `masters` statement in a zone clause. It is provided to simplify maintenance of situations in which common master servers are used for a number of zones.

masters Clause Syntax

```
masters "masters_name" [port pg_num] { ( "masters_list" | ip [port p_num] ↵
[key key-name] ) ; [...] } ;
```

The `masters_name` parameter (a quoted string) is the unique name by which this clause will be referenced. The `pg_num` parameter changes the port number used for zone transfers for all the listed servers (the default is port 53). The `p_num` parameter changes the port number for the specific IP address only. If present, `masters_list` references another list of masters defined in another `masters` clause. The optional `key-name` parameter defines the key to be used to authenticate the zone transfer and references a key clause with the same name. Any `masters` clause must be defined before it is referenced in a `masters` statement. The following example shows three masters for the zone, one of which will use port 1127 for zone transfers and one of which is an IPv6 address:

```
// defining masters
masters "common masters" {
    masters {192.168.2.7; 10.2.3.15 port 1127; 2001:db8:0:1::15;};
};
// using masters
zone "example.com" in{
  type slave;
  file "slave.example.com";
  masters {"common masters";};
};
zone "example.net" in{
  type slave;
  file "slave.example.net;
  masters {"common masters";};
};
```

BIND options Clause

The options clause is used to group statements that have global scope. The options clause may take a ferocious number of statements—see the list in Table 12–6.

options Clause Syntax

```
options {
    // options statements
};
```

The options clause has global scope, but many of the statements that can be used within an options clause can also appear within a view or zone clause, in which case they will override the statement in the options clause for the scope in which they appear (that is, for the whole view or the specific zone). The following example shows an also-notify statement (used to cause NOTIFY messages to be sent to servers other than the servers defined with NS RRs for the zone) being used globally but being overridden for a single zone:

```
// defining options clause
options {
    ....
    also-notify {192.168.2.3;192.168.2.4;};
    ....
};
// zones
zone "example.com" {
  // NOTIFY messages for this domain sent to global
  // also-notify list
  type master;
  file "master.example.com";
};
zone "example.net" {
  // NOTIFY messages NOT sent to global
  // also-notify list
```

```
    type master;
    file "master.example.net;
    also-notify {"none";};
};
```

BIND server Clause

The server clause defines the behavior BIND will use when accessing (incoming or outgoing) a remote server. It's typically used when the remote server has specific characteristics or protocol behavior, when it provides secure DNS (DNSSEC) services, or to stop handling requests from a specific server. The server clause can take a modest number of statements as defined in Table 12–6. The server clause may also be nested within a view clause.

server **Clause Syntax**

```
server ip_address {
     // server statements
};
```

The ip_address parameter can be either IPv4 or IPv6. The ip_address will only accept a single address—it can't take an IP prefix value (slash notation). If a group of servers have common behaviors, each one will require a separate server clause. If the remote server is a dual-stacked server (IPv4/IPv6), both addresses will need to be defined using separate server clauses. server clauses can appear independently (a global server clause) or within a view clause. If they appear within a view clause, the defined behavior is limited to that view clause only. Outside the view clause, they will use the behavior of the global server clause if it exists; if none exists, they will take the default for any statements that can appear inside the server clause. The following example shows a dual-stacked server that will only accept single messages in each TCP block during transfers and that can't support EDNS:

```
// named.conf fragment
....
// IPv4 server
server 10.2.3.15 {
    transfer-format one-answer;
    edns no;
};
// IPv6 addresses of same server
server 2001:db8:0:27::17 {
    transfer-format one-answer;
    edns no;
};
....
```

BIND statistics-channels Clause

The statistics-channels clause is used to define access control to server statistics. The statistics-channels clause only allows an inet statement type, though more than one inet statement may be defined in the clause. The inet statement is defined in the later section "BIND controls Statements."

```
statistics-channels {
   inet inet_spec [inet_spec]  ;
};
```

A statistics-channels clause is *never defaulted*; if remote access to server statistics is required, a statistics-channels clause *must* be defined. Statistics are provided only in XML format at this time using a suitable web browser. When used with the statistics-channels the inet statement's optional keys parameter is not permitted and will result in a fatal error. If no port number is specified on the inet statement, it will default to respond on port 80. The following example illustrates the use of the statistics-channels clause to allow access using port 80 (port) on any local server address (*) but only from the IPv4 address 192.168.2.1 (allow):

```
....
statistics-channels {
    inet * port 80 allow {192.168.2.1;};
};
```

To access the server statistics simply load a modern XML-capable browser such as Firefox or Internet Explorer and, assuming the name server is ns1.example.com, enter:

http://ns1.example.com

Clearly, for this to work, the same server can't be hosting any other service which responds to port 80, such as a web server. If this is the case, the inet statement should be modified to respond on a non-standard port, such as 2234, and the following line used in the browser:

http://ns1.example.com:2234

BIND 9 provides a significant amount of information using the statistics-channels feature; it's well worth experimenting with it as a source of information and as a potential diagnostic aid. The standard Ubuntu BIND 9 package doesn't support the feature (see the –"Building BIND from Source' section in Chapter 6) but FreeBSD offers it as a build option. BIND 9 statistics are not dynamically updated so the refresh feature of the browser must be used periodically to get the latest statistics.

BIND trusted-keys Clause

The trusted-keys clause contains one or more public keys that have been obtained by a secure process for use as trusted anchors in DNSSEC operations (see Chapter 11). The data defined in this clause will be the same as that of a DNSKEY RR defined at the apex or root of the domain or zone for which it is the trusted anchor and that has been used to sign the zone, most typically as a Key Signing Key (KSK). Thus, if the domain for which a trusted anchor is defined is example.com, then there *must* be a corresponding DNSKEY RR with a name of example.com. The public keys that appear in a trusted-keys clause must be obtained by a secure (non-DNS) procedure. While the key data contained in a trusted-key clause is public (and, unlike a key clause, requires no special protection), the reason it is obtained by a secure process lies with the need to authenticate the *source* of the data, not the data itself. If the DNSKEY RR was simply read from the DNS by an insecure query, it could have been spoofed in some way. Its presence in a trusted-keys clause indicates that it was received from a trusted (authenticated) source. Secure domains delegated from the domain for which this trusted anchor is defined, say sub.example.com (a child zone), will be authenticated by the presence of a DS RR at the delegation point in the domain example.com (the parent zone) and thus do not require a corresponding trusted anchor. The format of each trusted anchor in a trusted-keys clause is shown here:

"domain-name" flags proto algorithm "key-data"

The meaning and value of the flags, proto, and algorithm fields are as defined for the corresponding DNSKEY RR (see Chapter 13). The "domain-name" field is the name value from the DNSKEY RR, optionally enclosed in quotation marks (a quoted string), and must be the name of the domain that it will be used to verify. The key-data field is copied from the key-data field of the corresponding DNSKEY RR and is the base64 (RFC 3548) representation of the public key enclosed in quotation marks and terminated with the ubiquitous semicolon. The following example shows a DNSKEY RR with the zone signing and SEP (a.k.a. KSK) bits set, using the RSA-SHA-1 algorithm and the corresponding trusted-keys clause that would be derived from it:

```
example.com.          IN       DNSKEY 257  3  5 (
                               AQPSKmynfzW4kyBvO15MUG2DeIQ3
                               Cbl+BBZH4b/OPY1kxkmvHjcZc8no
                               kfzj31GajIQKY+5CptLr3buXA1Oh
                               WqTkF7H6RfoRqXQeogmMHfpftf6z
                               Mv1LyBUgia7za6ZEzOJBOztyvhjL
                               742iU/TpPSEDhm2SNKLijfUppn1U
                               aNvv4w==   )
```

The trusted-keys clause using the preceding DNSKEY RR would be as shown here:

```
trusted-keys {
"example.com"   257  3  5 "AQPSKmynfzW4kyBvO15MUG2DeIQ3
                          Cbl+BBZH4b/OPY1kxkmvHjcZc8no
                          kfzj31GajIQKY+5CptLr3buXA1Oh
                          WqTkF7H6RfoRqXQeogmMHfpftf6z
                          Mv1LyBUgia7za6ZEzOJBOztyvhjL
                          742iU/TpPSEDhm2SNKLijfUppn1U
                          aNvv4w==";
};
```

Any number of trusted anchors for different domains may be added to a trusted-keys clause. To allow for key-rollover procedures (see Chapter 11), it's permissible to have more than one trusted anchor with the same domain-name; thus in the preceding fragment, it's permissible to have a second (third, fourth, etc.) entry with the name "example.com", each of which will contain a different public key (key-data). The trusted-keys clause may be nested within a view clause.

BIND view Clause

The view clause allows the behavior of BIND to be based on any combination of the source IP address of the request, the destination address of the request, the recursive behavior of the request, or the keys used by the user. The view clause can take a vast number of statements, as defined in Table 12–6.

view Clause Syntax

```
view "view_name" {
    // view statements
};
```

The view_name (optionally a quoted string; mandatory if there is a space in the name) is an arbitrary name that uniquely identifies the view. A view clause matches when either or both of its match-clients and match-destinations statements match and when the match-recursive-only condition is met. If either or both of match-clients and match-destinations are missing, they default to any (all hosts match). The match-clients statement defines the address_match_list for the source IP address(es) of the incoming messages. The match-destination statement defines the address_match_list for the destination IP address of the incoming messages and may be used with multihomed servers or to differentiate, for example, localhost behavior from all other IP address sources. The match-recursive-only statement may be further used to qualify the view clause based on its query type (recursive or iterative). Both the match-clients and match-destinations statements can take an optional key parameter, which means that view selection can be based on a user rather than a physical IP address, or they can point to an acl clause, which defines the address_match_list. The view clause is unique in that all required zone clauses must be defined within each view clause such that a zone's behavior can be significantly different in each view. Any number of view clauses can be used. The majority, but not all, statements that may be used in an options clause may also be used in a view clause to control specific behavior (see Table 12–6). The following example shows a view clause being used based on the source addresses of the DNS transactions and the presence of recursive queries:

```
// named.conf fragment
view "recursive-external" {
    match-clients {!10.2.3.4/24;};
    match-recursive-only yes;
    // other view statements
    zone "example.com" in {
    ....
    };
};
view "internal" {
    match-clients {10.2.3.4/24;};
    // other view statements
    zone "example.com" in {
    ....
    };
};
```

In the preceding example, the second view clause is not strictly necessary since all conditions not satisfied by the first view will be defaulted to a zone definition outside the view clause. Many users, however, like to add the second view clause to avoid confusion. For further examples of the use of the view clause when used with stealth server configurations, see Chapter 7.

BIND zone Clause

The zone clause defines the characteristics of the zone. The zone clause may take a significant number of statements; see Table 12–6 for the full list.

zone Clause Syntax

```
zone "zone_name" [class] {
    // zone statements
};
```

The zone_name (optionally a quoted string) defines the name of the zone or domain being defined. The class parameter is optional; if not present, the default class IN (Internet) will be used. This book always defines the class parameter in examples to avoid confusion at the cost of two characters of typing per zone. zone clauses may also be defined inside a view clause, in which case the scope of the zone definition is limited to the view clause. If the zone is to be supported in another view clause or outside any view clause, the zone clause must be repeated even if its operational characteristics remain the same. The following example shows a zone clause being used inside two view clauses and outside the view clause:

```
// named.conf fragment
view "recursive-external" {
```

```
    match-clients {10.2.4.4/24;};
    match-recursive-only yes;
    // other view statements
    zone "example.com" in {
    ....
    };
};
view "internal" {
    match-clients {10.2.3.4/24;};
    match-recursive-only yes;
    // other view statements
    zone "example.com" in {
    ....
    };
};
// definition of zone behavior outside the views
zone "example.com" in {
....
};
```

BIND Statements

BIND provides a daunting list of statements to control its behavior. For convenience, they are provided in alphabetic order in Table 12–5 with each statement allocated to a generic category (for example, Transfers) that loosely describes its functionality and is briefly summarized with any default setting where applicable. Each statement is then described in detail within its category section. It is hoped that you may find this more useful when browsing to find statements to control specific behaviors. Thus, if you need to find statements that control query behavior, just scan through the BIND Query Statement section. Many statements can appear within more than one clause, and Table 12–6 lists each statement in alphabetic order and the clauses within which it may be used. A number of the statements use a generic structure called an address_match_list that was previously described. The general format of each statement's description is a brief summary of the statement's functionality followed by the syntax of each statement with an accompanying example. The syntax is then described in detail with additional examples as appropriate.

Table 12–5. BIND Statement Summary

Statement	Category	Summary
achache-cleaning-interval	Performance	Determines how frequently the additional section cache (*acache*) is cleaned. The default is 60 minutes.
achache-enable	Performance	Controls whether the additional section cache (*acache*) feature is enabled. The default is no.
additional-from-auth	Queries	Used in conjunction with additional-from-cache to control whether BIND will follow CNAME (and DNAME) out-of-zone references. The default is to follow references.

Statement	Category	Summary
additional-from-cache	Queries	Used in conjunction with additional-from-auth to control whether BIND will follow CNAME (and DNAME) out-of-zone references. The default is to follow references.
algorithm	Security	Defines the algorithm to be used in a key clause.
allow-new-zones	Operations	Placeholder for dynamic zone additions. Beta status (see Chapter 9 rndc).
allow-notify	Transfers	Applies to slave zones only and defines an address_match_list that is allowed to send NOTIFY messages for the zone in addition to those defined in the masters option for the zone. The default behavior is to allow NOTIFY messages only from the zone masters.
allow-query	Queries	An address_match_list defining which hosts are allowed to issue queries to the server. If not specified, all hosts are allowed to make queries.
allow-query-cache	Queries	Defines an address_match_list of addresses that are allowed to make queries that access the cache. Defaults to use allow-query or allow-recursion or recursion settings.
allow-query-cache-on	Queries	Defines an address_match_list of server addresses that will accept queries that can use the cache. The default is to accept such queries on all server addresses.
allow-query-on	Queries	Defines an address_match_list of server addresses that will accept queries. The default is to accept queries on all server addresses.
allow-recursion	Queries	Defines an address_match_list of source addresses that will be allowed to perform recursive queries. Defaults to *localhost* and *localnets*.
allow-recursion-on	Queries	Defines an address_match_list of server addresses that will accept recursive queries. The default is to accept recursive queries on all addresses.
allow-transfer	Transfers	Defines an address_match_list that is allowed to transfer the zone information from this server. The default behavior is to allow zone transfers to *any* host.
allow-update	Security	Defines an address_match_list that is allowed to submit dynamic updates for master zones. The default in BIND 9 is to disallow dynamic updates from all hosts.

Statement	Category	Summary
allow-update-forwarding	Transfers	Defines an address_match_list that is allowed to submit dynamic updates to a slave server for onward transmission to a master. The default is to disallow update forwarding.
allow-v6-synthesis		Obsolete statement.
also-notify	Transfers	Applies to zone masters only. Defines one or more hosts that will be sent NOTIFY messages when zone changes occur.
alt-transfer-source	Transfers	Applies to slave zones only. Defines an alternative local IPv4 address(es) to be used for inbound zone transfers by the server if that defined by transfer-source fails and use-alt-transfer-source is enabled.
alt-transfer-source-v6	Transfers	Applies to slave zones only. Defines an alternative local IPv6 address(es) to be used for inbound zone transfers by the server if that defined by transfer-source-v6 fails and use-alt-transfer-source is enabled.
attach-cache	Performance	Allows for caches to be shared by multiple view clauses. Default is that each view clause uses a separate cache.
auth-nxdomain	Queries	Controls whether the server will answer authoritatively on returning NXDOMAIN (domain does not exist) answers. The default behavior is not to answer authoritatively.
auto-dnssec	Security	Allows BIND 9 to perform various levels of automatic zone signing for dynamic zones including key management and generation. The default is off, which means the zone will not be automatically signed.
avoid-v4-udp-ports	Operations	Defines a list of IPv4 ports that BIND will not use when initiating queries. Used to avoid ports blocked by firewalls.
avoid-v6-udp-ports	Operations	Defines a list of IPv6 ports that BIND will not use when initiating queries. Used to avoid ports blocked by firewalls.
bindkeys-file	Security	Used to override the BIND 9 supplied managed-keys clause (DLV). Defaults to /etc/bind.keys.
blackhole	Queries	Defines an address_match_list that the server will not respond to or answer queries for. The default is none—all hosts are responded to.
bogus	Server	Defined in a server clause and allows a remote server to be ignored. The default is not to ignore.

Statement	Category	Summary
cache-file		Developer-only option.
category	Logging	Controls the type of data logged to a particular channel.
channel	Logging	Defines a stream of data that may be independently logged.
check-dup-records	Operations	Check for duplicate RRs. The default is warn.
check-integrity	Operations	Perform zone integrity checks when zone is loaded. The default is yes.
check-names	Zones/ Operations	Restricts the character set of host names to those defined by RFC 952 and 1123. Has different syntax in the view and options clause from that used in the zone clause and is described separately.
check-mx	Operations	Checks that MX RRs points to an IP address. The default is to warn if not the case.
check-mx-cname	Operations	Checks that MX RRs do not point to CNAME RRs. The default is to warn if they do.
check-sibling	Operations	Checks that if a subdomain delegation is present that glue RRs exist. The default is to warn if not.
check-srv-cname	Operations	Checks that SRV RRs do not point to CNAME RRs. The default is to warn if they do.
check-wildcard	Operations	Checks for non-terminal wildcards. The default is to warn if present.
cleaning-interval	Operations	The time in minutes when the server will remove expired resource records from the cache. The default is 60.
clients-per-query	Queries	Resolver. Defines the initial number of outstanding queries that are allowed by a resolver for the same name. The default is 10.
coresize	Operations	Defines the maximum size of a core dump.
database	Operations	Only used with BIND Simple Database (sdb) API and specifies the driver name and any initial parameters.
datasize	Operations	Defines the maximum memory size the server may use.
deallocate-on-exit		Obsolete statement.

Statement	Category	Summary
delegation-only	Queries	Applies to hint and stub zones only. Controls whether queries will always return a referral.
deny-answer-addresses	Security	Resolver. Defines IP addresses that will be rejected (and will not be cached) by the resolver if they appear in an answer. Default is to accept any IP address in an answer.
deny-answer-aliases	Security	Resolver. Defines CNAME or DNAME RRs that will be rejected (and will not be cached) by the resolver if they appear in an answer. The default is to accept any CNAME or DNAME in an answer.
dialup	Operations	Optimizes the behavior of certain operations to minimize connect time for dial-up links.
directory	Operations	A quoted string defining the base directory used for zone and other files. Defaults to the location of named.conf file on most systems.
disable-algorithms	Security	Disables DNSSEC algorithms from a specific zone.
disable-empty-zone	Operations	Allows selective disabling of BIND 9's built-in empty-zones used to minimize unnecessary external traffic. The default is to enable all built-in empty zones.
dnssec-accept-expired	Security	Resolver. Controls whether to accept expired RRSIG signatures. The default is no.
dnssec-enable	Security	Enables DNSSEC support in BIND. The default is yes, which enables DNSSEC support.
dnssec-dnskey-kskonly	Security	Controls whether only KSKs are used to sign the DNSKEY RRset at the zone apex. The default is no, meaning that both KSKs and ZSKs sign the DNSKEY RRset.
dnssec-lookaside	Security	Used with DNSSEC Lookaside Validation (DLV). Controls the method of validating DNSKEY RRs at the apex of a zone.
dnssec-must-be-secure	Security	Defines hierarchies that must/may not be secure (signed and validated).
dnssec-secure-to-insecure	Security	Allows a dynamic zone to change from secure to insecure by deleting (with, say, nsupdate) the DNSKEY RRs at the zone apex, which will cause the RRSIG and NSEC/NSEC3 RRs to be deleted. The default is no.

Statement	Category	Summary
dnssec-validation	Security	Resolver. Indicates that a resolver will perform DNSSEC validation. The default is yes if dnssec-enable is yes.
dual-stack-servers	Operations	Only valid on dual-stacked (IPv4/IPv6) servers and defines a method of reaching a server using one of the stacks.
dump-file	Operations	A quoted string defining the absolute path where BIND dumps the cache in response to an rndc dumpdb command. If not specified, the default is named_dump.db in the location specified by a directory statement.
edns	Server	Controls use of the EDNS0 (RFC 2671) feature. The default is to support EDNS0.
edns-udp-size	Performance	Defines the size of the UDP packet advertised by the server when using EDNS0. The default is 4096.
empty-contact	Operations	Defines value returned as the admin-mailbox (RNAME) field in the SOA for all empty zones. The default is . (dot), meaning no e-mail address supplied..
empty-server	Operations	Defines the value returned as the server-name (MNAME) field in the SOA for all empty zones. The default is the zone name.
empty-zones-enable	Operations	Controls use of BIND 9's built-in empty-zones used to minimize unnecessary external traffic. The default is yes (enable all built-in empty zones).
fake-iquery		Obsolete statement.
fetch-glue		Obsolete statement.
file	Zone	Generic file name definition—used by master or slave zone files and in logging clauses.
files	Operations	Defines the maximum number of files the server may have open concurrently. The default is unlimited.
filter-aaaa-on-v4	Operations	Allows AAAA RRs to be deleted from query responses when the client is not connected to an IPv6 network. Default is no. Only available if BIND is built using --enable-filter-aaaa=yes which is not the case with either Ubuntu Server or FreeBSD standard packages (see the "Building BIND from Source" section in Chapter 6). It's not described further.

Statement	Category	Summary
flush-zones-on-shutdown	Operations	Defines whether or not pending DDNS updates are flushed when the server is closed normally. The default is no.
forward	Queries	Defines the order in which forwarding is to be performed. Always used in conjunction with the forwarders statement.
forwarders	Queries	Defines one or more hosts to which queries will be forwarded. Always used in conjunction with the forward statement.
has-old-clients		Obsolete. Replaced with auth-nxdomain and rfc2308-type1.
heartbeat-interval	Operations	Only valid with the dialup statement. The server will perform zone maintenance tasks for all zones marked as dialup whenever this interval expires.
host-statistics		Not implemented.
host-statistics-max		Not implemented.
hostname	Operations	Only used with CHAOS (CH) class. The host name the server should report via a TXT query.
inet	Controls	Defines the control channel to be used for remote administration (rndc) of the server and to access server statistics.
interface-interval	Operations	Defines when periodic checks and update of server interfaces is performed.
ixfr-from-differences	Transfers	Controls how IXFR transfers are calculated.
ixfr-tmp-file		Obsolete statement.
journal	Operations	Overrides the default journal file name used in DDNS. Default is zone-file-name.jnl.
key-directory	Security	A quoted string defining the absolute path where the keys used in the dynamic update of secure zones may be found. Only required if this directory is different from that defined by a directory statement.
keys	Server	Specifies one or more key-names, defined within a key clause, to be used with a remote server.

Statement	Category	Summary
lame-ttl	Operations	Defines the number of seconds to cache a lame server indication.
listen-on	Operations	Defines the port and IPv4 address(es) on which BIND will listen for incoming queries. The default is port 53 on all server interfaces. Multiple listen-on statements are allowed.
listen-on-v6	Operations	Defines the port and IPv6 address(es) on which BIND will listen for incoming queries. The default is port 53 on all server interfaces. Multiple listen-on-v6 statements are allowed.
maintain-ixfr-base		Obsolete statement.
managed-keys-directory	Security	Used to override the default directory used for managed-key files. Default is directory statement.
masterfile-format	Zone	Defines if the zone file is in text or raw (output from named-compilezone; see Chapter 9) format. Default is text.
masters	Zone	Slave only. Defines one or more zone masters.
match-clients	Views	Controls the hosts that satisfy a view clause.
match-destinations	Views	Controls the hosts that satisfy a view clause.
match-mapped-addresses	Operations	Controls whether an IPv4 mapped address within an IPv6 address is used in an address_match_list.
match-recursive-only	Views	Controls the hosts that satisfy a view clause.
max-acache-size	Performance	Defines the maximum size of the additional section cache (acache). Default is 16MB.
max-cache-size	Operations	Defines the maximum amount of memory to use for the server's cache in bytes.
max-cache-ttl	Operations	Defines the maximum time in seconds for which the server will cache positive answers.
max-clients-per-query	Operations	Defines the maximum number of outstanding queries that are allowed by a resolver for the same name. Default is 100.
max-ixfr-log-size		Obsolete statement.

Statement	Category	Summary
max-ncache-ttl	Operations	Defines the maximum time in seconds for wIf defined overrides the SOA nx (ex min) field for all zones.
max-ixfr-log-size		Obsolete statement.
max-journal-size	Transfers	Controls the size of the journal files used in DDNS.
max-refresh-time	Transfers	Only valid for slave zones. The zone refresh time is normally defined by the SOA record refresh parameter. This statement will override the SOA and substitute the values defined.
max-retry-time	Transfers	Only valid for slave zones. The retry time is normally defined by the SOA record retry parameter. This statement will override the SOA and substitute the values defined.
max-transfer-idle-in	Transfers	Only valid for slave zones. Inbound zone transfers making no progress in the defined minutes will be terminated. The default is 60 (1 hour).
max-transfer-idle-out	Transfers	Only valid for master zones. Outbound zone transfers making no progress in the defined minutes will be terminated. The default is 120 (2 hours).
max-transfer-time-in	Transfers	Only valid for slave zones. Inbound zone transfers running longer than the defined minutes will be terminated. The default is 120 (2 hours).
max-transfer-time-out	Transfers	Only valid for master zones. Outbound zone transfers running longer than the defined minutes will be terminated. The default is 120 (2 hours).
max-udp-size	Performance	Defines the maximum size in bytes the server will use to send UDP packets. Default is 4096.
memstatistics	Operations	Defines if memory statistics are to be written on exit. Default is no.
memstatistics-file	Operations	The name of the file to which the server writes memory usage statistics on exit. If not specified, the default is named.memstats.
min-refresh-time	Transfers	Only valid for slave zones. The zone refresh time is normally defined by the SOA record refresh parameter. This statement will override the definition and substitute the values defined.

Statement	Category	Summary
min-retry-time	Transfers	Only valid for slave zones. The retry time is normally defined by the SOA record retry parameter. This statement will override the definition and substitute the values defined.
min-roots		Not implemented.
minimal-responses	Performance	Controls whether the server will only add records to the authority and additional data sections when they are required (such as delegations, negative responses). This may improve the performance of the server.
multi-master	Transfers	Applies to slave servers only. Controls how multiple masters' serial number errors are logged.
multiple-cnames		Obsolete statement.
named-xfer		Obsolete statement.
ndots	lwres	Controls how queries are constructed in the lightweight resolver.
notify	Transfers	Controls whether NOTIFY messages are sent from a zone master on zone changes.
notify-delay	Transfers	Allows control over the time between retries of NOTIFY messages. Default is 5 seconds.
notify-source	Transfers	Only valid for master zones. Defines the IPv4 address (and optional port) to be used for outgoing NOTIFY messages.
notify-source-v6	Transfers	Only valid for master zones. Defines the IPv6 address (and optional port) to be used for outgoing NOTIFY messages.
notify-to-soa	Transfers	Controls whether to send a NOTIFY to the name-server (MNAME) in the SOA RR for the domain. The default is no.
pid-file	Operations	A quoted string defining where the Process Identifier (PID) used by BIND is written. If not present, it is distribution or OS specific, typically /var/run/named/named.pid.
port	Operations	Controls the port BIND will use to provide UDP or TCP services. The default is 53. This statement is intended primarily for testing.
preferred-glue	Operations	Controls the order of glue records in a response (A or AAAA).

Statement	Category	Summary
provide-ixfr	Transfers	Controls whether a master will respond to an incremental (IXFR) zone request or will only respond with a full zone transfer (AXFR). The BIND 9 default is to use IXFR if possible.
pubkey		Obsolete statement.
queryport-pool-ports		Obsolete statement
query-port-pool-updateinterval		Obsolete statement
query-source	Queries	Controls the IPv4 address and port on which recursive queries are issued.
query-source-v6	Queries	Controls the IPv6 address and port on which recursive queries are issued.
querylog	Operations	Controls whether logging of queries is performed—overrides the logging clause category definition.
recursing-file	Operations	The file name used when the remote command rndc recursing is issued.
random-device	Security	The source of entropy to be used by the server for DNSSEC operations. If not specified, the default value is /dev/random (or equivalent) when present and none otherwise.
recursion	Queries	Defines whether recursion (caching) is allowed or not. The default is to provide recursive support.
recursive-clients	Queries	The maximum number of concurrent recursive queries the server may perform. The default is 1000.
request-ixfr	Transfers	Controls whether a server (acting as a slave or on behalf of a slave zone) will request an incremental (IXFR) zone transfer or will request a full zone transfer (AXFR). The BIND 9 default is to request IXFR.
request-nsid	Operations	Allows the server to respond to HOSTNAME.BIND or ID.SERVER with a class of CH. The default is no.
reserved-sockets	Operations	Defines the number of TCP sockets allocated. The default is 512.
rfc2308-type1	Queries	Not implemented.

Statement	Category	Summary
root-delegation-only	Queries	Used for root domains (gTLD and ccTLD) to indicate that all responses will be referrals (delegations).
rrset-order	Queries	Defines the order in which equal RRs (RRsets) are returned. Applies to all RR types.
search	lwres	Controls the operation of the lightweight resolver.
secret	Security	A base64-encoded string containing a shared secret in a key clause.
secroots-file	Security	Defines the file name that will be used when rndc secroots is issued. Defaults to named.secroots.
serial-queries		Obsolete statement.
serial-query-rate	Transfers	Defines the number of queries per second that will be issued by the server on behalf of slave zones when querying the SOA RRs. The default is 20 per second.
server-id	Operations	The ID supplied by a server when interrogated under the CHAOS (CH) class.
session-keyfile	Security	Overrides the default DDNS TSIG key file created with update-policy local. Defaults to /var/run/named/session.key.
session-keyname	Security	Overrides the default DDNS TSIG key name created with update-policy local. Defaults to local-ddns.
session-keyalg	Security	Overrides the default DDNS TSIG key algorithm created with update-policy local. Defaults to HMAC-SHA256.
sig-signing-nodes	Security	Defines the number of RRs that will be signed at any one time when a new DNSKEY RR is introduced. Default is 100.
sig-signing-signatures	Security	Defines the maximum number of signatures (new RRSIG RRs) that will be performed at any one time. The default is 10.
sig-signing-type	Security	Defines an alternative RR type value for the KEYDATA RR used in the DDNS zone when zones are managed using RFC 5011 procedures. The default is 65535.
sortlist	Queries	Controls the order in which equal RRs (RRsets) are returned to the client resolver. This is the client-side equivalent of the rrset-order statement.

Statement	Category	Summary
stacksize	Operations	Controls the stack size used by the server.
statistics-file	Operations	The name of the file the server appends statistics to when instructed to do so using rndc stats. If not specified, the default is named.stats.
statistics-interval		Not implemented.
support-ixfr		Obsolete statement.
suppress-initial-notify		Not implemented.
sig-validity-interval	Security	Controls the time in days when DDNS signatures will expire. The default is 30 days.
tcp-clients	Operations	By default, DNS uses UDP port 53 for queries but allows both TCP and UDP. tcp-clients allows the user to define the maximum number of TCP connections that may be supported. The default is 100.
tcp-listen-queue	Operations	Controls the number of outstanding TCP listen operations. The minimum value is 3.
tkey-dhkey	Security	The Diffie-Hellman key used by the server to generate shared keys.
tkey-domain	Security	The domain appended to the names of all shared keys generated with TKEY.
tkey-gssapi-credential	Security	Used with TKEY operations. The GSSAPI and the credentials required are defined by RFC 2743 and its Kerberos form is defined in RFC 1964.
topology		Not implemented.
transfer-format	Transfers	Only used by master zones. Controls how many records are packed into a message during zone transfers.
transfer-source	Transfers	Only valid for slave zones. Defines which local IPv4 address(es) will be bound to TCP connections used to fetch zones transferred inbound by the server.
transfer-source-v6	Transfers	Only valid for slave zones. Defines which local IPv6 address(es) will be bound to TCP connections used to fetch zones transferred inbound by the server.

Statement	Category	Summary
transfers	Server	Limits the number of concurrent zone transfers from any given server. If not present, the default for transfers-per-ns is used.
transfers-in	Transfers	Only used by slave zones. Controls the number of concurrent inbound zone transfers. The default is 10.
transfers-out	Transfers	Only used by master zones. Controls the number of concurrent outbound zone transfers. The default is 10.
transfers-per-ns	Transfers	Only used by slave zones. Defines the number of concurrent inbound zone transfers from any single name server. The default is 2.
treat-cr-as-space		Obsolete statement.
try-tcp-refresh	Operations	Defines whether to use TCP for refresh if UDP fails. The default is yes.
type	Zone	Defines the characteristic of a zone for example master or hint.
unix		Not implemented.
update-check-ksk	Security	Controls whether the DNSKEY RRs with the KSK will only sign the DNSKEY RRset. The default is yes.
update-policy	Security	Applies to master zones only. Controls the rules by which dynamic updates (DDNS) may be carried out. Mutually exclusive with allow-update.
use-alt-transfer-source	Transfers	Indicates whether alt-transfer-source and alt-transfer-source-v6 can be used or not.
use-id-pool		Obsolete statement.
use-ixfr		Obsolete. Use provide-ixfr.
use-v4-udp-ports	Security	Defines the range of IPv4 UDP ports to be used for outgoing queries. Defaults to 1024 - 655535.
use-v6-udp-ports	Security	Defines the range of IPv6 UDP ports to be used for outgoing queries. Defaults to 1024 - 655535.
view	lwres	Used to define resolver characteristics.

Statement	Category	Summary
version	Operations	Specifies the string that will be returned to a version.bind query when using the CHAOS (CH) class only. If not defined, the real BIND version number is returned.
zero-no-soa-ttl	Operations	Defines that an authoritative NXDOMAIN response to an SOA query will have a 0 TTL (do not cache) on the SOA RR returned, irrespective of the actual TTL of the SOA. The default is yes.
zero-no-soa-ttl-cache	Operations	Resolver. Defines that an authoritative NXDOMAIN response to an SOA query will cause the resolver to set a 0 TTL (do not cache) on the SOA RR returned irrespective of the actual TTL of the SOA. The default is no.
zone-statistics	Operations	Controls whether the server will collect statistical data on all zones (unless specifically turned off on a per-zone basis by specifying zone-statistics no; in the zone clause). These statistics may be accessed using rndc stats.

Table 12–6 lists all statements and identifies in which clauses they may be used.

Table 12–6. BIND Statements by Clause [1]

Statement	A	C	K	L	O	R	S	T	V	Z	X
acache-cleaning-interval					x				x		
acache-enable					x				x		
additional-from-auth					x				x		
additional-from-cache					x				x		
algorithm			X								
allow-new-zones					x				x		
allow-notify					x				x	x	
allow-query					x				x	x	
allow-query-cache					x				x		
allow-query-cache-on					x				x		
allow-query-on					x				x	x	

Statement	A	C	K	L	O	R	S	T	V	Z	X
allow-recursion					x				x		
allow-recursion-on					x				x		
allow-transfer					x				x	x	
allow-update					x				x	x	
allow-update-forwarding					x				x	x	
allow-v6-synthesis											O
also-notify					x				x	x	
alt-transfer-source					x				x	x	
alt-transfer-source-v6					x				x	x	
attach-cache					x				x		
auth-nxdomain					x				x		
auto-dnssec					x				x	x	
avoid-v4-udp-ports					x						
avoid-v6-udp-ports					x						
bindkeys-file					x						
blackhole					x						
bogus							x				
cache-file					x				x		
category				x							
channel				x							
check-dup-records					x				x	x	
check-integrity					x				x	x	
check-mx					x				x	x	

Statement	A	C	K	L	O	R	S	T	V	Z	X
check-mx-cname					x				x	x	
check-names					x				x	x	
check-sibling					x				x	x	
check-srv-cname					x				x	x	
check-wildcard					x				x	x	
cleaning-interval					x				x		
clients-per-query					x				x		
coresize					x						
database										x	
datasize					x						
deallocate-on-exit											O
delegation-only									x		
deny-answer-address					x				x		
deny-answer-aliases					x				x		
dialup					x				x	x	
directory					x						
disable-algorithms					x				x		
disable-empty-zone					x				x		
dnssec-accept-expired					x				x		
dnssec-dnskey-kskonly					x				x	x	
dnssec-enable					x				x		
dnssec-lookaside					x				x		
dnssec-must-be-secure					x				x		

Statement	A	C	K	L	O	R	S	T	V	Z	X
dnssec-secure-to-insecure					x			x	x		
dnssec-validation					x			x			
dual-stack-servers					x			x			
dump-file					x						
edns							x				
edns-udp-size					x		x	x			
empty-contact					x			x			
empty-server					x			x			
empty-zones-enable					x			x			
fake-iquery											O
fetch-glue											O
file									x		
files					x						
filter-aaaa-on-v4					x			x			CO
flush-zones-on-shutdown					x						
forward					x			x	x		
forwarders					x			x	x		
has-old-clients											O
heartbeat-interval					x						
host-statistics											NI
host-statistics-max											NI
hostname					x						

Statement	A	C	K	L	O	R	S	T	V	Z	X
inet	x	x									
interface-interval					x						
ixfr-from-differences									x		
ixfr-base											O
ixfr-tmp-file											O
journal									x		
key-directory					x				x	x	
keys							x				
lame-ttl					x				x		
listen-on					x	x					
listen-on-v6					x						
maintain-ixfr-base											O
managed-keys-directory					x						
masterfile-format					x				x	x	
masters									x		
match-clients									x		
match-destinations									x		
match-mapped-addresses					x						
match-recursive-only									x		
max-acache-size					x				x		
max-cache-size					x				x		
max-cache-ttl					x				x		
max-clients-per-query					x				x		

Statement	A	C	K	L	O	R	S	T	V	Z	X
max-ixfr-log-size										O	
max-journal-size					x			x	x		
max-ncache-ttl					x			x			
max-refresh-time					x			x	x		
max-retry-time					x			x	x		
max-transfer-idle-in					x			x	x		
max-transfer-idle-out					x			x	x		
max-transfer-time-in					x			x	x		
max-transfer-time-out					x			x	x		
max-udp-size					x		x	x			
memstatistics					x						
memstatistics-file					x						
min-refresh-time					x			x	x		
min-retry-time					x			x	x		
min-roots					x			x		NI	
minimal-responses					x			x			
multi-master					x			x	x		
multiple-cnames										O	
named-xfer										O	
ndots						x					
notify					x			x	x		
notify-delay					x			x	x		
notify-source					x		x	x	x		

Statement	A	C	K	L	O	R	S	T	V	Z	X
notify-source-v6					x		x		x	x	
notify-to-soa					x				x	x	
pid-file					x						
port					x						
preferred-glue					x				x		
provide-ixfr						x					
pubkey											O
queryport-pool-ports											O
queryport-pools-updateinterval											O
query-source					x		x		x		
query-source-v6					x		x		x		
querylog					x						
recursing-file					x						
random-device					x						
recursion					x				x		
recursive-clients					x						
request-ixfr					x		x		x		
request-nsid					x			x			
reserved-sockets					x						
rfc2308-type1					x			x			NI
root-delegation-only					x				x		
rrset-order					x				x		

Statement	A	C	K	L	O	R	S	T	V	Z	X
search						x					
secret		X									
secroots-file					x						
serial-queries					x						O
serial-query-rate					x						
server-id					x						
session-keyfile					x						
session-keyname					x						
session-keyalg					x						
sig-signing-nodes					x				x	x	
sig-signing-signatures					x				x	x	
sig-signing-type					x				x	x	
sig-validity-interval					x				x	x	
sortlist					x				x		
stacksize					x						
statistics-file					x						
statistics-interval					x						NI
support-ixfr											O
suppress-initial-notify											NI
tcp-clients					x						
tcp-listen-queue					x						
tkey-dhkey					x						
tkey-domain					x						

Statement	A	C	K	L	O	R	S	T	V	Z	X
tkey-gssapi-credential					x						
topology											NI
transfer-format					x		x		x		
transfer-source					x		x		x	x	
transfer-source-v6					x		x		x	x	
transfers							x				
transfers-in					x						
transfers-out					x						
transfers-per-ns					x						
treat-cr-as-space											O
try-tcp-refresh					x				x	x	
type									x		
unix		x									NI
update-check-ksk					x				x	x	
update-policy									x		
use-alt-transfer-source					x				x	x	
use-id-pool					x						O
use-ixfr					x						
use-queryport-pool											O
use-v4-udp-ports					x						
use-v6-udp-ports					x						
view						x					
version					x						

Statement	A	C	K	L	O	R	S	T	V	Z	X
zero-no-soa-ttl					x				x	x	
zero-no-soa-ttl-cache					x				x		
Zone-statistics					x				x	x	

[1]*Key:*

   A = Statistics-Channels clause

   C = Controls clause

   K = Keys clause

   L = Logging clause

   O = Options clause

   R = lwres clause

   S = Server clause

   T = Trusted-keys clause

   V = View clause

   Z = Zone clause

   X = Obsolete (O), Not implemented(NI) or Configure (Source build) Option (CO)

BIND controls Statements

The controls clause and the statistics-channels clause permit only the inet statement type, though multiple such statements can appear inside either clause. No default statistics-channel clause is assumed. If external access to statistics is required, an explicit statistics-channels clause must be defined. A default controls clause is always assumed in the absence of any definition, which causes a TCP listen operation to be placed on port 953 of the loopback address for IPv4 and/or IPv6 (127.0.0.1 and ::1 respectively). If the rndc utility will not be used, the controls interface can be disabled by using an empty controls clause as shown here:

controls {};

inet Statement

The inet statement defines a method to control access to the rndc (remote administration) utility and to server statistics using HTTP. More than one inet statement may be included in a controls or statistics-channels clause.

inet **Statement Syntax**

```
inet inet_spec [inet_spec] ..;
inet * allow {192.168.254.2;} keys {"rndc-key";};
```

Each inet_spec parameter has the following format:

```
inet_spec = ( ip_addr | * ) [ port ip_port ] allow {  address_match_list  }
                 keys {  key_list  };
```

The ip_address parameter defines the IP address of the local server interface on which rndc or statistics connections will be accepted. The wildcard value (*) will allow connection on any of the server's IPv4 addresses including the loopback address. The equivalent wildcard for IPv6 is ::. The optional ip_port parameter allows a specific port to be nominated for use by rndc connections; if not present, the default port of 953 will be used in a controls clause and port 80 (HTTP) in a statistics-channels clause. The address_match_list defines the permitted hosts that can connect to the rndc channel. The key_list parameter is only permitted with the controls clause (it is rejected if present in a statistics-channels clause) and contains one or more key-names (defined in a key clause) containing the list of permitted users who are allowed access. While address_match_lists can include a key parameter, if one is present in the referenced address_match_list, it is ignored; only keys defined in the key_list of the inet statement are permitted access. The key_list can be omitted, in which case the file rndc.key in the same directory as named.conf that contains a default key clause with the name "rndc-key" (rndckey for Fedora) will be used to provide default access. The rndc.key file is created by running the following command:

```
rndc-confgen -a
```

The following example shows that a user on the loopback address can use the default key for access, while all other users must use the "rndc-remote" key. In all cases, localhost will use port 953 (the default) and external connections will use port 7766. An acl clause is used as the source of the address_match_list:

```
// named.conf fragment
acl "rndc-users" {
    10.0.15.0/24;
    !10.0.16.1/24; // negated
    2001:db8:0:27::/64; // any address in subnet
 };
....
key "rndc-remote" {
    algorithm hmac-md5;
    secret "OmItW1lOyLVUEuvv+Fme+Q==";
};
controls {
    // local host - default key
    inet 127.0.0.1 allow {localhost;};
    inet * port 7766 allow {"rndc-users";} keys {"rndc-remote";};
};
```

Further examples of the inet statement are illustrated in the "rndc" section located in Chapter 9 and in the "statistics-controls Clause" section in this chapter.

■ **Caution** For security reasons, the key clause earlier would normally be placed in a separate file, secured with read access only for the UID of BIND (the named daemon), which is typically either named or bind, and then included in the named.conf using an include statement.

BIND logging Statements

The logging clause takes two statements: the first defines the channel, one or more physical paths to the output stream, and the second defines the category or type of data that will be output to the channels. Multiple channel and category statements can exist in a logging clause. If no logging clause is defined in the named.conf file, the following default definition is assumed:

```
logging {
      category default { default_syslog; default_debug; };
      category unmatched { null; };
};
```

The default means all categories (defined in Table 12–9), with the exception of queries and lame-servers, will be written to syslog (default_syslog) and, if the debug level is nonzero, to a file called named.run (default_debug) in the location defined by a directory statement and that this file will grow to unlimited size unless manually deleted. The values in the preceding logging clause will only make complete sense after having read the channel and category descriptions that follow.

channel Statement

The channel statement is optional; if not present, the four predefined channel_name values described in Table 12–8 are always available. One or more channel statements define the output streams to which logging data will be written. channel statements can only be used in a logging clause.

channel Statement Syntax

```
channel channel_name { channel_spec };
channel secure_log {file "/var/log/named/dnssec.log" version 3 size 1m;
                  severity info;};
```

The channel_name is a unique name that is used to identify a channel definition and is used by the category statement as the destination for a particular type or category of log information. It is traditionally written as a nonspace string without quotes but can be written as a quoted string. channel_spec defines the characteristics of the output stream and has the following format:

```
channel_spec = ( file "path-to-file"
                      [ versions ( number | unlimited ) ]
                      [ size size_in_bytes ]
                      | syslog syslog_facility | stderr | null );
```

```
[ severity (critical | error | warning | notice |
    info | debug [ level ] | dynamic ); ]
[ print-category yes | no; ]
[ print-severity yes | no; ]
[ print-time yes | no; ]
};
```

Table 12–7 describes the value of each parameter in the channel_spec.

Table 12–7. Channel Statement Parameters

Parameter	Values	Description
file	path-to-file	A quoted string defining the absolute or relative (to directory statement) path to the logging file; for instance, /var/log/named/named.log. From the preceding syntax, **file**, **syslog**, **stderr**, and **null** are mutually exclusive for a channel.
versions	number|unlimited	May take a number in the range 0 to 99 or unlimited (defaults to 99). This defines the number of file versions that should be kept by BIND. Versioned files are created by appending .0, .1, etc to the file name in the **file** parameter. Files are rolled (renamed or overwritten) so the base file name will contain the current log and .0 will contain the last log information prior to commencing the new log, .1 the next, and so on up to the limit defined by number or unlimited. Unless a **size** parameter is used, new log versions will only be rolled (or swapped) when BIND is restarted. If no **versions** statement is defined, a single log file of unlimited size is used; upon restart, new data is appended to the defined file. This can create a very big file, very quickly; it's not recommended.
size	size_in_bytes	Defines a size limit to the log file. May take the case-insensitive short forms K, M, or G; for example, 25m = 25000000 (25MB). **size** and **versions** are related as shown: **size** value and no **versions** parameter: When the size limit is reached, BIND will stop logging until the file size is reduced to below the threshold defined by manually deleting or truncating the file. **size** and a **versions** parameter: The log files will be rolled when the size limit is reached. No **size**, only a **versions** parameter: The log files will be rolled only when BIND is restarted.

Parameter	Values	Description
syslog	syslog_facility	Uses syslogd to write output. The syslog_facility parameter is the facility definition to be used when writing to **syslog** and may take any valid value defined for **syslog** (see man 3 syslog) and its handing will be defined in /etc/syslog.conf. The default syslog_facility is user. When running under Windows, this setting will use the Event Log, Applications category. From the preceding syntax, **file**, **syslog**, **stderr**, and **null** are mutually exclusive for a channel.
stderr		Writes to the current standard error location (normally the console) and would typically only be used for debug purposes. From the preceding syntax, **file**, **syslog**, **stderr**, and **null** are mutually exclusive for a channel.
null		Writes to /dev/null—the bit bucket—such that all data is discarded. From the preceding syntax **file**, **syslog**, **stderr**, and **null** are mutually exclusive for a channel.
severity	level	Controls the logging level and may take one of the values defined in the preceding section "channel Statement Syntax." Logging will occur for any message equal to or higher than the level specified (=>); lower levels will not be logged. Various debug levels can be defined (see -d argument in Table 12–1) and where level 0 is no debug information. The value dynamic means the value defined by either the -d command-line argument or by an rndc trace debug_level command.
print-time	yes|no	Controls whether the date and time are written to the output channel (yes) or not (no). The default is no.
print-severity	yes|no	Controls whether the severity level is written to the output channel (yes) or not (no). The default is no.
print-category	yes|no	Controls whether the category value is written to the output channel (yes) or not (no). The default is no.

BIND provides four predefined channel_name definitions. If these are used in a category statement, they don't need to be defined using a channel statement—they just exist. Table 12–8 shows the predefined channels and their implicit definition.

Table 12–8. Predefined Channels

channel_name	Implicit Definition
default_syslog	```channel default_syslog {
syslog daemon;
severity info
};```
default_debug	```channel default_debug {
file "named.run";
severity dynamic;
};```
default_stderr	```channel default_stderr {
stderr;
severity info;
};```
null	```channel null {
null;
};```

If no channel statement is defined, the four predefined channels in Table 12–8 are available by default. The default_debug channel has the unique property that data is written to it *only* if the debug level (defined by a category statement, the -d command-line argument, or an rndc trace debug_level) is nonzero. This channel and the default_syslog channel are used in the default logging clause described at the beginning of this section.

category Statement

The category statement defines the type of log messages to be sent to a particular channel. More than one category statement may be included.

category **Statement Syntax**

```
category category_name { channel_name ; [ channel_name ; ... ] };
category dnssec {secure_log;};
```

The channel_name may refer to either one of the predefined channel_name values (default_syslog, default_debug, default_stderr, or null) or one defined in a channel statement. More than one channel_name may be defined for any given category statement; in that case, the category is written to all the defined channel_name values. The category_name parameter defines the type of output to be sent to the defined channel_name. This may take one of the values defined in Table 12–9.

Table 12–9. Logging Category Types

Value	Description
client	Logs processing of client requests.
config	Logs configuration file parsing and processing.
database	Logs messages relating to the databases used internally by the name server to store zone and cache data.
default	Logs all values that are not explicitly defined in category statements. If this is the only category defined, it will log all categories listed in this table with the exception of queries, which are not turned on by default, and unmatched.
delegation-only	Logs queries that have returned NXDOMAIN as the result of a delegation-only zone type or a delegation-only statement in a hint or stub zone clause.
dispatch	Logs dispatches of incoming packets to the server modules where they are to be processed.
dnssec	Logs all DNSSEC, SIG(0), TKEY, and TSIG protocol processing.
edns-disabled	Logs queries that were forced to use normal DNS after an EDNS0 transaction timed out. This may indicate that the requestor was not standards-compliant (RFC 1034).
general	Logs anything that is not classified in this table; a catch-all category.
lame-servers	Logs all instances of lame servers (misconfiguration in the delegation of domains) discovered by BIND 9 when trying to obtain authoritative answers. If the volume of these messages is high, many users elect to send them to the null channel using, for instance, a category lame-servers {null;}; statement.
network	Logs all network operations.
notify	Logs all NOTIFY operations.
queries	Logs all query transactions. The querylog statement may be used to override this category statement. This entry can generate a substantial volume of data very quickly. This category is not turned on by default; hence the default type earlier will not log this information. This entry now logs the client's IP address and port number, the query name, class and RR type requested, whether a recursive query is requested (+ is recursive, - is iterative), whether it is EDNS0 (E), whether TCP was used (T), whether DNSSEC OK (DO bit) set = query validated (D), whether Checking Disabled (CD bit) set (C), or whether it is signed (S).
query-errors	Logs any errors relating to queries.

Value	Description
resolver	Logs name resolution information including recursive lookups performed on behalf of clients by a caching name server.
security	Logs approval and denial of requests.
unmatched	Logs no matching view clause or unrecognized class value. A one-line summary is also logged to the client category. By default, this category is sent to the null channel.
update	Logs all DDNS transactions.
update-security	Logs approval and denial of update requests used with DDNS.
xfer-in	Logs details of zone transfers the server is receiving.
xfer-out	Logs details of zone transfers the server is sending.

The category statement is optional; if not present BIND will assume the following default:

```
category default { default_syslog; default_debug; };
```

This means that all categories except queries and unmatched will be logged to syslog (or Windows Event Manager, under the Applications category). In addition, the same categories will *also* be logged to the file named.run in the directory statement location (or its default) if the debug level in a channel statement is nonzero. The following example shows a simple logging clause using a single file:

```
// named.conf fragment
logging{
    channel single_log {
    file "/var/log/named/bind.log" versions 3 size 2m;
    severity info;
    print-time yes;
    print-severity yes;
    print-category yes;
    };
    category default{
    single_log;
    };
    category lame-servers{
    null; // discard
    };
};
```

The following example shows streaming of NOTIFY and Dynamic DNS messages to separate log files. Assuming the view clause is being used, the unmatched category is also sent to stderr so the file can be quickly debugged.

```
// named.conf fragment
logging{
    channel main_log {
```

```
        file "/var/log/named/main.log" versions 3 size 2m;
        severity info;
        print-time yes;
        print-severity yes;
        print-category yes;
        };
        channel notify_log {
        file "/var/log/named/notify.log" versions 3 size 1m;
        severity info;
        print-time yes;
        print-severity yes;
        print-category yes;
        };
        channel ddns_log {
        file "/var/log/named/ddns.log" versions 3 size 1m;
        severity info;
        print-time yes;
        print-severity yes;
        print-category yes;
        };
        category default{
        main_log;
        };
        category lame-servers{
        null;  // discard
        };
        category notify{
        notify_log;
        };
        category update{
        ddns_log;
        };
        category update-security{
        ddns_log;
        };
        category unmatched {
        main_log; default_stderr;
        };
};
```

BIND `lwres` Statements

This section describes the statements that may be included in the lwres (lightweight resolver) clause. The listen-on statement, which may also be included in the lwres clause, is described in the "DNS BIND Operations" section later in this chapter. If the listen-on statement is omitted in the lwres clause, it defaults to port 921 on localhost (127.0.0.1).

view

```
view "view-name";
view "good guys";
```

The view statement allows the resolver to use the characteristics defined by a view clause. If the statement is not present and no view clauses are defined, it uses a default (hard-coded) view within BIND. This statement can only appear in an lwres clause.

search

```
search {domain-name; [domain-name; ...]};
search {example.com; example.org;};
```

This statement has the same meaning as the equivalent named parameter in the /etc/resolv.conf file and defines the domain-name that will be added to any name supplied to the resolver. The ndots statement that follows can be used to control when this process is invoked. If more than one domain-name is present, they will be tried one after the other in the order they were defined. In the preceding example statement, if a name of joe.example.net was supplied and no ndots statement was present, the resolver will try joe.example.net, and if that fails, joe.example.net.example.com, and then joe.example.net.example.org. If the name joe was supplied, then the resolver would try first with joe, and if that fails, joe.example.com, and if that fails, joe.example.org. This statement can only appear in an lwres clause.

ndots

```
ndots number;
ndots 2;
```

This statement has the same meaning as the equivalent named parameter in the /etc/resolv.conf file and defines the minimum number of dots that must be present in a name before it uses as an absolute name (it is assumed to be an FDQN). If there are fewer dots in the supplied name than number, each domain-name defined in a search statement will be added to the name. To illustrate the process, the ndots 2; from the example will be used together with the example defined in the search parameter earlier. If the resolver received the name joe.example.net, this has two dots in the name, and hence will be used in a query—only if this fails will the values defined in the search statement be appended to give joe.example.net.example.com, etc. If the name joe was supplied to the resolver, it has no dots and so will not be used directly in a query; but each value in the search statement will be appended to give joe.example.com, and if that fails, joe.example.org. This statement can only appear in an lwres clause.

BIND Transfer Statements

This section describes all the statements, in alphabetic order, that control or affect the behavior of zone transfers and Dynamic DNS updates.

allow-notify

```
allow-notify { address_match_list };
allow-notify { 10.2.3.2;10.2.3.7;192.168.2.0/24;};
```

allow-notify applies to slave zones only and defines an address_list_match for hosts that are allowed to send NOTIFY messages to this slave in addition to those hosts defined in the masters statement for the zone. The default behavior is to allow zone NOTIFY messages only from the hosts defined in the `masters` statement. This statement may be defined in zone or view clauses or in a global options clause. Example:

```
// named.conf fragment
....
zone "example.com" in{
    type slave;
    masters {192.168.254.2;};
    file "slave.example.com";
    // allows NOTIFY message from the defined IPs
    allow-notify (192.168.0.15; 192.168.0.16; 10.0.0.1;);
};
zone "example.net" in{
    type slave;
    file "slave.example.net";
    masters {192.168.254.3;};
    // allows no NOTIFY messages
    allow-notify (none;);
};
```

The zone example.com can receive NOTIFY messages from 192.168.254.2 and the listed IPs; example.net can only accept NOTIFY messages from 192.168.254.3.

allow-transfer

allow-transfer { address_match_list };
allow-transfer { 192.168.2.7;};

allow-transfer defines an `address_match_list` of hosts that are allowed to transfer the zone information *from* the server, master or slave, for the zone. The default behavior is to allow zone transfers to any host, which means that any host anywhere in the world can copy your zone file. While this may look excessively friendly, the assumption is that all zone data is public. If this isn't the required behavior, it must be disabled explicitly as shown in the following example fragment. This statement may be specified in zone or view clauses or in a global options clause. This example shows zone transfers disabled for all zones by default, but the zone example.com has decided to allow transfers to any host for reasons best known to the domain owner:

```
options {
....
    allow-transfer {none;}; // none by default
....
};
....
zone "example.com" in{
....
    allow-transfer {any;}; // this zone only
....
};
```

allow-update-forwarding

allow-update-forwarding { address_match_list };
allow-update-forwarding { none;};

allow-update-forwarding defines an address_match_list of hosts that are allowed to submit dynamic updates to a slave server for onward transmission to a master. By default, this behavior is not allowed; that is, "none" is assumed as an address_match_list. This backdoor route to DDNS should be used with extreme caution: if the allow-update on the master enables the zone slave to perform a DDNS update, this statement could expose the master to indirect attack. This statement applies to slave zones only and may be specified in zone or view clauses or in a global options clause.

also-notify

```
also-notify { ip_addr [port ip_port] ; [ ip_addr [port ip_port] ; ... ] };
also-notify { 10.0.3.7 port 1177;};
```

also-notify is applicable to master zones only and defines a list of IP address(es) and optional port numbers that will be sent a NOTIFY message when a zone changes, or a specific zone changes if the statement is specified in a zone clause. Any IP addresses are in addition to those listed in the NS RRs for the zone that will also be sent NOTIFY messages. The also-notify in a zone is *not* cumulative with any global also-notify statements. In addition, if a global notify no; statement is defined, this option may be used to override it for a specific zone; conversely, if the global options clause contains an also-notify list, setting notify no; in the zone will override the global option. This statement may be specified in a zone or view clause or in a global options clause.

```
options {
....
    also-notify {10.1.0.15; 172.28.32.7;}; // all zones
....
};
....
zone "example.com" in{
....
    also-notify {10.0.1.2;}; // only this host + those in NS RRs for zone
....
};
zone "example.net in{
....
    notify no; // no NOTIFY for zone
....
};
```

alt-transfer-source, alt-transfer-source-v6

```
alt-transfer-source ( ipv4_address | * ) [ port ( integer | * )];
alt-transfer-source-v6 ( ipv6_address | * ) [ port ( integer | * ) ];
alt-transfer-source 172.22.3.15; // assumed multihomed
alt-transfer-source-v6 2001:db8::2; // assumed multihomed
```

alt-transfer-source and alt-transfer-source-v6 apply to slave zones only. They define an alternative local IP address (on this server) to be used for inbound zone transfers by the server if that defined by transfer-source (transfer-source-v6) fails and use-alt-transfer-source is enabled. This address (and port) must also appear in the remote end's allow-transfer statement for the zone being transferred. This statement may be specified in zone or view clauses or in a global options clause.

ixfr-from-differences

```
ixfr-from-differences (yes | no);
ixfr-from-differences yes;
```

ixfr-from-differences defines how the name server calculates incremental zone changes. Normally, incremental zone transfers are only possible when used in conjunction with DDNS. ixfr-from-differences allows a zone master or slave to create incremental zone transfers for nondynamic zones. If set to yes, when the server receives (if a slave) or loads (if a master) a new version of a zone file, it will compare the new version to the previous one and calculate a set of differences. The differences are then logged in the zone's journal file (.jnl appended to zone file name) such that the changes can be transmitted to downstream slaves as an incremental zone transfer. This statement saves bandwidth at the expense of increased CPU and memory consumption. This statement may only be used in a zone clause.

max-journal-size

```
max-journal-size size_in_bytes;
max-journal-size 50k;
```

max-journal-size sets a maximum size in bytes (may take the case-insensitive K, M, or G short forms) for each journal file. When the journal file approaches the specified size, some of the oldest transactions in the journal will be automatically removed. The default is unlimited size. Journal files are used by DDNS when modifying the primary master zone file and when receiving IXFR changes on slave zones. The journal file uses a binary format; its name is formed by appending the extension .jnl to the name of the corresponding zone file.

All changes made to a zone using dynamic update are written to the zone's journal file. The server will periodically flush the complete contents of the updated zone to its zone file; this happens approximately every 15 minutes. When a server is restarted after a shutdown or crash, it will replay the journal file to incorporate into the zone any updates that took place after the last zone file update.

If changes have to be made manually to a dynamic zone, use the following sequence:

1. Disable dynamic updates to the zone using rndc freeze zone, which causes the zone file to be updated.

2. Edit the zone file.

3. Delete the .jnl file for the zone.

4. Run rndc thaw (unfreeze) zone to reload the changed zone and reenable dynamic updates. The current versions of BIND (9.3+) use the command rndc thaw zone; older versions use rndc unfreeze zone.

This statement may be used in a zone, view, or global options clause.

max-refresh-time, min-refresh-time

```
max-refresh-time seconds ;
min-refresh-time seconds ;
max-refresh-time 2w;
min-refresh-time 12h ;
```

max-refresh-time and min-refresh-time are only valid for slave or stub zones. The refresh time is normally defined by the SOA RR refresh parameter (defined in seconds). These statements allow the slave server administrator to override the definition and substitute the values defined, which are in seconds. The values may take the normal time shortcuts, for example, 35m or 2d55m. These statements may be specified in zone or view clauses or in a global options clause.

max-retry-time, min-retry-time

```
max-retry-time seconds ;
min-retry-time seconds ;
max-retry-time 3600 ;
min-retry-time 1800 ;
```

max-retry-time and min-retry-time are only valid for slave or stub zones. The retry time is normally defined by the SOA RR retry parameter. These statements allow the slave server administrator to override the definition and substitute the values defined. The values may take the normal time shortcuts, for example, 35m or 2d55m. These statements may be specified in zone or view clauses or in a global options clause.

max-transfer-idle-in

```
max-transfer-idle-in minutes ;
max-transfer-idle-in 10 ;
```

max-transfer-idle-in is only valid for slave zones. Inbound zone transfers making no progress in this many minutes will be terminated. The default is 60 (1 hour). The maximum value is 40320 (28 days). This statement may be specified in zone or view clauses or in a global options clause.

max-transfer-idle-out

```
max-transfer-idle-out minutes ;
max-transfer-idle-out 20;
```

max-transfer-idle-out is only valid for master zones. Outbound zone transfers running longer than this many minutes will be terminated. The default is 120 (2 hours). The maximum value is 40320 (28 days). This statement may be specified in zone or view clauses or in a global options clause.

max-transfer-time-in

```
max-transfer-time-in minutes ;
max-transfer-time-in 120;
```

max-transfer-time-in is only valid for slave zones. Inbound zone transfers running longer than this many minutes will be terminated. The default is 120 (2 hours). The maximum value is 40320 (28 days). This statement may be specified in zone or view clauses or in a global options clause.

max-transfer-time-out

```
max-transfer-time-out minutes ;
max-transfer-time-out 120;
```

max-transfer-time-out is only valid for master zones. Outbound zone transfers running longer than this many minutes will be terminated. The default is 120 (2 hours). The maximum value is 40320 (28 days). This statement may be specified in zone or view clauses or in a global options clause.

multi-master

```
multi-master ( yes | no) ;
multi-master yes ;
```

multi-master is relevant only when multiple masters are defined for a slave zone. It controls whether a log entry will be generated each time the serial number is *less* than that currently maintained by the slave (no) or not (yes). This situation can occur when the zone masters are out of sync with each other. The default is no. This statement may be specified in zone or view clauses or in a global options clause.

notify

```
notify ( yes | no | explicit );
notify explicit;
```

notify behavior is only applicable to authoritative (master or slave) zones. If set to yes (BIND default), when zone information changes, NOTIFY messages are sent to all servers defined in the NS RRs for the zone (with the exception of the primary master name server defined in the SOA RR, though this may be modified using the notify-to-soa statement) and to any IPs listed in also-notify options. If set to no, NOTIFY messages are not sent to any name server. If set to explicit, NOTIFY is only sent to those IP(s) listed in an also-notify statement.

If a global notify option is no, an also-notify statement may be used to override it for a specific zone; conversely, if the global options contains an also-notify list, setting notify to no in the zone will override the global option. This statement may be specified in zone or view clauses or in a global options clause. The following example illustrates that the zone example.net will *not* send NOTIFY messages to the name servers defined in its NS RRs but only those defined in the global also-notify statement:

```
options {
....
    also-notify {10.1.0.15; 172.28.32.7;}; // all zones
....
};
....
zone "example.com in{
....
    // NS RRs and global  also-notify
    // default behavior so could have been omitted
    notify yes;
....
};
zone "example.net in{
....
    // no NOTIFY to NS RRs
    // NOTIFY to global also-notify IPs
    notify explicit;
....
};
```

notify-delay

```
notify-delay seconds;
notify-delay 10;
```

When an authoritative server sends a NOTIFY message, it expects to receive a response (another NOTIFY message). If no response is received (the NOTIFY times out), notify-delay allows the user to define the interval between retries. The default value is 5 seconds. notify-delay is only relevant for authoritative (master or slave) zones. The statement may appear in zone or view clauses or in a global options clause.

notify-source, notify-source-v6

```
notify-source (ip4_addr | *) [port ip_port] ;
notify-source-v6 (ip6_addr | *) [port ip_port] ;
notify-source 192.168.254.3 ;
notify-source-v6 2001:db8:0:1::3 port 1178;
```

notify-source and notify-source-v6 are only relevant for authoritative (master or slave) zones. notify-source defines the IP address and optionally UDP port to be used for outgoing NOTIFY messages. The value * means the IP of this server (default). This IP address must appear in the masters or allow-notify statement of the receiving slave name servers. Since neither the masters nor allow-notify statements take a port parameter, if an optional UDP port value other than 53 is used, a transfer-source, transfer-source-v6, listen-on, or listen-on-v6 statement would be required on the slave. These statements are typically only used on a multihomed server and may be specified in zone,view, server, or a global options clause. The following example shows an IPv6 address being used to send NOTIFY messages to a Global Unicast address:

```
options {
....
    notify-source-v6 {2001:db8:0:1::3;}; // all zones
....
};
```

notify-to-soa

```
notify-to-soa ( yes | no );
notify-to-soa yes;
```

Normally an authoritative server sends NOTIFY messages to the servers listed in the NS RRs for the zone and doesn't send a NOTIFY to the name-server (MNAME) field of the SOA RR (see Chapter 13's "SOA Record" section). Especially in hidden master configurations, this server will typically not appear in any NS RR for the zone and thus will never receive a NOTIFY message when the zone changes. notify-to-soa yes; forces the server to check if the name-server in the SOA RR appears in any NS RR; if it does *not* (it is hidden), then a NOTIFY message will be send to this server. The default value is no, meaning that if the name server in the SOA RR does not appear in any NS RR for the zone it will not be sent a NOTIFY message. notify-to-soa is only relevant for authoritative (master or slave) zones. The statement may appear in zone or view clauses or in a global options clause.

provide-ixfr

provide-ixfr (yes| no) ;
provide-ixfr no ;

provide-ixfr only applies to master zones. The provide-ixfr option controls whether a master will respond to an incremental zone transfer request (IXFR)—parameter = yes—or will respond with a full zone transfer (AXFR)—parameter = no. The default is yes. This statement may be specified in server or view clauses or in a global options clause.

request-ixfr

request-ixfr (yes| no) ;
request-ixfr no;

request-ixfr applies only to slave zones. The request-ixfr option defines whether a server will request an incremental zone transfer (IXFR)—parameter = yes—or will request a full zone transfer (AXFR)—parameter = no. The default is yes. This statement may be specified in server or view clauses or in a global options clause.

serial-query-rate

serial-query-rate number;
serial-query-rate 5;

serial-query-rate applies to slave zones only and limits the number of simultaneous SOA queries to the number per second. The default is 20. This statement may only be used in a global options clause.

transfer-format

transfer-format (one-answer | many-answers);
transfer-format one-answer;

transfer-format is only used by master zones. It controls the format the server uses to transfer zones: one-answer places a single record in each message and many-answers packs as many records as possible into a maximum-sized TCP message. The default is many-answers, which is only known to be supported by BIND; if transferring zones to others servers, a transfer-format one-answer; statement *may* be required. This statement may be specified in server, zone, or view clauses or in a global options clause.

transfer-source, transfer-source-v6

transfer-source (ip4_addr | *) [port ip_port] ;
transfer-source-v6 (ip6_addr | *) [port ip_port] ;
transfer-source 172.15.2.3 port 1178;
transfer-source-v6 2001:db8::1;

transfer-source and transfer-source-v6 are only valid for slave zones on multihomed hosts (hosts with more than one IP address or interface). transfer-source defines which local IP address (on this server) will be bound to TCP connections used to fetch zones transferred inbound by this server. These statements also determine the source IP address, and optionally the UDP port, used for refresh queries and forwarded dynamic updates. If not set, it defaults to a value that will usually be the address of the interface "closest" to the remote end—generally the IP address on which the request arrived. This address must appear in the remote end's allow-transfer option for the zone being transferred. These statements may be used in zone, view, server or a global options clause. The following example shows a multihomed server with IP addresses of 192.168.254.2 and 192.168.254.4; traffic normally arrives on 192.168.254.2:

```
// named.conf fragment
zone "example.com" in {
    type slave;
    ...
    // force transfers onto one interface
    transfer-source 192.168.254.4;
};
```

The master server for the zone must permit the transfer, as shown here:

```
// named.conf fragment
zone "example.com" in {
    type master;
    ...
    // permit transfer
    allow-transfer 192.168.254.4;
};
```

transfers-in

```
transfers-in number ;
transfers-in 5 ;
```

transfers-in is only used by slave zones. This statement defines the number of concurrent inbound zone transfers. The default is 10. This option may only be used in a global options clause.

transfers-per-ns

```
transfers-per-ns number
transfers-per-ns 5
```

transfers-per-ns is only used by slave zones. This statement determines the number of concurrent inbound zone transfers from any remote name server. The default is 2. This option may only be specified in a global options clause.

transfers-out

```
transfers-out number ;
transfers-out 20 ;
```

transfers-out is only used by master zones. transfers-out defines the number of concurrent outbound zone transfers. The default is 10. Zone transfer requests in excess of this limit will be refused. This option may only be specified in a global options clause.

use-alt-transfer-source

```
use-alt-transfer-source ( yes | no );
use-alt-transfer-source yes;
```

use-alt-transfer-source specifies whether the alt-transfer-source statements are allowed (yes) or not (no). The statement is typically defined in a zone clause to control specific behavior over a globally defined alt-transfer-source statement. If view clauses are used, this statement defaults to no; otherwise it defaults to yes (for BIND 8 compatibility). This statement may be specified in normal zone or view clauses or in a global options clause.

BIND Operations Statements

This section describes the statements that affect operation of the server.

avoid-v4-udp-ports, avoid-v6-udp-ports

```
avoid-v4-udp-ports { port; ... };
avoid-v6-udp-ports { port; ... };
avoid-v4-udp-ports { 1178; 1183;1188 };
avoid-v6-udp-ports { 7734; };
```

avoid-v4-udp-ports and avoid-v6-udp-ports define a list of port numbers that will *not* be used by BIND when initiating queries or zone transfers. This list may be used to avoid ports that are blocked by a firewall. This option can only be defined in the global options clause.

check-names

```
check-names ( master | slave | response ) ( fail | warn | ignore );
check-names response warn;
```

The check-names statement will check any host (owner) name in A, AAAA, or MX RRs and the domain names in SOA, NS, MX, and PTR RRs for the defined type (master, slave, or response) for compliance with RFC 821, 952, and 1123 and result in the defined action (fail, warn, or ignore). Care should be taken when using this statement because RFC 2181 greatly liberalized the rules for names (see the "Resource Record Common Format" section in Chapter 13 for full details). The type of host name to be checked may be master, in which case the check only applies to master zones, slave applies only to slave zones, and response applies to names that arrive in response to a query from an authoritative server. The default is *not* to perform host name checks. check-names may be used in a view or options clause with the preceding syntax and in a zone clause, where it has a *different* syntax, shown here:

```
check-names ( fail | warn | ignore );
check-names warn;
```

check-dup-records, check-mx, check-wildcard

```
check-dup-record ( fail | warn | ignore );
check-mx ( fail | warn | ignore );
check-wildcard ( yes | no );
```

```
check-dup-record warn;
check-mx ignore;
check-wildcard warn;
```

These statements are applicable to authoritative servers with master zones (they make little, if any sense, for slave zones and no sense for resolvers) and provide granular control over various checks performed when a zone is loaded or reloaded. In all cases, the utility named-checkzone (see Chapter 9) performs the same extensive checks. The check-dup-records statement is only relevant to DNSSEC signed zones and checks for cases where a RR is different in a DNSSEC signed zone but the same for an unsigned zone. dnssec-signzone (see Chapter 9) removes such RRs before signing, so this statement is only effective for DDNS signed zones. Default is warn. check-mx verifies that an MX RR with an in-zone right-hand name only results in an A or AAAA RR (a check also carried out by check-integrity). Default is warn. check-wildcard checks for non-terminal wildcards and reports a warning if found. Non-terminal wildcards are syntactically allowed but are very unusual, extremely confusing, and may be the result of imperfect understanding of DNS wildcards. Non-terminal simply means the DNS wildcard value (*) is not on the extreme left of the RR; for example, joe.*.example.com is a non-terminal wildcard whereas *.joe.example.com is a terminal wildcard. The default is yes (check and warn if non-terminals are present). These statements can appear in an options, view, or zone clause.

check-integrity, check-mx-cname, check-sibling, check-srv-cname

```
check-integrity ( yes | no );
check-mx-cname ( fail | warn | ignore );
check-sibling ( yes | no );
check-srv-cname ( fail | warn | ignore );
check-integrity yes;
check-mx-cname warn;
check-sibling yes;
check-srv-cname fail;
```

These statements are applicable to authoritative servers with master zones (they make little sense for slave zones) and provide granular control over various checks performed when a zone is loaded or reloaded. In all cases, the utility named-checkzone provides the same extended checks. So, unless DDNS is being used, offline verification with named-checkzone will yield better results. The statements check-mx-cname, check-sibling, and check-srv-cname are ignored if check-integrity no; is present (check-integrity defaults to yes). check-integrity verifies that in-zone names (named-checkzone also verifies out-of-zone names) on NS, MX, and SRV RRs point to A or AAAA RRs and that glue RRs exist for delegations. A warning will be logged for any failure. The check-mx-cname statement will take the action defined if an MX RR right-hand name points to a CNAME RR (default is to warn), a technically illegal but common configuration. check-srv-cname performs the same function for right-hand names in SRV RRs. Glue RRs are already checked by check-integrity so the only function of check-sibling is to turn off the glue RR checks (check-sibling no;). These statements can appear in an options, view, or zone clause.

cleaning-interval

```
cleaning-interval minutes;
cleaning-interval 12h;
```

cleaning-interval defines the time in minutes when all expired records will be deleted from the cache. The default is 60 (1 hour); if specified as 0, *no* cleaning will be performed. The maximum value is

40320 (28 days). This statement does not affect the TTL interval but merely controls the size the cache may occupy on disk. This statement may be used in a view or global options clause.

coresize

```
coresize size_in_bytes;
coresize 2m;
```

The maximum size in bytes (may take the case-insensitive short forms K, M, or G) of a core dump if BIND crashes. This statement can only be used in a global options clause.

database

```
database "driver-name [param] [param] ..";
database "mysql param1 param2";
```

database defines information to be supplied to a database driver including using the Simple Database API. The data is enclosed in a quoted string and driver-name defines the name of the driver defined by the dns_sdb_register() function call (see Chapter 14). The optional param field may be any number of space-separated values that are passed as arguments (via argc/argv) to the included driver's create() callback to be interpreted in a way specific to the driver. This statement can only be used in a zone clause.

datasize

```
datasize size_in_bytes;
datasize 250m;
```

datasize specifies the maximum size in bytes (may take the case-insensitive short forms K or M) of memory used by the server. This is a hard limit and may stop the server from working. The statements max-cache-size and recursive-clients may also be used to limit memory usage. This statement can only be used in a global options clause.

dialup

```
dialup dialup_options;
dialup passive;
```

dialup optimizes behavior to minimize use of connect time on dial-up links. The default is no. This option can be defined in the view, zone, and options clauses.

The dialup statement's behavior concentrates activity into the heartbeat-interval and triggers NOTIFY and zone refresh operations based on the value of the dialup_option as defined in Table 12–10.

Table 12–10. *Dial-up Statement Parameters*

dialup_option	Normal Refresh	Heartbeat Refresh	Heartbeat Notify
No	Yes	No	No
Yes	No	Yes	Yes
Notify	Yes	No	Yes
Refresh	No	Yes	No
passive	No	No	No
notify-passive	No	No	Yes

directory

directory "path_name";
directory "/usr/local/var";

directory is a quoted string defining an absolute path, such as /var/named. All subsequent relative paths use this base directory. If no directory statement is specified, the directory from which the named.conf file was loaded is used (defined by –sysconfdir when BIND is configured). This option may only be used in a global options clause.

disable-empty-zone, empty-contact, empty-server, empty-zones-enable

disable-empty-zone "zone-name";
empty-contact name;
empty-server name;
empty-zones-enable (yes | no);
disable-empty-zone "127.in-addr.arpa";
empty-contact joe.example.com;
empty-server ns1.example.com;
empty-zones-enable no;

In order to reduce the volume of unnecessary traffic (mostly through badly configured name servers), BIND 9 contains a number of built-in empty zones that are enabled by default (empty-zones-enable defaults to yes). The current list of empty zones is:

0.IN-ADDR.ARPA
127.IN-ADDR.ARPA
254.169.IN-ADDR.ARPA
2.0.192.IN-ADDR.ARPA
255.255.255.255.IN-ADDR.ARPA
0.0.0.0.0.0.0.0.0.0.0.0.0.0.0.0.0.0.0.0.0.0.0.0.0.0.0.0.0.0.0.0.IP6.ARPA
1.0.0.0.0.0.0.0.0.0.0.0.0.0.0.0.0.0.0.0.0.0.0.0.0.0.0.0.0.0.0.0.IP6.ARPA

```
D.F.IP6.ARPA
8.E.F.IP6.ARPA
9.E.F.IP6.ARPA
A.E.F.IP6.ARPA
B.E.F.IP6.ARPA
```

All the built-in zones are reverse maps. It is likely that additional empty zones may be added to BIND 9 in the future. All built-in zones may be disabled using an `empty-zones-enable no;` statement. Individual zones can be disabled using `disable-empty-zone` as shown in the example above—one zone per statement. If the zone referenced is not built-in, the statement is silently ignored. In general, disabling zones should only be done if there is a local authoritative zone that will replace it (defined with a zone clause). However, if the server detects a zone clause with the same name as a built-in zone, its built-in empty zone is automatically disabled. `disable-empty-zone` is not strictly necessary in this case; indeed, it may be best not to use it. If, in the future, your local built-in replacement zone is removed, no further action is required to configure a well-behaved server.

Empty zones contain only an SOA RR and a single NS RR. They do not respond with meaningful answers (they are designed simply to stop unnecessary traffic). As an example, if you think that there will be a valid reverse queries for the loopback address (IPv4 127.0.0.1, IPv6 ::1), you may want to replace one or more built-in zones with valid reverse mapped zones. Empty zones will typically return an NXDOMAIN (name does not exist) status with an SOA RR for the domain in the ADDITIONAL SECTION. By default, this SOA RR has a `name-server` field (MNAME; see Chapter 13's "SOA RR" section) set to the zone name. This may be changed using the `empty-server` statement. The `email-address` (RNAME; again, see Chapter 13's "SOA RR" section) field is a single dot, which means no name. This may be changed with the `empty-contact` statement. In the example shown, this value is set to `joe.example.com`, which means that e-mail would be sent to joe@example.com. Multiple `disable-empty-zone` statements and a single `empty-zones-enable`, `empty-contact` and `empty-server` statement may be defined in an `options` or a `view` clause.

dual-stack-server

```
dual-stack-servers [ port pg_num ] { ( "host" [port p_num] |
              ipv4 [port p_num] | ipv6 [port p_num] ); ... };
dual-stack-servers port 1177 {192.168.2.3; "bill.example.net"};
```

`dual-stack-server` defines the IP address of one or more dual-stacked (IPv4/IPv6) servers that can be used by this server to resolve a query using a stack it does not support. In the preceding example, if only an AAAA (IPv6) RR is returned to a query, then this server (which is assumed to support only IPv4) can use the defined server or servers to resolve the query, since they support both stacks. On dual-stack servers, it is only effective if one of the stacks has been disabled on the command line. Using pg_num will act as a global port number for all subsequent server definitions, or they can be defined individually with the p_num field. The host field is a quoted string and is the FQDN of the host, which must be resolvable using the default protocol that is IPv4 in the preceding example. The ipv4 and ipv6 fields are the explicit IPv4 or IPv6 addresses that may be used as an alternative to the host format. This statement may be used in a view or global options clause.

dump-file

```
dump-file path_name;
dump-file "/var/cache/bind.cache";
```

dump-file is a quoted string defining the absolute path where BIND dumps the database (cache) in response to a rndc dumpdb (see Chapter 10). If not specified, the default is named_dump.db in the location specified by a directory option. This statement may only be used in a global options clause.

files

files max_files ;
files 200 ;

files specifies the maximum number of files the server may have open concurrently. The default is unlimited. This statement may be used in a global options clause.

flush-zones-on-shutdown

flush-zones-on-shutdown (yes | no);
flush-zones-on-shutdown yes ;

flush-zones-on-shutdown defines how DDNS zones behave when BIND is terminated normally. If set to no (the default), zones are not flushed. Thus, pending changes to the zone file are not written but remain in the .jnl file and will be applied to the zone file at some time after the server is restarted/reloaded. If set to yes, the outstanding operations in the .jnl file are written to the zone file before BIND exits. This can take some time depending on the number of zones supported but does have the merit that the zones are files are in a known and fully updated state on termination. This statement may only be used in a global options clause.

heartbeat-interval

heartbeat-interval minutes;
heartbeat-interval 2h;

heartbeat-interval defines the time in minutes when zones marked as dialup are updated. The default is 60 (1 hour); if specified as 0, no updating will be performed. The maximum value is 40320 (28 days). This statement may be used in a view or global options clause.

hostname

hostname ("host-name" | none);
hostname "myhost";

The host-name (a quoted string) the server should report when it receives a query of the name hostname.bind with type TXT and class CHAOS (CH). This defaults to the name found by gethostname() (the current host's name). While it may appear this statement is not relevant for normal non-CHAOS systems, using a command such as dig @192.168.2.3 hostname.bind txt ch to any name server this information may be easily discovered; so if such information is sensitive, specifying none disables processing of the queries. This statement may be used in a global options clause.

interface-interval

interface-interval minutes;
interface-interval 0;

interface-interval controls the time in minutes when BIND scans all interfaces on the server and begins to listen on new interfaces (assuming they are not prevented by a listen-on option) and stops listening on interfaces that no longer exist. This statement is only required in a dynamic environment where IP addresses may be changing. The default is 60 (1 hour); if specified as 0, no interface scan will be performed. The maximum value is 40320 (28 days). This statement may only be specified in a global options clause.

journal

journal "name-or-suffix;
journal ".dyn";

By default, when DDNS is active on a zone, it writes updates temporarily to a journal file that it periodically flushes to update the zone file. By convention, this journal file takes the name zone-file-name.jnl. This convention may be overridden on a zone-by-zone basis using the journal statement. The filename and suffix, or the suffix only, may be changed. The example shown only changes the suffix; the journal file for the zone will have a name of zone-file-name.dyn. If journal "master.dyn"; was used, the journal file name would become master.dyn. The only reason for wanting to make such a change would be if the name clashed with other files being used. Alternatively, one may have a pathological hatred of the name .jnl. This statement may only be specified in a zone clause. See also max-journal-size.

lame-ttl

lame-ttl seconds;
lame-ttl 15m;

lame-ttl defines the number of seconds to cache lame delegations or lame servers; that is, servers that are defined as authoritative (they appear in an NS RR) but do not respond as authoritative. The value 0 disables such caching and is *not* recommended. The default is 600 (10 minutes) and the maximum value is 1800 (30 minutes). This statement may be used in a view or global options clause.

listen-on

listen-on [port ip_port] { address_match_list };
listen-on { 192.168.254.2; };

listen-on defines the optional port and IP address(es) on which BIND will listen for incoming queries. The default is port 53 on all server interfaces. Multiple listen-on statements are allowed. This option may be used in a global options clause and an lwres clause where, if omitted, it defaults to port 921 on localhost (127.0.0.1).

listen-on-v6

listen-on-v6 [port ip_port] { address_match_list };
listen-on-v6 port 1234 { any; };

listen-on-v6 turns on BIND to listen for IPv6 queries. If this statement is not specified, the server will not listen for any IPv6 traffic, which is the default behavior. If the OS supports RFC 3493– and RFC 3542–compliant IPv6 sockets and the address_match_list uses the special any name, then a single listen is issued to the wildcard address. If the OS does not support this feature, a socket is opened for every required address and port. The port default is 53. Multiple listen-on-v6 statements are allowed. This option may only be used in a global options clause. The following examples show a number of definitions:

```
options {
....
    // turns on IPv6 for port 53
    listen-on-v6 {any;};
};
options {
....
    // turns off IPv6
    listen-on-v6 {none;};
};

options {
....
    // turns on IPv6 for port 53 for 16 IP range
    listen-on-v6 {2001:db8::/124;};
};
```

match-mapped-addresses

match-mapped-addresses (yes | no) ;
match-mapped-addresses yes   ;

If yes, match-mapped-addresses indicates that an address_match_list containing an IPv4 address will be checked against an IPv4-mapped IPv6 address (described in Chapter 5). This feature can incur significant CPU overheads and should be used as a workaround only where the OS software accepts such connections. This statement may only be used in a global options clause.

max-cache-size

max-cache-size size_in_bytes;
max-cache-size 50m;

max-cache-size defines the maximum amount of memory in bytes to use for the server's cache (case-insensitive short forms of K, M, or G are allowed). When the amount of data in the cache reaches this limit, the server will cause records to expire prematurely so that the limit is not exceeded. In a server with multiple views, the limit applies separately to the cache of each view. The default is unlimited, meaning that records are purged from the cache only when their TTLs expire. This statement may be used in a view or global options clause.

max-cache-ttl

max-cache-ttl seconds;
max-cache-ttl 3d2h5m;

max-cache-ttl sets the maximum time (in seconds) for which the server will cache positive answers and may be used to override (reduce) the actual TTL values on received RRs. Negative answer caching—NXDOMAIN—is defined by max-ncache-ttl. The default is one week (604800 seconds). Standard BIND time short forms may be used. This statement may be used in a view or global options clause.

max-journal-size

max-journal-size bytes;
max-journal-size 2m;

max-journal-size sets the maximum size in bytes for the journal file used by DDNS. If this statement is not present, the journal file has no size limitation. If the statement is present when the limit defined is approached, which can be terminated with k (1024 bytes) or m (1,048,576 bytes), older transactions will be deleted from the journal file. This statement may be used in a view, zone, or global options clause.

max-ncache-ttl

max-ncache-ttl seconds
max-cache-ttl 3h;

max-ncache-ttl sets the maximum time (in seconds) for which the server will cache negative (NXDOMAIN) answers (positive answers are defined by max-cache-ttl). The default max-ncache-ttl is 10800 (3 hours). max-ncache-ttl cannot exceed 7 days and will be silently truncated to 7 days if set to a greater value. This statement may be used in a view or global options clause.

memstatistics

memstatistics (yes | no);
memstatistics yes;

memstatistics yes: causes BIND to write its memory usage data to the location defined by the memstatistics-file statement (or its default) when it exits. The default value is no. Many of the statistics output by the statement are now also output—with significant enhancements—by the memstatistics-channels clause feature described previously in this chapter. This statement may only be used in a global options clause.

memstatistics-file

memstatistics-file "file.name";
memstatistics-file "/var/stats/named/bind.mem";

memstatistics-file defines the file.name (a quoted string) to which BIND memory usage statistics will be written when it exits if memstatistics yes; is present (or the -m argument was used to when BIND was loaded). This may be an absolute or relative (to directory) path. If the parameter is not present, the stats are written to named.memstats in the path defined by directory or its default. This statement may only be used in a global options clause.

pid-file

pid-file "path_name" ;
pid-file "bind.pid";

pid-file is a quoted string and defines where the Process Identifier used by BIND is written. It may be defined using an absolute path or path relative to the directory statement. If not present, it is distribution or OS specific, typically /var/run/named/named.pid. The appropriate permissions may be required to allow this file to be written. This option can only be defined in the global options clause.

port

port ip_port ;
port 1137;

ip_port defines on which port BIND will provide UDP and TCP services. The default is 53. This option is intended primarily for testing; setting it to a nonstandard value will not allow the server to communicate with normal DNS systems. It can also be used in stealth configuration between internal and external name servers to further disguise traffic that passes through a firewall (see Chapter 7). The option can only appear in the global options clause and must come before any other option that defines ports or IP addresses.

preferred-glue

preferred-glue A | AAAA;
preferred-glue AAAA;

preferred-glue defines the order in which glue records will be listed in the ADDITIONAL SECTION of the response (see Chapter 15) if they contain both IPv4 (A) and IPv6 (AAAA) RRs. If no order is specified, they will be listed in the order they appear in the zone file. This statement may be used in a view or global options clause.

querylog

querylog (yes | no) ;
querylog yes;

querylog may override the setting of the category statement of the logging clause and controls whether query logging should be started when named (BIND) starts. If querylog is not specified, query logging is controlled by the rndc querylog command or the logging category queries. This statement may only be used in a global options clause.

recursing-file

recursing-file "file.name";
recursing-file "bind.stats";

recursing-file defines the file.name to which data will be written when the command rndc recursing is issued. May be an absolute or relative (to directory) path. If the parameter is not present, the information is written to the file named.recursing in the path defined by directory or its default. This statement may only be used in a global options clause.

request-nsid

request-nsid (yes | no);
request-nsid yes;

Name servers are frequently used with anycasting. Sometimes it's useful or important to know which name server instance is being accessed. The Name Server ID (NSID) is the current method defined in RFC 5001. request-nsid (default is no) determines if the server will respond to a query with OPCODE = 3 (see the "DNS Message Header" section in Chapter 15) that requests an Name Server ID (NSID). If set to yes, the server will respond either with the value set by the server-id statement or, in its absence, with the servers hostname obtained by the gethostname() library call. This statement may be used in a options or view clause.

reserved-sockets

reserved-sockets number;
reserved-sockets 256;

reserved-sockets defines the number of TCP actions the server may handle at any one time, which includes listening (listen_on) and internal uses as well as active connections. The value must always be greater tcp-clients (or its default). The range allowed is from 128 to 128 less than the maximum number supported by the OS platform or that specified by the -S argument when named loads. The default value is 512. This statement should rarely need to be used; in fact, it's likely to be made obsolete. It may only be used in a global options clause.

server-id

server-id ("id-string" | none | hostname);
server-id "123";

server-id specifies the ID the server will return in response to a query for ID.SERVER with type TXT, under class CHAOS (CH) using a command such as dig @192.168.2.3 id.server txt ch. The ID is also returned when a NSID query with opcode = 3 (see Chapter 15) is received. The value id-string sets the ID to the defined (arbitrary) text string that may be used to identify the host in some useful way, the value hostname will cause the host name to be returned (obtained using a gethostname() library call). The objective of this feature is to allow identification of which host is responding in situations where anycast is being used. Specifying none (the default) disables processing of the queries (they return REFUSED). This statement may only be used in a global options clause.

stacksize

stacksize size_in_bytes;
stacksize 20k;

stacksize defines the maximum size in bytes (may take the case-insensitive short forms K, M, or G) of the stack memory used by the server. The default is no limit on stacksize. This statement may only be used in a global options clause.

statistics-file

```
statistics-file "file-name";
statistics-file "/var/stats/names/bind.stats";
```

statistics-file defines the file-name to which data will be written when the command rndc stats is issued. This may be an absolute or relative (to directory) path. If the parameter is not present, the information is written to the file named.stats in the path defined by directory or its default. The statistics-channels clause, described earlier in the chapter, provides an alternative and more efficient method of achieving the same result. This statement may only be used in a global options clause.

tcp-clients

```
tcp-clients number ;
tcp-clients 77;
```

By default, DNS uses UDP port 53 for queries, but allows both TCP and UDP. The tcp-clients statement allows the user to define the maximum number of TCP connections that may be supported. The BIND 9 default is 100. The option can only appear in the global options clause.

tcp-listen-queue

```
tcp-listen-queue number;
tcp-listen-queue 7;
```

tcp-listen-queue defines how many TCP listen operations are queued for incoming zone transfers. The default and minimum is 3; any value lower than this will be silently raised to 3. Depending on OS features, this also controls how many TCP connections will be queued in kernel space waiting for some data before being passed to TCP accept. This statement may only be used in a global options clause.

try-tcp-refresh

```
try-tcp-refresh ( yes | no );
try-tcp-refresh no;
```

When a slave server attempts to refresh the zone after it has detected a changed serial number (sn) field in the zone's SOA RR (see the "SOA Record" section in Chapter 13), it will use UDP. If this fails, it can retry using UDP or try using TCP. The try-tcp-refresh statement when set to yes (the default) allows the retry to use TCP; when set to no, it forces the retry to use UDP. This statement may be used in a global options, view, or zone clause.

version

```
version version_string ;
version "No Way";
```

The version statement defines the text that will be returned to a version.bind query for the CHAOS (CH) class only. The default is for BIND to return its real version number. This information, however, is easily discovered using the dig version.bind txt ch command, so by adding version_string and a quoted string such as "get lost", it may be possible to avoid exploitation of known weaknesses of specific software versions. This option can only be defined in the global options clause.

zone-statistics

```
zone-statistics ( yes | no ) ;
zone-statistics no;
```

zone-statistics defines whether zone statistics will be maintained. The default is no. The zone statistics may be accessed using rndc stats. This statement may be used in a view, zone, or global options clause.

zero-nosoa-ttl, zero-no-soa-ttl-cache

```
zero-no-soa-ttl ( yes | no ) ;
zero-no-soa-ttl-cache ( yes | no ) ;
zero-no-soa-ttl no ;
zero-no-soa-ttl-cache yes
```

When an NXDOMAIN (name does not exist) response is sent from an authoritative server, a copy of the domain's SOA is supplied in the ADDITIONAL SECTION (see Chapter 16). This feature is designed, among other uses, to allow the zone administrator to be contacted using the mail-address (RNAME) field from the SOA RR (see the "SOA Record" section in Chapter 13). NXDOMAIN responses are now cached for up to 3 hours (defined by the value of the nx field of the SOA). However, if the query that fails NXDOMAIN was for an SOA RR, this is most likely an error (an SOA query can only fail for a non-apex name). The zero-no-soa-ttl statement when set to yes (default) instructs an authoritative server to set the TTL value of the SOA RR in the response to 0 (which prevents caching at the resolver). The zero-no-soa-ttl-cache statement when set to yes instructs a resolver to assume the TTL of the SOA RR, in this case, is 0 (inhibiting caching). The default for zero-no-soa-ttl-cache is no, which means that if a non-zero TTL is present on the SOA RR, the response will be cached. The zero-no-soa-ttl statement may be used in a view, zone, or global options clause. The zero-no-soa-ttl-cache statement may only be used in a options or view clause.

BIND Performance Statements

This section describes statements that affect BIND 9 throughput and performance or memory utilization.

acache-cleaning-interval, acache-enable, max-acache-size

```
acache-cleaning-interval minutes;
acache-enable yes | no;
max-acache-size bytes;
acache-cleaning-interval 30;
acache-enable yes;
max-acache-size 5m;
```

These statements are only relevant for authoritative name servers. They control the operation of the additional cache (*acache*) that is used to speed up population of the ADDITIONAL SECTION in a query response (see the "DNS Message Formats" section in Chapter 15). The most significant performance effect will be in cases where there are large numbers of delegations (NS RRs) and their associated glue records (A or AAAA RRs) as in, for example, TLD servers. However, user domain servers that have significant numbers of subdomains may also see some performance improvements. In all other cases, minimal, if any, improvements will be obtained by using these statements.

The *acache* feature is activated by acache-enable (defaults to no). max-cache-size allows a hard limit to be placed on the amount of memory used for the *acache* and is defined in bytes but may take the case insensitive values k (1024 bytes) or m (1,048,576 bytes). acache-cleaning-interval defines the time in minutes (default is 60) between cache cleaning using a Least Recently Used (LRU) algorithm. When acache-enable yes; is present, the order of RRs is fixed, meaning that the setting of any rrset-order statement (default is cyclic) is ignored for the ADDITIONAL SECTION only. The statements may appear in either an options or view clause. Where multiple view clauses appear and acache-enable yes; is defined in a global options clause, each view creates a separate *acache*.

attach-cache

```
attache-cache cache-name;
attach-cache one-cache;
```

These statements are only relevant when one or more view clauses are present in a named.conf file. By default, each view maintains its own cache, which can cause significant memory usage. The attach-cache statement allows one or more caches to be combined. However superficially attractive such a policy may appear at first glance, extreme caution should be exercised before using this statement since the law of unintended consequences can easily arise. Consider a multi-homed server providing resolver (caching name server) services to two networks, each connected to a separate interface. The attraction of attach-cache is that having queried for, say, the address of a popular service on one network, it is immediately available to the other network, which would not be case otherwise—a separate query would result. However, the IP addresses of the hosts on both networks will also be present in the common cache and therefore are discoverable by the other network—and indeed, depending on naming policies, may even clash. Imaginative readers may care to consider even more doom-laden scenarios.

Assuming that all possible consequences have been considered and found to be benign, the attach-cache statement may be used in either a global options clause or a view clause. When used in an options clause, the cache-name parameter is entirely arbitrary or may be defaulted to the view-name when used only in the view clause. The following two fragments are functionally identical; the choice between the two forms may be either a matter of policy or it may be driven by a fetish for, or aversion to, typing:

```
options {
                ….
                attach-cache "big-cache";   // globally assigned cache name
                ….
};
view "one"{
                attach-cache "big-cache";
                ….
};
view "two"{
                attach-cache "big-cache";
                ….
};
```

Alternative usage, functionally equivalent:

```
options {
                ....
};
view "one"{
                        ....
};
view "two"{
                        attach-cache "one";  // cache name defaults to view name
                        ....
};
```

edns-udp-size

edns-udp-size size-in-bytes ;
edns-udp-size 1460;

edns-udp-size specifies the size-in-bytes that the server will advertise for an EDNS UDP buffer and defines the maximum incoming UDP block size that the server will accept. Valid values are 1024 to 4096; values outside this range will be silently adjusted. The default value is 4096. EDNS is primarily used with DNSSEC transactions, which typically contain 1500 to 2500 byte responses. The normal reason for changing the default size is to bypass a firewall or DNS proxy limitation. However, if the user defined value is smaller than a typical packet size, the server will use TCP for these larger blocks, which significantly slows down throughput and response times. This statement may be used in a view, server or global options clause. See also max-udp-size.

max-udp-size

max-udp-size bytes
max-udp-size 4096;

max-udp-size sets the maximum UDP block size in bytes the server will send (edns-udp-size sets maximum UDP block size the server can receive). The range allowed is 512 to 4096 and the default is 4096. The only reason not to use the default is if there are size limitations in firewalls or DNS proxies. If the size limit is lower than a typical send block, the server will use TCP for these larger blocks and thus slow down transaction response time and server throughput significantly. This statement may be used in a view, server or global options clause. See also edns-udp-size.

minimal-responses

minimal-responses (yes | no) ;
minimal-responses yes ;

If minimal-responses is set to yes, the server will only add records to the authority and additional data sections (see Chapter 15) when they are required by the protocol, specifically delegations and negative responses. Since the effect of this is to reduce the data volumes sent, it can significantly improve the performance of the server. The BIND default is no. This statement may be used in a view or global zone clause.

BIND Query Statements

This section describes all the statements available that relate to or control queries.

additional-from-auth, additional-from-cache

```
additional-from-auth ( yes | no ) ;
additional-from-cache ( yes | no ) ;
additional-from-auth yes ;
additional-from-cache no ;
```

additional-from-auth and additional-from-cache control when ADDITIONAL SECTION information is populated from other zones for which this server is also Authoritative (master or slave) and are relevant when a zone has additional (out-of-zone; sometimes called *out-of-bailiwick*) data or when following CNAME (or DNAME) RRs. Assuming this name server is Authoritative (master or slave) for example.com and example.net, then references between these zones is controlled by the use of the additional-from-auth statement while a reference to, say, example.org (for which this server is not Authoritative) is controlled by additional-from-cache. These options are used when configuring authoritative-only (noncaching) servers and are only effective when recursion no; is specified in a global options or view clause. The default for both statements is yes. The statements may be defined in a view or global options clause. The behavior is defined by Table 12–11.

Table 12–11. additional-from Statement Behavior

auth	cache	BIND Behavior
yes	yes	This is the default behavior. Assume a query for the MX RR for example.com. If this MX RR points to mail.example.net *and* this server is also Authoritative for example.net, the ADDITIONAL SECTION will be populated with the A or AAAA RRs from mail.example.net (additional-from-auth controlled). However, if the MX RR points to, say, mail.example.org (for which this server is not Authoritative) then the ADDITIONAL SECTION will *only* be populated if it exists in the cache (controlled by additional-from-cache).
no	no	Assume a query for the MX RR for example.com. If this MX RR points to mail.example.net *and* this server is also Authoritative for example.net, the ADDITIONAL SECTION will *not* be populated with the A or AAAA RRs from mail.example.net (additional-from-auth controlled). Similarly, if the MX RR points to, say, mail.example.org (for which this server is not Authoritative) then the ADDITIONAL SECTION will *not* be populated even if the data exists in the cache (controlled by additional-from-cache).
yes	no	Assume a query for the MX RR for example.com. If this MX RR points to mail.example.net *and* this server is also Authoritative for example.net, the ADDITIONAL SECTION will be populated with the A or AAAA RRs from mail.example.net (additional-from-auth controlled). However, if the MX RR points to, say, mail.example.org (for which this server is not Authoritative), the ADDITIONAL SECTION will *not* be populated even if it exists in the cache (controlled by additional-from-cache).

auth	cache	BIND Behavior
no	yes	Assume a query for the MX RR for example.com. If this MX RR points to mail.example.net *and* this server is also Authoritative for example.net then the ADDITIONAL SECTION will *not* be populated with the A or AAAA RRs from mail.example.net (additional-from-auth controlled). However, if the MX RR points to, say, mail.example.org (for which this server is not Authoritative), the ADDITIONAL SECTION will *only* be populated if it exists in the cache (controlled by additional-from-cache).

Never returning information in the ADDITIONAL SECTION (both statements are no) reduces the amount of data sent by the Authoritative name server and can thus have a significant effect on query throughput. However, this is somewhat misleading because if the data is available from this authoritative server, it will immediately result in an additional query from the resolver for the additional information—unless the resolver has previously cached the data.

Prior to BIND 9.7 referral behavior was also controlled by additional-from-cache. Thus, if the server was Authoritative for example.com and it received a query for any zone for which it was not Authoritative, it would provide a referral to the root (since this data would always be available in the cache). This root referral also occurs if the query was upward; for example, the same server received a query for .com or . (the root). Since such a root referral could trivially be used in an DoS amplification attack, BIND 9 now responds with REFUSED status to all such queries when recursion no; is present, irrespective of the setting of additional-from-cache. These statements may appear in a options or a view clause.

allow-query, allow-query-on

```
allow-query { address_match_list };
allow-query-on { address_match_list };
allow-query {!10.0.3/24;}; // allow queries from all IPs except 10.0.3.0 to 10.0.3.255
allow-query-on {localhost;}; // only allow queries arriving on 127.0.0.1
```

allow-query defines an address_match_list of hosts (source IP addresses) that are allowed to issue queries to this server. If not specified, all hosts are allowed to make queries. allow-query-on defines an address_match_list of server IP addresses that are allowed to receive queries. This statement allows an alternative form of control without having to know all the permitted IP addresses. Assume that the name server is multihomed with one interface, say 192.168.2.2, connected to the local LAN and another interface, say 10.0.0.5, used for external access. Defining allow-query-on {192.168.2.2;localhost;}; permits only queries arriving at the local LAN interface and 127.0.0.1, all others will receive a REFUSED status.. When used to control recursive queries (in a resolver configuration), these statements together with allow-query-cache, allow-query-cache-on, allow-recursion and allow-recursion-on determine the behavior. These statements may be used in a view, zone, or global options clause.

allow-query-cache, allow-query-cache-on

```
allow-query-cache { address_match_list };
allow-query-cache-on { address_match_list };
allow-query-cache {10.0.2/24;}; // allow cache access to queries from 10.0.2.0 to 10.0.2.255
allow-query-cache-on {192.168.2.1}; // only allow cache access to queries on 192.168.2.1
```

In order to make it more difficult to unwittingly configure an OPEN resolver (see "Resolvers" in Chapter 8) these two statements, introduced in BIND 9.4, control access to the cache and default to very restrictive values. Both statements are only relevant to resolvers; that is, a name server with recursion yes; specified or no recursion statement present (it defaults to yes).

allow-query-cache defines an address_match_list of hosts that are allowed to issue queries to this server that will cause a cache access; in essence, this defines those hosts that are allowed to issue recursive queries. If allow-query-cache is not present, only localnets (see "BIND address_match_list" in this chapter), hosts are allowed to issue recursive queries *unless* an allow-recursion statement is present, in which case its values are assumed. All other hosts will receive REFUSED status.

allow-query-cache-on defines an address_match_list of server IP addresses that are allowed to receive queries that access the cache (recursive queries). This statement allows an alternative form of control without having to know all the permitted IP addresses. Assume that the name server (resolver) is multihomed with one interface, say 192.168.2.2, connected to the local LAN and another interface, say 10.0.05, used for external access. Using allow-query-cache-on {192.168.2.2;}; permits only recursive queries arriving at this interface and the loopback address (127.0.0.1). All recursive queries arriving at any other interface will receive REFUSED status. If allow-query-cache-on is not defined, recursive queries are allowed on all server interfaces, including localhost (127.0.0.1), as limited by an allow-query-cache statement.

The intent of allow-query-cache is laudable (to stop open resolvers), but care must be exercised in its use. Both allow-query-cache and allow-recursion are permitted. This can easily lead to conflicts and should be avoided like the plague unless serious de-bugging is the desired outcome. One of the other statements should be used; in general, because allow-query-cache defaults to the allow-recursion value when present, allow-recursion should be used by preference to control recursive behavior.

allow-query-cache and allow-query-cache-on statements may be used in a view or global options clause.

allow-recursion, allow-recursion-on

allow-recursion { address_match_list };
allow-recursion-on { address_match_list };
allow-recursion {!192.168.2.7; 192.168.2/24;}; // allow 192.168.2.0 to 192.168.2.255 except
192.168.2.7
allow-recursion-on { 10.0.2.1;}; // allow arriving on 10.0.2.1

allow-recursion defines an address_match_list of hosts that are allowed to issue recursive queries to this server. In the absence of any allow-query-cache statement, the address_match_list defined for the allow-recursion statement also permits access to the cache. If both statements are present, inconsistencies can easily arise and this should be avoided. If neither statement is present, the default for allow-query-cache is used (localnets only).

allow-recursion-on defines an address_match_list of server IP addresses on which recursive queries can be received. If the statement is not present, recursive queries are permitted to arrive on any server interface but are subject to the limitations defined by allow-recursion, allow-query-cache, or its default value (localnets only). These statements may be used in a view or global options clause.

auth-nxdomain

auth-nxdomain (yes | no);
auth-nxdomain yes;]

If auth-nxdomain is yes, it allows the server to answer authoritatively (the AA bit is set) on returning NXDOMAIN (domain does not exist) answers. If no (the default), the server will not answer authoritatively. The current setting reverses the BIND 8 default. This statement may only be used in a global options clause.

blackhole

```
blackhole { address_match_list };
blackhole { none; };
```

blackhole defines an address_match_list of hosts that the server will *not* respond to nor answer queries for. This statement has the same effect as a series of server clauses with a bogus yes; statement but is significantly shorter! The default is none (all hosts are responded to). This statement may only be used in a global options clause.

clients-per-query, max-clients-per-query

```
clients-per-query number ;
max-clients-per-query number;
client-per-query 10;
max clients-per-query 20;
```

These statements are only applicable to resolvers and control the minimum (clients-per-query) and maximum (max-clients-per-query) number of queries for the same name that may be outstanding before being rejected (with SERVFAIL) by the name server. The default for clients-per-query is 10. Setting it to 0 indicates that no limits (neither min nor max) are applied and any number of queries for the same name may be outstanding up to the limit set by recursive-clients or its default value. max-clients-per-query defaults to 100. If set to 0, no upper limit is applied other than that imposed by recursive-clients or its default. These statements may appear in an options or a view clause.

delegation-only

```
delegation-only ( yes | no ) ;
delegation no;
```

delegation-only applies to hint and stub zones only, and if set to yes, indicates the zone will only respond with delegations (or referrals). (See the type statement for more information.) The default is no. This statement may only be used in a zone clause.

forward

```
forward ( only | first );
forward only;
```

forward is only relevant in conjunction with a valid forwarders statement. If set to only, the server will only forward queries; if set to first (the default), it will send the queries to the forwarder (defined by the forwarders statement); and if not answered, it will issue queries directly. This statement may be used in a zone, view, or global zone clause.

forwarders

```
forwarders { ip_addr [port ip_port] ; [ ip_addr [port ip_port] ; ... ] };
forwarders { 10.2.3.4; 192.168.2.5;};
```

forwarders defines a list of IP address(es) (and optional port numbers) to which queries will be forwarded. It is only relevant if used with the forward statement. This statement may be used in a zone, view, or global zone clause. See also "Forwarding (a.k.a. Proxy, Client, Remote) DNS Server" in Chapter 7.

query-source, query-source-v6

```
query-source [ address ( ip_addr | * ) ] [ port ( ip_port | * ) ];
query-source address 192.168.2.3 ;
query-source-v6 [ address ( ip_addr | * ) ] [ port ( ip_port | * ) ];
query-source-v6 address  * port 1188;
```

query-source and query-source-v6 define the IP address (IPv4 or IPv6) and optional port to be used as the source for outgoing queries from the server and are normally relevant only on multihomed servers (servers with multiple IP addresses or interfaces). The BIND default is any server interface IP address and a random unprivileged port (* port *;). The optional port field only controls UDP operations (not TCP) and should never be set to an explicit value to avoid cache poisoning attacks (see the discussion at use-v4-udp-ports and use-v6-udp-ports for details). Instead, the value port * should always be used to allow maximum port randomization. avoid-v4-udp-ports and avoid-v6-udp-ports can be used to prevent selection of defined ports. This statement may be used in a view, server, or global options clause.

recursion

```
recursion ( yes | no );
recursion no;
```

If recursion is set to yes (the default), the server will always provide *recursive query* behavior if requested by the client (resolver). If recursion is set to no, the server will only provide *iterative query* behavior. If the answer to the query already exists in the cache, it will be returned irrespective of the value of this statement but subject to any limits defined by allow-query-cache or allow-recursion statements. This statement essentially controls caching behavior in the server. The allow-recursion statement and the view clause provide fine-grained control over recursion services. This statement may be used in a view or global options clause.

recursive-clients

```
recursive-clients number;
recursive-clients 20;
```

Defines the number of simultaneous recursive lookups the server will perform on behalf of its clients. The default is 1000; that is, it will support 1000 simultaneous recursive lookup requests, which should be enough for most purposes! This statement may only be used in a global options clause.

root-delegation-only

```
root-delegation-only [ exclude { "domain_name"; ... } ];
root-delegation-only exclude { "com"; "net" };
```

If present, root-delegation-only indicates that all responses will be referrals or delegations. The optional exclude list consists of one or more domain_name (a quoted string) parameters. This statement is intended to be used for root and TLD domains (gTLDs and ccTLDs), but the delegation-only statement may be used to create the same effect for specific zones. This statement may be used in a view or global options clause.

rrset-order

```
rrset-order { order_spec ; [ order_spec ; ... ]
rrset-order { type A order cyclic; };
```

rrset-order defines the order in which RRsets are returned in the ANSWER and ADDITIONAL SECTION of responses. This statement applies to any RR type in which the records are similar (their name, class, and type are the same). The default is cyclic. The rrset-order defines the order in which similar RRs are returned from the name server. The sortlist statement controls the order in which the RRs are returned to a client, for instance, a resolver. An order_spec is defined as follows

```
[ class class_name ][ type type_name ][ name "domain_name"]
     order ordering
```

where class_name is the record class, such as IN (default is any); type_name is the RR type (defaults to any); and domain_name limits the statement to a specific domain suffix and defaults to root (all domains). ordering may take one of the following values: fixed—records are returned in the order they are defined in the zone file; random—records are returned in a random order; cyclic—records are returned in a round-robin fashion. fixed needs BIND to be built using the configure option --enable-fixed-rrset which is not the done on standard BIND packages for either Ubuntu or FreeBSD. For practical purposes, only random and cyclic ordering values are available. See also the acache-enable statement under "BIND Performance Statements" for additional restrictions. Only one such statement may appear in any clause—the last defined will be used in the case of multiple statements. This statement may be used in a view or global options clause.

The following example shows that MX RRs for example.com only will be returned in random order; all others responses will use the default cyclic order:

```
rrset-order { type MX name "example.com" order random; order cyclic;};
```

sortlist

The sortlist statement is used to order RRsets for use by a resolver (a client). It is the client-side equivalent of the rrset-order statement and can work *against* the rrset-order statement when being used as part of a load-balancing configuration: rrset-order carefully delivers RRsets in its order of preference to a remote resolver that may then proceed to reorder them with a sortlist statement when responding to its client resolver. The sortlist statement attempts to order returned records based on the IP address of the client that initiated the request.

sortlist Statement Syntax

```
sortlist { address_match_list };
sortlist { {10.2/16; } ;};
```

The address_match_list is used very differently from the way it is used in all other statements; it assumes that each element of the address_match_list is itself an address_match_list, that is, it is a nested address_match_list and is enclosed in braces. Processing depends on whether there is one or more than one element in the nested address_match_list. In the simple case of one element, as in the preceding example, if the client's IP address matches 10.2/16 (that is, lies in the range 10.2.0.0 to 10.2.255.255) and there are any IP addresses in the response in the same range, they will be the first records supplied in the response. Any remaining records will be sorted according to the rrset-order (default is cyclic). If no match is found, the records are simply returned in the order defined by the rrset-order or its default value (cyclic). If two elements are provided in the address_match_list, then the second element is assumed to be an ordered list of preferences. This is best illustrated by an example. Assume the zone example.com has a zone file with multiple A RRs for lots.example.com:

```
// zone file example.com
$ORIGIN example.com.
lots    IN  A  192.168.3.6
        IN  A  192.168.4.5
        IN  A  192.168.5.5
        IN  A  10.2.4.5
        IN  A  172.17.4.5
```

The client-side server has a sortlist statement, as shown here:

```
options {
    ....
    sortlist {
    {// 1st preference block start
     192.168.4/24;  // 1st client IP selection matches any of these
     {10.2/16;    // return any of these response IPs as 1st preference
      172.17.4/24;  // 2nd preference
     };
    }; // end first block
    { // second preference block
     192.168.5/24;  // 2nd client IP selection matches any of these
     {192.168.4/24;    // return any of these response IPs as 1st preference
      172.18.4/24;  // 2nd preference
      10.2/16;  // 3rd preference
     };
    }; // end second block
   }; // end sortlist

};
```

If the client, say a resolver with an IP address of 192.168.5.33, issues an A query for lots.example.com, then the RRs will be returned in the following order:

```
192.168.4.5
10.2.4.5
192.168.3.6
192.168.5.5
172.17.4.5
```

The preceding order is computed using the following process: The top level of the address_match_list is searched against the client IP (192.168.5.33) address and matches the IP address in the sortlist statement with a comment beginning with "2nd client IP selection"; the nested address_match_list of the second block is then treated as an ordered list for the A query result RRset IPs (not the client IP). The IP address in the sortlist statement with a comment ending with "1st preference" matches, so 192.168.4.5 becomes first in the returned list. The IP address in the sortlist statement with a comment of "2nd preference" does not match any of the returned IPs. The IP address in the sortlist statement with a comment of "3rd preference" matches, so 10.2.4.5 becomes second in the returned list. The remaining three RRs do not match, so they are returned according to the rrset-order statement or its default (cyclic) if not defined. The sortlist statement may be used in a view or global options clause.

BIND Security Statements

This section describes all the statements that relate to or control security.

algorithm

```
algorithm algorithm-name;
algorithm hmac-md5;
```

The algorithm statement defines the shared secret algorithm being used and may only take the value hmac-md5. The algorithm statement is only used in a key clause.

allow-update

```
allow-update { address_match_list };
allow-update { !172.22.0.0/16;};
```

allow-update defines an address_match_list of hosts that are allowed to submit dynamic updates for master zones, and thus this statement enables DDNS. The default in BIND 9 is to disallow updates from all hosts; that is, DDNS is *disabled* by default. This statement may be specified in zone, view, or an options clause. This statement is mutually exclusive with update-policy and applies to master zones only. The example shows DDNS for three zones: the first disables DDNS explicitly, the second uses an IP-based list, and the third references a key clause. The allow-update in the first zone clause could have been omitted since it is the default behavior. Many people like to be cautious in case the default mode changes.

```
// named.conf fragment
// key clause is shown only for illustration and would
// normally be included in the named.conf file
key "update-key" {
    ....
};
zone "example.net" in{
    type master;
    allow-update {none;}; // no DDNS by default
    ....
};
....
zone "example.com" in{
....type master;
    allow-update {10.0.1.2;}; // DDNS this host only
    ....
};
zone "example.org" in{
    type master;
    allow-update {keys "update-key";};
    ....
};
```

In the example.org zone, the reference to the key clause "update-key" implies that the application that performs the update, say nsupdate, is using TSIG and must also have the same shared secret *with the same key-name*. This process is described in Chapter 10.

auto-dnssec

```
auto-dnssec ( allow | maintain| create | off );
auto-dnssec maintain ;
```

BIND 9 supports a number of different DNSSEC models (see the "BIND Zone Signing Models" section in Chapter 11) involving more, or less, user involvement. auto-dnssec represents the highest level of automation and assumes that the maintained zone will be managed using DDNS. The statement may take the values allow, maintain, create, and off (the default). allow will use the keys located in a managed-keys-directory or a key-directory (or their defaults) to sign the zone when prompted by the user with an rndc sign zone command (see the "rndc Commands" section in Chapter 9). maintain will automatically sign the zone at appropriate intervals based on the values contained in the metadata of the keysets (see the –"dnssec-keygen Metadata Format" section in Chapter 9). The user must manually add (using dnssec-keygen) and revoke (using dnssec-revoke) keys in the defined key directory but it does not require initiating the zone signing process. create allows BIND to add and revoke keys automatically for the zone. No manual intervention is required. The auto-dnssec statement may be used in a options, view, or zone clause.

bindkeys-file

```
bindkeys-file "filename/or/path/and/filename";
bindkeys-file "/etc/named/working/root.keys";
```

By default, BIND 9 reads a file that is assumed to be in /etc/bind.keys (but the directory part may be changed by managed-keys-directory) containing a managed-keys clause (described earlier in the chapter) currently for the dlv.isc.org DNSSEC DLV site. The bindkeys-file statement allows the name of this file to be changed or a full path, including filename, as shown above. In either case, a quoted string format must be used. This statement may only be used in a options clause.

deny-answer-addresses, deny-answer-aliases

```
deny-answer-addresses { address_match_list } [except from { namelist } ];
deny-answer-aliases { namelist } [except from { namelist } ];
deny-answer-addresses {10./24;192.168/16;172.16/20} except from {example.com};
deny-answer-aliases {example.net;example.org} except from {example.com};
```

These statements are only applicable to resolvers; they allow them to filter information in the ANSWER SECTION of a response in order to prevent what is called a "rebinding" attack (in which a specially crafted web page coupled with a malicious authoritative server can cause a resolver to unwittingly participate in a DoS attack, including servers located on private network addresses (typically RFC 1918 addresses) behind a firewall or NAT gateway). The solution provided by the two statements allows the resolver to filter out RFC 1918 or any other known-to-be-invalid set of IP addresses from received answers since these should never be returned from any authoritative public server.

deny-answer-addresses allows an address_match_list of IP addresses to be filtered from the ANSWER SECTION from all domains. The optional except from parameter allows a namelist (a semicolon separated list of domain names) to be excluded from the checks. The example shown above disallows all private RFC 1918 IPv4 addresses from all responses except from example.com, which is assumed to be an internal domain, in which case a RFC 1918 address may be valid.

deny-answer-aliases performs the same function for CNAME and DNAME RRs appearing in the ANSWER SECTION. The example above disallows a CNAME or DNAME RR whose right-hand name contains either the name example.net or example.org. All names below this level are also disallowed; for instance, joe.example.net and fred.sub.example.org will also be disallowed by the example statement. Answers removed using either or both of these statements are not cached, and if the resulting ANSWER SECTION is empty, then SERVFAIL status is returned. As with all such solutions, if not carefully implemented, the cure can cause more problems than the disease. Multiple deny-answer-addresses and deny-answer-aliases statements may appear in a global options or view clause.

disable-algorithms

disable-algorithms domain {alg; [alg;]};
disable-algorithms example.net {hmac-md5; rsamd5;};

The disable-algorithms statement may be used to disable specific cryptographic algorithms used with the defined domain. The alg field (one or more is allowed in each statement) may take the case-insensitive values hmac-md5, rsamd5, rsasha1, dsa, rsasha256, rsasha512, nsec3rsasha1, nsec3dsa, or dh. Multiple disable-algorithm statements may appear in a global options or view clause.

dnssec-accept-expired

dnssec-accept-expired (yes | no);
dnssec-accept-expired yes;

dnssec-accept-expired is applicable only to validating resolvers (see Chapter 11) and takes the default value no. When a DNSSEC zone is signed, all RRsets have signatures in the form of RRSIG RRs (see the "RRSIG Record" section in Chapter 13). All RRSIG RRs have a signature expiration time. If the zone is not resigned before the signatures expire, it will not validate. A validating resolver will classify any responses from the zone as bogus and will typically return SERVFAIL to the client (default BIND behavior). The zone becomes unreachable (in the jargon, it becomes a *dark zone*) when accessed through a validating resolver—a fairly serious situation for all concerned. Under normal circumstances, signatures should not expire; the zone owner's normal procedures or DNSSEC tools should not allow such an event. However, it could happen; mistakes are made; tools have bugs. The dnssec-accept-expired yes; statement will allow the validating server to accept expired signatures that in all other respects pass the validation process (they cryptographically validate). While this may seem like a neighborly act, it does open the validating resolver to the possibility of a zone replay attack, which may be even more serious than the dark zone problem, which can be fixed. It should be considered carefully before being used; however, as a temporary feature used during internal DNSSEC testing, it may have a role to play. This statement may be used in a view or global options clause.

dnssec-dnskey-kskonly

dnssec-dnskey-kskonly (yes | no);
dnssec-dnskey-kskonly yes;

dnssec-dnskey-kskonly only applies when update-check-ksk yes; is set or omitted (the default is yes). It is otherwise ignored. When both update-check-ksk and this statement are set to yes, then when a DDNS zone is signed, any KSKs will only be used to sign the DNSKEY RRset (as normal) but ZSKs will *only* sign all other RRsets and not the DNSKEY RRset (not normal but standard-compliant nonetheless). This is equivalent to using dnssec-signzone with the -x argument. It has the effect of removing arguably unnecessary signatures, reducing both CPU use (important when online DDNS signing is being used), and reducing the number of RRs sent during DNSSEC query responses. If this statement is no (its default) then KSKs will only sign the DNSKEY RRset, as normal, but ZSKs will sign all zone RRsets *and* the DNSKEY RRset. This statement may be used in an options, view, or zone clause; consequently, care must be taken that the scope of this statement is covered by an update-check-ksk statement:

```
options{
    ….
    update-check-ksk no;
    ….
};
zone "example.com{
    ….
    dnssec-dnskeys-kskonly yes;   // ignored - needs an update-ckeck-ksk in this zone clause
    …
};
```

dnssec-enable

```
dnssec-enable (yes | no);
dnssec-enable yes;
```

From BIND 9.5 onward, DNSSEC features are enabled by default. dnssec-enable yes; enables any secure (cryptographic) operations such as TSIG, TKEY, SIG(0), or DNSSEC. Any name server with dnssec-enable yes; advertises its ability to support secure operations by including an OPT meta-RR (or pseudo-RR) in the ADDITIONAL SECTION of any query and implicitly enables EDNS0 (RFC 2671) features. If DNS security features are not required, they must be explicitly disabled using a dnssec-enable no; statement. This statement may be used in a view or global options clause. See also the dnssec-validation statement.

dnssec-lookaside

```
dnssec-lookaside auto | domain trust-anchor dlv-domain
dnssec-lookaside .com trust-anchor dlv.isc.org;
```

The dnssec-lookaside statement is used with the experimental DNSSEC Lookaside Validation service and provides an alternative method for verifying a chain of trust using experimental DLV RRs. The objective of the DLV is to provide equivalent capabilities to a signed TLD zone *without* the registry operator having to sign the TLD zone. Any secure zone that lies at or below domain and that does not have a local trusted-keys clause may interrogate the dlv-domain to search for a DLV RR (which is similar in every respect to a DS RR). To verify the dlv-domain, a trusted anchor must be present (in a trusted-keys clause) for this dlv-domain. The dlv-domain may also be specified using the -l option to the dnssec-signzone command (see Chapter 9) to generate DLV RRs when the zone is signed. In the preceding example statement, any .com domain that does not have a configured trusted anchor will interrogate the domain dlv.isc.org.

When set to the value auto (assuming dnssec-enable yes; and dnssec-validation yes; are set; both default to yes) BIND will use the managed-keys clause contained in the file bind.keys to start DNSSEC validation of all queries using the DLV service at dlv.isc.org. Neither Ubuntu nor FreeBSD install the bind.keys file using their standard packages; however, BIND contains a compiled-in version of the managed-keys clause contained in this file. This statement may be used in a view or global options clause. DLV is explained further in Chapter 11.

dnssec-must-be-secure

```
dnssec-must-be-secure domain (yes | no);
dnssec-must-be-secure example.com yes;
```

The dnssec-must-be-secure statement indicates whether domain must be secure or not. If the yes option is defined, domain must be signed and must have a trusted anchor (in a local trusted-keys clause) or a verifiable chain of trust (through a DS RR at the parent), or dnssec-lookaside must be active at or above domain. The default is no. This statement may be used in a view or global options clause.

dnssec-secure-to-insecure

```
dnssec-secure-to-insecure (yes | no);
dnssec-secure-to-insecure yes;
```

The dnssec-secure-to-insecure statement only applies to DDNS signed zones. It has a default of no which indicates that the zone will remain signed even if all the DNSKEY RRs at the apex are deleted (using nsupdate or a similar tool). It is assumed that at some future time a new DNSKEY RR will be added that will immediately cause the zone to be signed appropriately with the new key(s). If set to yes and all DNSKEY RRs at the zone apex are deleted, the zone will be unsigned (it will become insecure); this will include removal of all NSEC chains. However, if the zone was signed with NSEC3 (see Chapter 11), then to remove the NSEC3 chains will also require the user to delete the NSE3PARAM RR at the zone apex (see Chapter 13). This statement may be used in an options, view, or zone clause.

dnssec-validation

```
dnssec-validation (yes | no);
dnssec-validation no;
```

dnssec-validation is applicable only to resolvers and is used in conjunction with dnssec-enable. By default, dnssec-validation yes; is assumed if either dnssec-enable yes; is specified or is not present (it defaults to yes). When both statements are set (or defaulted), the resolver will use any trusted-key or managed-key clause to cryptographically validate any signed zone (see Chapter 11). BIND distributes a standard managed-keys clause in the file bind.keys currently for use with the ISC DLV service, though this may change in the future. Neither Ubuntu Server 10.04 nor FreeBSD install this file as standard and under these circumstances the default setting is relatively benign. If even a modest overhead is unacceptable, for example, on an authoritative only server with no out-of-zone references, the feature may be explicitly disabled using a dnssec-validation no; statement. This statement may be used in a view or global options clause.

key-directory

```
key-directory "path_name";
key-directory "/var/named/keys";
```

key-directory is a quoted string defining the absolute path where the private keys used in the dynamic update (DDNS) of secure (signed) zones may be found. It is only required if this directory is different from that defined by a directory statement. This statement may be used in a zone, view, or global options statement.

managed-keys-directory

```
managed-keys-directory "path/to/directory";
managed-keys-directory "/etc/named/managed-keys";
```

When DNSSEC zones are being managed by RFC 5011 procedures (see the "Key Handling Automation" section in Chapter 11), a special DDNS zone and journal files are created. In non-view configurations, the zone file is called `managed-keys.bind`; when used in a `view` clause, the zone file takes the SHA256 hash of the view name with the suffix `.mkeys`. The default location of these files is the current working directory or that defined by the `directory` statement. However, a suitable directory that requires both read and write permission for the UID of `bind` (named for FreeBSD) may be allocated by the `managed-keys-directory` statement and may be either absolute or relative to the working directory. Further, by default, BIND 9 tries to read a file called `bind.keys`, containing a `managed-keys` clause, that is assumed to be in `/etc` but may be located in the directory defined by `managed-keys-directory`. This statement may only be used in a global `options` clause.

random-device

```
random-device "path_to_device";
random-device "/dev/random";
```

`random-device` defines a source of randomness (or entropy) within the system and defaults to `/dev/random`. This device is needed for DNSSEC operations such as TKEY transactions and dynamic update of signed zones. Operations requiring entropy will fail when the specified source has been exhausted. The `random-device` option takes effect during the initial configuration load at server startup time and is ignored on subsequent reloads. This statement may only be used in a global `options` clause.

secret

```
secret key-data;
secret BLAH….BLAH;
```

The `secret` statement can only appear in a key clause. The `key-data` field contains base64-encoded (RFC 4648) data, frequently referred to as *keying material*, that constitutes the *shared secret*. It is typically produced by the `dnssec-keygen` or `rndc-confgen` utilities (see Chapter 9). Chapter 10 shows how this statement is constructed from the `.private` file created when the `dnssec-keygen` utility is run. This statement contains *extremely sensitive* data, so the `secret` statement and its enclosing key clause is normally placed in a separate file (with minimal read permission), and the `include` statement is used to embed it into the `named.conf` file at run time.

secroots-file

```
secroots-file "file.name";
secroots-file "/var/run/trusted.keys";
```

Defines the file that will be used (absolute or relative path) to write all security root information (trusted anchors) when `rndc secroots` is issued. The default is `named.secroots`. The statement may only appear in an `options` clause.

session-keyfile, session-keyname, session-keyalg

```
session-keyfile "/path/to/file";
session-keyname "key-name";
session-keyalg algorithm;
session-keyfile "/etc/named/dynamic/tsig.key";
```

```
session-keyname "key-to-the-highway";
session-keyalg hmac-md5;
```

Applicable to authoritative master zones only. When DDNS is being used, updates to the zone file may be protected by either allow-update or policy-update statements. policy-update is significantly more secure but requires cryptographic key generation. To simplify the process update-policy local; will automatically generate a suitable TSIG key (see the –"TSIG DDNS Configuration" section in Chapter 10). The key is, by default, placed in /var/run/named/session.key; the key-name is "local-ddns"; and the MAC session algorithm is HMAC-SHA256. All these defaults may be changed. session-keyfile will change the name and/or the location of the default session.key file, as shown in the example above. session-keyname may be used to change the "local-ddns" default to a suitable or interesting name, as also shown in the example above. session-keyalg may be used to change the session MAC algorithm from its default of hmac-sha256 to any of the case-insensitive values hmac-md5, hmac-sha1, hmac-sha224, hmac-sha384, or hmac-sha512. These statements may only be used in a global options clause. See also update-policy statement.

sig-signing-nodes, sig-signing-signatures

```
sig-signing-nodes number;
sig-signing-signatures number;
sig-signing-nodes 50;
sig-signing-signatures 8;
```

When DDNS is being used with DNSSEC signed zones or when zones are being signed on-line using RFC 5011 procedures (see the "Key Handling Automation" section in Chapter 11) and new ZSK keys are introduced, the zone must be resigned. This is a processor-intensive operation that interferes with throughput and performance. To minimize the impact, the signing is done in bite-sized pieces (quaintly called a *quantum* by BIND). The server then returns to normal processing for a period and then returns to the signing task for another bite-sized piece (quantum) and so on until signing is complete. The duration of this quantum is determined by the number of inspected RRs (nodes) and the number of signatures generated. The number of signatures generated is defined by the sig-signing-signatures statement (default is 10) and the number of RRs (nodes) examined is defined by the sig-signing-nodes statement (default is 100). In general, either or both parameters should be reduced if performance seems excessively sluggish. These statements may be used in a zone, view, or global options clause.

sig-signing-type

```
sig-signing-type rr-type-number;
sig-signing-type 65280;
```

When zones are being managed using RFC 5011 procedures (see the "Key Automation" section of Chapter 11), they are controlled using a managed-keys clause. A special DDNS zone is created containing one or more KEYDATA RR(s) that are not currently standardized by any RFC. The KEYDATA RR currently uses a type number of 65535 (see the "User Defined RRs" section of Chapter 13). The sig-signing-type may be used to change the type number if this clashes with an existing RR type and may take any currently unused value from the list maintained at www.iana.org/assignments/dns-parameters . When the KEYDATA RR is defined by an RFC and allocated a specific type value, this statement will become obsolete. This statement may be used in a zone, view, or global options statement.

sig-validity-interval

sig-validity-interval days ;
sig-validity-interval 30 ;

sig-validity-interval specifies the number of days into the future when DNSSEC signatures (using RRSIG RRs) automatically generated as a result of dynamic updates to signed zones will expire. The default is 30. The maximum value is 3660 (10 years). The signature inception time is unconditionally set to one hour before Universal Coordinated Time (UTC) to allow for a limited amount of clock skew. All DNSSEC operations rely on a correct time zone value and network clock synchronization using ntpd. This statement may be used in a zone, view, or global options statement.

tkey-dhkey

tkey-dhkey "host-name" key-tag;
tkey-dhkey "fred.example.com" 45312;

The tkey-dhkey statement defines the file containing the Diffie-Hellman private key to be used in TKEY operations and must be located in the directory defined using a directory statement. In the preceding example, the key would be generated using the command shown here:

dnssec-keygen -a dh -b 1024 -n host fred.example.com
Kfred.example.com.+002+45312

The dnssec-keygen utility outputs a single line identifying the files containing information; Kfred.example.com.+002+4531 in the preceding example. The value K is a fixed identifier; fred.example.com. is the name of the host KEY RR reflected from the dnssec-keygen arguments (see Chapter 9); the number 002 indicates the Diffie-Hellman algorithm; the number 45312 is known as the key-tag or *fingerprint* and is algorithmically generated to uniquely identify this key when the dnssec-keygen utility is run. The TKEY feature is not widely used and is not described further in this book. This statement may only be used in a global options clause.

tkey-domain

tkey-domain domain-name;
tkey-domain "example.com";

The tkey-domain statement defines the domain name that will be added to the names of all keys generated by a TKEY sequence. When a name server requests a TKEY exchange, it can optionally indicate the required name for the key. If present, the name of the shared key will be the client's supplied name with the domain-name appended to it; thus, if the client supplied a name of fred, the name server will return fred.example.com. If the client does not supply a name, a random series of hex digits will be used as the client part of the name. TKEY is not widely implemented and is not described further in this book. This statement can only be used in a global options clause.

tkey-gssapi-credential

tkey-gssapi-credential "kerberos-principal";
tkey-gssapi-credential "USER/example.com";

tkey-gssapi-credential defines the credential associated with a Generic Security Services API (GSSAPI). The GSSAPI and the credentials required are defined by RFC 2743 and its Kerberos form is defined in RFC 1964 and 4121. TKEY is not widely implemented at this time and is not described further in this book. This statement may only appear in a global options clause.

update-check-ksk

```
update-check-ksk ( yes | no );
update-check-ksk no;
```

Only applicable when using DDNS with DNSSEC signed zones. Normally, when a zone is signed, the KSK is used to sign only the DNSKEY RRset at the zone apex. The ZSK signs all RRsets in the zone including the DNSKEY RRset. If this statement is set to yes (the default), the normal KSK and ZSK signing procedure is followed. If set to no, a KSK, if found, will be treated like a ZSK and used to sign all the RRsets in the zone. In general, this statement would be used if only a single key is being used for zone signing, which is allowed for by the DNSSEC standards but is not currently recommended. If update-check-ksk is yes (or not present), there must be two keys (a KSK and a ZSK) present for every algorithm being used to sign the zone. If this is not the case, the zone RRsets will be signed with any suitable key, irrespective of whether it is a KSK or ZSK. This statement may be used in a global options, view, or zone clause and is equivalent to dnssec-signzone with the -z argument. See also dnssec-dnskey-kskonly.

use-v4-udp-ports, use-v6-udp-ports

```
use-v4-udp-ports { range low high };
use-v6-udp-ports { range low high };
use-v4-udp-ports { range 1024 33791 };
use-v6-udp-ports { range 32767 65535 };
```

When a resolver issues queries, the destination port is usually the normal DNS port number 53. The source port number is arbitrary. However, if this source port is predictable, then it's trivial for an attacker to spoof a response and poison the resolver's cache. The source port should therefore be randomized across a sufficiently large set of available ports to make guessing as difficult as possible. Port numbers on both IPv4 and IPv6 are in the range 0 to 65535 (16 bits), but on most systems ports less than 1024 are reserved for special applications. Extreme care should be exercised when using either of these statements to allow a minimum of 16384 ports, providing 14 bits of randomization and higher if possible (specific ports can always be excluded by using avoid-v4-udp-ports and avoid-v6-udp-ports). By default, the values for both use-v4-udp-ports and use-v6-udp-ports is { range 1024 65535 };, providing the maximum practical range. This statement may only be used in a global options clause.

update-policy

```
update-policy ( local | { update-policy-rule; } );
update-policy { grant fred.example.net name example.net MX;};
```

update-policy only applies to master zones. This statement defines the rules by which DDNS updates may be carried out. This statement may only be used with a key (TSIG or SIG(0)) that is used to cryptographically sign each update request and may be specified only in a zone statement. It is mutually exclusive with allow-update in any single zone clause. The statement may take the keyword local or an update-policy-rule structure. The keyword local is designed to simplify configuration of secure updates using a TSIG key and limits the update source to only to localhost (loopback address, 127.0.0.1 or ::1), thus both nsupdate and the name server must reside on the same host. When BIND encounters a update-policy local; statement, it generates a TSIG key (with the algorithm HMAC-SHA256) and a private key file only in /var/run/named/session.key (location may be modified using the session-keyfile statement) and with a key-name of "local-ddns". This session key is also used by nsupdate when the -l argument is supplied (see Chapter 9). The local keyword is expanded to an equivalent update-policy-rule, as shown:

```
update-policy local;
// expanded by BIND to
update-policy {grant local-ddns subzone any;};
```

The effect of this statement is to allow any DDNs update signed with the key-name "local-ddns" to update any RRs with the name of the zone file or a subdomain of the zone name (as it appears in the zone clause) in which the update-policy local; statement appears. Thus, if update-policy local; appears in the example.com zone clause, any update from localhost is allowed to update RRs with a name of example.com, www.example.com, joe.example.com, etc.. The update-policy local; statement may be used in one or more zone clauses, while other zone clauses may use the update-policy update-policy-rule; format. See the following section for a full explanation of all the fields in the expanded update-policy statement.

update-policy-rule takes the following format:

```
update-policy-rule permission identity matchtype [tname] [rr]
```

Table 12–12 describes the various fields used in the update-policy-rule.

Table 12–12. Update Policy Rules

Parameter	Description
permission	May be either grant or deny.
identity	A key name as it appears in a key clause for TSIG or the name of a KEY RR for SIG(0). Can also take the DNS wildcard value * which is expanded to mean anything matches.
matchtype	Can take any of the following values: 6to4-self: Only applicable to reverse-mapped zones updates. The RR name to be updated must match the 6to4 (48 bits only) reverse mapped name of the IPv4 address that initiated this update session. Thus, if the source of the update session is 192.168.2.3, this is added to the IPv6 6to4 prefix (always 2002::/16) to create the address 2002:C0A8:0203::/48 (C0A80203 is the hex format of 192.168.2.3); when reversed, it will yield an RR name of 3.0.2.0.8.A.0.C.2.0.0.2.IP6.ARPA and thus allow any RR names at this zone apex, such as NS or DNAME, to be modified or added. name: The RR name being updated must match the tname field exactly. That is, if tname is joe.example.com., then this update-policy can only update an RR with the name joe.example.com. self: The RR name being updated must match the identity field exactly, including the DNS wildcard value(*). Thus, if identity is *, this update-policy will update an RR with any name; if identity is example.com, only an RR with the name example.com may be updated The optional tname field should be the same as identity.

selfsub: The RR name being updated must match the identity field or a subdomain of identity. Thus, if identity is example.com, this update-policy will update any RR with the name example.com or joe.example.com etc. The optional tname field should be the same as identity.

selfwildcard: The RR name being updated can only match a subdomain of the identity field. Thus, if identity is example.com this update-policy can only update RRs with a name of joe.example.com or sheila.example.com, etc. but not RRs with a name of example.com. The optional tname field is ignored but should be the same as identity.

subdomain: The RR name being updated matches anything containing (is a subdomain of) the tname field. Thus, if the tname is example.com., this update-policy will match any RRs with a name of bill.example.com, sheila.example.com etc. as well as example.com.

tcp-self: Only applicable to reverse-mapped zones updates. The RR name to be updated must match the reverse mapped name of the IP address (IPv4 or IPv6) that initiated this update session. Thus, if the source of the update session is 192.168.2.27 and the update-policy appears in a zone 2.168.192.IN-ADDR.ARPA, the RR name must match 127 that when fully expanded (using ORIGIN substitution) becomes 27.2.168.192.IN-ADDR.ARPA. If the source address is IPv6, the reverse mapping occurs in the IP6.ARPA reverse map domain.

wildcard: The RR name being updated will match the tname field after any DNS wildcard expansion has been applied. The tname field must contain at least one wildcard (*) and may be a single *, in which case this update can apply to *any* RR name.

zonesub: The RR name being updated must match anything containing the zone name (as it appears in the zone clause containing this update-policy), including subdomains of this zone name. The optional tname field must be omitted when using this form.

tname	Optional. The name of the target or part of the target RR name (depending on the value of matchtype) that will be allowed by this update-policy. Can take the value * which means any RR name.
rr	Optional. Defines the RR types that may be updated including ANY (all RR types except NSEC/NSEC3). If omitted, the default allows all RR types except RRSIG, NSEC, NSEC3, SOA, and NS. Multiple entries may be defined using space-separated entries; for instance, A MX PTR.

The matchtype field may also take the values krb5-self, krb5-subdomain, and ms-self that only apply when GSS-TSIG is being used with Kerberos V; this lies outside the scope of this book.

The following example shows the use of update-policy whereby each host can update its own A RR but no others:

```
zone "example.com" in {
    type master;
    ....
    update-policy { grant * self * A;};
};
```

The policy says that any KEY RR name or key-name as it appears in a key clause (the first *) with the same name (self) as the A RR it is trying to update (the second *) will be allowed (grant) to do so.

The next example shows mixed use of the local and update-policy-rule formats:

```
zone "example.com" in {
    type master;
    ....
    update-policy local;  // allow updates to any RR but only from localhost
};
zone "example.net" in {
    type master;
    ....
    update-policy { grant "remote-key" name example.com MX;};

};
```

The first zone clause allows DDNS updates to any RR in the zone but only from localhost. The second (example.net) zone allows updates from any TSIG signed transaction with the key-name of "remote-key" (there must be a key clause with the name "remote-key" in this named.conf) but only to the MX RR at the zone apex.

Further examples of update-policy are described in the "Securing Dynamic Updates" section in Chapter 10, including the necessary zone file entries.

BIND server Statements

This section describes statements that may *only* be used in the server clause. The server clause can take additional statements that are described in other sections; consult Table 12–6 for a complete list.

bogus

```
bogus ( yes | no );
bogus ( yes | no );
```

bogus indicates that traffic from this server should be ignored (yes) if known to be giving bad data, suffering a DoS attack, or some other reason. The same effect may be obtained using the blackhole statement. The default is no. This option can only be defined in the server clause.

edns

```
edns ( yes | no ) ;
edns no  ;
```

edns defines whether to use EDNS0 (RFC 2671) with a specific server (yes) or not (no). The default is yes. This statement may only be used in a server clause.

keys

```
keys "key-name";["key-name"; ...;];
keys "serv1-zone-transfer-key";
```

The key-name field of the keys statement references a key clause with the same key-name and mandates that transactions secured by TSIG (zone transfer or dynamic update) will use this key. In the case of zone transfers, the peer host must have an equivalent key clause with the same key-name. When used with nsupdate, key-name appears in the -k argument (see Chapter 9). This statement can only appear in a server clause, and while the formal syntax allows for more than one key-name as of the current releases of BIND, only one key-name is supported per server. The "Securing Zone Transfers" section in Chapter 10 shows the use of the keys statement in a server clause.

transfers

transfers number ;
transfers 5;

transfers limits the number of concurrent zone transfers from any given server. If not present, the default for transfers-per-ns is used (the default is 2). This option may be used only in a server clause.

BIND view Statements

This section describes statements that may only be used in the view clause. The view clause can take many more statements; consult Table 12–6 for a complete list.

match-clients

match-clients { address_match_element; ... };
match-clients { 10.2.3.0/8;172.16.30.0/16;!192.168.0.0/16; };

A view clause matches when either or both of its match-clients and match-destinations statements match and when the match-recursive-only condition is met. If either match-clients or match-destinations or both are missing, they default to any (all hosts match). The match-clients statement defines the address_match_list for the source IP address of the incoming messages. Any IP address that matches will use the defined view clause. This statement may only be used in a view clause. An example showing the use of all three statements is described in the "BIND view Clause" section in this chapter.

match-destinations

match-destinations { address_match_element; ... };
match-destinations { 192.168.0.3; };

The match-destination statement defines the address_match_list for the destination address of the *incoming* message. It is one of three statements that can be used to match a view clause. The relationship between the statements is described under match-clients. This statement may only be used in a view clause.

match-recursive-only

match-recursive-only (yes | no);
match-recursive-only yes;

If an incoming query requests recursion and `match-recursive-only` is yes, the condition is met. It is one of three statements that can be used to match a view clause. The relationship between the statements is described under the `match-clients` entry. This statement may only be used in a view clause.

BIND zone Statements

This section describes the zone-only statements. The zone clause can take many more statements than described here; consult Table 12–6 for a complete list.

check-names

check-names (warn|fail|ignore) ;
```
check-names fail;
```

The `check-names` statement may also appear in a view or global options clause where its syntax is different. The behavior controlled by this statement, which allows certain names to be limited to compliance with the name format defined in RFCs 821, 952, and 1123, is described under `check-names` in the "BIND Operations Statements" section in this chapter.

file

file "file.name";
```
file "slave.example.com";
```

file defines the file used by the zone in quoted string format; for example, "slave.example.com"—or whatever convention you use. The `file` entry is mandatory for master and hint; is optional—but highly recommended—for slave; and is not required for forward zones. The file may be an absolute path or relative to the `directory` statement. The following example shows the use of the `file` statement:

```
// named.conf fragment
zone "example.com" in {
    type slave;
    // defines an optional file used to save slave zone data
    file "slave.example.com";
    ...
};
zone "example.net" in {
    type master;
    // defines a master zone file
    file "master.example.net";
    ....
};
```

masterfile-format

```
masterfile-format (text | raw );;
masterfile-format raw;
```

This is only applicable to servers with type master; in the zone clause. By default, BIND 9 reads zone files in text format. Loading many text zone files and converting them into a format suitable for internal use can take some time. BIND 9 provides a utility named-compilezone (see the "named-compilezone" section in Chapter 9) whose output may be optionally in raw (binary) format. The masterfile-format statement is used to indicate which format is being used and may take the values raw (zone file has been created by named-compilezone) or text (standard text zone file). The statement may be omitted if standard text zone files are being used since this is the default. Zone files in raw format are not subject to the same checks as text files when loaded; therefore, it's advised that, prior to using named-compilezone, the utility named-checkzone be used to verify the zone file. The statement may be used in a global options, view or zone clause as required.

```
// named.conf fragment
....
zone "example.net" in {
    type master;
    // defines a master zone file in raw format
    masterfile-format raw;
    file "master.example.net";
    ....
};
```

masters

```
masters [ port pg_num ] { ( masters_list | ipv4
            [port p_num] | ipv6 [port p_num ] ) [ key "key-name" ]; ... };
masters {192.168.3.5;};
```

The masters statement is valid only with slave zones and defines one or more IP addresses and optional port numbers of servers that hold the master zone file. The slave will use the defined IP address(es) to update the zone file when the SOA RR refresh parameter is reached. The pg_num parameter changes the port number used for zone transfers for all the listed servers (the default is port 53). The p_num parameter changes the port number for the specific IP address only. masters_list may be used to reference a list of masters defined in a masters clause. The key-name field defines the key to be used to authenticate the zone transfers when using TSIG and references the name of the key clause; a corresponding key clause with the same key-name must be present in the master server for the zone. The following example shows three masters for the zone, one of which will use port 1127 for zone transfers and one of which is an IPv6 address:

```
// named.conf fragment
zone "example.com" in {
    type slave;
    file "slave.example.com";
    masters {192.168.2.7; 10.2.3.15 port 1127; 2001:db8:0:1::15;};
};
```

type

```
type zone_type;
type delegation-only;
```

The type statement defines the characteristics of the zone and may take one of the values defined in Table 12–13.

Table 12–13. Type Statement Values

Value	Description
master	The server has a master copy of the zone data (which is loaded from a local filestore) and provides authoritative answers for the zone.
slave	A slave zone is a replica of the master zone and obtains its zone data by zone transfer operations. The slave will respond authoritatively for the zone as long as it has valid (not timed out) zone data. The masters statement specifies one or more IP addresses of master servers that the slave contacts to refresh or update its copy of the zone data. When the TTL specified by the refresh parameter of the zone's SOA RR is reached or a NOTIFY message is received, the slave will query the SOA RR from the zone master. If the sn parameter (serial number) is greater than the current value, a zone transfer is initiated. If the slave can't obtain a new copy of the zone data when the SOA expiry value is reached, it will stop responding for the zone. Authentication of the master can also be done with per-server TSIG keys (see the entry for the masters statement earlier). By default, zone transfers are made using UDP on port 53, but this can be changed using the masters statement. If a file statement is defined, the zone data will be written to this file whenever the zone is changed and reloaded from this file on a server restart. If no file statement is defined, the slave will require a zone transfer from the zone master before it can start responding to queries for the zone. Slave zones are permitted to transfer zones if requested and are subject to any controlling allow-transfer statements.
forward	A zone of type forward is simply a way to configure forwarding, perhaps to a unique name server, on a per-domain or per-zone basis. To be effective, both a forward and forwarders statement should be included. If no forwarders statement is present or an empty list is provided, no forwarding will be done for the domain, canceling the effects of any forwarders in the global options clause.
hint	The initial set of root-servers is defined using a hint zone. When the server starts up, it uses the hint's zone file to find a root name server and get the most recent list of root name servers. If no hint zone is specified for class IN, the server uses a compiled-in default set of root servers. Classes other than IN have no built-in default hints. The hint zone is only required for a name server that provides recursive services or a master or slave server that sends NOTIFY messages to any out-of-zone servers defined in NS RRs for the zone.
stub	A stub zone is similar to a slave zone except that it replicates only the NS records of a master zone instead of the entire zone. Stub zones are not a standard part of the DNS—they are a feature specific to the BIND implementation and should not be used in general.
delegation-only	This indicates that only referrals (or delegations) will be made for the zone; it's recommended only for use with TLDs, *not* leaf (non-TLD) zones. The generation of referrals in leaf zones is determined by the use of the delegation-only statement and the RRs contained in the zone file; that is, a zone consisting of an SOA RR, NS RRs, and glue records will *only* be able to generate referrals (see also Chapter 9).

Summary

This chapter is a reference for the command-line options used when BIND is loaded and for all the entities used in a named.conf file—the file that controls the detailed behavior of BIND.

The named.conf file statements were defined to be of three types—comments, clauses, or statements. This book rigorously uses the term *clause* to refer to a collection or group of *statements* in the interest of clarity and consistency. Much BIND documentation uses a variety of terms such as *sections*, *clauses*, *statements*, *options*, and *phrases* to define the two entity types (excluding comments) contained in the named.conf file. Advanced readers may well be comfortable with different terms being applied to the same type of entity or, even worse (but depressingly frequent), the same term being applied to completely different entities. Such an environment, however, is neither edifying nor conducive to creating safe, error-free BIND configurations—the ultimate objective of this book. The terms were selected after consulting *Merriam-Webster Online* and BIND's source code.

The available clauses are listed alphabetically in Table 12–3. Statements are listed alphabetically in Table 12–5, together with very short descriptions and categorization. The individual statements are then described in detail in alphabetic order within each category, with a simple example in every case and more complex examples where appropriate. It is hoped that such categorization will allow the reader to dip into the specific section required and also to allow browsing of statements when looking to control or affect the behavior of similar types of operations such as queries. Many statements can be used in more than one clause; Table 12–6 lists each statement alphabetically and the clauses in which it can be used.

The next chapter contains reference material on zone files and the directives and RRs that may be used in them.

Zone File Reference

This chapter is intended to be a reference for zone file directives and resource records. Table 13–1 contains a list of all current RRs defined by IANA (www.iana.org/assignments/dns-parameters), their support status within BIND and Windows DNS software, the RFCs that define them, and a very brief description of the RR type. This provides you with a quick overview of the formidable list of RRs available and will enable you to browse them more effectively. This chapter features descriptions of the syntax for each directive and resource record; in most cases their use is illustrated with one or more examples.

RRs have two representations: a textual form, in which they appear in a zone file as described in this chapter, and a binary format, also called the *wire format*, used when one or more RRs are transmitted in a query, query response, or similar network operation. The binary format of RRs is defined in Chapter 15. The following section reviews the zone file format rules and is then followed by material on the zone file directives and finally the resource records descriptions.

DNS Zone File Structure

Zone files describe a domain's characteristics—the hosts and services supported—in a form that may be used by DNS software. The files are textual and may be read or edited using any standard text editor. They can contain three types of entries:

1. *Comments*: All comments start with a ; (semicolon) and continue to the end of the line. Comments can occupy a single line or be added to any of the following record types.

2. *Directives*: All directives start with $ and are used to control processing of the zone files.

3. *Resource Records*: RRs are used to define the characteristics, properties, or entities contained within the domain or zone. RRs are contained on a single line with the exception that entries enclosed in parentheses can spread across multiple lines.

The following is a zone file fragment that illustrates the preceding points and record types:

```
; this is a full-line comment
$TTL 12h    ; directive - comment terminates the line
$ORIGIN example.com.
; Start of Authority (SOA) record defining the zone (domain)
; illustrates an RR record spread over more than one line
; using the enclosing parentheses
@  IN  SOA  ns1.example.com. hostmaster.example.com. (
            2010121500 ; sn = serial number
            3h         ; ref = refresh
```

```
            15m        ; ret = refresh retry
            3w         ; ex = expiry
            3h      ; nx = nxdomain ttl
            )
; single line RR
    IN  NS  ns1.example.com. ;with a comment
...
```

You can also write the preceding SOA RR a single line, in which case there's no need for the parentheses:

```
@  IN  SOA  ns1.example.com. hostmaster.example.com. 2003080800 3h 15m 3w 3h
```

If parentheses are used, the ((open parenthesis) must appear on the first line.

DNS Directives

Zone file directives control the processing of zone files. There are three standardized directives: $TTL, $ORIGIN, and $INCLUDE (RFC 1035). A fourth directive, $GENERATE, is supported by BIND but is not standardized.

The $ORIGIN Directive

The $ORIGIN directive was standardized in RFC 1035 and defines the domain name that will be appended to any name that appears in an RR and does not end with a dot—frequently called a *relative* or an *unqualified* name—to create a *fully qualified domain name* (FQDN). This process is called the $ORIGIN substitution rule throughout this book.

The $ORIGIN Substitution Rule

If a name appears in a Resource Record and does *not* end with a dot, then the value of the last, or only, $ORIGIN value will be appended to the name. If the name does end with a dot, then it is a fully qualified domain name and nothing will be appended to the name. The terminating dot in an FQDN is interpreted as the root of the domain tree or hierarchy. An FQDN unambiguously defines a name to the root.

$ORIGIN Syntax

```
$ORIGIN domain-name
```

domain-name is usually an FQDN—it ends with a dot—to avoid confusion. However, it obeys the normal rules of $ORIGIN substitution if it does not end in a dot. The "Define a DKIM Record" section in Chapter 8 shows an example of non-FQDN usage. $ORIGIN directives can appear anywhere in a zone file and will be used from the point they are defined onwards until replaced with another $ORIGIN, like so:

```
$ORIGIN example.com.
; unqualified names from here will append example.com.
www             IN  A 192.168.2.2 ; unqualified
; www expands to www.example.com.
...
ftp.example.com. IN A 192.168.2.3 ; FQDN
```

```
...
$ORIGIN us.example.com.
; unqualified names from here will append us.example.com.
www              IN  A 192.168.254.2 ; unqualified
; www expands to www.us.example.com.
...
```

The $ORIGIN directive is not mandatory. If an $ORIGIN directive is not present, BIND will assume that the $ORIGIN value is the name of the zone clause that defines the zone file in named.conf (described in Chapter 12). This book always uses $ORIGIN directives in zone files for three reasons:

1. With the $ORIGIN directive present, a zone file is self-descriptive and self-contained; it requires no reference to any external information.

2. The $ORIGIN substitution rule (defined previously) is much less confusing. The value to be substituted is immediately apparent—the last $ORIGIN directive.

3. Not all software may use the same default assumptions about the $ORIGIN directive as does BIND. Zone files are more portable when the $ORIGIN directive is included.

Tip For a further insight into the use of the $ORIGIN directive, have a look at a zone file on a slave server after the zone file has been transferred (assuming the file statement was used in the slave definition). You will see that BIND 9 constructs its zone files with an $ORIGIN directive at every level of the hierarchy.

The $INCLUDE Directive

The $INCLUDE directive allows inclusion in situ of an external file containing additional directives or RRs. It's typically used in maintenance of larger zone files; that is, individual parts of a single zone file can be modified by clients without exposing the global parameters or other client parts to either inspection or corruption. Alternatively, it can be used to add RRs to a zone file that were created externally such as KEY or DNSKEY RRs generated by the dnssec-keygen utility for use in secure DNS operations. Unlike the include statement used in the named.conf file, which is typically used to secure sensitive (private) keys, there is no corresponding need for the $INCLUDE in the zone file—any keys appearing in a zone file will always be public. This directive is standardized in RFC 1035. The RFC is silent on the topic of embedded $INCLUDE directives in the included files, so to err on the side of safety they should not be used.

$INCLUDE Syntax

```
$INCLUDE filename [domain-name]
```

The filename parameter may be an absolute path (for example, /absolute/path/to/file) or a relative path (for example, relative/path/to/file). If the relative path format is used, then the base directory is assumed to be the same location as the zone file. The optional domain-name parameter may be used to set an explicit $ORIGIN to be used in the included file; however, an included file can also contain one or more $ORIGIN directives as shown in the fragments that follow. The scope of $ORIGIN directives when used with an included file is limited to the included file only. On termination of the include operation, the value of $ORIGIN is restored to the value before the $INCLUDE directive.

The first zone file fragment shows an included file with no $ORIGIN directives. In this case, the included file will use the current $ORIGIN directive in operation at the point of inclusion, like so:

```
$ORIGIN us.example.com.
...
mail      IN     A   192.168.35.12
; expands to mail.us.example.com.
$INCLUDE /var/named/zones/sub.example.com ; absolute path no $ORIGIN
ftp       IN     A   192.168.35.16
; expands to ftp.us.example.com.
```

The following fragment shows expansion of the /var/named/zones/sub.example.com include file:

```
; INCLUDE file statements
www       IN     A  192.168.23.15
; expands to www.us.example.com
...
; end of included file
```

The following fragment shows the use of an explicit $ORIGIN on the $INCLUDE directive:

```
$ORIGIN us.example.com.
...
mail      IN     A   192.168.35.15
; expands to mail.us.example.com.
$INCLUDE sub.example.com uk.example.com. ; overrides current $ORIGIN
; $ORIGIN reverts to value before the $INCLUDE directive
ftp       IN     A   192.168.35.16
; expands to ftp.us.example.com
```

The included fragment in sub.example.com uses the explicit $ORIGIN on the $INCLUDE directive:

```
; INCLUDE file statements
www       IN     A  192.168.23.15
; expands to www.uk.example.com
...
; end of included file
```

The following fragments achieve the same result as the previous ones but may be less confusing because of the explicit use of an $ORIGIN directive in the included file:

```
$ORIGIN us.example.com.
...
mail      IN     A   192.168.35.15
; expands to mail.us.example.com.
$INCLUDE sub.example.com ; no $ORIGIN
; $ORIGIN reverts to value before the $INCLUDE directive
ftp       IN     A   192.168.35.16
; expands to ftp.us.example.com
```

The included fragment uses an explicit $ORIGIN directive:

```
; INCLUDE file statements
$ORIGIN uk.example.com.
www       IN     A  192.168.23.15
; expands to www.uk.example.com
...
; end of included file
```

The preceding fragment is self-contained and self-descriptive.

The $TTL Directive

Every resource record may take an optional Time to Live (TTL) value specified in seconds. The $TTL directive was standardized in RFC 2038 and defines the default TTL value applied to any RR that does not have an explicit TTL defined. TTL in the context of DNS means the time in seconds that a record may be cached (stored) by another name server acting as a resolver. (Caching is explained in Chapter 4.)

$TTL Syntax

$TTL time-in-seconds

The following shows a typical $TTL directive:

$TTL 172800 ; 2 days

BIND provides a short format to allow the time value to be written without resorting to a calculator or some strenuous mental arithmetic. The case-insensitive values are m = minutes, h = hours, d = days, w = weeks. This book uses the standard BIND short format throughout simply to make the time values easy to understand quickly. While most DNS software has adopted the BIND short form convention, it's not universal; and if zone files are to be ported between BIND and other DNS software, the short forms should be used with care. The preceding $TTL could be written in any of the following forms when using the BIND short format:

$TTL 2d
$TTL 48h
$TTL 2880m
$TTL 1d24h

The time-in-seconds value may be in the range 0, which indicates the record should never be cached, to a maximum of 2147483647 (roughly 68 years). The current best practice recommendation (RFC 1912) suggests a value greater than one day; on RRs that rarely change, longer values should be considered. This book typically uses a $TTL value of 172800 (2 days), which represents a reasonable balance between name server load and speed of change. The " DNS TTL and Time Values" section in Chapter 8 describes other considerations that may affect TTLs in certain RR types.

The $TTL directive must appear before any RR to which it will be applied and for that reason it is normally defined at the beginning of the zone file. A $TTL directive continues in force until superseded by another $TTL directive.

Note In older versions of BIND (prior to BIND 9), the default $TTL was defined in the SOA RR (described later in this chapter), which reflected the standards then in force. RFC 2308 defines both implementation of the $TTL directive and the revised use of the last field (previously known as the min field) in the SOA RR to mean the NXDOMAIN (negative) caching time and is commented throughout this book as nx = nxdomainttl to reflect current usage.

The $GENERATE Directive

The $GENERATE directive is BIND-specific and should not be used if zone files will be ported between BIND and other RFC-compliant DNS software.

$GENERATE is provided to ease generation of repetitive sequences of RRs. Only NS, PTR, A, AAAA, DNAME, and CNAME RRs are supported. The most obvious use for $GENERATE is when creating zone files used in delegation of reverse subnet maps. The reverse-map zone files involve a series of RRs that increment by a single value. The following fragment shows an extract from the reverse delegation zone file described in Chapter 8:

```
$ORIGIN 199.168.192.IN-ADDR.ARPA.
.....
65          IN  CNAME   65.64/26
66          IN  CNAME   66.64/26
67          IN  CNAME   67.64/26

....
125         IN  CNAME   125.64/26
126         IN  CNAME   126.64/26
```

The following $GENERATE directive would create the preceding full sequence:

```
$GENERATE 65-126 $ CNAME $.64/26
```

$GENERATE Syntax

```
$GENERATE start-stop[step] lhn type rhn
```

In the $GENERATE syntax, start is the starting value of the generated sequence and stop is the ending value. step is optional and indicates the value to be added on each iteration; if omitted, 1 is assumed. lhn indicates the value of the left-hand name. An lhn value of $ indicates the current iteration value that will be substituted as shown in the example. The type field is the RR type, and only CNAME, NS, A, AAAA, DNAME, and PTR are supported. rhn is the left-hand name; again, $ indicates the current iteration value will be substituted. The rhn and lhn values will have normal $ORIGIN substitution rules applied.

The corresponding PTR records used in normal reverse-map zone files will typically have unique host names that can't be used with the $GENERATE directives; for example, bill, fred, www, etc. do not have an iterator relationship, but if host names were sequentially numbered, such as PC65 to PC126, the $GENERATE directive could be applied to them. Occasionally one wishes life was that simple!

DNS Resource Records

A large number of resource records have been defined over the life of the DNS specifications. These RRs are of two types: *real* RRs (for want of any better terminology) that appear in a zone file, and meta (or pseudo) RRs that only appear in the QUESTION SECTION or ADDITIONAL SECTION of queries (see Chapter 15). Table 13–2 describes the meta (or pseudo) RRs. Table 13–1 shows the currently assigned RRs (they appear in zone files) from IANA (www.iana.org/assignments/dns-parameters) and their current support status in BIND and Windows DNS (Windows Server 2008 R2). The code column identifies the RR type, which is used only in the binary format when the RR is transmitted and does not appear in the text version of the RR; it's provided for information and cross-referencing purposes only. Table 13–1 also shows the documentation status in this book (Reference column). The RRs are shown in alphabetic order for convenience.

Table 13–1. Resource Record Status

RR Name	Code	Reference	BIND	Windows	Specification	Notes
A	1	Yes	Yes	Yes	RFC 1035	Forward map. Host to IPv4 address.
A6	38	Yes	Yes	No	RFC 2874	Experimental. Forward map. Host to IPv6 address.
AAAA	28	Yes	Yes	Yes	RFC 3596	Forward map. Host to IPv6 address.
AFSDB	18	Yes	Yes	Yes	RFC 5864, 1183	AFS Database location.
APL	42	Yes	Yes	No	RFC 3123	Experimental. Stands for Address Prefix Lists. Supplies lists of IP addresses for any required purpose.
ATMA	34	Yes	No	No	None	Private. Stands for ATM Address. Defined by the ATM forum (document reference af-saa-0069.000.pdf).
CERT	37	Yes	Yes	No	RFC 4398	CERT RRs define various security certificate formats, such as X.509, for storage in the DNS.
CNAME	5	Yes	Yes	Yes	RFC 1035	Stands for Canonical Name (Alias). Maps an alias name to another name.
DHCID	49	Yes	Yes	No	RFC 4701	Used by DCP Servers to ensure only a single host can update A or AAAA RRs.
DLV	32769	Yes	Yes	No	RFC 4431	Functionally equivalent to DS, used by DNSSEC in alternative trust chains
DNAME	39	Yes	Yes	No	RFC 2672, 4592	Experimental. Used for reverse-map delegation, especially IPv6.

RR Name	Code	Reference	BIND	Windows	Specification	Notes
DNSKEY	48	Yes	Yes	Yes	RFC 4034	DNSKEY RRs define the public key used in DNSSEC operations only. The KEY RR is used for all other public keys.
DS	43	Yes	Yes	Yes	RFC 4034	Delegation Signer RRs are only used in DNSSEC operations and are placed in parent zones at the point of delegation to a child zone to create chains of trust.
EID	31	No	No	No	None	Private RR. Stands for Endpoint Identifier.
GPOS	27	No	Yes	No	RFC 1712	Stands for Geographical Position. Made obsolete by LOC RR.
HINFO	13	Yes	Yes	Yes	RFC 1035	Textual host OS and hardware description.
HIP	55	Yes	Patch	No	RFC 5205	Host Identity Protocol
IPSECKEY	45	Yes	No	No	RFC 4025	IPSECKEY RRs define keys and other properties used in IPSec operations.
ISDN	20	Yes	Yes	Yes	RFC 1183	Maps a host to an ISDN E.164 address.
KEY	25	Yes	Yes	No	RFC 4034, 3755, 3445	KEY RRs define public keys for use in cryptographic security operation, such as SIG(0). The exception: DNSSEC (DNSSEC), which uses the DNSKEY RR exclusively.
KX	36	Yes	Yes	No	RFC 2230	Key Exchanger. Returns an alternative host name.

RR Name	Code	Reference	BIND	Windows	Specification	Notes
LOC	29	Yes	Yes	No	RFC 1876	Experimental but historically widely used. Provides longitude, latitude, and altitude information for a name.
MB	7	Yes	Yes	Yes	RFC 1035	Experimental. Mailbox Name. Not widely used.
MD	3	No	No	Yes	RFC 1035	Mail Destination. Obsolete. Replaced by MX.
MF	4	No	No	Yes	RFC 1035	Mail Forwarder. Obsolete. Replaced by MX.
MG	8	Yes	Yes	Yes	RFC 1035	Experimental. Mail Group Member. Not widely used.
MINFO	14	Yes	No	Yes	RFC 1035	Experimental. Mail list information. Not widely used.
MR	9	Yes	Yes	Yes	RFC 1035	Experimental. Mail Rename. Not widely used.
MX	15	Yes	Yes	Yes	RFC 1035	Mail Exchanger. Defines the domain's incoming mail servers.
NAPTR	35	Yes	Yes	No	RFC 3403	Naming Authority Pointer. This is a general-purpose RR that defines rules to be applied to application data.
NIMLOC	32	No	No	No	None	Private. NIMROD Locator.
NS	2	Yes	Yes	Yes	RFC 1035	Name Server RRs define the authoritative name servers for the domain.

RR Name	Code	Reference	BIND	Windows	Specification	Notes
NSAP	22	Yes	Yes	No	RFC 1706	Maps a host to an NSAP (OSI address).
NSAP-PTR	23	No	No	No	RFC 1348	NSAP reverse map. Made obsolete in RFC 1706.
NSEC3	50	Yes	Yes	No	RFC 5155	Used in DNSSEC as alternative to NSEC for proof of nonexistence (PNE).
NSEC3PARAM	51	Yes	Yes	No	RFC 5155	Used in DNSSEC to provide global information when NSEC3 used.
NSEC	47	Yes	Yes	Yes	RFC 4034	NSEC RRs are used in DNSSEC operations to provide PNE.
NULL	10	No	Yes	No	RFC 1035	Experimental. Can't be defined in a master zone file.
NXT	30	No	Yes	No	RFC 3755	Next Domain. Made obsolete by RFC 3755.
PTR	12	Yes	Yes	Yes	RFC 1035	IP to host (reverse mapping) used by IPv4 and IPv6.
PX	26	Yes	Yes	No	RFC 2163	X.400 to RFC 822 mail mapping.
RP	17	Yes	Yes	Yes	RFC 1183	Experimental. Responsible Person. Supplies textual information about a host or name.
RRSIG	46	Yes	Yes	Yes	RFC 4034	RRSIG RRs are used in DNSSEC operations to contain the digital signatures of RRsets.

RR Name	Code	Reference	BIND	Windows	Specification	Notes
RT	21	Yes	Yes	Yes	RFC 1183	Experimental. Route Through. Defines the route to one host via another host.
SIG	24	Yes	Yes	No	RFC 4034, 3755, 2535	Security Signature. This RR is now limited to use as a meta (or pseudo) RR when securing public key transactions. SIG(0) used in Dynamic DNS (DDNS).
SINK	40	No	No	No	None	Private RR.
SOA	6	Yes	Yes	Yes	RFC 1035/2308	Start of Authority. Defines global information about the domain.
SPF	99	Yes	Yes	No	RFC 4408	May be used as an alternative or in addition to SPF TXT RR for antispam protection.
SRV	33	Yes	Yes	Yes	RFC 2782	Services Record. Allows discovery of services provided by hosts.
SSHFP	44	Yes	Yes	No	RFC 4255	Secure Shell Fingerprint. Keys for use with Secure Shell (SSH).
TXT	16	Yes	Yes	Yes	RFC 1035	Arbitrary text associated with a domain. Also used for SPF and DKIM antispam records.
WKS	11	Yes	Yes	Yes	RFC 1035	Deprecated. SRV provides more powerful features.
X25	19	Yes	Yes	Yes	RFC 1183	Maps a host to an X.25 address.

In addition to the above list Microsoft Server 2008 R2 supports the proprietary RRs WINS and WINSR which are not described further in this book.

Table 13–2 lists meta (or pseudo) RRs and describes their use. Meta RRs do not appear in zone files but may appear in the QUESTION SECTION, ANSWER SECTION, or ADDITIONAL SECTION of a query (see Chapter 15). Meta RRs are defined in the IANA list.

Table 13–2. Meta RRs

RR Name	Code	Description
ANY	255	Appears in the QUESTION SECTION of a query and requests all records associated with the query name. If the associated name is the zone or domain name, then only those records having that name are supplied; for example, SOA, MX, NS RRs, not the entire zone file.
AXFR	252	Appears in the QUESTION SECTION of a query and requests a transfer of the entire zone.
IXFR	251	Appears in the QUESTION SECTION of a query and requests an incremental zone transfer, that is, only changed records.
MAILB	253	Appears in the QUESTION SECTION of a query and requests all MB, MG, and MR RRs for the associated name.
OPT	41	Appears in the ADDITIONAL SECTION of a query and response. Used to indicate EDNS0 (RFC 2671) is in use when either dnssec-enable yes; (default) is set in the options clause or edns yes; is defined in a server clause of named.conf. The OPT meta RR format is described in the "EDNS0 Transactions" section in Chapter 15 and is used to negotiate a larger UDP block size, among other things.
SIG	24	Appears in the ADDITIONAL SECTION when using public key secured transmissions. See the Notes column in Table 13–1.
TKEY	249	Appears only in the ADDITIONAL SECTION of a query or response. The Transfer KEY RR contains the computed Diffie-Hellman key exchange material.
TSIG	250	Appears only in the ADDITIONAL SECTION of a query or response. The Transfer SIG RR contains the Message Authentication Code (MAC) for use with either zone transfers or Dynamic DNS updates in shared secret transactions.

Resource Record Common Format

The first part of textual RRs is common to all types; the various fields are described in detail here to avoid repetition within the individual RR descriptions:

```
name    ttl    class    type    type-specific-data
```

The name Field

The name field, frequently called the *owner* name or the *left-hand name* to differentiate it from names that can appear on the *right-hand* or type-specific-data side of the RR, may take any of the following values:

- A fully qualified domain name (ends with a dot).

- An unqualified name (does not end with a dot), in which case the $ORIGIN substitution rule is applied as described previously for the $ORIGIN directive.

- A single @ character, in which case the current value of $ORIGIN is substituted.

- A blank (tab) or space, in which case the name from the previous RR. If no name field has been defined, then the $ORIGIN is substituted. The following code illustrates this point:

```
; zone file
    $TTL 2d
    $ORIGIN example.com.
    ; $ORIGIN is substituted in the following RR
            SOA ns1 hostmaster (....)
    ; could also be written as
    @       SOA ns1 hostmaster (....)
    ...
    www     A 192.158.2.1
    $ORIGIN sub.example.com.
        NS   ns1
    ; in the above RR the name (label) substituted will be www.example.com
    ; NOT sub.example.com
    ; in order to force the $ORIGIN an @ must be used as follows
    @   NS  ns1
; in the above RR the label substituted will be sub.example.com
```

Each dot-separated value in a name can be up to 63 characters in length (limited to 59 characters when using IDNA – see below) and is called a label. The label field may now use a very liberal set of characters; however, the original specifications (RFCs 821, 952, and 1123) limited the character set to the following:

- Any upper- or lowercase alpha character—a to z and A to Z

- Any numeric value from the range 0 to 9

- The - (hyphen or minus sign)

- Labels may not start or end with a – (hyphen or minus)

The preceding list is the safest set to use under all conditions (and can be enforced by using the check-name statement in BIND's named.conf file if required). The rule for the permissible character set was liberalized by RFC 2181, which essentially says any ASCII (IRA5) character in context is permissible and it's up to the client application to validate the name format before using it. The justification for this change is that the DNS can be used for the storage of many types of data, not just domain names, each of which may need to use a unique character set. The biggest single effect of this RFC was to formally allow _ (underscore), which is used in the SRV RR, and the / (forward slash), which can be used in the delegation of reverse subnet maps (see Chapter 8). There appears to be only two remaining hard limitations on names. First is the use of the terminating . (dot) in a name, the absence of which will invoke the $ORIGIN substitution rule. Second, a single @ (commercial at sign) will explicitly substitute the $ORIGIN name. While hostname labels may be use the more liberalized interpretation of RFC2181, delegated domain names from gTLDs and ccTLDs are constrained to use the original a-z, A-Z, 0-9 and hyphen limits (see also IDNA below), thus _hostname.example.com is valid but _example.com is invalid and would never be delegated. DNS labels are case insensitive for comparison and other purposes, thus example is equivalent to EXAMPLE or ExamplE, but case should be preserved when stored or between a query and response.

In practice, to avoid reaching the historic 512-byte limit of UDP transactions in cases where multiple records are returned, smaller labels are better! A practical limit could be 10 to 20 characters per label and indeed, certain libraries limit host name parts (labels) to 32 characters, but as noted, up to 63 characters (or 59 in the case of IDNA) can be used where necessary. If the host name part is also used as a NETBIOS name, it should be limited to 15 characters or less due to NETBIOS limits. The sum of all labels in a name, including the separating dots, must not exceed 255 characters.

Internationalized Domain Names for Applications (IDNA)

As noted, the DNS specifications permit domain names to be constructed from a series of labels, each of which uses a set of ASCII (IRA5) characters implicitly ordered from left to right. This is a major impediment to the majority of the world's population who use character sets that don't lie within this range and/or employ a right-to-left character order. To overcome these limitations, a set of algorithms (called *Punycode*) was defined in RFC 3492 to encode/decode Unicode (www.unicode.org) characters into ASCII equivalence for use in DNS operations. The current implementation of IDNA (known informally as IDNA2008 to differentiate it from earlier work) is described in RFCs 5890 (definitions), 5891 (protocol), 5892 (Unicode conversion), 5893 (right-to-left names), 5894 (rationale) and 5895 (mappings).

The process of creation of IDNA labels for use as internationalized domain names (IDN) consists of:

- The national registry (country manager) for each country that wishes to use IDNA defines a list of special characters that will be allowed in its IDNA labels from a defined set (RFC 5892 and www.iana.org/assignments/idnabis-tables). The country specific list is maintained by IANA at www.iana.org/domains/idn-tables.

- A label to be used in a country specific IDN is defined using Unicode (www.unicode.org) in Normalized Format C (NFC) from the set defined in the first step and then encoded using, say, UTF-8 to create what IDNA calls a U-label.

- The U-label is then compressed and converted using the *ToASCII* algorithm of the Punycode definition (RFC 3492) and prepended with the string xn-- to create an ASCII compatible encoding (ACE) called an A-label. The addition of xn-- is the reason IDNA labels are limited to 59 characters rather than the normal 63. The string output from the *ToASCII* Punycode algorithm consists only of lowercase letters, numbers, and the hyphen (minus).

- Care is taken that resulting A-labels do not clash with existing registered names (at the appropriate registration level) and that, where possible, letters (Unicode code points) do not look like others and thus increase the possibly of simple phishing or phrming attacks. This process is usually called Nameprep/String prep.

- The A-label, to be valid, must be capable of being reversed using the Punycode *ToUnicode* (RFC 3492) algorithm.

- Domain names (combinations of labels) may use a mixture of normal and IDNA labels as required.

Despite appearing a relatively simple concept, handling of character sets and generation of appropriate IDNA A-labels involves a stunning amount of detail that is well beyond the scope of this book. Readers who need to be familiar with IDNA are urged to take a deep breath and then consult the relevant RFCs and noted web sites for the details. As of the end of 2010, 11 IDNA ccTLDs were fully operational and a further 12 were awaiting final delegation (`www.icann.org/en/topics/idn/fast-track/string-evaluation-completion-a-en.htm`). Current versions of the major browser families all support IDNA, either directly or using plug-ins. In the case of e-mail, the domain part of an RFC 822 format address is covered by IDNA but internationalization of e-mail is still at the experimental stage within the IETF (end 2010) under the generic title of Email Address Internationalization (EAI).

Due to the use of ACE, BIND will support the use of IDNA transparently. However, tools, such as dig, nslookup etc. that accept and display native language values by performing the correct conversions to/from IDNA require BIND to be built using the configure variable --with-idn, which is not standard on Ubuntu but is selectable as a build option with FreeBSD (see the "Building BIND from Source" section of Chapter 6).

The `ttl` Field

The `ttl` field defines the time in seconds that the RR to which it applies may be cached. The field is optional; if not present, the zone default (defined by the $TTL directive) is used. If the field is present, it will be used whether it is lower or higher than the zone default. The `ttl` field is an unsigned 32-bit integer and may take a value in the range 0 (do not cache) to 2147483647. BIND allows its standard short format to be used in any `ttl` field. The case-insensitive values are m (minutes), h (hours), d (days), and w (weeks); for example, 3w2d1h5m5 is equivalent to 1991705 seconds. This book uses the BIND short format throughout because it is clearer, but if zone files are to be ported between BIND and other DNS applications, the short format should be used with care. The value of the TTL field was clarified in RFC 2181. The "DNS TTL and Time Values" section in Chapter 8 contains further discussion about TTL values for specific RR types or groups.

The `class` Field

The `class` field may take the case-insensitive values of IN = Internet class, CH = CHAOS (an MIT LAN protocol), or HS = Hesiod (an information service used at MIT). The latter two seem mostly of historic interest, but the use of the CHAOS class in a dig command (see Chapter 9) is the only way in which the BIND version number may be interrogated remotely (the version statement in named.conf may be used to reply with arbitrary information to disguise the version number).

The `type` Field

The type field designates the RR type such as AAAA (an IPv6 address RR). Each type is described in alphabetic order under its RR name in the "Resource Record Descriptions" section later in this chapter.

The `type-specific-data` Field

The type-specific-data field may consist of one or more parameters and is unique to the RR. The type-specific-data textual representations for each RR are described in the following sections. Chapter 15 defines the binary (*wire format*) representation.

Bit Labels

RFC 2673 introduced a new *bit label* (or *bit-string label* field) that was optimized for the definition of IPv6 addresses when used in reverse-map delegation where the volume of textual data can be brutal. This bit label, which currently has EXPERIMENTAL status (its status was changed by RFC 3363), is described here for completeness, but is otherwise not used throughout this book. The bit-label field is designed to be used as a left-hand (or owner) name field only. It can't appear in a right-hand name expression.

Bit Label Syntax

`\[string]`

In the bit-label syntax, \ is a literal to indicate the beginning of a bit label. The characters [and] are used to enclose the bit-string label definition. The `string` field may be used to define a binary, octal, hexadecimal, or IPv4 format address field as shown here:

`type-string[/length]`

The `type-string` field begins with a literal that defines the string format and takes one of the following values:

- x indicates hexadecimal format and is followed by as many hexadecimal characters as required to enclose that part of the address being defined by the bit label. The `/length` field is mandatory and indicates the number of bits contained within the hexadecimal field. Any unused bits must be set to 0. The first hexadecimal character is assumed to begin the field; thus the hexadecimal format can only be used on 4-bit boundaries.

- o indicates octal format and is followed by as many octal characters as required to enclose that part of the address being defined by the bit label. The `/length` field is mandatory and indicates the number of bits contained within the octal field. Any unused bits must be set to zero. The first octal character is assumed to begin the field; thus the octal format can only be used on 3-bit boundaries.

- b indicates binary format and is followed by as many binary characters as required to enclose that part of the address being defined by the bit label. The `/length` field is not required with the binary format. The binary format can be used on any bit boundary.

- The absence of any literal defines that the field is in *dotted-quad* format (IPv4 address format) and must contain all four parts of the address. The `/length` field is mandatory and indicates the number of bits contained within the dotted-quad field. The dotted-quad format can only be used on 32-bit boundaries.

The following fragments show a *Global Unicast* IPv6 address of 2001:db8:3d::1 being fully delegated using an aggregator hierarchy that is no longer actively supported by the regional Internet registries (RIRs). Each $ORIGIN directive is assumed to start a separate zone file.

```
$ORIGIN IPV6.ARPA.
; first 16 bits
.....
\[x2001/16]              IN   DNAME   tla.example.org.
.....
```

```
$ORIGIN tla.example.org.
; next 13 bits
.....
\[x0db8/13]                 IN    DNAME   nla.example.net.
.....

$ORIGIN nla.example.net.
; next 19 bits only possible with binary format
.....
\[b0010000000000111101]  IN    DNAME   ip6.example.com.
.....

$ORIGIN ip6.example.com.
; last 80 bits
.....
\[x000100000001/80]       IN    PTR    bill.example.com.
.....
```

The labels are significantly shorter than the textual equivalents but are probably significantly less comprehensible. Bit labels are fully supported by BIND (9.3+), but if used with DNS software that does not support them (including previous versions of BIND), such software will reject queries containing bit labels as invalid (SERVFAIL or REFUSED error).

RRsets

RRs with the same name, class, and type are collectively called an RRset. By extension of this definition, a singleton RR is also an RRset! The following is an example of an RRset using MX RRs:

```
; zone file fragment
$TTL 2d ;172800 seconds
$ORIGIN example.com.
....
    3w  IN  MX 10 mail.example.com.
    4h  IN  MX  10 mail.example.com.
        IN  MX  20 mail.example.net.
....
```

The type-specific-data and ttl fields are explicitly excluded from the definition of an RRset. However, RFC 2181 does not allow RRsets to have different TTL values. If they are different, only one TTL, typically the lowest, will be used to cover the RRset. In the preceding example, the TTL values are not all the same, and the lowest (4h or 14400 seconds) would typically be used for the RRset.

Resource Record Descriptions

The following sections describe each RR type defined in Table 13–1. Examples are provided where appropriate to illustrate the RR usage.

> ■**Note** While it may appear that a number of the RR types described have very specific or even exotic use, this need not be the case. As long as the RR syntax is satisfied, the RR could be used for any purpose. As an example, the AFSDB RR could be used to differentiate between, say, two types of MySQL servers. The client application would clearly need to issue the appropriate AFSDB DNS query to obtain the required results from the name server. An alternative strategy would be to define a specific user-defined MySQL RR type. This process is described in the "User-Defined RRs" section later in the chapter.

IPv4 Address (A) Record

The Address RR forward maps a host name to an IPv4 address. The IPv6 equivalent is an AAAA RR. The A RR is defined in RFC 1035. The only parameter is an IPv4 address in dotted decimal format.

A RR Syntax

```
name  ttl  class  rr    ipv4
joe        IN     A     192.168.254.3
```

If multiple addresses are defined with the same name, then BIND will respond to queries with all the addresses defined (an RRset), but the order may change depending on the value of the rrset-order statement in BIND's named.conf file. The default order is cyclic or round-robin. The same IP address may be defined with different names. IP addresses don't have to be in the same IP address class or range. The order in which A RRs are defined is not significant, but it may be easier to define them in either an ascending or descending order of IP address, as this can prevent unintentional duplicate definition of IP addresses. Since the ipv4 field is an address, not a name, there is no terminating dot. The following zone file fragment illustrates various uses of the A RR:

```
; zone fragment for example.com
$TTL 2d ; zone default = 2 days or 172800 seconds
$ORIGIN example.com.
....
joe        IN     A     192.168.0.3  ; joe & www = same ip
www        IN     A     192.168.0.3
; could be rewritten as
; www.example.com.  A      192.168.0.3
fred 3600 IN     A     192.168.0.4  ; ttl overrides $TTL default
ftp        IN     A     192.168.0.5 ; round-robin with next
           IN     A     192.168.0.6
mail       IN     A     192.168.0.15  ; mail = round-robin
mail       IN     A     192.168.0.32
mail       IN     A     192.168.0.33
squat      IN     A     10.0.14.13  ; address in another range & class
```

In the preceding example, BIND will respond to A queries for mail.example.com as follows—assume use of the rrset-order {order cyclic;}; statement or no rrset-order statement, in which case it defaults to cyclic:

```
1st query 192.168.0.15, 192.168.0.32, 192.168.0.33
2nd query 192.168.0.33, 192.168.0.15, 192.168.0.32
3rd query 192.168.0.32, 192.168.0.33, 192.168.0.15
4th query 192.168.0.15, 192.168.0.32, 192.168.0.33
```

Multiple names may be used to define the same IP address as shown in the preceding example for joe and www. Many people prefer to use a CNAME RR (defined later in this chapter) to achieve the same result. There is no functional difference between the two definitions except that multiple A RRs are marginally faster since they involve less work when processing a query.

Note This book uses both FQDN and unqualified name formats when defining left-hand and right-hand names to expose the reader to a variety of styles. It is recommended that a single style be used throughout zone files to avoid confusion; for example, FQDN in right-hand names, unqualified in left-hand names, or whatever style you find less confusing. Do not be tempted to adopt a style solely because it is shorter. If the style is short and less confusing—bliss.

Experimental IPv6 Address (A6) Record

The A6 RR is an experimental RR used to forward map host names to IPv6 addresses. RFC 3363 changed the status of the A6 RR, defined in RFC 2874, from a PROPOSED STANDARD to EXPERIMENTAL due primarily to performance and operational concerns. The current IETF recommendation is to use AAAA RRs to forward map IPv6 addresses. It is not clear at this time when (or if) the A6 RR will ever be restored to recommended usage by the IETF, even though it is fully supported by BIND. It is described here because it does significantly reduce the effort required to define an IPv6 address by recognizing the hierarchical nature of IPv6 addresses and allowing various parts of addresses to be defined in separate zone files or as separate parts of the same zone file. The default behavior of current BIND versions is to issue AAAA RR queries for IPv6 or A RR and AAAA RR queries when using dual-stack implementations. The only way to force use of A6 RRs at this time is to use BIND 9.2.1 or lower. IPv6 addresses are described in Chapter 5.

A6 RR Syntax

```
name    ttl  class  A6  prefix  ipv6 [next-name]
joe          IN     A6  64      ::1  subnet1.example.com.
```

The prefix field defines the number of bits (0 to 128) that are *not* defined by the A6 RR. In the preceding example, 64 bits are defined by this A6 RR, and 64 bits will be defined by another A6 RR. If the prefix is 0, then no additional A6 RRs are required, the complete IPv6 address is defined in this RR, and the A6 RR has the same functionality as an AAAA RR.

The ipv6 field contains that part of the IPv6 address that is defined by this A6 RR, which in the preceding example is 64 bits (128 – prefix). A full 128 bits must be defined in each A6 RR; bits that are not defined within any A6 RR should by convention be set to 0 as in the preceding example.

The optional next-name field defines the name of another A6 RR, which will define the remaining bits (64 in the preceding example) of the IPv6 address. This field is mandatory if the prefix field is not 0; that is, the IPv6 address in this A6 RR is not completely defined.

A6 RRs may be chained such that an A6 record pointed to by one A6 RR may itself point to another A6 RR that describes the next part of the address. This process is illustrated in the following fragment where the zone file separates the subnet definition (bits 48 to 63) from the interface ID and in turn defines an additional A6 pointer for a target IPv6 address of 2001:dba:ddef:1::1:

```
; zone fragment for example.com
$TTL 2d ; zone default = 2 days or 172800 seconds
$ORIGIN example.com.
....
joe          IN A6 64      ::1  subnet1.example.com.
....
; the next A6 RR defines the subnet ID only (16 bits) and
; references a further A6 RR for the remaining 48 bits
subnet1      IN A6 48      0:0:0:1:: example-com.example.net.
....
```

In the preceding fragment, the second A6 RR contains only 16 valid bits (128 – 64 – 48 = 16) and leaves a further 48 bits to be defined at the A6 RR with the name example-com.example.net., which is contained in an external domain (example.net). The second A6 RR defines a full 128-bit address (0:0:0:1::) with the relevant part (the subnet ID of 1) in the correct position (bits 48 to 63); all other bits in the address are 0.

The A6 RR at example-com.example.net could define the remaining 48 bits or further chain to the Internet registry that assigned the address blocks. In the following fragment, the remaining A6 RRs are shown in a series of zone files reflecting the IPv6 hierarchy—each $ORIGIN directive is assumed to be a separate zone file:

```
$ORIGIN example.net.
; NLA assigns 19 bits
example-com  IN A6  29  0:2:ddef:: ipv6.example.org.

$ORIGIN example.org.
; SLA assigns remaining 29 bits
ipv6         IN A6  0  2001:db8::
```

The resulting address of joe.example.com is 2001:dba:ddef:1::1. Once established, the A6 RR chains should be stable, but the address values contained within them can be easily and readily changed, allowing network renumbering to be a fairly painless process.

The concerns expressed by the IETF, which led to the A6 RR being relegated to EXPERIMENTAL status, are that a single address lookup can result in a significant number of DNS transactions, any one of which could fail; the chains can take some time to debug and are potentially error-prone; and it is also possible to create A6 RR loops.

IPv6 Address (AAAA) Record

The AAAA RR is used to forward map hosts to IPv6 addresses and is the current IETF recommendation for this purpose. IPv6 is described in Chapter 5. The AAAA (colloquially referred to as Quad A) RR is functionally similar to the A RR used for IPv4 addresses and is defined in RFC 3596.

AAAA RR Syntax

```
name ttl class  rr   ipv6
joe      IN     A    2001:db8::1
```

If multiple addresses are defined with the same name, then BIND will respond to queries with a list of the addresses, but the order may change on successive queries depending on the value of the rrset-order statement in BIND's named.conf file. The default order is cyclic or round-robin. The same IP may be defined with different names. IP addresses do not have to be in the same subnet or use the same global routing prefix. The order in which AAAA RRs are defined is not significant, but it may be easier to define them in either an ascending or descending order of IP address since this can prevent unintentional duplication of IP addresses. Since the ipv6 field is an address and not a name, there is no terminating dot. The following zone file fragment illustrates various uses of the AAAA RR:

```
; zone fragment for example.com
$TTL 2d ; zone default = 2 days or 172800 seconds
$ORIGIN example.com.
....
joe           IN      AAAA        2001:db8::3  ; joe & www = same ip
www           IN      AAAA        2001:db8::3
; functionally the same as the preceding record
www.example.com.      AAAA        2001:db8::3
fred  3600 IN         AAAA        2001:db8::4  ; ttl =3600 overrides $TTL default
ftp           IN      AAAA        2001:db8::5 ; round robin with next
              IN      AAAA        2001:db8::6
mail          IN      AAAA        2001:db8::7  ; mail = round robin
mail          IN      AAAA        2001:db8::32
mail          IN      AAAA        2001:db8::33
squat         IN      AAAA        2001:db8:0:0:1::13  ; address in another subnet
```

IPv6 and IPv4 RRs can be freely mixed in the zone file, as shown the following fragment:

```
; zone fragment for example.com
$TTL 2d ; zone default = 2 days or 172800 seconds
$ORIGIN example.com.
....

www           IN      A       192.168.0.3
mail          IN      A       192.168.0.32
www           IN      AAAA    2001:db8::3
mail          IN      AAAA    2001:db8::32
```

Blank name substitution can also be used in mixed configurations if this is more convenient or understandable:

```
; zone fragment for example.com
$TTL 2d ; zone default = 2 days or 172800 seconds
$ORIGIN example.com.
....
www           IN      A       192.168.0.3
              IN      AAAA    2001:db8::3
mail          IN      A       192.168.0.32
              IN      AAAA    2001:db8::32
```

In both preceding fragments, it is assumed that the hosts, www.example.com and mail.example.com, are running dual (IPv4/IPv6) IP stacks.

AFS Database (AFSDB) Record

The AFS Database RR defines a host that provides an AFS Database service (AFS was originally the Andrew File System). The purpose of this RR is to allow hosts within the domain to discover the host or hosts that provide both the AFS service and the type of service. The AFSDB RR is experimental and is defined in RFC 1183. RFC 5864 deprecates the use of the AFSDB RR in favor of the generic SRV RR but continues to allow for the use of AFSDB RRs when used with older clients that may not recognize the SRV RR type.

AFSDB RR Syntax

```
name    ttl class AFSDB  sub-type host
joe          IN    AFSDB 2          joe.people.example.com.
```

The sub-type field may be either 1 = the AFS version 3.0 of the service or 2 = the OSF DCE/NCA (no longer used) version of the AFS VLDB service. The host field defines the host name that provides the sub-type service. The following fragment shows the use of the AFSDB RR:

```
; zone file fragment for example.com
$TTL 2d ; zone TTL default = 2 days or 172800 seconds
$ORIGIN example.com.
...
@           IN  AFSDB  1  joe.example.com.
            IN  AFSDB  1  bill.example.com.
joe         IN  A      192.168.254.3
bill        IN  A      192.168.254.4
....
```

In the preceding fragment, multiple hosts providing the same sub-type are shown—the order of use is not defined in the RFC.

RFC 5864 allows for two separate AFS services (VLDB and PTS) to be discovered through the use of the _service field of the SRV RR (described later in this chapter) which have been allocated the values of _afs3-vlserver (VLDB service) and _afs3-prserver (PTS service), in both cases using a _proto value of either _udp (the normal case) or _tcp (possible future use). The SRV RR, since it returns a port number, allows non-standard ports to be used to provide either of the AFS service types.

Address Prefix List (APL) Record

The Address Prefix List RR is an RR that may be used to define one or more IP addresses or IP address ranges for any required purpose. The APL RR is experimental and is defined in RFC 3132.

APL RR Syntax

```
name     class  ttl  rr  [!]af:address/prefix
router1  IN          APL 1:192.168.38.0/24 !1:192.168.38.0/26
```

The ! field is optional and, if present, indicates negation; that is, the following address or address range is explicitly excluded. The negation feature can greatly reduce the number of entries required to define a given address range. To illustrate this point, in the preceding example, the first value (192.168.38.0/24) defines an IPv4 address range from 192.168.38.0 to 192.168.38.255. The negated part (!192.168.38.0/26) excludes 64 IPv4 addresses (192.168.38.0 to 192.168.38.63) that lie in this range. If the negation value was not used, then this definition would require all the positive ranges to be defined, which in the preceding case would result in 192.168.38.64/26, 192.168.38.128/26, and 192.168.38.192/26. The af field defines the address family as defined by IANA (`www.iana.org/assignments/address-family-numbers`); from this list, IPv4 = 1 and IPv6 = 2. The `address/prefix` value is the IP address, whose format is defined by af value, written in the IP prefix (or slash) notation.

The following fragment shows the use of the APL RR to indicate the range of private addresses IPv4 used by a NAT-PT (IPv4 to IPv6) gateway and the corresponding public (Global Unicast) IPv6 addresses:

```
; zone file fragment for example.com
$TTL 2d ; zone TTL default = 2 days or 172800 seconds
$ORIGIN example.com.
...
nat-pt    IN  A     192.168.254.3
          IN  AAAA  2001:db8::17
          IN  APL   (
                    1:192.168.254.0/27  ; IPv4 = 32
                    2:2001:db8::0/122   ; IPv6 = 64
                    !2:2001:db8::37/128 ; excluding 1 IPv6
                    )
....
```

The APL RR does not define any specific application or requirement for the address lists. The preceding example, which is entirely fictitious, shows a possible use of the APL RR.

ATM Address (ATMA) Record

The Asynchronous Transfer Mode Address RR is the equivalent of an A RR for ATM endpoints. It associates an ATM address in either E.164 format or the AESA (ATM End System Address, defined in ISO8348/AD 2). The ATMA RR is a private RR type. It has been allocated an ID value by IANA, though it is not defined by an RFC, but by the Broadband Forum standards document (`www.broadband-forum.org/technical/atmtechspec.php`), document reference `af-saa-0069.000.pdf`, which is available at no charge. This specification defines both forward and reverse mapping. The ATMA RR is not supported by the any BIND release.

Certificate (CERT) Record

The Certificate RR may be used to store either public key certificates or certificate revocation lists (CRL) in the zone file. The CERT RR is defined in RFC 4398.

CERT RR Syntax

```
name ttl class  rr   type key-tag algorithm cert-crl
joe      IN     CERT 1    12179   3         (
                         AQPSKmynfzW4kyBvO15MUG2DeIQ3
                         Cbl+BBZH4b/OPY1kxkmvHjcZc8no
                         kfzj31GajIQKY+5CptLr3buXA1Oh
                         WqTkF7H6RfoRqXQeogmMHfpftf6z
                         Mv1LyBUgia7za6ZEzOJBOztyvhjL
                         742iU/TpPSEDhm2SNKLijfUppn1U
                         aNvv4w==  )
```

For the CERT RR, the type field defines the certificate format and may take one of the following values:

0 = Reserved
1 = X.509 Certificate (RFC 5280)
2 = SKPI - Simple Public Key Certificate (RFC 2693)
3 = OpenPGP Packet(RFC 4880, 5581)
4 = IPKIX   The URL of an X.509 data object
5 = ISPKI   The URL of an SPKI certificate
6 = IPGP The fingerprint and URL of an OpenPGP packet (RFC 4398)
7 ACPKIX   Attribute Certificate (RFC 5755)
8 IACPKIX The URL of an Attribute Certificate
9–252 = Currently unassigned
253 = Private URI (see the text that follows)
254 = Private OID (see the text that follows)
255 = Reserved
256-65279 = Available for IANA assignment
65280-65534 = Experimental
65535 = Reserved

The value 253 specifies that the format of the cert-crl field will commence with a URI that defines the address such as a host name of the location that may be interpreted by the recipient to define the format of the certificate. The URI must be followed by a single space and then a certificate whose representation format is defined by the URI.

The value 254 specifies that the format of the cert-crl field will commence with an object identifier (OID) that defines an object that may be interpreted by the recipient to define the format of the certificate. The OID must be followed by one or more spaces and then the certificate whose representation format is defined by the OID. In general, the indirect form (URL of…) should only be used when including the certificate directly in the RR will result in a total DNS packet of > 512 bytes, though with the increasing use of DNSSEC this limit is now somewhat academic.

The key-tag field is generated by the dnssec-keygen utility to identify the key embedded in the certificate. The algorithm field defines the cryptographic algorithm being used and is now aligned to be the same list as defined in the algorithm field for DNSKEY, DS, and RRSIG (see the "DNSKEY RR" section later in this chapter).

The cert-crl field contains the certificate or a certificate revocation list entry (see also text preceding this list if the type field is either 253 or 254) in the format defined by the relevant RFC associated with the type field. The CERT RR X.509 cert-crl field data may be generated using tools such as OpenSSL and GnuTLS and then edited into the RR.

RFC 4398 makes a number of recommendations as to the name value used to store the CERT RR (Section 3). In particular, it identifies a content-based method where the querying party has some knowledge of the certificate content and a purpose-based method where the querying party has some knowledge of the purpose for which the certificate is being used. In the later case, it identifies appropriate names for three purposes:

1. *S/MIME Certificate:* In this case, the name would be derived from the mail address. Thus, if mail originates from the address user@example.com, then the corresponding CERT RR would be located at user.example.com.

2. *TLS (SSL) Certificate:* Any CERT RR would be located at the host name supplying the service. Thus, if the TLS certificate were being used with www.example.com, then the CERT RR would appear at this name. The current TLS specification (RFC 5246) does not allow certificates to be obtained other than through either a Server or Client Certificate message; thus a CERT RR obtained using this method would currently only provide for additional verification of any server supplied x.509 (SSL) certificate.

3. *IPsec Certificate:* In this case, the CERT could appear either at the host name, if known, or at the reversed IP (IPv4 or IPv6) address associated with the domain. Thus, if an IPsec service were provided by the host `ipsec.example.com` at IP address 192.168.2.1, the corresponding CERT RR could be provided at either `ipsec.example.com` or `1.2.168.192.example.com`.

Canonical Name (CNAME) Record

A canonical name record maps an alias to the real or canonical name that may lie inside or outside the current zone. *Canonical* simply means the expected or real name. The CNAME RR is defined in RFC 1035.

CNAME RR Syntax

```
name  ttl  class  rr     canonical-name
www        IN     CNAME  server1.example.com.
```

The most common use of CNAME RRs is where a host has more than one possible name; for example, assume a server has a real name of `server1.example.com` but also hosts a web and an FTP service; then both `www.example.com` and `ftp.example.com` must be *resolvable* (must translate) to the same IP address as `server1.example.com`. This can be done using multiple A records as shown previously, but many people elect to use an A RR for the real name, `server1.example.com`, and use CNAME RRs for `www.example.com` and `ftp.example.com`, both of which alias `server1.example.com`, as shown in the following fragment:

```
; zone fragment for example.com
$TTL 2d ; zone default = 2 days or 172800 seconds
$ORIGIN example.com.
....
server1  IN   A      192.168.0.3
www      IN   CNAME  server1
ftp      IN   CNAME  server1
```

A name defined with a CNAME RR is only allowed to have a NSEC/NSEC3, KEY, DNSKEY, and RRSIG RR (used in DNSSEC only) using the same name; thus, it's not permissible, for example, to define a TXT RR or an RP RR using the left-hand name defined in the CNAME RR.

CNAME RRs incur performance overheads. The most common DNS query is for an A RR, or an AAAA RR if IPv6—the end system typically needs an address that is only defined with these RR types. In the preceding example, if a query for the address of `www.example.com` is received (an A or AAAA query), two lookup operations are performed on the master or slave server. The first lookup finds `www`, which is a CNAME; this is followed by a lookup for `server1.example.com` to obtain the IP address. In other words, the CNAME *chain* is followed to attempt to resolve the original request for an IP address. On low-volume name servers, the additional resources used are probably not significant, but on high-volume servers the additional load can become nontrivial. The user must make a choice to balance what many see as the convenience of using CNAME RRs against the possible performance degradation involved.

While use of CNAME RRs with NS and MX records is widely implemented and normally generates a working configuration, it is theoretically not permitted (RFC 1034 section 3.6.2) since it can result in lost names. This fragment illustrates a widely used but technically invalid configuration:

```
; zone fragment for example.com
$TTL 2d ; zone default = 2 days or 172800 seconds
$ORIGIN example.com.
....
         IN    MX  10  mail.example.com.
```

```
mail      IN      CNAME   server1
server1   IN      A       192.168.0.3
```

In the preceding configuration, when a query is issued for the A RR of mail.example.com, the result will return both the mail.example.com CNAME RR and the server1.example.com A RR. When the A RR is used by a mail application, the name associated with the CNAME can be lost; for instance, there may be a valid MX record referencing the host mail.example.com and elsewhere an A RR referencing server1.example.com, but nothing joining the two records. The following fragment, by reordering the RRs, will achieve the same result and allow a valid mapping of the MX name to the A RR name:

```
; zone fragment for example.com
$TTL 2d ; zone default = 2 days or 172800 seconds
$ORIGIN example.com.
....
          IN      MX 10   mail.example.com.
server1   IN      CNAME   mail
mail      IN      A       192.168.0.3
```

For many users, the preceding simply feels uncomfortable because the *real* host name is server1.example.com, not mail.example.com, but it is a perfectly legitimate definition that will cause no problems.

It is permitted for one CNAME RR to alias another CNAME RR, but this considered bad practice due to the additional lookup loads involved and because it can lead to CNAME loops (that is, a CNAME RR references a CNAME RR, which references a CNAME RR, and so on, ad infinitum).

CNAME RRs are the only way to handle references to RRs that lie in another domain, sometimes referred to as an *out-of-bailiwick* or *out-of-zone reference*. The following fragment shows that ftp.example.com is actually provided by ftp.example.net:

```
; zone fragment for example.com
$TTL 2d ; zone default = 2 days or 172800 seconds
$ORIGIN example.com.
....
ftp       IN      CNAME   ftp.example.net.
```

The following fragment allows URLs of the form www.example.com and example.com to both access the same web service—in this case, one that also uses DNS load-balancing or resilience since three IP addresses will be returned:

```
; www.example.com and example.com access
$TTL 2d ; zone default = 2 days
$ORIGIN example.com.
; resolves example.com to an IP
....
@         IN      A       192.168.254.8
          IN      A       192.168.254.9
          IN      A       192.168.254.10
www       IN      CNAME   example.com.
```

As in all such cases, the above could also have been accomplished with A RRs for www; however, in this case three such A RRs would be required to provide similar capabilities.

Delegation of Reverse Names (DNAME) Record

The Delegation of Reverse Name RR is designed to assist the delegation of reverse mapping by reducing the size of the data that must be entered. The DNAME RR is designed to be used in conjunction with a bit label (described in the "Bit Labels" section earlier in the chapter) but does not strictly require a bit label. The DNAME without a bit label is equivalent to a CNAME when used in a reverse-map (or delegation) zone file, an example of which is provided in the "Delegate Reverse Subnet Maps" section of Chapter 8. RFC 3363 changed the status of the bit label and the A6 RR from PROPOSED STANDARD to EXPERIMENTAL due to concerns over performance and that the new bit labels would require a change to all DNS software in the root and gTLD servers before the bit label could become active. Because the DNAME RR without bit labels is functionally equivalent to CNAME, its use is deprecated. The current IETF recommendation is to use text labels (names) with PTR records under the IP6.ARPA domain for the reverse mapping of IPv6 addresses. The DNAME RR is defined in RFC 2672 and its use with wildcards was clarified by RFC 4592.

DNAME RR Syntax

```
name            ttl  class  rr  next-name
1.0.0.0         IN     DNAME  ipv6.example.org.
```

An example of the use of DNAME RRs to delegate reverse mapping of IPv6 addresses is illustrated in the "Bit Labels" section earlier in the chapter.

DHCID Record

The Dynamic Host Control ID (DHCID) RR is designed to prevent DHCP Servers from using DDNS (see the "Securing Dynamic Updates" section of Chapter 10) to update the same A or AAAA RR (and consequently the associated PTR RRs) for multiple hosts by creating a unique host ID. DHCID RRs would not normally be manually added to a zone file but rather be added as part of a DDNS update cycle described later in this chapter. The DHCID RR is defined by RFC 4701 and has been supported since BIND 9.5+.

DHCID RR Syntax

```
name ttl class DHCID dhcid-data
bill.example.com. IN DHCID (AAIBY2/...
                            ...OjxfNuVAA2kjEA=)
```

The dhcid-data is a unique host identifier and contains three fields (source-type, digest-type, digest) but whose presentational (text) format is defined by RFC 4701 to be entirely base64. The values and meanings of the three fields is defined in the "DNS Binary RR Format" section of Chapter 15.

When a DHCP Server attempts to update an A or AAAA RR on behalf of a client, it first checks to see if a DHCID RR exists at the desired FQDN of the client, and if so, verifies that the dhcid-data is the same as that for the current client. If no DHCID RR exists or the dhcid-data field is different, the DHCPserver should either fail the operation or restart with a new client FQDN. While DHCID RR may be used with PTR RRs, it will typically only be used with A and AAAA RRs since it assumed that any DHCP DDNS update cycle will start with these RR types.

DLV Record

The DNS Lookaside Validation (DLV) RR is functionally identical to the DS RR (defined below) with the exception of the RR type code value and is only used in DLV implementations (alternative trust chains, described in Chapter 11's "DNSSEC Lookaside Validation" section). The DLV RR may be optionally created by the dnssec-signzone utility (Chapter 9) and is defined by the INFORMATIONAL RFC 4431.

DNSKEY Record

The DNSKEY RR describes the public key of a public key (asymmetric) cryptographic algorithm used with DNSSEC (see Chapter 11). It is used to authenticate signed keys (if a Key Signing Key [KSK]) or zones (if a Zone Signing Key [ZSK]). The DNSKEY RR is typically generated by the dnssec-keygen utility (see Chapter 9) and is defined in RFC 4034.

DNSKEY RR Syntax

```
name ttl class   rr    flags proto algorithm key-data
example.com. IN   DNSKEY 256   3       5 (
                        AQPSKmynfzW4kyBvO15MUG2DeIQ3
                        Cbl+BBZH4b/OPY1kxkmvHjcZc8no
                        kfzj31GajIQKY+5CptLr3buXA1Oh
                        WqTkF7H6RfoRqXQeogmMHfpftf6z
                        Mv1LyBUgia7za6ZEzOJBOztyvhjL
                        742iU/TpPSEDhm2SNKLijfUppn1U
                        aNvv4w==   )
```

The flags field is the decimal representation of a 16-bit field that has the following bit-significant values (bit numbering is the normal IETF standard of left-to-right base 0):

- *Bits 0 to 6*: Currently unused and must be zero.

- *Bit 7*: If set, this indicates a ZSK, and the name field must be that of the apex or root of the zone being signed, as shown in the preceding example. If not set, the key may not be used to sign zones, and the name field will typically reference a host record to which the DNSKEY applies.

- *Bit 8*: If set (1), this indicates the key-data field of this DNSKEY RR has been revoked and therefore must not be used to authenticate signatures (RRSIG RRs). It is relevant only to RFC 5011-compliant (Trust Anchor Automation; see the "Key Handling Automation" section of Chapter 11) resolvers and is relevant only to KSKs. If not set (0), this key may be used, subject to RFC5011 acceptance periods if applicable, by validating resolvers to authenticate signatures (RRSIG RRs).

- *Bits 9 to 14*: Currently unused and must be set to zero.

- *Bit 15*: If set, this is a Secure Entry Point key, and in this case, bit 7 must also be set to 1. This indicates for administrative purposes only that the key is a KSK; consequently, this bit is frequently referred to as the KSK bit.

The only valid hexadecimal combinations of the flags field are 0000, 0100, and 0101, which yield decimal values used in the RR of, respectively 0, 256, and 257.

The proto field can only take the value of 3 at this time; all other values are invalid.

The algorithm field may take one of the following values (www.iana.org/assignments/dns-sec-alg-numbers):

```
0 = Reserved
1 = RSA-MD5—not recommended (RFC 2537)
2 = Diffie-Hellman (RFC 2539)
3 = DSA/SHA-1—optional (RFC 3755, 2536)
4 = Elliptic curve—not currently standardized
5 = RSA/SHA-1—mandatory (RFC 3755, 3110)
```

6 = DSA-NSEC3-SHA1 (RFC 5155)
7 = RSASHA1-NSEC3-SHA1 (RFC 5155)
8 = RSA/SHA-256 (RFC 5702)
9 = unassigned
10 = RSA/SHA512 (RFC 5702)
11 = unassigned
12 = GOST R 34.10-2001 (RFC 5933)
13 - 122 = Currently unassigned
123 - 251 = Reserved
252 = Indirect (see the "Alternative Cryptographic Algorithms" section later in this chapter)
253 = Private URI (see the "Alternative Cryptographic Algorithms" section later in this chapter)
254 = Private OID (see the "Alternative Cryptographic Algorithms" section later in this chapter)
255 = Reserved

The algorithm values 6 = DSA-NSEC3-SHA1 and 7 = RSASHA1-NSEC3-SHA1 are aliases for the values 3 and 5, respectively, in the list above. However, the values 6 and 7 must be used if the signed zone uses NSEC3 to avoid problems with incompatibility in NSEC3-unaware DNSSEC validating resolvers. If NSEC3 is not being used within a zone, then the values 3 and 5 must be used. The gory details associated with this point are further explained in Chapter 11's "NSEC3/Opt-Out" section.

The key-data field is the base64 (RFC 4648) representation of the public key data. As shown in the example, if enclosed in the parentheses, whitespace is allowed for layout purposes.

Note RSA-MD5 is no longer recommended due to a number of discovered weaknesses published in February 2005. The weaknesses do not invalidate use of the algorithm.

Delegation Signer (DS) Record

The Delegation Signer RR is used in DNSSSEC (see Chapter 11) to create the chain of trust or authority from a signed parent zone to a signed child zone. The DS RR contains a hash (or digest) of a DNSKEY RR at the apex of the child zone. By convention, this DNSKEY RR has the SEP bit set (it has a flags field value of 257), but this is not a requirement of the DNSSEC protocol. If a chain of trust is required for the zone sub.example.com (the child), the DS RR is added to the zone example.com (the parent) at the point of delegation—the NS RRs that point to sub.example.com. Both the parent and child zones must be signed. The DS RR is optionally generated by the dnssec-signzone utility (described in Chapter 9) and is defined in RFC 4034.

DS RR Syntax

```
name  ttl  class  rr  key-tag algorithm digest-type digest
joe        IN     DS  13245   5 1       (E0B4B11D0FCE00E3F
                                        FA89FA873F40DC51281BF34)
```

The key-tag field is generated algorithmically by the dnssec-keygen utility and identifies the particular DNSKEY RR at the child zone; this is required because more than one DNSKEY RR may be present at the child zone apex either because separate KSK and ZSKs are used or due to key-rollover operations. The algorithm field defines the algorithm used by the key-tag-identified DNSKEY RR at the child zone, which is recommended to be a KSK, and takes the same values defined for the algorithm field of the DNSKEY RR above.

The digest-type field defines the digest algorithm being used and may take one of the following values:

0 = Reserved
1 = SHA-1—mandatory
2 = SHA-256 (RFC 4509)
3–255 = Currently unassigned

The digest field is the base64 encoding of the digest of the KSK DNSKEY RR at the child zone.

The dnssec-signzone utility will optionally generate the DS RR with a file name of dsset-zonename; for example, if the zone being signed is sub.example.com, the resulting file is called dsset-sub.example.com.

As previously stated, the DS RR is included in the parent (signed) zone, which must then be re-signed following its addition. The experimental DNSSEC Lookaside Validation (DLV) system provides an alternative method of creating chains of trust using a DLV RR, which is functionally identical to the DS RR with the exception of the RR type code. DLV is described further in Chapter 11.

System Information (HINFO) Record

The System Information RR allows the user to define the hardware type and operating system (OS) in use at a host. The HINFO RR was defined in RFC 1035. For security reasons, these records are rarely used on public servers.

HINFO RR Syntax

```
name ttl  class  rr      hardware      OS
          IN     HINFO   PC-Intel-700mhz "Ubuntu 10.04"
```

If a space exists in either the hardware or OS field, that field must be enclosed in quotes. There must be at least one space between the hardware and OS fields. The preceding example illustrates that quotes are not required with the hardware field—the spaces have been replaced with - (hyphen)—but are required with the OS field, since it contains spaces within the field. No validation is performed on the field contents other than the space rules defined previously, which means this record can be used for any purpose; for instance, the fields could contain the name and phone number of technical support for the system. The following example shows the use of the HINFO RR:

```
; zone file fragment for example.com
$TTL 2d ; zone default = 2 days
$ORIGIN example.com.
....
www       IN     A      192.168.254.8
          IN     HINFO  "AMD 64 4.8GHZ 10TB" "FreeBSD 8.1"
```

The preceding HINFO record is associated with www.example.com.

Host Identity Protocol (HIP) Record

The Host Identity Protocol (RFC 5201), which has EXPERIMENTAL status, is concerned with trying to abstract the IP address/Name relationship by essentially creating a new namespace. In HIP, the Host Identity (HI), roughly equivalent to a host name, is defined to be a public key; the Host Identity Tag (HIT) is a shorter hash of the public key. An end-point (a host) may have one or more unique Host Identities. The HI is assumed to be enduring in the HIP model (though it *may* change) whereas the IP address is assumed to be ephemeral (short lived). The HI, being a public key, may be directly used with, say, IPsec's Encapsulating Security Payload (ESP) protocol. Within HIP, Host Identities may communicate using one or more third parties called Rendezvous Servers (RVSs). In particular, HI will do this when the IP address may change or is changing continuously; for example, in a mobile environment, the HIP uses a DNS HIP RR (defined in the EXPERIMENTAL RFC 5205) to maintain translation information.

HIP RR Syntax

```
name    ttl class rr  algorithm hit hi [rvs …]
joe         IN   HIP  (
                                     2                                     ; algorithm = RSA
                                     200100…. 1D578         ; HIT
                                     AwEAAbdx…. dXF5D ; HI
                                     rvs.example.com.)        ; optional RVS name
```

The algorithm field defines the asymmetric encryption method used in the hi field. The values are limited to those defined for IPSECKEY RR (described later in the chapter).

The hit field is the hash (SHA1) of the hi field encoded in base16 (RFC 4648). The hi field is the base64 (RFC 4648) encoded public key, whose format is defined by algorithm and which represents the Host Identity. The rvs field is optional. When present, it is the name of a Rendezvous Server used to contact this HI. Multiple space separated RVSs may be defined; they are used in the order defined for this RR only.

In the case where an RVS name is not present in the HIP RR, there would be a corresponding A or AAAA RR at the same name, as shown by the following fragment:

```
; zone example.com
…
joe         IN    A     192.168.2.1
            IN    HIP   (
                                     2                                     ; algorithm = RSA
                                     200100…. 1D578         ; HIT
                                     AwEAAbdx…. dXF5D) ; HI
…
```

In the case where an rvs field is present, an corresponding A or AAAA RR would be present at the rvs name, as shown in the following fragment:

```
; zone example.com
…
joe         IN    HIP   (
                                     2                                     ; algorithm = RSA
                                     200100…. 1D578         ; HIT
                                     AwEAAbdx…. dXF5D ; HI
                                       rvs.example.com.)        ; rvs
…
rvs         IN    A     192.168.2.17
```

While the name of the RVS server in the above example lies within the domain (*rvs.example.com*), it could equally be an *out-of-zone* name such as rvs.example.net. In this case, obviously, the corresponding A or AAAA RR would lie in the example.net domain.

The HIP RR is not supported by any BIND9 release version but a BIND patch to support the HIP RR may be obtained from openhip.cvs.sourceforge.net/openhip/patches/bind.

Integrated Services Digital Network (ISDN) Record

The Integrated Services Digital Network RR is the equivalent of an A RR for ISDN Customer Premise Equipment (CPE). It associates the telephone number of the ISDN CPE to a host name. The ISDN RR has EXPERIMENTAL status and is defined in RFC 1183.

ISDN RR Syntax

```
name   ttl class  rr  isdn-number    sa
joe        IN    ISDN 1441115551212 001
```

The isdn-number is in E.164 format (a telephone number). The telephone number is assumed to begin with the E.164 international dial sequence. There must be no spaces within the field.

The sa field defines an optional subaddress used with ISDN multidrop configurations and, if present, is separated from the isdn-number field by one or more spaces. If not used, it is omitted. Since the isdn-number is an address, not a name, there is no terminating dot.

IPSEC Key (IPSECKEY) Record

The IPSEC Key RR is used for storage of keys used specifically for IPSec operations. Originally, the KEY RR was designed to store such keys generically using an application subtype value. RFC 3445 limited the KEY RR to DNS security uses only. Using this new RR type means that an application that wishes to establish a VPN (an IPSec service) to a specific host name can query the DNS for an IPSECKEY RR with the host name it wishes to connect to and obtain the relevant details such as the optional gateway and the cryptographic algorithm being used. The IPSECKEY RR is defined by RFC 4025.

IPSECKEY RR Syntax

```
name ttl  class    rr   prec gwt algorithm gw key-data
joe        IN    IPSECKEY 256   1     2   192.168.2.1 (
                      AQPSKmynfzW4kyBvO15MUG2DeIQ3
                      Cbl+BBZH4b/OPY1kxkmvHjcZc8no
                      kfzj31GajIQKY+5CptLr3buXA1Oh
                      WqTkF7H6RfoRqXQeogmMHfpftf6z
                      Mv1LyBUgia7za6ZEzOJBOztyvhjL
                      742iU/TpPSEDhm2SNKLijfUppn1U
                      aNvv4w==   )
```

The prec (precedence) field is used the same way as the preference field of an MX RR to define the order of priority. Lower numbers take the highest precedence. Values may lie in the range 0 to 255 only.

The gwt field defines the type of gateway and may take one of the following values:

0 = No gateway (the host supports the IPSec service directly).
1 = An IPv4 gateway is defined; it should be used to access this host.
2 = An IPv6 gateway is defined; it should be used to access this host.
3 = A named host is present; it should be used to access this host.

The algorithm field may take one of the values defined here:

0 = No key is present.
1 = DSA (RFC 2536).
2 = RSA (RFC 3110).

3–255 = Not assigned.

The gw field defines the gateway and may be either a single . (dot) if the qwt field = 0, an IPv4 address if qwt = 1, an IPv6 address if qwt = 2, or a host name if qwt = 3.

The key-data field contains the base64-encoded public key of the algorithm defined in the algorithm field. Where the IPsec service requires a certificate rather than a simple public key the CERT RR may be optionally used.

Public Key (KEY) Record

The Public Key RR was originally defined in RFC 2535 to be used for the storage of public keys for use by multiple applications such as IPSec, SSH, etc., as well as for use by DNS security methods including the original DNSSEC protocol. RFC 3445 limits this RR to use in DNS security operations such as DDNS and zone transfer due to the difficulty of querying for specific uses—DNS queries operate on the RR type field, whereas the application functionality was defined in the proto field (described in the upcoming text) and was therefore not *directly* obtained by a query operation. IPSec (IPSECKEY) and SSH (SSHFP) both have new RR types that allow applications to directly query for the relevant RR.

KEY RR Syntax

```
name ttl class  rr     flags proto algorithm key-data
joe      IN     KEY    256    3        5 (
                       AQPSKmynfzW4kyBvO15MUG2DeIQ3
                       Cbl+BBZH4b/OPY1kxkmvHjcZc8no
                       kfzj31GajIQKY+5CptLr3buXA10h
                       WqTkF7H6RfoRqXQeogmMHfpftf6z
                       Mv1LyBUgia7za6ZEzOJBOztyvhjL
                       742iU/TpPSEDhm2SNKLijfUppn1U
                       aNvv4w==   )
```

The original definition of this RR was significantly reduced by RFC 3445 as noted previously. The definitions that follow reflect the current RFC 3445 status, and previous values where appropriate are also shown but noted as deprecated. The flags field consists of 16 bits in which only bit 7 is now used. In the textual format, this field is represented as a decimal value of either 0 (no flag bits set), in which case the key is used with the SIG(0) or TKEY meta RR to secure DDNS or zone transfer operations, or 256 (bit 7 = 1), which allows it to still be used in zone signing or verification operations (see Chapter 11) though functionally replaced with the DNSKEY RR in DNSSEC. All other values will be ignored by DNS systems. The proto field may only take the value 3, all other values being deprecated. For historical reasons, previous versions may still exist and are defined here for completeness:

0 = Reserved
1 = TLS (deprecated by RFC 3445)
2 = E-mail (deprecated by RFC 3445)
3 = DNSSEC (only value allowed by RFC 3445)
4 = IPSEC (deprecated—replaced by IPSECKEY RR)
5–255 = Reserved

The algorithm field may take one of the following values:

0 = Reserved
1 = RSA-MD5—not recommended (RFC 2537)
2 = Diffie-Hellman—optional, key only (RFC 2539)
3 = DSA—mandatory (RFC 2536)

4 = Elliptic curve—not currently standardized

5 = RSA-SHA-1—mandatory (RFC 3110)

6–251 = Available for IANA allocation

252 = Reserved for indirect keys (see the "Alternative Cryptographic Algorithms" section later in this chapter)

253 = Private URI (see the "Alternative Cryptographic Algorithms" section later in this chapter)

254 = Private OID (see the "Alternative Cryptographic Algorithms" section later in this chapter)

255 = Reserved

Note The original specification of the KEY RR (RFC 2535) only allowed algorithm types 1 to 4 defined previously and was apparently not revised; however, the dnssec-keygen utility allows algorithm 5 to be specified. Indeed, this algorithm can be used in SIG(0) operations that use the KEY RR, so it's shown in the preceding supported list.

KEY RRs are typically generated by the dnssec-keygen utility (see Chapter 9), which creates an RR that may be included if appropriate (see Chapters 10 and 11), either directly in the zone file or through the $INCLUDE directive.

While various RFCs limit the use of this RR type in a variety of ways, there is in principle nothing to stop the user from using it, and the dnssec-keygen utility that creates it, as a general-purpose public key RR for specialized applications such as secure e-mail where the functionality is known to the application and the presence of a KEY RR with the same name as, say, an RP RR could provide some unique functionality.

Key Exchanger (KX) Record

The Key Exchanger RR is provided to allow a client to query a destination host and be provided with one or more alternative hosts. It is primarily intended for use in secure operations such as creation of an IPSec VPN or similar service, though its applicability is much wider. The destination host may not be capable of providing the particular service, but in its corresponding KX RR it can nominate another host that will support the service such as a secure gateway or router, which can be used to route packets to the target host. The IPSECKEY RR replaces many of the functions of this RR type for the particular example described in the defining RFC. The KX RR is defined in RFC 2230.

KX RR Syntax

```
name  ttl  class   rr    preference alt-host
joe         IN      KX    2    rt1.example.com.
```

The preference field has exactly the same meaning and use as in the MX RR. It may take a value in the range 0 to 65535, with lower values being the most preferred. The alt-host field defines the host name where a VPN or some other service may be obtained for the current host.

Location (LOC) Record

The Location RR allows the definition of geographic positioning information associated with a host or service name. The LOC RR allows longitude, latitude, and altitude to be defined using the WGS-1984

(NAD-83) coordinate system—a US DoD standard for the definition of geographic coordinates. The LOC RR, which is experimental, was defined in RFC 1876 and was widely deployed, for instance, to allow geographic analysis of Internet backbones. Due to increased security concerns, LOC RRs are becoming significantly less common. The LOC RR can take a large number of parameters and most often uses the standard parentheses framing to allow them to be written on more than one line for clarity, as shown in the following text. Location data may be acquired using GPS equipment or from a number of websites (to varying degrees of accuracy) such as GEOnet Names Server (GNS—http://earth-info.nga.mil/gns/html/index.html), US Geological Survey's Geographic Names Information System (GNIS—http://geonames.usgs.gov), or the *Getty Thesaurus of Geographic Names Online* (www.getty.edu/research/conducting_research/vocabularies/tgn/).

LOC RR Syntax

```
name  ttl  class   rr  (
                         lat-d
                         [lat-m [lat-s]]
                         n-s
                         long-d
                         [long-m [long-s]]
                         e-w
                         alt["m"]
                         [size["m"] [hp["m"] [vp["m"]]]]
                         )
example.com.   IN   LOC  37 23 30.900 N 121 59 19.000 W 7.00m 100m 100m 2m
```

The lat-d field defines the location latitude in degrees. lat-m and lat-s are optional fields defining the minutes (lat-m) and seconds (lat-s) and, if omitted, default to zero. The field n-s is mandatory and can take the value N (north) or S (south).

The long-d field defines the location longitude in degrees. long-m and long-s are optional fields defining the minutes (long-m) and seconds (long-s) and, if omitted, default to zero. The field e-w is mandatory and can take the value E (east) or W (west).

The alt field defines the location altitude and can be either positive or negative in the range -100000.00 to 42849672.95 meters.

The size field is optional and is the diameter of the circle that encompasses the location; it represents the positional accuracy. If omitted, 1m is assumed.

The hp field is the optional horizontal accuracy and defaults to 10,000m (meters). The vp field is the vertical accuracy and, if omitted, defaults to 10m (meters). The defaults selected in these two parameters represent the typical size of zip/postal code data.

■**Note** The datum (base reference) used by the LOC record is WSG-1984 or NAD-83 (North American Datum) used by the GPS system. In some cases, geographic data uses NAD-27 as the datum, which is not the same—always verify the datum being used. Geographic data can be presented in decimal degrees. To convert decimal degrees to minutes and seconds, multiply the fractional part by 60 to get minutes and fractional minutes, and then multiply the fractional minutes by 60 to get seconds and fractional seconds.

The LOC record can be associated with any host or the domain. The following shows individual LOC RR examples using published records or publicly available data from the preceding sources and including a number of formats:

```
; Stamford, CT, US - Harbor Lighthouse
            IN    LOC  41 00 48 N 73 32 21 W 10m
; Kilmarnock, Scotland UK
            IN    LOC  (
                        55 ;latitude
                        38 ; seconds omitted
                        N
                        4 32 W ; longitude
                        100m  ; altitude - pure guess
                       )
```

The example RRs were created using random locations from the databases referenced previously. There are, as far as the author knows, no registered domains for either the Stamford Harbor Lighthouse or the town of Kilmarnock in Scotland, nor does either entity publish a LOC RR! The preceding databases typically do not provide altitude data, and while it is reasonable to suppose a lighthouse is close to sea level, the height of the town of Kilmarnock is entirely fictitious. The required accuracy of the data will depend on the reason for publishing an LOC RR, and in many cases, the longitude and latitude may suffice to give location data.

Mailbox (MB) Record

The Mailbox RR defines the location of a given domain e-mail address. The MB RR has EXPERIMENTAL status and is defined in RFC 1035. The MB record is not widely deployed; the MX RR is the dominant mail record.

MB RR Syntax

```
name    ttl class rr  mailbox-host
joe           IN   MB  fred.example.com.
```

The `mailbox-host` field defines the host where the mailbox is located. The `mailbox-host` must have a valid A RR. The name field is the mailbox name written in the standard DNS format for mailboxes: the first . (dot) is replaced with an @ (commercial at sign) when constructing the e-mail address. The example fragment that follows illustrates that the mailbox for the domain administrator, `hostmaster.example.com.` (defined in the SOA record), is located on the host `bill.example.com`, whereas the normal mail host is `mail.example.com`. The mail address, when constructed, is the normal RFC 822 format, which is hostmaster@example.com in the following example:

```
; zone file fragment for example.com
$TTL 2d ; zone TTL default = 2 days or 172800 seconds
$ORIGIN example.com.
example.com. IN      SOA  ns1.example.com. hostmaster.example.com. (
              2010121500 ; serial number
              3h         ; refresh =  3 hours
              15M        ; refresh retry = 15 minutes
              3W12h      ; expiry = 3 weeks + 12 hours
              2h20M      ; nx = 2 hours + 20 minutes
              )
             IN  MX     10  mail.example.com.
```

```
hostmaster    IN  MB        bill.example.com.
bill          IN  A         192.168.254.2
mail          IN  A         192.168.254.3
....
```

This example requires the mail system to look for an appropriate MB record—almost none do. Most mail software looks for the presence of an MX RR and delivers mail to this specified host, which is mail.example.com in this fragment. To achieve the same result in the preceding case, the mail system at mail.example.com would be configured to forward mail to the mailbox hostmaster on the host bill.example.com.

Mail Group (MG) Record

The Mail Group RR defines a group name and the mail boxes that are members of that group. The MG RR has EXPERIMENTAL status and is defined in RFC 1035. The MG record is not widely deployed; the MX RR is the dominant mail record.

MG RR Syntax

```
name    ttl class rr  mailbox-name
admins    IN   MG  fred.example.com.
```

The mailbox-name field defines the mailbox names that are part of the mail group. Mail sent to the group will be sent to each mailbox in the group. Each member of the mail group must be defined using an MB RR. The mailbox-name field is written in the standard DNS format for mailboxes, that is, the first . (dot) is replaced with an @ (commercial at sign) when constructing the e-mail address. The following fragment illustrates that the mailbox for the domain administrator, hostmaster.example.com. (defined in the SOA record), is a mail group and will cause mail to be sent to phil.example.com (phil@example.com) and sheila.example.com (sheila@example.com), both of whose MB RRs define the final destination for the mail:

```
; zone file fragment for example.com
$TTL 2d ; zone TTL default = 2 days or 172800 seconds
$ORIGIN example.com.
example.com. IN       SOA   ns1.example.com. hostmaster.example.com. (
                 2010121500 ; serial number
                 3h         ; refresh =  3 hours
                 15M        ; refresh retry = 15 minutes
                 3W12h      ; expiry = 3 weeks + 12 hours
                 2h20M      ; nx = 2 hours + 20 minutes
                 )
              IN  MX    10  mail.example.com.
hostmaster    IN  MG        phil.example.com.
              IN  MG        sheila.example.com.
phil          IN  MB        bill.example.com.
sheila        IN  MB        pc.example.com.
....
pc            IN  A         192.168.254.4
bill          IN  A         192.168.254.2
mail          IN  A         192.168.254.3
....
```

This example needs the mail system to look for appropriate MG and MB RRs—almost none do. Most mail software looks for the presence of an MX RR and delivers mail to this specified host, which is `mail.example.com` in this fragment. To achieve the same result in this case, the mail system at `mail.example.com` would have to be configured to forward mail for the mailbox `hostmaster` to both `phil@example.com` and `sheila@example.com`.

Mailbox Renamed (MR) Record

The Mailbox Renamed RR allows a mailbox name to be aliased (or forwarded) to another mailbox name. The MR RR has EXPERIMENTAL status and is defined in RFC 1035. The MB record is not widely deployed; the MX RR is the dominant mail record.

MR RR Syntax

```
name   ttl class rr  real-mailbox
joe         IN   MR  fred.example.com.
```

The `real-mailbox` field defines the aliased, or real, mailbox that must be defined with an MB RR. Mail sent to `name` will be forwarded to `real-mailbox`. The `name` and `real-mailbox` fields are the mailbox names written in the standard DNS format for mailboxes: the first . (dot) is replaced with an @ (commercial at sign) when constructing the e-mail address. The following fragment illustrates that the mailbox for the domain administrator, `hostmaster.example.com.` (defined in the SOA record), is forwarded to `phil.example.com`, located on the host `bill.example.com`, whereas the normal mail host is `mail.example.com`. The mail address when constructed is the normal format, which is `hostmaster@example.com` in the following example:

```
; zone file fragment for example.com
$TTL 2d ; zone TTL default = 2 days or 172800 seconds
$ORIGIN example.com.
example.com. IN      SOA   ns1.example.com. hostmaster.example.com. (
                2010121500 ; serial number
                3h         ; refresh =  3 hours
                15M        ; refresh retry = 15 minutes
                3W12h      ; expiry = 3 weeks + 12 hours
                2h20M      ; nx = 2 hours + 20 minutes
                )
             IN  MX     10  mail.example.com.
hostmaster   IN  MR         phil.example.com.
phil         IN  MB         bill.example.com.
....
bill         IN  A          192.168.254.2
mail         IN  A          192.168.254.3
....
```

This example needs the mail system to look for both MR and MB RRs—almost none do. Most mail software looks for the presence of an MX RR and delivers mail to this specified host, which is `mail.example.com` in this fragment. To achieve the same result in this case, the mail system at `mail.example.com` will be configured to forward mail for the mailbox `hostmaster@example.com` to `phil@example.com` on the host `bill.example.com`.

Mailbox Mail List Information (MINFO) Record

The Mailbox Mail List Information RR defines the mailbox administrator for a mail list and, optionally, a mailbox to receive error messages relating to the mail list. The MINFO RR is experimental and is defined in RFC 1035.The MINFO RR is not widely deployed; the MX RR is the dominant mail record.

MINFO RR Syntax

```
name    ttl class rr    admin-mailbox     [error-mailbox]
users      IN MINFO  fred.example.com. joe.example.com.
```

The admin-mailbox field defines the mailbox to which mail related to the mail list name will be sent. The optional error-mailbox will receive mail concerning errors relating to the mail list name. Both admin-mailbox and error-mail-box must be defined with an MB RR. The name, admin-mailbox, and error-mailbox fields are mailbox names written in the standard DNS format for mailboxes: the first . (dot) is replaced with an @ (commercial at sign) when constructing the e-mail address.

```
; zone file fragment for example.com
$TTL 2d ; zone TTL default = 2 days or 172800 seconds
$ORIGIN example.com.
example.com. IN       SOA   ns1.example.com. hostmaster.example.com. (
               2010121500 ; serial number
               3h         ; refresh =  3 hours
               15M        ; refresh retry = 15 minutes
               3W12h      ; expiry = 3 weeks + 12 hours
               2h20M      ; nx = 2 hours + 20 minutes
               )
               IN  MX    10  mail.example.com.
people         IN  MINFO     admin.example.com. broken.example.com.
admin          IN  MB        bill.example.com.
broken         IN  MB        bill.example.com.
....
bill           IN  A         192.168.254.2
mail           IN  A         192.168.254.3
....
```

This example needs the mail system to look for both MINFO and MB RRs—almost none do. Most mail software looks for the presence of an MX RR and delivers mail to this specified host, which is mail.example.com in this fragment. Mail software typically treats mail list management as a separate or loosely coupled function.

Mail Exchange (MX) Record

The Mail Exchanger RR specifies the name and relative preference of mail servers (mail exchangers in the DNS jargon) for the zone. The MX record was defined in RFC 1035.

MX RR Syntax

```
name             ttl class  rr preference name
example.com.         IN     MX 10   mail.example.com.
```

The preference field is relative to any other MX record for the zone and may take the value in the range 0 to 65535. Low values are *more* preferred. The common preferred value of 10 is just a convention and allows more preferred servers to be added without changing any other records; that is, if the most preferred server was set to 0 (again a common practice) and then an *even more preferred* server was introduced, two records would have to be changed! Any number of MX records may be defined with either different or equal preference values. The effect of using multiple MX RRs with an equal preference is described in the "DNS Load Balancing" section in Chapter 8. If the mail host lies in the same zone, it requires an A RR. The right-hand name used in an MX RR should not point to a CNAME record (see the discussion of this point in the "Canonical Name (CNAME) Record" section earlier). MX records frequently use the wildcard * (asterisk) in the name field, which is described in Chapter 8. The following example shows a domain using three mail servers, two of which are hosted within the domain. The third and least preferred is hosted externally.

```
; zone fragment for example.com
; mail servers in the same zone
$TTL 2d ; zone default = 2 days or 172800 seconds
$ORIGIN example.com.
example.com. IN      SOA    ns1.example.com. hostmaster.example.com. (
                2010121500 ; serial number
                3h         ; refresh =  3 hours
                15M        ; refresh retry = 15 minutes
                3W12h      ; expiry = 3 weeks + 12 hours
                2h20M      ; nx = 2 hours + 20 minutes
                )
                IN      MX     10  mail  ; unqualified name
; the line above is functionally the same as the line that follows
; example.com. IN      MX     10  mail.example.com.
; any number of mail servers may be defined
                IN      MX     20  mail2.example.com.
; an external back-up
                IN      MX     30  mail.example.net.
; the local mail servers need an A record
mail    IN      A      192.168.0.3
mail2   IN      A      192.168.0.3
```

The following fragment shows two mail servers, neither of which is located in the domain and hence do not require A RRs:

```
; zone fragment for example.com
; mail servers not in the zone
$TTL 2d ; zone default = 2 days or 172800 seconds
$ORIGIN example.com.
example.com. IN      SOA    ns1.example.com. root.example.com. (
                2010121500 ; serial number
                3h         ; refresh =  3 hours
                15M        ; refresh retry = 15 minutes
                3W12h      ; expiry = 3 weeks + 12 hours
                2h20M      ; nx = 2 hours + 20 minutes
                )
; mail servers not in zone - no A records required
                IN      MX     10  mail.example.net.
                IN      MX     20  mail.example.org.
```

Subdomain MX Records

Subdomains can be fully delegated, in which case the mail servers are defined in the subdomain zone files. This process is described in Chapter 8. This book uses the term *virtual* (or *pseudo*) subdomains, which use a single zone file to provide subdomain style addressing. The following example shows a *virtual* subdomain—the domain and all subdomain definitions are contained in a single zone file:

```
; zone fragment for example.com
; subdomain name servers
$TTL 2d ; zone default = 2 days or 172800 seconds
$ORIGIN example.com.
example.com. IN      SOA   ns1.example.com. hostmaster.example.com. (
               2010121500 ; serial number
               2h         ; refresh =  2 hours
               15M        ; refresh retry = 15 minutes
               3W12h      ; expiry = 3 weeks + 12 hours
               2h20M      ; nx = 2 hours + 20 minutes
               )
....
; mail server for main domain
               IN      MX 10  mail.example.com.
; A record for mail server earlier
mail           IN      A       192.168.0.5
; other domain level hosts and services
....
; subdomain definitions
$ORIGIN us.example.com.
               IN      MX 10  mail
; preceding record could have been written as
; us.example.com.   IN MX 10 mail.us.example.com.
; optional - define the main mail server as backup
               IN      MX 20 mail.example.com.
; A record for subdomain mail server
mail           IN      A       10.10.0.29
; the preceding record could have been written as
; mail.us.example.com. A 10.10.0.29 if it is less confusing
....
; other subdomain definitions as required
```

An alternative way of defining the preceding groups the MX records together, like so:

```
; zone fragment for example.com
; subdomain mail servers
$TTL 2d ; zone default = 2 days or 172800 seconds
$ORIGIN example.com.
example.com. IN      SOA   ns1.example.com. hostmaster.example.com. (
               2010121500 ; serial number
               2h         ; refresh =  2 hours
               15M        ; refresh retry = 15 minutes
               3W12h      ; expiry = 3 weeks + 12 hours
               2h20M      ; nx = 2 hours + 20 minutes
               )
....
; mail server for main domain
               IN      MX 10  mail.example.com.
```

```
; mail server for subdomain 'us'
us              IN      MX 10  mail.us.example.com.
us              IN      MX 20  mail.example.com.
; A record for main mail server earlier
mail            IN      A       192.168.0.5
; other domain level hosts and services
....
; subdomain definitions
$ORIGIN us.example.com.
; A record for subdomain mail server
mail            IN      A       10.10.0.29
; the record above could have been written as
; mail.us.example.com. A 10.10.0.28 if it is less confusing
....
; other subdomain definitions as required
```

Naming Authority Pointer (NAPTR) Record

The Naming Authority Pointer Record RR is part of the Dynamic Delegation Discovery System (DDDS), which is defined in RFCs 3401, 3402, 3403, and 3404. The NAPTR RR is a generic record that defines a rule that may be applied to private data owned by a client application (for example, the ENUM telephony application) to yield a result that is meaningful to that application. The private client data is referred to as the *Application Unique String (AUS)*. Multiple NAPTR RRs may be present to create a *rule set*. NAPTR RRs are meaningful only in the context of the application that uses them. The following example illustrates the use of the rules in the context of a client application, ENUM telephony, to illustrate one use of the NAPTR RR. You are, however, cautioned that other client applications can and do exist and that appropriate documentation for the target application will describe how the result of applying the NAPTR rule will be used. It is further possible that the target application may redefine the use of certain fields within the NAPTR RR. The NAPTR RR is defined in RFC 3403.

NAPTR RR Syntax

```
name    ttl class rr      order pref flag svc regexp replace
users           IN  NAPTR (
                        10  ; order
                        10  ; preference
                        "u" ; flag
                        "E2U+sip"  ; service
                        "!^.*$!sip:1234@sip.example.com!"  ; regexp
                        .  ; no replacement
                        )
```

The order field defines the order in which NAPTR RRs should be processed. It is a 16-bit unsigned value and may take the range 0 to 65535, with low values having the highest priority. If two NAPTR RRs have the same order, then the pref field is used to select the first NAPTR RR to be processed.

The pref field defines the preference within order to select the NAPTR RR to process first. It is a 16-bit field and may take the values 0 to 65535, the lowest value being the most preferred. The sense in which pref and order are used is that NAPTR RRs of higher order are not used until the client has examined all those of the lower order, and only if none is acceptable (for example, the protocol is not supported) should it use the higher order values, whereas pref indicates a user preference that the client is free to ignore if it wishes.

The optional flag field may be used to indicate an action to be taken by the application. The flag is a *quoted string* (it is enclosed in quotes) and may take any case-insensitive value from the set A to Z or 0 to 9; if no flag is present, an empty string ("") is used. The flag field's values are defined by the application and not by the NAPTR RR specification. The following values are *conventions* used by the ENUM (RFC 3761), SIP (RFC 3263), and URN (RFC 3404) applications and illustrate the functionality that may be provided by the flag field. The flag "a" defines a *terminal condition* (this NAPTR RR generates a complete result) and indicates that the result of the processing of this NAPTR rule will yield a name that can be used in a query for an address record (either A or AAAA RRs). The flag "s" defines a terminal condition where the result is a name that may be used to query for an SRV RR. The flag "u" defines a terminal condition where the result will be a URI. The flag "p" indicates that this is the last rule that obeys the NAPTR RR specification. On the surface this might imply a terminal condition, but the client application is free to continue processing using any private rules that lie outside the definition of the NAPTR RR, so it is terminal only as far as the NAPTR record is concerned, not necessarily the client application.

The optional svc field defines the service parameters used by the application. The parameters are contained within a quoted string, and their meaning is defined by the client application, not the NAPTR RR. If not present, an empty string ("") must be defined. As an example of the use of this field, the ENUM telephony application (RFC 3761) defines the svc field to be of the format

```
rs+protocol[+protocol]
```

where the rs field defines a *resolution service*, usually a mnemonic that indicates a transformation rule known to the client application and that is applied to the client data (the AUS). In the ENUM example that follows, the rs value is E2U (which defines the rules for ENUM-to-URI transformation). This field may be 1 to 32 alphanumeric characters in length and must start with an alphabetical character. The + (plus sign) is a separator and must be present. The protocol field may be any protocol known to the client application, such as SIP, H323, or goobledeygook. This field may be a maximum of 32 alphanumeric characters and must start with an alphabetical character. More than one such protocol field may be present, each separated by a + (plus sign). To illustrate the point that this field is application defined, the URN application (RFC 3404) and SIP (RFC 3263) use the same format but *currently* reverse the order of the rs and protocol element!

The optional regexp field is a quoted string enclosing a POSIX Extended Regular Expression (ERE— defined in IEEE POSIX 1003.2 Section 2.8), augmented with a substitution expression defined in RFC 3402 (and loosely based on that used in the sed Unix utility), which is used to transform the client data (AUS). If the field is not present, an empty string ("") must be present. The formal grammar of the regexp field is

```
delim ere delim repl delim flag
```

where delim is a delimiting character (it may be / or !) used to separate parts of the field. The same delimiting character must be used throughout any single regexp field. The ere field is a valid Extended Regular Expression. repl is the replacement string. flag is optional and may take the value i to indicate a case-insensitive ere is to be used. The resulting repl field *may* also be normalized to lowercase as a consequence of using this flag. The regexp supports a back-reference feature whereby strings found within enclosing parentheses in the ere field may be substituted in the repl field by a numeric reference (1 to 9) indicating the order in which they were found. The following example illustrates this process. Assume the ere field contains the following:

```
(A(B(C)DE)(F)G)
```

The following back references in the repl field may be used to access the values:

```
\1   = ABCDEFG
\2   = BCDE
\3   = C
```

```
\4  = F
\5..\9  = error - no matching subexpression
```

The optional `replace` field is a domain name that will replace the client data. If the field is not used, a single . (dot) must be present.

The `replace` and `regexp` fields are mutually exclusive. It is an error for both to be present in the same NAPTR RR.

The NAPTR RR is a complex and powerful RR that provides generic capability to any client application. Its functionality can only be understood in the context of the application that uses it. To illustrate how the NAPTR RR can be used, the following summarizes the order of processing of an NAPTR RR by the ENUM application:

1. The client application, say a VoIP SIP User Agent (UA), receives an E.164 telephone number (the client data or AUS—in this example, we assume +44-111-555-1212). The ENUM application within the SIP UA applies what is called the First Well Known Rule (a private rule known by the ENUM application), which in this case creates a domain name by stripping all nonnumeric values, reversing the number, and appending `E164.ARPA` to the end of it to create `2.1.2.1.5.5.5.4.4.E164.ARPA`.

2. The client ENUM application issues a DNS query for NAPTR RRs with this domain name.

3. Zero or more NAPTR RRs may be returned.

4. Assuming at least one NAPTR RR is returned, the `order` and `pref` fields defined earlier are inspected to determine which NAPTR will be processed first.

5. If a `regexp` file is present, it will be applied to the private client data (the AUS).

6. The `svc` field will then be inspected and the E2U transformation algorithm applied to the results of the `regexp` output to create a URI. The resulting URI will then be used to find the target.

7. The `protocol` field within `svc` is used to indicate the protocol to be used to communicate with the target.

The zone fragment shown here illustrates the use of the NAPTR with the ENUM service (RFC 3761) and defines an NAPTR RR for the number +44-111-555-1212 (an E.164 format number) within a zone file describing the NXX (exchange code) 555, within area code (111), within the country code (44). As noted previously, the ENUM application transforms the number +44-111-555-1212 into a DNS query for `2.1.2.1.5.5.5.1.1.1.4.4.E164.ARPA`. The various fields are further described following the fragment.

```
; zone file fragment for example.com
$TTL 2d ; zone TTL default = 2 days or 172800 seconds
$ORIGIN 5.5.5.1.1.1.4.4.E164.ARPA.
....
2.1.2.1    NAPTR (
    10    ;order
    100   ; preference
    "u" ; flag - only one allowed by ENUM
    "E2U+sip" ;svc
    "!^\\+44111555(.#)$!sip:7\\1@sip.example.com!"
    . ; no replace field
    )
            NAPTR 10 101 "u" "E2U+pres" "!^.*$!mailto:sheila@example.com!" .
....
```

In this example, all the order fields are the same, so the pref field will be used to determine which record is used first—here, the NAPTR with a pref of 100. The regexp field !^\\+44111555(.#)$!sip:7\\1@sip.example.com!, when applied to 441115551212 (the AUS), will result in sip:71212@sip.example.com—in this case, a 7 is appended to the last four digits of the supplied phone number (using the extracted back-reference of \1), but it could be any appropriate algorithm. The application will then inspect the svc field (E2U+sip in the preceding example) and initiate a SIP session using the URI sip:71212@sip.example.com to contact the user. If this fails, it may decide to process the NAPTR RR with a pref of 101, which will result in a contact to sheila@example.com using a presence service of some kind.

Note RFC 3403, which defines the NAPTR, describes an ENUM telephony example that has been updated by RFC 3761. The ENUM example shown is compatible with RFC 3761, whereby the order of resolution services (rs and protocol) have been reversed.

Name Server (NS) Record

Name Server RRs are used to list all the name servers that will respond authoritatively for the domain. NS RRs for a given zone are defined in two places: the child zone (where they are authoritative) and the parent zone (where they are not authoritative). Thus, the zone example.com (the child zone) contains NS RRs defining the authoritative name servers for the zone, and the .com zone (the parent) has corresponding NS RRs, called the *delegation point*, that are used to create a referral to the authoritative name servers for the domain or zone. The requirement is that there should be a minimum of two authoritative name servers and hence a minimum of two NS RRs for every operational zone. The number two is not a hard and fast rule, rather a simple but effective form of resilience. There is nothing to stop, say, a subdomain delegation using a single NS RR. It may not be wise, but it is not illegal. The NS RR was defined in RFC 1035.

NS RR Syntax

```
name            ttl  class  rr    name
example.com.         IN     NS    ns1.example.com.
```

NS RRs for the zone are defined at the zone apex or root; that is, they have the same name as the domain or zone as shown in the preceding example. By convention, name servers are defined immediately after the SOA record, but they can be defined anywhere convenient in the zone file. The name server defined in the SOA record, the so-called *primary master*, must have a corresponding NS RR. There is no requirement that any name servers, including the name server defined in the SOA RR for the zone, are contained within the domain for which they are authoritative. NS RRs define name servers that respond authoritatively for the zone; since both master (primary) and slave (secondary) servers perform this function, they are not differentiated in any way in NS RRs. The designation of master and slave is a purely operational decision. The NS RRs defined in the zone file (and in its parent) are publicly visible name servers. There is no need or requirement to define all the name servers in NS RRs for a specific zone file—it is possible to hide, say, a zone master name server while making only the slaves publicly visible as long as the requirement for two visible name servers is satisfied.

If the name server lies within the domain, it should have a corresponding A (or AAAA) record as would be defined for any host in the domain. The A RRs that define name servers that lie within the domain are frequently called *glue records*. Glue records are essential only for referrals from a parent zone. In practice, glue records are used for two purposes:

1. To speed up queries—and reduce DNS load—by providing the name and IP addresses (the glue) for all authoritative name servers, both within and external to the domain. The root and TLD servers, for example, provide this information in all referrals to remove the need for a subsequent query for an IP address of the name server. In the case of the TLD servers, the glue data is not obtained from the domain's zone file but from the registrar when the domain name is registered.

2. To break the query deadlock for referrals that return name servers within the domain being queried. Assume a query for a domain, say the A RR for www.example.com, returns a referral containing the name but not the IP address of a name server, say ns1.example.com, which lies *within the domain* example.com. Since the IP address of the name server is not known, this will naturally result in a query for the A RR of ns1.example.com, which will return, again, a referral with the name but not the IP of ns1.example.com! When the glue record (an A or AAAA RR) is provided, both the name and the IP address are returned.

When dealing with any zone file, the A (or AAAA) RRs for the name servers that lie within the domain are not strictly glue records—they are conventional A RRs. However, if a subdomain is being delegated from the zone file, the A (or AAAA) RRs for the subdomain name servers that lie inside the subdomain are glue records and are absolutely essential. This point is illustrated in the example fragments that follow.

■**Note** It is worth stressing what may be to most readers an obvious point. The name servers referenced in NS records must all be zone masters or slaves. That is, they must respond *authoritatively* for the domain. They must have been positively configured to perform this function (for BIND this means type slave or type master in the zone clause) and must have a full copy of the zone file obtained from the local filesystem (master or primary) or via zone transfer (slave or secondary). *A caching server can't perform this function.* Name servers defined in NS RRs that do not respond authoritatively are said to be lame servers or the zone is said to have lame delegation and will generate lots of nasty log entries on DNS servers across the world—this configuration error is very visible to the DNS community.

The following zone file fragment shows two name servers, both of which lie within the domain:

```
; zone fragment for example.com
; name servers in the same zone
$TTL 2d ; default TTL is 2 days
$ORIGIN example.com.
example.com.    IN      SOA    ns1.example.com. hostmaster.example.com. (
                2010121500 ; serial number
                3h          ; refresh =  3 hours
                15M         ; refresh retry = 15 minutes
                3W12h       ; expiry = 3 weeks + 12 hours
                2h20M       ; nx = 2 hours + 20 minutes
                )
                IN      NS     ns1  ; unqualified name
; the preceding line is functionally the same as the line that follows
; example.com. IN      NS     ns1.example.com.
; at least two name servers must be defined
                IN      NS     ns2.example.com. ;FQDN
; the in-zone name server(s) should have an A record
ns1             IN      A      192.168.0.3
ns2             IN      A      192.168.0.3
```

This fragment shows two name servers, both of which lie outside the zone:

```
; zone fragment for example.com
; name servers not in the zone
$TTL 2d ; default TTL is 2 days
$ORIGIN example.com.
example.com.   IN     SOA    ns1.example.net. hostmaster.example.com. (
                2010121500 ; serial number
                3h          ; refresh =  3 hours
                15M         ; refresh retry = 15 minutes
                3W12h       ; expiry = 3 weeks + 12 hours
                2h20M       ; nx = 2 hours + 20 minutes
                )
; name servers not in zone - no A records required
                IN     NS     ns1.example.net.
                IN     NS     ns2.example.net.
```

The following zone file delegates a subdomain us.example.com and shows the use of glue records:

```
; zone fragment for example.com
; name servers in the same zone
$TTL 2d ; default TTL is 2 days
$ORIGIN example.com.
@              IN     SOA    ns1.example.com. hostmaster.example.com. (
                2010121500 ; serial number
                2h          ; refresh =  2 hours
                15M         ; refresh retry = 15 minutes
                3W12h       ; expiry = 3 weeks + 12 hours
                2h20M       ; nx = 2 hours + 20 minutes
                )
; main domain name servers
                IN     NS     ns1.example.com.
                IN     NS     ns2.example.com.
; A records for name servers above - not glue records
```

```
ns1             IN      A       192.168.0.3
ns2             IN      A       192.168.0.4
....
; subdomain definitions
$ORIGIN us.example.com.
; two name servers for the subdomain
@               IN      NS      ns3.us.example.com.
; the record above could have been written as
; us.example.com. IN NS ns3.us.example.com.
; OR as simply
;       IN NS   ns3
; the next name server points to ns1 above
                IN      NS      ns1.example.com.
; address record for subdomain name server - essential glue record
ns3             IN      A       10.10.0.24 ; glue record
; the record above could have been written as
; ns3.us.example.com. A 10.10.0.24 if it is less confusing
```

In this fragment, the NS RRs at the zone apex (the first two NS RRs) are part of the authoritative data for the zone example.com. The NS RRs for the subdomain us.example.com (the last two NS RRs shown) and the corresponding A RR is not part of the authoritative data for the zone example.com.

Network Service Access Point (NSAP) Record

The Network Service Access Point RR is the equivalent of an A RR for ISO's Open Systems Interconnect (OSI) system in that it maps a host name to an endpoint address. The NSAP is the OSI equivalent of the IP address and is hierarchically structured. The NSAP RR has informational status and is defined in RFC 1706. The NSAP address format is defined in ISO/IEC 8348 (www.iso.org). NSAP addresses are vaguely similar to IPv6 addresses in that they have a hierarchical organization, use a hexadecimal representation format, and are 128 bits long.

NSAP RR Syntax

```
name    ttl class rr  nsap-address
joe         IN    NSAP   0x47.0005.80.005a00.0000.0001.e133.ffffff000161.00
```

The nsap-address is the NSAP address of the end system. The NSAP address field begins with the literal string "0x", which will be familiar to C/C++ programmers and indicates the following field is hexadecimal. The dots within the nsap-address field are used for readability reasons only and do not appear in the binary representation. Since the nsap-address is an address, not a name, there is no terminating dot.

The following fragment shows a dual-stack (OSI/IP) host, fred.example.com, which is reachable by an IPv4 address and an NSAP address:

```
; zone file fragment for example.com
$TTL 2d ; zone TTL default = 2 days or 172800 seconds
$ORIGIN example.com.
example.com. IN      SOA    ns1.example.com. hostmaster.example.com. (
            2010121500 ; serial number
            3h         ; refresh =  3 hours
            15M        ; refresh retry = 15 minutes
            3W12h      ; expiry = 3 weeks + 12 hours
```

```
                2h20M       ; nx = 2 hours + 20 minutes
                )
                IN  MX    10  mail.example.com.
....
fred            IN  A     192.168.254.2
                IN  NSAP  0x47.0005.80.005a00.0000.0001.e133.ffffff000161.00
....
mail            IN  A     192/168.254.3
....
```

NSAPs may be reverse mapped using the domain NSAP.INT and normal PTR RRs. The reverse map is constructed in a similar manner to that defined for IPv6 (see Chapter 5 for full explanation) using a *nibble* format in which each character of the address is reversed, separated with a . (dot), and placed under the NSAP.INT domain. The example that follows shows a reverse-map fragment for the NSAP defined in the previous fragment:

```
; reverse zone file fragment for example.com
$TTL 2d ; zone TTL default = 2 days or 172800 seconds
$ORIGIN 3.3.1.e.1.0.0.0.0.0.0.0.0.0.a.5.0.0.0.8.5.0.0.0.7.4.NSAP.INT.
example.com. IN      SOA   ns1.example.com. hostmaster.example.com. (
                2010121500 ; serial number
                3h         ; refresh =  3 hours
                15M        ; refresh retry = 15 minutes
                3W12h      ; expiry = 3 weeks + 12 hours
                2h20M      ; nx = 2 hours + 20 minutes
                )
....
0.0.1.6.1.0.0.0.f.f.f.f.f.f  IN    PTR  fred.example.com.
```

In the example forward-mapping zone file, the host fred.example.com was shown as supporting a dual OSI/IP stack. The reverse maps for the IPv4 address and the NSAPs are constructed as separate zone files.

Next Secure (NSEC) Record

The NSEC RR is part of DNSSEC (see Chapter 11) and is designed to provide two forms of what is called *proof of nonexistence* (PNE) or *denial of existence*. The first form allows a query to verify that a host name does *not* exist. Each host name has a corresponding NSEC RR that points to the next valid host name in the zone. The NSEC RRs provide a chain of valid host names—by implication anything not in this chain does not exist. In the second form, the NSEC RR contains a list of RR types that have the same name as the NSEC RR—again by implication, any RR type not in the list does not exist. NSEC RRs are generated automatically by the dnssec-signzone utility (described in Chapter 9). The NSEC RR is defined in RFC 4034.

NSEC RR Syntax

```
name ttl class  rr     next-name rr-list
joe       IN    NSEC   joes      A TXT RRSIG NSEC
```

The next-name field defines the next host name in the zone file. NSEC RRs are added during the dnssec-signzone process to each RR with a particular name to form a continuous chain through the zone file. If the RR to which the NSEC is added is the last in the file, the next-name points back to the SOA RR (the zone apex), thus creating a loop. Once the zone file is signed (see Chapter 11), it is possible to verify that any name does, or does not, exist in the zone file. The rr-list field defines all the RR types that exist with the same name as the NSEC RR. Since the NSEC RR is used only in DNSSEC signed zones (see Chapter 11), the rr-list will always contain as a minimum the NSEC RR and its accompanying RRSIG RR. The rr-list makes it possible to verify that there is, say, an A RR for a host name but not, say, a KEY RR. The example that follows shows how the NSEC RR is used, including the loopback to the beginning of the zone file: if a user-defined RR exists at a particular host name (see the "User-Defined RRs" section later in the chapter), then it will be included in the list of RR types using the normal syntax, such as TYPE6235.

```
; zone fragment for example.com
$TTL 2d ; zone default = 2 days or 172800 seconds
$ORIGIN example.com.
....
mail        IN      A       192,168.2.3
            IN      AAAA    2001:db8::3
            IN      TXT "one upon a time"
            IN      KX   10 bill.example.com.
            IN      RRSIG ...
            IN      NSEC www.example.com.  A TXT KX AAAA RRSIG NSEC
www         IN      AAAA    2001:db8::4
            IN      A       192.168.2.4
            IN      RRSIG ...
            IN      NSEC   example.com. A AAAA RRSIG NSEC ; loops back to SOA
```

The NSEC RR is generated as part of a zone signing process, for example, using the utility dnssec-signzone (see Chapter 9). Since the NSEC RR is only used with negative (name error - NXDOMAIN) results, its ttl is *always* taken from the nx field of the SOA RR. By following the NSEC chain for a particular domain, the entire domain may be trivially enumerated. Without the NSEC RR, the domain can still be enumerated by exhaustive search, which can take some time and is more likely to be caught by intrusion detection systems. It is worth emphasizing, however, that data can't be hidden in a publicly visible name server—after all, the point of it being in the DNS is that it can and will be used. If DNS records need to be protected, then techniques such as stealth servers must be used (see Chapter 4). Nevertheless, to mitigate the trivial enumeration possibilities of the NSEC RR (especially in delegation-centric domains such as TLDs) while continuing to provide PNE features, an alternative RR called the NSEC3 RR was standardized; it's described below.

Next Secure 3 (NSEC3) RR

The NSEC3 RR is a DNSSEC RR (see Chapter 11), which provides an alternative method of generating proof of nonexistence (PNE) responses by returning a hashed name value instead of the normal name of the next RR in the zone (as is the case for NSEC RRs), thus reducing the probability of zone enumeration. The NSEC3 RR is created by a zone signing utility, such dnssec-signzone (see Chapter 9), using the -3 argument or when an NSEC3PARAM RR is present at the zone apex. If an NSEC3PARAM RR is not present in a signed zone, then NSEC RRs (described previously) are generated for PNE. The NSEC3 RR is described in RFC 5155.

NSEC3 RR Syntax

```
name ttl class   rr      hash-alg flag iterations salt hashed-next-name rr-list
K3PE...IG88.example.com.  10800 IN      NSEC3   (
                                        1 ; hash-alg
                                        1 ; flag Opt-Out set
```

```
                    20 ; iterations
                    abcdef12 ; salt
                    4JSK….67P8;  hash-next-name
                    A TXT RRSIG;  rr-list)
```

The left-hand name of the NSEC3 RR is computed by taking the normal, fully expanded, left-hand label of the RRs at this name (which appear in the rr-list field), adding the salt field from the zone's NSEC3PARAM RR, hashing the result using the hash-alg from the zone's NSEC3PARAM RR, repeating the hash operation as defined in NSEC3PARAM RR iterations field, and appending the name of the zone. Since the NSEC3 RR is only used with negative (name error - NXDOMAIN) results, its ttl value is *always* taken from the nx field of the zone's SOA RR. hash-alg may currently only take the value 1 (SHA1) and is copied from the hash-alg field of the NSEC3PARAM RR for the zone. flag may be either 0 = no Opt-Out or 1 = Opt-Out (defined by the –A argument to dnssec-signzone; see Chapter 9). iterations is a copy of the iterations field from the zone's NSEC3PARAM. salt is a copy of the salt field from the zone's NSEC3PARAM RR. hashed-next-name is a base32 encoded (RFC 4648) name created by adding the salt field to the next fully expanded left-hand name, hashing the result using the algorithm defined by hash-alg, and repeating the hash operation the number of times defined by iterations. rr-list is the list of RR types (see NSEC rr-list for more information) that appear at the normal left-hand name for RRs that are covered by this NSEC3. When the zone-signing operation is complete, the resulting zone file is sorted into canonical (alpha-numeric) name order, which means that the normal left-hand name RRs and their corresponding NSEC3 RR will not appear adjacently in the zone file. This is illustrated with operational examples in the "NSEC3/Opt-Out" section of Chapter 11.

Next Secure 3 Parameter (NECS3PARAM) RR

The NSEC3PARAM RR is a DNSSEC RR (see Chapter 11) that is typically added to a zone by a zone signing utility such as dnssec-signzone; the various fields are constructed by arguments to the utility. It may be added or edited manually using, say, nsupdate (see Chapter 9) when online signing is being used. The NSEC3PARAM RR can only appear at the zone apex. The NSEC3PARAM RR is only used operationally by authoritative name servers (never by validating resolvers) when supplying proof of nonexistence (PNE) responses when using NSEC3. The NSEC3PARAM RR *always* has a ttl of 0 to prohibit resolver caching. The NSEC3PARAM RR is defined in RFC 5155.

NSEC3PARAM RR Syntax

```
name ttl class   rr     hash-alg flag iterations salt
example.com.  IN   NSEC3PARAM   1 0 50 abcdef12
```

hash-alg defines the hash algorithm used to generate hashed name fields (used in the name and hashed-next-name field of the NSEC3 RR) from the normal left-hand names in the zone file. This field may take the following values:

0 = Reserved
1 = SHA1
2 – 255 = Unassigned

flag defines the Opt-Out status and may only be set to 0 when used with NSEC3PARAM (Opt-Out status is only relevant in the NSEC3 RR). iteration defines the number of hash iterations used to obscure names in the zone. This value is a trade-off and determines both how effectively the names are disguised (the higher the better) and the processor power used to generate the name and hashed-next-name field of the NSEC3 RR (the lower the better). RFC 5155 recommends a maximum value based on the keysize used by the ZSK DNSKEY RRs for the zone as follows:

Keysize in ZSK DNSKEY = 1024 Maximum Iterations = 150
Keysize in ZSK DNSKEY = 2048 Maximum Iterations = 500
Keysize in ZSK DNSKEY = 4096 Maximum Iterations = 2,500

Zone-signing (dnssec-signzone) software should reject values higher than these (or reduce to the maximum value) and DNSSEC validators (resolvers) should treat zones with higher values as insecure. The above list defines the recommended maximum value; in practice, significantly lower values can be sensibly used with perhaps 3-10 being a reasonable range (dnssec-signzone defaults to 10). salt is optional and is appended to each left-hand zone name before hashing is performed to make dictionary attacks more difficult. If required, it's defined by 2-512 hex characters (case-insensitive, two per octet) without white space. RFC 5155 recommends a minimum of 8 octets (64 bits or 16 hex characters) of salt is used. If salt is not required, a single – (dash) is used. An operational NSEC3PARAM RR is illustrated in the "NSEC3/Opt-Out" section of Chapter 11.

Pointer (PTR) Record

The Pointer RR is used to reverse map an address to a host name. PTR RRs are used for both IPv4 and IPv6 addresses, as well as others such as NSAP addresses. Pointer records are the opposite of A RRs (or AAAA RRs for IPv6), which are used to forward map hosts to IP addresses. The PTR RR was defined in RFC 1035.

PTR RR Syntax

```
name ttl  class   rr     host-name
15        IN      PTR     www.example.com.
```

The left-hand name field in a PTR RR typically looks like a number but is always a name; that is, if it's not terminated with a dot, it's an unqualified name, and $ORIGIN substitution takes place. The right-hand host-name field *must* be an FQDN; otherwise very bizarre results will occur. This is illustrated in the examples that follow. The $ORIGIN directive in a reverse-map zone file is essential if you wish to remain sane. The following fragment defines a reverse-map zone file for the IPv4 address range 192.168.23.0 to 192.168.23.255:

```
; Reverse map for 192.168.23.0
$TTL 2d
$ORIGIN 23.168.192.IN-ADDR.ARPA.
@           IN    SOA   ns1.example.com. hostmaster.example.com. (
                        2010121500 ; serial number
                        3h         ; refresh
                        15m        ; refresh retry
                        3w         ; expiry
                        3h         ; nx
                        )
            IN    NS    ns1.example.com.
            IN    NS    ns2.example.com.
....
2           IN    PTR   joe.example.com. ; right-hand FQDN names
; 2 is an unqualified name and could have been written as
; 2.23.168.192.IN-ADDR.ARPA. IN PTR  joe.example.com.
....
15          IN    PTR   www.example.com.
....
```

```
17              IN      PTR     bill.example.com.
....
254             IN      PTR     fred.mydomain.com.
```

In this fragment, the IP address 192.168.23.2 will return the host name joe.example.com to a PTR query. As noted earlier, the right-hand name must be an FQDN (it must end with a dot) because of the $ORIGIN. If the dot were erroneously omitted, then joe.example.com would become joe.example.com.23.168.192.IN-ADDR.ARPA.—not the desired result. While it's good practice, it's not essential to define all IP addresses in the reverse-map zone file. The addresses 0 and 255 in the preceding example file (it's based on a Class C private address range) are designated the multicast (0) and broadcast (255) addresses for the class and are not defined in the reverse map. If either of these IP addresses was queried, they would result in a Name Error (NXDOMAIN) result.

IPv6 and IPv4 addresses can't be mixed in the same file as they can for forward-map zone files. IPv6 addresses are mapped under the domain IP6.ARPA, whereas IPv4 addresses are mapped under the IN-ADDR.ARPA domain. IPv6 reverse maps use a nibble domain name format defined in Chapter 5. The following fragment illustrates the use of the PTR RR to reverse map the IPv6 addresses 2001:db8:0:1::1, 2001:db8:0:1::2, 2001:db8:0:2::1, and 2001:db8:0:2::1:

```
; reverse IPV6 zone file for example.com
$TTL 2d    ; default TTL for zone
$ORIGIN 0.0.0.0.8.b.d.0.1.0.0.2.IP6.ARPA.
@           IN      SOA     ns1.example.com. hostmaster.example.com. (
                            2010121500 ; sn = serial number
                            12h        ; refresh = refresh
                            15m        ; retry = refresh retry
                            3w         ; expiry = expiry
                            2h         ; nx = nxdomain ttl
                            )
; name servers Resource Recordsfor the domain
            IN      NS      ns1.example.com.
; the second name server is
; external to this zone (domain).
            IN      NS      ns2.example.net.
; PTR RR maps a IPv6 address to a host name
; hosts in subnet ID 1
1.0.0.0.0.0.0.0.0.0.0.0.0.0.0.1.0.0.0          IN      PTR     ns1.example.com.
2.0.0.0.0.0.0.0.0.0.0.0.0.0.0.1.0.0.0          IN      PTR     mail.example.com.
; hosts in subnet ID 2
1.0.0.0.0.0.0.0.0.0.0.0.0.0.0.2.0.0.0          IN      PTR     joe.example.com.
2.0.0.0.0.0.0.0.0.0.0.0.0.0.0.2.0.0.0          IN      PTR     www.example.com.
```

Chapter 5 defines alternative methods by which the IPv6 reverse maps may be organized to reduce the sheer size of the host addresses required.

X.400 to RFC 822 E-mail (PX) Record

The X.400 to RFC 822 E-mail RR allows mapping of ITU X.400-format e-mail addresses (a largely extinct e-mail system) to RFC 822-format (IETF) e-mail addresses using a MIXER-conformant gateway. The PX RR is defined in RFC 3163. The X.400 mail address format is defined by X.400 and X.402 (www.itu.int). X.400 uses an addressing scheme that ends with a country code and has no equivalent of a generic noncountry code entity such as .com or .org; the address mappings defined within the RFC are thus limited to country code–based domains (ccTLDs) or require an explicit mapping of the gTLD to a country code.

PX RR Syntax

```
name          ttl class rr  pref 822-domain x.400-name
*.example.com.    IN   PX  10    example.com. PRMD-example.ADMD-p400.C-nl.
```

The pref field is the same as used by the MX RR in that it takes the value 0 to 65535 and indicates the relative preference of an X.400 name. Lower values are the most preferred; that is, 10 is more preferred than 20. The 822-domain field is the domain name to which this PX RR applies. The x.400-name field defines the X.400 address to which mail will be sent by the MIXER gateway.

The following fragment sends all of example.com's incoming mail to an X.400 mail system in Holland:

```
; zone file fragment for example.com
$TTL 2d ; zone TTL default = 2 days or 172800 seconds
$ORIGIN example.com.
example.com.     IN  SOA   ns1.example.com. hostmaster.example.com. (
                 2010121500 ; serial number
                 3h          ; refresh =  3 hours
                 15M         ; refresh retry = 15 minutes
                 3W12h       ; expiry = 3 weeks + 12 hours
                 2h20M       ; nx = 2 hours + 20 minutes
                 )
                 IN  NS    ns1.example.com.
                 IN  NS    ns2.example.com.
*.example.com.   IN  PX  10    example.com.  PRMD-example.ADMD-p400.C-nl.
ns1              IN  A     192.168.254.2
ns2              IN  A     192.168.254.3
www              IN  A     192.168.254.4
```

In this example, the DNS wildcard is used to map every name that doesn't have another record in the zone file to the X.400 gateway function. In the preceding zone file, every name except ns1.example.com, ns2.example.com, and www.example.com will be sent to the MIXER gateway. Because of the wildcard, the zone does not *require* an MX RR, but the sending mail system does need to be aware of, and explicitly request, the PX RR—most mail systems only check for an MX RR, which may significantly reduce the effectiveness of the PX RR. An alternative strategy would be for the domain to publish a normal MX RR and for the receiving MTA to send to the MIXER gateway via a local mapping or configuration option. A PX RR can be constructed to use a single mailbox mapping, rather than the wildcard mapping, as shown in the line that follows:

```
fred.example.com.  IN  PX  10    fred.example.com.  O-ab.PRMD-net2.ADMDb.C-nl.
```

Responsible Person (RP) Record

The Responsible Person RR allows an e-mail address and some optional human-readable text to be associated with a host. The RP RR is experimental and is defined in RFC 1183. Due to privacy and spam considerations, RP records are not widely used on public servers but can provide very useful contact data during diagnosis and debugging network problems.

RP RR Syntax

```
name   ttl class RP  email txt-rr
joe          IN   RP  fred.example.com. joe.people.example.com.
```

The email field is constructed in the normal method for e-mail addresses within the DNS where the first
. (dot) is replaced with a @ (commercial at sign) when constructing the mail address; so in the preceding
example `fred.example.com` would result in the e-mail address of `fred@example.com`. This format is used
because @ has a special significance in the RR: it's a short form for the `$ORIGIN`.

The `text-rr` field defines the name of an optional TXT RR that may contain human-readable text
such as a name and phone number. If no TXT is present, the `text-rr` field is replaced with a single dot.
Multiple RP records may be associated with any host. The following fragment shows the use of the RP
RR:

```
; zone file fragment for example.com
$TTL 2d ; zone TTL default = 2 days or 172800 seconds
$ORIGIN example.com.
...
www        IN  A    192.168.254.2
           IN  A    192.168.254.3
           IN  RP   bill.example.com. bill.people.example.com.
; could have been written as
;          IN  RP   bill bill.people
; line that follows uses an e-mail external to the domain
; and has no corresponding text record (replaced with a single dot)
           IN  RP   fred.example.net. .
...
; all people records organized under people
bill.people  IN  TXT "Bill Someone - pager = 111-1111"
....
```

The line beginning `bill.people` does not strictly define a subdomain structure, but in this case is
used simply as a convenient method of grouping people records in the zone file for the organization.

Resource Record Signature (RRSIG) Record

The Resource Recordset Signature RR is a DNSSEC (see Chapter 11) record that contains the digital
signature of the RRset being signed. RRSIG RRs operate on RRsets—defined as being any record whose
name, `class`, and `rr` type fields are the same—not individual RRs. The RRSIG RRs (the digital signatures)
for the zone's RRsets are generated automatically by a zone-signer, such as the `dnssec-signzone` utility
(described in Chapter 9) using the private key whose public key is stored in a DNSKEY RR defined at the
zone apex or root. The RRSIG RR is defined in RFC 4034.

RRSIG RR Syntax

```
name ttl class  rr     (type algorithm labels ottl expire
                        start key-tag signer signature)
joe  2d  IN     A      192.168.22.22
joe      IN     RRSIG (A    ; rr type covered
                       5    ; algorithm (RSA-SHA-1)
                       3    ; labels at this name
                       172800 ; original ttl of RRs covered
                       20050414000000 ;expiry time
                       20050314000000 ; start time
                       24567 ; key tag
                       example.com. ; signer
                       blah....blah) ; signature data
```

In this example, both the RR being signed (the A RR) and the RRSIG RR (its digital signature) are shown to clarify the use of the RRSIG record.

The type field defines the RRset type being signed. In this example an RRset comprising a single A RR is shown, but any number of such RRs could have been included in the RRset.

The algorithm field may take one of the values defined here:

0 = Reserved
1 = RSA-MD5—not recommended (RFC 2537)
2 = Diffie-Hellman (RFC 2539)
3 = DSA/SHA-1—optional (RFC 3755, 2536)
4 = Elliptic curve—not currently standardized
5 = RSA/SHA-1—mandatory (RFC 3755, 3110)
6 = DSA-NSEC3-SHA1 (RFC 5155)
7 = RSASHA1-NSEC3-SHA1 (RFC 5155)
8 = RSA/SHA-256 (RFC 5702)
9 = unassigned
10 = RSA/SHA512 (RFC 5702)
11 = unassigned
12 = GOST R 34.10-2001 (RFC 5933)
13 - 122 = Currently unassigned
123 – 251 = Reserved
252 = Indirect (see the "Alternative Cryptographic Algorithms" section later in this chapter)
253 = Private URI (see the "Alternative Cryptographic Algorithms" section later in this chapter)
254 = Private OID (see the "Alternative Cryptographic Algorithms" section later in this chapter)
255 = Reserved

The labels field defines the number of labels in the FQDN version of the name field, excluding any wildcard values. In the preceding example, the number is 3 since the FQDN corresponding to joe is joe.example.com. If the name had been * (the DNS wildcard value), then the value of the label field would have been 2, thus excluding the wildcard from the label count. This allows verification software to know whether the RRSIG was or was not synthesized and thus re-create the conditions by which successful verification can take place.

The ottl field defines the TTL of the RRset being covered. In the preceding example, this is shown explicitly as 2d (172800 seconds) in the A RR, but if not present would have been taken from the last $TTL directive in the zone file.

The expire field defines the time at which the RRSIG is no longer valid, and the start field indicates when the RRSIG record becomes valid. In their textual form, both have the format YYYYMMDDHHMMSS where YYYY is a four-digit year number, MM a two-digit month number, DD a two-digit day within a month number, HH a two-digit hour within a day, MM a two-digit minute within an hour, and SS a two-digit second within an hour. Time and date values use Universal Coordinated Time (UTC).

The key-tag field identifies the DNSKEY RR used to generate the digital signature. Since multiple DNSKEY RRs may be present with the same name in a zone file, this field is used to find the correct key. The key-tag field is generated by the dnssec-keygen utility and uses a variant on the zone's complement checksum algorithm and can thus be rapidly reproduced by verification software to find the correct key.

The signer field is the name of the DNSKEY RR whose private key was used to generate the signature; in the example, it's a DNSKEY RR with a name of example.com.

The signature field is the base64 (RFC 3548) representation of the digital signature. In the example shown, the digital signature is generated using the digest function SHA-1, which is then encrypted with the RSA algorithm using a private key whose public key is defined in the DNSKEY RR with a host name of example.com.

The RRSIG RR is unique in that it does *not* form an RRset; otherwise recursive processing would occur when signing a zone.

Route Through (RT) Record

The Route Through RR defines an intermediate host through which all datagrams should be routed. The intermediate host would typically be a gateway or protocol converter. The RT RR is experimental and is defined in RFC 1183. The RT RR is not widely used.

RT RR Syntax

```
name    ttl class RT  preference intermediate
joe          IN   RT  10         bill.example.com.
```

The preference field is a value in the range 0 to 65535 and is used in a similar way to the MX record. The lower the value, the more preferred the route. The intermediate field defines the host name to which datagrams destined for name should be sent. The following fragment shows how the RT RR is used:

```
; zone file fragment for example.com
$TTL 2d ; zone TTL default = 2 days or 172800 seconds
$ORIGIN example.com.
...
fred        IN  A    192.168.254.2
joe         IN  A    192.168.254.3
bill        IN  A    192.168.254.4
            IN  RT  10  fred.example.com.
            IN  RT  20  joe.example.com.
....
```

In this fragment, in order to reach bill.example.com, fred.example.com. would be used; if not available, then joe.example.com. would be used.

Signature (SIG) Record

The Signature RR was defined as part of the first generation of DNSSEC (RFC 2535). It is no longer used for this purpose; it's now limited to specific use as a meta (or pseudo) RR containing the digital signature when securing transactions such as dynamic update using public key (asymmetric) cryptographic techniques. The equivalent RR for shared secret transaction security is TSIG, another meta RR. The revised use of what is now called SIG(0) is defined in RFC 2931.

SIG RR Syntax

```
name ttl class  rr (type algorithm labels ottl
                    expire start key-tag signature)
joe       IN   SIG  (0    ; identifies SIG(0)
                    5  ; algorithm (RSA-SHA-1)
                    3  ; labels at this name
                    172800 ; original ttl of RRs covered
                    20050414000000 ;expiry time
                    20050314000000 ; start time
                    24567 ; key tag
                    example.com. ; signer
                    blah….blah) ; signature data
```

The field values and meaning of the SIG RR are exactly the same as those of the RRSIG RR defined earlier with the exception of the type field, which in this usage is always set to 0; hence this RR type is commonly referred to as a SIG(0) RR.

The SIG(0) RR is generated at run time (it is a meta or pseudo RR) by the name server and is added to the ADDITIONAL SECTION (see Chapter 15) of the query or its response to carry the digital signature that both authenticates and ensures the integrity of the transaction. The public key used by SIG(0) is stored in the zone file using a KEY RR.

Start of Authority (SOA) Record

The Start of Authority RR describes the global properties for the zone (or domain). There is only one SOA record allowed in a zone file and it must be the first RR entry. The SOA RR was defined in RFC 1035 and the use of the min(imum) field of the RR was redefined in RFC 2308.

SOA RR Syntax

```
name        ttl class rr     name-server admin-mailbox  sn refresh retry expiry min
@               IN    SOA    ns.example.com. hostmaster.example.com. (
                             2010080800 ; se = serial number
                             43200      ; refresh = refresh retry = 12h
                             900        ; retry = 15m
                             1209600    ; expiry = 2w
                             3600       ; nx = nxdomain ttl= 1h (ex minimum field
                             )
```

The SOA RR is the most important RR and takes one of the largest numbers of fields of any RR. To assist in readability, it's usually written using the standard parentheses method to enable the various fields to be written one per line for clarity, as shown in the preceding example. Table 13–3 describes the fields unique to this record; note that the common fields were described previously.

Table 13–3. SOA RR Fields

Field	Description
name-server	This is a name server for the domain and is referred to as the primary master, which has a meaning only in the context of Dynamic DNS (described in Chapter 3) and designates the server that can be updated by DDNS transactions. If DDNS is not being used, it may be *any* suitable name server that will answer authoritatively for the domain. The name server may lie within the domain or in an external or foreign domain. The name server referenced, however, must be defined using an NS RR. The name-server is most commonly written as an FQDN (ends with a dot). If the name-server is an external server (does not lie in this zone), it *must* be an FQDN. In the DNS jargon, this field is called the MNAME field, which is why this book uses the term name-server.

Field	Description
admin-mailbox	The e-mail address of the person responsible for this zone. In the jargon, this is called the RNAME field, which is why this book calls it the admin-mailbox. It is the e-mail address of a suitable administrator or technical contact for the domain. By convention (in RFC 2412), it is suggested that the reserved mailbox hostmaster be used for this purpose, but any sensible and stable e-mail address can be used. The format is mailbox-name.domain; for example, hostmaster.example.com, using a . (dot), not the more normal @ (commercial at sign), which has other uses in the zone file. When e-mail is sent to the admin-mailbox, the normal format of hostmaster@example.com is used. There is no requirement that this mailbox lie inside the domain—it can use any suitable mail address such as hostmaster.example.org. It is most commonly written as an FQDN (ends with a dot), but if the e-mail address lies in the domain, it can be written as simply hostmaster without the dot and $ORIGIN substitution will occur as normal.
sn (serial number)	Unsigned 32-bit value in range 1 to 4294967295 with a maximum increment of 2147483647. In BIND implementations, this is defined to be a ten-digit field. The sn value must be incremented (must be greater) when any resource record in the zone file is updated. By convention, a date format is used to simplify the task of updating the sn value; the most popular date convention is YYYYMMDDSS, where YYYY is the four-digit year number, MM is the two-digit month, DD is the two-digit day, and SS is a two-digit sequence number, starting from 00, used when the zone file changes more than once in the day. Using this date format, the value 2010061504 would mean the last update was done on 15 June 2010 and it was the fifth update that day. The date format is just a convention, not a requirement; consequentially, no validation is performed on this value, so it's easy to use incorrect date values. Extreme care should be taken when working with this number. Chapter 8 describes how to fix out-of-sequence errors. The value, range, and arithmetic operations performed on the serial number is defined in RFC 1982.
refresh	Signed 32-bit time value in seconds. It indicates the time after which the slave will try to refresh the zone from the master. RFC 1912 recommends a range of 1200 to 43200, 1200 (20 minutes) if the data is volatile or 43200 (12 hours) if it is not. If NOTIFY (described in Chapter 3), the BIND default is being used; this can be set to a much higher value such as one or more days or greater than 86400. When using BIND, the normal time short format can be used.
retry	Signed 32-bit value in seconds. It defines the time between retries if the slave (secondary) fails to contact the master after refresh has expired. Values will depend upon local knowledge of the network speed and reliability of the master (primary) servers. Typical values would be 180 (2 minutes) to 900 (15 minutes) or higher. When using BIND, the normal time short format can be used.

Field	Description
expiry	Signed 32-bit value in seconds. It indicates when the zone data is no longer authoritative. This field applies to slave (secondary) servers only. In BIND, slaves stop responding to queries for the zone when this time has expired and no contact has been made with the master. Thus, when the refresh value expires, the slave will attempt to read the SOA record for the zone—and request a zone transfer (AXFR) if the sn field has changed. If contact is made, the expire and refresh values are reset and the cycle begins again. If the slave *fails* to contact the master, it will retry the operation every retry interval, but it will continue to supply authoritative data for the zone until the expiry value is reached, at which point it will stop responding to queries for the domain. RFC 1912 recommends 1209600 to 2419200 (2 to 4 weeks) to allow for major outages of the master. When using BIND, the normal time short format can be used.
nx	Signed 32-bit value in seconds. RFC 2308 redefined this value to be the negative caching time—the time a NXDOMAIN (name error) record is cached. The field was, and still is, called min (minimum) in most DNS documentation. It is renamed throughout this book as nx to reflect its current use and to remove confusion caused by ongoing use of an obsolete term. The maximum value allowed for this parameter is 10800 (3 hours). This field *was* the zone TTL default (in BIND versions 4 and 8). RFC 2308 makes the $TTL directive mandatory in a zone file and consequentially allows the min field to be reused for negative caching time. Older documentation or zone file configurations may reflect the old usage and have time values greater than 3 hours in this field. In this case, BIND will log a nasty error message when the zone is loaded but continue with a 10800 value. When using BIND, the normal time short format can be used.

The following zone file fragment illustrates that one or all name servers may be external to the domain:

```
; zone file fragment for example.com
$TTL 2d ; zone TTL default = 2 days or 172800 seconds
$ORIGIN example.com.
@       IN      SOA   ns.example.net. hostmaster.example.com. (
                2010121500 ; serial number
                1d12h      ; refresh =  1 day 12 hours
                15m        ; refresh retry = 15 minutes
                3w12h      ; expiry = 3 weeks + 12 hours
                2h20m      ; nx = 2 hours + 20 minutes
                )
        IN      NS    ns.example.net. ;name servers
        IN      NS    ns.example.org.
```

The e-mail address in the preceding example is inside the domain, so it could have been rewritten to use the unqualified name form as shown here:

```
; zone file fragment for example.com
$TTL 2d ; zone TTL default = 2 days or 172800 seconds
$ORIGIN example.com.
@       IN      SOA   ns.example.net. hostmaster (
                2010121500 ; serial number
                1d12h      ; refresh =  1 day 12 hours
```

```
                15m         ; refresh retry = 15 minutes
                3w12h       ; expiry = 3 weeks + 12 hours
                2h20m       ; nx = 2 hours + 20 minutes
                )
        IN      NS      ns.example.net. ;name servers
        IN      NS      ns.example.org.
```

The following fragment shows use of two name servers, one inside the domain and the other external:

```
; zone file fragment for example.com
$TTL 2d ; zone TTL default = 2 days or 172800 seconds
$ORIGIN example.com.
@       IN      SOA     ns.example.com. hostmaster.example.com. (
                2010121500 ; serial number
                1d12h       ; refresh =  1 day 12 hours
                15m         ; refresh retry = 15 minutes
                3w12h       ; expiry = 3 weeks + 12 hours
                2h20m       ; nx = 2 hours + 20 minutes
                )
        IN      NS  ns.example.com.
        IN      NS  ns.example.net.
...
; A record required for internal name server
ns      IN      A    192.168.2.1
```

The following fragment rewrites the preceding fragment and uses unqualified names wherever possible:

```
; zone file fragment for example.com
$TTL 2d ; zone TTL default = 2 days or 172800 seconds
$ORIGIN example.com.
@       IN      SOA     ns  hostmaster (
                2010121500 ; serial number
                1d12h       ; refresh =  1 day 12 hours
                15m         ; refreshretry = 15 minutes
                3w12h       ; expiry = 3 weeks + 12 hours
                2h20m       ; nx= 2 hours + 20 minutes
                )
        IN      NS  ns
        IN      NS  ns.example.net.
...
; A record required for internal name server
ns      IN      A    192.168.2.1
```

Sender Policy Framework (SPF) Record

The SPF RR is defined by RFC 4408. The format and functionality of the SPF RR (described in the "Define an SPF Record" section of Chapter 8) is identical to that when used with a TXT RR with the single exception that the RR type code is 99. For SPF to be used with SPF libraries and DNS software that may not support the SPF RR, RFC 4408 recommends that a TXT RR always be used. If the DNS software that supports the zone file (master and slave) also supports SPF, then both a TXT and SPF RRs should be defined with identical parameters. The SPF RR has been supported since BIND 9.4.

Services (SRV) Record

The Services RR allows a service to be associated with a host name. A user or application that wishes to discover where a service is located can interrogate for the relevant SRV RR that describes the service. The result of a successful SRV query will be one or more host names, the port that provides the service, and two values that can be used to select the relative priority and performance of the service. Having obtained the host name, a further A (or AAAA) query will be required to obtain the IP address of the selected service. The SRV RR is being increasingly supported as the means by which the location of a service at a particular domain may be discovered, notably with VoIP and LDAP applications. OpenLDAP (www.openldap.org) in particular supports the SRV record (and its domain publishes an SRV RR) to discover the location of the LDAP service at a domain. The SRV RR is defined in RFC 2782.

SRV RR Syntax

```
srvce.prot.name  ttl  class   rr  pri  weight port target
_http._tcp            IN      SRV 0    5      80   www.example.com.
```

Table 13–4 describes the various fields unique to the SRV RR.

Table 13–4. SRV RR Fields

Field	Description
srvce	The srvce field defines the *symbolic service name*. Standard symbolic service name values are listed by IANA (under the port number list at www.iana.org/assignments/port-numbers), but there is a specific SRV list currently being maintained (see note that follows) outside of IANA. Service names are case insensitive and are always prepended with _ (underscore). Common values are _http for web service, _ftp for File Transfer Protocol, _sip for Session Initiation Protocol, and _ldap for LDAP service. This srvce field may also take a *local* value—its scope is local to the user and therefore may take any desired value that does not conflict with the IANA list. The IANA list also defines the port assigned to the service, but the port field within the SRV RR allows this port number to be changed for the particular service instance if required.
prot	The prot field defines the case-insensitive protocol name (see www.iana.org/assignments/service-names) prepended with _ (underscore). Common values are _tcp for the TCP protocol and _udp for the UDP protocol.
name	The name field is optional. If not present, then normal $ORIGIN substitution rules will occur. See the examples that follow.
pri	The pri field defines the relative priority of this service (range 0 to 65535). Lower numbers are higher priority as in the MX RR type.
weight	The weight field is used when more than one service with same priority is available. weight is a 16-bit unsigned integer in the range 0 to 65535. The value 0 indicates no weighting should be applied. If the weight is 1 or greater, it is a relative number in which the highest is most frequently delivered; that is, given two SRV records, both with a priority of 10 but one with a weight of 1 and the other a weight of 6, the one with weight 6 will have its RR delivered first six times out of seven by the name server.

Field	Description
port	The port field defines the port number that delivers the service on the target (see the target entry). This would normally be the port assigned to the symbolic service (srvce field), but this is not a requirement; for instance, it is permissible to define an _http service with a port number of 8100 rather than the more normal port 80.
target	The target field defines the name of the host that will provide this service and will typically require a query to obtain the IP address (A or AAAA RR query). The target host may lie within this domain or in an external or out-of-zone domain.

The following fragment shows use of the priority and weight fields to define a web service with load balancing:

```
; zone file fragment for example.com.
$TTL 2d ; zone TTL default = 2 days
$ORIGIN example.com.
@              SOA server.example.com. hostmaster.example.com. (
               2010121500 ; serial number
               1d12h      ; refresh =  1 day 12 hours
               15m        ; refreshretry = 15 minutes
               3w12h      ; expiry = 3 weeks + 12 hours
               2h20m      ; nx= 2 hours + 20 minutes
               )
...
_http._tcp    SRV 10 1 80 slow.example.com.
              SRV 10 3 80 fast.example.com.
; if neither slow or fast available, switch to
; an external backup web server but use port 8100 not port 80
              SRV 20 0 8100 backup.example.net.
slow          A   192.168.254.3
fast          A   192.168.254.4
```

In this fragment, both fast.example.com and slow.example.com have equal priorities; the weight values are 1 and 3, respectively, which will result in fast.example.com being returned three times to every one return of slow.example.com. Thus fast.example.com will theoretically receive 75% of the load. If neither fast nor slow is available, the externally hosted backup.example.net should be used with port 8100, not the more normal HTTP port of 80. The following fragment shows use of the SRV RR to discover the host for the LDAP service at example.com:

```
; zone file fragment for example.com.
$TTL 2d ; zone TTL default = 2 days
$ORIGIN example.com.
....
; defines an ldap service available at the host jim.example.com
_ldap._tcp.example.com.  IN  SRV 0 0 389 ldap.example.com.
; the preceding record could have been written as
; _ldap._tcp            IN  SRV 0 0 389 ldap
....
ldap                     IN  A   192.168.254.2
....
```

To discover whether an LDAP service is available at example.com, an SRV query would be sent for _ldap_.tcp.example.com, which in this case would return 0 0 389 ldap.example.com; ldap.example.com would then be queried for its A RR (or AAAA RR if IPv6) and communication could commence.

Note IANA, for some unaccountable reason, is not currently maintaining a registry of SRV symbolic service names. As a consequence, a number of impromptu web sites are springing up to try to maintain such a registry, the objective being to hand it over to IANA at the appropriate time. One such site is maintained at www.dns-sd.org/ServiceTypes.html.

SSH Key Fingerprint (SSHFP) Record

The SSH Key Fingerprint RR allows a host to obtain the fingerprint (hash or digest) of the public key for use in an SSH session by using a DNS query. This functionality was originally provided using the subtype of the KEY RR but subsequently removed by RFC 3445. The SSHFP RR is defined in RFC 4255.

Note The current list of algorithms and fingerprint (hash) types supported by the SSHFP RR is defined at www.iana.org/assignments/dns-sshfp-rr-parameters.

SSHFP RR Syntax

```
name  ttl  class   rr      alg fpt  fingerprint
joe         IN      SSHFP   2   1 (123456
                                   789abcdef67890123456
                                   789abcdef67890)
```

The alg field defines the SSH algorithm and may take one of the following values:

    0 = Reserved
    1 = RSA
    2 = DSS (DSA)

The fpt field is a message-digest algorithm used to create the fingerprint of the SSH key and may take one of the following values:

    0 = Reserved
    1 = SHA-1

The fingerprint field is the base64 (RFC 3548) material created by the digest (hash) algorithm.

```
; zone fragment for example.com
$TTL 2d ; zone default = 2 days or 172800 seconds
$ORIGIN example.com.
....
www         IN      A       192.168.0.3
            IN      SSHFP   1 1 (AABB12AA334477
```

```
                                CD1234a57890)
....
```

In this example, the SSH key for the host www.example.com uses the RSA algorithm and may be computed by decoding the fingerprint using the SHA-1 message digest.

The current (BIND 9.3+) versions of BIND support the SSHFP RR type natively. The SSHFP RR may be created using the ssh-keygen utility (OpenSSH 3.6.1+) using a command such as the following:

```
ssh-keygen -f /etc/ssh/ssh_host_rsa_key.pub \
-r host.example.com. >> master.example.com
```

The \ indicates the line has been broken solely for presentation reasons and should appear as a single line when entered on the command line. The preceding command generates the SSHFP RR from the default OpenSSH (www.openssh.com) RSA key (the -f argument) with a name of host.example.com (the -r argument) and appends it to the zone file master.example.com.

The ssh-key utility is also capable of generating an SSHFP RR using the generic RR format (see the "User-defined RRs" section later in the chapter) if the BIND version being used does not support the SSHFP RR (any release prior to 9.3). In this case, the following command will create a TYPE44 RR of the correct format by using the -g argument:

```
ssh-keygen -g -f /etc/ssh/ssh_host_rsa_key.pub \
-r host.example.com. >> master.example.com
```

The \ indicates the line has been broken solely for presentation reasons and should appear as a single line when entered on the command line.

Text (TXT) Record

The Text RR provides the ability to associate arbitrary text with a name; for example, it can be used to provide a description of the host, service contacts, or any other required information. The TXT RR was defined in RFC 1035.

TXT RR Syntax

```
name  ttl  class  rr    text
joe        IN     TXT   "Located in a black hole"
```

The text field may be any arbitrary text and is enclosed in quotes. The TXT RR is also used to define the Sender Policy Framework (SPF) and DKIM information used to validate legitimate e-mail from a domain, as described in Chapter 8. In these cases, the content and format of the text field are defined by the SPF specification. The following example shows the use of a TXT record to contain truly meaningful data for a host:

```
; zone file fragment for example.com
$TTL 2d ; zone default = 2 days
$ORIGIN example.com.
....
@         IN    A      192.168.254.8
          IN    A      192.168.254.9
          IN    A      192.168.254.10
          IN    TXT "example.com web service is really here"
www       IN    CNAME  example.com.
```

The text "example.com web service is really here" is associated with example.com and will be returned on a TXT query for example.com. The associated CNAME RR, as noted in the "Canonical Name (CNAME) Record" section, does not allow TXT RRs to be defined with the same name.

Well-Known Service (WKS) Record

The Well-Known Service RR is used to define the services and protocols supported by a host. Clients can discover the location of the desired service by inspecting the WKS for the domain. The WKS RR was defined in RFC 1035. Its use is deprecated and replaced by the SRV RR, which provides a more general-purpose mechanism.

WKS RR Syntax

```
name  class ttl  rr   ipv4         proto svc1 svc2 ...
@     IN         WKS  192.168.0.1  TCP   telnet http
```

The ipv4 field is the IPv4 address to which the following list of services applies. The proto field defines the protocol supported by the following services and may take the case-insensitive value tcp or udp. The svc1 and svc2 fields are an arbitrary long list of the services provided at the ipv4 address. The services list may use any name from the IANA registered port numbers list (www.iana.org/assignments/port-numbers). This list may be enclosed in the standard parentheses notation if it extends over more than a single line, as illustrated in the fragments that follow.

WKS RRs are normally defined at the domain level such that a domain query for the WKS RRs will return all the available records and the client must then find the appropriate host to provide the service. The fragment that follows shows a number of services provided on two separate hosts. The RFC is silent on the topic of selecting a host when two hosts provide the same service.

```
; zone file fragment for example.com
$TTL 2d ; zone default = 2 days
$ORIGIN example.com.
....
@          IN   WKS  192.168.254.2 TCP telnet http
           IN   WKS  192.168.254.3 {
                telnet
                smptp   ;some comment about this service
                ftp
           }
....
bill       IN   192.168.254.2
fred       IN   192.168.254.2
...
```

The first preceding WKS RR could be replaced with two SRV RRs, as shown here:

```
_telnet._tcp   IN   SRV 10 0 23   bill.example.com.
_http._tcp     IN   SRV 10 0 80   bill.example.com.
```

X.25 Address (X25) Record

The X.25 Address RR is the equivalent of an A RR for an X.25 (packet-switched network) address. It associates the address of an endpoint (DTE) in an X.25 network with a given host name. The X25 RR has EXPERIMENTAL status and is defined in RFC 1183.

X25 RR Syntax

```
name   ttl class x.25-address
joe         IN   X25  311061700956
```

The x.25-address field is the numeric Packet-Switched Data Network (PSDN) address in X.121 format. It must start with the four-character Data Network Identification Code (DNIC—similar to the regional code in a phone number). Since x.25-address is an address, not a name, there is no terminating dot.

Alternative Cryptographic Algorithms

The cryptographic RR types that define or reference cryptographic algorithms, specifically CERT, DNSKEY, DS, KEY, and RRSIG, allow for additional algorithms other than those specified within the RFC that defines each RR type. This is accomplished using the algorithm field values 252, 253, and 254.

The value 252 denotes an indirect value where the key-data or signature field of the RR is located elsewhere. As of the publication of this book, no further definition of this field has been introduced, and it must currently be regarded as unused. The value 253 denotes that the key-data or signature field will commence with a host name that will be used by the recipient to interpret the content of the space-separated key-data or signature field. The value 254 denotes that the key-data or signature field will start with an object identifier. The OID is assumed to define the cryptographic algorithm being used and allows the recipient to interpret the following space-separated key-data or signature fields. The following example shows a standard DNSKEY RR using the RSA-SHA-1 algorithm (5):

```
example.com.        IN      DNSKEY 256    3        5 (
                            AQPSKmynfzW4kyBvO15MUG2DeIQ3
                            Cbl+BBZH4b/OPY1kxkmvHjcZc8no
                            kfzj31GajIQKY+5CptLr3buXA1Oh
                            WqTkF7H6RfoRqXQeogmMHfpftf6z
                            Mv1LyBUgia7za6ZEzOJBOztyvhjL
                            742iU/TpPSEDhm2SNKLijfUppn1U
                            aNvv4w==   )
```

The following shows the same RR using an OID (254) format:

```
example.com.        IN      DNSKEY 256    3      254 (1.3.6.1.4.1.X.22.55.4.3
                            AQPSKmynfzW4kyBvO15MUG2DeIQ3
                            Cbl+BBZH4b/OPY1kxkmvHjcZc8no
                            kfzj31GajIQKY+5CptLr3buXA1Oh
                            WqTkF7H6RfoRqXQeogmMHfpftf6z
                            Mv1LyBUgia7za6ZEzOJBOztyvhjL
                            742iU/TpPSEDhm2SNKLijfUppn1U
                            aNvv4w==   )
```

The OID shown in the preceding example (1.3.6.1.4.1.X.22.55.4.3) represents one possible format and is comprised of two parts. The first part, 1.3.6.1.4.1, is the base OID of the private enterprise group assigned by IANA (www.iana.org). The value X would be replaced by an enterprise unique number that may be obtained from IANA (www.iana.org/cgi-bin/enterprise.pl). This is followed by an enterprise-assigned number (22.55.4.3) that would define the algorithm to be used.

User-Defined RRs

It is possible to extend the DNS with user-defined RRs. User-defined RRs may be used to add a new RR type not defined in the current IANA list (www.iana.org/assignments/dns-parameters), to define a standardized RR that is not currently supported by the name server software, or to supply the normal type-specific data in an alternative format. Such RRs can be stored in zone files, transferred to slaves, and queried by clients. The method by which DNS software handles user-defined RRs is specified by RFC 3597.

The standard syntax of an RR is defined as follows:

```
name    ttl  class   type  type-specific-data
```

The class, type, and type-specific-data fields may all be defined using the mechanism described below.

- The class field may be user defined by using the word "CLASS" immediately followed by the decimal value of the class type being defined; for instance, CLASS15 defines a new class type that will have a decimal value of 15. No whitespace is allowed between CLASS and the decimal number. Existing classes may be represented using this format; for example, CLASS1 = IN (or Internet class).

- The type field may be user defined by using the word "TYPE" immediately followed by the decimal value of the type being defined, for example, TYPE555 defines a new type that will have a decimal value of 555. No whitespace is allowed between TYPE and the decimal number. Existing RRs types may be represented using this format, for example, TYPE1 is an A RR.

- User-defined type-specific-data is indicated by using the literal sequence \#, followed by whitespace, followed by the number of octets in the field. The fields are written as two hexadecimal characters per octet. If an RR does not have any data, it must be written with a data length of zero. If whitespace is required for clarity, the values must be enclosed in (and) (parentheses). The following example illustrates the possible definitions:

```
$ORIGIN example.com.
....
a       CLASS32     TYPE731         \# 6 abcd (
                                            ef 01 23 45 )
b       HS          TYPE62347       \# 0  ; no data format
e       IN          A               \# 4 0A000001 ;hex version of IP address
f       CLASS1      TYPE1           10.0.0.2 ; A RR
....
```

If a known RR is defined using the TYPEx format, such as TYPE1 for an A RR, or the data with a known type is defined using the \# format, then those formats are used for the purposes of converting the data to a binary format. Thereafter, the RR is treated as normal for that type; that is, it becomes a *known RR type*. It is not possible to alter the *operational* treatment of an existing RR using the user-defined RR textual syntax earlier.

Summary

This chapter has provided a reference with examples where appropriate for all zone file directives and most RRs defined in the current IANA list (www.iana.org/assignments/dns-parameters). The RRs not described are either privately defined (NIMLOC, EID, and SINK), formally obsolete (GPOS, MD, MF, and NSAP-PTR), or not useful in a production environment (NULL, which is experimental and can't be defined in a master zone file). Definitive RFC references are provided for all RRs.

The RRs supported by both the current version of BIND (9.7.2-P2) and Windows (Windows 2008 Server R2) are presented in Table 13–1.

The current IETF policy regarding IPv6 addresses, forward mapping using AAAA RR, and reverse-mapping using PTR RRs, is documented, and the experimental A6 RR is shown with examples. The NAPTR RR is illustrated with some examples. You are reminded that this brutally complicated RR only makes sense when read in conjunction with the application that will make use of the NAPTR RR.

The descriptions of the RRs concerned with DNS security (DS, DNSKEY, KEY, NSEC, and RRSIG) should be read in conjunction with Chapters 10 and 11 as appropriate. A number of the RRs described are rarely used; you are cautioned that those defined as experimental may be withdrawn or changed at any time. RFC 3597 defines a method by which user-defined DNS RR types may be added to DNS zone files and queried by clients. Using this procedure, it is possible for users to extend DNS capabilities using standard software. BIND 9.3+ supports the user-defined RR capability.

Programming

Properties

## CHAPTER 14

BIND APIs and Resolver Libraries

This chapter is primarily intended for programmers and designers who wish to modify the basic functionality of BIND, need to interface to the libraries available with BIND, or need to interface to the standard DNS-related POSIX calls supported by libc. Reasonable knowledge of the C language is required to make sense of most of the information in this chapter.

DNS Libraries and APIs

A confusing number of library functions are available with BIND. They fall into three categories:

- Standard BIND 9 libraries, including from BIND 9.7 a library called libirs which may now be separately built and exported. It uses /etc/resolv.conf but optionally adds a new file (dns.conf) to support addition functionality. This library includes DNSSEC-aware versions of the POSIX standard getaddrinfo(), getnameinfo(), gai_strerror() and freeaddrinfo() and is intended to support third party developers. See the "BIND 9 DNS Libraries" section later in this chapter.

- The historic so-called res_ library set has been available for some time as libbind9, but it has been updated with newer BIND 9 and DNSSEC features. These library functions are controlled by resolv.conf (normally /etc/resolv.conf). This library is primarily concerned with providing programmatic access to the construction of DNS queries. This library is not described further in this edition, having been superseded by other libraries.

- An lwres library set is new with BIND 9. This library is not widely implemented and is not described further in this book.

In addition to the above BIND and standard libraries, the NSD project (open source Authoritative only name server) has also released a DNS library (ldns) that provides many features of interest to the DNS programmer; it may be obtained from www.nlnetlabs.nl/projects/ldns/.

Although all the samples and most of the code descriptions use C, there are several language wrappers such as Python, Java, and Ruby. A number of these language wrappers are listed on the author's website for this book at www.netwidget.net/books/apress/dns.

POSIX Library

The POSIX DNS calls are defined in IEEE 1003.1 - 2004 - POSIX.1. However, because IETF documents are freely available (unlike the IEEE documents), they are also described in RFC 3493, which has a status of INFORMATIONAL and defers to the IEEE specification as being definitive. The available POSIX DNS functions are listed with brief notes about their status, as follows:

- gethostbyname(): Name to Address translation. IPv4 only. Not thread safe.

- gethostbyaddr(): Number to Name (reverse-map) translation. IPv4 only. Not thread safe.

- getaddrinfo(): Name to Address translation. IPv4 and IPv6. Thread safe.

- freeaddrinfo(): Free resources used by getaddrinfo(). Thread safe.

- getnameinfo(): Address to Name translation. IPv4 and IPv6. Thread safe.

The functions gethostbyname2() and gethostbyaddr2() were tactical updates to enable a basic IPv6 service and are now deprecated in favor of getnameinfo() and getaddrinfo(). The functions gethostbyname_r() and gethostbyaddr_r() were, again, tactical implementations to provide thread safe calls and were never defined formally. The functions getipnodebyname() and getipnodebyaddr() were defined in RFC 2553 and are deprecated in favor of getnameinfo() and getaddrinfo(), respectively. getnameinfo() and getaddrinfo() should be used for all new implementations (IPv4 or IPv6) using the interface described by RFC 3493. BIND 9 supplied non-standard but entirely compatible DNSSEC-aware versions of getaddrinfo() and getnameinfo() that are further described below in the "DNSSEC Aware getaddrinfo() and getnameinfo()" section.

BIND 9 DNS Libraries

The DNS user libraries (consisting of libdns, libisc, and libisccfg) are built by standard BIND builds and packages (Ubuntu and FreeBSD), but a new library, libirs, may be separately built (exported) to make it accessible to applications (see "Building BIND 9 Libraries"). The libraries provide four feature sets:

- *POSIX enhancements*: DNSSEC-aware replacements are provided for the getaddrinfo(), getnameinfo(), gai_strerror(), and freeaddrinfo() standard C library calls (part of the IRS system below). Provided by libirs.

- *Information Retrieval System (IRS):* Provides functions to access to the various configuration files (resolv.conf and dns.conf) used by the library. Provided by libirs.

- *DNS client*: Provides basic DNS name resolution access including programmatic access to DDNS. Provided by libdns, libisc and libisccfg.

- *Event Framework*: Not described further in this book.

The functionality of this set of library calls is partly controlled by resolv.conf (normally /etc/resolv.conf) commands, whose format and use is described later in this section; some functionality (getaddrinfo() and getnameinfo() in libirs) is supported by a new configuration file called dns.conf. The dns.conf file is only applicable when the BIND 9 library is used and plays no role in normal BIND (named) operation.

Building BIND 9 Libraries

Most standard packages, such as FreeBSD and Ubuntu server, will build and install the various libraries including libdns, libisc, libisccfg, libbind9, and liblwres normally in /usr/lib and with headers in /usr/include. These are installed as static libraries (with suffix .a, such as libdns.a) in all cases and as both static and dynamic (or shared) libraries (with suffix.so, such as libdns.so) when the configure option --with-libtool is used (Ubuntu). However, to use any of the IRS library functions, including the DNSSEC aware getaddrinfo() and getnameinfo() involves building bind from source (see the –"Building BIND from Source" section in Chapter 6) using the --enable-export, --with-export-libdir, and --with-export-includedir configure options, which are not included in standard Ubuntu or FreeBSD packages This build will, by default, *replace* the current version of named and its associated tools. If only the libraries are desired, this can be done by going to the directory lib/export and issuing the make install from there to create a partial install.

■**Caution** Use of a partial library-only installation is not the official BIND policy. It is potentially dangerous; if the library versions being installed using this procedure are different from those currently installed for BIND, incompatibilities can arise. If this procedure is used, it's recommended that non-standard directories be used for both libraries and header files, as shown in the configure options below.

The following sequence shows building from a source tarball on an Ubuntu Server 10.04 system using its normal build configure options with the addition of those to create the export libraries in **bold**. If BIND is already installed, issuing named -V will list all the configure options used; unless there's a good reason, they should replace or be added to the configure line below, especially if a full install is being attempted. FreeBSD users should consult the –"Building BIND from Source" section in Chapter 6 for the equivalent set of standard configure options, but should also note that either a full or partial install will require GNU make, thus the command gmake install must be used.

```
# cd /bind/source/dir
# ./configure --prefix=/usr --mandir=/usr/share/man --infodir=/usr/share/info --
sysconfdir=/etc/bind --localstatedir=/var --enable-threads --enable-largefile --with-libtool -
-enable-shared --enable-static --with-openssl=/usr --with-gnu-ld --enable-ipv6 --enable-
exportlib --with-export-libdir=/usr/lib/test --with-export-includedir=/usr/include/test
'CFLAGS=-fno-strict-aliasing -DDIG_SIGCHASE -O2' 'LDFLAGS=-Wl,-Bsymbolic-functions'
'CPPFLAGS='
# make install // install full named release
#cd lib/export
# make install // install libraries and headers only
```

This code will install the libraries as /usr/lib/test/libdns.a (and .so), libirs.a (and .so), libisc.a (and .so) and libisccfg.a (and .so), and the header files used when invoking the library in /usr/include/test with subdirectories dns, dst, irs, isc, isccfg. These are non-standard locations on most systems and will require -I /usr/include/test (for headers) and -L/usr/lib/test when compiling and linking against the library with gcc. The standard locations on most systems are /usr/lib and /usr/include, respectively. A number of sample files are included to illustrate the use of the various library calls and are worth the time investment in perusing the modest but very useful source code if the library functions are to be used. There are few things in life more rewarding than source code inspection if you are of that disposition. The samples are *only* compiled when make or make install is executed either from lib/export or from lib/export/samples (or gmake or gmake install for FreeBSD). The sample applications and source code are located in /bind/source/dir/lib/export/samples. The most useful sample applications are described in Table 14–1

Table 14–1. BIND Library Sample Applications

Name	Parameters	Notes
sample-gai	fqdn-name	sample-gai www.example.com.
		Will attempt a forward map (getaddrinfo) using IPv4, IPv6, and Unspecified sockets followed by a socket->name lookup (getnameinfo) for the supplied fqdn-name. DNSSEC aware if dns.conf configured.
sample-request	[-t type] server hostname	sample-request NS ns1.example.com example.com
		Send a request for hostname of RR type (A is default) to server (IPv4) and prints the response. DNSSEC aware if dns.conf configured.

Additional samples include sample-update (dynamic updates using the libdns/libisc/libirs library functions), nsprobe (checks for RFC 4074 compliance using libdns/libisc/libirs library functions), sample (a simple stub-resolver using libdns/libisc/libirs library functions), each of which may be DNSSEC aware if dns.conf is configured. sample-async is an asynchronous stub-resolver (using libdns/libisc) that is not DNSSEC-aware. In all case, running the sample with the -h argument will list the available options.

DNSSEC Aware getaddrinfo() and getnameinfo()

The library libirs.a or libirs.so provides, in addition to other functions noted below, DNSSEC-aware versions of the POSIX standard getaddrinfo() and getnameinfo(), freeaddrinfo() and gai_strerror() calls. The calling interface remains identical to that defined for the standard (more information may be obtained using man getaddrinfo and man getnameinfo or from RFC 3493). These functions will look for the file dns.conf in the location defined by --sysconfdir in the configure options (/etc/bind/dns.conf for Ubuntu or /etc/namedb/dns.conf for BSD). This file has a format equivalent to the named.conf; it currently only takes a trusted-keys clause containing an appropriate trust-anchor for validation (see Chapter 12 for the "trusted-keys Clause" section). If this file is present and contains a trusted-anchor with appropriate scope, DNSSEC validation will occur. If the DNS response validates, the function will return success as normal (0). If the functions fail, a text version of the error-code may be obtained using the function gai_strerror(error-code) as normal. Specifically, if the functions fail DNSSEC validation of the response (assuming the zones have been signed; see Chapter 11), the error code EAI_INSECUREDATA (15) (corresponding to a bogus DNSSEC state) will be returned. If the functions fail to find a dns.conf file or it does not contain a trusted-keys clause with the appropriate scope, the function will behave exactly like the POSIX standard; that is, no DNSSEC validation will take place. These functions could be used in, for example, building a validating stub-resolver.

■**Note** The enhanced functions do not provide status information on whether the zone was signed, insecure, or indeterminate; in essence, they provide DNSSEC validation with minimal changes to the current interface.

DNSSEC POSIX enhanced Calls

The following calls are defined in the irs/netdb.h header, provided in libirs, and are unchanged from the POSIX standard calls.

```
int getaddrinfo(const char *hostname, const char *service,
                    const struct addrinfo *hints, struct addrinfo **results)
```

The example above is used to obtain forward mapping information; thus, given a hostname, it will return the associated address(es) in results:

```
int getnameinfo(const struct sockaddr *sa, socklen_t slen, char *hostname,
                    size_t hostnamelen, char *service, size_t servicelen, int flags)
```

That is used to obtain reverse mapping information, thus given a socket address structure sa (normally an addrinfo structure obtained from getaddrinfo()), it will return a hostname of length hostnamelen and optionally a service name of length servicelen.

```
void freeaddrinfo(struct addrinfo *results)
```

This function is used to free the dynamically allocated addrinfo structure created when using getaddrinfo().

```
const char * gai_strerror(int)
```

This is used to return a textual representation of any error code returned by either getaddrinfo() or getnameinfo(). The function provides the extended error code EAI_INSECUREDATA (see header in irs/netdb.h).

The structure addrinfo, used in getaddrinfo(), has the following format:

```
struct addrinfo {
  int                      ai_flags;                 /* AI_PASSIVE, AI_CANONNAME,
AI_NUMERICHOST */
  int                      ai_family;            /* PF_xxx */
  int                      ai_socktype;          /* SOCK_xxx */
  int                      ai_protocol;              /* 0 or IPPROTO_xxx for IPv4 and IPv6 */
  socklen_t         ai_addrlen;         /* length of ai_addr */
  char*                 ai_canonname;     /* canonical name for hostname */
  struct sockaddr  *ai_addr;          /* binary address */
  struct addrinfo  *ai_next;                 /* next structure in linked list */
};
```

The following code snippet illustrates the use of the functions:

```
/* sample use of getaddrinfo() call to obtain A/AAAA RRs
 * do_getaddrinfo takes a pointer to a null terminated name string as input
 * and either:
 * 1. prints the RR if successful
 * 2. prints an error message if not
 * Notes:
 * No hints addrinfo is used which means it will default to AF_UNSPEC
 * (Tries to find IPv4 and IPv6 addresses)
 * function returns GOOD or BAD
 */

#include <sys/types.h>  /* standard location */
#include <sys/socket.h> /* standard location */
```

```
#include <irs/netdb.h>  /* if irs headers in standard location else use
                           #include "irs/netdb.h" and use -I /usr/include/test
                           in compile/linker if using the sample test locations*/
#include <netinet/in.h> /* for sockaddr_in and sockaddr_in6 */
#include <arpa/inet.h>  /* for inet_ntop */
#include <stdio.h>      /* for printf */
/* other includes as necessary */

#define GOOD 0          /* good return code */
#define BAD  1          /* fail return code */

int do_getaddrinfo(char *hostname)
{
    struct addrinfo *results=NULL;
    struct addrinfo *loop=NULL;      /* addrinfo structure pointers - defined in netdb.h */
    int      code;                   /* getaddrinfo return code */
    struct sockaddr_in  *sa4;        /* to manipulate IPv4 addresses */
    struct sockaddr_in6 *sa6;        /* to manipulate IPv6 addresses */
    char                v6[42];      /* for max IPv6 address */

    code = getaddrinfo(hostname, NULL, NULL, &results); /* no hints */
    if(code != 0)
    {
        /* failed */
        printf("getaddrinfo for %s failed=%s", hostname,gai_strerror(code));
        return BAD;
    }else{
        for (loop = results; loop != NULL; loop = loop->ai_next)
        {
            switch(loop->ai_family)
            {
            case AF_INET: /* IPv4 type */
                sa4 = (struct sockaddr_in *)loop->ai_addr; /* cast to IPv4 socket type */
                printf("IPv4 name=%s A=%s", hostname, inet_ntoa(sa4->sin_addr) );
                break;
            case AF_INET6: /* IPv6 type*/
                sa6 = (struct sockaddr_in6 *)loop->ai_addr; /* cast to IPv6 socket type */
                printf("IPv4 name=%s AAAA=%s", hostname,
                            inet_ntop(loop->ai_family, &sa6->sin6_addr, v6,42) );
                break;
            default:
                printf("Unknown family %d", loop->ai_family);
                break;
            }
        }
    }
    freeaddrinfo(results);
    return GOOD;
}
```

getaddrinfo() uses the default order of searching (defined in /etc/nsswitch.conf) so local files such as hosts will always be searched before using DNS.

Configuring for DNSSEC Validation

In order to enable the enhanced functions to validate DNSSEC responses, a file called dns.conf must be created in the directory defined by --sysconfdir (in the example build, this is /etc/bind). This file takes a standard trusted-keys clause (see the "BIND trusted-keys Clause" section in Chapter 12). The trust-anchor used was the root key (obtained using the process defined in the "Obtaining the Root Key" section in Chapter 11) and thus the format of /etc/bind/dns.conf in this case was:

```
trusted-keys{
"." 257 3 8 "AwEAAagAIKlVZrpC6Ia7gEzahOR+9W29euxhJhVVLOyQbSEWOO8gcCjF
FVQUTf6v58fLjwBdOYIOEzrAcQqBGCzh/RStIoO8gONfnfL2MTJRkxoX
bfDaUeVPQuYEhg37NZWAJQ9VnMVDxP/VHL496M/QZxkjf5/Efucp2gaD
X6RS6CXpoY68LsvPVjROZSwzz1apAzvN9dlzEheX7ICJBBtuA6G3LQpz
W5hOA2hzCTMjJPJ8LbqF6dsV6DoBQzgul0sGIcGOYl7OyQdXfZ57relS
Qageu+ipAdTTJ25AsRTAoub8ONGcLmqrAmRLKBP1dfwhYB4N7knNnulq QxA+Uk1ihz0=";
};
```

Additional trust-anchors may be added as required to this trusted-keys clause. The POSIX functions require the use of a resolver (they are stub-resolver functions and do not provide recursive query support) and the host's resolv.conf file (normally /etc/resolv.conf) will be used to obtain the resolver address. With the dns.conf file present, the following command will provide DNSSEC validated results, assuming the target zone is signed:

```
cd /bind/source/dir/lib/export/samples
sample-gai www.example.com
www.example.com (www.example.com/192.168.2.1)=www.example.com:0
getaddrinfo failed for www.example.com, family=10:8
www.example.com (www.example.com/192.168.2.1)=www.example.com:0
```

sample-gai cycles through getaddrinfo() using a socket type of AF_INET (only IPv4), then AF_NET6 (only IPv6), and finally AF_UNSPEC (any or both IPv4 or IPv6). In the above case, both AF_INET and AF_UNSPEC provided valid results. AF_NET6 failed with error code=8, EAI_NONAME, indicating that an IPv6 address (AAAA RR) does not exist for www.example.com in the zone file, which was correct in the test case shown.

Note Finding publically available DNSSEC signed zones can be a tad difficult. A useful trick is to look at the TLD zones that are signed and then use www.nic.tld or www.register.tld. You can confirm that they are part of a signed zone with dig +dnssec www.nic.tld or dig +dnssec www.register.tld, in which case the RRSIG RRs will be supplied. What if you want to find all of the signed TLDs? Use dig @xfr.lax.dns.icann.org . axfr > root-zone-file followed by grep DS root-zone-file. Every TLD name that publishes a DS RR in this file is signed.

Including Enhanced POSIX Functions in Applications

The enhanced POSIX functions are designed to replace the standard functions supplied in libc (C standard Library). This is a non-trivial process, especially when using shared libraries.

The samples are built by the make files supplied with BIND. If --with-libtool is *not* used during configure, only a static library is produced and all required functions are included into the application samples. The sample applications may then be moved to any suitable directory as required. However, if

--with-libtool is used, a shared library is built and libtool provides appropriate bindings (a script wrapper) to ensure that the POSIX functions are picked up from the required library within the directory system in which BIND was built. The sample applications, in this case, *can't* be moved to any other location.

To compile and link an application statically (this assumes the availability of libraries and headers in /usr/lib/test/ and /usr/include/test), use the following commands to pick up the required libraries and headers:

```
gcc testapp.c -c -I /usr/include/test -o testapp.o
```

This only compiles the application (-c); other flags and include directories should be used as required. The resulting object file is testapp.o and it's used as input to the link operation:

```
gcc testapp.o /usr/lib/test/libirs.a /usr/lib/test/libdns.a /usr/lib/test/libisc.a
/usr/lib/test/libisccfg.a
```

The above command, in which the testapp.o module *must* come first, directly links the static libraries into the final executable (testapp by default) and thus ensures the required functions (the POSIX replacements especially) are included from the BIND libraries. Only the BIND libraries containing functions used by the application are required (see Table 15-1). Any functions required from other libraries will be statically included from standard library locations. Other linker flags should be included as required. Because it is statically built, the resulting application will be of significant size and will obviously need to be rebuilt every time a new static library is introduced.

When using dynamic or shared (.so) libraries, the compile procedure is the same, but the link process is significantly different, as you can see here:

```
gcc testapp.o -L/usr/lib/test --rpath -Wl,/usr/lib/test
```

The resulting executable (testapp by default) should be examined using ldd /path/to/testapp which will display the various libraries and their paths used by the application. An example output line from the ldd command is shown for illustration:

```
libirs.so.60 => /usr/lib/test/libirs.so.60
```

In this case, this shows that libirs.so.60 (60 is just the version number associated with this library) is being picked up from the install location. The various functions that are unique to BIND can only, obviously, be obtained from the BIND libraries, so few problems should arise. However, in the case of getaddrinfo(), getnameinfo(), gai_strerror(), and freeaddrinfo(), these functions will be sourced as standard from libc if the previous procedure was not used. It is particularly important to check that libirs.so is both referenced and uses the expected path since this library contains the replacement functions (as well as others; see Table 14–2). In the event that the above process doesn't work, you are of a profoundly distrusting nature, or you want to vary the library from which the calls are sourced at run-time, environmental variables may be set before running the application, like so:

```
export LD_PRELOAD=/path/to/BIND/library/libirs.so.60
export LD_LIBRARY_PATH=/path/to/BIND/library:$LD_LIBRARY_PATH
sample-gai www.example.com.
```

This assumes a BASH family shell; for those of a c-shell preference, use setenv instead of export. This has a similar effect to the linker options by forcing the run-time loader responsible for dynamically linking the libraries to look first in libirs.so.60 before looking at libc, effectively overriding its normal selection procedure.

BIND Library Functions

Table 14–2 shows the functions provided as well as their header file locations. The header files have varying degrees of description from comprehensive to incomprehensible.

Table 14–2. BIND IRS Library Functions

Name	Library	Header	Notes
freeaddrinfo	Libirs	irs/netdb.h	POSIX replacement
gai_strerror	Libirs	irs/netdb.h	POSIX replacement
getaddrinfo	Libirs	irs/netdb.h	POSIX replacement
getnameinfo	Libirs	irs/netdb.h	POSIX replacement
irs_context_create	Libirs	irs/context.h	
irs_context_destroy	Libirs	irs/context.h	
irs_context_get	Libirs	irs/context.h	
irs_context_getappctx	Libirs	irs/context.h	
irs_context_getdnsclient	Libirs	irs/context.h	
irs_context_getdnsconf	Libirs	irs/context.h	
irs_context_getmctx	Libirs	irs/context.h	
irs_context_getresconf	Libirs	irs/context.h	
irs_context_gettask	Libirs	irs/context.h	
irs_context_gettaskmgr	Libirs	irs/context.h	
irs_context_gettimermgr	Libirs	irs/context.h	
irs_dnsconf_destroy	Libirs	irs/dnsconf.h	dns.conf
irs_dnsconf_gettrustedkeys	Libirs	irs/dnsconf.h	dns.conf
irs_dnsconf_load	Libirs	irs/dnsconf.h	dns.conf
irs_resconf_destroy	Libirs	irs/resconf.h	resolv.conf
irs_resconf_getnameservers	Libirs	irs/resconf.h	resolv.conf
irs_resconf_getndots	Libirs	irs/resconf.h	resolv.conf
irs_resconf_getsearchlist	Libirs	irs/resconf.h	resolv.conf
irs_resconf_load	Libirs	irs/resconf.h	resolv.conf

BIND API Overview

BIND provides two APIs. One is an Advanced Database API (called *adb* for convenience), which has been available since BIND version 8. It allows user-written routines to replace BIND's internal database function for both nominated and all zones. Only a brief synopsis of the adb is included in this chapter. From BIND version 9.1 onward, a Simple Database API, termed *sdb*, has also been provided. It allows a user-written driver to supply zone data either from alternate data sources (for instance, a relational database) or using specialized algorithms (for instance, for load-balancing). A complete description of this API, including an example driver, is presented in the chapter. Neither the adb nor the sdb APIs allow zones to be added or deleted dynamically at this time.

■**Caution** Before contemplating the use of either of these APIs, it is important to be aware that they are statically linked. Simply put, this means the BIND source files and `Makefile.in` are edited and BIND is rebuilt to include the user-written source and header files. If anything goes wrong with the added routines, it's likely that BIND will crash and stop serving DNS queries. No supervisory functionality is provided by the BIND API functions. This is unlike, say, Apache, where modules can be dynamically loaded, and in the event of an error in the loaded module, the basic server will likely continue to function.

Advanced Database API (adb)

Use of the adb is a nontrivial task because all the DNS protocol functionality that is required must be supported by user-written software routines. These may include zone transfer, Dynamic Update (DDNS), and DNSSEC as well as the basic service of providing zone data. The adb API provides a total of 36 functions to implement the capability of the interface. The definitive reference for the adb is the commented C header file `db.h`. It's located in the directory `bind-release/lib/dns/include/dns/db.h`, where `bind-release` should be replaced with the location and version number where you unpacked the source distribution (for example, `/usr/src/bind-9.3.0`). Although this source file is well documented, it doesn't contain enough information to implement fully all the capability required to support this interface. Any potential developer needs to spend time with the BIND source to understand the subject and all its nuances fully before starting any implementation. The adb API is not described further in this book.

Simple Database API (sdb)

The sdb is a relatively simple abstraction consisting of five callbacks and a small handful of RR writing functions. It is optimized to enable zone data to be supplied via a user-written driver from alternative data sources such as a relational database or a Lightweight Directory Access Protocol (LDAP) service, or to manipulate zone data in a user-defined way, for instance, to allow load balancing of A RRs or MX RRs. Information for the sdb API is documented in typical minimalist style in the C header file `bind-release/lib/dns/include/dns/sdb.h`, where `bind-release` should be replaced with the location and version number where you unpacked the source distribution (for example, `/usr/src/bind/9.7.2-P2`). A number of sdb API examples are also provided in the directory `bind-release/contrib/sdb`, covering PostgreSQL, LDAP, and Berkeley Database (BDB). The sdb API provides the following functionality:

- Responses may be in textual RR format (though binary alternates are provided), and hence are optimized for user-interface–style databases.

- Parameters can be passed to the sdb driver when the zone is initialized (defined in the database statement of named.conf and illustrated in the example later in this chapter).

- The sdb driver may register up to five callback types, which cover zone initialization (create()), zone termination (destroy()), zone transfer (allnodes()), zone authority information (authority()), and zone query (lookup()).

- Zones that use the sdb driver interface can't also be dynamically updated.

The functionality of the sdb interface is described with an illustrative example in the following sections.

The Simple Database API (sdb)

The functionality of the sdb API is illustrated with a sample driver that simply reads a standard zone file, whose name is supplied as an initialization parameter, into a memory buffer that it subsequently uses to respond to queries. The comments in the code fragments and the accompanying notes indicate the kind of functionality that could be provided at each callback. The sample driver used in this book is contained in a single module called example.c; has an accompanying header file called example.h; and has a driver name of "example". The code for the sample driver is shown in extracted fragments as required. The listing for both the C module and the header file are shown in the section called "sdb Sample Driver."

Before starting, it is assumed that a copy of the latest tarball for BIND has been downloaded from the ISC site (www.isc.org) and unpacked into a suitable location. The following sample assumes that version 9.7.2-P2 was downloaded and unpacked into /usr/src. Thus, the base directory of BIND (called bind-release from here on) is /usr/src/bind-9.7.2-P2.

Note The sample application is a viable, if not very useful, driver application that reads a standard zone file and serves it via the sdb API. Its primary purpose is to illustrate the functionality of the interface, not the back-end file-system interface, which is inevitably user specific. The code sample should be viewed entirely from this perspective, and by no means as a real-world, ready-to-go driver application. The author pleads brevity as the sole justification for any egregious shortcuts.

Callback Overview

The sdb API provides five callback functions, only one of which is mandatory; these callback functions are introduced here.

create()

The create() callback function is optional and is invoked when the zone is initialized by BIND. It is therefore called for each instance of the driver. The use of a specific sdb driver is defined using the database statement in a zone clause of named.conf. Any mixture of zone clauses may be configured to support one or more sdb drivers, as shown in the following fragment:

```
// named.conf fragment
....
zone "example.com" in {
    // invokes the driver named "example" with one argument
    database "example master.example.com";
};
zone "example.net" in{
    type master;
  // normal zone definition - no driver used
    file "master.example.net";
};
zone "example.org" in {
    // uses another driver for this zone
    database "another-driver";
};
....
```

In this fragment, the zone example.com uses the sample driver, whose name is "example", and is passed the master.example.com parameter (any number of which may be supplied, each being space-separated) on the create() callback in a standard command-line argc/argv structure. The example.net zone is a normal master zone that does not use any sdb driver functionality. The example.org zone uses another (fictitious) sdb driver called "another-driver", which does not require any parameters to be passed.

destroy()

The destroy() callback is optional and is invoked when the zone is unloaded. It is typically used to perform any tidy-up functions, such as terminating database connections, closing files used, freeing memory allocated, and so on.

lookup()

The lookup() callback is mandatory and is invoked on receipt of a query for the domain for which the driver has been registered. The driver supplies results to be included in the ANSWER SECTION of the query (see Chapter 15) by using either the dns_sdb_putrr (a text RR) or the dns_sdb_putrdata (a binary RDATA section only; see Chapter 15) functions. Both of these functions are described in the "Returning RRs" section of this chapter. If the driver always returns SOA and NS RRs for all queries at the zone apex, the authority() callback function is not required. If the driver maintains these records in a separate structure for some reason, then an authority() callback is required. The lookup() callback does not request a type of record (for instance, an A or AAAA RR); instead, all RRs for the queried name must be returned.

authority()

The authority() callback is optional and is invoked for a received query at the zone apex when the preceding lookup() callback did not return the zone SOA and NS RRs. It requests the SOA and NS RRs for the zone apex used to populate the AUTHORITY SECTION (see Chapter 15) of the query response. The authority() callback returns the required NS and SOA using either the dns_sdb_putrr() or dns_sdb_putrdata() functions, or the SOA RR may be optionally returned using the dns_sdb_putsoa() function. Each function is described later in the chapter.

allnodes()

The allnodes() callback is optional and is invoked when a transfer zone request (AXFR) is received by the name server for the zone for which the driver is registered. It may not be appropriate depending on the application type. Each RR in the zone is returned using the dsn_sdb_putnamedrr() or dns_sdb_putnamedrdata() functions, or in the case of the SOA, only the dns_sdb_putsoa() function.

Registering the Callbacks

Registering the callbacks involves calling the dns_sdb_register() function from a driver-initialization function, which in turn is invoked by a manual edit to the bind-release/bin/named/main.c BIND module. To keep matters as simple as possible, the example.c and example.h files reside in the same directory as main.c (bind-release/bin/named). The following fragment from the example.c module contains example_init(), which registers four of the five callback interfaces for illustration purposes. However, recall that only the lookup() callback is mandatory. The fragment also shows the example_clear() function, which performs the corresponding dns_sdb_unregister() function:

```
// example.c fragment
....
// list of callback functions in dns_sdbmethods_t structure
PRIVATE dns_sdbmethods_t example_callbacks = {
    example_lookup, // lookup callback function - mandatory
    NULL, // authority callback function - optional
    example_allnodes, // allnodes callback function - optional
    example_create, // create callback function - optional
    example_destroy // destroy callback function - optional
};
// pointer to handle allocated by BIND and supplied to dns_sdb_unregister
PRIVATE dns_sdbimplementation_t *namedhandle = NULL;

....

/*********************
*
* example_init
* register callbacks for the example driver
* Note: In this driver the DNS_SDBFLAG_RELATIVERDATA flag
* is not strictly needed and is used only to illustrate the use of multiple flags
* the variable 'directory' is used to illustrate that
* parameters may be supplied to this function
* equally the function may or may not return a value
*********************/
isc_result_t  example_init (char directory[])
{
    // initialize flags
    unsigned int flags = DNS_SDBFLAG_RELATIVEOWNER |
                     DNS_SDBFLAG_RELATIVERDATA;
    return (dns_sdb_register(DRIVERNAME,&example_callbacks,
            directory,flags,ns_g_mctx, &namedhandle));
```

```
};
/********************
*
* example_clear
* unregister callbacks for this driver
*
********************/

void example_clear(void)
{
    if (namedhandle != NULL){
        dns_sdb_unregister(&namedhandle);
    };
};
```

The significant point to note in this fragment is that because the calls to initialize and terminate any driver are under control of the driver developer, zero or more parameters can be supplied and a value can be optionally returned that may be tested in the main.c code. The initialization function typically performs global (driver-level) initialization (for example, open one or more database connections). The termination function typically performs any global (driver-level) clean-up processing.

dns_sdb_register() Function

The dns_sdb_register() function is called once from the driver initialization function to register all the supported callback functions. In the sample driver, dns_sdb_register() is called from the function example_init(). The prototype statement is shown here:

```
isc_result_t dns_sdb_register(const char *drivername,
    const dns_sdbmethods_t *methods,
    void *driverdata, unsigned int flags, isc_mem_t *mctx,
    dns_sdbimplementation_t **sdbimp);
```

As you can see, this function accepts numerous parameters. Let's introduce each:

- isc_result_t is the standard return code, whose values are described in the "isc_result_t Return Codes" section later in the chapter.

- drivername is a standard null-terminated string containing the name of the driver; it corresponds to that defined in the database statement in the zone clause of named.conf. In the sample driver, this is "example".

- methods is the dns_sdbmethods_t structure used to contain the address of the callback functions in the order lookup(), authority(), allnodes(), create(), and destroy(). Only the lookup() callback is mandatory. Any of the others may be set to NULL to indicate it is not supported.

- driverdata is an optional driver-allocated parameter. The type and value are determined by the driver. This value is returned on the create() and destroy() callbacks. This parameter is driver specific, not zone specific. An equivalent zone (or instance) parameter (dbdata) provides a similar function and may be supplied using the optional create() callback when the zone is initialized. The driver-level parameter is a way of passing parameters to each zone's create() callback. This parameter could, as an example, store a time value that would be used to compute elapsed time in all zones handled by the driver. In the sample driver, a directory-string variable is used to illustrate its usage. If not required, the variable should be set to NULL.

- flags defines any required flags, which may take one or more of the following values:

    - _SDBFLAG_RELATIVEOWNER: If present, it indicates that the lookup() and authority() callbacks will be called with relative domain names. If not present, the callbacks will use absolute names (FQDN). If the zone is example.com and the DNS_SDBFLAG_RELATIVEOWNER flag is present, the name joe would be supplied on a lookup to indicate joe.example.com. If the DNS_SDBFLAG_RELATIVEOWNER flag were not present, the same call would need to supply a name of joe.example.com. (with the dot).

    - NS_SDBFLAG_RELATIVERDATA: If present, it indicates that responses in a dns_sdb_putnamedrdata() or a dns_sdb_putrdata() function may contain labels with relative names in the binary string supplied (see the "NAME Field Format" section in Chapter 15). If this flag is not present, only fully expanded names (FQDNs) are allowed in RDATA fields.

    - NS_SDBFLAG_THREADSAFE: If present, it indicates that the driver is capable of handling multiple parallel requests. If not present, only one request is sent at a time, and the next request is issued only when the driver has returned from that callback.

- mctx is a pointer to a BIND memory context and should take the value ns_g_mctx in all drivers. This pointer is also used in the memory management functions isc_mem_free(), isc_mem_put(), isc_mem_get(), and isc_mem_strdup() (see the "Memory Management for Drivers" section).

- sdbimp is a pointer to a *handle pointer* allocated by BIND when the dns_sdb_register() function is invoked, and it must be returned by the driver when it issues the dns_sdb_unregister() function. The driver is responsible for defining the storage location to contain this pointer in a dns_sdb_implementation_t structure. It should be initialized as shown in the preceding sample driver fragment.

dns_sdc_unregister() Function

This function is called to unregister the driver's callback functions. In the sample driver, this is done from the example_clear() function, which in turn is called from BIND's main.c module on termination of BIND. example_clear() is always called after all destroy() callback functions. The prototype is shown here:

```
void dns_sdb_unregister(dns_sdbimplementation_t **sdbimp);
```

The sdbimp pointer is the same as the one supplied by the driver when the dns_sdb_register() function was invoked, and it's the handle used by BIND to recognize this driver.

isc_result_t Return Codes

The following return codes may be used with all the driver functions—including callbacks—to indicate the return type:

- ISC_R_SUCCESS: Good return.

- ISC_R_FAILURE: The function failed for some unspecified reason.

- ISC_R_NOTFOUND: The specified hostname or authority RRs were not found.

- ISC_R_NOMEMORY: Memory allocation failure. See the "Memory Management for Drivers" section.

Adding the Driver to BIND

The functions example_init() and example_clear() must be triggered from BIND's main.c module and the driver's header file added to support the calls. The following example uses BIND 9.7.2-P2 main.c (in bind-release/bin/named/main.c). Finally, all the modules that comprise the driver must be added to the BIND Makefile.in to be included in the final build.

Header File Insertion

The driver header file should be kept to an absolute minimum to minimize nesting complexity and it should contain only prototypes and necessary definitions to support the calls from this module. The header file should be placed in the bind-release/bin/named directory. The insertion point for headers is well documented (line 74 in main.c for 9.7.2-P2), as shown in the following code:

```
#include <named/lwresd.h>
#include <named/main.h>

/*
 * Include header files for database drivers here.
 */
/*
#include "example.h"  // header for example driver inserted
```

Initialization Function Insertion

The initialization function example_init() must now be inserted to call the driver. Any number of drivers may be included, each of which is added to the function setup() in a well-documented location before the call to ns_server_create() (line 838 in main.c for 9.7.2-P2), as shown in the following code:

```
ns_builtin_init();
/*
 * Add calls to register sdb drivers here.
 */
/* xxdb_init(); */
```

```
example_init("/var/named/zones/");  // call to example to register the callbacks
….
```

Termination Function Insertion

Finally, the termination function example_clear() needs to be added to main.c in the cleanup() function, after the call to ns_server_destroy(). Again, the location is well documented in the source (line 862 in 9.7.2-P2), as shown in the following code:

```
ns_server_destroy(&ns_g_server);
ns_builtin_deinit();
/*
 * Add calls to unregister sdb drivers here.
 */
/* xxdb_clear(); */
example_clear();  // unregister callback function
```

Makefile.in Insertion

The Makefile.in file (bind-release/bin/named/Makefile.in) must be modified to include all the driver modules during the BIND build. The insertion point for source (DBDRIVER_SRCS) and object (DBDRIVER_OBJS) is well documented (line 29 in 9.7.2-P2), as shown in the following code:

```
#
# Add database drivers here.
#
DBDRIVER_OBJS = example.@O@
DBDRIVER_SRCS = example.c
DBDRIVER_INCLUDES =
DBDRIVER_LIBS =
```

The sample driver has no special requirements for either library or include locations.

The Callback Functions

As defined previously, there are five callback functions: lookup() (mandatory), authority() (optional), allnodes() (optional), create() (optional), and destroy() (optional). In the following sections, each callback function is described and illustrated using the sample application.

create() Callback Function

The create() callback is called for each zone in which a database statement exists for this driver. Thus, it is called to create an *instance* of the driver and provides the opportunity to initialize any zone-specific data. For instance, the create() callback could allocate memory, initialize SQL queries, and so on. The prototype is as follows

```
isc_result_t (*dns_sdbcreatefunc_t)(const char *zone, int argc, char **argv,
        void *driverdata, void **dbdata);
```

which breaks down as

- isc_result_t is the result code—see the "isc_result_t Return Codes" section earlier in the chapter.

- zone is a null-terminated string containing the zone name.

- argc is the standard count of arguments supplied in the database statement of this zone clause. In the example database statement used previously (database "example master.example.com";), the count is 2.

- argv is a null-terminated string array with one entry for each of the supplied arguments. In the example database statement (database "example master.example.com";), arg[0] contains "example" and argv[1] contains "master.example.com".

- driverdata is the optional value supplied in the dns_sdb_register function that may be used as a driver global.

- dbdata is optional and allows this instance of the driver to create unique information that is returned with every allnodes(), authority(), destroy(), and lookup() callback. It is used in the sample driver to contain the zone data in a memory location that has been dynamically allocated.

The following is an extracted fragment from the sample driver application showing some of the possible functionality of the create() callback:

```
// sdb driver fragment
/*********************
*
* example_create()
* handle create callback for the example driver
* 1. call example_read_zone
* 2. update dbdata if OK
* 3. driverdata contains /var/named/zones/
* 4. on good exit dbdata contains memory based zone structure
*********************/
PRIVATE isc_result_t example_create(const char *zone, int argc, char **argv,
        void *driverdata, void **dbdata)
{
  isc_result_t result = ISC_R_FAILURE;
  if (argc != 2){
    isc_log_write(ns_g_lctx, NS_LOGCATEGORY_GENERAL,NS_LOGMODULE_SERVER,
ISC_LOG_ERROR, "Example Driver: No file defined for %s", zone);
        return result;
        };
  *dbdata = example_read_zone(driverdata, argv[1],zone);
  if(*dbdata == NULL){ // failed
    return result;
  };
  return ISC_R_SUCCESS;
};
```

The sample driver uses a file name argument (argv[1]) supplied as part of the create() callback and defined in the database statement for the zone. The driverdata variable that was set up during the dns_sdb_register() function call is used as a parameter to example_read_zone(). The function uses the logging service (see the "Logging for Drivers" section later in the chapter) to log an error if the required file name parameter is not present. The function example_read_zone() allocates a block of memory in which it stores the complete parsed zone file (in a structure called RRSET). This memory structure is returned as the dbdata value, which is subsequently returned on all lookup(), authority(), allnodes(), and destroy() callbacks for this zone.

destroy() Callback Function

The destroy() function is called when the zone is closed and provides the opportunity to release memory, close files, terminate database connections, and so on. The prototype is as follows

```
void (*dns_sdbdestroyfunc_t)(const char *zone, void *driverdata, void **dbdata);
```

where

- zone is the null-terminated string containing the zone name.

- driverdata is the global data that was optionally supplied in the dns_sdb_register() function call.

- dbdata is the instance-specific data that was optionally supplied on the create() callback.

The following fragment shows use of the destroy() function:

```
/********************
*
* example_destroy
* handle destroy callback for the example driver
* deallocate memory allocated at create
********************/
PRIVATE void example_destroy(const char *zone, void *driverdata, void **dbdata)
{
  isc_mem_free(ns_g_mctx, dbdata);
  return;
};
```

In the sample driver, the dbdata parameter is a dynamic memory chunk allocated during the create() callback in the function example_read_zone()) and is freed in the example_destroy() function.

lookup() Callback Function

The lookup() callback is invoked on receipt of a query for any zone that uses the nominated driver; that is, it has a database statement in the zone clause that references the "name" of this driver. The lookup prototype is shown here

```
isc_result_t  (*dns_sdblookupfunc_t)(const char *zone, const char *name,
                void *dbdata, dns_sdblookup_t *lookup);
```

where

- isc_result_t is the result code—see the "isc_result_t Return Codes" section earlier in the chapter.

- zone is a null-terminated string containing the zone name.

- name is the required hostname in the query. This value may be a relative (unqualified) name if the DNS_SDBFLAG_RELATIVEOWNER flag was present in the dns_sdb_register() function call (the relative name of the zone apex is represented as "@"). If this flag was not present, an FQDN would be supplied; for instance, joe.example.com. (with a dot). The driver should return *all* RRs using the dsn_sdb_putrr(), dns_sdb_putrdata(), or dns_sdb_putsoa() functions with the supplied name. It is left to BIND to select and return the appropriate RRs.

- dbdata is the value that was optionally supplied in the create() callback and may be NULL.

- lookup is a dns_sdblookup_t structure that is used to return the results of the lookup() callback.

The lookup (dns_sdblookup_t) structure is referenced in any dns_sdb_putrr(), dns_sdb_putsoa(), or dns_sdb_putrdata() calls used to return RRs, as shown in the following fragment:

```
/*********************
*
* example_lookup
* handle lookup callback for the example driver
* trivial exhaustive scan of the whole memory structure
*
*********************/
isc_result_t  example_lookup(const char *zone, const char *name,
                void *dbdata, dns_sdblookup_t *lookup)
{
  RRSET_ID rrs = dbdata;
  isc_result_t result = ISC_R_NOTFOUND; // default
  while(*(&rrs->owner[0]) != '~') // ~ is EOZ marker
  {
    if(strcmp(name,rrs->owner))
    {
      result = ISC_R_SUCCESS;
      result = dns_sdb_putrr(lookup,rrs->type,rrs->ttl, rrs->rdata);
      if (result != ISC_R_SUCCESS)
      {
        return result;  // error exit
      };
    };
    ++rrs;
  };
  return result;
};
```

In the sample driver, each RR is returned using dns_sdb_putrr(), which is a purely textual interface. This includes the SOA and NS RRs, so in this driver the authority() callback is not required.

authority() Callback Function

The authority() callback is optional. It is invoked upon receipt of a query for the zone apex if the SOA and NS RRs were not returned with the preceding lookup() callback. The authority() prototype is shown in the following code

```
isc_result_t  (*dns_sdbauthorityfunc_t)(const char *zone, void *dbdata,
    dns_sdblookup_t *authority);
```

where

- isc_result_t is the result code—see the "isc_result_t Return Codes" section earlier in the chapter.

- zone is a null-terminated string containing the zone name.

- dbdata is a user-created value that was optionally supplied in the create() callback. This value is returned on all lookup(), allnodes(), authority(), and destroy() calls.

- authority is a dns_sdblookup_t structure that contains the RRs returned by the authority() callback and is referenced in any dns_sdb_putrr(), dns_sdb_putrdata(), or dns_sdb_putsoa() calls used to return RRs. Each function is described in the "Returning RRs" section later in the chapter.

allnodes() Callback Function

The allnodes() callback is optional. It is invoked on receipt of a zone transfer request for the zone. The allnodes() prototype is shown here

```
isc_result_t (*dns_sdballnodesfunc_t)(const char *zone, void *dbdata,
                  dns_sdballnodes_t *allnodes);
```

where

- isc_result_t is the result code—see the "isc_result_t Return Codes" section earlier in the chapter.

- zone is a null-terminated string containing the zone name.

- dbdata is a user-created value that was optionally supplied in the create() callback. This value is returned on all lookup(), allnodes(), authority(), and destroy() calls.

- allnodes is a dns_sdblookup_t structure that contains the RRs returned by the allnodes() callback.

The allnodes dns_sdblookup_t structure is referenced in any dns_sdb_putnamedrr() or dns_sdb_putnamedrdata() calls used to return RRs, as shown in the following fragment:

```
/*********************
*
* example_allnodes
* handle allnodes callback for the example driver
*
*********************/
```

```
PRIVATE isc_result_t example_allnodes(const char *zone, void *dbdata,
                      dns_sdballnodes_t *allnodes)
{
  RRSET_ID rrs = dbdata;
  isc_result_t result = ISC_R_SUCCESS; // default
  while(*(&rrs->owner[0]) != '~'){ // ~ is EOZ marker
    result = dns_sdb_putnamedrr(allnodes,rrs->owner,rrs->type,rrs->ttl, rrs->rdata);
    if (result != ISC_R_SUCCESS){
      return result;  // error exit - error code from dns_sdb_putrr
    };
    ++rrs;
  };
  return result;
};
```

The sample driver's `allnodes()` function simply iterates through the memory version of the zone file and returns all RRs. In the event of any error, it returns the error code returned by the failing function, which all use the "isc_result_t Return Codes" values defined earlier in the chapter.

Returning RRs

Five functions are supplied for returning RRs; these are described in this section.

dns_sdb_putrr() Function

This function may be used to return RRs by either the `lookup()` or `authority()` callbacks when the data is purely textual. The prototype is as follows

```
isc_result_t  dns_sdb_putrr(dns_sdblookup_t *lookup, const char *type,
                dns_ttl_t ttl, const char *data);
```

where

- isc_result_t is the result code—see the "isc_result_t Return Codes" section earlier in the chapter.

- lookup() is the address of the dns_sdblookup_t structure supplied in either the lookup() or authority() callback.

- type is a null-terminated string containing the returned RR type.

- ttl is the binary TTL associated with the RR.

- data is a single null-terminated string containing the RDATA for the RR type. Thus, if the RR type being returned is an MX RR, this field would contain both the *preference* field and the *name* (for example, "10 mail" or "10 mail.example.com."). Either a relative name or an FQDN is acceptable and does not depend on the setting of the DNS_SDBFLAG_RELATIVEOWNER, which refers to the owner (or left-hand name only). This function may be used to return the SOA; alternatively, the optimized function dns_sdb_putsoa() may be used. In either case, it is important that the serial number is incremented if zone data has changed since the last callback. This function is used to return all the RRs in the sample application.

dns_sdb_putrdata() **Function**

This function may be used to return RR records to the lookup() or authority() callbacks in binary format. The prototype is as follows

```
isc_result_t  dns_sdb_putrdata(dns_sdblookup_t *lookup,
        dns_rdatatype_t type, dns_ttl_t ttl,
        const unsigned char *rdata, unsigned int rdlen);
```

where

- isc_result_t is the result code—see the "isc_result_t Return Codes" section earlier in the chapter.

- lookup is the address of the dns_sdblookup_t structure supplied in either the lookup() or authority() callback.

- type is the binary RR number.

- ttl is the TTL associated with the RR.

- rdata is a binary representation of the RDATA field for the RR type. Relative names (containing labels with the top two bits set to 11; see "NAME Field Format" section in Chapter 15) can only appear in this binary field if the DNS_SDBFLAG_RELATIVERDATA flag that was supplied in the dns_sdb_register() function has been set. Otherwise, it is assumed that all names are labels (top two bits set to 00) and must be FQDNs (end with a dot).

dns_sdb_putsoa() **Function**

This function is optimized to simplify returning SOA RRs and may be used by either the lookup() or authority() callbacks. The prototype is as follows

```
isc_result_t  dns_sdb_putsoa(dns_sdblookup_t *lookup, const char *mname,
        const char *rname, isc_uint32_t serial);
```

where

- isc_result_t is the result code—see the "isc_result_t Return Codes" section earlier in the chapter.

- lookup is the address of the dns_sdblookup_t structure supplied in either the lookup() or authority() callback.

- mname is a null-terminated string containing the MNAME field—the name of the primary-master server for the zone.

- rname is a null-terminated string containing the RNAME field (the e-mail address of the zone administrator), and by convention uses hostmaster.example.com.

- serial is the binary serial number for the zone.

All the other fields in the SOA RR are defaulted; that is, refresh, expiry, and so on. The sample driver does not use this function call, but the following fragment shows how it could be used in the lookup() callback function:

```
dns_sdb_putsoa(lookup, "ns1.example.com", "hostmaster.example.com", 2005042900);
```

dns_sdb_putnamedrr() **Function**

This function may be used when returning text RRs during an allnodes() (zone transfer) callback. The prototype is as follows:

```
isc_result_t dns_sdb_putnamedrr(dns_sdballnodes_t *allnodes, const char *name,
    const char *type, dns_ttl_t ttl, const char *data);
```

The fields used in this function are in every respect the same as those used in the dns_sdb_putrr() function described previously.

dsn_sdb_putnamedrdata() **Function**

This function may be used when returning binary (wire-format) RRs during an allnodes() (zone transfer) callback. The prototype is as follows:

```
isc_result_t dns_sdb_putnamedrdata(dns_sdballnodes_t *allnodes, const char *name,
    dns_rdatatype_t type, dns_ttl_t ttl,
    const void *rdata, unsigned int rdlen);
```

The fields used in this function are in every respect the same as those used in the dns_sdb_putrdata() function described previously.

Memory Management for Drivers

Memory for use in driver instances should be allocated via BIND's memory allocation functions to assist in any debug problems and to allow BIND to manage all memory usage. Memory management functions are defined in bind-release/lib/isc/include/isc/mem.h, and this header should be included into the driver module if these functions are required. Although a number of functions are provided, the following may be used to obtain memory and to free memory.

isc_mem_get() **Function**

This BIND function may be used to allocate any required memory for use by the driver

```
void *isc_mem_get(isc_mem_t *context, size_t size);
```

where

- void * is the start address of the allocated memory. If set to NULL on return, it means that no memory is available and the requesting callback function should return with a status of ISC_R_NOMEMORY.

- context is the name-server memory context and should be set to ns_g_mctx.

- size is the size in bytes of the memory required.

isc_mem_free() **Function**

This BIND function de-allocates the memory obtained by the corresponding isc_mem_get() function

```
void isc_mem_free(isc_mem_t context, void *memory);
```

where

- context is the name-server memory context and should be set to ns_g_mctx.

- memory is the address of the start of memory allocated by an isc_mem_get() function.

Logging for Drivers

Drivers may invoke BIND's logging services. The available functions are accessed via the header named/log.h, which must be included in the driver module if any logging function is used. The following describes isc_log_write(), the most useful generic log function, which is used in the sample code.

isc_log_write() Function

This isc_log_write() function may be used to write a log entry. The prototype, contained in bind-release/lib/isc/include/isc/log.h, is as follows

```
void isc_log_write(isc_log_t *lctx, isc_logcategory_t *category,
    isc_logmodule_t *module, int level,
    const char *format, ...);
```

where

- lctxt indicates a BIND logging context and should be set to ns_g_lctx.

- category is the log category as defined in the category statement (see the "BIND logging Statements" section in Chapter 12) of a logging clause. It takes the following values:

  - NS_LOGCATEGORY_GENERAL: General—default

  - NS_LOGCATEGORY_CLIENT: Client

  - NS_LOGCATEGORY_NETWORK: Network

  - NS_LOGCATEGORY_UPDATE: Update

  - NS_LOGCATEGORY_UPDATE_SECURITY: Update security

  - NS_LOGCATEGORY_QUERIES: Query

  - NS_LOGCATEGORY_UNMATCHED: Unmatched

- The most useful logging value is NS_LOGCATEGORY_GENERAL, which is written to the default logging category. However, to assist in debugging, a seldom-used category such as *unmatched* could be used with appropriate category and channel statements in the logging clause.

- module defines the module being used and should be set to NS_LOGMODULE_SERVER.

- level defines the log level number and should be set to ISC_LOG_ERROR.

- format is a field that accepts normal printf arguments.

The following shows an example of a log message:

```
isc_log_write(ns_g_ltcx, NS_LOGCATEGORY_GENERAL,
   NS_LOGMODULE_SERVER, ISC_LOG_ERROR,
   "Example zone %s: Failed status=%d", zone,status);
```

Here, zone would be defined as a null-terminated string variable and status as an integer variable.

Testing the Driver

The following line test compiles the example.c module. The -I argument is necessary to pick up various BIND header files, the -o argument defines the output file name, and the -c argument limits the operation to compile only:

```
# gcc example.c -o example.o -c -I include
```

To test compile BIND's main.c module in isolation, use the following line (the -I and -D directives suppress BIND environment errors):

```
# gcc main.c -o main.o -c -I include -I unix/include -I ../../lib/bind9 \
-I ../../lib/isc/include \
-DNS_SYSCONFDIR="" -DNS_LOCALSTATEDIR="" -DVERSION=__VERSION__ -DCONFIGARGS=NULL
```

The "\" splits the line for presentation purposes only, and the command should appear on a single line.

Building BIND

The following command sequence configures and makes BIND in a test location of /var/etc for the named.conf file. This test location keeps it separate from any current installation version of named.conf:

```
# make distclean
# ./configure --prefix=/usr --sysconfdir=/var/etc --localstatedir=/var \
--disable-threads  --with-openssl
# make
```

The above is a simplified set of configure parameters that will work on most systems; see the "Building BIND from Source" section in Chapter 6 for the full set used with either Ubuntu or FreeBSD standard packages (or use named -V to display them if BIND is already installed). If you are of a suspicious disposition and want to verify that your module was included in the BIND build, replace the make command above with the following:

```
# make > build.out
# OR to have both console and file output
# make |tee build.out
```

Next, look for the name of your module in the build.out file:

```
grep example build.out
```

Replace example with whatever you called your module.

If an existing version of BIND 9 has been installed on the system, there is no need to run make install until the new software has been fully tested. The following command line runs BIND from the bind-release directory (assumed to be /usr/src):

```
# /usr/src/bind-9.7.2-P2/bin/named/named -u named
```

The command-line arguments should be the same as those used on the existing BIND installation. Only when the software is production ready should it be built with the final locations and installed, as shown in the following code:

```
# make distclean
# ./configure --prefix=/usr --sysconfdir=/etc --localstatedir=/var \
--disable-threads  --with-openssl
# make
# make install
```

Again, a simplified configure set that should work on most systems is shown. To replicate those used for standard package builds for Ubuntu and FreeBSD, see the "Building BIND from Source" section in Chapter 6, or, if BIND is already installed, issue named -V.

sdb Sample Driver

The listings for the sample application driver are shown in the following sections.

Source Module (example.c)

The following listing is the complete source module for example.c. Fragments of this module were used to illustrate various functions throughout the preceding sdb API function descriptions. It is presented here for completeness only.

```
// example sdb driver for BIND
// reads and parses zone file into ram structure
// INCLUDES
// add any required std function includes used by driver
#include <stdio.h> // for fopen etc.

// BIND includes
#include <isc/mem.h> // required for isc_mem_t structure
#include <isc/result.h> // result codes
#include <dns/sdb.h> // std headers for all sdb functions
#include <named/globals.h> // BIND globals
#include <named/log.h> // for isc_log_write
// driver includes
#include "example.h"  // header for sample driver

// DEFINES and MACROS
#define DRIVERNAME "example"
#define PRIVATE static
#define EXAMPLE_ZONE_SIZE (2 * 1024) // fixed memory allocation
#define FILENAME_SIZE 50
#define BUFFER_SIZE 200
// STRUCTURES
/* trivial structure to hold RRs */
typedef struct rrset_tag{
  char        owner[30];  // owner name
  unsigned int ttl;       // TTL
  char        type[10];  // RR type
  char        rdata[50];  // rdata
}RRSET, *RRSET_ID;
```

```
// PRIVATE PROTOTYPES
PRIVATE isc_result_t example_create(const char *zone, int argc, char **argv,
        void *driverdata, void **dbdata);
PRIVATE void example_destroy(const char *zone, void *driverdata, void **dbdata);
PRIVATE isc_result_t  example_lookup(const char *zone, const char *name,
                void *dbdata, dns_sdblookup_t *);
PRIVATE isc_result_t example_allnodes(const char *zone, void *dbdata,
                    dns_sdballnodes_t *allnodes);
PRIVATE void * example_read_zone(char *directory, char *file,const char* zone);
// PRIVATE VARIABLES
// list of callback functions in dns_sdbmethods_t structure
PRIVATE dns_sdbmethods_t example_callbacks = {
    example_lookup, // lookup callback function - mandatory
    NULL, // authority callback function - optional
    example_allnodes, // allnodes callback function - optional
    example_create, // create callback function - optional
    example_destroy // destroy callback function - optional
};
// pointer to handle allocated by BIND and supplied to dns_sdb_unregister
PRIVATE dns_sdbimplementation_t *namedhandle = NULL;

// PRIVATE FUNCTIONS
/*********************
*
* example_create()
* handle create callback for the example driver
* 1. call example_read_zone
* 2. update dbdata if OK
* 3. driverdata contains /var/named/zones/
* 4. on good exit dbdata contains memory based zone structure
********************/
PRIVATE isc_result_t example_create(const char *zone, int argc, char **argv,
        void *driverdata, void **dbdata)
{
  isc_result_t result = ISC_R_FAILURE;
  if (argc != 2){
    isc_log_write(ns_g_lctx, NS_LOGCATEGORY_GENERAL,
    NS_LOGMODULE_SERVER, ISC_LOG_ERROR,
      "Example Driver: No file defined for %s", zone);
       return result;
      };
  *dbdata = example_read_zone(driverdata, argv[1],zone);
  if(*dbdata == NULL){ // failed
    return result;
  };
```

```
    return ISC_R_SUCCESS;
};
/********************
 *
 * example_read_zone
 * 1. read zone file
 * 2. allocate fixed memory chunk (2K)
 * 3. add count of RRs
 * 4. populate RR structure
 * return NULL = error else address of buffer containing zone file
 ********************/
PRIVATE void * example_read_zone(char *directory, char *file, const char* zone)
{
  char filename[FILENAME_SIZE];  // zone file name
  char buffer[BUFFER_SIZE];   // zone file line buffer
  FILE *fp;
  RRSET_ID rrs;
  strcpy(filename, directory);
  strcpy(&filename[0] + strlen(directory), file);
  if(!fopen(filename,"r")){
    isc_log_write(ns_g_lctx, NS_LOGCATEGORY_GENERAL,
      NS_LOGMODULE_SERVER, ISC_LOG_ERROR,
      "Example Driver: Zone %s File %s does not exist", zone, filename);
    return NULL;
  }
  // allocate fixed memory for file
  // very crude for example purposes only
  rrs = (RRSET_ID)isc_mem_get(ns_g_mctx,EXAMPLE_ZONE_SIZE);
  if (rrs == NULL){ // failed
  isc_log_write(ns_g_lctx, NS_LOGCATEGORY_GENERAL,
      NS_LOGMODULE_SERVER, ISC_LOG_ERROR,
      "Example Driver: isc_mem_get fail");
    return NULL;
  }
  while(fgets(buffer, BUFFER_SIZE, fp) != NULL){
    /* read file discard comments
     *  populate structure rrs
     * all zone apex RRs will have @ in owner name */
  };
  ++rrs; // point to next structure entry
  // add dummy end record
  *(&rrs->owner[0]) = '~'; // special end name
  fclose(fp);  // close file
  return rrs;  // return dbdata containing zone file
};
/********************
 *
 * example_lookup
 * handle lookup callback for the example driver
 * trivial exhaustive scan of the whole memory structure
 *
 ********************/
```

```
isc_result_t  example_lookup(const char *zone, const char *name,
                void *dbdata, dns_sdblookup_t *lookup)
{
  RRSET_ID rrs = dbdata;
  isc_result_t result = ISC_R_NOTFOUND; // default
  while(*(&rrs->owner[0]) != '~')
  {
    if(strcmp(name,rrs->owner))
    {
      result = ISC_R_SUCCESS;
      result = dns_sdb_putrr(lookup,rrs->type,rrs->ttl, rrs->rdata);
      if (result != ISC_R_SUCCESS)
      {
        return result;  // error exit
      };
    };
    ++rrs;
  };
  return result;
};


/*******************
*
* example_allnodes
* handle allnodes callback for the example driver
*
*******************/
PRIVATE isc_result_t example_allnodes(const char *zone, void *dbdata,
                    dns_sdballnodes_t *allnodes)
{
  RRSET_ID rrs = dbdata;
  isc_result_t result = ISC_R_SUCCESS; // default
  while(*(&rrs->owner[0]) != '~'){
    result = dns_sdb_putnamedrr(allnodes,rrs->owner,rrs->type,rrs->ttl, rrs->rdata);
    if (result != ISC_R_SUCCESS){
      return result;  // error exit
    };
    ++rrs;
  };
  return result;
};
/*******************
*
* example_destroy
* handle destroy callback for the example driver
* deallocate memory allocated at create
*******************/
PRIVATE void example_destroy(const char *zone, void *driverdata, void **dbdata)
{
  isc_mem_free(ns_g_mctx, dbdata);
  return;
};

// PUBLIC FUNCTIONS
```

```
/********************
*
* example_init
* register callbacks for the example driver
* Note: In this driver the DNS_SDBFLAG_RELATIVERDATA flag
* is not strictly needed and is used only to illustrate the use of multiple flags
* the variable 'directory' is used to illustrate that
* parameters may be supplied on this call
* equally the function may or may not return a value
*
********************/
isc_result_t  example_init (char directory[])
{
    // initialize flags
    unsigned int flags = DNS_SDBFLAG_RELATIVEOWNER | DNS_SDBFLAG_RELATIVERDATA;
    return (dns_sdb_register(DRIVERNAME,&example_callbacks,
        directory,flags,ns_g_mctx, &namedhandle));
};
/********************
*
* example_clear
* unregister callbacks for this driver
*
********************/

void example_clear(void)
{
    if (namedhandle != NULL){
        dns_sdb_unregister(&namedhandle);
    };
};
```

Header File (example.h)

example.h follows:

```
// example sdb driver for BIND
// reads and parses zone file into ram structure
// header file
isc_result_t example_init (char directory[]);
void example_clear(void);
```

Summary

BIND 9 provides a number of libraries that may be used to build DNS-aware applications. The user libraries are contained in libdns, libisc, and libisccfg; these are built as standard by Ubuntu (dynamic and static) and FreeBSD (static only). No further action is required to use these libraries. In addition, BIND 9 provides DNSSEC-aware replacements for the standard POSIX functions getaddrinfo(), getnameinfo(), gai_strerror(), and freeaddrinfo(). These functions and others are provided in the library libirs, which needs to be specially built using specific configure options. The process of building and installing the library using the replacement functions and incorporating them into user applications is described and illustrated with examples.

BIND 9 provides two APIs to allow the user to add functionality to the basic name server. Both interfaces are statically linked and require manual editing of core BIND modules. Unlike most dynamically loaded extensions, such as those used in Apache, any failure in the user-supplied functions will likely result in a failure of the named daemon and a consequent loss of DNS service.

The adb interface allows complete replacement of the core zone-processing functionality of BIND. adb must support all the required capabilities of the production system, including zone transfers, dynamic updates, and DNSSEC operations. Use of this API requires a significant outlay of time and resources, with 36 functions being supported. This interface is documented in bind-release/lib/dns/include/dns/db.h. The adb API is not described in this book.

The sdb API is an abstracted interface that allows one or more zones to be replaced with one or more drivers. These drivers supply the appropriate data in response to DNS queries for the zones to which the driver applies. The interface operates using up to five callback functions, of which only one, the lookup() callback, is mandatory. The sdb interface, as well as additional interfaces that may be used for logging and allocating memory, is described with a sample driver used to illustrate key points.

The next chapter describes the DNS binary or wire-format messages. The chapter is appropriate for those of a curious disposition, those doing serious debugging, or for those using the binary version when returning RRs via the sdb interface.

## CHAPTER 15

DNS Messages and Records

This chapter describes the binary messages and resource record (RR) formats that pass between DNS servers. These messages comprise what is sometimes called the *wire format* because it is the format sent across the network, or *wire*, in the understated slang of the network professional. While it's primarily a reference section with copious descriptions of bits and bytes, this chapter is also answers the following questions and more for the naturally curious reader: What is a referral? When a dig command is issued, just what are the ANSWER SECTIONs and AUTHORITY SECTIONs that are returned? Why are there only 13 root-servers (because of packet size considerations)?

The chapter is laid out in two sections. The first section details the layout and format of the binary data that passes between servers. The second section defines the binary format of each resource record as it appears in a message. In most cases, the fastest and most convenient way to analyze the format of these messages is to use a network or protocol sniffer. These applications typically capture raw network frames. Most will provide differing levels of protocol interpretation—translating the various messages into a somewhat understandable form. There are many excellent packages available from a variety of sources, including the superb open source Wireshark network analyzer (www.wireshark.org) that runs on Linux, Unix, and Windows platforms.

DNS messages depend on whether or not the server initiating the transaction is using Extended DNS (EDNS0—RFC 2671) features. EDNS is used by security transactions such as TSIG and SIG(0) and security-aware servers in DNSSEC transactions (see Chapter 11). In the interest of clarity, EDNS and normal messages are clearly separated. If you are not running secure transactions (secure zone transfers, secure DDNS, or DNSSEC), the "EDNS0 Transactions" section later in this chapter may not be relevant. There are three situations where the information contained in this chapter may be of more than superficial interest:

1. First, during network debugging when name servers from multiple vendors or even differently configured name servers from the same source may be experiencing interworking problems. In this situation, it is important to identify which server is, or may be, causing the problem. Having a general understanding of normal traffic is an essential prerequisite to accomplish this analysis.

2. Second, during testing of new or beta software where sniffer analysis software may not be available to perform interpretation of the various formats being used.

3. And finally, the DNS specifications allow new RRs to be created for any user-defined purpose using the special syntax described in the "User-Defined RRs" section in Chapter 13. These RRs will most certainly not have sniffer analysis support, and verification of the correct format during testing will of necessity be an entirely manual process.

To understand this chapter, you should be reasonably familiar with hexadecimal, binary, and decimal representations. The "Binary, Decimal, and Hexadecimal" sidebar is provided as a quick refresher.

BINARY, DECIMAL, AND HEXADECIMAL

The contents of any 8-bit byte (an octet) may be expressed in decimal (base 10), yielding a value in the range 0 to 255; binary (base 2), yielding a value in the range 0000 0000 to 1111 1111; or hexadecimal (base 16), yielding two hex characters in the range 00 to FF. Each hexadecimal character may take values from 0 to 9 and A to F, allowing a total of 16 values to be represented. The following table shows a number of arbitrary values represented in all three bases:

Decimal	Hexadecimal	Binary
0	00	0000 0000
65	41	0100 0001
187	BB	1011 1011
255	FF	1111 1111

To convert a dotted decimal IP, for instance, 192.168.0.5 to hexadecimal, take each dotted decimal value and convert it using a hex calculator (the standard Windows calculator, gcalc on Gnome 2 and kcalc on KDE, will all do the job when scientific mode is selected). Thus, 192.168.0.5 will yield C0.A8.0.5. When representing a hexadecimal number, it's normal to show both hexadecimal characters, so this value would be normally written as C0.A8.00.05. The separating dots are just an easy way to make the number more readable but otherwise have no significance—the value could have been written as C0A80005. To convert from hexadecimal to dotted decimal, simply reverse the process and omit any leading zeros; thus 005 or 05 would normally be written simply as 5 in decimal mode.

Bit Numbering

Bit numbering can be very confusing, and various standard bodies have adopted different conventions. The following are all valid and current bit-numbering conventions for describing an 8-bit byte.

Left-to-right base 0 (IETF)	0	1	2	3	4	5	6	7
Left-to-right base 1	1	2	3	4	5	6	7	8
Right-to-left base 1 (ITU)	8	7	6	5	4	3	2	1
Power of 2	7	6	5	4	3	2	1	0

Always check what convention is used on any specification. The convention used by the IETF and in this book is a left-to-right number starting from 0.

DNS Message Formats

When a dig is issued, it generates a corresponding DNS query and typically responds with a lot of data. The response is essentially a translation of the binary message—the answer—that is received to the dig command's question. The following dig command is a simple query for the IPv4 address of www.example.com using the recursive server at 192.168.254.2 (the full syntax of the dig command is described in Chapter 9).

```
# dig @192.168.254.2 example.com a

; <<>> DiG 9.7.2-P2 <<>> @192.186.254.2 www.example.com a
;; global options:  printcmd
;; Got answer:
;; ->>HEADER<<- opcode: QUERY, status: NOERROR, id: 1947
;; flags: qr rd ra; QUERY: 1, ANSWER: 2, AUTHORITY: 2, ADDITIONAL: 2

;; QUESTION SECTION:
;www.example.com.          IN    A

;; ANSWER SECTION:
www.example.com.        172800    IN    CNAME    joe.example.com.
joe.example.com.        172800    IN    A        192.168.200.4
;; AUTHORITY SECTION:
example.com.        172800    IN    NS    ns2.example.net.
example.com.        172800    IN    NS    ns1.example.com.

;; ADDITIONAL SECTION:
ns1.example.com.        172800    IN    A    192.168.200.8
ns2.example.net.        172800    IN    A    192.168.254.10

;; Query time: 312 msec
;; SERVER: 192.168.254.2 #53(192.168.254.2)
;; WHEN: Wed Mar 09 22:17:44 2005
;; MSG SIZE  rcvd: 124
```

The response is divided into four parts (sections):

- The QUESTION SECTION reflects the original query that is being answered, which in this case was a query for the A RR of www.example.com.

- The ANSWER SECTION provides two answers to the query. The first indicates that www.example.com is a CNAME, and since the server follows the CNAME chain because the dig requested an A RR (not a CNAME RR), it supplies the A RR of the canonical (or real) host; in this case, the A RR of joe.example.com.

- The AUTHORITY SECTION provides the name of the servers that are authoritative for the domain example.com.

- The ADDITIONAL SECTION provides information that may be useful to the server; in this case, it is the A RRs of the name servers.

Note When used with DNSSEC, a fifth section titled OPT PSEUDOSECTION is displayed. This is simply a reformatting of the OPT meta (pseudo) RR used in DNSSEC transactions from the ADDITIONAL SECTION.

The next dig command is the same A query for www.example.com, but in this case the target server is 128.8.10.90, which is one of the 13 root-servers (D.ROOT-SERVERS.NET in this case).

```
# dig @128.8.10.90 www.example.com A

; <<>> DiG 9.7.2-P2 <<>> @128.8.10.90 www.example.com a
;; global options:  printcmd
;; Got answer:
;; ->>HEADER<<- opcode: QUERY, status: NOERROR, id: 42
;; flags: qr rd; QUERY: 1, ANSWER: 0, AUTHORITY: 13, ADDITIONAL: 14

;; QUESTION SECTION:
;www.example.com.             IN    A

;; AUTHORITY SECTION:
com.      172800    IN    NS    A.GTLD-SERVERS.NET.
com.      172800    IN    NS    G.GTLD-SERVERS.NET.
com.      172800    IN    NS    H.GTLD-SERVERS.NET.
com.      172800    IN    NS    C.GTLD-SERVERS.NET.
com.      172800    IN    NS    I.GTLD-SERVERS.NET.
com.      172800    IN    NS    B.GTLD-SERVERS.NET.
com.      172800    IN    NS    D.GTLD-SERVERS.NET.
com.      172800    IN    NS    L.GTLD-SERVERS.NET.
com.      172800    IN    NS    F.GTLD-SERVERS.NET.
com.      172800    IN    NS    J.GTLD-SERVERS.NET.
com.      172800    IN    NS    K.GTLD-SERVERS.NET.
com.      172800    IN    NS    E.GTLD-SERVERS.NET.
com.      172800    IN    NS    M.GTLD-SERVERS.NET.

;; ADDITIONAL SECTION:
A.GTLD-SERVERS.NET.      172800    IN    A    192.5.6.30
G.GTLD-SERVERS.NET.      172800    IN    A    192.42.93.30
H.GTLD-SERVERS.NET.      172800    IN    A    192.54.112.30
C.GTLD-SERVERS.NET.      172800    IN    A    192.26.92.30
I.GTLD-SERVERS.NET.      172800    IN    A    192.43.172.30
B.GTLD-SERVERS.NET.      172800    IN    A    192.33.14.30
D.GTLD-SERVERS.NET.      172800    IN    A    192.31.80.30
L.GTLD-SERVERS.NET.      172800    IN    A    192.41.162.30
F.GTLD-SERVERS.NET.      172800    IN    A    192.35.51.30
J.GTLD-SERVERS.NET.      172800    IN    A    192.48.79.30
K.GTLD-SERVERS.NET.      172800    IN    A    192.52.178.30
E.GTLD-SERVERS.NET.      172800    IN    A    192.12.94.30
M.GTLD-SERVERS.NET.      172800    IN    A    192.55.83.30
A.GTLD-SERVERS.NET.      172800    IN    AAAA 2001:503:a83e::2:30

;; Query time: 46 msec
;; SERVER: 128.8.10.90#53(128.8.10.90)
```

```
;; WHEN: Wed Mar 09 22:28:53 2005
;; MSG SIZE  rcvd: 492
```

In this case, the QUESTION SECTION is a simple reflection of the dig command—the query or question that was sent. There is no ANSWER SECTION, because this query is for a user domain (example.com), and root-servers do not provide recursive query support. There is, however, an AUTHORITY SECTION indicating the next closest name servers that may be able to answer the query—in this case, the .com gTLD servers. Finally, the ADDITIONAL SECTION provides the A RRs and, in one case, an AAAA (IPv6) RR of the name servers listed in the AUTHORITY SECTION. These RRs will save an additional transaction, since without this information the next step would be to find the A RR of one or more of the supplied servers. This response is a *referral*—it contains no errors (NOERR status) and no ANSWER SECTION, just information in the AUTHORITY SECTION and usually—from the root and TLD servers always—information in the ADDITIONAL SECTION.

Note The AAAA RR is perfectly reasonable in the preceding list since, as you saw in Chapter 13, zone files can mix AAAA and A RRs freely. In the particular case shown, the server that issued the dig was dual stacked with IPv4 and IPv6, but an IPv4-only server would also have received the AAAA RR.

DNS Message Overview

Message formats are defined in RFC 1035 and were extended by RFC 2671 (EDNS0). To help explain this section, the following dig command was issued:

```
# dig @192.168.235.2 www.example.com A
```

The command returned the following text response:

```
; <<>> DiG 9.7.2-P2 <<>> @192.168.235.2 www.example.com a
;; global options:  printcmd
;; Got answer:
;; ->>HEADER<<- opcode: QUERY, status: NOERROR, id: 146
;; flags: qr aa rd ra; QUERY: 1, ANSWER: 6, AUTHORITY: 2, ADDITIONAL: 1

;; QUESTION SECTION:
;www.example.com.       IN    A

;; ANSWER SECTION:
www.example.com.       86400   IN   A   10.1.2.1
www.example.com.       86400   IN   A   192.168.3.1
www.example.com.       86400   IN   A   192.168.4.1
www.example.com.       86400   IN   A   172.16.2.1
www.example.com.       86400   IN   A   172.17.2.1
www.example.com.       86400   IN   A   192.168.2.1

;; AUTHORITY SECTION:
example.com.    86400   IN   NS   ns1.example.com.
example.com.    86400   IN   NS   ns2.example.net.

;; ADDITIONAL SECTION:
```

```
ns1.example.com.    86400   IN   A   192.168.2.6

;; Query time: 0 msec
;; SERVER: 192.168.235.2 #53(192.168.235.2)
;; WHEN: Thu Mar 10 15:47:05 2005
;; MSG SIZE  rcvd: 192
```

This answer indicates a successful response (NOERR) with an ANSWER SECTION—in this case, many A RRs—and both AUTHORITY and ADDITIONAL SECTIONs. A packet sniffer namely Wireshark was used to capture the question packet content, as shown in Figure 15–1. The content shown *excludes* all IP and UDP packet framing and is just the raw DNS message.

```
0000   05 5e 01 00 00 01 00 00 00 00 00 00 03 77 77 77   .............www
0001   07 65 78 61 6d 70 6c 85 03 63 6f 6d 00 00 01 00   .example.com....
0002   01                                                .
```

Figure 15–1. DNS query question

The corresponding answer packet is shown in Figure 15–2 and was again captured using a packet sniffer. This content excludes all IP and UDP packet framing.

```
0000   05 5e 85 80 00 01 00 06 00 02 00 01 03 77 77 77   .............www
0001   07 65 78 61 6d 70 6c 85 03 63 6f 6d 00 00 01 00   .example.com....
0002   01 c0 0c 00 01 00 01 00 01 51 80 00 04 0a 01 02   .........Q......
0003   01 c0 0c 00 01 00 01 00 01 51 80 00 04 c0 a8 03   .........Q......
0004   01 c0 0c 00 01 00 01 00 01 51 80 00 04 c0 a8 04   .........Q......
0005   01 c0 0c 00 01 00 01 00 01 51 80 00 04 ac 10 02   .........Q......
0006   01 c0 0c 00 01 00 01 00 01 51 80 00 04 ac 11 02   .........Q......
0007   01 c0 0c 00 01 00 01 00 01 51 80 00 04 c0 a8 02   .........Q......
0008   01 c0 10 00 02 00 01 00 01 51 80 00 11 03 63 73   .........Q....ns
0009   32 07 65 78 61 6d 70 6c 65 03 6e 65 74 00 c0 10   2.example.net...
000a   00 02 00 01 00 01 51 80 00 06 03 6e 73 31 c0 10   ......Q....ns1..
000b   c0 aa 00 01 00 01 00 01 51 80 00 04 c0 a8 02 06   ........Q.......
```

Figure 15–2. DNS query response

These two messages will be used throughout this chapter to illustrate the explanations that follow.

■**Note** The data highlighted in gray in Figures 15–1 and 15–2 indicates the message header, which is explained in the next section.

DNS Message Format

The good news is that each message has the same generic format with five sections, as shown in Table 15–1.

Table 15–1. DNS Message Format

Section	Meaning/Use
Section 1	Message header
Section 2	The QUESTION SECTION: the DNS query for which a response is being sought
Section 3	The ANSWER SECTION: the resource record(s) that answer the question
Section 4	The AUTHORITY SECTION: the resource record(s) that point to the domain authority
Section 5	The ADDITIONAL SECTION: the resource record(s) that may hold additional information

Not every section is present in every message, and this is indicated in the message header this chapter covers next.

DNS Message Header

The message header is present in all messages. It contains various flags and values that control the transaction. Figure 15–3 shows the format of the message header and uses the standard IETF bit numbering convention throughout.

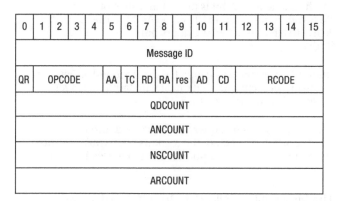

Figure 15–3. DNS message header

Table 15–2 defines the field values listed in Figure 15–3.

Table 15–2. DNS Message Header Values

Section	Bits	Explanation
Message ID	16	The message ID supplied by the requestor (the questioner) and reflected back unchanged by the responder (answerer). Identifies the transaction. Appears as a value of 055e in Figures 15–1 and 15–2.
QR	1	Query-Response bit. Set to 0 by the questioner (query) and to 1 in the response (answer). Not set in Figure 15–1 and set in Figure 15–2.
OPCODE	4	Identifies the request/operation type. Currently assigned values are 0 = QUERY. Standard query. 1 = IQUERY. Inverse query. Made obsolete by RFC 3425. 2 = STATUS. DNS status request. 3 = NSID Request (RFC 5001). 4 = NOTIFY. 5 = DDNS update. 6–15 = Unused. Available for assignment. In a response, this field reflects the user's request. In Figures 15–1 and 15–2, this field is 0 (a query).
AA	1	Authoritative Answer. Valid in responses only. Set if the response was received from a zone master or slave. It is also set the first time the response is received from a master or slave by a resolver (caching name server), but when subsequently read from the cache the AA bit is not set. Because of aliases (CNAME RRs), multiple owner names may exist, so the AA bit corresponds to the name in the ANSWER SECTION that matches the query name. Set in Figure 15–2 to indicate an authoritative response.
TC	1	Truncation. Specifies that this message was truncated due to length greater than that permitted on the transmission channel. Set on all truncated messages except the last one. Not set in Figures 15–1 or 15–3.
RD	1	Recursion Desired. This bit may be set in a query and is copied into the response if recursion is supported. If rejected, the response (answer) does not have this bit set. Recursive query support is optional. Set in Figures 15–1 and 15–2.
RA	1	Recursion Available. This bit is valid in a response (answer) and denotes whether recursive query support is available (1) or not (0) in the name server. Set in Figure 15–2.
res	1	Reserved by IANA for future use.
AD	1	Authenticated Data. Used by DNSSEC. Indicates that the data was reliably authenticated. A chain of trust was verified (see Chapter 11). Not set in Figures 15–1 or 15–2, and since the target server used in the example was a security-aware name server, it means the zone was not signed.

Section	Bits	Explanation
CD	1	Checking Disabled. Used by DNSSEC. If set, it means the initiator of the request (either a server or a resolver) will take responsibility for all security processing. It disables DNSSEC validation at the receiving name server, which will simply pass back all the necessary information such as RRSIG and DNSKEY RRs to the resolver to allow it to perform the transaction validation.
RCODE	4	Identifies the response type to the query. Ignored on a request (question). Currently assigned values include the following: 0 = NOERR. No error condition. 1 = FORMERR. Format error. The name server was unable to interpret the query. 2 = SERVFAIL. Server failure. The name server was unable to process this query either due to a problem with the name server or a requested feature can't be satisfied by the current configuration. 3 = NXDOMAIN. Name error. Meaningful only for responses from an authoritative name server, this code signifies that the domain name referenced in the query does not exist. The negative responses are cached by a resolver for the period defined by the nx (min) value of the SAO RR for the zone. 4 = NOTIMP. Not implemented (versions of BIND prior to 9.3 would respond with NOTIMPL). The name server does not support the requested operation. 5 = REFUSED. The name server refuses to perform the specified operation for policy reasons. For example, a name server may not wish to provide the information to the particular requester, or a name server may not wish to perform a particular operation such as a zone transfer for a particular zone. 6 = YXDomain. Name exists when it should not (RFC 2136). 7 = YXRRSet. RR set exists when it should not (RFC 2136). 8 = NXRRSet. RR set that should exist does not (RFC 2136). 9 = NotAuth. Server not authoritative for zone (RFC 2136). 10 = NotZone. Name not contained in zone (RFC 2136). 11–15 = Unused. Available for assignment. Extended RCODE values with EDNS0 only (see the "EDNS0 Transactions" section later in this chapter): 16 = BADVERS. Bad OPT version number (not 0) (RFC 2671). 16 = BADSIG. TSIG signature failure (RFC 2845). 17 = BADKEY. Key not recognized. (RFC 2845). 18 = BADTIME. Signature out-of-time window (RFC 2845). 19 = BADMODE. Bad TKEY mode (RFC 2930) or invalid key name. 20 = BADNAME. Duplicate key name (RFC 2930). 21 = BADALG. Algorithm not supported (RFC 2930). 22–3840 = Not used. Available for assignment. 3841–4095 = Private use. 4096–65535 = Not used and available for assignment. The RCODE is 0 (NOERR) in Figure 15–2.

Section	Bits	Explanation
QDCOUNT	16	Defines the number of entries in the QUESTION SECTION. This field is 1 in Figures 15–1 and 15–2.
ANCOUNT	16	Defines the number of resource records in the ANSWER SECTION. May be 0, in which case no answer records are present in the message. This field is 0 in Figure 15–1 and 6 in Figure 15–2.
NSCOUNT	16	Defines the number of resource records in the AUTHORITY SECTION. May be 0, in which case no authority records are present in the message. This field is 0 in Figure 15–1 and 2 in Figure 15–2.
ARCOUNT	16	Defines the number of resource records in the ADDITIONAL SECTION. May be 0, in which case no additional records are present in the message. This field is 0 in Figure 15–1 and 1 in Figure 15–2.

DNS QUESTION SECTION

It is permissible to have only one question per message (defined by QDCOUNT earlier). A question has the generic format defined in Table 15–3.

Table 15–3. DNS QUESTION Format

Field Name	Meaning/Use
QNAME	The domain name being queried such as www.example.com.
QTYPE	The RR type being requested. Values are defined by IANA (www.iana.org/assignments/dns-parameters) such as A, ANY, or NAPTR.
QCLASS	The RR class being requested; for instance, Internet, CHAOS, etc.

Figure 15–4 shows the highlighted QUESTION SECTION.

```
0000   05 5e 01 00 00 01 00 00 00 00 00 00 03 77 77 77   .............www
0001   07 65 78 61 6d 70 6c 85 03 63 6f 6d 00 00 01 00   .example.com....
0002   01                                                 .
```

Figure 15–4. QUESTION *section*

Each field has the format defined in Table 15–4.

Table 15–4. DNS QUESTION Fields

Name	Explanation
QNAME	Defines the name being queried. The name being queried is split into *labels* by removing the separating dots. Each label is represented as a length (one octet) followed by a variable number of characters—the label string—defined by length:
	length: A single octet defining the number of characters in the label that follows. The top 2 bits of this number must be 00 (to indicate the label format is being used), which gives a maximum label name length of 63 bytes (octets). A value of 0 indicates the end of the name field.
	label string: A string containing the characters in the label. In Figure 15–1, the question name is comprised of three labels, with lengths 3, 7, and 3, respectively, terminated with a 00 value, as shown here:
	03 77 77 77 07 65 78 61 6D 70 6D 65 03 63 6F 6D 00 w w w e x a m p l e c o m
	The final 00 (a zero label length) indicates the end of the name.
QTYPE	Unsigned 16-bit value. The RR type being requested. These values are assigned by IANA (www.iana.org/assignments/dns-parameters). The values are also listed in Chapter 13, Table 13-1. In Figures 15–1 and 15–2, the value is 1 (indicating an A RR).
QCLASS	Unsigned 16-bit value. The class of resource records being requested; for instance, Internet, CHAOS, etc. These values are assigned by IANA. The currently assigned values are:
	1 = IN or Internet
	2 = Obsolete
	3 = CH (CHAOS)
	4 = HS (HESIOD)
	In Figures 15–1 and 15–2, this value is 1 (Internet).

DNS ANSWER, AUTHORITY, and ADDITIONAL SECTIONS

The ANSWER, AUTHORITY, and ADDITIONAL SECTIONs contain RR records that all share the same format. Which section the RR appears in is determined solely by the count of records in each section that is contained in the message header. Thus, an A RR can appear in an ANSWER or an ADDITIONAL SECTION. So far, this stuff has been relatively straightforward if slightly messy—take a deep breath before reading on. The generic binary, or wire format, of all RRs is shown in Table 15–5.

Table 15–5. ANSWER, AUTHORITY, and ADDITIONAL SECTION RR Format

Field Name	Explanation
NAME	The name being returned; for instance www or ns2.example.net. If the name is in the same domain as the question, then typically only the host part (label) is returned and a pointer record used to construct an FQDN; if not, then an FQDN is present. This process is described and illustrated later in this section.
TYPE	The RR type being returned; for instance, NS or AAAA.
CLASS	The RR class being returned; for instance, Internet, CHAOS, etc.
TTL	The TTL of the RR being returned in seconds; for instance, 2800.
RDLENGTH	The length in octets of the RDATA field being returned.
RDATA	The RR-specific data length defined by RDLENGTH; for instance, 192.168.254.2.

NAME **Field Format**

The NAME field, including those with individual labels in Internationalized Domain Name for Applications (IDNA) ACE (ASCII Compatible Encoding - see Chapter 13), takes one of three formats depending on the value of the top 2 bits. Table 15–6 shows the meaning and layout of the three types based on the value of the top 2 bits.

Table 15–6. NAME Field Format

Value	Size of Field	Explanation
00	6	This indicates the label format described for the QUESTION SECTION earlier and comprises a series of variable strings whose length is indicated by the low 6 bits of each octet (see Figure 15–4. The sequence is always terminated with a zero length value. The remaining fields of this record format are defined in Table 15–7.
11	14	The pointer format. The following 14 bits are assumed to be the offset from the start of the message of a name that must be in standard label format. Figure 15–5 shows a highlighted ANSWER SECTION commencing with a pointer format with an offset of x0c (12 octets) into the message that points to the label record for www.example.com. The remaining fields of this record format are defined in Table 15–7.
01	6	This denotes an EDNS0 format message (RFC 2671). The low order 6 bits of this field contains an extended TYPE field that, together with the rest of the record format, is described in the "EDNS0 Transactions" section.

The format of the subsequent data is determined by the top 2 bits and is described next for non-EDNS0 values (top 2 bits either 00 or 11) and EDNS0 format data (top 2 bits are 01).

```
0000   05 5e 85 80 00 01 00 06 00 02 00 01 03 77 77 77   ............wwww
0001   07 65 78 61 6d 70 6c 85 03 63 6f 6d 00 00 01 00   .example.com....
0002   01 c0 0c 00 01 00 01 00 01 51 80 00 04 0a 01 02   ................
0003   01 c0 0c 00 01 00 01 00 01 51 80 00 04 c0 a8 03   ................
0004   01 c0 0c 00 01 00 01 00 01 51 80 00 04 c0 a8 04   ................
0005   01 c0 0c 00 01 00 01 00 01 51 80 00 04 ac 10 02   ................
0006   01 c0 0c 00 01 00 01 00 01 51 80 00 04 ac 11 02   ................
0007   01 c0 0c 00 01 00 01 00 01 51 80 00 04 c0 a8 02   ................
0008   01 c0 10 00 02 00 01 00 01 51 80 00 11 03 63 73   ..............ns
0009   32 07 65 78 61 6d 70 6c 65 03 6e 65 74 00 c0 10   2.example.net...
000a   00 02 00 01 00 01 51 80 00 06 03 6e 73 31 c0 10   ...........ns1..
000b   c0 aa 00 01 00 01 00 01 51 80 00 04 c0 a8 02 06   ................
```

Figure 15–5. Highlighted ANSWER SECTION

Non-EDNS0 Record Format

The format of a non-EDNS response record—one that has the top 2 bits set to either 00 or 11—is described in Table 15–7.

Table 15–7. Non-EDNS Record Format

Name	Explanation
TYPE	Unsigned 16-bit value. The RR type that determines the content of the RDATA field (see RDATA entry). These values are assigned by IANA (www.iana.org/assignments/dns-parameters). In Figure 15–5, the highlighted record has a value of 00 01 = A type RR.
CLASS	Unsigned 16-bit value. The class of RR; for instance, Internet, CHAOS, etc. These values are assigned by IANA. In Figure 15–5, the highlighted record has a value of 00 01 = Internet class.
TTL	Unsigned 32-bit value. The time in seconds that the record may be cached. A value of 0 indicates the record should not be cached. In Figure 15–5, the highlighted record has a value of 00 01 51 80 (hex) = 86,400 seconds (2 days).
RDLENGTH	Unsigned 16-bit value that defines the length in bytes (octets) of the RDATA record. In Figure 15–5, the highlighted record has a value of 00 04, meaning the following record has a length of 4 octets.
RDATA	Each RR type has a specific RDATA format, whose length is defined by RDLENGTH, which is defined in the "DNS Binary RR Format" section later in this chapter. In Figure 15–5, the highlighted record has a value of 0a 01 02 01 (hex) = 10.1.2.1. Since this is an A RR, it defines a 4-octet (32-bit) IPv4 address.

All records create FQDNs, sometimes using chained (pointer) constructs to minimize the amount of data returned. Figure 15–6 shows a highlighted additional section containing an A RR.

```
0000   05 5e 85 80 00 01 00 06 00 02 00 01 03 77 77 77   .............www
0001   07 65 78 61 6d 70 6c 85 03 63 6f 6d 00 00 01 00   .example.com....
0002   01 c0 0c 00 01 00 01 00 01 51 80 00 04 0a 01 02   ................
0003   01 c0 0c 00 01 00 01 00 01 51 80 00 04 c0 a8 03   ................
0004   01 c0 0c 00 01 00 01 00 01 51 80 00 04 c0 a8 04   ................
0005   01 c0 0c 00 01 00 01 00 01 51 80 00 04 ac 10 02   ................
0006   01 c0 0c 00 01 00 01 00 01 51 80 00 04 ac 11 02   ................
0007   01 c0 0c 00 01 00 01 00 01 51 80 00 04 c0 a8 02   ................
0008   01 c0 10 00 02 00 01 00 01 51 80 00 11 03 63 73   ................ns
0009   32 07 65 78 61 6d 70 6c 65 03 6e 65 74 00 c0 10   2.example.net...
000a   00 02 00 01 00 01 51 80 00 06 03 6e 73 31 c0 10   ...........ns1..
000b   c0 aa 00 01 00 01 00 01 51 80 00 04 c0 a8 02 06   ................
```

Figure 15–6. A RR using chained pointers

The preceding record (highlighted in gray) starts with a pointer format (top 2 bits are 11) containing an offset of 00 aa (decimal 170) that points to a label name type containing 03 6e 73 31 (for ns1), which is followed by a pointer type (c0 10) with offset of 00 10 (decimal 16), which in turn points to example.com. The last label in the chain is zero length, which stops the label generation phase. The record contains type = 00 01 (A), class = 00 01 (IN), ttl = 00 01 51 80 (28,600 seconds—2 days), an RDLENGTH of 00 04 octets, and RDATA of c0 a8 02 06, which being an A RR represents an IP of 192.168.2.6, resulting in the A RR that follows:

```
ns1.example.com.   28600   IN   A   192.168.2.6
```

This is the A RR in the ADDITIONAL SECTION of the dig result shown in the "DNS Message Overview" section earlier.

EDNS0 Transactions

EDNS0 is normally used only in security transactions, but it can be forced by defining a server clause with the statement edns yes; in BIND's named.conf file (see Chapter 12). Since BIND 9.5+ DNSSEC is now turned on by default, so unless action is taken (dnssec-enable no;), EDNS0 is the normal wire format used by BIND 9. The server will advertise its ability to participate in EDNS transactions by sending an OPT pseudo RR in the ADDITIONAL SECTION field of a query but is displayed by dig under the title OPT PSEUDOSECTION (see the "Verifying the Signed Zone" section of Chapter 11 for an example). If the receiving server can't support such a service or does not recognize the OPT RR, it will respond with a failure in the RCODE field of the message header (NOTIMP, FORMERR, or SERVFAIL). In this case, the initiating server may continue without using EDNS services. Figure 15–7 shows the original dig command (presented earlier in Figure 15–1) after the server was configured to use EDNS services through the use of the following named.conf fragment:

```
// named.conf fragment
options {
    ....
    forward only;
    forwarders {192.168.2.3;};
};
```

```
server 192.168.2.3 {
    edns yes;
};
....
```

The captured query packet is shown in Figure 15–7.

```
0000   01 51 01 00 00 01 00 00 00 00 00 01 03 77 77 77   .............www
0001   07 65 78 61 6d 70 6c 85 03 63 6f 6d 00 00 01 00   .example.com....
0002   01 00 00 29 10 00 00 00 80 00 00 00               ...........
```

Figure 15–7. EDNS0 query

The query differs from that shown in Figure 15–1 by having a count of 1 in the ADDITIONAL SECTION of the message header and contains an OPT pseudo RR whose format is defined in Table 15–8.

The corresponding response packet also contains an OPT pseudo RR, as shown in Figure 15–8.

```
0000   05 5e 85 80 00 01 00 06 00 02 00 02 03 77 77 77   .............www
0001   07 65 78 61 6d 70 6c 85 03 63 6f 6d 00 00 01 00   .example.com....
0002   01 c0 0c 00 01 00 01 00 01 51 80 00 04 0a 01 02   ...............
0003   01 c0 0c 00 01 00 01 00 01 51 80 00 04 c0 a8 03   ...............
0004   01 c0 0c 00 01 00 01 00 01 51 80 00 04 c0 a8 04   ...............
0005   01 c0 0c 00 01 00 01 00 01 51 80 00 04 ac 10 02   ...............
0006   01 c0 0c 00 01 00 01 00 01 51 80 00 04 ac 11 02   ...............
0007   01 c0 0c 00 01 00 01 00 01 51 80 00 04 c0 a8 02   ...............
0008   01 c0 10 00 02 00 01 00 01 51 80 00 11 03 63 73   ..............ns
0009   32 07 65 78 61 6d 70 6c 65 03 6e 65 74 00 c0 10   2.example.net...
000a   00 02 00 01 00 01 51 80 00 06 03 6e 73 31 c0 10   ...........ns1..
000b   c0 aa 00 01 00 01 00 01 51 80 00 04 c0 a8 02 06   ...............
000c   00 00 29 10 00 00 00 80 00 00 00                  ...........
```

Figure 15–8. EDNS0 response message

The number of ADDITIONAL SECTION records is now 2 (it is 1 in Figure 15–2) and the OPT pseudo RR is present as highlighted. Rather than modifying the named.conf file, the same result may be obtained using the dig command with the option +dnssec, which turns on DNSSEC services that always use the EDNS0 service:

```
dig @192.168.235.2 www.example.com A +dnssec
```

OPT Pseudo RR Format

The OPT pseudo RR is created dynamically by the server and does not appear in a zone file. Its format uses the standard RR format defined in Table 15–5 but redefines the use of each field, as shown in Table 15–8.

Table 15–8. OPT RR Format

Field Name	Explanation
NAME	Always 00 (root).
TYPE	16 bits unsigned. The OPT RR type = 29 (41 decimal) in Figures 15–7 and 15–8.
CLASS	16 bits unsigned. The maximum size of a UDP message that can be accepted by this server. This is defined to be a minimum of 1220 octets and its default size is 4096 (Figures 15–7 and 15–8 both show 10 00 = 4096 decimal).
TTL	32 bits unsigned. This field is laid out as follows:
	Field 1: 8 bits unsigned. Extended RCODE (values defined in Table 15–2 earlier).
	Field 2: 8 bits unsigned. Version (must be 0).
	Field3: 16 bits unsigned. Flags as shown here:
	Bit 0 = DO (DNSSEC OK).
	Bits 1–15 = Unused.
RDLENGTH	The length in octets of the RDATA field being returned.
RDATA	The RDATA may be used to carry any number of extended optional data sets, each of which has the following format:
	Field 1: 16 bits unsigned. OPTION-CODE (none currently assigned).
	Field 2: 16 bits unsigned. OPTION-LENGTH. Length in octets of option data.
	Field 3: Option data. Length defined by OPTION-LENGTH and format defined by OPTION-CODE.

EDNS0 allows for extended label formats by setting the top 2 bits of the NAME field (see Table 15–6) to the value 01. The low 6 bits of this field contain an extended label code. The binary or bit label type (defined in RFC 2673 and discussed in Chapter 13) uses an extended label code value of 1 (binary 00 0001). This label type was changed to *experimental* status by RFC 3363 and is not discussed further. The value 63 (binary 11 1111) has been reserved for further extensions to the EDNS format.

DNS Binary RR Format

Each RR type has an RR-specific RDATA content. Table 15–9 shows the binary format (RDATA) of each RR type described in Chapter 13.

Table 15–9. RDATA Field

RR Name	Type Code	Specification	RDLENGTH	RDATA
A	1	RFC 1035	4	Field 1: Unsigned 32-bit integer. IPv4 address.
A6	38	RFC 2874	Var	May contain two or three fields defined by RDLENGTH and the value of the Prefix Length. If 0, the third (Prefix Name) field is not present; if 128, the Address Suffix field is not present.
				Field 1: Prefix Length. Unsigned 8-bit integer with a value between 0 and 128 inclusive. Defines the number of bits not included in this record. If 0, the third field is not present and the second field defines the full IP address.
				Field 2: Address Suffix. Optional. There must be exactly enough octets in this field to contain a number of bits equal to 128 minus Prefix Length, with 0 to 7 leading *pad bits* to make this field an integral number of octets. Pad bits, if present, must be 0. Length in range 0 to 16 defined by Prefix Length.
				Field 3: Prefix Name. Optional. Present if Prefix Length field is nonzero. The domain name of the prefix (the A6 record that defines the next part of the address).
AAAA	28	RFC 3596	16	Field 1: 128 bits (16 octets). IPv6 address.
AFSDB	18	RFC 1183	Var	Field 1: 16-bit integer—subtype.
				Field 2: Variable-length host name in label format.*

RR Name	Type Code	Specification	RDLENGTH	RDATA
APL	42	RFC 3123	Var	Field 1: 16-bit address family (www.iana.org/assignments/address-family-numbers).
				Field 2: 7-bits length of prefix (address family specific).
				Field 3: 1-bit negation. 1 = negated.
				Field 4: Address type determined by Field 1. If IPv4 (1), it is 32 bits unsigned; if IPv6 (2), it is 16 octets (128 bits).
				Fields 1 to 4 may be repeated any number of times to allow for multiple address ranges and is defined by RDLENGTH.
CERT	37	RFC 4398	Var	Field 1: 16 bits unsigned. Type of certificate. Values:
				0 = Reserved
				1 = PKIX (X.509 as per PKIX)
				2 = SPKI cert
				3 = PGP cert
				4–252 = Available for IANA assignment
				253 = Private URI
				254 = Private OID (ASN.1)
				255–65534 = Available for IANA assignment
				65535 = Reserved
				Field 2: 16-bit unsigned key-tag.
				Field 3: 8-bit unsigned algorithm type. Values (RFC 4034):
				0 = Reserved
				1 = RSA-MD5 (recommended)
				2 = Diffie-Hellman optional, key only
				3 = DSA
				4 = Reserved for elliptic curve cryptography
				5–251 = Available for IANA assignment
				252 = Reserved for indirect keys
				253 = Private URI
				254 = Private OID (ASN.1)
				255 = Reserved
				Field 4: Base64-encoded key string (for format, see RFC 3548).

RR Name	Type Code	Specification	RDLENGTH	RDATA
CNAME	5	RFC 1035	Var	Field 1: Variable-length host name in label format.*
DHCID	49	RFC 4701	Var	Field 1: 16 bit unsigned source-type. Values: 0 = use htype and chaddr (typically MAC) fields from DHCPREQUEST 1 = use the Type and Client Identifier field from DHCPREQUEST 2 = use DUID (data only value from Client Identifier) 3 – 65535 = Unassigned Field 2: 8 bit unsigned. Values: 0 = unassigned 1 = SHA-256 2 – 255 = Unassigned Field 3: Variable based on digest type. Hashed value covers the identifier (defined by source-type) concatenated with the FQDN of the host (client).
DLV	32769	RFC 4431	Var	Functionally identical to DS, defined below.
DNAME	39	RFC 2672	Var	Field 1: Variable-length host name in label format.*
DNSKEY	48	RFC 4034	Var	Field 1: 16-bit unsigned flags (see Chapter 13). Field 2: 8-bit unsigned protocol (must be 3 per RFC 4304). Field 3: 8-bit unsigned algorithm (see the "DNSKEY Record" section of Chapter 13). Field 4: Public key data—format depends on algorithm.†
DS	43	RFC 4034	Var	Field 1: 16-bit unsigned key-tag. Field 2: 8-bit unsigned algorithm (see the "Delegation Signer (DS) Record" section of Chapter 13). Field 3: 8-bit unsigned digest. Values: 0 = Reserved 1= SHA-1 2 = SHA-256 3–255 = Unassigned Field 4: Digest data.
HINFO	13	RFC 1035	Var	Field 1: Variable-length hardware description (nominal) in label format.* Field 2: Variable-length OS description (nominal) in label format.*
HIP	55	RFC 5205	Var	Field 1: hit (Host Identity Tag) length. 8 bit unsigned.

RR Name	Type Code	Specification	RDLENGTH	RDATA
				The length of hit (field 4).
				Field 2: hi (Host Identity) algorithm. 8 bit unsigned. Takes same values defined for IPSECKEY RR field 3.
				Field 3: hi length. 16 bit unsigned. The length of hi (field 5).
				Field 4: hit. Hash of hi (field 5). Length defined by Field 1.
				Field 5: hi. Public key in format defined by field 2.
				Field 6: (Optional) rvs. When present may consist of one or more names (in label format *) which define the Rendezvous Servers used to contact the host defined by hi (field 5)
IPSECKEY	45	RFC 4025	Var	Field 1: 8-bit unsigned preference.
				Field 2: 8-bit unsigned gateway type. Defines the contents and format of Field 4. Values:
				0 = No gateway is present.
				1 = A 4-byte IPv4 address is present in Field 4.
				2 = A 16-byte IPv6 address is present in Field 4.
				3 = Domain name in Field 4 in label format.*
				Field 3: 8-bit unsigned algorithm type. Values:
				0 = No key is present.
				1 = A DSA key is present (defined in RFC 2536).
				2 = A RSA key is present (defined in RFC 3110).
				Field 4: Variable gateway. Content defined by Field 2.
				Field 5: Variable-length base64-encoded data defined by Field 3.
ISDN	20	RFC 1183	Var	Field 1: Variable-length ISDN E.164 number in label format.*
				Field 2: Variable-length ISDN subaddress in label format.*
KEY	25	RFC 2535	Var	Field 1: 16-bit unsigned flags (see the "Public Key (KEY) Record" section of Chapter 13).
				Field 2: 8-bit unsigned protocol (must be 3 per RFC 3445).
				Field 3: 8-bit unsigned algorithm (see the "Public Key (KEY) Record" section of Chapter 13).
				Field 4: Public key data—format depends on algorithm.†
KX	36	RFC 2230	Var	Field 1: 16-bit unsigned preference.
				Field 2: Variable-length of exchange host name in label format.*

RR Name	Type Code	Specification	RDLENGTH	RDATA
LOC	29	RFC 1876	28	Field 1: 8-bit unsigned version (must be 0).
				Field 2: 8-bit size. The diameter of a sphere enclosing the described entity, in centimeters, expressed as a pair of 4-bit unsigned integers, each ranging from 0 to 9; the most significant 4 bits represent the base and the second number represents the power of 10 by which to multiply the base.
				Field 3: 8-bit horizontal precision of the data, in centimeters, expressed using the same representation as size (earlier). This is the diameter of the horizontal "circle of error."
				Field 4: 8-bit vertical precision of the data, in centimeters, expressed using the same representation as size (earlier) This is the total potential vertical error.
				Field 5: Unsigned 32-bit integer. The latitude of the center of the sphere described by the SIZE field in thousandths of a second of arc. 2^31 represents the equator; numbers above that are northern latitude.
				Field 6: Unsigned 32-bit integer. The longitude of the center of the sphere described by the SIZE field, in thousandths of a second of arc, rounded away from the prime meridian. 2^31 represents the prime meridian; numbers above that are eastern longitude.
				Field 7: Unsigned 32-bit integer. The altitude of the center of the sphere described by the SIZE field, in centimeters, from a base of 100,000m below the (WGS 84) reference spheroid used by GPS (semimajor axis a = 6378137.0, reciprocal flattening rf = 298.257223563).
MB	7	RFC 1035	Var	Field 1: Variable-length mailbox name in label format.*
MG	8	RFC 1035	Var	Field 1: Variable-length group mailbox name in label format.*
MINFO	14	RFC 1035	Var	Field 1: Variable-length mailbox name responsible for mailbox or group in label format.*
				Field 2: Variable-length error mailbox name in label format.* If not used, contains a single zero length label.
MR	9	RFC 1035	Var	Field 1: Variable-length mailbox name in label format.*

RR Name	Type Code	Specification	RDLENGTH	RDATA
MX	15	RFC 1035	Var	Field 1: 16-bit unsigned preference. Field 2: Variable-length mail host name in label format.*
NAPTR	35	RFC 3403	Var	Field 1: 16-bit unsigned order. Field 2: 16-bit unsigned preference. Field 3: Variable-length alphanumeric flags in label format.* Flag values are defined by the application (see the "Naming Authority Pointer (NAPTR) Record" section of Chapter 13). Field 4: Variable-length service name in label format.* Services values are defined by the application (see Chapter 13). Field 5: Variable-length regular expression in label format.* Field 6: Variable-length replacement host name in label format.*
NS	2	RFC 1035	Var	Field 1: Variable-length name server in label format.*
NSAP	22	RFC 1706	Var	Field 1: Variable-length binary-encoded NSAP.
NSEC3	50	RFC 5155	Var	Field 1: Hash Algorithm. 8-bit unsigned. Values: 0 = Reserved 1 = SHA1 2 – 255 = Unassigned Field 2: Flags. 8-bit unsigned. Bit significant values (IETF format, left to right starting with bit 0): Bits 0 – 6 = unassigned must be 0 Bit 7 = Opt-Out. 0 = Name is covered by NSEC3, 1 = Name may not be covered by NSEC3. Field 3: Iterations. 16-bit unsigned. Field 4: Salt-Length. 8-bit unsigned. Range 0 – 255. Field 5: Salt. Length defined by Field 4. Field 6: Hash length. 8-bit unsigned. Range 0 – 255. Field 7: Next Hashed Owner Name. Length defined by Field 6. Field 8: Bitmap of RR present at the host name of the NSEC3 RR (for format, see the "NSEC Bitmap Format" section later).

RR Name	Type Code	Specification	RDLENGTH	RDATA
NSEC3PARAM	51	RFC 5155	Var	Field 1: Hash Algorithm. 8-bit unsigned. Values: 0 = Reserved 1 = SHA1 2 – 255 = Unassigned Field 2: Flags. 8-bit unsigned. Bit significant values (IETF format, left to right starting with bit 0): Bits 0 – 7 = must be 0 Field 3: Iterations. 16-bit unsigned. Field 4: Salt-Length. 8-bit unsigned. Range 0 – 255. Field 5: Salt. Length defined by Field 4.
NSEC	47	RFC 4034	Var	Field 1: Variable-length next host name (or name of SOA RR if this is the last in the zone) in label format.* Field 2: Bitmap of RR present at the host name of the NSEC RR (for format, see the "NSEC Bitmap Format" section later).
OPT	41	RFC 2671	Var	The OPT is a pseudo RR; it does not appear in a zone file but is created by the server. Its format is defined in Table 15–8.
PTR	12	RFC 1035	Var	Field 1: Variable-length host name in label format.*
PX	26	RFC 2163	Var	Field 1: Unsigned 16-bit preference value. *Field 2:* Variable-length mailbox (RFC 822 format) name in label format.* Field 3: Variable-length X.400 name in label format.*
RP	17	RFC 1183	Var	Field 1: Variable-length mailbox name in label format.* Field 2: Variable-length name of Text RR containing additional information in label format.* If not used, contains a single zero length label.
RRSIG	46	RFC 4034	Var	Field 1: Unsigned 16-bit type covered (the RR type being signed). Field 2: Unsigned 8-bit algorithm (see the "Resource Record Signature (RRSIG) Record" section of Chapter 13). Field 3: Unsigned 8-bit labels (number of labels in the host name excluding root and wildcard). Field 4: Unsigned 32-bit original TTL. Field 5: Unsigned 32-bit signature expiration. Field 6: Unsigned 32-bit signature inception (when valid). Field 7: Unsigned 16-bit key tag. Field 8: Variable-length of the name of the DNSKEY RR used to sign the RRSIG. In label format.* Field 9: Signature data. Format depends on algorithm.†

RR Name	Type Code	Specification	RDLENGTH	RDATA
RT	21	RFC 1183	Var	Field 1: Unsigned 16-bit preference value.
				Field 2: Variable-length host name in label format.*
SIG	25	RFC 2931/2535	Var	A meta (pseudo) RR used in SIG(0) transactions.
				Field 1: Unsigned 16-bit type covered (the RR type being signed). Must be 0.
				Field 2: Unsigned 8-bit algorithm (see Chapter 13).
				Field 3: Unsigned 8-bit labels (number of labels in the host name excluding root and wildcard).
				Field 4: Unsigned 32-bit original TTL.
				Field 5: Unsigned 32-bit signature expiration.
				Field 6: Unsigned 32-bit signature inception (when valid).
				Field 7: Unsigned 16-bit key-tag.
				Field 8: Variable length of the name of the DNSKEY RR used to sign the RRSIG. In label format.*
				Field 9: Signature data. Format depends on algorithm.†
SOA	6	RFC 1035/2308	Var	Field 1: Variable-length name of the primary name server (MNAME) in label format.*
				Field 2: Variable-length group mailbox name (RNAME) in label format.*
				Field 3: Unsigned 32-bit serial number.
				Field 4: Unsigned 32-bit refresh value.
				Field 5: Unsigned 32-bit retry value.
				Field 6: Unsigned 32-bit expiry value.
				Field 7: Unsigned 32-bit negative response (NXDOMAIN) TTL.
SRV	33	RFC 2782	Var	Field 1: Unsigned 16-bit priority.
				Field 2: Unsigned 16-bit weight.
				Field 3: Unsigned 16-bit port number.
				Field 4: Variable-length target host name in label format.*

RR Name	Type Code	Specification	RDLENGTH	RDATA
SSHFP	44	Draft	Var	Field 1: Unsigned 8-bit algorithm (values as for RRSIG RR; see the "Resource Record Signature (RRSIG) Record" section of Chapter 13).
				Field 2: Unsigned 8-bit fingerprint type. Values:
				0 = Reserved
				1 = SHA-1
				Field 3: Public key data. Format depends on algorithm.†
TXT	16	RFC 1035	Var	Field 1: Variable-length text in label format.*
WKS	11	RFC 1035	Var	Deprecated (use SRV):
				Field 1: Unsigned 32-bit IPv4 address.
				Field 2: Unsigned 8-bit protocol (www.iana.org/assignments/protocol-numbers).
				Field 3: Variable-length field that contains a single bit for all the ports used by the protocol, where bit 0 = port 0, etc. Must be an integral number of octets. Length is defined by RDLENGTH—length of Field 1 and Field 2 (5).
X25	19	RFC 1183	Var	Field 1: Variable-length X.25 PSDN address (X.121) in label format.*

* See Table 15–6.

† See the "Security Algorithm Formats" section later in this chapter

Security Algorithm Formats

Each security algorithm used in the RRSIG, DS, DNSKEY, SIG, and KEY RRs has an identifying value as defined here:

0 = Reserved.
1 = RSA-MD5 (RFC 2537). Not recommended by IETF
2 = Diffie-Hellman (RFC 2539).
3 = DSA/SHA-1. Optional [Z] (RFC 3755, 2536)
4 = Elliptic Curve. Not currently standardized for DNS
5 = RSA/SHA-1. Mandatory [Z] (RFC 3755, 3110).
6 = DSA-NSEC3-SHA1 (RFC 5155).
7 = RSASHA1-NSEC3-SHA1 (RFC 5155).
8 = RSA/SHA-256 [Z] (RFC 5702).
9 = Unassigned.

10 = RSA/SHA512 [Z] (RFC 5702).
11 = Unassigned.
12 = GOST R 34.10-2001 (RFC 5933).
13 - 122 = Currently unassigned.
123 – 251 = Reserved.
252 = Indirect.
253 = Private DNS [Z]. Optional.
254 = Private OID [Z]. Optional.
255 = Reserved.

The public key data area is encoded uniquely for each type as defined by the RFC listed earlier: the algorithms marked [Z] may be used as Zone Signing Keys (see Chapter 11). The mandatory algorithm (type 5) is defined later for convenience since this is expected to be used most frequently.

The algorithm value 253 contains a host name in label format (see the "NAME Field Format" section earlier). This entry is assumed to describe the actual algorithm and encoding format being used. The algorithm 254 is an ASN.1 OID and starts with a single octet length followed by a BER-encoded (ITU X.690) ASN.1 OID that describes the algorithm and key encoding format.

Algorithm 5 (RSA-SHA-1) and 7 (RSASHA1-NSEC3-SHA1)

The binary part of the RDATA field containing the key data is encoded as shown here:

- LENGTH: Length of the exponent. May be either 1 or 3 octets.

- EXPONENT: Defined by length.

- MODULUS: Remaining size of RDATA = RDLENGTH – (other fields in RDATA + LENGTH + EXPONENT).

The LENGTH field is one octet if the exponent length is in the range 1 to 255. If greater than 255, the first octet is 0 and octets 2 and 3 define the length. Both the EXPONENT and MODULUS fields have a maximum length of 4096 bits (512 octets) and are unsigned numbers (binary string).

NSEC/NSEC3 Bitmap Format

The NSEC/NSEC3 RR uses a bitmap format in its binary RDATA field to minimize data volume, and its format is described in this section. The NSEC/NSEC3 RR requires a list of all the RR types with the same host name. The RR TYPE field is an unsigned 16-bit integer allowing 65,535 possible values—the vast majority of which will be unused. In order to remove as much redundant information as possible, the RDATA Field 2 format is defined as shown here:

```
window | length | bitmap1 [ | bitmapn]
```

The total available TYPE field space (65,535) is divided into 256 (0 to 255) windows, each of 256-bit values (32 octets), each bit representing a record type and numbered from 0 to 255. Thus, the first window (window 0) will describe RRs from 0 to 255, the second window (window 1) will describe RRs from 256 to 511, and so on. Only those windows that contain any RRs are required to be present. If there are no RRs in window 1, then it need not be present. Each window has up to 32 octets containing the bitmap for the 256 values. The number of octets may be truncated at the last nonzero octet of the bitmap and the length field used to indicate the number of octets available in the window description. The following is a simple example containing an A RR (type value = 1), an AAAA RR (type value = 28), an RRSIG RR (type value = 46), and an NSEC RR (type value = 47) to illustrate the mechanism:

```
bill    IN    NSEC next.example.com (A AAAA RRSIG NSEC)
```

The hexadecimal representation of Field 2 only of this RR is

```
00 06 40 00 00 08 00 03
```

where the first 00 is the window (window 0 covering RR types 0 to 255). The length is 06, indicating that only 6 octets (of the possible 32) are present. The first octet of the bitmap represents RR types from 0 to 7 and is 40, indicating type 1 (bit 1) is present (an A RR), and the fourth octet represents RR types 24 to 31 and is 08, indicating type 28 (bit 28) is present (an AAAA RR). Similarly, the RRSIG and NSEC RRs occupy the relevant bit positions in the sixth octet, which describes types 40 to 47. Since this is the last RR type in this record, all other values are omitted.

The next example shows a more complex type using the user-defined RR syntax described in Chapter 14 to define a TYPE517 RR:

```
bill    IN    NSEC  next.example.com (A AAAA RRSIG NSEC TYPE517)
```

The hexadecimal representation of Field 2 only of this RR is shown here:

```
00 06 40 00 00 08 00 03
02 01 04
```

The first line is the same as the previous example and is not described further. The second line indicates window 2 (RRs from 512 to 767). Window 1 has no entries and has been omitted. The length value is 01, indicating only a single octet is present. The octet represents RR types 512 to 519 and has bit 517 set—indicating the TYPE517 RR.

Summary

This chapter described the protocol messages that pass between DNS servers; this is sometimes called the wire format. In most cases the message, or wire, format can be interpreted using a packet sniffer; there are times, however, when even the best tools either don't support the latest version or provide less-than-complete interpretation so the user has to resort to trusted manual methods. Each message has the same format consisting of a message header followed by QUESTION, ANSWER, AUTHORITY, and ADDITIONAL SECTIONs. EDNS0 message formats add further complexity to the wire format and are used with security transactions such as TSIG, SIG(0), TKEY, and DNSSEC.

■ ■ ■

## PART V

Appendixes

◼ ◼ ◼

DNS Registration and Governance

In order to use a domain name, it must be registered. Where and how it is registered depends on the top-level domain (TLD). For instance, in example.com, .com is the TLD. To those of a particular disposition, the topic of DNS governance (who controls what) is always endlessly fascinating, but under certain circumstances, it can provide essential background. The following information may be useful when registering or planning to register domain names and is presented in the form of frequently asked questions (FAQs).

1. What is a domain name?

2. What is a TLD (or gTLD or ccTLD or sTLD) domain name?

3. Who is responsible for domain names?

4. What TLDs are available?

5. I thought www.example.com was my domain name.

6. What is a URL (or URI or URN)?

7. What is an SLD?

8. How do I register a .com or .org or .net domain name?

9. How do I register a domain in Malaysia (or any other country)?

10. Can I register my domain name in any country?

11. How do I register a US (.us) or state (for instance, ny.us) domain name?

12. How do I register a Canadian (.ca) or provincial (for instance, bc.ca) domain name?

13. If I register a .com, do I automatically register in every country?

14. What happens when I register a domain name?

15. What do the primary and secondary DNS server names do and why are they necessary?

16. How do I change my domain name information?

17. How do I register an .edu (or .mil or .gov or .int) name?

18. How do I check my (or some else's) registration information?

19. What is IANA and how does it relate to ICANN and the IETF?

20. Who controls the .ARPA domain name?

21. Who Controls ICANN?

22. What are WGIG, IGF, and IGP?

23. What is re-delegation of ccTLDs?

24. How do I get an IDN (Internationalized Domain Name) ccTLD?

Answers

What is a domain name?

A domain name is a unique identifier registered by an individual or organization and is composed in a hierarchical fashion. For example, if the web site for a registered domain name is www.example.com, then example is the domain name, .com is the top-level domain (TLD), and www is a server, host, or service name. When an individual or organization registers a domain name, they are delegated control and responsibility for that domain name. Specifically, they are responsible for the operation of at least two name servers that will respond authoritatively for information about the domain. This may be provided in-house or by a third party, such as an ISP or hosting service. The domain owner controls all naming to the left of the domain name. If the domain name registered is example.com, then depending on the individual or organizational requirements, the domain owner could create (and give public or private access to) systems with names like myhost.example.com or us.example.com or plant1.us.example.com or anything the domain owner chooses.

What is a TLD (or gTLD or ccTLD or sTLD) domain name?

A TLD is a top-level domain; for example, in www.example.com, .com is the TLD. It is the highest point in the domain hierarchy and appears on the right. gTLD is used to describe the generic top-level domains such as .com, .net, .edu, etc. ccTLD is used to denote the country code top-level domains such as .us for United States and .tv for Tuvala. sTLD is used to describe a sponsored, limited registration TLD such as .aero (aeronautical industry) and .travel (travel industry).

Who is responsible for domain names?

Since 1998, the organization responsible for all top-level domains (TLDs) is ICANN (The Internet Corporation for Assigned Names and Numbers, www.icann.org), an independent, nonprofit corporation. TLDs are split into generic TLDs (gTLDs) such as .com, and .org; country code TLDs (ccTLDs) such as .us, .uk, and .my; and sponsored TLDs (sTLDs) such as .aero, .museum, and .travel. ICANN sets the rules for domain name disputes, authorizes new TLDs, and oversees through contractual agreements the registration and operational processes. ICANN also maintains the list of root-servers and oversees their operation. In the case of the gTLDs and sTLDs, ICANN contracts the registration of domain names to accredited registrars (www.icann.org/en/registrars/accredited-list.html). Operation of the gTLD and sTLD DNS servers is contracted to registry operators. In the case of ccTLDs, a country-code manager is designated who is responsible for the specific policies. A list of country-code managers is maintained by IANA (Internet Assigned Number Authority) on behalf of ICANN (www.iana.org/domains/root/db/).

What TLDs are available?

The available TLDs are controlled by two processes. For country code TLDs, the list is controlled by ISO 3166. Each nation in ISO 3166 is automatically assigned a two-letter code. The remaining TLDs, the generic TLDs (gTLDs) and sponsored TLDs (sTLD), are controlled by ICANN (www.icann.org). The list of available TLDs changes from time to time but currently comprises the original list available prior to the establishment of ICANN, which is shown here:

gTLD	Use	Registry Operator	Registrars
.com	Generic. Historically the abbreviation for company.	VeriSign, Inc. until 20-12	ICANN-accredited registrars
.net	Generic. Historically for use by network operators.	VeriSign, Inc. until 2011	ICANN-accredited registrars
.org	Generic. Historically a nonprofit organization.	Public Interest Registry (www.pir.org) DNS operated by Afilias Limited	ICANN-accredited registrars
.mil	Sponsored. Reserved exclusively for use by the US military.	US DOD Network Information Center	US DOD Network Information Center
.gov	Sponsored. Reserved exclusively for use by the US government.	Data Mountain Solutions, Inc. (www.datamtn.com)	US General Services Administration (GSA) (www.dotgov.gov)
.int	Sponsored. Reserved exclusively for use by organizations established by international treaty.	IANA	IANA (www.iana.org/domains/int/)
.arpa	Special domain name reserved for use in reverse mapping.	IANA	Not available for registration
.edu	Special TLD reserved for use by certain US educational institutions.	EDUCAUSE (www.educause.edu)	EDUCAUSE (www.educause.edu)

On November 16, 2000, ICANN authorized the following TLDs:

TLD	Use	Sponsor	Registry Operator
`.aero`	Sponsored. Reserved for use by the airline industry.	SITA (Société Internationale de Télécommunications Aéronautiques— `www.sita.aero`)	Afilias Ltd (`www.afilias.info`)
`.museum`	Sponsored. Reserved for use by museums.	Museum Domain Management Association (`www.musedoma.museum`)	Museum Domain Management Association (`www.musedoma.museum`)
`.biz`	Generic but restricted business name domain.	NeuLevel, Inc. (`www.neulevel.biz`)	NeuLevel, Inc. (`www.neulevel.biz`)
`.info`	Generic information resources.	Afilias Limited (`www.afilias.info`)	Afilias Limited (`www.afilias.info`)
`.coop`	Sponsored. Reserved for use by cooperatives.	Dot Cooperation LLC (`www.cooperative.org`)	The Midcounties Co-operative Domains Ltd (`www.mcd.coop`)
`.pro`	Generic but restricted to certified professionals.	RegistryPro (`www.nic.pro`)	Registry Services Corporation (`www.registrypro.pro`)
`.name`	Generic but restricted for use by individuals—vanity domain names.	VeriSign, Inc. (`www.name`)	VeriSign, Inc. (`www.verisign.com`)

On April 8, 2005, ICANN announced the availability of two new sTLDs:

TLD	Use	Sponsor	Registry Operator
`.travel`	Sponsored. Reserved for use by the travel industry.	Tralliance Corporation (`www.travel.travel`)	NeuLevel Inc. (`www.neulevel.biz`)
`.jobs`	Sponsored. Reserved for use by employment companies and human resources organizations.	Employ Media LLC (`www.goto.jobs`)	Employ Media LLC (`www.employmedia.com`)

On April 28, 2005, ICANN announced the availability of a new sTLD:

TLD	Use	Sponsor	Registry Operator
.mobi	Sponsored. Reserved for users and providers of mobile services.	mTLD Top Level Domain Ltd (www.mtld.mobi)	Afilias Ltd (www.afilias.info)

On September 15, 2005, ICANN announced the availability of a new sTLD:

TLD	Use	Sponsor	Registry Operator
.cat	Sponsored. Reserved for Catalan linguistic community.	Fundacio puntCAT (www.domini.cat)	Fundacio puntCAT (www.domini.cat)

On May 10, 2006, ICANN announced the availability of a new sTLD:

TLD	Use	Sponsor	Registry Operator
.tel	Sponsored. Reserved for professional and business contact information.	Telnic Ltd (www.telnic.org)	Telnic Ltd (www.nic.tel)

On October 18, 2006, ICANN announced the availability of a new sTLD:

TLD	Use	Sponsor	Registry Operator
.asia	Sponsored. Reserved for legal entities in Asia/Australia/Pacific region.	DotAsia Organisation Ltd.(www.registry.asia)	Afilias Ltd.(www.afilias.info)

Whois services are typically, but not always, available using www.whois.tld, for example, www.whois.aero.

A revised gTLD policy was adopted by ICANN's board on June 16, 2008 and is based on the report produced by the ICANN GNSO (Generic Names Supporting Organization) Working Group (gnso.icann.org/issues/new-gtlds/pdp-dec05-fr-parta-08aug07.htm). This report recommends (author's selected highlights only) that essentially an unlimited number of new gTLDs should be permitted, that a proportion must be IDNs (Internationalized Domain Names), that the technical and financial resources of the applicant must be verified to ensure DNS stability, that applications for new gTLDs must be judged against pre-existing criteria (Application Guidebook www.icann.org/en/topics/new-gtlds/dag-en.htm), and that only ICANN accredited Registrars can sell the new domain names.

I thought www.example.com was my domain name.

The URL www.example.com is simply the name of a service (or resource). The www is the host or service name, in this case www is World Wide Web; example is the domain name part that was registered by the user and frequently called the second-level domain (SLD); and .com is the top-level domain (TLD). Once you own the domain name, it is *delegated* to you. You can do anything to the left of example.com, so depending on your company, you could create resources (and provide appropriate public or private access) with names like myhost.example.com or us.example.com or plant1.us.example.com or anything you choose.

What is a URL (or URI or URN)?

A Uniform Resource Locator (URL) is the string of letters that define the location of a resource and how to access it; for example, http://www.example.com is conventionally the URL of a web service for the example.com domain, which is accessed using the HTTP protocol. Part of the URL, www.example.com, is used (resolved) by a DNS and an IP address returned from an authoritative DNS for the domain. A Uniform Resource Identifier (URI) is the generic, or high-level, term that defines the syntax and rules for both URLs and Universal Resource Names (URNs).

What is an SLD?

An SLD is a second-level domain. It describes the second name in the domain naming hierarchy below the TLD. In example.com, .com is the TLD (in this case a gTLD) and example.com is the SLD. SLD is frequently used as a generic expression to denote a user domain name, which works fine for the gTLDs (for instance, example.org, example.net); however, it's rarely appropriate when dealing with ccTLDs where the user domain name is frequently a third-level domain name such as example.md.us, example.co.uk, or example.com.br.

How do I register a .com or .org or .net domain name?

ICANN (The Internet Corporation for Assigned Names and Numbers) has subcontracted the registration of domains names to accredited registrars (www.icann.org/en/registrars/accredited-list.html).

How do I register a domain in Malaysia (or any other country)?

IANA (Internet Assigned Numbers Authority) maintains a list of current country code top-level domain (ccTLD) registration authorities for all recognized countries (www.iana.org/domains/root/db/). Each country defined in ISO 3166 is automatically assigned a two-letter TLD such as .my, .au, and .se. You can also try www.nic.ccTLD, for example www.nic.se which works for many (but unfortunately not all) countries.

Can I register a domain name in any country?

There is no single standard for the registration of ccTLDs such as .us or .my. To register a ccTLD, most countries require that you satisfy some local qualifications such as being a citizen or a registered business, maintaining country offices, or other criteria specific to the particular country registration authority. Consult the IANA list of country registration authorities (www.iana.org/domains/root/db/), and then follow the country link for detailed information.

How do I register a US (.us) or state (for instance, ny.us) domain name?

Historically, the US delegation policy was defined by RFC 1480, which described a locality-based method administered via delegation managers. Since April 24, 2002, NeuStar, Inc. has been the official registry operator for the .us domain (www.nic.us) with the idea of expanding the use of the name space. Prior to April 2002, it was only possible to register a locality based (third or higher level) domain in the .us domain (for instance, mynameis.md.us). As of now, with certain exceptions, it is possible to also register a second-level domain such as mynameis.us. The locality-based method is still supported for historic reasons but new locality registrations appear to be limited only to government entities; www.nic.us defines current locality domain name policies though you have to look hard for the information.

How do I register a Canadian (.ca) or provincial (for instance, bc.ca) domain name?

Since November 1, 2000, the Canadian Internet Registration Authority (www.cira.ca) has moved to a distributed model (like ICANN) in which the process of registration is handled by certified registrars. A list of these registrars can be found at the CIRA web site (www.cira.ca). The new registration procedure covers both national (mynameis.ca) and provincial (mynameis.qc.ca) registrations.

If I register a .com, do I automatically register in every country?

Your .com (or .net or .org, etc.) domain name is accessible from every country in the world as is every other domain name, but registering a .com (or .net or .org or .coop) domain name does not grant any rights in another country. For instance, if example.com is registered, then anyone can still register example.us (United States) or example.tv (Tuvala) or example.net, assuming they are available for registration.

What happens when I register a domain name?

When you register a domain name, four types of information are normally requested:

Registrant contact details: This section defines the owner of the domain name and requires the full name, address, telephone number, fax number, and e-mail address. When you register a domain name, it's vital that the e-mail address in particular is correct, accessible by you, and preferably not in your own domain name—in the event that you are either disputing the ownership of the domain or changing suppliers—the very time that you need this e-mail address—it may not be working or available.

Administration contact details: The administration contact controls (and approves) any changes to the rest of the domain name details and is thus the party responsible for the domain. While this will typically be the same as the registrant if a domain is licensed to a third party, the third party's information would be included here. This section requires the full name, address, telephone number, fax number, and e-mail address. The administration contact controls (and approves) any changes to the rest of the domain name details.
Technical contact details: Generally, the technical contact also supplies the DNS service for convenience, but this is *not* essential. This section requires the full name, address, telephone number, fax number, and e-mail address of the technical or DNS delegation authority.
Billing contact details: The location where registration fee invoices are sent. This section requires the full name, address, telephone number, fax number, and e-mail address. Certain registration organizations will send regular mail invoices and reminders, so having correct information here is vital.

Primary and secondary name servers (DNS): This section usually requires both the name and IP address of the name servers that will be authoritative for your domain. Generally, but not always, these will be the responsibility of the technical contact.

During the registration process, you may be asked for an authentication method—typically you have a choice of e-mail or web interface with a username and password. If e-mail is selected, whenever a change is made to the registration record, the registrar will send an e-mail to the address specified in the registrant/administrative contact record and request confirmation of the change. It is vital that this e-mail address is valid and accessible under all conditions. Since the e-mail address is the piece of information most likely to be needed, it is recommended that this e-mail address not be in your domain (that is, use a free Hotmail, Gmail, or Yahoo! account and keep it active).

Many ISPs and service providers offer to register domain names on behalf of their clients. If this is done, the registration should be verified immediately, using a whois service, to confirm that the registrant/administration contact (the domain owner) is the real owner and not the ISP or other third party. If the ISP or third party is the registrant/administration contact, then they effectively control the domain, and it may not be possible, in the event of a dispute, to change or move the domain name.

What do the primary and secondary DNS server names do and why are they necessary?

When you register a domain name with a certified or accredited registrar, the authority for management of that domain is delegated to you. As the delegated party, you are responsible for providing at least two DNS servers that will respond authoritatively for your domain—they will provide answers to questions such as "What is the IP address of your web site?" The DNS service can be provided by running your own DNS servers, or it can in turn be delegated to a third party such as an ISP or a specialized DNS hosting service. Increasingly, many registrars also offer domain parking services to satisfy the minimum registration requirements. The DNS names and/or IP addresses of the authoritative servers are defined in the registration record for your domain (a minimum of two, but can be more) and are used by the registry operator for the TLD involved to refer queries for your domain's web site such as www.example.com to your domain's DNS. When a local DNS looks for a name, say, www.example.com, and can't find it locally, it will ask one of the root-servers for the information, which will cause a referral to the TLD server for the domain, in this case .com. The .com DNS will return a referral containing the name and IP addresses of the DNSs that contain the authoritative information for your domain, for instance, ns1.example.com. The local DNS will then interrogate the authoritative DNS for the domain, ns1.example.com, for the specific service or server, such as www.example.com, and get back its IP address. The reason for having primary and secondary (and even tertiary or more) DNS names and IPs is for redundancy purposes. A single DNS may become overloaded or fail, so if the first DNS is not available, the second is tried, then the third, and so on.

How do I change my domain name information?

To change your domain information, you must go to the registrar with whom you registered the domain name and follow their procedure for changes or modifications. Depending on the procedures defined by the registrar, the administration contact associated with the domain may have to authorize any changes via e-mail or some other procedure selected when the domain name was originally registered. Increasingly, the process of domain change is being provided via secure registrar web interfaces, and the owner of the username and password (used to secure access to the domain information) are assumed to have the rights to perform modifications without any other verification.

How do I register an .edu (or .mil or .gov or .int) name?

All these TLDs are sponsored (sTLDs) and have restricted use. The .edu gTLD is available only for educational institutions in the United States, and registration is handled exclusively by EDUCAUSE (www.educause.edu). The .gov gTLD is reserved exclusively for the United States government, and registration is handled by the General Services Administration (GSA) at www.dotgov.gov. The .mil TLD is reserved exclusively for use by the United States military, and registration is handled by the US DOD

Network Information Center. The .int TLD is reserved exclusively for organizations created by international treaties, such as www.un.int and www.itu.int, and is registered through IANA (www.iana.org/domains/int/).

How do I check my (or some else's) registration information?

Most Registrars operate a search facility that will let you know if a specific domain name is available or not (www.icann.org/en/registrars/accredited-list.html). The registration data is also made available via a whois service, which can be accessed by a whois utility or via a web interface provided by a number of third parties. Unfortunately, spammers and others misuse these whois services, so many whois service operators now have restrictive access policies or limit the number of requests allowed over time in an attempt to minimize abuse.

What is IANA and how does it relate to ICANN and the IETF?

The Internet Assigned Numbers Authority, or IANA, was assigned to ICANN as part of its establishment in 1998. A number of the services performed by IANA relate to the storage and administration of protocol and other values that are defined in RFCs, which are controlled by the Internet Engineering Task Force (IETF) overseen by the Internet Architecture Board. Both the IETF and IAB are under the umbrella of the Internet Society (ISOC www.isoc.org)—a separate organization from ICANN. The relationship between the IETF/IAB and IANA is defined in RFC 2860.

Who controls the .ARPA domain name?

The domain .ARPA—which has now been renamed Address and Routing Parameter Area—is reserved exclusively for use in the Internet infrastructure. It includes the currently assigned domains IN-ADDR.ARPA (IPv4 reverse mapping), IP6.ARPA (IPv6 reverse mapping), E164.ARPA (ENUM), URI.ARPA (Uniform Address Identifiers), and URN.ARPA (Uniform Resource Names). The domain is administered by IANA (ICANN) under the guidance of the IETF/IAB as defined in RFC 3172. The latest list of assigned domains may be found at www.iana.org/domains/arpa/.

Who controls ICANN?

Prior to 1998, responsibility for running and managing the root domain lay ultimately with the US Department of Commerce (DOC). ICANN was established on November 21, 1998 as a US-based nonprofit public benefit corporation (essentially a charity under US tax laws) and was charged with assuming the direction and control of the Internet root domain (operations and policy) under what was termed the Memorandum of Understanding/Joint Project Agreement initially signed on November 25, 1998 and modified a number of times over the following years (http://www.icann.org/en/general/agreements.htm). The purpose of the MOU/JPA was "to privatize the management of the domain name system (DNS) in a manner that increases competition and facilitates international participation in its management." The net of the MOU/JPA was that ICANN would be controlled by its elected board but that the DOC could still be required to approve unspecified decisions acting in its governmental role. On September 29, 2006 the MOU/JPA was again modified (http://www.icann.org/en/general/JPA-29sep06.pdf). This modification included the addition of Annex A: "Affirmation of Responsibilities" in which ICANN's role was defined. Notably, this included increased recognition of ICANN's Governmental Advisory Committee (GAC) (http://gac.icann.org).
The GAC was initially established in 1999, but it underwent a significant change and upgrade of status in April 2005. On September 30, 2009, a document called the "Affirmation of Commitments" (http://www.icann.org/en/documents/affirmation-of-commitments-30sep09-en.htm) replaced the

MOU/JPA. In this document, the DOC confirmed its support for ICANN's multi-stakeholder, private sector role; its willingness to see new TLDs; and its ongoing participation in ICANN's GAC. ICANN committed itself to three yearly reviews of its effectiveness (the first of which is due by December 31, 2010), multi-stakeholder transparency, on-going operation of the DNS, and a replacement WHOIS system. The following is a direct quotation from section 8 of this agreement "ICANN is a private organization and nothing in this Affirmation should be construed as control by any one entity." The Affirmation of Commitments, unlike the previous MOU/JPA, assumes the agreement will continue indefinitely and thus currently has no end date.

What are WGIG, IGF and IGP?

ICANN controls the worldwide policy affecting all TLDs (gTLDs and ccTLDs). Such a critical role and ICANN's relationship with the US government (via U.S. Department of Commerce) has always attracted an element of suspicion (real or imagined) and controversy. The United Nations at the World Summit on Information Systems (WSIS) in Geneva (December 10-12, 2003) established the Working Group on Internet Governance (WGIG) comprising 40 representatives from " governments, private sector and civil society, who all participated on an equal footing and in their personal capacity." The WGIG produced its first report (www.wgig.org/docs/WGIGREPORT.pdf) in June 2005 which proposed four possible Internet Governance models and eventually led to the establishment of what is now called the Internet Governance Forum (IGF) in 2006. The IGF (www.intgovforum.org) whose mandate is described on its website (www.intgovforum.org/cms/index.php/aboutigf) holds annual public meetings whose agenda is set by a Multistakeholder Advisory Group (MAG) comprising "50 Members from governments, the private sector and civil society, including representatives from the academic and technical communities" that meets three times per year in Geneva.

The Internet Governance Project (IGP) is an alliance of academics that contribute ideas on Internet governance, among others, to various organizations including ICANN and the IGF. The IGP (www.internetgovernance.org) is allied to the School of Information Studies, Syracuse University.

What is re-delegation of ccTLDs

Long ago when the Internet was young, many ccTLDs (especially, but not exclusively, smaller countries) were tactically delegated to a sponsoring authority (in the majority of cases, these were academic institutions reflecting the dominant Internet usage at that time) that created the necessary zone files and DNS operational capacity to allow access to the ccTLDs. In some cases, the sponsoring authority delegated the ccTLD at the request of a local enterprise or organization at a time when the eventual importance of the Internet was little understood. As the Internet has grown, many countries now see the importance of controlling their own ccTLDs, which frequently requires a change to the current delegation. To accomplish such a change, countries must undergo a process known as re-delegation, which involves an investigation by IANA personnel into all the circumstances surrounding the historic delegation and the proposed changes. IANA's final report on the requested re-delegation must be approved by the ICANN board. Information about the process and about making applications for re-delegation may be obtained from www.iana.org/domains/root/delegation-guide/. IANA follows the guidelines defined in RFC 1591 as modified by the ICANN document ICP-1 (www.icann.org/en/icp/icp-1.htm).

How do I get an IDN (Internationalized Domain Name) ccTLD?

ICANN, through its country code names supporting organization (ccNSO ccnso.icann.org), opened a three-stage fast-track approval process on November 16, 2009 to allow countries whose national language(s) do not use Latin languages to obtain an IDN (Internationalized Domain Name) variant. The fast track is defined to be a temporary process which will, at some stage, be replaced by a standard policy (being developed by the ccNSO). As of the time of writing, the fast track is the only available process to acquire IDN ccTLDs. IDN ccTLDs are designed only to augment the existing ccTLDs by providing national language(s) support, and it is anticipated that applications will only be accepted from existing ccTLD operators or applicants who can demonstrate some level of governmental approval and support. More information may be obtained from `www.icann.org/en/topics/idn/fast-track/`. As of the end of 2010, 11 IDN domains had been fully delegated and operational with 12 more awaiting final delegation. The current status of approved IDNs and their IDN strings may be obtained from `www.icann.org/en/topics/idn/fast-track/string-evaluation-completion-z-en.htm`.

APPENDIX B

■ ■ ■

DNS RFCs

There are a significant number of RFCs that define the DNS or are relevant to it as befits its status as a core Internet technology. The main repository for RFCs is maintained by the IETF (http://www.ietf.org/rfc.html), which provides a keyword-searchable list (https://datatracker.ietf.org/doc/) covering both published and draft RFCs. There are two IETF Working Groups (WGs) concerned with developing DNS RFCs. The dnsext WG (http://datatracker.ietf.org/wg/dnsext) is primarily concerned with development of DNS protocol standards and extensions and the dnsop WG (https://datatracker.ietf.org/wg/dnsop) is concerned with operational procedures and practices.

The following is the current list of DNS or DNS-related RFCs and their status. RFCs are being published on a regular basis so the latest RFC index maintained by the IETF should be consulted (http://www.ietf.org/download/rfc-index.txt). The relevant RFCs are generally referenced in the text where appropriate.

RFC	Title, Author, and Status
RFC 1034	"Domain Names—Concepts and Facilities." P. V. Mockapetris. 1 November 1987. Makes obsolete RFC 0973, RFC 0882, RFC 0883. Updated by RFC 1101, RFC 1183, RFC 1348, RFC 1876, RFC 1982, RFC 2065, RFC 2181, RFC 2308, RFC 2535, RFC 4033, RFC 4034, RFC 4035, RFC 4343, RFC 4035, RFC 4592, RFC 5936 (Also STD0013) Status: STANDARD. Still the classic work on the subject.
RFC 1035	"Domain Names—Implementation and Specification." P. V. Mockapetris. 1 November 1987. Makes obsolete RFC 0973, RFC 0882, RFC 0883. Updated by RFC 1101, RFC 1183, RFC 1348, RFC 1876, RFC 1982, RFC 1995, RFC 1996, RFC 2065, RFC 2136, RFC 2181, RFC 2137, RFC 2308, RFC 2535, RFC 2845, RFC 3425, RFC 3658, RFC 4033, RFC 4034, RFC 4035, RFC 4343, RFC 5936, RFC 5966 (Also STD0013) Status: STANDARD.
RFC 1183	"New DNS RR Definitions." C. F. Everhart, L. A. Mamakos, R. Ullmann, P. V. Mockapetris. 1 October 1990. Updates RFC 1034, RFC 1035. Updated by RFC5395, RFC5864 Status: EXPERIMENTAL.
RFC 1591	"Domain Name System Structure and Delegation." J. Postel. March 1994. Status: INFORMATIONAL.
RFC 1706	"DNS NSAP Resource Records." B. Manning, R. Colella. October 1994. Makes obsolete RFC 1637. Status: INFORMATIONAL.

RFC	Title, Author, and Status
RFC 1794	"DNS Support for Load Balancing." T. Brisco. April 1995. Status: INFORMATIONAL.
RFC 1876	"A Means for Expressing Location Information in the Domain Name System." C. Davis, P. Vixie, T. Goodwin, I. Dickinson. January 1996. Updates RFC 1034, RFC 1035. Status: EXPERIMENTAL.
RFC 1912	"Common DNS Operational and Configuration Errors." D. Barr. February 1996. Makes obsolete RFC 1537. Status: INFORMATIONAL.
RFC 1918	"Address Allocation for Private Internets." Y. Rekhter, B. Moskowitz, D. Karrenberg, G. J. de Groot, E. Lear. February 1996. Obsoletes RFC 1627, RFC 1597 (Also BCP0005). Status: BEST CURRENT PRACTICE.
RFC 1995	"Incremental Zone Transfer in DNS." M. Ohta. August 1996. Updates RFC 1035. Status: PROPOSED STANDARD.
RFC 1996	"A Mechanism for Prompt Notification of Zone Changes (DNS NOTIFY)." P. Vixie. August 1996. Updates RFC 1035. Status: PROPOSED STANDARD.
RFC 2136	"Dynamic Updates in the Domain Name System (DNS UPDATE)." P. Vixie, Ed.; S. Thomson; Y. Rekhter; J. Bound. April 1997. Updates RFC 1035. Updated by RFC 3007, RFC 4035, RFC 4033, RFC 4034. Status: PROPOSED STANDARD.
RFC 2181	"Clarifications to the DNS Specification." R. Elz, R. Bush. July 1997. Updates RFC 1034, RFC 1035, RFC 1123. Updated by RFC 2535, RFC 4343, RFC 4033, RFC 4034, RFC 4035, RFC 5452. Status: PROPOSED STANDARD.
RFC 2230	"Key Exchange Delegation Record for the DNS." R. Atkinson. November 1997. Status: INFORMATIONAL.
RFC 2308	"Negative Caching of DNS Queries (DNS NCACHE)." M. Andrews. March 1998. Updates RFC 1034, RFC 1035. Updated by RFC 4035, RFC 4033, RFC 4034. Status: PROPOSED STANDARD.
RFC 2317	"Classless IN-ADDR.ARPA delegation." H. Eidnes, G. de Groot, P. Vixie. March 1998. Also BCP0020. Status: BEST CURRENT PRACTICE.
RFC 2536	"DSA KEYs and SIGs in the Domain Name System (DNS)." D. Eastlake, III. March 1999. Status: PROPOSED STANDARD.
RFC 2539	"Storage of Diffie-Hellman Keys in the Domain Name System (DNS)." D. Eastlake, III. March 1999. Status: PROPOSED STANDARD.
RFC 2540	"Detached Domain Name System (DNS) Information." D. Eastlake 3rd. March 1999. Status: EXPERIMENTAL.

RFC	Title, Author, and Status
RFC 2606	"Reserved Top Level DNS Names." D. Eastlake, III, A. Panitz. June 1999. Also BCP0032. Status: BEST CURRENT PRACTICE.
RFC 2671	"Extension Mechanisms for DNS (EDNS0)." P. Vixie. August 1999. Status: PROPOSED STANDARD.
RFC 2672	"Non-Terminal DNS Name Redirection." M. Crawford. August 1999. Updated by RFC 4592. Status: PROPOSED STANDARD.
RFC 2673	"Binary Labels in the Domain Name System." M. Crawford. August 1999. Updated by RFC 3363, RFC 3364. Status: EXPERIMENTAL.
RFC 2694	"DNS Extensions to Network Address Translators (DNS_ALG)." P. Srisuresh, G. Tsirtsis, P. Akkiraju, A. Heffernan. September 1999. Status: INFORMATIONAL.
RFC 2782	"A DNS RR for Specifying the Location of Services (DNS SRV)." A. Gulbrandsen, P. Vixie, L. Esibov. February 2000. Makes obsolete RFC 2052. Status: PROPOSED STANDARD.
RFC 2845	"Secret Key Transaction Authentication for DNS (TSIG)." P. Vixie, O. Gudmundsson, D. Eastlake, III, B. Wellington. May 2000. Updates RFC 1035. Updated by RFC 3645. Status: PROPOSED STANDARD.
RFC 2874	"DNS Extensions to Support IPv6 Address Aggregation and Renumbering." M. Crawford, C. Huitema. July 2000. Updates RFC1886. Updated by RFC3152, RFC3226, RFC3363, RFC3364. Status: EXPERIMENTAL.
RFC 2930	"Secret Key Establishment for DNS (TKEY RR)." D. Eastlake, III. September 2000. Status: PROPOSED STANDARD.
RFC 2931	"DNS Request and Transaction Signatures (SIG(0)s)." D. Eastlake, III. September 2000. Updates RFC 2535. Status: PROPOSED STANDARD.
RFC 3007	"Secure Domain Name System (DNS) Dynamic Update." B. Wellington. November 2000. Makes obsolete RFC 2137. Updates RFC 2535, RFC 2136. Updated by RFC 4033, RFC 4034, RFC 4035. Status: PROPOSED STANDARD.
RFC 3110	"RSA/SHA-1 SIGs and RSA KEYs in the Domain Name System (DNS)." D. Eastlake, III. May 2001. Makes obsolete RFC 2537. Status: PROPOSED STANDARD.
RFC 3123	"A DNS RR Type for Lists of Address Prefixes (APL RR)." P. Koch. June 2001. Status: EXPERIMENTAL.
RFC 3225	"Indicating Resolver Support of DNSSEC." D. Conrad. December 2001. Updated by RFC 4033, RFC 4034, RFC 403. Status: PROPOSED STANDARD.

RFC	Title, Author, and Status
RFC 3226	"DNSSEC and IPv6 A6 Aware Server/Resolver Message Size Requirements." O. Gudmundsson. December 2001. Updates RFC 2535, RFC 2874. Updated by RFC 4033, RFC 4034, RFC 4035. Status: PROPOSED STANDARD.
RFC 3363	"Representing Internet Protocol Version 6 (IPv6) Addresses in the Domain Name System (DNS)." R. Bush, A. Durand, B. Fink, O. Gudmundsson, T. Hain. August 2002. Updates RFC 2673, RFC 2874. Status: INFORMATIONAL.
RFC 3401	"Dynamic Delegation Discovery System (DDDS) Part One: The Comprehensive DDDS." M. Mealling. October 2002. Makes obsolete RFC 2915, RFC 2168. Updates RFC 2276. Status: INFORMATIONAL.
RFC 3402	"Dynamic Delegation Discovery System (DDDS) Part Two: The Algorithm." M. Mealling. October 2002. Makes obsolete RFC 2915, RFC 2168. Status: PROPOSED STANDARD.
RFC 3403	"Dynamic Delegation Discovery System (DDDS) Part Three: The Domain Name System (DNS) Database." M. Mealling. October 2002. Makes obsolete RFC 2915, RFC 2168. Status: PROPOSED STANDARD.
RFC 3404	"Dynamic Delegation Discovery System (DDDS) Part Four: The Uniform Resource Identifiers (URI)." M. Mealling. October 2002. Makes obsolete RFC 2915, RFC 2168. Status: PROPOSED STANDARD.
RFC 3405	"Dynamic Delegation Discovery System (DDDS) Part Five: URI.ARPA Assignment Procedures." M. Mealling. October 2002. (Also BCP0065). Status: BEST CURRENT PRACTICE.
RFC 3425	"Obsoleting IQUERY." D. Lawrence. November 2002. Updates RFC 1035. Status: PROPOSED STANDARD.
RFC 3492	"Punycode: A Bootstring encoding of Unicode for Internationalized Domain Names in Applications (IDNA)." A. Costello. March 2003. Updated by RFC 5891. (Status: PROPOSED STANDARD.
RFC 3596	"DNS Extensions to Support IP Version 6." S. Thomson, C. Huitema, V. Ksinant, M. Souissi. October 2003. Makes obsolete RFC 3152, RFC 1886. Status: DRAFT STANDARD.
RFC 3597	"Handling of Unknown DNS Resource Record (RR) Types." A. Gustafsson. September 2003. Updates RFC 2163, RFC 2535. Status: Updated by RFC 4033, RFC 4034, RFC 4035, RFC 5395. PROPOSED STANDARD.
RFC 3645	"Generic Security Service Algorithm for Secret Key Transaction Authentication for DNS (GSS-TSIG)." S. Kwan, P. Garg, J. Gilroy, L. Esibov, J. Westhead, R. Hall. October 2003. Updates RFC 2845. Status: PROPOSED STANDARD.

RFC	Title, Author, and Status
RFC 3761	"The E.164 to Uniform Resource Identifiers (URI) Dynamic Delegation Discovery System (DDDS) Application (ENUM)." P. Faltstrom, M. Mealling. April 2004. Makes obsolete RFC 2916. Status: PROPOSED STANDARD.
RFC 3833	"Threat Analysis of the Domain Name System (DNS)." D. Atkins, R. Austein. August 2004. Status: INFORMATIONAL.
RFC 3958	"Domain-Based Application Service Location Using SRV RRs and the Dynamic Delegation Discovery Service (DDDS)." L. Daigle, A. Newton. January 2005. Status: PROPOSED STANDARD.
RFC 4025	"A Method for Storing IPsec Keying Material in DNS." M. Richardson. March 2005. Status: PROPOSED STANDARD.
RFC 4033	"DNS Security Introduction and Requirements." R. Arends, R. Austein, M. Larson, D. Massey, S. Rose. March 2005. Makes obsolete RFC 2535, RFC 3008, RFC 3090, RFC 3445, RFC 3655, RFC 3658, RFC 3755, RFC 3757, RFC 3845. Updates RFC 1034,RFC 1035, RFC 2136, RFC 2181, RFC 2308, RFC 3225, RFC 3007, RFC 3597, RFC 3226. Status: PROPOSED STANDARD.
RFC 4034	"Resource Records for the DNS Security Extensions." R. Arends, R. Austein, M. Larson, D. Massey, S. Rose. March 2005. Makes obsolete RFC 2535, RFC 3008, RFC 3090, RFC 3445, RFC 3655, RFC 3658, RFC 3755, RFC 3757, RFC 3845. Updates RFC 1034, RFC 1035, RFC 2136, RFC 2181, RFC 2308, RFC 3225, RFC 3007, RFC 3597, RFC 3226. Updated by RFC 4470. Status: PROPOSED STANDARD.
RFC 4035	"Protocol Modifications for the DNS Security Extensions." R. Arends, R. Austein, M. Larson, D. Massey, S. Rose. March 2005. Makes obsolete RFC 2535, RFC 3008, RFC 3090, RFC 3445, RFC 3655, RFC 3658, RFC 3755, RFC 3757, RFC 3845. Updates RFC 1034, RFC 1035, RFC 2136, RFC 2181, RFC 2308, RFC 3225, RFC 3007, RFC 3597, RFC 3226. Updated by RFC 4470. Status: PROPOSED STANDARD.
RFC 4255	"Using DNS to Securely Publish Secure Shell (SSH) Key Fingerprints." J. Schlyter, W. Griffin. January 2006. Status: PROPOSED STANDARD.
RFC 4343	"Domain Name System (DNS) Case Insensitivity Clarification." D. Eastlake 3rd. January 2006. Updates RFC 1034, RFC 1035, RFC 2181. Status: PROPOSED STANDARD.
RFC 4367	"What's in a Name: False Assumptions about DNS Names." J. Rosenberg, Ed., IAB. February 2006. Status: INFORMATIONAL.
RFC 4398	"Storing Certificates in the Domain Name System (DNS)." S. Josefsson. March 2006. Obsoletes RFC2538 Status: PROPOSED STANDARD.
RFC 4408	"Sender Policy Framework (SPF) for Authorizing Use of Domains in E-Mail, Version 1." M. Wong, W. Schlitt. April 2006. Status: EXPERIMENTAL.

RFC	Title, Author, and Status
RFC 4431	"The DNSSEC Lookaside Validation (DLV) DNS Resource Record." M. Andrews, S. Weiler. February 2006. Status: INFORMATIONAL.
RFC 4470	"Minimally Covering NSEC Records and DNSSEC On-line Signing." S. Weiler, J. Ihren. April 2006. Updates RFC 4035, RFC 4034. Status: PROPOSED STANDARD.
RFC 4472	"Operational Considerations and Issues with IPv6 DNS." A. Durand, J. Ihren, P. Savola. April 2006. Status: INFORMATIONAL.
RFC 4501	"Domain Name System Uniform Resource Identifiers." S. Josefsson. May 2006. Status: PROPOSED STANDARD.
RFC 4592	"The Role of Wildcards in the Domain Name System." E. Lewis. July 2006. Updates RFC 1034, RFC 2672. Status: PROPOSED STANDARD.
RFC 4635	"HMAC SHA (Hashed Message Authentication Code, Secure Hash Algorithm) TSIG Algorithm Identifiers." D. Eastlake 3rd. August 2006. Status: PROPOSED STANDARD.
RFC 4641	"DNSSEC Operational Practices." O. Kolkman, R. Gieben. September 2006. Obsoletes RFC2541. Status: INFORMATIONAL.
RFC 4648	"The Base16, Base32, and Base64 Data Encodings." S. Josefsson. October 2006. Obsoletes RFC3548. Status: PROPOSED STANDARD.
RFC 4697	"Observed DNS Resolution Misbehavior." M. Larson, P. Barber. October 2006. (Also BCP0123) Status: BEST CURRENT PRACTICE.
RFC 4701	"A DNS Resource Record (RR) for Encoding Dynamic Host Configuration Protocol (DHCP) Information (DHCID RR)." M. Stapp, T. Lemon, A. Gustafsson. October 2006. Updated by RFC5494. Status: PROPOSED STANDARD.
RFC 4725	"ENUM Validation Architecture." A. Mayrhofer, B. Hoeneisen. November 2006. Status: INFORMATIONAL.
RFC 4871	"DomainKeys Identified Mail (DKIM) Signatures." E. Allman, J. Callas, M. Delany, M. Libbey, J. Fenton, M. Thomas. May 2007. Obsoletes RFC4870. Updated by RFC5672. Status: PROPOSED STANDARD.
RFC 4892	"Requirements for a Mechanism Identifying a Name Server Instance." S. Woolf, D. Conrad. June 2007. Status: INFORMATIONAL.
RFC 4955	"DNS Security (DNSSEC) Experiments." D. Blacka. July 2007. Status: PROPOSED STANDARD.
RFC 4956	"DNS Security (DNSSEC) Opt-In." R. Arends, M. Kosters, D. Blacka. July 2007. Status: EXPERIMENTAL.

RFC	Title, Author, and Status
RFC 4986	"Requirements Related to DNS Security (DNSSEC) Trust Anchor Rollover." H. Eland, R. Mundy, S. Crocker, S. Krishnaswamy. August 2007. Status: INFORMATIONAL.
RFC 5001	"DNS Name Server Identifier (NSID) Option." R. Austein. August 2007. Status: PROPOSED STANDARD.
RFC 5011	"Automated Updates of DNS Security (DNSSEC) Trust Anchors." M. StJohns. September 2007. Status: PROPOSED STANDARD.
RFC 5016	"Requirements for a DomainKeys Identified Mail (DKIM) Signing Practices Protocol." M. Thomas. October 2007. Status: INFORMATIONAL.
RFC 5067	"Infrastructure ENUM Requirements." S. Lind, P. Pfautz. November 2007. Status: INFORMATIONAL.
RFC 5074	"DNSSEC Lookaside Validation (DLV)." S. Weiler. November 2007. Status: INFORMATIONAL.
RFC 5076	"ENUM Validation Information Mapping for the Extensible Provisioning Protocol." B. Hoeneisen. December 2007. Status: PROPOSED STANDARD.
RFC 5155	"DNS Security (DNSSEC) Hashed Authenticated Denial of Existence." B. Laurie, G. Sisson, R. Arends, D. Blacka. March 2008. Status: PROPOSED STANDARD. NSEC3 Definition
RFC 5158	"6to4 Reverse DNS Delegation Specification." G. Huston. March 2008. Status: INFORMATIONAL.
RFC 5205	"Host Identity Protocol (HIP) Domain Name System (DNS) Extensions." P. Nikander, J. Laganier. April 2008. Status: EXPERIMENTAL.
RFC 5358	"Preventing Use of Recursive Nameservers in Reflector Attacks." J. Damas, F. Neves. October 2008. (Also BCP0140) Status: BEST CURRENT PRACTICE.
RFC 5359	"Domain Name System (DNS) IANA Considerations." D. Eastlake 3rd. November 2008. Obsoletes RFC 2929. Updates RFC 1183, RFC 3597. (Also BCP0042) Status: BEST CURRENT PRACTICE.
RFC 5452	"Measures for Making DNS More Resilient against Forged Answers." A. Hubert, R. van Mook. January 2009. Updates RFC 2181. Status: PROPOSED STANDARD.
RFC 5483	"ENUM Implementation Issues and Experiences." L. Conroy, K. Fujiwara. March 2009. Status: INFORMATIONAL.
RFC 5507	"Design Choices When Expanding the DNS." IAB, P. Faltstrom, Ed., R. Austein, Ed., P. Koch, Ed.. April 2009. Status: INFORMATIONAL.

RFC	Title, Author, and Status
RFC 5526	"The E.164 to Uniform Resource Identifiers (URI) Dynamic Delegation Discovery System (DDDS) Application for Infrastructure ENUM." J. Livingood, P. Pfautz, R. Stastny. April 2009. Status: INFORMATIONAL.
RFC 5564	"Linguistic Guidelines for the Use of the Arabic Language in Internet Domains." A. El-Sherbiny, M. Farah, I. Oueichek, A. Al-Zoman. February 2010. Status: INFORMATIONAL.
RFC 5585	"DomainKeys Identified Mail (DKIM) Service Overview." T. Hansen, D. Crocker, P. Hallam-Baker. July 2009. Status: INFORMATIONAL.
RFC 5617	"DomainKeys Identified Mail (DKIM) Author Domain Signing Practices (ADSP)." E. Allman, J. Fenton, M. Delany, J. Levine. August 2009. Status: PROPOSED STANDARD.
RFC 5625	"DNS Proxy Implementation Guidelines." R. Bellis. August 2009. (Also BCP0152) Status: BEST CURRENT PRACTICE.
RFC 5672	"RFC 4871 DomainKeys Identified Mail (DKIM) Signatures—Update." D. Crocker, Ed.. August 2009. (Updates RFC4871. Status: PROPOSED STANDARD.
RFC 5679	"Locating IEEE 802.21 Mobility Services Using DNS." G. Bajko. December 2009. Status: PROPOSED STANDARD.
RFC 5730	"Extensible Provisioning Protocol (EPP)." S. Hollenbeck. August 2009. Obsoletes RFC4930. (Also STD0069) Status: STANDARD.
RFC 5731	"Extensible Provisioning Protocol (EPP) Domain Name Mapping." S. Hollenbeck. August 2009. Obsoletes RFC 4931. (Also STD0069) Status: STANDARD.
RFC 5732	"Extensible Provisioning Protocol (EPP) Host Mapping." S. Hollenbeck. August 2009. Obsoletes RFC 4932. (Also STD0069) Status: STANDARD.
RFC 5733	"Extensible Provisioning Protocol (EPP) Contact Mapping." S. Hollenbeck. August 2009. Obsoletes RFC 4933. (Also STD0069) Status: STANDARD.
RFC 5734	"Extensible Provisioning Protocol (EPP) Transport over TCP." S. Hollenbeck. August 2009. Obsoletes RFC 4934. (Also STD0069) Status: STANDARD.
RFC 5782	"DNS Blacklists and Whitelists." J. Levine. February 2010. Status: INFORMATIONAL.
RFC 5863	"DomainKeys Identified Mail (DKIM) Development, Deployment, and Operations." T. Hansen, E. Siegel, P. Hallam-Baker, D. Crocker. May 2010. Status: INFORMATIONAL,
RFC 5864	"DNS SRV Resource Records for AFS." R. Allbery. April 2010. Updates RFC 1183. Status: PROPOSED STANDARD.

RFC	Title, Author, and Status
RFC 5890	"Internationalized Domain Names for Applications (IDNA): Definitions and Document Framework." J. Klensin. August 2010. Obsoletes RFC 3490. Status: PROPOSED STANDARD.
RFC 5891	"Internationalized Domain Names in Applications (IDNA): Protocol." J. Klensin. August 2010. Obsoletes RFC 3490, RFC 3491. Updates RFC 3492. Status: PROPOSED STANDARD.
RFC 5982	"The Unicode Code Points and Internationalized Domain Names for Applications (IDNA)." P. Faltstrom, Ed.. August 2010. Status: PROPOSED STANDARD.
RFC 5893	"Right-to-Left Scripts for Internationalized Domain Names for Applications (IDNA)." H. Alvestrand, Ed., C. Karp. August 2010.Status: PROPOSED STANDARD.
RFC 5894	"Internationalized Domain Names for Applications (IDNA): Background, Explanation, and Rationale." J. Klensin. August 2010. Status: INFORMATIONAL.
RFC 5895	"Mapping Characters for Internationalized Domain Names in Applications (IDNA) 2008." P. Resnick, P. Hoffman. September 2010. Status: INFORMATIONAL.
RFC 5910	"Domain Name System (DNS) Security Extensions Mapping for the Extensible Provisioning Protocol (EPP)." J. Gould, S. Hollenbeck. May 2010. Obsoletes RFC 4310. Status: PROPOSED STANDARD.
RFC 5933	"Use of GOST Signature Algorithms in DNSKEY and RRSIG Resource Records for DNSSEC." V. Dolmatov, Ed., A. Chuprina, I. Ustinov. July 2010. Status: PROPOSED STANDARD.
RFC 5936	"DNS Zone Transfer Protocol (AXFR)." E. Lewis, A. Hoenes, Ed.. June 2010. Updates RFC1034, RFC1035. Status: PROPOSED STANDARD.
RFC 5966	"DNS Transport over TCP - Implementation Requirements." R. Bellis. August 2010.Updates RFC1035, RFC1123. Status: PROPOSED STANDARD.
RFC 5992	"Internationalized Domain Names Registration and Administration Guidelines for European Languages Using Cyrillic." S. Sharikov, D. Miloshevic, J. Klensin. October 2010. Status: INFORMATIONAL.

Index

■ ■ ■

■ J

■ K

CPSIA information can be obtained
at www.ICGtesting.com
Printed in the USA
LVHW101933210420
654208LV00006B/83